The Silent Sex

The Silent Sex

GENDER, DELIBERATION, AND INSTITUTIONS

Christopher F. Karpowitz
and
Tali Mendelberg

PRINCETON UNIVERSITY PRESS
PRINCETON AND OXFORD

Published by Princeton University Press, 41 William Street,
Princeton, New Jersey 08540

In the United Kingdom: Princeton University Press, 6 Oxford Street,
Woodstock, Oxfordshire OX20 1TW

press.princeton.edu

Jacket photograph © Africa Studio/Shutterstock. Jacket design by Lorraine Doneker.

Library of Congress Cataloging-in-Publication Data

Karpowitz, Christopher F., 1969–

The silent sex : gender, deliberation, and
institutions / Christopher F. Karpowitz, Tali Mendelberg.
pages cm
Summary: "Do women participate in and influence meetings equally with men? Does gender shape how a meeting is run and whose voices are heard? The Silent Sex shows how the gender composition and rules of a deliberative body dramatically affect who speaks, how the group interacts, the kinds of issues the group takes up, whose voices prevail, and what the group ultimately decides. It argues that efforts to improve the representation of women will fall short unless they address institutional rules that impede women's voices.Using groundbreaking experimental research supplemented with analysis of school boards, Christopher Karpowitz and Tali Mendelberg demonstrate how the effects of rules depend on women's numbers, so that small numbers are not fatal with a consensus process, but consensus is not always beneficial when there are large numbers of women. Men and women enter deliberative settings facing different expectations about their influence and authority. Karpowitz and Mendelberg reveal how the wrong institutional rules can exacerbate women's deficit of authority while the right rules can close it, and, in the process, establish more cooperative norms of group behavior and more generous policies for the disadvantaged. Rules and numbers have far-reaching implications for the representation of women and their interests.Bringing clarity and insight to one of today's most contentious debates, The Silent Sex provides important new findings on ways to bring women's voices into the conversation on matters of common concern"—Provided by publisher.
Includes bibliographical references and index.
ISBN 978-0-691-15975-1 (hardback) — ISBN 978-0-691-15976-8 (paperback) 1. Corporate meetings. 2. Women. 3. Social participation. 4. Social interaction. 5. Social groups 6. Social psychology. I. Mendelberg, Tali. II. Title.
HD2743.K295 2014
302.3'5—dc23
2014008938

British Library Cataloging-in-Publication Data is available

This book has been composed in Minion and Avant Garde

Printed on acid-free paper. ∞

Printed in the United States of America
1 3 5 7 9 10 8 6 4 2

To Caleb, Quinn,
Cami, and Zach,
and to Leora and Dani—
our children, whose beloved voices are created equal.

Contents

Illustrations

Tables

Acknowledgments

THIS PROJECT HAS BEEN A LONG-TERM UNDERTAKING, and we are extremely grateful to the many people who made it possible. First we thank our families for their love and support. Tali wishes to thank her parents, Hava and Uri Mendelberg, her brother and sister-in-law, Gabi and Jill Mendelberg, and her daughters, Leora and Daniella Paradise. She also thanks her dear friends Gil Blitz and Jody Kirtner for their encouragement. Chris thanks his parents, Dennis and Diane Karpowitz, his five siblings, his children Caleb, Quinn, Cami, and Zach, and above all his unfailingly supportive wife, Jordan.

We want to thank our coauthors on parts of this book that originate in papers: Lee Shaker on verbal participation, Nick Goedert on issue mentions, and Baxter Oliphant on interruptions. We owe Baxter an extra debt of gratitude for the many difficult hours he put in to assist with the challenging coding of interruptions. Each started out as a dedicated research assistant and transitioned into a collaborator, and we are very grateful for each phase of our association with them.

We received invaluable feedback and encouragement from colleagues. First we wish to thank Marty Gilens, an exemplary colleague and friend who read every word, took the time to really think things through, and provided essential guidance. We are also extremely grateful to Amy Lerman, Chris Achen, Markus Prior, Susan Fiske, and Pat Egan, who read the draft manuscript and spent a full day discussing it with us. The faculty research seminar at Brigham Young University provided especially helpful early feedback on several chapters, and the enthusiasm of the BYU faculty for the project encouraged us to press forward. Valerie Hudson and Jessica Preece served as insightful discussants at these events, and Dan Nielson offered generous and wise insights on early versions of several chapters. BYU colleagues Jeremy Pope, Quin Monson, and Kelly Patterson provided unstinting support and encouragement at multiple points along the way. Kathy Cramer Walsh, Michele Epstein, Amaney Jamal, Cindy Kam, Yanna Krupnikov, Nan Keohane, Jane Mansbridge, and Steve Macedo also provided helpful comments on parts of this project. Additional helpful comments came from the West Coast Experiments Conference, the NYU CESS Experiments Conference, Princeton University's CSDP seminar, and participants at various meetings and workshops, including the Harvard Kennedy School Women in Public Policy Program. We thank our former editor Chuck Myers for his ongoing interest in the project and for an insightful conversation that prompted us to conduct our analysis of school boards. Two reviewers for the Princeton University Press provided extremely helpful suggestions for revision. Tali also wishes to thank Lynn Sanders and Oliver Avens for early stimulating conversations on deliberation, and Don Kinder and Virginia Sapiro for formative teaching. We both thank Larry Bartels for his generous mentorship.

Funding was generously provided by the Center for Advanced Study in the Behavioral Sciences, BYU (including a Mentored Environment Grant and substantial support from the College of Family, Home, and Social Sciences, the Political Science Department, and the Center for the Study of Elections and Democracy), and Princeton University (we especially thank former chairs Jeff Herbst and Helen Milner, the Bobst Center and the CSDP). Money can't buy you love, but it buys nearly everything else—labor, which leads to time, which leads to mental focus, which leads to creativity and productivity.

We were also fortunate to have the help of talented undergraduate and graduate assistants. We thank Dan Myers, Lisa Argyle, and Oleg Bespalov for running many of the sessions. Quite simply, our rich data set would not exist without their long hours and commitment to the project. Early assistance came from Steve Howell, Dusan Zaric, and Jason Teeple. We are indebted to Jesse Mudrick for spending a year of his life listening to and deciphering phrases such as "yeah, you know, that thought, but what if, I agree, we wouldn't want, not that, you know, umm, [unintelligible]." Kabir Khanna provided careful, smart, and extremely helpful edits on the final manuscript. We also thank Matt Barnes, Joy Yang, Adriana Estor, Lois Lee, Oliver Bloom, Dan Chen, Alex Simon, Gabriela Gonzalez, Hayden Galloway, Josephine Borich Shipley, Bobby Purks, Krista Frederico, Greg Baker, Alex Bitter, Ashley Erickson, Jason Harrington, Kris Mahoney, Brooke Rieder, Michael Sheflo, Katherine McCabe, Luke Bell, the invaluable Chris McConnell, and Kyrene Gibb, who is suited to run a country or at least a corporation—we are incredibly lucky that she put her formidable talents to work managing our challenging though comparatively puny school boards project.

Article-length versions of several chapters were published in scholarly journals, and we thank the editors of those journals for their helpful guidance. An earlier version of chapter 5, co-authored with Lee Shaker, appeared in *The American Political Science Review* (2012, volume 106, issue 3, 533–547). A previous iteration of chapter 7, co-authored with Nicholas Goedert and employing controls for liberalism instead of egalitarianism, was published in *The American Journal of Political Science* (2014, volume 58, issue 2, 291–306), and an earlier version of chapter 8, written with Baxter Oliphant, can be found in *Perspectives on Politics*' special issue on gender and politics (2014, volume 12, issue 1, 18–44). In addition, portions of the description of our experimental research design in chapter 4 are inspired by similar descriptions found in these various journals. We are grateful to the publishers of these articles for permission to draw upon them here.

The Silent Sex

Introduction

THE TITLE OF THIS BOOK TAKES OFF FROM Simone de Beauvoir's classic tome *The Second Sex*, originally published in 1949. That book was the first ambitious piece of research on the problem of women's lower status in society. Although we have come a long way since 1949, women remain second-class citizens in reality if not in law. How this status plays out in a key arena of politics and society—public discussion—and what to do about it is the focus of our book. Women are not the "silent sex" in all domains. However, we show that they are less likely than men to talk and to influence others when discussing matters of common concern. This gender gap is far larger than women's tremendous progress in Western society would indicate. In the most powerful settings where common affairs are decided, where women are often few and discussion is governed by competitive norms, the average woman participates at only two-thirds of the average man's rate. Along with this quiescence, women are perceived as less influential, women set the agenda less effectively, and women more often fail to move the decision toward their preferences. That is, women tend to enter—and to exit—with less authority than men.

Authority is the expectation of influence, and society typically grants less of it to women than to men.[1] So men and women tend to enter the room with different levels of expected influence. However, a person can act in ways that enhance or detract from their authority. By the same token, others can act in ways that enhance or detract from another's authority. In both cases, these actions affect others' and one's own expectation that one can or should carry influence. Therefore, the actions that people exchange during discussion affect the authority gender gap.[2]

[1] We depart somewhat from the standard Weberian definition of authority as the legitimate exercise of power (Weber 1947), but our definition may be closer to the original one Weber himself offered, which is "the probability that a command with a specific content will be obeyed by a given group of persons, despite resistance, regardless of the basis on which that probability rests" (Uphoff 1989). We define authority as the expectation of influence, retaining Weber's emphasis on the probability of obedience, and following Weber, we focus on ways in which social roles and expectations confer authority.

[2] We use the term *gender* rather than *sex* to refer to the comparison of men and women, following the common practice in political science.

And those actions are in turn shaped by the rules, procedures, and the social composition of the group. Some procedures and compositions can affect the interaction in ways that elevate women's status in the group, thereby remedying the authority deficit women face. But other rules and compositions create dynamics of conversation that further erode women's low standing, and then, women tend to exit with even less than they had when they began.

The final twist is that the rules interact with the number of women present, so that the same rule works very differently depending on who is in the room. That is, the discussion group's gender composition and decision rule matter a great deal, but the effect of the former depends on the latter. When groups are composed of many women and the group uses majority rule, women's authority rises and sometimes equals that of men. But even when women are few, the right rules for collective decision making can ameliorate the gender gap in authority. Women can achieve a higher status and authority in part by their own actions—namely, by participating and articulating their preferences at rates equal to men. They also achieve this status and authority in part as a consequence of others' actions: women's authority is boosted when the degree of warmth and affirmation they receive rises. When women's status has been instantiated in these ways during discussion, women are more likely to voice their distinctive concerns and preferences and to gain influence in their own and in others' eyes. And this increased voice has an effect on collective outcomes: the group sets policies that are more generous toward the poor and vulnerable. Thus, attending to the joint consequences of who is in the room and the rules by which groups make decisions allows us to offer new insights about gender and authority.

Gender is a key theme of the book, and we use the concept of gender in several ways. First, and most obvious, gender refers to a social identity as a man or a woman. However, gender is not simply a characteristic of the individual man or woman, nor is it reducible merely to average differences between men and women. It is also a dimension of the style of interaction between individuals, which can be more masculine or more feminine. When the interaction tilts toward a style associated with men, or toward a style associated with women, it is "gendered." Similarly, gender is also a characteristic of settings. When a setting is structured in a way that emphasizes overt competition, or in a way that stresses cooperation, it is gendered, since these modes are associated with men and women, respectively.[3] These gendered aspects of interactions and of settings in turn can have an additional gendering effect by affecting the authority of women. Some of the gendered effects of interactions and settings affect women's authority by shifting the behavior of women, and some affect that authority indirectly, by shifting the behavior of men. Women can enhance

[3] See Winter (2008) for the idea that structures of discourse can be gendered without mentioning gender.

their authority by speaking more; men can lend women authority by validating their speech and supporting what they say. Our goal is to bring together these various ways in which gender matters to better understand the effects of gender on authority. We aim to do as Burns recommends: "The most successful work combining context and gender has done two things simultaneously. It has employed theories and measures placing gender in context, and it has deployed theories and measures of individual-level mechanisms, usually from psychology. In the end, this work has helped us understand not just that context enables gender to matter, but it has allowed us to begin to specify why and exactly how" (Burns 2007, 115–16).[4]

However, this book also addresses a number of issues beyond gender. First, we are exploring how people talk about economic redistribution, and therefore, our study sheds light on the determinants of policy on a salient issue of our time. Topics ranging from income inequality to poverty, to taxes, to the obligations of government, to the needs of children—all these are implicated in the discussions we investigate, and so are the policies that address these themes.

As a study of politics and public discussion, our book also speaks to those concerned with public opinion and political participation. We find that group discussion is a formidable force in shaping public opinion. But unlike many of the proliferating studies of deliberation, we attend to one very important fact about discussion: it occurs in small groups.[5] Our definition of small groups draws on a part of Verba's: "groups in which face-to-face communication is possible among all members" (1961, 12). This definition includes gatherings attended by as few as three and as many as dozens of people, and it is thus useful for capturing the dynamics of a large number of settings affecting many people. From the school board to the church committee, small groups are a defining characteristic of civic life. Yet while small groups are ubiquitous in our politics, studies of public opinion have neglected the impact of the characteristics of small groups on citizens.

Such neglect is all the more puzzling because several large literatures in economics, sociology, and psychology point to the importance of a group level of

[4] We treat gender as a category of analysis (Beckwith 2005; Ritter 2008; Scott 1986). The concept of gender invites attention to men as well as women, to men's and women's interaction within their own sex as well as with the opposite sex, to masculine and feminine styles and settings, and to ways that actions vary along a continuum from more feminine to more masculine. While it is convenient to refer in shorthand to a discrete category of femininity or masculinity, they are more useful as end points on a continuum. For example, we inquire about the conditions of deliberation that move men's and women's priorities and preferences from the feminine to the masculine, or the reverse. Making these conceptual moves carries the additional benefit of allowing us to avoid essentializing or oversimplifying gender as nothing more than fixed and unchangeable stereotypes. While we recognize enduring differences between men and women, we also want to understand how priorities and patterns of interaction between and among men and women change as the features of the group change.

[5] For some explorations of deliberation and small group dynamics, see Gastil (1993; 2010).

analysis. One of the most robust and strong findings of the literature on social dilemmas and games is that small group discussion converts a loose collective of individuals acting in their narrow self-interest into a cooperative unit acting for the common good of its members (Mendelberg 2002; Ostrom 1998). That literature finds that the group unit of analysis is crucial; for example, the group's voting rules and agenda-setting procedures significantly affect the behavior of its members (Meirowitz and Landa 2009). Using quite different paradigms, social psychologists have documented over decades the crucial impact of group factors on individual members, including the group's initial distribution of views and the persistent norms it develops (Mendelberg 2002). A group's dynamics thus operate independently of the individuals in it and can shape those individuals in important ways. The group is, to paraphrase Kurt Lewin (1951), more than the sum of its parts.

Most importantly for scholars of political behavior, as we unpack the processes of deliberation and small-group interaction, we come to understand how people communicate and how this process of communication shapes not only attitudes and policy preferences but also the fundamental bedrock of political power—the authoritative exercise of voice. We provide the largest-scale analysis to date of how the specifics of interaction build or erode power, and these insights point to the importance of social factors in constructing the currency of politics. The key insights we offer scholars of political behavior are: first, the specific nature of interaction matters by shaping the authority of group members and, thereby, the weight of their opinion in the discussion; second, social identity must be taken into account, because who is interacting with whom also matters; and third, institutions and their procedures deserve a central place in attempts to understand how group dynamics construct authority and how authority affects group decisions.

This book's focus on the social and institutional construction of authority in groups thus contributes not only to our understanding of gender and of political behavior but also to analyses of institutions. It investigates how institutions reinforce, or eliminate, social inequalities. Institutional procedures that appear neutral can in fact be systematically biased in favor of half the population. However, some rules can inoculate against the disadvantages created by society and level the playing field of political power. People walk through the door with stable differences shaped by social mechanisms, and institutions must take them as they are, but if the institution understands the nature of the social inequality it is dealing with, it can shape the way people interact, for good or for bad. The key is to recognize what scholarship on institutions seldom does: that institutions carry different effects depending on the composition of their members, and that the effects vary depending on the social identity of the member. We show this by undertaking an unusually systematic analysis of how members interact under the constraints of different rules and different social compositions.

Our focus on the group and on authority also allows us to speak to advocates —and critics—of democratic deliberation. Deliberation provides a potential remedy for the troubling ills of modern democracies. The average citizen's woefully low levels of political knowledge, reasoning, and interest in politics call out for reform. Inviting people to participate in town-meeting-style forums and revitalizing the vibrant grassroots associations of the past are promising ideas that rightly give observers and practitioners hope. But deliberation rests on the foundation of the small group. Small groups, as scholars have long known, have their own serious pitfalls. We show that one of the pitfalls most advocates of deliberation neglect is gender inequality. Women are highly disadvantaged in many deliberative settings, and this disadvantage affects everything from how long they speak, to the respect they are shown, to the content of what they say, to the influence they carry, to their sense of their own capacity, and to their power over group decisions. All the more troubling, these problems can emerge even when the terms of discussion do not, at first glance, appear to disadvantage women. The problem is not that women are disliked or formally discriminated against; rather, the problem is that while women are liked, they are not given equal authority.

We demonstrate how to use the potential of deliberation without incurring its liabilities. Deliberation can come closer to the aspirations of its advocates, but only if its practitioners attend closely to the nature of the group and the rules by which group members interact. The key lies in who is deliberating and the rules and norms of deliberation. Deliberation requires careful institutional design, and we offer guidelines for that design.

To move beyond the existing literatures on deliberation, we rely on speech-act theory rather than on the philosophical assumptions of deliberation's advocates. This theory is a general approach to the study of language that emphasizes its social meaning and functions (Holtgraves 2002, 5–6). While scholars of deliberation tend to focus on rationality, and thus on the truth-value, logic, and evidence that talk communicates, we take a different tack. We are not studying the types of phenomena that scholars of political behavior tend to study: knowledge gains, increasing tolerance of cultural difference, the group's polarization to an extreme decision, or the effects of diverse preferences. Because we treat language as an act that conveys social meaning, such as status, or human connection, we analyze its social impact rather than the quality of the information or the level of reasoning contained in language.[6] Because speech is a social act, it shapes rapport and connection as well as efficacy and influence. We

[6]Developments in the philosophy of language have helped to recast the notion of language as a conduit of logical meaning into the notion of language as a form of social action. Speech act theory, propounded by the philosophers John Searle and J. L. Austin, claims that language is a set of rules that people use to enact their intention. Relatedly, Ludwig Wittgenstein argued that the meaning of language derives from the associations people form between it and their social contexts. See the discussion by Maynard and Peräkylä (2003).

examine speech as a form of symbolic political or civic participation that may reflect and contribute to the sense of political efficacy and authority—in short, as a political act that creates civic standing.

Our book brings not only renewed attention but also innovative methods to the question of how to create such standing for women. While some leaders and moderators of such groups, and scholars of small group settings, have long assumed that gender matters, and taken steps to include women, our findings can make several new contributions.[7]

First, this book uses controlled experiments that randomly vary the conditions of discussion, using many groups. Those results are validated with a study of naturally occurring groups. These methodological moves represent an advance, showing rigorously the depth of the problem and the great success of the solutions. While some practitioners and scholars understand the perils of the gender inequality we document, many do not fully do so. The most recent study on this subject, by Hickerson and Gastil, concludes that gender inequality is not a big problem, and that its findings "shift the burden of evidence somewhat by challenging deliberation's critics to find compelling examples of difference effects in well-structured and consequential deliberative spaces" (2008, 300). Our evidence establishes that gender inequality is deep and pervasive despite the steps commonly assumed to guard against it.

Second, the group's formal procedures are often neglected in these literatures yet turn out to matter a great deal. We show when and why unanimous decision rule, and the consensus process it can generate, improves gender equality in deliberation—and when it does not do so. Third, in previous studies, group gender composition is often overlooked, or measured inseparably from individual gender, or hampered by inconclusive tests or inconsistent findings. We explain these inconsistencies and show when they disappear. Fourth, we have put all these elements together and added to the picture a fine-grained analysis of actual interaction and the contents of speech, at the level of the individual member. To our knowledge, no previous study has done so. Finally and most important, some of the practices deemed to alleviate the problem of inequality, such as a consensus process, do not work in all cases, because they do not take into account the combination of gender composition and the rules of discussion.[8] We offer an explanation for the successes of procedures that have a long tradition in the practice of small group discussion—and for the problems of those same procedures, problems that many dialogue practitioners have failed to notice.

Potential applications for our findings are found in all corners of civic life. In that sense, this book intends to shed light not only on deliberation preced-

[7] This paragraph is elaborated and supported in the conclusion chapter.

[8] Specifically, consensus building and inclusive processes may actually backfire for women when they are the majority, a problem not recognized in any scholarship but one we document. For more on such processes, see Gastil (1993; 2008).

ing a formal decision but also on dialogue groups, work meetings, investigative committees, boards of civic associations, classrooms, and many settings where people convene and converse over matters of common concern. The gender dynamics of groups play out anywhere people gather and interact with each other in more formal settings.

Our own experiences in academia have provided numerous opportunities to observe such interactions, and it is clear to us that the number of women present and the group's norm of interaction matter. In Karpowitz's department, women's representation is a salient issue. In Mendelberg's department, one notable experience reinforces this conclusion.

Every year, Mendelberg's academic department at Princeton assembles committees of its faculty to make initial decisions about hiring and promotion. Women compose approximately 25% of the faculty in the department. On a typical hiring committee, women are a minority, and the interaction tends to be competitive. But once in a while, the gender composition veers off this average. On one committee, Mendelberg served entirely with other women. The group consisted of five people, the same size as the groups assembled for our experiment. All were tenured. None was a shrinking violet. Yet in this group, unlike any of the other committees, the interaction took on what can only be described as a norm of niceness. The members affirmed each other's statements. They smiled and nodded. Each person spoke, and at length. The group did not lack for deep disagreements; the members each came from a different field within the department, and their research paradigms were as disparate as can be found in the social sciences. But the general tenor of the interaction was geared toward validating the speaker's basic worth as a group member. By the end, the group had reached agreement, not through conformity, but out of mutual respect. What happened at this meeting? How exactly did the group generate warmth, and how does that rapport lead to inclusion and genuine consensus? Why was this meeting different from all the others? And how can groups composed of both men and women institutionalize procedures that replicate this dynamic? This book tells the story of this meeting writ large.

CHAPTER 1

The Problem

New Jersey's Governor Chris Christie was a darling of the Republican Party when he rolled into the town of Princeton for a public relations blitz in November 2011. The governor had just declined calls to run for the highest office in the land and was riding high in opinion polls. On this day, he was putting his political capital to work in a town meeting with some 150 residents. Christie lumbered into the local public library's common room and spoke in his trademark pugnacious style. He voiced some themes of his agenda and then opened the floor to the residents of Princeton. The lowliest, the poorest, and the most powerless people in the town now had the chance to tell the governor directly whatever they wished him to know.

Christie chose a public meeting as the optimal setting to publicize his agenda and score political points. Even in today's mass media society, meetings are a backbone of politics. Not only do they air pressing matters, they also symbolize the heart and soul of a community. In a recent national survey, when Americans were asked "the best way for officials to learn what the majority of people in our country think about important issues," they gave a resounding approval to town meetings, choosing them as their favorite means. By a ratio of 2 to 1 they preferred town meetings to the second favorite, opinion polls.[1] Americans want their political system to be a meeting democracy.

This is not merely wishful talk. Between a quarter and a third of American citizens participate in deliberative settings in any given year—as many as contribute to campaigns, far more than the number who work for a political campaign or engage in protest, and nearly as many as the percentage who contact a public official.[2] Aside from all this discourse directed by or at government,

[1] By a ratio of 4 to 1 they would rather see officials talking to people in town meetings than "talking to people at malls or on the street" or to people who "call, write, or e-mail" the official. The telephone poll was conducted by the Kaiser Family Foundation and Princeton Survey Research Associates from January to March 2001, with 1,206 randomly sampled adults, and reported in the *Public Perspective* July/August 2001.

[2] Various estimates converge to show that the percentage of Americans who attend a public meeting at least once a year is between 25% and 38%. The numbers of attendance compared to

it seems that everywhere Americans turn, a meeting of their fellows is waiting for them.[3] Americans talk in groups with their compatriots at work, at their religious institutions, or in their voluntary associations—clubs, charities, homeowner associations, neighborhood groups, professional and trade organizations, and PTAs. Of the three-quarters of Americans who belong to an association of some kind, over a quarter serve on its board (Burns, Schlozman, and Verba 2001, 76).[4] Most Americans affiliate with a church, and most of them serve on its board at some point (90).[5] Americans are committed to committees. Long ago, the famous French observer Alexis de Tocqueville noted that Americans love to gather together, talk, and act for a common purpose (Tocqueville [1835] 2006, 192).[6] The iconic moment in the birth of our nation, the Boston

---

other activities are from the 2000 National Election Study; 27% of respondents report attending a meeting in the past twelve months. The 1990 Citizen Participation study finds that 77% of women and 80% of men are members of an organization (political or not), and of these, 49% and 50% respectively report attending a meeting of the organization at least once in the past year, meaning that about 38% of Americans attend a meeting of their organization at least once a year (based on Burns, Schlozman, and Verba 2001, 76, table 3.2). American attendance in public meetings has declined (Karpowitz 2006), but about 75% of Americans report attending a public meeting at some point in their lives (Karpowitz 2006, chapter 2). Conover, Searing, and Crewe estimate a similar number (29%) for Americans and a slightly lower number for British citizens (Conover, Searing, and Crewe 2002, table 3). Jacobs, Cook, and Delli Carpini (2009) found that 25% of Americans engaged in face-to-face deliberation ("attending a formal or informal meeting in the past year to discuss a local, national, or international issue," 37–40); 68% informally discussed issues ("informal face-to-face or phone conversations or exchanges with people you know about public issues that are local, national, or international concerns" at least "a few times a month," 36); and 81% engaged in at least one form of discursive participation within the last year (38; see generally Jacobs, Cook, and Delli Carpini 2009, 42). When they are invited to participate in a face-to-face deliberation, 25% of Americans are willing to do so (Neblo et al. 2010). By contrast, the heralded age of online discussion has not yet materialized; the best and most recent estimate is that a mere 4% of Americans participate in online deliberation (Jacobs, Cook, and Delli Carpini 2009, 40). Finally, the median meeting size is forty (Jacobs, Cook, and Delli Carpini 2009, 60). In all, then, deliberation still occurs in groups small enough for face-to-face interaction, and with sufficient frequency to make its study worthwhile.

[3] This phrase is an allusion to Tocqueville, cited below.

[4] Serve on the board, or been an officer, in the past five years.

[5] Percent affiliated with a religious institution: 74% and 58% of women and men respectively; served on board or as officer within past five years: 49% and 61% respectively.

[6] On his observational tour of the upstart new democracy across the Atlantic, Tocqueville chronicled a political culture bustling with meetings, discussion, and other indicators of vibrant civic life: "The political activity that pervades the United States must be seen to be understood. No sooner do you set foot upon American ground than you are stunned by a kind of tumult . . . here the people of one quarter of a town are meeting to decide upon the building of a church; there the election of a representative is going on; a little farther, the delegates of a district are hastening to the town in order to consult upon some local improvements; in another place, the laborers of a village quit their plows to deliberate upon a project of a road or a public school . . . To take a hand in the regulation of society and to discuss it is the biggest concern and, so to speak, the only pleasure an American knows" (Tocqueville [1835] 2006, 249–50). Contrary to this portrait, the average contemporary American taking in the weekend game or carousing on a night out does seem to know pleasures aside from discussion. But Tocqueville was on to something. We take from him

Tea Party, came to life at a public meeting in Old South Meeting House (Young 2011). Americans are still joiners, lamentations of declining bowling leagues notwithstanding. But they are more than joiners; they are meeters. The organizations they join still rest on the foundation of the public meeting. And what people do at meetings is talk.

But what no one noticed at the meeting with Governor Christie is that in this poster child of democracy, where all could speak their mind to all, one-half of the population spoke *twice as much* as the other half. That quiescence mattered; the louder half received over twice the governor's time in response.[7] And perhaps surprisingly, this pattern had nothing to do with race or class or political party; the quieter half—the population that spoke little and to whom little was said—was the female half.

Two speakers illustrate the dynamic at the meeting, and the pattern we will document in this book. One speaker was a twenty-something student, liberal, articulate, and passionate. The other speaker was also a twenty-something student, also liberal, articulate, and passionate. Both voiced clear positions and stated relevant facts. Both struck a civil tone as they challenged the governor on a salient issue of the day. But the female speaker took only 63% of the floor time of the male. And she received 29% of the response time devoted to the male. While all the citizens in attendance were equal, some were more equal than others—but not for the reasons we commonly suspect.

It is one of the best documented facts of American politics that groups with less power and authority in society are less likely to participate in politics (Verba, Schlozman, and Brady 1995). But we typically think of these groups as defined by lines of race, ethnicity, language, income, age, or education. In modern America, observers of politics focus on the political disadvantages of groups with less resources: those left out of the privileges of class, those still stigmatized by race, those struggling as new arrivals from far-off places. But the quiescent half at the meeting was none of these groups. To the contrary, as residents of one of the wealthiest towns in America, they were members of the country's moneyed and social elite. They were the "1%," or close to it. But they were the *female* "1%."

The women of Princeton are members of some of the top households of the most powerful nation in the world, yet in the setting that Americans idealize as the heart of democracy, they took half the floor time of the men and got half the attention of the highest official of their state. When Ralph Waldo Emerson described the meetings in his town of Concord, Massachusetts, he wrote that every person "has his fair weight in the government" (Mansbridge 1983, 133). By our notions of fairness, Emerson was wrong about the men

---

the insight that democracy rests on active meetings attended by all, and that part of the key to their success is their cultivation of social bonds among participants.

[7]The governor took eight minutes to reply to the quieter half, and twenty minutes to the talkative half. A later town hall meeting with the governor in a different part of the state exhibited a similar pattern, e.g., male audience members took more turns, made more follow-up comments, and received more speaking turns back. These findings are from our direct observations.

of Massachusetts, most of whom were denied the ability to carry any weight in government by exclusions of property, race, or age (132–33). Clearly, at a time when women were excluded from eligibility, he was not even thinking of women. The America of today is not the America of Emerson. But what goes with little notice is that even now, in a historical age when women have made great strides in American society, and when women vote in greater numbers than men, America's female citizens greatly underparticipate relative to men in key areas of politics and other public settings of decision making.[8] Women lack a "fair weight in the government."

Princeton is not your typical American town, but its gender inequality is far from an anomaly. The only comprehensive study of "open, face-to-face, legislative democracy in general purpose governments" is Frank Bryan's book, *Real Democracy* (2004, 216). Bryan, a political scientist and fan of New England, took it upon himself to crisscross every last acre of Vermont out of sheer passion for town meetings. He and his students can recount in loving detail what transpired in each of a jaw-dropping 1,389 meetings in that state. Bryan found that although women composed 46% of attenders, they contributed only 28% of the speaking turns to the average meeting. Most men speak; most women don't.[9] In only 8% of the meetings Bryan studied were women more likely to speak than men.[10] Attending the meeting is not the same as speaking up. Speech is an act of political participation in its own right. And while women are dutifully showing up, they are not actively participating.

Gender Inequality and Descriptive Representation in Deliberative Settings

Women make up 50.1% of the world's adult population, but 20% of its leaders.[11] At first thought, this massive gap is easily discounted as yet another unfortunate dysfunction of the many third-world countries that populate the globe. But

[8] We review studies of women's underparticipation in chapters 2 and 3.

[9] To be exact, 52% of men speak; 34% of women do.

[10] Calculated from numbers on pages 216–17. "Women's speech exceed men's speech in 105 meetings" (Bryan 2004, 216), combined with the overall number of meetings reported under figure 9.1 (217). Women compose 36% of the speakers (Bryan 2004, 214). The sample was drawn randomly from Vermont towns, but some towns were repeatedly sampled. The large majority of the sample has between two hundred and five thousand residents. The data set has 1,435 meetings. As a point of comparison, Mansbridge found a similar pattern of gender inequality in her study of face-to-face deliberation (1983).

[11] The figure of the adult population is from United States Census Bureau—International Data Base. http://www.census.gov/population/international/data/idb/region.php?N=%20Region%20Results%20&T=1&A=both&RT=0&Y=2012&R=1&C=. The 20% figure is from Crowder-Meyer 2010. The most up-to-date figure for leaders is 19.5%. http://www.un.org/apps/news/story.asp?NewsID=41445&Cr=un+women&Cr1. (See also Dahlerup 2012, vii). http://www.cnn.com/2012/06/28/world/europe/women-politics-global-power/index.html?iid=article_sidebar.

the gap does not naturally go away as a society achieves economic and social progress.[12] Twenty percent is just as accurate in the United States as in Turkmenistan.[13] And 20% is the number not only in the highest level of national government, where the ranks of women might be thinnest, but at the local level as well, in towns all across the United States and many other developed nations (Crowder-Meyer 2010).[14]

Sounding the alarm, the United Nations declared that all member states should adopt 30% minimum targets for women in all political bodies by 1995.[15] A who's who of leading international institutions has issued similar proclamations. The European Union, the Organization of American States, and the African Union have all declared that their continent should adopt specific compositions of women in their official decision making (Krook 2009).

The movement toward women's descriptive representation—that is, increasing women's physical presence in decision making (Pitkin 1967)—is not mere rhetoric. Of the fifty-nine countries holding elections in 2011, seventeen mandated quotas in their legislatures.[16] As of that year, fifty-two countries had introduced legal gender quotas of some kind in elections, and in approximately forty more, at least one political party uses voluntary gender quotas to choose its candidates (Dahlerup 2012, vii; see also Krook 2008, table 2; Krook 2009). Most countries have implemented a political quota for women of some kind (Pande and Ford 2011, 8). Similar efforts are being implemented in quasi-public or private domains, such as laws requiring minimal female representation on corporate boards, enacted in Spain, Iceland, the Netherlands, Norway, and France (10).[17]

[12] Inglehart and Norris's comparative study finds that, at least during the mid-1990s, the gender gap in political representation was closing more slowly than the gender gap in other areas of society, including education, legal rights, and economic opportunities (2000).

[13] http://www.ipu.org/wmn-e/classif.htm. The United States and Turkmenistan are tied at 78 in this ranking of percentage of women in the lower or single House.

[14] In some cases the percentage is closer to 25%. Significant exceptions to the 20% figure are the Nordic countries, where women compose 42% of the national legislatures, and the Arab states, with 11%. http://www.cnn.com/2012/06/28/world/europe/women-politics-global-power/index.html?iid=article_sidebar.

[15] The 30% figure was endorsed by the United Nations Economic and Social Council as a goal to be achieved by 1995 (Report of the Fourth World Conference on Women, Beijing, September 4–15, 1995, http://www.un.org/womenwatch/daw/beijing/platform/decision.htm, accessed June 14, 2013). The United Nations Fourth World Conference on Women, which met in Beijing, included a reference to this 30% goal in its report and issued the Beijing Declaration and Platform for Action, signed unanimously by all 189 member states. This conference approved a resolution stating "[Governments should] commit themselves to establishing the goal of gender balance in governmental bodies and committees, as well as in public administrative entities, and in the judiciary, including, *inter alia*, setting specific targets and implementing measures to substantially increase the number of women with a view to achieving equal representation of women and men, if necessary through positive action, in all governmental and public administration positions" (paragraph 190, part a).

[16] http://www.un.org/apps/news/story.asp?NewsID=41445&Cr=un+women&Cr1.

[17] Other countries have quotas for state-owned companies, including Israel, South Africa, Denmark, Finland, Ireland, and Switzerland (Pande and Ford 2011, 11).

Unlike some reforms adopted on a world scale, this one has not entirely bypassed the United States. Although the United States has fewer and weaker requirements than many other countries, public and quasi-public efforts have been made to increase women's presence. The state of Iowa, for example, has passed several rounds of legal mandates for "gender balance" in response to the low numbers of women on its appointed boards (Hannagan and Larimer 2011a). Federal law requires that boards be representative of "social identities" (Mansbridge 1999).[18] Both the Democratic and Republican parties have used gender in choosing party representatives for committees or national convention delegates (Baer 2003, 127–31).[19]

As public officials made a concerted effort to bring women into their representative bodies, another equally ambitious democratic reform effort was taking off around the globe. Along the length of the Americas, in island nations off the coast of Africa, in the heart of Europe, in remote villages throughout India, and even in communist China, ordinary people are finding themselves invited to participate in official attempts to bring power to the people. The setting in each case would look strikingly familiar to Emerson and his compatriots in their New England town meetings. What these groups are doing, each in their own way, is deliberating about the pressing issues of the day. Citizens have gathered in locations as disparate as Porto Alegre, Brazil; British Columbia, Canada; Rajasthan, India; São Tomé and Príncipe; Benin; and the state of Texas.

[18]The issue of gender representation on corporate boards has received attention recently; for example, Catalyst conducts regular counts of women's numbers on Fortune 500 boards (in 2012, women composed 17% overall, and fewer than 20% of boards had at least 25% female directors. http://www.catalyst.org/knowledge/2012-catalyst-census-fortune-500-women-board-directors. The Securities and Exchange Commission required in 2010 that corporate boards disclose their formal efforts to achieve diversity. http://online.wsj.com/article_email/SB10001424052702303990604577368344256435440-lMyQjAxMTAyMDMwMDEzNDAyWj.html. Women's presence on corporate boards does not automatically rise with women's growing education or income. According to Pande and Ford, "increased education and labor participation rates among women are only weakly correlated with the number of women in leadership positions in the corporate sector. Despite the increase to over 50% women currently working in high-paying management and professional positions in the U.S., the percent of female CEOs in the Fortune 500 companies only increased from 0.2% in 1995 to 3% in 2009. While women constitute 15.2% of board directors in the U.S. and 12.2% in the UK, the percentage of women directors in the top companies (Fortune 500 and the FTSE 100) increased by less than 0.5% average per year over the last 10 to 15 years. The trends are not much different in developing countries" (2011, 5).

[19]According to Krook, Lovenduski, and Squires: "Soon after women gained the right to vote in 1920, the Democratic party mandated that the Democratic National Committee (DNC) be composed of one man and one woman from each state and territory. The Republican party adopted a similar measure that same year, which they abandoned in 1952 but replaced in 1960 with a rule calling for 50–50 representation in all convention committees. . . . the DNC later ratified guidelines requiring state parties to select women as national convention delegates in proportion to their presence in the state population. When these reforms came under attack in 1972, the party rewrote delegate selection rules to ban 'quotas' in favour of 'affirmative action.' The Republicans, in contrast, chose not to regulate the state parties, although some states mandated 50–50 representation on their state central committees" (2009, 792–93).

Anywhere from a handful of individuals all the way up to 6% of the adult population of the country has participated in these forums. People are not merely spewing hot air at these meetings; they are actually governing. The citizens of British Columbia used a face-to-face assembly to recommend a new electoral system to their fellow citizens. Indian village meetings are constitutionally empowered to decide many of the issues that directly affect quality of life in the most basic way. And the list goes on.[20]

The best evidence we have for the broad scope of deliberative settings comes from the United States. As many as 97% of American cities hold public meetings, and most large cities rely on active neighborhood councils (Macedo et al. 2005, 66; Karpowitz 2006). Over one thousand towns conduct formal New England–style town meetings in the United States (Bryan 2004, 3). Some states, such as Oregon, use citizen deliberation groups to plan state budgets; environmental protection assessments routinely include citizen meetings; and important policy domains, such as medical research priorities, are informed by citizen deliberation (Gastil 2000; Ryfe 2004; Simonsen and Robbins 2000). Well over three million US citizens serve on deliberating juries each year (Gastil et al. 2010, 4), and approximately a third will have served on a jury at some point in their lives (Devine et al. 2001, 622; Gastil et al. 2010, 4, note 3). Over fifty million people belong to one of over one-quarter million homeowners associations (Macedo et al. 2005, 102).

But while deliberative democracy is being cultivated in the grass roots, women's representation in these settings has been wallowing in the backwater. Few have applied the question of women's equality from the arena of legislatures to these forums for the people.[21] Seldom do we ask how to design these deliberations so that half the population can find equal voice.[22]

[20] See Ban and Rao 2009; Besley et al. 2005a; and Chattopadhyay and Duflo 2004. In 1993 the Indian constitution was amended to require the Indian states to grant full power over the allocation of expenditures to the most local level—village councils (Gram Panchayats), which decide on the provision of local services such as drinking water, irrigation, public buildings, roads, social services such as pensions for widows and the aged, and in some cases, informal education. It also required that one-third of village council seats, and of the council heads, be set aside for a woman. These are also set aside for Scheduled Castes and Scheduled Tribes, who are disadvantaged populations in India, in proportion to their district population. In every major state since then, at least 25% of council heads are female. The village council must hold village meetings open to any voter in that village (Gram Sabhas or Gram Sansads) to report its activities, bring its budget to a vote, and decide on recipients of social programs, at a minimum of two to four yearly village-wide meetings. Finally, the council head must "set up regular office hours where villagers can lodge complaints or requests" (Chattopadhyay and Duflo 2004, 1412).

[21] While the British Columbia Citizens' Assembly explicitly secured equal descriptive representation of men and women (James 2008, 110), we are not aware of reports of women's substantive or symbolic representation.

[22] It would be easy to assume that a random sample of the population will provide adequate descriptive representation, and it may do so (see Fishkin 1995), but as we show, that will not necessarily secure equal substantive or symbolic representation for women.

And when scholars ask this question, they often cannot produce a clear answer. In studies of participation in Indian village meetings, a team of researchers has concluded, "it is clear that Gram Sabhas (village meetings) are not a forum for women in their current form" (Besley et al. 2005a, 656).[23] The usual variables that enhance the attendance rates of disadvantaged groups including the landless, illiterate, and Scheduled Castes and Tribes—such as village literacy—actually *depress* women's participation significantly (Besley et al. 2005a, 653, table 2). Similarly, Pamela Conover, Donald Searing, and Ivor Crewe included controls on a host of possible variables that could explain why British and American women report engaging in fewer political discussions than men, but the gender gap persisted nonetheless (2002, table 7).[24] Not only do we seldom study women's representation in deliberative democracy, when we do, we are left scratching our heads. Frank Bryan, one of the few scholars to rigorously study this question in the United States, has recently declared, "for the life of me and after thirty years of research, I remain stumped when it comes to predicting women's involvement" in public meetings (Bryan 2004, 249).[25]

The best hopes for women's equal representation have come from "critical mass" theory. Elegantly formulated by Rosabeth Moss Kanter, the theory predicts that where women compose less than 15%, men's culture dominates. Women function there as mere tokens. They have little influence or agency and must conform to masculine ways. But where women's percentage climbs well beyond 15% and reaches up to 40%, women can begin to make a difference. Indeed, the United Nations justified its 30% female target on the premise of this notion. Its formal language states, "The figure of 30 percent forms the so-called 'critical mass,' believed to be necessary for women to make a visible impact on the style and content of political decision-making."[26] And should women reach a balance with men, their experience and power improves further still. Or so the theory goes.

[23] Ban and Rao (2009) studied speaking in 121 Indian village meetings constitutionally empowered to make important local distributional decisions. The transcripts were matched with data from household surveys conducted in the village before the meeting, allowing them to see whose preferences were expressed and implemented.

[24] Conover, Searing, and Crewe's (2002) measure of participation in political discussion includes discussion in public meetings or in informal situations in public places such as workplaces and churches.

[25] Policy makers and nonprofit organizations have become interested in deliberation as a means of democratization and addressing corruption. In India, village meetings are constitutionally empowered to make important local decisions that affect private and public goods. The idea is that meetings can increase the transparency and accountability of government overall. In a society permeated by political corruption, these are urgent goals. But the risk of grassroots, local participation in decision making is that those with disproportionate influence will "capture" these processes and undermine the reform (Ban and Rao 2009). As Cornwall put it, women "are those most likely to lose out, finding themselves and their interests marginalized or overlooked in apparently 'participatory' processes" (2003, 1325; Guijt and Kaul Shah 1998; Mayoux 1995; and Mosse 1995).

[26] http://www.un.org/womenwatch/daw/egm/eql-men/, accessed June 14, 2013.

The problem is that women's percentage in deliberating bodies matters little —in itself. At issue is that descriptive representation may not translate into substantive representation—the actual expression and implementation of women's preferences. Nor will it unfailingly translate into symbolic representation—the sense that women can and should exercise power. There is puzzlingly mixed support for the prediction that increasing numbers yield increasing rates of participation or influence. In fact, in some settings, such as Vermont's town meetings, the higher women's percentage in the deliberating body, the *lower* is their share of the speakers (Bryan 2004, 222). Even reaching the promised land of gender balance seems woefully insufficient. Princeton's women made up 53% of those present at the town hall meeting with the governor, but 25% of the speakers, a pattern that mirrors Bryan's results from Vermont town meetings (cited earlier in this chapter; Bryan 2004, 216–17). A study of New York City's online discussions among city residents, held to consider rebuilding the World Trade Center, found similar results. While women's proportion of participants mirrored the city's population (around 50%), it dropped by about 10 points among active contributors to discussion—the upper quartile of participants, who posted about 80% of the posts (Trenel 2009).[27] That is, even in today's United States, where women are better educated than men and even outpace men in voter turnout, meetings are characterized by a significant gap between women's physical presence in deliberation and their participation in it, especially their active participation.

The weak or inconsistent effect of critical mass in citizen forums is not limited to the northeastern United States. The pattern repeats in midwestern college towns, in Israeli kibbutzim, and in Indian villages.[28] For example, while some studies find that village leadership quotas for Indian women "benefit their villages while providing the public goods preferred by women," others find that increasing women's descriptive representation matters little (Ban and Rao 2008b; 2009, 6).[29]

Numbers alone do not determine the active use of voice, and this is a familiar refrain in recent legislative studies of women. Specifically, larger numbers of women in the legislature do not consistently increase women's influence, or the substantive representation of women's distinctive priorities and perspectives (for example, Carroll 2001; Franceschet, Krook, and Piscopo 2012; Reingold 2000; 2008, 132, 140).[30] The reasons include the overriding influence of party membership (and the allocation of power according to the party's position in the legislature), women's lack of seniority, the imperative to represent constitu-

[27] This held particularly in bare-bones facilitated settings but not in actively facilitated settings; however, the study has methodological issues that make conclusions about facilitation difficult.

[28] Bryan 2004, 214, note 2, and 216, note 6; Ban and Rao 2009.

[29] Positive findings are reported by Chattopadhyay and Duflo (2004).

[30] Reingold concludes that "there is no clear, positive relationship between sex ratios in legislative rosters and 1) the frequency or magnitude of sex differences in legislative behavior or 2) overall levels of policy activity or outcomes promoting women's political interests" (2008, 140).

ency interests rather than women's distinctive concerns, women's heavy dependence on male elites and patrons who are the gatekeepers to elected positions or resources, and male legislators' backlash against women's legislative gains.[31]

For example, even after female members of the British Labour Party crossed well over the 15% threshold of elected members of the House of Commons, they still perceived hostility from male colleagues when they attempted to use a more feminine style, reporting pressure "to conform to the traditional norms of the House" (Childs 2004a). Or in New Zealand, though women's numbers increased to around 30%, their feminizing effect on decision making and policy remained negligible (Grey 2002). Even as women near an even split, they do not always advance. In Rwanda, women have composed nearly half the legislators, yet their balanced number made no apparent difference to policy outcomes (Devlin and Elgie 2008). That is, despite rising numbers, the institution often remains steeped in a masculine culture, and women fail to achieve the voice and authority predicted by theories of critical mass (Lovenduski 2005).

Not only do numbers often fail to advance women's representation, but also studies in various settings document a backlash as women's numbers increase. For example, in US state legislatures, as the proportion of women increased, male committee chairs became more verbally dominant and less inclusive of women (Kathlene 1994; Rosenthal 1998, 90). As Kathlene concluded: "women legislators, despite their numerical and positional gains, may be seriously disadvantaged in committee hearings and unable to participate equally" (1994, 572). Validating this backlash notion with an entirely different type of action—US House members' campaign contributions to fellow members—Kanthak and Krause found that as the proportion of women increases in the member's party, men decrease their contributions to women while increasing them to men (Kanthak and Krause 2010). These discouraging patterns obtain in a variety of countries. In New Zealand, for example, the representation of women's issues was set back as women increased from approximately 15% to 30% (Grey 2006).

Taking stock of the research on women's numbers, Beckwith and Cowell-Meyers argue that "critical mass theory is both problematic and under-theorized," its mechanism "unspecified," and the power of small numbers of women "neglected" (2007, 553). Dahlerup finds that "the number of women in parliaments is probably not the most crucial factor" in women's ability to exercise political power (2006, 520).[32] Htun and Weldon find that feminist movements and organizations in civil society affect social policy much more

[31] Beckwith 2007; Bratton 2005; Dodson 2006; Franceschet, Krook, and Piscopo 2012, 237–41; Walsh 2012.

[32] Dahlerup typifies the conclusions of many studies in arguing that more important than critical mass are the standard factors predicting any type of policy success, such as the "political context," the strength of relevant social movements and interest groups, and the "prevailing discourses" and frames (2006, 520). See also Htun and Weldon (2012) and Weldon (2002), who find that in policies that combat violence against women, feminist movements matter more than women in legislatures or other factors.

than "intra-legislative political phenomena such as . . . women in government" (2012, abstract). And as Franceschet, Krook, and Piscopo sum it up, raising women's numbers "may have positive, mixed, and sometimes even perverse effects on women's political representation" (2012, 13). That is, increasing numbers do not always help, and sometimes backfire.

Not only do women fail to reach consistent gains by exceeding the 15%, or even the 40% threshold, they may accomplish more when they are few. In some state legislatures, female "tokens" are more likely to sponsor and enact women's issue bills than men in that legislature, and may be as successful as the more numerous women in more gender-balanced legislatures (Bratton 2005). A critical mass may do little that a few exceptional "token" women accomplish as well or even better, according to some cross-national studies (Childs and Krook 2006; Crowley 2004; Kittilson 2008, 324). Such findings lead some to suggest that scholars "give up" on the notion that critical mass matters and instead study "critical actors" (Childs and Krook 2006). In sum, small numbers may not be fatal, just as large numbers may not be sufficient.

When do numbers change the masculine environment, give women a more equal effective voice, and lead to meaningful increases in women's substantive representation? Why do small numbers of women sometimes succeed?

The common denominator from many of these studies is the notion that the features of political institutions and contexts can determine whether, and how, women's numbers matter. For example, larger numbers help when women use institutional mechanisms to work collaboratively (Duerst-Lahti 2002a, 380; Thomas 2005, 253–54; Thomas and Welch 2001). Conversely, when the institution's incentives or structures tie women's fortunes to male party elites and make a women's coalition unlikely or weak, women have trouble turning their larger numbers into change (Franceschet, Krook, and Piscopo 2012). Numbers also help when they are accompanied by explicit efforts to empower women, such as through the advance of feminist movements and organizations, or when the discourse environment is receptive to women's voices (Beckwith and Cowell-Meyers 2007, 557; Studlar and McAllister 2002; Grey 2006). That is, the effects of numbers depend on institutional features. Not every study explicitly draws this conclusion, but these studies' evidence is consistent with it.

In this book we show why numbers do not matter on their own in formal discussions and why the combined effects of numbers and institutions help us to solve the puzzle of women's representation in deliberating bodies. Large numbers need particular institutional norms and rules in order to work. Moreover, we explain when and why small numbers can work quite well. The key is that the factors of numbers and institutional norms or rules jointly shape the status of deliberators within the group. Deliberation is a site of power and authority. It is one way that people with power exercise that power, and one place where people without authority can gain it. The numbers and the rules shape women's position in deliberation, and the very nature of deliberation itself, such that women's authority falls, or rises, accordingly. By unpacking the black box of deliberation, we can come to understand women's participation, influence, and authority.

We began with a puzzle. Women are more likely to be absent than present in the settings where public decisions are discussed and made. Moreover, even when they sit at the table in increasing numbers, they often participate and influence at low rates. Despite considerable study, the key to the puzzle has remained elusive. The problem has gained urgency as the effort to democratize has cultivated more opportunities for citizen deliberation, supplementing discussion in official bodies. The main remedy pursued so far is to raise the number of women to a critical mass. But that remedy seems to fail on its own. We show how, why, and what to do about it.

Why Does Women's Low Voice and Authority Matter?

Women's underrepresentation matters for a number of reasons. These reasons are grounded in one big starting point: women and men tend to differ in important respects. To be sure, the large variance within gender tends to exceed the typically small differences between the two sexes (Sapiro 2003). Yet despite the considerable diversity of women's views, a host of scholarly findings point to persistent average gender differences in some priorities and perspectives. Regardless of the sources of these differences, they are bolstered by the fact that society continues to be structured in part by gendered social roles, occupations, and divisions of labor. People tend to internalize the expectations that correspond to their assigned gender. Women and men are socialized from birth into respective feminine and masculine ways of acting, thinking, and feeling. Women's formal and implicit roles, their values, and even their core motives and personality are thus shaped in the mold of what society defines as feminine.[33]

Feminine habits of mind tend to be defined as cooperative and caring for others, so it is no surprise that women on average exhibit a stronger tendency in that direction. Women tend to have more empathy than men (Baron-Cohen 2003).[34] They are more likely than men to cooperate when there are no strategic incentives to do so (Eckel and Grossman 1998) and generally display somewhat more communal orientations (Huddy, Cassese, and Lizotte 2008, 33). Women are much more reluctant to endorse force and coercion than are men (Conover and Sapiro 1993). Women tend to be more religious and more oriented to community standards and morals (Burns, Schlozman, and Verba 2001; Clark and Clark 1993; Eagly et al. 2004; Huddy, Cassese, and Lizotte 2008, 44) and more responsive to social sanctions (Barr 2004).

[33] We elaborate and support these claims in chapters 2 and 3.

[34] But see Huddy, Cassese, and Lizotte (2008, 39).

Consequently, while women and men share much in common, and while women disagree with one another on many issues, women nevertheless tend to have some political priorities that differ from men's. Women, more than men, tend to favor, and to prioritize, the needs of those who are vulnerable, disadvantaged, poor, exploited, or stigmatized (Andersen 1996; Gilens 1988; Huddy, Cassese, and Lizotte 2008; Shapiro and Mahajan 1986; Sears and Huddy 1990).[35] These tendencies hold true for elites, such as officials in legislatures, as well as for ordinary citizens (Childs 2004b; Miguel 2012; Poggione 2004; Swers 1998; Thomas 1991, 1994).

Such preferences represent an important set of political viewpoints that are valuable in their own right, and if women do not participate fully, their distinctive concerns and perspectives may not find full representation. When women's voices are absent, those distinctive considerations are likely to be lost, to the detriment of the group.

By extension, greater participation from women could affect the decisions and outcomes that emerge from institutions. Policy can look very different when made by women—the needs of vulnerable populations tend to be placed front and center, and the poor become less destitute. When women are empowered under the right conditions, they are more likely than men to speak for, sponsor and advocate, or vote for policies that assist women, children, families, stigmatized or disadvantaged minorities, and the vulnerable in society, for more generous policies on a number of social service measures, or for policies that serve the common good (Beaman et al. 2009; Bolzendahl 2011; Childs 2004b; Duflo and Topalova 2004; MacDonald and O'Brien 2011; Miguel 2012; Poggione 2004; Swers 1998; 2002; Thomas 1991, 1994; Walsh 2002). To be sure, exceptions exist. Margaret Thatcher, for example, was well known for her masculine style and policy goals. She and a few others like her remind us that the effect of individual gender is far from deterministic or inconstant. However, on average, women do tend to exhibit a central tendency that differs from men's priorities.[36] Gender matters because if women are not adequately represented, their distinctive preferences cannot enrich the mix of views and shape collective decisions.

Full participation by women can affect not only *what* decisions are made but also *how* they are made. Put differently, if institutions were to adequately include women, the very nature of the institution could change (Carroll 2001; Phillips 1995). Some feminist theorists argue that "women make representative institutions more democratic" (Dovi 2008, 157) or deliberative (Mansbridge

[35] The gender gap persists even after controlling for partisanship and demographic variables (Crowder-Meyer 2010; Huddy, Cassese, and Lizotte 2008, 38). This is consistent with the framework of Carol Gilligan (1982). Women also tend to prioritize the needs of women, but inconsistently, though female legislators do appear to do so fairly consistently (Dodson 2006). We will discuss these issues more fully in later chapters, especially chapter 7.

[36] We develop this discussion more fully in the conclusion chapter.

1994; Norris 1996). As Norris put it, women "introduce a kinder, gentler politics," one that is "characterised by co-operation rather than conflict, collaboration rather than hierarchy" (1996, 91). Women are said to be "more willing to listen to the other side" and "less adversarial" (Bochel and Briggs 2000, 66). They even "make less noise in the [legislative] chamber" (G. Young 2001, 8; quoted in Childs 2004a, 3); as one study summed it up, "heckles are primarily a men's affair" (Grünenfelder and Bächtiger 2007, 16).[37] Raising the authority of women can thus alter a decision-making institution to make it more democratic (in the sense of more inclusive) and also more deliberative—more focused on listening, cooperating, and collaborating (Grünenfelder and Bächtiger 2007).

This combination of more inclusive and more deliberative interaction can create a feedback loop for women's representation, further increasing the authority of the women who are present. Norms of interaction that emphasize warmth and cooperation can encourage women to participate actively and to exercise influence. Some studies have suggested that predominantly male settings tend to produce a masculine style of interaction that negatively affects women, even among political elites (Kathlene 1994; Mattei 1998). The masculine forms of interaction in these settings can send a strong negative signal to women about their expected role in the discussion and thus may lower women's participation in it. If interaction becomes more feminine—that is, more deliberative and democratic—then women's authority can rise. One way to transform interaction is to increase women's descriptive representation in combination with the appropriate decision-making rule. Thus women's low numbers matter in part because they allow a less deliberative and democratic interaction style, which in turn depresses women's authority. Elevating the numbers can change that interaction style, increasing the probability that women will not be mere bystanders, but will instead become active, authoritative voices in the group.

In addition, women's low representation matters for democratic legitimacy and public engagement. Increasing women's participation in political institutions affects how observers—especially women—think and feel about those institutions and their place in them. For example, women's descriptive representation can elevate the legitimacy of the political institution that purports to represent them and can strengthen some citizens' democratic attitudes or civic orientations (Mansbridge 1999). Men and women view government as more legitimate and trustworthy where women are more numerous in it (Schwindt-Bayer and Mishler 2005). Women who are represented by women tend to view their members of Congress in a more positive light (Lawless 2004). Where women are visible on the ballot, or when the number of women in office increases, women tend to have higher levels of political efficacy, political knowledge, and

[37] Studies based on interviews with leaders in various countries often verify that this view holds at least in leaders' perceptions of female colleagues (Norris 1996; Childs 2004b).

engagement in a variety of political jurisdictions and countries.[38] When Americans were asked in 2000 whether they think the country would be governed better or worse if more women held public office, most said "governed better," and only a small minority said "governed worse" (Simmons 2002, cited in Dolan and Sanbonmatsu 2009).[39] Thus increasing the number of women in office may increase the level of political engagement by women and the overall legitimacy of government in the eyes of both women and men.

A rise in the number of women in government can also raise the status of women in the polity more generally. For example, as women occupy more leadership roles in Indian villages, voters' negative stereotypes of female as inadequate to lead decrease, and their willingness to vote for women rises (Beaman, Pande, and Cirone 2012). A study of twenty-five countries found that women's descriptive representation increases women's belief in "women's ability to govern" even after controlling for other competing explanations (Alexander 2012, 460). Women's authority in the eyes of others may rise as they prove by their cumulative performance that they can in fact govern competently.

More broadly, women's participation in public settings carries important symbolic meaning. Participation in the life of one's community and its public affairs signifies not only specific power over particular decisions but also a more general authority in public life, and authority in turn shapes the most fundamental sense of human worth. That sense goes by various names—honor, respect, standing, esteem, and so on. We see these as all referencing the notion of worth embodied most famously in the Declaration of Independence, which, modified, continues to resound today: all people are created equal. Women will not be viewed as equal in that basic sense of worth until they carry equal authority in the public discourse that governs their community. To participate fully is to take one's place in the ranks of those who govern, and in a democracy, where every member of the community governs, one must govern to be a member of the community. Mansbridge justifies the use of descriptive representation in part precisely on these grounds; when a social group has been excluded from governance, and its ability to govern questioned, then measures should be taken to include its members in deliberation so as to establish its "ability to rule" (1999, 628).

The notion that full participation in deliberative institutions constitutes one's standing in the community applies not only to the formal forums that directly govern, such as juries, formal community boards and councils, or committees selected by the state and invested with governing power; it also applies to the informal associations that make up civil society. Theorist Mark Warren writes

[38] Atkeson and Carrillo 2007; Barnes and Burchard 2012; Burns, Schlozman, and Verba 2001; Reingold and Harrell 2010; Smith, Reingold, and Owens 2012; Wolbrecht and Campbell 2007; but see Karp and Banducci 2008.

[39] The American public even endorses gender balance in government. The plurality articulates the equal balance ideal (Dolan and Sanbonmatsu 2009, 419).

that civil society is not divorced from the operation of government and politics (2000, 32–33). When citizens gather for private purposes their actions resonate outward. The life of neighborhood associations, parents' organizations, and even entertainment clubs shapes the orientation that the members adopt toward the role of government and their own efficacy to affect their political system (Eliasoph 1998). Civic associations can powerfully determine citizens' ability to affect their government, for example, by the way that they distribute and organize their own power internally (Skocpol, Ganz, and Munson 2000). The power relations of informal civic life—including the norms and patterns of discursive interaction in these settings—shape authority in the more formal institutions of politics and government. Thus women's standing in civic associations also bears on their standing in the polity.

Fundamentally, gender inequality is worth studying because gender continues to be a dimension of political underrepresentation.[40] As Burns, Schlozman, and Verba (2001) note, politics is still a "man's game." To be sure, women now enjoy equal formal legal rights in the United States and many countries. They have increased their income, occupational status, workforce participation, and most of all, education. Despite huge progress, individuals are still heavily sorted into gendered roles based on their biological features, and this sorting has profound implications for how political power is understood and used. As the psychologist Susan Fiske argues, with these roles come a bifurcation of social esteem into two opposing dimensions of regard; women's roles confer upon them love, or appreciation, or liking, or attraction—but not authority. Women may find "feminine" ways to get what they want, by leveraging their distinctive gender roles, yet still lack authority.

The problem for women is that while they can achieve some of their aims by being liked for their sociability, loved for their nurturing, appreciated for their cooperation and teamwork, or desired for their sexuality, they may still lack in basic respect and authority in public life and group decision making.[41] Women are expected to talk, and carry influence, on topics directly dealing with women's domains of expertise. But not so in other domains. It is no surprise, then, that gender gaps reveal themselves in many forms of political participation and representation. Even when women gain ground in society, their representation does not necessarily follow, because society continues to revolve around highly gendered notions of where and how women should exercise overt influence and who deserves authority.

Given that participation in public discussions has far-reaching implications, women's status in these discussions is of the utmost importance. Often, women

[40] The arguments in this paragraph are more fully developed and documented in chapters 2 and 3.

[41] See the extensive literature on ambivalent sexism and the notion that women, and other social groups, are independently rated as high on warmth but low on competence (Eagly and Carli 2007).

are not perceived, or perceive themselves, as influential or valued to the same extent as men during public discussions. This low status interferes with women's representation in a myriad of significant ways.

Deliberative Theory and the Question of Social Equality

Women's low authority is not only a problem for the ideal of democratic inclusion. It is also an Achilles heel for advocates of deliberation.

Political philosophy has experienced an explosion of interest in deliberative democracy. Many normative theorists have advocated more citizen deliberation.[42] As Gutmann and Thompson write, "no subject has been more discussed in political theory in the last two decades than deliberative democracy" (2004, vii; see also Dryzek 2007, cited in Thompson 2008).

The most influential theorist and advocate of the ideal of deliberative democracy is the eminent philosopher Jürgen Habermas (1996). Habermas's core concept is reason. For him the ideal speech situation is one that establishes reason through "intersubjectivity," the exchange and development of logic and evidence among deliberators. Justifying one's position through reasons that anyone can accept is the basis of deliberation. As Chambers puts it, in Habermasian fashion, deliberation "ought to spark active reasoning and thoughtfulness" (2009, 335). Deliberation can encourage people to question, to think more deeply about, and to articulate their fundamentals—why they believe what they do and wish what they want. In deliberation people are prompted to examine their presuppositions and their assumptions, their values and beliefs, and revisit them, reconstruct them, and come to a better understanding of what to do with them. The discourse of "practical reason" carries the Enlightenment project forward and forms the foundation of democratic practice. Habermas's theory is thus grounded in the notion that deliberation occurs through justification and rational discourse (1996; Chambers 1996).

Inspired by Habermas, a number of normative theorists have listed required preconditions for deliberation. One of the key dimensions of desirable deliberation as articulated by many theorists is social equality in participation and influence. A minimum requirement is equal access to the floor, but that is only the beginning. Knight and Johnson offer the standard of equal opportunity to influence the discussion, not merely the formal opportunity to deliberate (1997). For most theorists, equality does not require that each and every person should speak the same amount and carry the same influence. But following Habermas, many theorists posit that each person should speak and influence the same amount unless their arguments differ in quality. And this implies that

[42] See, for example, Barber 1984; Bohman 1997; Chambers 1996, 2003; Fishkin 1995; Gutmann and Thompson 1996, 2004; Habermas 1989, 1996; Macedo 1999.

factors other than quality should *not* play a role, whether they are based on concrete resources or more intangible status.

Gutmann and Thompson state, for example, that deliberation rightly constructed will "diminish the discriminatory effects of class, race, and gender inequalities" (2004, 50). Not only do theorists wish to see the equal opportunity to deliberate, they also posit an ideal where status or power inequalities in society do not affect the deliberation itself. In the article that in many ways sparked the deliberative turn in political theory, Joshua Cohen writes that in ideal deliberation the "existing distribution of power and resources does not shape [deliberators'] chances to contribute to deliberation, *nor does that distribution play an authoritative role in their deliberation*" (1996, 74; emphasis added). Dennis Thompson further specifies that "the discussion is better deliberation to the extent that *the participation is equally distributed*," and "most [theorists] agree that the more the deliberation is influenced by unequal economic resources and social status, the more deficient it is" (2008, 501 and 506; emphasis added). Thus several influential theorists of deliberation offer a standard of social equality of actual participation and influence, and not merely equal opportunity to talk.

However, a chief concern about implementing deliberation is that it will fall far short of equality and perhaps even exacerbate social inequalities. Some critics have argued that deliberation as actually practiced tends to reflect or even magnify existing disadvantages of status or power (Sanders 1997; Young 2000). In response, the later writings of advocates acknowledge that "unequal resources are likely to produce unequal participation in the deliberative forum" (Thompson 2008, 509). Still, as Thompson puts it, "we do not . . . know whether it is true, as some theorists plausibly argue, that under many conditions deliberation is less affected by prevailing inequalities than power-based modes of decision making" (2008, 509). So while advocates recognize that social inequalities are a barrier in actual deliberation, they do not explore the most serious ways that inequalities might undermine participation and influence, and some argue that actual deliberation is still more egalitarian than actual alternative modes of politics.[43] While the advocates make a strong case for the need to have gender-egalitarian deliberation, they have not yet provided an analysis of how or why patterns of inequality in society interfere with egalitarian deliberation, or what the appropriate solutions might be.

The critics have provided such an analysis, drawing attention to the specific mechanisms of voice and authority (Fraser 1992; Sanders 1997; Williams 2000; Young 1996; 2001). These critics worry that groups with less status or authority in society may speak less, be heard less, and, relatedly, carry less authority in deliberation than members of groups with more authority in society (Mansbridge 1983). Moreover, they argue that the very nature of language, through its

[43] On this latter point, see, for example, Gutmann and Thompson 2004 and Fishkin 1995; but see Hibbing and Theiss-Morse 2002.

rhetorical elements, either enhances inequality during deliberation or can remedy it. They claim that marginalized groups are more likely to express emotion, to offer personal testimony, and to structure their contributions as narratives rather than as logical "if-then" statements; consequently, their contributions may not seem to be based on the right kind of evidence, to be objective and universally relevant, and otherwise reasonable.

So it is not simply a problem of women's contributions being valued less because women speak them. Rather, the types of considerations women tend to articulate, and how they articulate them, are valued less because they reflect ways of thinking and self-expression that have been socially constructed as less authoritative (Sanders 1997; Williams 2000; Young 1996, 2000). As the philosopher Fricker (2007) argues, not only might women be devalued for who they are, but they also may be devalued for how they think, feel, and express themselves (see also Allen 2012, 22). In other words, because their social identity as women carries less authority, and because women's psychological modes and social styles tend to carry less authority, women as a whole will not be able to participate or be heard in the way that advocates of deliberation would wish. So while Habermas values the transformative potential of deliberation, deliberation will fail to achieve that transformation, because not all reasons, forms of expression, and modes of interaction are socially constructed to be equally authoritative. Thus the normative requirement of equal participation and influence can only be achieved when the devalued communication styles of marginalized groups are validated. From our perspective, this critique is extremely important because it argues that deliberation must enable groups such as women, who enter the deliberation with less authority, to build their authority during deliberation.

To their credit, many theorists have incorporated this critique of deliberation. They have included the types of rhetorical styles said to characterize the cultures of marginalized groups as part of their definition of what counts as quality discourse (Chambers 2003). For example, Dryzek expands deliberation to allow for rhetorical forms such as gossip and storytelling (2005, 224; so do Mansbridge et al. 2010). As Chambers summarizes the current state of the theoretical landscape: "Gone, with only a few exceptions . . . is the narrow, highly rationalistic view of reason-giving that stresses a model of impartiality rising above all difference" (2003, 321).

However, even with these more capacious understandings of deliberation, the deliberative vision remains incomplete and inadequate. What is still missing is a full reckoning with the problem of how authority gaps can be overcome. Both the advocates and the critics have yet to explain how to build equal authority within deliberative settings. A group that comes to the deliberation with lower stores of authority will not elevate its authority in the eyes of high-authority deliberators by using its distinctive styles of communication, because those styles signal low authority. For example, why would a low-authority member who tells a story be given a hearing by high-authority members inclined to dismiss this form of communication as nonauthoritative? Women are viewed as less authoritative when they express emotion, so why would their use of emotion remedy their lack of authority? Testimony and emotional expression may create a sense of authentic self-expression for disadvantaged groups, but if such expressions are not also a means to build real authority among discussion partners, then the goal of deliberative equality is not likely to be realized.

For that reason, encouraging devalued forms of deliberation may fail to close the authority gap, and may even reinforce it. That is, deliberation may not merely fail to live up to its promise; unless it guarantees equal authority within itself, it reinforces social inequality and risks becoming an actively negative force. As Honneth puts it, "recognition must precede cognition" (2005, 119). When it does not, the attempt to generate an exchange of reason, and perhaps even an exchange of emotions and personal experience, may become antiegalitarian. This is the point we seek to highlight in this book. By accepting that deliberation rests on authority, that unequal authority infiltrates deliberation itself, and that deliberation can thus reproduce and enhance unequal authority (at least under some conditions), advocates can then move to exploring ways to remedy this problem.[44]

In addition to authority, we also highlight the importance of another dimension: social and emotional connection. Not only does social inequality come from, and in turn affects, authority, it also shapes the nature of social interaction during discussion. Women are socialized to be more interdependent than men. While there is much variance within genders, there are also cultures of gender, as we mentioned and will elaborate in chapter 3. Consequently, women may not feel able or motivated to articulate their perspectives when the form of interaction lacks an interdependent character. This dimension of discussion may affect men's contribution on the whole less negatively. In other words, women may be less likely to feel comfortable and competent than men do in competitive discussions that lack active signals of emotional warmth and connection between deliberators. Deliberative equality thus requires attention to the style of discussion, and specifically to social warmth.

The position Anderson and Honneth articulate takes these arguments into account and provides a useful starting point. They put it as follows: "the conditions for autonomously leading one's own life turn out to be dependent on the establishment of relationships of mutual recognition. Prominent among these relationships are (1) legally institutionalized relations of universal respect for the autonomy and dignity of persons (central to self-respect); (2) close relations of love and friendship (central to self-trust); and (3) networks of solidarity and

[44] Some critics of deliberation argue that in place of deliberation, what subordinate groups need is a competition of ideas. However, this model is at least as disadvantageous to women as the criticized model of Habermasian deliberation. If the exchange resembles "a vibrant clash of democratic political positions," as Mouffe advocates, that will disadvantage people who do better under conditions of interdependence, including many women (Mouffe 2000).

shared values within which the particular worth of members of a community can be acknowledged (central to self-esteem)" (2005, 131).

Deliberation can offer the interweaving of Anderson and Honneth's three strands. Specifically, by interacting under the right circumstances, people can: (1) be subject to institutional conditions that encourage universal respect for each person's autonomy and dignity, (2) create relations of warm regard, and (3) establish solidarity and hence affirm the worth of each member of the group. In our view, the central concept of deliberation, and what it can offer the cause of equality, is "empathetic engagement" (to use Honneth's phrase [2005, 113]). But it is not enough for listeners to adopt a private mentality of empathy; they should convey to their conversation partners that they are experiencing empathy for the speaker. The speaker needs to sense that the listeners are empathizing with her. That is, empathy is not only necessary as a quality of the listener but also as a quality of the communication—the listener must signal it effectively enough for the speaker to perceive. Through this process, deliberation must first establish a socially connected and socially valued person before it can lead that person to engage in the pursuit of rationality. When deliberative settings carry out this social function, they not only enhance their mission of pursuing reason, they also enhance the equality of women with men. Empathy is not only the precursor to reason, it is also the precursor to equality.

We can now spell out the characteristics of settings that will produce gender equality. Settings that promote interactions high on social affiliation and "warm regard" are beneficial to women. These interactions should create for women the sense of "solidarity" and "friendship" Anderson and Honneth identified as important. In addition, these settings should create authority for women, the dimension on which women are particularly disadvantaged. Settings that do so would meet the requirement of "universal respect for the autonomy and dignity" of each member. In sum, we now have the guideposts that will chart our path here—women need settings that foster rapport and respect, because these affirm their sense of belonging and their competence, and these are prerequisites for women's authoritative participation and representation—in short, for their influence.

In sum, philosophers justify deliberation on various laudable grounds, but our argument privileges one of these justifications in particular. We view deliberation as a practice that cultivates citizenly virtues, that raises the knowledge, reasoning, and general cognitive competence of the typical disengaged, low-capacity voter. Nor is its most important justification its ability to cast democratic government in the glow of legitimacy. More important, egalitarian deliberation can establish and maintain the equal authority of each person as a citizen. The deliberative setting is not only a school for democracy that informs the masses, pacifies intolerance, and instills in the free rider a sense of duty to the community. Deliberative meetings are also a social institution that delineates the individual's standing as a respected member of that community.

And it is through that standing that the other beneficial effects of deliberation can come about for disadvantaged groups. Yes, deliberation can raise the citizen's motivation to engage in the life of the community, so crucial to the person's level of knowledge and interest in public affairs. But that motivation is rooted deeper, in the person's sense that she is the kind of person who is entitled to do so, expected to do so, capable of doing so, valued for doing so, and, therefore, does so. So deliberation can engage the unengaged, and thereby school them in the skills and attitudes of democracy, when it recasts who is entitled to carry authority in deliberation. By giving women authority, deliberation can signal to women that they are worthy of the full rights of citizenship and raise their competence in the process. When that occurs, deliberation can shape in fundamental ways the life, the dynamics, and ultimately the decisions of the polity.

The Argument of This Book

The key questions we aim to answer should now be clear: under what conditions will women achieve an effective voice in deliberating bodies?[45] Does equalizing the number of women help to equalize women's participation and representation? What can institutions do to facilitate women's authority? What needs to happen in order for the distinctive priorities of women—priorities such as the inclination to help others—to be heard and to influence fellow deliberators?

Our answer is: higher numbers of women do aid women's representation, but it all depends. It depends on the decision rule and the norms of discussion that such rules generate. The reason that having more women helps women is the same reason that decision rules matter: discussion is an act of communication, and therefore it is governed by implicit but powerful norms. These norms are rooted in gendered cultures, in conventions of interaction among women, among men, and between men and women, and they are rooted in unspoken rules of social inclusion or competition. Unanimous rule signals the need to include everyone. Majority rule produces a more competitive dynamic that aids each gender when it is the majority in the group. While we know a great deal about how these rules affect the inclusion of a *generic individual's* preferences and ideas, we know very little about how they affect gendered interaction and the inclusion of *women's* preferences and ideas. Our study explains why these decision rules affect men and women as men and women.

We set the stage for our analysis in chapter 2 by detailing why women continue today to be the "silent sex" in political participation broadly, and in authoritative discursive acts specifically, despite substantial gains in education, concrete resources, and formal rights. We derive expectations for women's participation and influence in group discussion in chapter 3.

[45] Chambers posed a similar question (2003, 322).

As we explain in chapter 4, we use an experimental design because we wish to avoid the unavoidable pitfall of observational studies—the effect of greater numbers of women, or of institutional arrangements, is shaped by other factors, making it impossible to know if what appear to be the effects of numbers or institutional rules are in fact due to something that causes these or that is correlated with them. We vary two features of deliberation: the group's gender composition and the group's decision rule. We create a norm of inclusive interaction by assigning groups to deliberate with unanimous rule, and we contrast these groups with others assigned to deliberate with majority rule. We replicate our results in two very different sites, one a religious and socially conservative city in the Mountain West (Provo, Utah), and the other a secular, wealthy, predominantly liberal town in the eastern seaboard (Princeton, New Jersey). The basic patterns of gendered interaction hold regardless of location.

In chapter 5 we show that numbers and rules jointly elevate or depress women's participation in discussion, and that the more women speak, the more influential they become. Conditions that prompt women to speak thus equalize their influence. The reason that speech is a civic act that reflects and creates one's standing in the community become clear in this chapter—speech affects the sense of personal efficacy and others' views of the person's authority. In chapter 6, we explore the reasons for this gender gap in speech participation, testing various statistical moderators to see what it is about a person's gender that causes the inequalities. We show in chapter 7 that settings that equalize women's voice also tilt the agenda toward talk of women's distinctive concerns: children, family, schools, the poor and the needy. Deliberation matters because it sets the terms of the decision, and women's lack of standing robs them of their ability to shape that agenda. In chapter 8, we show how the minute dynamics of conversational engagement deny equal status for women in the group. But we also demonstrate how these dynamics can foster a warm climate of social affiliation that helps women. In chapter 9, we find that the same conditions that foster equal participation, equal perceived influence, and an agenda devoted to women's distinctive concerns also produce more compassionate policies for the poor, vulnerable, and disadvantaged. Women's influence on collective generosity is measurable in precise dollar amounts, and settings that empower women generate significant increases in the standard of living of the poorest members of the society.

Our main findings are that majority rule is bad for women's substantive, symbolic, and authoritative representation as long as women are the gender minority. Conversely, majority rule is a boon for women when they make up a large majority of the group. Unanimous rule aids women when women are the gender minority, as they benefit from the norms of inclusion that unanimous rule produces. However, unanimous rule provides no advantage to women when they are the gender majority, as it also empowers the male minority. Putting these findings together, we conclude, in a departure from prior studies, that the effects of one factor—gender composition—depend upon the other factor—rules and procedures. That is, the effect of gender and the level of gender inequality depend on the structure of the group setting, and that structure is shaped by who deliberates and under what rules.

What these findings tell us is that rules that are unbiased on their face actually produce deep social inequalities, but rules can also remedy the inequality people bring with them into deliberation. Who deliberates matters, because it creates norms of social interaction and ways of talking, but deliberators are not trapped in the constraints society imposes on them.

Despite drawing heavily on our controlled experiment, we can take some comfort that our results hold up in the real world. To beef up the confidence in our findings—to increase our external validity—we replicate the key results in a natural setting. There are over 14,000 school boards in the United States. Among these we find an enormous variety of gender compositions. Many boards have an even mix of men and women, but many are lopsided, including all-female and all-male groups, what we call gender "enclaves." A sample of meetings from these boards allows us to test our lab findings in locations small and large, in rural, suburban, and urban settings, in places where gender roles have been slow to change and where women have advanced far. We present these findings in chapter 10.

While this book is about gender inequality, its framework can be used to study other forms of inequality. Some dynamics are probably special to the case of gender, as we explain in chapters 2 and 3. But other dynamics may not be. Unfortunately, we are unable to give a full treatment to the question of race, class, and other inequalities. In fact, school boards contain very small numbers of nonwhites, as do many other deliberative settings in the United States (Jacobs, Cook, and Delli Carpini 2009).[46] Although at the end of chapter 10 we do provide some small hints about the gender dynamics in racially diverse groups, our experiment is confined to Anglo whites in the United States. We hope that future studies carry on the important work of investigating the interaction dynamics of race, class, and other forms of inequality and marginalization.

Even with this important caveat, our study can provide a set of tools that enables scholars to look rigorously at how key features of the group—whether its composition, its decision rule, or other structures—shape the dynamics, content, and outcomes of group deliberation. It also fills the gap in studies of deliberation by conducting a large-scale systematic analysis of the details of political discussion itself, providing the first combined study of the words people use, the preferences they express, and the pattern of interruptions they receive. These then become data that we link to other data on participants' views on

[46] See chapter 10 for further discussion.

the matter at hand, their decisions, the level of influence they carry over the final outcome, and the perceptions of that influence.[47] It is only by carefully unpacking the ways in which men and women interact with each other in the process of making collective decisions that we begin to understand how gendered dynamics affect the individual and the group. Our study can offer other scholars of deliberation a set of ways to investigate authority in groups, gender notwithstanding.

Our theme is how and why women become the "silent sex" and how increased voice and authority for women are possible. We proceed to set the stage for women's participation in politics in the next chapter.

[47] Partial analyses include Stromer-Galley and Muhlberger 2009; Stromer-Galley 2007. Partial qualitative studies include Walsh 2007 and Rosenberg 2007b.

CHAPTER 2

The Sources of the Gender Gap in Political Participation

For too long, the history of women has been a history of silence.

—HILLARY CLINTON[1]

ARE WOMEN THE "SILENT SEX"? At first glance, the answer would seem to be no. It is difficult to call to mind a scene in which men outtalk women in everyday life. Women are often thought to be more sociable than men, not less. But when it comes to politics and public affairs, there is reason to take a closer look. Women are much less likely than men to take action to directly influence others. There is reason to wonder, then, whether women are also more passive than men when it comes to public discussion.

The notion that in advanced countries women tend to be less active than men in deciding matters of common concern may strike some as outdated. The voter registration rolls in America reveal clear gender parity. And women are no strangers to volunteerism in public life. Women are not reluctant to take up the cause of civic duty. But the equality we see in these modes of participation disappears when we turn to the forms of participation most concerned with the exercise of power and authority. Thus we have a puzzle on our hands: why do women participate less than men in some ways but not in others, and do so despite massive advances in their standing in society?

Our answer in this chapter is that women have the ability to participate equally, but do not use it. By ability, we mean concrete resources such as time, money, access to social networks, a store of relevant knowledge, and appropriate experience and skills (Verba, Schlozman, and Brady 1995). But ability is not enough. What active political participants need that women tend to lack is the motivation and the opportunity to engage in actions that society associates with authority. Women tend to be more passive than men in stating controversial

[1] "Women's Rights Are Human Rights," speech by Hillary Clinton, United Nations Fourth World Conference on Women, Beijing, China, September 5, 1995. http://www.columbia.edu/cu/augustine/arch/hrclinton.txt.

opinions and directing others to implement those views. That is, they are less motivated to carry influence in the allocation of values and resources, because that activity is deemed masculine territory.

The motivation to be political is socially acquired, and the process of acquisition runs through social identity. "The gender difference in the taste for politics," Nancy Burns and her colleagues write, may be "rooted in the fact that men have a basis for identifying with the vast majority of the key players in politics" (Burns, Schlozman, and Verba 2001, 341). Because it sends important messages about women's place in the political world, "the gender composition of the political environment . . . has consequences for women's engagement with politics" (356). The result is that women tend to view themselves as outsiders in the locker room of politics, and they do not engage as fully—as authoritatively—as they might across the complete set of participatory activities available to them. In this sense, they are not full citizens. Much the same can be said about women's participation in public meetings; the political environment may send the message that women are expected to be only partial participants.

Thus women may enter public discussions already inclined against making the full contribution of which they are capable. While women are now better educated and more civically experienced than men, they remain the less authoritative, and therefore relatively "silent," gender in public affairs. Women have plenty to say in formal meetings, but they do not say it as often as men do, because they have learned to avoid being the leaders—in other words, they have been motivated to be the followers.

The Gap Exists, but It's Not Based in Ability

Are women in fact less likely to participate in authoritative political acts? That is, are women less likely to attempt to voice their opinions to others, to direct others in their implementation, and in various ways, to attempt to influence others to act on them? For our initial answer, we turn to the most comprehensive treatment of gender inequality in political participation to date: Burns, Schlozman, and Verba's *Private Roots of Public Action* (*PROPA*).[2] When they combine together a variety of types of participation, such as voting, contributing money to a political campaign, or working on a community problem, they find a moderate gender gap.[3] This gap appears to be caused by an accumulation

[2]The previous classic work on the subject, *Voice and Equality*, reported that women participate only slightly less than men overall (Verba, Schlozman, and Brady 1995, 254).

[3]Other acts included in this participation measure are working on a campaign, serving as a volunteer on a local government board, contacting public officials, membership or contributions to organizations that take stands in politics (Burns, Schlozman, and Verba 2001, 64). In this chapter, quantitative reports of individuals' patterns of political activity or psychological engagement are typically based on a person's self-report of their activity and engagement (e.g., their level of politi-

of small differences in the resources that shape "pathways" to participation. For example, a white collar occupation gives skills that allow a person to write a letter to their representative. Earning more income enables political contributions. Education gives people skills, knowledge, and motivations that turn on their radar for politics, enable them to process political information, and drive them to participate. Education gets people to turn on, tune in, and drop in, to modify a phrase from 1960s counterculture.

However, women's continued lag in participation is puzzling given that women have made enormous strides in employment, earnings, and education. While women are still less likely to be employed full time than men, they now make up about half of the labor force. They still earn less, but now they earn 80% of men's income when they are employed (US Department of Commerce 2011).[4] In fact, according to the US Bureau of Labor Statistics, women now compose just over half of workers in "high-paying management, professional, and related occupations."[5] Consistent with this pattern, young women lag behind young men in political contributions but exceed them in contributing money for charities (Marcelo, Lopez, and Kirby 2007). Women do not have a problem accessing and using money in politics—they have a problem with politics. And the same holds for many of the forms of engagement we wish to see in the citizenry. As we will see, the biggest variable of all—education—now should offset the disadvantages from the small disparities in employment and income, positioning women to equal if not exceed men in political engagement. Given the enormous strides women have made in employment, education, and income, we need to look further for an explanation for why their political participation continues to lag. Only then can we accept the possibility that women may participate less than men in public discussions, and do so despite overall equal resources.[6]

Adding to the puzzle is that women have completely closed the gender gap in some modes of participation and engagement even as they continue to lag in others. Women have been voting at slightly higher rates than men since the 1980s. This holds not only in the United States but in Western Europe too, and

cal interest). The exception is the level of political knowledge, which is usually measured by asking factual questions and noting the accuracy of the answer. When self-reported turnout is validated by checking actual turnout records, the same variables that affect one affect the other, albeit somewhat less so (Achen and Blais 2010). We do not know if actual vote matches self-reported vote in the same way for women and men.

[4] According to a Bureau of Labor Statistics report, in 2010, 59 percent of working-age women in the United States were in the labor force—employed or actively seeking employment (US Department of Labor 2011).

[5] According to Pande and Ford 2011, 2, citing US Department of Labor, Bureau of Labor Statistics, Employment and Earnings, 2009 Annual Averages and the monthly Labor Review, November 2009.

[6] We can also rule out an additional possibility—that women are too busy with their domestic duties. This plays only a small role in explaining the gender gap in participation (Jennings and Stoker 2000; Burns, Schlozman, and Verba 2001).

in the 1990s the gender gap in turnout disappeared in a variety of countries worldwide.[7] Because women are slightly more numerous than men, women are actually a majority of the electorate—a reversal unthinkable to the suffragists of a century ago (Marcelo, Lopez, and Kirby 2007). Young women outvote young men by more than older women outvote older men, so women's advantage as voters is trending up (Godsay and Kirby 2010). That is, women today are dutiful when it comes to voting.

But *duty* may be a key word here, since it is a chief reason for the decision to turn out to vote (Achen and Blais 2010). In fact, when asked the reason for their voting turnout, 90% of women mention civic duty. Policy, social, or material motivations come in an eye-squinting distant second, third, and fourth place, respectively (Burns, Schlozman, and Verba 2001, 116).[8] Consistent with the duty explanation for women's political activity is the fact that among the youngest cohort of citizens, women are somewhat more likely than men to participate in charitable activities, but men are more likely than women to participate in electoral activities other than voting (Marcelo, Lopez, and Kirby 2007). That is, women no longer underparticipate men at the ballot box or in other duty-driven acts, but the gender parity does not extend to other types of participation.

Further underscoring the puzzle is the fact that women also have as much as or more than men by way of early experience that trains people to get moving in politics. Women are as likely as men to report that they were "very active" in student government or in clubs during college (Burns, Schlozman, and Verba 2001, 149). Women are more likely than men to recall having been "very active" in high school clubs. They are just as likely as men to recall having been "very active" in high school student government and to take civics classes. In real time, high school girls actually report *more* of these feeder activities, including taking part in student government, and being active in academic clubs and student publications (Burns, Schlozman, and Verba 2001, 148). That girls are advantaged here, by rates of 50% or even 100%, is surprising. These are powerful factors in fostering an interest in politics in adult life, even decades later (Shani 2010).

And yet women do not seem to be leveraging these formative experiences to the same extent as men, at least not consistently across the forms of political engagement. Burns, Schlozman, and Verba found that the same young women

[7]Desposato and Norrander 2009; Inglehart and Norris 2003; Verba, Schlozman, and Brady 1995, 255.

[8]The importance of duty also applies to men. Women are also about as likely as men to work on campaigns and to protest (Burns, Schlozman, and Verba 2001, 65; Verba, Schlozman, and Brady 1995). Women are *no more* likely to participate in local affairs than men, less likely to discuss local politics than men, and are less efficacious than men about local politics, even though they are as *interested* in local affairs as men and are more likely than men to know the name of the local head of the school system (Burns, Schlozman, and Verba. 2001, 67, 102–3). Women are equally knowledgeable with men regarding local politics (Delli Carpini and Keeter 2005).

whose participation rates in student clubs and government equal men's are far less likely than men to indicate that they are interested in "what is going on in government" (a gender gap of 15 points—among the biggest gender gaps one sees [Burns, Schlozman, and Verba 2001, 150]). Niemi and Junn's large national study found, similarly, that school-age boys are more likely than girls to enjoy civics classes, and boys score higher on measures of political knowledge, despite appropriate statistical controls (1993). While young women are civically active, they are not politically interested. Put differently, women have the resources, the experiences, and the sense of civic duty, and these factors cause them to participate actively in activities deemed dutiful, but women still lack the motivation to engage in activities that are not construed as dutiful.

When we look beyond actions that women may view as their civic duty or which fit closely with women's existing role as support staff to men, we see continuing trouble spots in women's steady march forward. These trouble spots tend to occur in the more authoritative political acts. Women are less likely than men to discuss politics, to try to persuade someone to vote for their preferred candidate, or to offer opinions about politics. This pattern conforms to the notion that the difficulty extends to psychological engagement—that is, to motivation. Women are less likely than men to indicate an interest in politics, to learn about politics, to enjoy political discussion, and to feel a sense of political efficacy (the sense that one can do something about politics).[9] The magnitude of the gender gap is modest—about 10 percentage points. But it is persistent and difficult to explain (Burns, Schlozman, and Verba 2001, 102–3).[10] And in some settings, the gender gap is massive. For example, women submit just 10% of op eds to prestigious news outlets in the United States.[11] And even when individual differences between men and women are modest, they cumulate significantly.

[9]These gender gaps in discussion, persuasion, opinionation, and psychological engagement are documented in Atkeson and Rapoport 2003; Burns, Schlozman, and Verba 2001, 102–3; Conover, Searing, and Crewe 2002; Delli Carpini and Keeter 1996; Delli Carpini and Keeter 2005; Hansen 1997; Huckfeldt and Sprague 1995. Not only does gender affect the average level of engagement, it also affects extremes: men are more likely to be news and political junkies (Burns, Schlozman, and Verba 2001, 105). Women are also far less likely to make big campaign donations (Burns, Schlozman, and Verba 2001; and here is one anecdote from 2008: http://www.usatoday.com/news/politics/election2008/2008-07-30-gender_N.htm).

[10]Women score higher on measures of knowledge based on visual recognition of political actors than on verbal measures (Prior 2004, 19). On verbal measures, men's knowledge is frequently at least 1.5 times greater than women's (Delli Carpini and Keeter 2005). A very important caveat is that when studies contain sufficient numbers to analyze separately African American and Hispanic youths, they find that the gender gap reverses, with girls more politically knowledgeable and efficacious than boys (Gimpel, Lay, and Schuknecht 2003, 87, 92).

[11]The 90% figure comes from a study by the *Washington Post* that tracked five months of submissions to the op ed pages of that publication. This was originally reported in the *Post* by Deborah Howell in May 2008, according to http://www.theopedproject.org/index.php?option=com_content&view=article&id=70&Itemid=82. The Op Ed Project reports similar percentages at other prestigious news outlets.

Women's relative lack of voice can add up: public officials receive approximately two million more letters or calls from men than from women (Campbell and Wolbrecht 2006, 234). In sum, women lag in areas that constitute the core of political influence—perceiving themselves as influential (as efficacious), expressing opinions about public affairs, and attempting to direct those affairs.

Neither is this gender gap going away any time soon. In a striking illustration of how the more things change the more they stay the same, Atkeson and Rapoport found in their review of a half century of American public opinion surveys that women are less likely than men to offer an opinion when asked by a survey interviewer what they like or dislike about the parties or candidates (2003). They don't even muster the same level of opinionation as men when asked about candidates for president, many of whom were incumbent presidents. And if any political figure is going to elicit an opinion, it is likely the president. Women are less likely to offer any opinion at all, and offer fewer opinions when they do offer something. As the authors put it, "it is interesting that this difference has shown little change over the past 50 years." Interesting indeed. Even more telling for our purpose, Atkeson and Rapoport could not make the gender gap go away even after controlling on every political and psychological resource under the sun (Atkeson and Rapoport 2003). Still more interesting, the less respondents talked during the interview about their likes and dislikes about electoral politics, the less they reported trying to persuade others to vote for their preferred candidate—and this effect obtains especially among women. Atkeson and Rapoport conclude that the willingness to express an opinion has important consequences for involvement in discussion and for agenda setting. As *PROPA* summarizes in its two-decade review of the trajectory of the gender gap in participation, "the lines for women and men move in tandem and almost never converge or cross" (Burns, Schlozman, and Verba 2001, 69). While voting is an exception, the most leader-like activities—offering opinions, attempting to persuade, feeling that it is possible to effect change or make a difference—show little progress despite the dramatic rise in women's position in society.

When it comes to the focus of our study—public meetings—we find strong confirmation of these trends. In their 1990 Citizen Participation Survey, for example, Verba, Schlozman, and Brady asked respondents to imagine that they were attending "a community meeting and people were making comments and statements." They then asked each respondent to tell them whether he or she could "speak well enough to make an effective statement at such a meeting." Using these data, Karpowitz (2006) finds that men are significantly more likely to believe that they could effectively speak up at meetings than women, even after controlling for political knowledge, education, vocabulary, and past experience, such as making speeches at work, church, or in other organizations. In other words, the gap in willingness to participate in public meetings has nothing to do with ability or intelligence. And it persists despite the fact that the gender gap in meeting *attendance* weakens or evaporates in the presence of controls for civic skills and social connectedness.[12] Thus even when we control for the factors that help to explain many other types of participation, women are less likely than men to believe themselves capable of speaking up and effectively contributing to the discussion. In this sense too, we see that women participate less than men when it comes to the more authoritative acts, those that carry the most influence.

But what about education? No resource matters more to political participation than education. Surely women close the engagement gap when they close the education gap? Well, actually, not so. Even when women have high levels of education they remain far behind men when it comes to feeling entitled or qualified to talk about and to take meaningful action in politics. In fact, when Hansen (1976) studied the effect of education on women in the 1972 election, she found that education made women *less* likely to participate relative to their male counterparts (Hansen 1997, 74). This is a head scratcher in political science if ever there was one. If political scientists awoke one morning to the news that social science dictators had taken over the academy and they would be allowed to study just one cause of citizens' behavior, most would choose education. It is the single most important predictor of political action (Wolfinger and Rosenstone 1980). And yet we see that in some cases, it utterly fails to move women to act. Young women closed and then reversed the college degree gap in the late 1990s.[13] Overall, today's women have the same rate of college graduation as men—30% (2010 US Census).[14] But the things that education is supposed to give them—knowledge, interest, and efficacy—did not show a commensurate elevation. Young women are significantly less likely than their male cohort to try to persuade others in an election and to follow news about politics—even though they tend to have *more* education.[15]

[12] In their 1990 Community Participation Survey, Verba, Schlozman, and Brady ask about attendance at "any official local government board or council that deals with community problems and issues such as a town council, a school board, a zoning board, a planning board, or the like." With these data, Karpowitz (2006) finds that men are more likely to report attending such meetings than women, but the gap falls just short of statistical significance in the presence of controls for political experience and social connectedness. These data are self-reports of meetings generally and do not necessarily reflect the gender composition of any single meeting.

[13] Burns, Schlozman, and Verba 2001, 144; US Department of Commerce 2011.

[14] http://www.census.gov/newsroom/releases/archives/education/cb11-72.html. The percentage is among those twenty-five years or older. Women twenty-five and older were more likely than men twenty-five and older to have completed at least high school, at 87.6% versus 86.6%. Among the youngest cohort (ages twenty-five to twenty-nine), women finish college more than men (36% vs. 28%). Interestingly, a study by the National Bureau of Economic Research finds that women are returning to pre–World War II levels in this regard; women composed about half of college students from 1900 to 1930, mainly in teacher-training colleges. The low point for women in college attendance was shortly after World War II, when the GI Bill subsidized (mostly) men; men exceeded women by 2.3 to 1 (Goldin, Katz, and Kuziemko 2006).

[15] Results from a 2006 national survey of young people conducted by CIRCLE at the University of Maryland. The Civic and Political Health of the Nation Survey (2006 CPHN) interviewed

Put differently, women lag behind men primarily because the resources that forcefully propel men to take action merely give women a gentle nudge. When a man completes college, he becomes much more informed about politics; when a woman completes college, she becomes only a little more informed. Economists talk about this effect as "differences in the returns" on education, since they think of education as an investment that yields high profit to some and low profit to others. For example, Dow found that the primary reason for the 10-percentage-point gap between men's and women's political knowledge from the mid-1990s to the mid-2000s is that women enjoy lower "returns" from education (Dow 2009).[16] The point is that despite having closed—and even reversed—the gap in higher education, women have yet to benefit fully from this achievement when it comes to politics. College educated women remain behind college educated men in their level of engagement.[17] Lower education is not the reason that women are less engaged than men. Women are now better educated, but even at the same level of education, women are less politically engaged than men.[18]

Much the same applies in the other primary route to political participation—civic organizations. Churches are powerful mobilizers in American politics, and they provide skills to ordinary people who, because of class or race, would otherwise tend to be even more quiescent and politically passive (Verba, Schlozman, and Brady 1995). However, a recent study of gender in churches finds that "the social conditions that at first glance offer the chance for more recruitment of women turn out to have the opposite effect" (Djupe, Sokhey, and Gilbert 2007, 917). Women are not given the same chance as men to participate in politics via churches, even though women are more numerous in the membership, and more active within churches (Djupe, Sokhey, and Gilbert 2007). Access to social networks that recruit people to participate in politics is one of

---

1,674 young people and 547 adults on civic and political activities performed over the past twelve months, measuring nineteen activities. It oversampled nonwhite youth (Marcelo, Lopez, and Kirby 2007).

[16]When we calculate the gender gap in political knowledge from table 5.5 of Delli Carpini and Keeter, we see clearly that at every education level, women know less than men, by a magnitude of 7 to 18 percentage points. For example, the chance of a college educated person correctly naming both of their US senators is 18 percentage points higher for men than for women (1996, 198).

[17]Delli Carpini and Keeter 1996, table 5.5, 197–98.

[18]One possible solution to the puzzle we have been describing is that education may not have much of an effect on anyone, man or woman. Instead, the causal arrow may run the other way; it may be that people already inclined to participate, engage with, and know about politics are also the people who tend to choose higher education (Highton 2009). That might explain why getting educated does not drive women very much—perhaps, while men who choose to obtain more education are also more active in politics to start with, women who choose more education are not more politically active than women who forego education. Regardless, this leaves us back where we started: why don't women participate as much as men despite having similar resources? And why do we see "continued and unabated differences between men and women in their willingness to openly express political attitudes" (Atkeson and Rapoport 2003, 495)?

the important resources that form the ability to participate. By providing that access, churches act as an important institution for overcoming the participatory deficits of other social cleavages, such as race and class (Verba, Schlozman, and Brady 1995). But women are not gaining the benefits from their ready access to that resource.

To further test the notion that the gender gap in engagement persists despite equal resources, let us look at the youngest cohort of Americans, ages fifteen to twenty-five. These women are more likely to be educated than the men of the cohort. Moreover, they have not yet experienced the suppressing effects of lower workforce participation and less income characteristic of the cohorts aged thirty+.[19] These are women who match, or out-participate, men in student associations and government, who are voting more than men, and who are more active in civic associations—all of which should be directly increasing their involvement in other venues of political participation. We should see these women out-participating men in every form of political engagement.

And yet while these young women do outvote men and participate in charitable activities more than men, they are less likely than men to try to persuade someone during an election and to follow politics in the news.[20] Higher rates of young men than young women report that they "follow what is going on in government and public affairs 'most of the time,'" while higher rates of women than men report "rarely or never." That more of these women than men report "rarely or never" following public affairs in the aftermath of 9/11 is a particularly urgent warning bell that we are missing an important factor shaping women's engagement with their society (Marcelo, Lopez, and Kirby 2007, 16). On the important question of whether the "government typically responds to the genuine need of the public," women were 11 points more likely to decline to give their opinion, choosing instead to indicate that they "haven't thought much about it" (Marcelo, Lopez, and Kirby 2007, 15).[21]

[19]One factor that does not affect women's participation, surprisingly, is having children, even young children, and time spent on household chores also has no effect (Burns, Schlozman, and Verba 2001, 320, 331).

[20]Results in this paragraph come from Marcelo, Lopez, and Kirby 2007 and Zukin et al. 2006.

[21]That is the single biggest gender difference across the nineteen forms of civic or political engagement in the survey. One other explanation that may at first seem decisive also falls flat. Perhaps women believe that government is not a likely, or appropriate, venue to address the needs of the polity. Perhaps women are more cynical or distrusting of government, and that is why they are less interested in what it does and less involved in its activities. This hypothesis turns out to have no support. Young women actually exceed young men in their desire to see the government do more to address problems and are more likely than men to reject the notion that government does "too many things" (Marcelo, Lopez, and Kirby 2007). (In both 2002 and 2006, CPHN survey of fifteen- to twenty-five-year-olds conducted by CIRCLE.) Young women are no more likely than young men to endorse the notion that "government is not responsive to the genuine needs of the public" (Marcelo, Lopez, and Kirby 2007, 15). They are slightly more likely than men to indicate that "government often does a better job than people give it credit for," as opposed to "government is almost always wasteful and inefficient" (13).

Most relevant to our argument, young women's motivation gap is evident in self-perceptions of political competence. Rapoport (1981) studied teenagers' expressions of opinion on issues, some of which were political and others not. He found no gender differences in the proclivity to express opinions on *non*political issues. However, boys were more likely than girls to express their views about politics—*even when controlling on their actual level of information.* Rapoport's analysis further found that these patterns persist into adult life.[22]

The heart of the problem is not really women's inequality of concrete resources, sense of civic duty, faith in government, or skills, whether obtained from education, civic participation, or elsewhere; rather, the problem is women's lower motivation to be politically authoritative. In predicting overall participation with all the variables that may matter, Burns, Schlozman, and Verba found that concrete resources explain only one-third of the gender gap. Another one-third is unexplained, and the remaining one-third is explained by psychological engagement—interest, knowledge, and efficacy.[23] The gender gap is not rooted primarily in the standard pathways to participation. Even when equal to or exceeding men in all these pathways, women are less motivated to engage with politics. Women are notably less likely to think about politics, to seek information about politics, to have opinions about politics, to enjoy politics, to try to influence others about politics, and crucially, to consider themselves able to speak effectively about political issues in public meetings. And that engagement is itself largely unexplained by concrete resources and structural pathways. After conducting the most comprehensive study of political knowledge to date, Delli Carpini and Keeter found that resources and similar structural factors explain only half of women's shortage of political knowledge (Delli Carpini and Keeter 2005, 29, 205–6). As Atkeson concludes her own study, "Political resources, though important in understanding political engagement, are not enough" (Atkeson 2003, 1052–53). What can explain the gender gap in political engagement is motivation. Because politics involves the exercise of authority, and authority is gendered, women are less likely than men to be motivated to be political.

Women out-participate men in voting and in civic acts of various kinds—even in financial contributions to charities—but not in the activities central to the exercise of political authority. It is not the nature of the act that explains the current gender gap; we see that women perform the same actions when the target is not political. Women are less likely to have opinions and information about politics and to talk about politics and public affairs. As Sapiro argues, this renders women more subjects than citizens (Sapiro 1983). Subjects are dutiful; citizens are willful.

[22] His subsequent study of "Don't Know" (DK) responses found significant sex differences in DK response rates as well (Rapoport 1982).

[23] Burns, Schlozman, and Verba 2001, 268, table 10.10.

This conclusion raises further, and more difficult, questions. Why are women more prone than men to act as subjects? Why are women the "quiet sex" in public affairs?

Inadequate Opportunity Depresses the Motivation to Exercise Power

To understand the gendered nature of the motivation to carry political power, we can begin by asking why women are less motivated from their access to the pathways of participation. A clue to what may be preventing women from benefiting from the feeder activities is what goes on in these settings. As Hansen writes, education may not empower women as expected because "the content of that education and the social setting in which it occurs continue to devalue women's experiences" (Hansen 1997, 78). We go further than Hansen; these experiences are not only devaluing women's experiences, they also construct women as less authoritative than men, and that has pernicious civic and political consequences.

In that sense, higher education and civic associations are not reaching their potential as opportunities to inculcate in women the motivation to participate in meaningful political activities. Instead of assisting women in establishing authority in their community, they may be doing the reverse. Here we draw on Delli Carpini and Keeter's helpful framework for understanding the sources of political knowledge (1996). They argue that political knowledge is based on three factors: (1) the ability to understand politics, (2) the motivation to gain knowledge and to reason about it, and (3) the opportunity to do so. In this section, we argue that as women gain ability—by obtaining higher education and participating in civic organizations—they lose motivation. That is because the gendered experiences in these settings reinforce women's gendered lack of authority.

A number of reports by academic organizations have suggested that the experience of many girls and women in educational settings is less empowering than men's. The American Association of University Women, for example, reported that women are less likely to speak in class, and that teachers are more likely to call on boys than girls (AAUW 1992). The general conclusion of the study is that standard practices in educational institutions are better at inviting or recognizing male than female speech (Hansen 1997). These settings represent an opportunity to buttress women's sense of competence, confidence, and thus, authority. As one female student put it, "Every class discussion where my ideas are respectfully listened to and validated, I grow in confidence and in my grasp of the subject."[24]

[24]Reader comment by Taffy C, September 19, 2012. http://jezebel.com/5944642/women-speak-75-less-when-theyre-surrounded-by-dudes-and-thats-bad?post=52822328.

Several reports on elite universities second this conclusion. We delve in depth into these reports for several reasons. First, they provide apt illustrations of the general phenomenon of the gender gap in educational settings. Second, they suggest what it is about the experience of higher education in particular that may be keeping women back. Third, they offer a revealing glimpse into the group-level dynamics in speaking behavior that will become the heart of our analysis in later chapters.

For example, studies of actual participation in Yale Law School class discussions, conducted in 2002 and again ten years later, find that men are as likely to outtalk women in 2012 as they did in 2002.[25] Interviews with female law students suggest that the class dynamics cause some women to lower their self-confidence. As one student said, law school holds up as the ideal lawyer an "image of the dominant male lawyer." Furthermore, as women grow more silent and men more talkative over the course of their law school experience, this may create a sense among women that the successful and influential members of their milieu are male and that women are outside on the margins. As one female student said, "There's very much this male in-group here . . . I feel it's very fratty and very insular, even more so than the Law School itself." In other words, women's experience becomes one of looking on as men talk with other men. This in itself could reinforce women's feelings of low confidence and failure. Again, we see that despite gains in women's status in society generally and education in particular, women's unequal participation in public discussion remains. The gender gap does not disappear with education or among the privileged and elite segments of the population. It is reinforced by the interaction between men and women in settings where talk carries influence, and unequal talk becomes an indicator of unequal status.

An official report by Princeton University also sheds light on current gender gaps and possible reasons why women do not translate experiences in education settings into equal political engagement. Princeton, like the other Ivies, was all male for most of its history. While the university has closed the gap in undergraduate female enrollment, women's status within the institution continues to lag behind men's (Princeton University 2011, 21).[26] While women do a "large proportion of the important work" in student groups, and while some run for elected office in those groups, women are less likely to run for the most visible posts of these organizations, such as president, and far less likely to occupy the most prestigious campus-wide positions (Princeton University

[25] The study observed participation in 113 sessions of twenty-one Law School courses, and surveyed 62% of the Law School students. "Yale Law School Faculty and Students Speak Up about Gender: Ten Years Later," by Yale Law Women, cited in http://www.yaledailynews.com/news/2012/apr/20/gender-imbalances-found-in-law-school/ and in Carol Bass, *Yale Alumni Magazine*, July/August 2012, p. 26.

[26] Women went from 0% in 1968 to 50% in the class of 2013.

2011, 5, 67).[27] In the 2000s, even as women's proportion of students was close to 50%, women held only 14% of the most important undergraduate elected posts on campus; this figure represents a 50% *decline* over the previous decade and a significant decline from the decade before that.[28] That is, women's leadership status declined as women's presence in the student body rose. As noted in the report, Princeton is far from alone; Harvard's student government recently passed a resolution to address the large gender gap in its ranks (Princeton University 2011, 71).

All the more striking is the fact that when the entire Princeton freshman class of '14 was surveyed before arriving on campus (in a survey that enjoyed unusually high response rates), there was no gender difference in intent to seek leadership positions in campus organizations, and women were more likely than men to indicate that they planned to seek leadership roles in campus activities after arriving on campus (Princeton University 2011, 39).[29] However, a mere eight weeks later, in their reinterviews, women were about 10 percentage points more likely than men to have changed their minds about seeking leadership posts, and this effect held across income groups (Princeton University 2011, 41). The gender gap had reared its head.

The possible reasons are several. Women who express an interest in prominent leadership positions are "sometimes actively discouraged by other students" (Princeton University 2011, 5). Some women explicitly state that they don't run because they don't think they'll win (69), much as women in politics are more reluctant than comparably qualified men to run for office (Fox and Lawless 2011).[30] Women may also be more likely to make self-effacing statements, while men may be more likely to make self-promoting ones, which may explain why people may take women less seriously. For example, men in classes may tend to "speak up more quickly" and express thoughts before they are fully formed, while women may be more likely to speak after they have figured out what to say and how to say it best (Princeton University 2011, 60).

Echoing the findings of the Yale study, students report that in some classes, participation is highly unequal by gender and that those tend to be more conflictual; as one student put it, "there are two kinds of precepts [discussion sections]. Some where everyone participates, and some that are just two people screaming at each other. The two people screaming scenario is always two men" (Princeton University 2011, 60). As in the Yale study, women may be particularly alienated

[27] Some of the men holding the top posts joked in focus groups that while they take the credit, they rely on women holding the supporting positions below them to ensure that "work gets done" (Princeton University 2011, 68).

[28] That is 14% of 70 (the 7 most important offices, assuming one person per office per year, times 10 years, equals 70) (Princeton University 2011, 27, 67).

[29] Women were slightly less likely than men to "strongly agree" that "I consider myself to be a leader," but only by 5 percentage points (Princeton University 2011, 40).

[30] We develop this point in chapter 3.

when men dominate discussion because men are taking the floor and because women tend to dislike conflict (more on this in subsequent chapters). Finally, the gap does not come from lower capacity. At Princeton, female GPA slightly exceeds male GPA, and the worst performers are predominantly male (Princeton University 2011, 60). That holds as a general finding at universities: women on average exceed men in academic achievement, suggesting that women are not falling behind in leadership because they are less academically capable (Heckman and LaFontaine 2007).[31] A final possible reason for the gender gap in leadership in higher educational institutions is that women may need more mentoring and peer support before they are willing to seek leadership, to enter competitions for fellowships or awards, and to think of themselves as meritorious. Women may especially need support and "affiliation with other women."

As in studies of national samples, so too in this Ivy League school, we see that women are at least as active as men in some parts of the life of the community but are far less likely than men to lead that community. Women may be less likely than men to self-promote, and more likely to self-efface. Especially relevant to our study, women may often find themselves as observers in classroom discussions, while men carry on the academic debate. Women may also need more encouragement and messages of affiliation than men do. For these reasons, they are not leveraging school experiences with civic participation into adult participation and interest in politics. In the settings where men are gaining authority and preparing to take leadership roles, women are not developing authority or building influence to the same extent.

The Media and Elections as a Missed, or Realized, Opportunity

Women's motivation to exercise power rests not only on their interactions within civic institutions but also on the subtle signals they receive from the information environment. The lag in women's motivation is rooted in part in the gendered portrayals of who exercises power. Despite progress over time, the media, and election campaigns, still frequently links authority with men. On the flip side of the coin, the opportunity to gain motivation can come in the face-to-face settings that women frequent and in the cues that trickle down to them as they consume the news or entertainment media.

Women continue to be portrayed in the news and entertainment media in heavily gendered ways. Although the overt sexism of the past has weakened, media coverage of candidates tends to be quite gendered. Coverage of gubernatorial, senatorial, and presidential candidates dwells more on women's than on comparable men's politically irrelevant personality traits, family, and appear-

[31] Professors, who were also surveyed by Princeton, responded that some of their most quiescent students are female. Shy women may compensate by going to office hours and doing their work more diligently (Princeton University 2011, 60).

ance.[32] Striking examples include commentary in the *Washington Post* and *New York Times* on presidential candidate and senator Hillary Clinton's low neckline and "over-reliance" on suits. Similarly, media commentator Bill Maher commented on Clinton's display of emotion during the 2008 primaries, that "the first thing a woman does, of course, is cry" (Lawless 2009, 71). This emphasis can be so skewed that coverage of the candidate's appearance or personal behavior can dominate the coverage of her issue positions (Aday and Devitt 2001). The amount of coverage can fall short of the candidate's standing in the polls, as in the case of Elizabeth Dole, who in the 2000 primaries was the first prominent female candidate to seek the Republican nomination for president (Heldman, Carroll, and Olson 2006). Female candidates' viability appears more fragile than comparable men's.[33]

These media representations matter. Kim Kahn's experimental evidence shows that this "distorted" media coverage shapes perceptions of women's authority (Kahn 1992; 1994b; 1996). The typical media stories of male candidates produce higher viability ratings and leadership ability ratings than the typical media stories of female candidates, which emphasize lack of viability and give relatively little attention to the candidate's issue positions (Kahn 1992). This evidence is consistent with the notion that voters tend to view men as more quintessentially leader-like in part because they view coverage that emphasizes this trait. Not surprisingly, while female candidates are perceived by voters as better able to handle care issues (health, education, social welfare), they are viewed as less capable on issues deemed men's domain (crime, military, foreign affairs, financial matters); and most important for our point, female candidates are viewed as having a more compassionate personality than men, while men are viewed as more assertive and confident, "tougher and more decisive"—that is, men are deemed better at the core traits of authority.[34] The masculine traits are perceived as better indicators of competence on a wider range of issues, that is, they are closer to the traits of a desirable leader (Huddy and Terkildsen 1993a; 1993b). Masculine traits are also deemed a more important qualification than feminine traits for the most powerful positions—national and executive offices (Huddy and Terkildsen 1993a, 518). Finally, even the seemingly positive coverage of female heads of state as the "first woman" in a high-level office could backfire by presenting women as anomalies in the masculine domain of power (Norris 1997a; 1997b). While the personnel who operate the news media often attempt to adopt a gender-neutral approach, the media continues to send often-subtle signals that women and political power fit together uneasily (Braden 1996).

[32] Devitt 2002; Kahn and Goldenberg 1991; Kahn 1992, 1994a, 1994b, 1996; Heldman, Carroll, and Olson 2005.

[33] Kahn 1992, 1994a, 1994b, 1996; Kahn and Goldenberg 1991.

[34] Burrell 1994; Dolan 2004; Heldman, Carroll, and Olson 2005; Huddy and Terkildsen 1993a, 1993b; Kahn 1996; Norris 1997b; Sapiro 1983; Watson and Gordon 2003.

At least as much as news coverage of leaders, everyday popular culture affects women's motivations to exercise power. As Murphy put it, "Perhaps nowhere is the view of minorities and women more partial and inadequate than in the mass media. . . . Moreover, the women who do appear are typically portrayed as passive, overemotional, dependent on men, and inordinately concerned with 'getting rings out of collars and commodes.'"[35] As one scholar of gender and media summarizes, "the media reinforces the notion that for women the secret to true power lies not in personal achievement or economic independence but in the guise of beauty" (Roessner 2012, 330).[36] Moreover, Murphy's experiments demonstrate that stereotypic media portrayals of women prompt people to make more gender-stereotypic judgments of specific individual women in prominent cases of males accused of wrongdoing. And the clincher is that even when told that the female characters they viewed are fictitious, the effect persisted (1991).

Further evidence that media representations undermine women's authority comes from a clever social psychology experiment—one with special relevance to our interest in discussion groups—in the tradition known as "stereotype threat." Paul Davies, Steven Spencer, and Claude Steele (2005) showed college students either a set of television product ads without people, or the same set of ads plus ads displaying women in traditional gender roles, such as women who aspired to be a homecoming queen. Then the students were asked to work in small groups to solve a common problem. They were asked whether they were interested in functioning as either a leader or a follower in the group. The women exposed to the gender-stereotyped ads indicated less interest in serving as the group leader and more interest in being a follower, while the ads had no effect on men. Merely reminding women in a subtle, indirect way that women fill feminine roles may signal to women that society values them for their femininity and that they are expected to engage in feminine behaviors. This may depress their motivation to take leadership roles. Society may be continually sending such signals to women and thereby creating the sense that leadership is not feminine and thus not valued for women. The opportunity available to women to view themselves, and to be viewed, as properly exercising authority is often limited.

However, there are cases where women do enjoy the opportunity to raise their sense of authority. That women's motivation to engage with politics can rise with opportunity is keenly apparent in the effect of visible female candidates. When women run for a high-level office, female voters increase their sense of efficacy and their level of political information, while men do not (Burns, Schlozman, and Verba 2001; Hansen 1997). The higher the number of

[35] Murphy 1998, 167, quoting Wood 1994, 232.

[36] Progress can be gleaned, with greater diversity of female characters and plot lines, but even when women are portrayed as powerful, they are also portrayed as conforming to feminine traits of beauty and sexuality (Roessner 2012, 331).

women who run for important offices, the stronger this effect becomes (Burns, Schlozman, and Verba 2001). The visibility of female candidates influences the behavior we have focused on as an indicator of the exercise of authority—political proselytizing (Atkeson 2003; Hansen 1997). Even more telling for our argument, Campbell and Wolbrecht found that "over time, the more that women politicians are made visible by national news coverage, the more likely adolescent girls are to indicate an intention to be politically active" as adults (2006, 233). The effect works in part by elevating adolescent girls' political discussion, especially within the family.[37] These results add to the evidence we have reviewed so far to form a consistent pattern. Women benefit from opportunities to view their influence as women as legitimate. These opportunities do their work by signaling to women that they do have the necessary authority. As Atkeson writes, "Despite women's legal ability to participate in the political system for over 80 years, the lack of visible female political players has helped the gender gap in political engagement to persist. The cues provided by minimal female representation in politics and campaigns are that women are not full citizens and that they are not welcome in the political world" (2003, 1053).

Conclusion

Women have certainly come a long way in Western society and politics. American women, like their counterparts in other advanced economies, have narrowed or even reversed the gap in important resources that form the prerequisites of political participation. Women have become reliable voters and civic activists. In other words, they are the foot soldiers of democracy. But they are not the generals. Women lag considerably on the more consequential forms of political activity. They have not turned their growing progress along the pathways to political participation into commensurate political influence. Why is that?

In this chapter we argued that the answer does not lie primarily in the standard list of participatory resources. The United States has experienced a shrinking gender gap in workforce participation, occupational status, and income. When it comes to the single most important antecedent of participation, namely, education, American women have even achieved a higher level than men. In addition, they are more involved than men with voluntary associations during childhood and adulthood. So women are actually advantaged over men in these two crucial pathways to participation. All these resources and opening pathways have given women the ability to participate. Education and

[37] The study found that the effect of visible women does not work by elevating women's endorsement of equal female participation in politics. However, that simply means that girls no longer adhere to the notions of explicit sexism (4% of girls endorse such views). It does not test our argument that girls are likely to view themselves as less influential when women are portrayed that way.

civic experiences have provided women with cognitive resources and skills that enable them to engage with politics—should they choose to do so. Yet women continue to lag behind men in making that choice. Put differently, there is no longer a gender gap in ability, but there remains a gender gap in motivation and opportunity.

The opportunities to participate in the public sphere have bifurcated effects on women. The institutions that provide women the ability to exercise political influence may interfere with their motivation to do so. By implication, women can close the gender gap with men in participation and influence when the institution provides an opportunity to do so. The key is to structure the institution so that it elevates women's motivation to participate. The way to do so is by elevating women's authority in those institutions and to provide women with opportunities to view women as properly exercising power.

Our story in the next chapter takes off from this point of departure. We turn back from an analysis of participation in general to focus on participation in public discussion specifically. We will explore in greater depth how and why women may have a motivation gap with men, and why they may experience an opportunity deficit relative to men. Moreover, we will explore how opportunity and motivation could work in tandem. As the college studies showed, lower motivation to engage, and relative passivity in public discussions, may arise from women's reactions to the gender dynamics they experience in the discussion itself. We then turn to the question of how the opportunity to contribute to discussion is structured by the group itself, and what types of motivations may contribute to the gender gap.

CHAPTER 3

Why Women Don't Speak

This is slavery, not to speak one's thought.

—EURIPIDES, THE PHOENICIAN WOMEN

Now that we have located the sources of women's relative political inactivity in general, we can home in on what specifically holds women back from exercising their voice in public discourse. We argued in the previous chapter that motivation and opportunity are the places to search. Here we ask, how, specifically, do motivation and opportunity depress—or elevate—women's authority in discussion? If we can identify the types of motivations and the forms of opportunity that affect women, we can better understand how women can make a full contribution to the public meeting, the lifeblood of democracy.

We begin by reviewing studies of gender in order to identify what differentiates men from women.[1] Our purpose is to identify motivations that could depress women's participation in discussion relative to men's. We identify characteristics of gender that tend to weaken people's sense of entitlement to exercise influence. That is, we explore the notion that women influence less than men because they are less likely to have a key motivation for doing so—a sense of entitlement to authority. In addition, women may tend to participate and influence less than men because they may be socialized to avoid conflict or to maintain social bonds. We then focus on opportunity—how the group structure and dynamic may either cue women's lower motivation to participate or erase the effects of those motivations. A key aspect of group structure and process is gender composition. We explore what differentiates groups with more men from groups with more women. We derive the hypothesis that when women are a

[1]We make no assumptions about the sources of stable gender differences, and we are not in a position to evaluate arguments about biological versus socially constructed sources of those differences. However, the literature on gender and social behavior supports the notion that much of what we seek to understand is shaped by social processes. As Leaper and Ayres conclude, "biologically oriented researchers investigating gender-related social behaviors generally acknowledge that first, biological predispositions can be altered over time through experience, and second, existing dispositions can be mitigated or overridden by situational demands" (2007, 331). For recent work on the interaction of biology and social practices, see Eagly and Wood (2012).

minority, the group dynamic operates to the detriment of women, and when women are a large majority, particularly without any men, the dynamic helps women. But equally important is the effect of institutional arrangements. The hypotheses we derive about gender composition are fully qualified by the effects of the group's decision rule.[2] Numbers matter depending on rule; put differently, we argue that procedures and gender composition interact to enlarge or neutralize the problem of women's lower authority.

Differences between Men and Women

Our general framework for understanding gender and authority begins with gender role theory.[3] The foundational idea is parsimonious: society classifies people into the categories of man or woman based on their biological differences and expects each category to engage in particular types of thought, feeling, and behavior.[4] These expectations are reflected in, and reinforced in, many small but cumulative ways, through daily experience, in the course of countless interactions with other people, in many settings. The expectations are widespread and carry a moralistic charge, and in that sense form a prescription, or a norm of behavior. And so women learn to behave in feminine ways that signal accommodation, and men to engage in behaviors deemed masculine, signaling assertiveness.[5] Thus gender role theory provides an overarching framework for understanding why women and men walk into formal discussions with different proclivities to engage in what society views as a core masculine behavior: to exercise authority.

Direct evidence for the explanatory power of gender role theory is plentiful in studies of leadership behavior. Women tend to be more reluctant to put

[2] We do not wish to signal that rule is less important than composition simply by the length of the respective sections. The only reason for the relative brevity of our discussion of rule is that much less relevant scholarship has been published on it.

[3] The sociological variant is known as Expectation States Theory (Ridgeway 2001; Ridgeway et al. 2009). Its core concept is "status beliefs." These beliefs constitute a widely shared norm that identifies women (or ethnic minorities) with a particular set of skills, motivations, and abilities and grants them lower status and overall lower social worth. Joseph Berger and colleagues proposed the Expectation States Theory to explain why some group members have more influence and participate more actively than others. It argues that these inequalities are caused by and in turn reinforce the status inequalities in society more generally. We view this theory as similar to Eagly's theory of gender roles, although there are some differences between the theories (Ridgeway and Diekema 1992).

[4] Eagly 1987; Eagly and Wood 2012; Ridgeway 2001; Ridgeway et al. 2009. See also the literature on gender stereotypes, e.g., Glick and Fiske 1996.

[5] People may be socialized into gender roles through self-esteem. One study found that two types of adolescents experienced a rise in self-esteem between the ages of seventeen and twenty-three: girls who viewed themselves as primarily communally oriented, and boys who viewed themselves as primarily self-oriented (Stein, Newcomb, and Bentler 1992, 465–83). These results suggest that when people conform to society's gendered expectations, they may experience approval and their self-esteem may rise accordingly.

forward their opinions or assert their preferences in formal situations. Women are less likely than men to engage in leadership behaviors in group interaction, such as giving opinions and making suggestions.[6] It is no accident that women tend to shy away from taking overt leadership roles in formal settings. As we detail below, when they do so, they often experience adverse consequences, and these consequences testify to the operation of a powerful norm of a gendered division of authority.

To be clear, we are not arguing that the feminine style is inferior and that women should therefore adopt masculine styles. In fact, there are significant advantages to the individual leader and to the group from the more feminine style of leadership. There are at least two reasons why the masculine style is not necessarily optimal. First, leaders who pursue the kind of leadership for which women are rewarded—a cooperative, inclusive, and caring type of leadership—can be highly effective at meeting the group's collective goals and simultaneously create a high-quality experience for all individual group members. An environment where subordinates are cultivated and supported, credit is shared, and conflict is handled through honest and open communication can be quite positive for everyone involved. Second, a style that moves beyond assertion and into aggression detracts even from men's authority under some circumstances (Ridgeway and Diekema 1989). Thus masculine leadership styles are in some ways risky not only for women but also for the men who engage in them because they may veer into excessive dominance and backfire.

However, neither the benefits from the feminine style nor the fact that men's style may carry a penalty if taken too far, negate the main point. As we will show, women tend to suffer adverse social consequences *as women* when they attempt to exert authority. These negative effects on women can explain why women, on average, may be less motivated to exercise influence in a discussion. The general conclusion from gender role theory, then, is that society tends to create expectations of lower authority for women.

But in addition to the overarching claim that women learn to avoid displays of authority, gender role theory offers three specific psychological mechanisms that pinpoint the sources of women's influence gap in group discussion. We proceed by discussing each of three pathways by which gender may matter: confidence, conflict aversion, and orientation to social bonds.

Gender Pathway I: Women May Participate Less Because They Have Less Confidence

It is tempting to conclude that women are equal to men in American society. Women have made enormous strides, as detailed in the previous chapter. But women still differ from men in an important respect. They are much more likely than men to underrate their competence, qualifications, and achievement. And

[6]See, for example, Wood and Karten 1986.

as we will see below, their performance is, in turn, more sensitive to this self-rating—women who underrate their ability also perform less well than women who do not, holding constant actual, objective ability. This gap between the performance of underraters and others is greater among women than men. Thus low self-confidence is a more potent negative force among women than men.[7] In sum, despite objectively similar ability, the sexes tend to diverge in matters related to confidence, in two ways: (1) in their level of self-confidence, and (2) in the degree to which low confidence and signals of ambiguous performance suppress the performance of achievement-oriented behaviors and authoritative actions.

Especially powerful demonstrations of the gender gap in self-confidence come from studies that measure objective competence. Women tend to underrate their competence when considered against objective indicators of ability (Beyer and Bowden 1997). For example, boys tend to rate their mathematical ability higher than girls do, even given the same objective level of ability (Wigfield, Eccles, and Pintrich 1996). Even in verbal ability, where women are more likely than men to excel, female students rate their ability at the same level as male students do (Pajares 2002). A striking illustration comes from the study of Princeton undergraduates described in chapter 2. At Princeton, women's GPA is slightly higher than men's, and women have a higher chance than men of graduating with honors, yet women graduate as they entered—rating their "intellectual self-confidence as compared to the average person your age" lower than men do theirs (Princeton University 2011, 49, 55).

Low self-confidence is not merely a problem for underachieving women, or when it comes to skills that are unfamiliar to women. As the informal study of Yale Law School suggested, women tend to feel less confident than men even at the highest levels of achievement, and in the most verbal of all professions. This illustrative evidence obtains in more rigorous studies in a variety of settings. For example, a study of doctoral students who won prestigious postdoctorate awards found that 70% of the men considered their ability to be above average, but only 52% of the women did so (Babcock and Laschever 2003, 77). The gender gap in confidence reaches to the top of the ability spectrum.

Women's proclivity to underestimate their ability can be so extreme that it has been dubbed the "impostor syndrome." Peggy Orenstein, an influential journalist and writer, recalled that when she was writing her senior thesis she "became paralyzed . . . convinced that my fraudulence was about to be unmasked. . . . I told [my advisor] of the fears that were choking me. 'You feel like an impostor?' she asked. 'Don't worry about it. All smart women feel that way'" (Babcock and Laschever 2003, 78). Even highly accomplished women can suffer intense doubts about their ability.

[7] As well, the gender gap in confidence is due in part to men's overconfidence. As Fox and Lawless put it, men are "more likely to express confidence in skills they do not possess and overconfidence in skills they do possess" (2011, 61–62).

Women are not only generally less likely than men to view themselves as competent and meritorious, they are also specifically less likely than men to view themselves as qualified to engage in leadership roles. This flows from the fact that women's confidence tends to plummet all the more when it comes to masculine actions and roles stereotypically associated with men (Beyer and Bowden 1997). In one experiment, psychologists Debra Instone, Brenda Major, and Barbara Bunker (1983) assembled students into task groups of four members and assigned one of them to supervise the work of the others. Ahead of time they asked the supervisors to indicate their level of confidence in their ability to supervise. On that self-report, the men scored a third higher than the women. Furthermore, the higher the score, the more that the supervisors attempted to exercise influence over the student workers. In other words, assertive, authoritative behavior was correlated with participants' feelings of confidence and efficacy. The confidence gender gap may explain the authority gender gap.

In addition to the gender gap in confidence stemming from beliefs about competence, there is a related gender gap in resilience in the face of negative feedback. Women tend to be more sensitive to negative cues about their performance, and even to the absence of positive ones. For example, a study of students in introductory economics classes found that among students who received a grade lower than B in the course, the men were more likely than the women to continue in the economics curriculum (Horvath, Beaudin, and Wright 1992). That is, given the identical low grade, women tend to be less persistent. Men have a stronger set point or anchor of perceived competence, which is less likely to move in response to negative information from the environment.[8] Similar patterns obtain among Princeton undergraduates. Women's self-evaluations were more affected by the valence of others' feedback, perhaps because they are more likely than men to view others' perceptions as accurate and valuable information about themselves (Roberts 1991).

Compared to men, women tend to need more explicit assurances that they are deserving of praise or reward. Several studies have demonstrated that women tend to have a lower sense of entitlement than men to benefits such as job pay. Women pay themselves less money in laboratory settings than men do and believe they should work longer, harder, better, and more efficiently than men believe they should for a given level of pay (Major, McFarlin, and Gagnon 1984). That is, men tend to have a higher sense of entitlement than women. This gender norm shows up quite early. The same gender gap in self-confidence and entitlement that we see among adults is found in children as young as six years old. In one study, first grade girls awarded themselves between 30 and

[8]The results are also consistent with the possibility that men's confidence drops as far as women's, but remains higher than women's after the negative feedback only because men begin at a higher confidence level. Regardless, the main point is that men tend to have more confidence in one sense or another.

78% fewer chocolates than boys gave to themselves, for the same level of performance (Callahan-Levy and Messe 1979). Moreover, girls' low self-payment correlated with a preference for feminine over masculine occupations; girls who indicated an interest in becoming a nurse or a secretary gave themselves less than girls who preferred to be a firefighter or astronaut (Callahan-Levy and Messe 1979).

Given the gender gap in perceptions of self-worth, it is no surprise that women, in a more vulnerable position to start with, are more susceptible to cues about their value. The psychologists Wayne Bylsma and Brenda Major (1992) conducted an experiment in which women and men were either given direct assurances of their worth, or not. When not given assurances, women felt entitled to lower wages than men did. But the gender gap closed when women were told that they had performed well at the job. Women tend to be less confident than men about their value and thus to be more sensitive than men to the absence of clear positive signals that they are meritorious.

A recent brain imaging study further reinforces the notion that the sexes differ in the proclivity to hold steady despite negative signals about performance. The study exposed subjects to information about their relative performance in IQ test questions. Beforehand, subjects took the same test individually, to establish their baseline performance. Then subjects were asked to answer the same questions, this time as part of a group task. After they answered each question, these subjects were told how their performance ranked relative to others in their test-taking group. Of the twenty-seven subjects, thirteen recovered their original performance level while fourteen did not.[9] What distinguishes the "breakdowns" from the "resilients"? Gender. The rates of resiliency were 21% for women and 77% for men. As one journalist summarized, "If we think others in a group are smarter, we may become dumber, temporarily losing both our problem-solving ability and what the researchers call our 'expression of IQ'" (Kishida et al. 2012). Becoming temporarily "dumber" may be a problem that women tend to experience more than men. It is a response to a signal that cues what many women have learned to internalize—that they are not valuable actors in society.

This does not mean that women—and men—who are sensitive to their relative performance lack ability and thus can offer less valuable contributions to the group. In the brain imaging study, the people more likely to experience the performance breakdown were the subjects with a high IQ. In other words, it is the members most valuable to the group and those who can best contribute to its mission whose capacities are lost because of group dynamics that cue women's sense of inferiority. Group interaction that causes some people to feel inadequate, because their views are not supported or are ignored, may undermine the group's chief goal. And women are more likely than men to suppress

[9]The number of subjects is small because the study used fMRI scans, which are quite expensive. The scan results are not important to our point here.

their potential contribution to the group in the presence of negative feedback or in the absence of positive affirmations.

Because it is all about power and authority, politics is an arena where the confidence gap, and its effects, might be especially pronounced. Various studies support the notion that women tend to have less confidence than men in political life and link it to the finding that women shy away from leadership positions.[10] In studies of potential candidates, women report less politically relevant experience than similarly qualified men do (Fox and Lawless 2011; Lawless and Fox 2010). As the authors put it, "Despite comparable credentials, backgrounds, and experiences, accomplished women are substantially less likely than similarly situated men to perceive themselves as qualified to seek office. Importantly, women and men rely on the same factors when evaluating themselves as candidates, but women are less likely than men to believe they meet these criteria" (Fox and Lawless 2011, 59). Confidence is the single biggest factor accounting for the gender gap in the decision to run for office (Lawless and Fox 2010). That is, women are far less likely than men to run for office, even when women and men share high levels of professional experiences that would qualify them for public office, and even when women have good social connections that facilitate running (Fox and Lawless 2011). Confidence affects women's participation in the leadership positions of politics.

Experimental evidence reinforces the notion that low confidence is a powerful negative motivation for women, overriding the positive effect of high qualifications. That is, even highly qualified women are more reluctant than comparable men to put themselves forward in a competition for the most competent member of the group. Kristin Kanthak and Jonathan Woon simulated the decision to run for office in a lab setting (2011). First they assigned subjects to perform a nongendered task and measured the person's objective performance. Then they asked participants if they were willing either to volunteer or to run against other group members for the position of the group's representative. The participants were told that the representative would perform the task on behalf of the group. The researchers found that the person's objective competence in performing the task had a great deal to do with *men's* decision to run to represent the group; but competence on the task had *no* effect on *women's* decision to do so. Furthermore, while women were more reluctant than men to *compete*, they were no more reluctant than men to *volunteer* to be the group's representative. Women were thus especially hesitant to take on a leadership role when it involved direct comparison with others—and the attendant possibility of negative feedback that might accompany such comparative judgments.[11]

[10] An extended discussion of these issues can be found in chapter 2.

[11] Participants were college students, again reinforcing the notion that the gender gap in political participation is not going away on its own anytime soon, and that it is not primarily caused by women's deficits in the workplace or earned income.

Both experimental and observational evidence thus point to the same conclusion: women are reluctant to compete for a leadership position even when their ability is high; confidence is a key element in the gender gap in leadership and authority.

At issue is not only women's confidence in general or in their political competence and desire to run for public office but also women's specific confidence in public speaking. That specific form of confidence may be particularly consequential for participation in public discussion. And here too we see the familiar pattern where women are shyer than men, on average. As one female city council member told an interviewer, "Men have more authority when they speak, not because they know more, but because they're more comfortable. Women are nervous because people say, 'what does she know?'" (Beck 2001, 59). While this comment may be rooted in different levels of confidence about political knowledge, it also refers specifically to speaking to an audience. And systematic studies of accomplished women confirm the interview results: Potential female candidates indicate less confidence than similar men do in their public speaking ability (Lawless and Fox 2011).[12]

If women have less confidence than men do while engaging in formal speech, it is not because women have a lower ability to speak. Verba, Schlozman, and Brady's Citizen Participation Study, based on a nationally representative sample, included a measure of the respondent's vocabulary. The authors found that women's vocabulary is better than men's, to a significant degree (Verba, Schlozman, and Brady 1995, 434). That is, women are not at a loss for words.

And yet studies consistently find that women are less confident than men about public speaking. Women show higher anxiety in the days leading up to an oral presentation (Behnke and Sawyer 2000). Among eighth graders, girls are less comfortable than boys when it comes to asking questions in class (Daly, Kriesler, and Roghaar 1994). Self-reports of general attitudes about communication produce the same pattern (Lustig and Anderson 1990). As an American woman in Conover and colleagues' cross-national study of public discussion noted, "I'm not going to bring it up because I have not studied it; I've not read about it. And I don't want to be made to look dumb." Even more succinct is this pithy summary by a British woman: "I'm not that brave" (Conover, Searing, and Crewe 2002, 53). The gender gap in general and in political confidence goes hand in hand with the gender gap in public speaking confidence.

Why do women tend to be less confident and assertive? In part because they are likely to face social sanction for asserting themselves and attempting to ex-

[12] Along these lines, a study of gendered speech among university professors found that women tend to use more tentative speech styles and men assertive forms. For example, men tended to say things like "I have two midterms and a final" or "I'm gonna ask you to do one midterm," while women tended to state the same content in indirect form: "there are two papers" or "there is going to be a midterm and a final" (Tannen 1994, 175–76). The men in the study tended to make clear that they are personally issuing requirements, while the women tended to avoid doing so.

ercise authority. Specifically, such actions are seen as violating norms of what society constructs as "feminine," and women are taught that they are valued primarily for their femininity. In the words of Babcock and Laschever, "An assertive personal style can be a gender-norm violation for a woman" (2003, 86).

A series of experiments relying on trained confederates has established that women who engage in a more assertive style tend to receive lower performance and/or likability ratings than either men who use the identical style or women who use a cooperative, accommodating style.[13] Men's ratings are unaffected; that is, men can be assertive without incurring a social cost (Carli 1990). Moreover, the same assertive behavior is more likely to be perceived as aggressive or irrational when performed by female rather than by male leaders (Heilman, Block, and Martell 1995). These effects hold in various settings, including group interactions. When the sociologist Cecilia Ridgeway trained female confederates to interact with other members of decision-making groups, she found that women exercised the most influence when they used a stereotypically defined feminine style: friendly, cooperative, caring, but nonconfrontational (1982, 81).[14] Women who attempt to exercise influence in the overt ways associated with men experience the failure that comes from norm violation—negative evaluation of their abilities and social rejection in the form of dislike.

For example, one experiment assigned either a male or a female leader to a decision-making group. All the leaders were confederates of the investigators. These female and male confederates had been trained to engage in the same leadership style during the group decision-making task. Nevertheless, the participants in the study rated the female leaders as more domineering than their male counterparts and gave them lower ratings on ability and skill. They also exhibited more negative facial expressions toward the female than the male leader, despite professing to have no more negative attitudes toward female leaders (Butler and Geis 1990). That is, when women use explicit markers of influence, they elicit powerful signals of social disapproval. Men do not. It is no surprise that powerful gender norms are typically well internalized, and few women test their boundaries. When a social identity group consistently encounters rejection when using power, it comes to question its competence to do so, and to believe that it lacks authority.[15]

The negative effects of women's violation of the norm are sufficiently powerful that they may be triggered even by the seemingly trivial use of nonverbal signals. A study by Carli, LaFleur, and Loeber (1995) exposed undergraduates to either a woman or a man who made the identical persuasive appeal to an

[13] Eagly and Carli 2007; Eagly, Makhijani, and Klonsky 1992; Heilman and Okimoto 2007; Rudman 1998; Rudman and Glick 2001.

[14] See also Ridgeway 2001.

[15] This process is not necessarily, or even likely, reflected in explicit ideology, nor is it necessarily recognized consciously. In fact, today there exists an ideology of gender equality in the public sphere. But gender roles, and socialization into them, continue to exist.

unpopular view. The content was identical. But the gender of the messenger varied, and so did the nonverbal communication style of the speaker; in one version the message was filmed using a "task-oriented" style using frequent eye contact, calm hand motions, and fluid speech, and in the other, the speaker used a "social style" communicating "friendliness and affiliation" by smiling, leaning forward, and using unintrusive body language. Male speakers gained most influence with the task-oriented communication style, but women did best with a social style. Moreover, the reason women succeeded best with the social style is that it best elevated their likability—and likability mattered more to women's influence than it did to men's (when the audience was male). Women fare worse when they act confidently than when they do not, because confidence is associated with masculinity.

And that fear of acting confidently, whether conscious or not, works preemptively to silence women and to distort the preferences they express. One experiment found that indeed, women's fear of being perceived to be "a pushy person" and triggering punishment for "being too demanding" explains why they shy away from acting assertively in financial negotiation (Amanatullah and Morris 2010, 260). In the study, men and women set the same financial goals before negotiation, but women acted on them less assertively—so much so that they lost 20% of their starting salary in just the first round. As Eagly and Carli sum it up, "People penalize women for immodesty more than they penalize men, and women respond by displaying modesty" (2007, 168). Put differently, women perceive the existence of a norm that expects them to act like women; that defines feminine behavior as demure, modest, accommodating, and cooperative; and that defines masculine behavior as assertive and dominant (Eagly and Karau 2002). Women tend to conform to this norm, because when they don't, they experience adverse social consequences—they are disliked more and respected less (Rudman 1998; Rudman and Fairchild 2004).[16]

These studies are often conducted in artificial settings with college students, but the same dynamic can be found in actual settings populated by "real" adults, as recounted by the economist Linda Babcock and the journalist Sara Laschever (2003). In interviews with successful women, the authors discovered a common refrain—the women were aware that they were expected to act deferentially and unassumingly. For example, one senior law partner told them that as a teenager her father admonished her to self-monitor: "Honey, you know you can't act like a tiger. You have to act like a kitten" (104). Another woman, capturing a common perception, said: "[an assertive woman] can often . . . come across as a bitch to people" (86).

[16]To be sure, women may tend to be more concerned with others' views of them and thus seek approval more intensely; perhaps consequently, they may try harder to avoid alienating others and maintain the connection with those in a position to judge them. But these studies also suggest that women try harder to avoid assertive communication styles because they experience negative consequences from doing so.

Most vividly, Babcock and Laschever learned of a firm that provides a "Bully Broads" service to companies seeking to "modify" businesswomen whose assertive style is viewed negatively. The firm attempts to teach these women to be "nicer" and become "ladies first" (Babcock and Laschever 2003, 85). A representative of the firm explains the problem: "a male executive . . . has more permission to be an ass. But when women speak their minds, they're seen as harsh" (85). As we have seen above, women face a particular difficulty when they speak their minds. The "Bully Broads" program trains women to speak hesitantly, self-deprecatingly, and apologetically. Most men sent to the program are sent to learn how to reduce stress or to delegate more; by contrast, almost every woman is sent to become "nicer."

Women are, therefore, socialized by positive and by negative reinforcements; they can observe the negative effects of their masculine actions and the positive effects of their feminine ones on how others in turn treat them. A woman who violates the gender norm may find herself sent to "nice" boot camp under the threat of losing her job—symbolically, in the form of social sanctions, if not literally. And this more anecdotal evidence is seconded by national surveys showing that while women are no longer expected to occupy themselves primarily in the domestic sphere, taking care of their family, they are nevertheless disfavored in positions of power. For example, a national Gallup poll found that Americans who prefer a male boss outnumber those who prefer a female boss by two to one.[17]

This reluctance to assert one's self and one's preferences lest one violate the norm of feminine behavior extends to various situations where people attempt to reach a formal agreement. Women are less likely to negotiate at all, to negotiate energetically, and to reap the rewards of negotiation (Eagly and Carli 2007, 169; Babcock and Laschever 2003). When researchers asked MBA students to simulate a job interview and then asked the students if they knew their worth during the salary negotiation, they found that 85% of the men indicated that they knew their worth, while 83% of the women indicated that they were unsure of their worth (Baron 2003). Fully 70% of the men believed they were entitled to above-average pay, while only 30% of the women did. As one woman said to the researcher, "it's hard to talk about yourself . . . you tend to just be humble and hope that people can see that you're a great person" (Eagly and Carli 2007, 170).[18] On average, women are not only less sure of the value of

[17] Cited in Pande and Ford 2011, 4. Original results at http://www.gallup.com/poll/24346/americans-prefer-male-boss-female-boss.aspx.

[18] Even more telling of the presence of a gender norm, women behave in more self-sacrificing and self-effacing ways when observed than when in private. In one experiment, participants were told to work as long and hard as it takes to "earn" four dollars. The investigators did not define "earn," allowing them to see if women set a higher standard for themselves than men did. They found that women indeed worked longer and harder than men, but doubly so when they were observed than when in private (Major, McFarlin, and Gagnon 1984). Women ask for lower salaries in

their abilities, but also they are more reluctant to communicate that value to others.[19] Women are trained to view self-assertion as self-promotion and are conditioned to avoid both.

In sum, women tend to be less confident, more sensitive to negative signals about their ability, qualifications, and value, and more reluctant to assert themselves in formal situations than men. They are also specifically less confident about their political competence and more shy about expressing their opinions in public than men. Yet they tend to have stronger verbal abilities than men. In general, women's confidence gap is not explained by lower objective aptitude. The solution to this apparent puzzle is societal norms about gender. Women's relative reluctance to assert their views in public meetings comes not from ability but from opportunity and motivation. If the conditions of deliberation do not address the gender gap in confidence, they may create a participation and representation deficit for women.

We have dwelt at length on confidence because it is the most direct hypothesis from gender role theory. In addition, many studies support the hypothesis that the gender gap in influence and achievement is rooted in confidence. However, gender role theory is also consistent with two other hypotheses.

Gender Pathway II: Women May Participate Less Because They Dislike Competition or Conflict

Even if politics were a woman's game, it might not invite women to participate if it was played like a man's game. Women may be more reluctant than men to engage in a discussion of public matters when it is conflictual. Eagly found that women are more likely than men to use cooperative and collaborative conflict resolution while men tend to take a winner-take-all, competitive approach to conflict (Eagly, Johannesen-Schmidt, and Engen 2003). In a comprehensive review of gender differences in economic behavior, Croson and Gneezy concluded that women are less likely than men to participate in contests, auctions, and bargaining, and they tend to prefer compensation by piecework over compensation that involves competition (2009).

For example, Niederle and Vesterlund ran a laboratory study in which subjects were assembled in groups of four, two men and two women, and had to complete tasks for rewards (2007). In the first round, the participants were given their payments as they completed the tasks, without competition. In a later round, they performed the tasks again, but this time their rewards de-

---

the presence of another person than in private (Wade 2002, cited in Babcock and Laschever 2003). Women act as if they are conforming to a gendered norm of behavior. That norm teaches them to defer to others' wishes and to avoid direct assertion of their own views.

[19] As in the previous chapter, we note that these gender gaps are not going away with time. The negotiation studies find just as massive a gender gap among young people (Babcock and Laschever 2003, 67).

pended on a competitive tournament. They learned their absolute performance after each task, but not how well they did relative to other participants. Then the subjects were given a choice—to be rewarded by tournament or by piecework. Most men (73%) chose the tournament, and most women did not (35%). The investigators found that one reason for this sizable gender gap is men's overconfidence in their performance, but the other cause is women's reluctance to compete even when they perform well. As the authors summarize it, "low-ability men enter the tournament too much, and high-ability women do not enter it enough" (Niederle and Vesterlund 2007, 1069). One factor that did not explain most of the gender gap was actual performance, which was the same for men and women. Again we see that women's lagging participation is not due to ability.[20] While this study confirms the importance of confidence, it also points to competition aversion by most women, and competition seeking by most men.

Two possible explanations for women's aversion to competition, especially against men, have emerged from existing research. First, unlike men's performance, women's performance is rated lower when they engage in competitive rather than accommodating behavior (Croson and Gneezy 2009; Eagly and Carli 2007), suggesting that women's interests are negatively affected when they emphasize conflict and competition over other alternatives. Second, the gender difference emerges early in life and may reflect long-term patterns of gender socialization. Girls and boys tend to pursue different patterns of play, with boys more likely than girls to engage in competition and conflict (Miller, Danaher, and Forbes 1986; Maccoby 1988).

A further clue that these processes are driven by cultural norms of gendered behavior comes from an intriguing study of gender and competition in two cultures that differ in women's status and role expectations. Gneezy and colleagues compared gender differences in the decision to enter a competition in two societies, one patrilineal (the Masai in Tanzania) and one matrilineal (the Khasi in India). They found the usual male proclivity to enter competitions in the patrilineal society, but a reversal in the matrilineal society, where women are much more likely than men to enter competitions (Gneezy, Leonard, and List 2009). If women are socialized to be more cooperative and interdependent with others, then women may dislike situations where there is conflict or competition, or even merely a lack of cooperation. When they are in such situations, women may tend to withdraw from the interaction in order to distance themselves from the conflict. The common denominator for these preferences may be the aversion to situations where the social ties of the participants are frayed.

As Hansen puts it, "women tend to be the peace-keepers and consensus-builders" (1997, 79). A number of studies specifically point to the deterring or silencing consequences of conflict for women: "women are especially likely to

[20] They also ruled out as important factors a person's level of risk aversion and sensitivity to negative feedback.

remain silent if they anticipate opposition."[21] Consistent with the reports from Yale Law School and Princeton University, for example, Houston and Kramarae observe that the aggressive, competitive nature of discussion in traditional classrooms discourages female students from contributing (Houston and Kramarae 1991). Recall, too, that in the Kanthak and Woon study we described earlier, women were no less likely than men to *volunteer* to represent their team, but were less likely than men to choose to run in an election to obtain a representative position. One difference between these two acts revolves around the possibility of competition and conflict. As Atkeson and Rapoport write, "conflict may be particularly problematic for women who are often more interdependent socially and thus less inclined to engage in activities that might 'rock the boat'" (Atkeson and Rapoport 2003, 499). This is seconded by Susan Beck's study of local council members. The women interviewed mentioned partisan conflict as their least favorite part of the job (Beck 2001, 62). The practice of accusing political opponents of misdeeds, launching attacks, and denying credit to meritorious opponents out of political strategy, all seemed to these women to be hateful (Beck 2001, 62).

Women may not only tend to be averse to conflict but may perform less well than men under competitive conditions. A study of students at a selective Israeli engineering school that rewarded students for solving difficult puzzles found that as the level of competition in the testing environment increased, male performance improved significantly, but female performance dropped (Gneezy, Niederle, and Rustichini 2003).

In politics specifically there are hints that women tend to prefer consensus modes of interaction. Kathlene (1994) found that female committee chairs in the Colorado legislature tended to use their positions to facilitate open discussion among many of those present, including committee members, witnesses, and bill sponsors. By contrast, male chairs tended to exercise more of their individual agency and ran the hearings to maximize their own preferences. National samples of state legislative leaders yield similar findings. Women are more likely than men to prefer collaboration in lawmaking. Men committee chairs tend to place less emphasis than female chairs do on a process of inclusion and consensus.[22] At the city level, unelected city managers exhibit a similar gendered pattern (Fox and Schuhmann 1999).

These findings for political settings echo findings from other settings. In firms and organizations, women tend to prefer and to practice more consensual

[21] Belenky et al. 1986; Margolis 1992; Houston and Kramarae 1991; Noelle-Neumann 1993.

[22] Dodson and Carroll 1991; Jewell and Whicker 1994; Rosenthal 1998 and 2005. For example, Rosenthal (1998) finds that women are more likely to emphasize an "integrative" style. This style is characterized by "trust, affection, a team orientation, moderation, and a commitment to process and task" (1998, 57). It highlights inclusion and relationships. She finds that men are more likely to engage in "aggregative" leadership that features "dominance, competitiveness, ambition, a drive to control, and opportunism" (1998, 57).

styles. A large survey of managers found that women are more likely than men to follow managerial practices such as "people development" and "participative decision-making," while men are more likely than women to use an individualistic decision-making style and seek more control.[23] In general, women tend to use a more democratic and participatory style and to focus on educating and improving those in their charge (Eagly and Carli 2003).

In sum, women may tend to prefer—and to thrive in—conditions of cooperation and to do less well than men in conditions of conflict. The conditions of discussion may well entail more or less cooperation or conflict. Attending to these conditions is, therefore, key because the level of harmony in the discussion may be especially consequential to women's participation.

Gender Pathway III: Women May Participate Less Because They Are More Sensitive to Social Bonds

Some of the findings we have reviewed so far not only support the notion that women tend to prefer consensus and to dislike conflict, but also that women may tend to be more oriented to social bonds. Disagreement can find more expression—and better resolution—when people feel connected to each other in bonds of cooperation, affection, or acceptance (Mansbridge 1983). As we saw in chapter 1, recent writing in political philosophy argues that in order to raise the quality of discussion, the first item of business is to establish these bonds. There is little productive exchange of reason without cooperation, according to this theory; the social precedes the cognitive. Exchange across lines of political difference, as Diana Mutz (2006) found, depends heavily on the nature of the social relationships in which people are embedded. We speculate that this effect may be particularly important to women.

The broad reason for this hypothesis is that women may tend to be more sensitive to the presence or absence of social ties. The foundational text on this thesis is Carol Gilligan's *In a Different Voice* (1982). This book argued that men and women, from a young age, exhibit different orientations to moral thought and action. Most generally, men tend to prioritize and think along lines of rights, and the regulation or freedom of those rights, while women tend to be motivated more by need for help and by their perceived ties to others, and to approach the world with empathy.

While valid criticisms have been launched against that particular book, the general point has received considerable support.[24] Other scholars, working from a different theoretical framework, have argued similarly that society tends to socialize women to "affirm their identities as members of a collective by

[23] McKinsey 2008 cited in Pande and Ford 2011, 21.

[24] See, for example, Walker 1984 and Jaffee and Hyde 2000 cited in Huddy, Cassese, and Lizotte 2008, 39.

attending to others" (Amanatullah and Morris 2010). Women tend to prioritize relationships in their lives more than men do, and they do so across the life span and regardless of class (Cross and Madson 1997). As we noted above, societies convey the expectation that a person should conform to gender roles. Men are expected and trained to have the attributes that go hand in hand with masculine roles, such as agency, assertion, and independence; women are expected to exhibit caring for and interdependence with others. Some studies support the notion that women tend to be more empathetic than men (Baron-Cohen 2003; Feldman and Steenbergen 2001). Women read nonverbal cues such as facial expressions more accurately (Falk 1997, cited in Hannagan and Larimer 2010), supporting the idea that women are especially attuned to the reactions of others. Women are more affected than men by the social context and by social cues in economic game experiments (Croson and Gneezy 2009). Women also conform to social pressures more than men when individuals meet face to face and are instructed to communicate their preference to other members (Bond and Smith 1996; Cooper 1979; Eagly and Carli 1981). Women score lower than men on Social Dominance Orientation, a stable personality tendency that undergirds a desire to dominate others (Sidanius and Pratto 1999). In Western cultures, women tend to orient toward interdependence and cooperation and to prioritize the principles of equality or need over merit even at the expense of their own self-interest, while men in turn tend to emphasize autonomy and to behave hierarchically.[25] Again, we emphasize that these often tend to be small differences between individuals, with variance within each gender, but may be amplified by characteristics of the setting (Hannagan and Larimer 2010).

One clue affirming this hypothesis can be found in Susan Beck's observations and interviews of men and women serving on municipal councils (2001). This study is especially useful for our purpose because these are people who attend public meetings about politics—and therefore the setting and the participants represent the types of settings and participants with which we are centrally concerned. Beck's interviews with these council members suggest that while men and women share much in common, the women tend to be less comfortable in this setting than men. Women tend to respond more than men to others' needs, and they "strive for collegiality" (Beck 2001). As one councilman said to Beck, "women . . . will avoid positions that will offend a group in town. They respond to feeling and people" (Beck 2001, 567). Other councilmen echoed this notion of women being more emotional, intuitive, and concerned for the feelings of others. While this notion may come from an attitude of denigration toward

[25] Aries 1998; Babcock and Laschever 2003; Babcock et al. 2003; Cross and Madson 1997; Eagly 1987; Eagly and Johnson 1990; Knight and Dubro 1984; Josephs, Markus, and Tafarodi 1992; Leventhal and Lane 1970; Scott et al. 2001; Schwartz and Rubel 2005; Sidanius and Pratto 1999. Studies find this across many countries (e.g., Schwartz and Rubel 2005) but not in all (Prince-Gibson and Schwarz 1998).

women, or from a stereotype about women's emotionality, women may in fact be more tuned in to the emotions of the people around them, on average.

In addition, as we saw above, women tend to pursue more facilitative styles of interaction in legislative settings. This may indicate not only a preference for cooperation but also a deeper underlying orientation to connect with others. Women endorse or use a more facilitative leadership style, on average (Dodson and Carroll 1991; Flammang 1985; Kathlene 1994). Beck found that female city council members saw themselves as more oriented to listening rather than finding a "quick management solution" (2001, 58). Sue Thomas concludes, "[among] women . . . influence is used for responsiveness to colleagues and constituents rather than for personal gain" (Thomas 2005, 252). These conclusions are consistent with those from a broad array of studies of female leadership in lab and organizational settings (Eagly and Johnson 1990). As Eagly and Carli summarize, women are somewhat more likely than men to adopt a democratic style, even when they fill the same leadership position (2007, chapter 8). As a colleague of the female speaker of New York's City Council said of her, "she has injected more democracy, with a little 'd', into the council; every single council member has a say in the budget" (Eagly and Carli 2007, 126).

A noteworthy illustration of women's tendency to connect with others comes, again, from the work of Lyn Kathlene. She conducted a fascinating analysis of the words Colorado state legislators use during a scholarly interview to describe the resources they draw upon in formulating bills. She found that only women mentioned "citizens, community, country, district, parents, or world" and "city council, county commissioners, leaders, legislators, mayor/s"; while only men mentioned "advisers, clients, consultants, experts, industry" (Kathlene 2001). Women were more likely than men to see their key political actions as linked to their community, including their legislative or political community. During legislative debate, these legislators talked in ways that reflected gender differences in views about autonomy versus connectedness. Men tended to articulate the view that criminals are autonomous individuals making bad choices for which they should be held accountable; women tended to express the view that criminals are embedded in a structure that denies them opportunity, including unhealthy families, inadequate economic opportunity, or poor education (Kathlene 2001).[26] The differences are not merely the result by party. All these threads woven together create a pattern pointing toward women's greater emotional and psychological interdependence with others. The small, narrow sample precludes generalization, but the results are suggestive of the hypothesis that women may tend to prioritize social bonds.

[26] Even when men took the liberal position, they tended to introduce bills that focused on rules regulating infringement on individual rights, such as those governing new evidence in criminal cases. While some women sponsored bills that toughened policy, only women introduced bills that focused on prevention.

Suggestive evidence in this direction also comes from Beck's interviews of suburban council members. A common refrain among her female, but not male, interviewees was that the politics surrounding them was "distasteful." Partisanship bothered and even enraged some of the women. They viewed it as "backstabbing," "political junk" (Beck 2001, 62). Again, this could be a preference for cooperation over conflict, but it could also stem from the desire to be part of a unified whole. What these women wanted above all, according to Beck, is to be part of a community of representatives. The "hardest thing" for these women was, in one woman's words, "not working together" (2001, 63). By contrast, men's most common complaint was against citizens voicing their views at council meetings (2001, 63). Men tended to resent citizen input; women tended to lament the lack of community. Put differently, on average, women may lean toward communitarianism rather than simply wishing to avoid conflict and live in peace.

Consistent with this finding, Karpowitz and Frost (2007) find that in public hearings about Walmart, women were significantly more likely than men to invoke the collective identity of the town and the connections among citizens when testifying before the town council. Instead of these communitarian appeals, men, by contrast, talked more about the merits of the legal arguments or about how Walmart might affect government revenues.

In sum, women tend to be more motivated than men by social ties and frequently do more to form and maintain connections to other people. On average, they may need and seek a heightened sense of community in their environment. They may respond more strongly to the absence of that sense of community. Situations in which people are not interacting cooperatively may trigger a sense of alienation or distance for women more than for men.

It stands to reason, then, that the deliberating group's displays of regard for its members will affect women more than men, on average. Part of what discussion can do to encourage women's participation is to signal to members that other members have an interdependent orientation. Discussions in which these expressions of social bonds are weak may expand the gender gap in participation; those with stronger positive ties, or warmer tone, may shrink it.

So far we have asked how women may differ from men, on average. We have developed three mechanisms or gender pathways that could explain why women may exercise less authority in discussion than men: because they are less confident, because they are more averse to conflict, and because they are more sensitive to social bonds. These three mechanisms are not mutually exclusive, but they are distinct enough that we can test each one.

However, the more central task of this book is to understand when differences between men and women mute. Put differently, what we really want to know is: what group-level conditions enlarge the gender gap in participation and influence? And what conditions shrink it, thereby helping women to achieve their potential for full citizenship?

Gender Composition

When Women Interact with Men

Deliberation occurs in groups. This may seem to be an obvious fact, but it has received little systematic attention from studies of deliberation.[27] If we want to understand the gender gap in authority, we need to pay attention to ways that groups produce that gender gap and consider the possibility that group dynamics can affect women and men differently. By understanding how groups can create or reinforce gender gaps, we can also come to understand how groups could mute or erase those gaps.

To set the scene in broad strokes, we rely on the notion that gender is a characteristic not only of an individual, but also of a situation. Gender signals expectations about social interaction as much as it does about the characteristics of a person. That insight may be the most important development to come from the study of gender so far.[28] To be sure, we need to attend to the gender gap in the sources of participation and influence, which may lie in the fact that women are more likely than men to underestimate their competence, to alter their confidence in response to social feedback, to avoid asserting their opinions, to minimize conflict, and to prioritize their connection with those around them. But while it matters that women tend to have proclivities that differ from men's, it matters even more that the effect of those gendered proclivities *depends heavily on the setting*. Our interest in particular lies with the ways that interaction within a discussion group may elicit gendered attitudes and behaviors, and how those gendered attitudes and behaviors produce a gender gap in participation and influence—in other words, in substantive and symbolic representation, in authority, standing, and power.[29] The way that groups are set up, and how they interact, can either facilitate or neutralize the detrimental effect of insecurity, reactivity, conformity, and conflict aversion on women's speech. The composition of the group, and its procedures, can shape the norm of interaction, and the result is that gender roles may strongly determine individuals' behavior, or conversely, be neutralized.

The first question to ask in our study of gender in groups, then, is who is in the room. Put differently, a key aspect of gender in groups is the relative

[27] Some studies discuss what goes on in group discussions but have not systematically studied the effects of different characteristics of groups and have not focused on gender (e.g., Walsh 2007; Gastil 1993, 2010).

[28] See, for example, Aries 1996, 1998; Deaux and Major 1987; Eagly 1987; LaFrance, Hecht, and Paluck 2003; Leaper, Anderson, and Sanders 1998; Leaper and Smith 2004; Ridgeway and Smith-Lovin 1999; Eagly, Wood, and Diekman 2000; Leaper 2000.

[29] Here we draw on the general assumptions of Expectation States Theory (Ridgeway 2001; Ridgeway et al. 2009) and on the interactionist theory of gender, which argues that gender roles become more or less salient with the situation (Eagly and Carli 2007).

number of men and women in the group. Scholarship on group composition suggests that gender composition has a variety of powerful effects on the group decision and on individual attitudes.[30] For example, gender composition affects judges' decisions, and the level of respect in legislative debates—even when individual gender does not affect preferences, and even after controlling on ideology and other factors.[31]

Why would gender composition matter? One possible reason is the gender gap in perceived competence and in confidence. As we indicated, men still tend to be perceived as more competent in areas not clearly denoted as women's domain, and that includes matters of common concern in general and public affairs specifically. And as we also noted, women not only tend to view themselves as less competent than men do, but they have less confidence in a variety of skills, and in formal situations, including public speaking. When women interact with men, they may view themselves as less qualified than the men in the group and be less motivated to assert their views. Consequently, when women discuss matters of common concern in mixed-gender groups, they may speak less, feel less confident, exercise less influence than men, and feel less free or able to express views or raise topics not articulated or shared by men, and the more men there are, the more this gender gap is likely to grow.[32] The signal that gender composition sends about women's status in the group may be subtle and

[30] Aries 1976, 1996; Hannagan and Larimer 2010; Johnson and Schulman 1989; Smith-Lovin and Brody 1989; Mendelberg and Karpowitz 2007.

[31] Boyd, Epstein, and Martin 2010; Farhang and Wawro 2004, 2010; Grünenfelder and Bächtiger 2007; Massie, Johnson, and Gubala 2002; Peresie 2005. While few strong or consistent gender effects are evident in individual-level analyses of the decisions of women serving on the bench (Ashenfelter, Eisenberg, and Schwab 1995; Segal 2000; Songer, Davis, and Haire 1994; Walker and Barrow 1985), much larger effects emerge when examining the gender composition of judicial panels. These effects of gender composition appear to hold even after controlling on ideology and other factors. In a sample of cases over a nearly twenty-year period, Massie, Johnson, and Gubala (2002) find, for example, that judicial panels with at least one woman are more likely to take pro-plaintiff positions in criminal procedure and civil rights cases. Similar gender-composition effects show up in Farhang and Wawro's (2004) study of employment discrimination cases, with panels that include women again proving more likely to take pro-plaintiff positions. These effects extend to the individual judge's opinions as well as the overall decision of the panel. The most powerful effects are reported by Peresie (2005), who finds that in sex discrimination and sexual harassment cases, the more women on the panel, the more likely the panel is to find in favor of the plaintiff, even after controlling for ideology and a variety of other factors. More sophisticated and rigorous studies echo these findings (Boyd, Epstein, and Martin 2010; Farhang and Wawro 2010). These studies and others support Sapiro's general conclusion: Differences between the average man and woman may be small and inconsistent, especially in comparison to large variances within gender, but these differences can become large and consequential when amplified by group-level forces (Sapiro 2003). It is not the case, though, that we already know that gender composition increases ordinary women's participation and influence, as we explain in the appendix to chapter 4. In addition, there is little work on the mechanism explaining gender composition effects or the process by which judges interact.

[32] Aries 1998; Bowers, Steiner, and Sandys 2001; Croson and Gneezy 2009; Eagly 1987; Giles et al. 1987; Hastie, Penrod, and Pennington 1983; Huckfeldt and Sprague 1995; Ridgeway 1982; Strodtbeck, James, and Hawkins 1957.

indirect, yet powerful. Experimental studies show that men enjoy a higher status than women in discussions, unless the subject is commonly perceived to be a feminine one (Ridgeway and Smith-Lovin 1999). This would apply to discussions of most public affairs topics or matters of common concern to the group.

For example, Wood and Karten's experiments show that when four-member, mixed-gender groups are asked to reach a unanimous decision in a hypothetical ethical dilemma, men are more likely than women to engage in leadership behaviors such as offering information, making suggestions, and giving opinions, and to be perceived as competent. Moreover, in another experiment they show that this gender gap goes away when the investigators supply the same (false) competence feedback to the men and the women before discussion (Wood and Karten 1986). The overall pattern suggests that the reason men exercise more authority and are perceived as more authoritative is that they are viewed, and view themselves, as relatively more competent than women. Thus when women interact with men on such topics, women's relatively low status may translate into inequality in participation, representation, and influence. In mixed-gender situations, the group thus becomes a site for the enactment, and reinforcement, of gender role expectations that posit that women have less authority than men.

An example of a study that underscores the effects on women when they interact with men is the Israeli engineering study of Gneezy, Niederle, and Rustichini (2003). Gneezy and his colleagues assigned men and women at a highly selective engineering school to solve maze problems. We noted above that the more competition, the worse women did and the better men did. However, competition is not the end of the story. Our point here is that in addition, the effect of competition was highest when women had to compete against men. In fact, when women competed exclusively against other women, they solved more mazes than they did without competition of any kind. So women may not do worse in conditions of competition per se. Rather, they may react negatively to competition when they compete with men. Because men are viewed as more competent engineers, having to compete with men depresses women's performance.[33] Similarly, in discussion with men on subjects other than those considered women's special purview, women are likely to view their competence as inferior to men's, and make fewer attempts to express their views or influence the group.[34]

[33] Another study, by Barbara Ritter and Janice Yoder, also finds that even women with a dominant personality are unlikely to assume leadership roles in dyads when paired with a man. The researchers assigned unacquainted students to task pairs, such that one member was selected based on having a higher dominant-personality score than the other member. They found that in same-sex pairs, the dominant member emerged as the leader of the pair. But in mixed-gender pairs, dominance had no effect, and the man was more likely than the woman to emerge as leader regardless of their dominance level. So even when women are inclined toward leadership by having a dominant personality, they will be less likely to act accordingly than men are (Ritter and Yoder 2004).

[34] Women may also wish to avoid outperforming men out of a fear that they will be rejected as romantic partners. Two female MBA students at Harvard on CBS's *60 Minutes* stated in 2002 that

Not only are women likely to take the group composition as a signal about their relative competence and authority, those around them are also likely to alter their behavior accordingly. The more men in the group, the higher the number of individuals who are likely to signal to women that their contributions are less adequate. A recent review of psychology studies of leadership found that stereotypes that associate leadership with masculinity are more commonly held by men than by women; that is, men are especially likely to view leadership as a masculine role and to see men as more fit to lead (Koenig et al. 2011). Along these lines, men are also more likely than women to negatively evaluate women who engage in leadership acts even when these acts are identical to those undertaken by men (Eagly, Makhijani, and Klonsky 1992). Similarly, not only are men less likely to choose women than to choose men for political discussion,[35] men are also less inclined than women to attribute influence to authoritative women when they speak in public. Specifically, men in churches whose clergy is a woman rate the political influence of the clergy on the members much lower than do female members of those churches, and underestimate the amount of political speech issued by the clergy member (Djupe, Sokhey, and Gilbert 2007).

These patterns matter to the level of influence that women can exercise when speaking with many men. They demonstrate that men are likely to infer that women are less competent than they are in discussions of matters not deemed feminine, and as a consequence of that evaluation accept less influence from women than they do from men. And that in turn means that when women are interacting with many men, they will carry less influence than when interacting with many women. A set of studies on gendered double standards and influence find that men tend to devalue women's competence, and as a consequence are less likely to accept influence from them. Furthermore, women do not devalue men's competence, and consequently they are likely to accept influence from them. In these studies, pairs first individually performed a task that is not viewed as feminine. They were then informed either that they outperformed or underperformed their partner. They were then observed interacting about disagreements prearranged by the investigators, and the level of influence from one to another is recorded. The findings show that men are less influenced by a female partner than women are by a male partner, unless she outperformed him in the first round. A woman accepts influence from the male partner even when he underperforms her, while a man accepts influence from his female

they no longer tell men that they go to Harvard so as not to squash potential romantic relationships (cited in Babcock and Laschever 2003, 103).

[35] Djupe, McClurg, and Sokhey 2010; Huckfeldt and Sprague 1995. In addition, in studies of actual car sales interactions using trained confederate consumers, women are quoted higher prices than men in anticipation of women's weaker negotiation behavior, and in lab studies of ultimatum games, women receive lower offers from their partners than men do and are expected to make higher offers than men (Babcock and Laschever 2003).

partner only if she outperforms him. Men are more likely than women to expect less of women's ability and consequently tend to accept less influence from women than from men.[36]

These results suggest that when men are women's predominant conversation partners, women will receive signals that they have less to contribute than the men in the group. They will be expected to behave in less assertive and more accommodating ways than they would if surrounded by many women. As one respondent told interviewers in Conover and colleagues' study of public discussions, "the men are talking, and the ladies and, you know, the wives or whatever, and we are almost spoken down to—because they know better than us! So I think we've had to keep quiet, you know [nervous laughter]" (Conover, Searing, and Crewe 2002, 56). The more men present, the greater the number of members likely to hold stereotypes that regard authority as men's purview and who thus may act in ways that send negative signals to women who engage in acts of authority.[37] Even when the signals are subtle, women may pick up on these expectations to remain relatively quiescent and unassertive during discussion with men.

Finally, when women interact with many men, they are also less likely to engage in assertive behaviors than they do when they interact with women. For example, women who have a personality that seeks dominance take dominant positions primarily with respect to their female conversation partners. Women who score high on dominance measures attempt to assert dominance over women who scored low on dominance, but not over men who scored low in dominance.[38]

All this is to say that interactions between men and women tend to be characterized by unequal authority. We can tell that authority is at work here, because when status is equalized between the sexes, their inequality disappears. For example, in studies of the conversations of intimate heterosexual couples, members of couples characterized by an equal relationship exhibit equal talk times (Kollock, Blumstein, and Schwartz 1985). Similarly, women who fill clearly legitimized leadership roles, such as managers in an organization, engage in leadership acts as often as men do in these roles (Eagly and Johnson 1990). By default, gender is entangled with authority; when authority is equalized, gender differences tend to deflate and even disappear.

In mixed-gender discussion of matters of common concern, women may defer to men's perceived expertise, and the result may be less talk, less talk of women's distinctive concerns, less talk about women's preferences, less affirmation of women's speech, less perceived influence over the discussion, and more adverse consequences for women's sense of efficacy.

[36] Pugh and Wahrman 1983; Ridgeway 1982; Wagner et al. 1993; see the review by Foschi and Freeman 1991.

[37] Similar implications derive from research on social dominance orientation (Pratto, Sidanius, and Levin 2006) and on sexism (Glick and Fiske 1996).

[38] Aries 1998; Carbonell 1984; Davis and Gilbert 1989; Nyquist and Spence 1986.

The Minority Status Hypothesis

The foregoing leads to what we call the "minority status" hypothesis: numerical minority status affects women's status in the group (see table 3.1). That status in turn affects their participation in discussion, their substantive representation—how much they speak to their particular concerns and preferences—and their symbolic representation—whether they are viewed as full citizens with equal authority to govern. Women have the most standing in groups with many women, and they face the greatest disadvantage when they are heavily outnumbered, especially when one woman is surrounded by men. In general, the more sparse women are, the lower their status, and the wider the gender gap in participation and representation.[39] Support for this notion comes from various studies. For example, Johnson and Schulman (1989) found that while both men's and women's influence is rated lower when they are in a numerical minority, women incur a greater disadvantage.[40] A study of small groups' evaluation of candidates for promotion at a utility company found similar effects on evaluations of competence (Schmitt and Hill 1977).[41]

This effect may be due to the inferences people draw about gender and competence when women are scarce. Women in male-dominated work groups experience more sex stereotyping than women in female-dominated groups (Konrad, Winter, and Gutek 1992, 131). In one study, students working on Masters of Business Administration (MBA) degrees were more likely to attribute stereotypically feminine traits to women in an applicant pool for a hypothetical job, and to rate them more negatively, when the pool included fewer than three women out of eight than when the pool included a larger proportion of women (Heilman 1980). In addition, in an analysis of 486 jobs across several firms, the percentage of women in blue-collar and clerical jobs in a given firm was positively related to supervisors' ratings of women's performance, even after accounting for women's education and ability (Sackett et al. 1991, 265). These studies imply that women's disadvantage when they are a numerical minority is at least partially caused by the stereotypes primed by their minority

[39] For statements of this notion that rest on the claim that women have less power and status in society, see Kanter 1977a; Lakoff 1975, 1990; O'Barr 1982; O'Barr and Atkins 1980.

[40] One may wonder about the threat hypothesis, which would predict that increasing numbers of women provoke a sense of threat among men and a backlash against women. However, a recent review of the literature in workplace settings concludes that there is no strong evidence for a threat thesis when it comes to women's level of participation or evaluations of women; it is low rather than high numbers that hinder women. The authors conclude: "many studies are preliminary, and there is rarely a set of consistent findings based on well-specified models from which to draw final conclusions" (Reskin, McBrier, and Kmec 1999, 55.)

[41] According to Schmitt and Hill's study, the greater white men's share of the group, the more positive were evaluators' assessments of other individual white men. There were no effects on evaluations of white women, but the evaluations of black women in the group were negatively and significantly correlated with the number of white men in the group.

Table 3.1: Main Hypotheses about Gender Composition and Decision Rules of Small Groups

Hypothesis	Explanation
Minority Status Hypothesis	The average woman in the numerical minority occupies a lower status and hence participates and influences less than the average woman in a numerical majority. Consequently, the gender gap in the group shrinks as women's numbers increase. Men may be negatively affected by being a minority gender, but not as much as women.
Enclave Hypothesis	The average woman's participation and influence is greatest in all-female groups, where women are less constrained by the gender role expectation to avoid authoritative behavior, and which build women's confidence and employ cooperative norms. There are no clear expectations for male enclaves.
Interaction Hypothesis	Under *majority* rule, the average woman participates and influences more as women's numbers increase, shrinking the gender gap in the group. Men may be negatively affected by being a minority gender, but not as much as women. Under this rule, the minority status hypothesis is accurate. Under *unanimous* rule, the group develops an inclusive interaction norm that elevates the participation and influence of both gender minorities. When women are few, that norm increases the average woman's participation and influence. Thus the average minority woman participates and influences considerably more under unanimous than majority rule. But the inclusive norm also raises the average minority man's participation and influence. Therefore, under unanimous rule, the average woman's participation and influence remains the same, or even decreases, as women's numbers increase, enlarging the gender gap in the group. That is, the effects of women's higher numbers are neutralized, or even exceeded, by the boost minority men received from being the gender minority under consensus norms of interaction.

status per se. When people see few women, they may implicitly assume that the task at hand is not going to be well performed by women. That is, the number of women may act as a cue to gender stereotypes about the kinds of actions that women are well suited to undertake.

Once these gender stereotypes are cued, they may implicitly affect women's actions. Experiments conducted on "stereotype threat" demonstrate that even seemingly minor signals about women's relative competence compared to men can significantly affect women's performance on tasks viewed as more masculine. For example, one set of Michigan undergraduates was told that there were usually no gender differences on a difficult math test they were about to take. Another set was told that the test usually produced gender differences. Women scored less than half as well in the second than in the first group. Men moved in the opposite direction, gaining a performance boost from the gender signal (Spencer, Steele, and Quinn 1999). The idea behind findings such as these is that others' expectations reside in the person's mind in the form of stereotypes and associations between who they are and what they are capable of. People learn these associations over the course of countless small, often subtle interactions with their environment. Men and women know about these and are affected even when they are unaware of that effect and even when they have not internalized the stereotypes, indeed, even when the stereotypes are rejected (Aronson et al. 1999). When these expectations are made salient, or "primed"—for example, by the scarcity of members of the person's social category—the person's confidence in their competence drops. And the less confidence individuals feel, the less likely they are to attempt the action, to execute it well, and to feel good about their attempt. This is the theory of stereotype threat, and it has been validated over many settings (Steele and Aronson 1995). When women are under conditions of stereotype threat, their performance relative to men on masculine-typed tasks suffers (Kray, Thompson, and Galinsky 2001).

This effect of women's relative numbers is likely to be all the more powerful when people interact. Not only will women observe many men around them and draw the implicit conclusion that they are not suited to the task at hand. The men are likely to *act* confidently, exacerbating women's drop in self-confidence. The journalist Sara Laschever recalls that after having worked as an executive, she took a temporary job as a store clerk where she was required to perform mental arithmetic calculations. Her (male) boss, however, did not know of her competence and believed that he was much better at the task. He exhibited high competence, and he was, well, a man. Although she had always done well at math, she found herself making mistakes and feeling unsure of her ability (Babcock and Laschever 2003, 80). The economist Linda Babcock recounts a similar story. While serving as an interim dean, Babcock made a presentation at an important meeting with university officers. She had always felt well respected and valued by these colleagues, but in this meeting, she found herself the only woman. She grew "uncharacteristically nervous," and "when it was her turn to speak" she found herself "petrified" (81). Her self-confidence dropped and negatively affected her performance. She spoke less well than she believed herself capable. The effects of others' expectations work through women's own self-confidence.

The key point is that who is in the room can have a powerful effect on what women think, feel, and ultimately do during the group's discussion. When the situation cues women's sense that they may not belong, and that they may not be as competent as men, their lowered self-confidence may thus prompt them to underperform and perhaps to withdraw. They may lessen their participation in discussion, raise issues only if they believe the others are likely to view those issues as relevant, express preferences only if they anticipate that they are shared by others in the group, and respond strongly to negative signals by other deliberators. As the research on stereotype threat shows, and in line with the general literature on stereotypes, this process may not be conscious and may occur despite a woman's rejection of gender stereotypes.

There is reason to expect women to participate less and to achieve lower levels of substantive representation in groups where women are a minority. In these settings, women's low numbers, and the presence of active, confident male participants, will place women in a lower status relative to men. Women will perceive themselves to have less authority than men, and consequently they will speak less, speak less to their distinctive concerns, articulate their preferences less often, and carry less influence over the group.

This is what we mean by opportunity and the motivation to participate. Women need discussion settings that do not cue their relative lack of confidence, relative lack of assertion, and sense of relative incompetence in comparison with men. Even when the signals are not overtly hostile, the absence of positive reassurance can act as a negative cue. Society defines women as members of a lower-status category; when women are a minority, that status becomes salient, and the consequences follow predictably.

Gendered Norms of Interaction

The prediction of the "minority-status" hypothesis is seconded by another literature. Women may participate less and carry less authority in discussions with many men than in discussions with many women not only because of a gender difference in perceived expertise and confidence, but also because gendered norms of interaction vary with gender composition and facilitate or hinder women's participation. Specifically, predominantly female groups tend to adopt more inclusive and cooperative norms of interaction, while predominantly male groups tend to accent individual agency. Women tend to be deterred by the latter and encouraged by the former.

We have already discussed the fact that women are socialized to interact in more expressive, cooperative, and warm ways, but our point here is that small group interaction amplifies this tendency. The more cooperative and warm individuals are present, the more the norm tilts in that direction. In settings with many men, the norm of interaction tends to take on more stereotypically masculine characteristics of individual assertion, agency, competition, and dominance; in settings with many women, people tend to interact in a more stereotypically feminine style that emphasizes cooperation, intimacy, and the inclusion of all participants.[42] This, too, is what we mean when we say that gender is a feature of the context, not just of individuals. People take their cues about gendered behavior from the gender of those around them. When surrounded by many men, both men and women are likely to shift their own behavior in a more masculine direction, emphasizing individual agency and assertion. It's as if people note the gender of those around them and conclude that the setting calls for acting like a member of that gender. Composition signals the social expectation of conforming to the behavioral style of the numerically prevalent gender.

A high-level female executive in a male-dominated industry illustrates how individuals shift in response to the perceived masculine norm: "I learned that you had to . . . put on a more serious demeanor, to establish credibility more quickly . . . you stop trying to be warm, wonderful, and nice" (Eagly and Carli 2007, 124). Female leaders tend to adopt a stereotypically masculine style in predominantly male settings, pursuing task-oriented rather than democratic or nurturing leadership to the same extent as the men in these settings, and adopting a more tough and domineering manner with subordinates (Eagly and Carli 2007, 126). As we noted earlier, this style tends to trigger social dislike, and yet despite the social cost, women in highly masculine settings, and occupying a role with heavily masculine expectations, tend to find it necessary to exercise power in the ways defined as masculine. Examples of this phenomenon are well known: Indira Gandhi, Golda Meir, and Margaret Thatcher.[43] In less male settings, however, female leaders tend to behave in ways that are "caring, supportive and considerate" (Eagly and Carli 2007, 130). When surrounded by many women, people expect themselves and others to behave in more stereotypically feminine fashion—to interact in ways that are more warm, expressive, and cooperative.

Evidence that the gender composition of the setting affects gendered norms and behavior comes from a variety of studies. For example, levels of self-disclosure during group discussion increase as the number of women in the group increases (Dindia and Allen 1992). For another example, men in all-male university departments express the least cohesion, and men in predominantly female departments express the most (Bird and Wharton 1996, 109; Reskin, McBrier, and Kmec 1999, 347). All-male groups establish hierarchy more quickly than all-female groups, and when women are the majority, the group develops less hierarchy (Berdahl and Anderson 2005; Mast 2001). Similarly, when a confederate acts in a dominant, aggressive manner during group discussion, all-male groups are more likely to gang up on the aggressor with dominance behavior of their own, relative to all-female groups (Ridgeway and Diekema 1989). A study of interruption patterns in simulated work groups found that both men and

[42] Aries 1976; Dindia and Allen 1992; Ellis 1982; McCarrick, Manderscheid, and Silbergeld 1981; Miller 1985; Smith-Lovin and Brody 1989; Mendelberg and Karpowitz 2007.

[43] We discuss the case of masculine female leaders in the conclusion chapter.

women issued more hostile interruptions as the proportion of men increased (Karakowsky, McBey, and Miller 2004).[44]

These findings are consistent with the culture theory of gender. A key piece of this theory is that gendered cultural scripts of behavior are triggered by gender composition. That is, a gendered cultural convention is acted out when the individual interacts with others who follow the same cultural convention. An individual surrounded by many women will adopt the conventions of women in the same way that an individual surrounded by many Americans will adopt the conventions of Americans. The more homogenous the gender of the small group, the more that every member will conform to the social conventions of the predominant gender. An all-female group signals implicitly that members will interact according to a feminine style; the same holds for all-male groups and their cue to use a masculine style (Maltz and Borker 1982; Tannen 1990; Thorne and Luria 1986). These gendered subcultures are said to be learned early; some of the same gender composition differences scholars find in adult groups show up in girls' and boys' play patterns (Maccoby 1998). As we mentioned earlier, for example, girls' playgroups tend to avoid conflict within the group and to reach agreement more than boys' groups do (Miller, Danaher, and Forbes 1986). Thus the theory argues that girls and boys are socialized to different gendered cultures of interaction and carry these implicit scripts of behavior with them into adulthood. This theory can explain not only why gender composition shapes gendered norms of interaction but also highlights the independent and differential effect of those norms on women versus men.

The theory of gendered subcultures is consistent with the findings of several studies we reviewed above. For example, it predicts women's proclivity to dislike conflict and their sensitivity to affiliative social ties, and that women respond to settings that highlight conflict or cold relations by reducing their participation. The prediction is grounded in the notion that women do so out of a sense of cultural alienation. Other settings highlight cooperation and warm interactions, and these may encourage women to take full part. Again, this positive boost is grounded in women's cultural milieu, which creates a sense of comfort and cultural familiarity with settings where individuals work to create rapport.

One example of how gendered norms play out is in social science classrooms. A study of Harvard undergraduates identified a style of discussion called "gov talk" (Margolis 1992). "Gov talk" is depersonalized, focuses on abstractions, and is rationalistic, according to the author. A number of women interviewed in the study claimed that this style made them uncomfortable, depressed their frequency of speaking during class discussion, and caused them to be "unwilling to challenge others' views in public" (Hansen 1997). These suggestive findings are

[44] An overview of the literature on work groups concludes that "women in the minority in their work groups felt more isolated than either women who were in the majority, or men regardless of their share of group members" (Aries 1976, 15; Carlock and Martin 1977; Reskin, McBrier, and Kmec 1999, 346).

consistent with the findings we reviewed in chapter 2, which show that women participate less than men in activities that express clear opinions despite their balanced numbers in many educational and civic settings. Other evidence we reviewed earlier also fits this theory. For example, the theory is fully consistent with Kathlene's (1994) findings about predominantly male legislative committees exhibiting a competitive, aggressive communication behavior that tends to inhibit women's participation more than it does men's. The theory predicts that such behavior will not only be found in university classrooms or formal legislative committees; rather, in a broad swath of settings with more masculine interaction norms, women will participate and influence less, and speak less about what's on their mind.

Men may also be affected by gendered norms of interaction around them, although to a lesser extent.[45] As women's status in the group grows, men's may lessen. Men may participate less and be less likely to raise issues of distinctive concerns to men. The evidence, however, is sparse, and the effects tend to be small. Some indirect evidence comes from studies of the effect of women's candidacies on citizens. Susan Hansen found that during the 1992 presidential election year, men were somewhat less likely to engage in political proselytizing—attempts to persuade others to vote for one's preferred candidate—if women were on the ballot (Hansen 1992). As discussed in chapter 2, the effect of female candidates is positive on women; as it turns out, men experience a slight drop in engagement as women rise in it. These findings hold after controls for the person's partisanship, age, party, and issue positions, so they seem to be genuine gender effects rather than spurious consequences (Hansen 1997).

The gendered culture theory argues that mixed-gender settings are characterized by a norm that deviates from the one to which women were acculturated, and that this bad fit depresses women's sense of belonging to the group. Women may thus experience a greater sense of comfort in predominantly female settings with their more stereotypically feminine norms of interaction and feel ill at ease in settings with predominantly male norms. There are far less clear expectations for the effects of gender composition and of masculine or feminine norms on men. Thus the literature on gendered norms seconds the "minority-status" hypothesis—women will participate less, and engage in other forms of substantive and symbolic representation less, in predominantly male groups, and increase their involvement as their proportion increases.

The Enclave Hypothesis

Existing studies of group gender dynamics also support an "enclave" hypothesis: women flourish in all-female settings. This follows from the logic of the work on minority status. Because women are disadvantaged in political discus-

[45] For this general argument see Burns, Schlozman, and Verba 2001.

sions with men, they may do best without any interactions with men and may benefit most from their own discussion space. Thus women's talk time, their references to women's issues, and their perceived and actual influence will be higher in all-female than in mixed-gender deliberating groups (see table 3.1).[46]

Support for the enclave hypothesis emerges from a variety of sources. For example, the philosopher Habermas might approve of female enclaves. As we noted in chapter 2, feminist theorists criticize Habermas for paying inadequate attention to ways that gender inequality undermines women in deliberation (Fraser 1990). But Habermas was quite taken with what he viewed as protected social spaces for people, located away from the influence of political power—namely, the church and the government. For Habermas, civil society is the "nervous system" of democracy for this reason (McCarthy 1994). The salons of the French enlightenment, and the coffeehouses of eighteenth-century Britain, served for Habermas as a key historical lesson about the need in democracy for deliberative spaces that the authorities cannot infiltrate. In these spaces, citizens could develop a public opinion independent enough of entities that hold disproportionate power to be able to hold these powers accountable.[47]

Nancy Fraser has specifically argued that women have long formed their own civil society and recommended these protected enclaves as a form of "subaltern counterpublics." The idea is similar to Habermas's notion that people with less power need to interact with each other as a way to form opinions uncontaminated by coercion, or worse still, by the more implicit but insidious influence of others who control the hegemonic ideology of the day.

Karpowitz, Raphael, and Hammond (2009) take on the notion of enclaves directly, arguing that the goals of deliberative democracy are well served by protected spaces in which homogenous groups—especially those who have been traditionally disempowered—can congregate, talk among themselves, and explore the issues of the day from their own unique perspectives. Enclaves are not, as those who worry about group polarization often assume, only groups with common views; they should also be understood as groups that might share a structural location with respect to an issue or a common predeliberation identity. In fact, one of the values of enclave deliberation is that it allows groups with such a common identity not just to practice civic skills but also to more fully understand their similarities and their differences. By allowing

[46] Hannagan and Larimer argue from an evolutionary perspective that group composition matters because women are more likely to seek consensus in a group and are more likely to both (indirectly, nonverbally) signal their wishes and to read those of others. Thus groups with more women are more likely to effectively converge on the median. See Hannagan and Larimer 2010.

[47] Habermas believes that such spaces are still necessary and laments what he sees as their erosion by the mass media and large, powerful organizations. These entities, he believes, attempt to manufacture consensus through advertising and public relations. In addition, by preempting face-to-face meetings, they rob people of the opportunity to develop their ability to discuss notions that check domination.

such exploration of the diversity of views within groups that are homogeneous in other ways, enclave deliberation "can thus serve the larger cause of a fully inclusive public discourse by giving disempowered or marginalized groups an opportunity to develop their own unique perspectives and arguments, which might otherwise be overlooked or ignored" (Karpowitz, Raphael, and Hammond 2009, 582). This can be the first step in more effective and successful engagement in mixed settings as part of the larger deliberative landscape.

Do American Women Congregate in Enclaves?

Of course, the benefits of enclaves are only possible if women do, in fact, congregate among themselves. And on that score, women in the United States have a rich tradition of enclave endeavors; in part because of their formal exclusion from some aspects of civic life, women joined all-female associations through much of American history. In Skocpol's words, "voluntary associations have always rivaled voting as pathways Americans follow into community and public affairs" (Skocpol 1999, 462). A key feature of these groups is that their members interacted. As Theda Skocpol describes it, their watchword was "interact or die" (Skocpol 1999, 491). The point we want to emphasize is that in these all-female settings women interacted only with each other. Here they had the chance to develop their political skills and aptitudes. They were trained to lead, whether through a general sense of capacity and support from fellow women or by learning practical acts—"giving a speech, running a meeting, keeping the books" (Burns, Schlozman, and Verba 2001, 73). The first women to become prominent political leaders were members of all-female associations.[48] And Skocpol (1992) recounts how women used women's associations to achieve meaningful policy change, including the rise of the Children's Bureau, mother's pensions, and other elements of the early welfare state. Even today, women's associations have a great deal to do with whether women in their area run for local office (Crowder-Meyer 2010).[49]

As women mobilized for gender equality in the 1970s and 1980s, they did so largely in all-female groups. These included the National Organization for

[48] Theda Skocpol writes that for many decades in the nineteenth century, educated, higher status women were "mainstays of voluntary membership federations" (Skocpol 1999, 482). She also argues that the associations of that time were much more mixed along class lines, though much more segregated along lines of race.

[49] There is also a literature on single-sex education. It offers mixed results and suffers from a shortage of rigorous studies. For an example of positive findings regarding women's colleges, see Smith 1990. Some reports find that women's colleges tend to engage in a concerted program of leadership education for its students, presumably more so than co-ed colleges do, though that is not tested (Whitt 1994). A recent report by the US Department of Education concluded that girls in all-girl schools tend to have a higher level of academic achievement and career aspirations. However, many of these studies are confounded by comparing Catholic with public schools. http://eric.ed.gov/PDFS/ED486476.pdf.

Women, which was based in local chapters where women met with their neighbors and members of their community (Skocpol 1999, 468), and other new organizations, some of which also included interaction among female members. They joined women's groups with a long-established tradition of local meetings, including the YWCA, League of Women Voters, the American Association of University Women, the General Federation of Women's Clubs (GFWC), and the National Congress of Parents and Teachers (Skocpol 1999, 465–66). The GFWC alone had nearly a million members and over 15,000 clubs at its peak (Skocpol 1999, 479).[50] While old civic groups declined, a trend well documented—and well lamented—by Robert Putnam in *Bowling Alone*, new groups oriented to advancing disadvantaged people surged (Skocpol 1999, 468–72). Women's rights groups, composed almost entirely of women, were at the crest of the surge. One scholar found that while various racial, ethnic, and women's associations proliferated in that period, women's groups did so exponentially.[51]

Women still belong to all-female or predominantly female groups. Evidence on this comes from the 1990 Citizen Participation Study, the backbone of *PROPA*. Burns, Schlozman, and Verba asked their respondents to which organizations they belonged, defined as being either a member or a contributor (2001).[52] Then they asked respondents to indicate which one of these organizations is the "most important" to them. Finally, they asked about the gender composition of this "most important" organization. Of women, 17% report that their most important organization is all female, another 17% report belonging to a mostly female group, 60% report that their group is "mixed," and only 4% report "few" women (Burns, Schlozman, and Verba 2001, 76).[53] While women are not in all-female groups as a rule, there are certainly still settings where women do interact exclusively with each other.

Burns and her colleagues report that many men also belong to a "most important" group composed entirely or predominantly of men. In fact, men are more likely than women to belong to a "most important" group composed "mostly" of the same sex. The percentages of men reporting all male, mostly male, mixed gender, and few men are, respectively: 13, 26, 56, and 2%. Men, too, have opportunities to interact exclusively with other men.[54]

[50] For extensive documentation of the role of local meetings in women's groups around the United States, see Skocpol 1992.

[51] Minkoff, cited in Skocpol 1999, 470.

[52] Before asking gender composition, they also filtered out people who were not at least minimally active in the organization by asking if the person had donated at least $25 or given some time to the organization (Burns, Schlozman, and Verba 2001, 229, note 7).

[53] These percentages are 2 points different in table 9.4 (page 228), perhaps because of the treatment of missing responses—19, 15, and 62, in order.

[54] For men: 24% of all-male groups are service/fraternal or veterans', 31% are unions/business/professional, 16% are hobby/sports clubs. All-female groups: 16% service/fraternal, 13% religious, 10% business/professional, 9% educational, including PTAs (Burns, Schlozman, and Verba 2001, 228, note 6).

The workplace also continues to be a place where some people interact in predominantly same-sex groups. A national survey of American organizations found that 11% of businesses had over 90% male employees, and 7% of businesses were more than 90% female (Reskin, McBrier, and Kmec 1999, citing Kalleberg et al. 1996).[55] Approximately 90% of businesses in the United States employ fewer than twenty employees, a number small enough to generate interaction among the employees.[56] So in nearly 20% of businesses, people are interacting almost exclusively with members of the same sex.

These findings underscore an important point for our purpose—there is considerable variety in the gender compositions of American organizations, from work groups to political boards and councils to voluntary organizations of various kinds. While a majority of Americans are in mixed-gender groups, a sizable minority of Americans are in groups where one gender or the other predominates. This means that it makes sense to ask, as we do, what is the effect of this variety on its participants?

What Happens in Enclaves?

What happens to women who associate with women?[57] Burns, Schlozman, and Verba (2001) can tell us a great deal, at least, about what people report is happening to them in their civic associations. They asked their respondents a series of questions about their activities in their "most important" organization. In gender-mixed organizations, women are less likely than men to report activity.

The gender gap in mixed-gender groups is largest on the activities that are most relevant to leadership of discussion: whether the person has written a letter, the number of times the person has been asked for their opinion, the number of times the person has expressed an opinion at a meeting, the number of times the person went to a decision-making meeting. And the biggest gender gap of all obtains on whether the person made a speech (men exceed women by 12 percentage points).[58] In other words, where women trail men the most in gender-mixed groups is on the act that most requires a confident, public statement of views—in other words, the most leader-like act on the list—making a speech.

By contrast, "plan a meeting" produces only the tiniest of gender gaps. A general indifference to meetings is not the reason why women are less likely

[55] Percentages are of full-time employees.

[56] Eighty-seven percent of businesses had fewer than twenty employees (Reskin, McBrier, and Kmec 1999, 346, citing US Census Bureau).

[57] See also the sociology literature: Smith-Lovin and McPherson 1993, page 238; Mcpherson and Smith-Lovin 1986; McPherson and Smith-Lovin 1982; McPherson and Smith-Lovin 1987; Ridgeway and Smith-Lovin 1999.

[58] The numbers in this section are drawn from table 9.5, page 230, in Burns, Schlozman, and Verba 2001.

to express an opinion at a meeting, attend meetings where decisions are made, or make a speech at a meeting. Women are not averse to getting involved with meetings, but they tend to engage in meetings more as support staff than as influential members or leaders. Women might send out mailings announcing a meeting, or figure out where to seat the participants, or provide other logistical aid. Support fits women's traditional gender role much more than does leadership. And that feminine gender role may get in the way of women's full exercise of voice in the life of their communities.

But this gender gap reveals itself only when we compare women and men in mixed-gender organizations. In same-sex associations, these gender differences disappear or even reverse.[59] The consistency across the various activities is striking; there is not a single activity that sustains women's disadvantage to men in same-sex groups. The gender gap disappears even though men increase their activities in same-sex groups. That is, women gain so much from same-sex groups that they close the gap with men despite men's own gains from their same-sex groups.[60]

Even more telling of the empowerment of enclaves, the activities on which they elevate women's participation the most are those most relevant to authority. The activities with the five biggest increases in women's percentages are as follows, with the percentage point increase from mixed to all-female groups noted in parenthesis:

- Went to a meeting where respondent took part in making decisions (31%)
- Opinion has been asked (19%)
- Expressed opinion at meeting (18%)
- Wrote a letter (16%)
- Made a speech (15%)
- Served on board or as officer (15%)

The magnitude of these enclave effects is remarkable. A 30+ percentage point effect, which is what we see for attending decision-making meetings, is nearly impossible to unearth in the study of participation.[61] But that effect is specific. The

[59] Here, we are comparing women in all-female groups to men in all-male groups.

[60] Whether men, too, benefit from their own enclaves is a possibility we can examine in our data. The evidence from existing studies is inconclusive. For example, in contrast to Burns, Schlozman, and Verba's positive finding, according to Bird and Wharton (1996), men in predominantly male and mixed-sex work groups were more satisfied than men in all-male groups. All-male groups exhibit the highest levels of dominance behavior (Aries 1976). However, Smith-Lovin and Brody found that men offer more positive interruptions to other men in all-male than in mixed-gender groups (1989). These findings are not directly contradictory, of course.

[61] The most discussed ascriptive variables in studies of inequality and political participation are age and race/ethnicity. The voting turnout gap between youngest and oldest is about 20 points, and the gap between the most- and least-participating racial groups is 15 points (reported by Michael Macdonald, based on the 2008 Current Population Survey. The percentages for the age and the race gap, respectively, are 22 and 20 in 2004. http://elections.gmu.edu/CPS_2008.html). The biggest

massive shifts occur mostly in women's involvement in decisions made for the collective. One has to think of oneself as entitled to and responsible for contributing to and influencing decisions in order to attend meetings where decisions are made. Making decisions is at the heart of authority.[62]

In sum, as *PROPA* describes it, "organizations of women provide the kinds of experiences that have been attributed to them: providing opportunities for leadership, facilitating the exercise of voice in organizational matters and the development of civic skills, and generating requests for political activity" (Burns, Schlozman, and Verba 2001, 230). But in our view, what is significant about the findings is less that they locate the source of women's civic skills, but more that they point toward a particular mechanism—authority. Women need more than the knowledge of how to plan a meeting; they need, far more, the sense that they are entitled to power. The results from that study's data confirm the importance of looking at all-female groups for the development of authority.

However, as important as these findings are for their implications, they require some caveats. They emerge from a research design that serves some purposes quite well, but which leaves some doubts for our purposes, as we will explain in greater detail in chapter 4. For now we note that the data come from self-reports rather than objective measures of gender composition and of the person's experiences in their group; that a person who ends up in an enclave may differ in important respects from one who does not, and this initial difference could explain the apparent effects of enclaves; and that enclaves may differ from mixed groups in any number of ways that could account for the differences we observed.

---

effect in the whole literature is for education, which moves the probability of voting by approximately 45 points. The gender gap in voting turnout is much more modest; men and women differ far less than the young and old or white and Latino Americans. Yet as powerful as age and race are in American political participation, far more powerful is the effect of gender composition on authoritative participation in civic groups. And that effect dwarfs the effect of individual gender. However, we do not wish to put much weight on this contrast, since comparing the effect of composition on organizational participation against the effect of other demographics on voter turnout is comparing two different predictors on two different outcomes. The ideal comparison would be on the same participatory variables, but we are not aware of findings reporting those. In any case, our point is that no matter what type of participation is examined and what type of predictor, gender composition effects are large by comparison.

[62] When we compare female enclaves to male enclaves, the pattern is also consistent with the notion that enclaves strengthen women's authority. There are two experiences that produce more than a 3-point gap favoring women when we compare all-female and all-male groups (we set a gap of more than 3 percentage points as our threshold here as a proxy for statistical significance): Opinion was asked, and feel some control over policy. Women's enclaves help women (above the help that male enclaves give to men) in these two respects. One of them implicates the exchange of opinions—women's opinion is solicited more in all-female groups than men's is in all-male groups. The other is a general sense of empowerment.

The problem of self-reported experiences, and of spurious differences between enclaves and others, can be addressed with controlled experiments. Existing experimental studies provide support for the observational findings from surveys. In general, single-sex groups generate larger gender differences than do mixed-sex groups (Aries 1996). Similarly, in their study of how much individuals disclose about themselves in group settings, Dindia and Allen use a meta-analytic approach to show that all-female groups display high levels of self-disclosure, all-male groups very low levels, and mixed groups fall in between these extremes (1992). Studies of negotiation also show that in all-female dyads, negotiators share more information, do so earlier in the exchange, attend more to the needs of the other party, and the agreements they reach are more likely to serve the common good, relative to mixed-gender or all-male pairs (Babcock and Laschever 2003, 168–72). A similar pattern emerges in studies of dominance behavior.[63] Women in enclaves are more likely than women in mixed groups to initiate interaction and to be addressed (Aries 1976, 15).[64] Women are more likely to express emotion and to read other people's emotion accurately from nonverbal signals, especially when reading women's signals. The implication of this is that women will be more tuned in to other group members in a mutually reinforcing cycle of emotional sensitivity, leading to more group solidarity.[65] While these studies have their own methodological problems, detailed in the next chapter, they do offer enough support for the enclave hypothesis that it is worth testing.

The enclave hypothesis is worth further investigation. There are enough all-female and all-male groups in American public life that they are worth studying. Existing research points to the possible qualitative differences between mixed-gender and all-female groups. These differences suggest that all-female groups may be a place of particular empowerment for women. The existing studies leave methodological gaps, but we proceed with their working hypothesis: levels of women's participation and representation rise from mixed-gender groups to all-female enclaves.

In summary, we will test several implications of the notion that women's numbers matter. One is the "minority status hypothesis," that women in a numerical minority occupy a lower status. The other is the "enclave hypothesis," that women in all-female groups are especially empowered. We wish to see if these variables affect the level of women's participation and representation in group discussion.

[63] Aries 1976.

[64] For observational or quasi-experimental studies, see Carlock and Martin 1977; Reskin, McBrier, and Kmec 1999, 346.

[65] Buck et al. 1972; Hall 1984; Wagner, Buck, and Winterbotham 1993; for a nonexperimental study, see Falk 1997.

Decision Rule

Gender role theory, including the minority status hypothesis and the enclave hypothesis, dominates the literature on gender and discussion, but we view it as incomplete. Specifically, the proportion of women in a group is not the only important factor that affects gendered patterns of speech participation. Institutions—by which we mean the rules and procedures that organize group functioning—can eliminate the disadvantages of low numbers; similarly, they can block the power of high numbers. Among the neglected procedural or institutional factors that shape group norms is the group's decision rule.

A rule that governs the group can determine far more than the substance of its decision. It can set in motion a set of social scripts, cancel individual habits, and produce particular styles of interaction. In other words, rules can help to shape a group's norms and dynamics, and as we have argued, these norms in turn can elevate or depress the authority of group members.

A rule is a relatively small intervention that carries large potential effects. Groups can often have a say over their own procedures. Gastil claims that "most small groups have considerable leeway in establishing at least some—if not all—of their procedures" (2010, 101). It can be far easier to adopt than a dramatic elevation in the physical presence of an underrepresented group. It can be adopted by the group itself, or imposed by those empowered to design the discussion. It is a reform that can be imported into many different settings, is easy to understand, and does not prompt contentious debates about quotas or difficult controversies about the appropriate remedies to the low status of a social group. It is easy to implement and far-reaching in its benefits.[66]

No rule is a panacea. Any given rule carries advantages and disadvantages, as we elaborate in the conclusion chapter. In fact, we leverage the contingent effect of a rule to spell out when a rule will benefit women, and when it will further erode their standing. Despite the caveats just noted, our point stands: some rules are likely to generate a process that can build the authority of women.

The two most common rules are majority rule and unanimous rule. Majority rule is commonly used in formal settings of politics. Unanimous rule has been investigated in recent years primarily in the context of jury decision making and groups with close bonds.[67] But unanimous rule and its variants are common in various settings, including formal institutions with a great deal of power, such as the UN Security Council and the US Courts of Appeals.[68]

Unanimous rule holds out a significant potential to elevate the authority of women, because it can create group norms that enhance consensus and inclu-

[66] We do not mean to overstate the case for ease. Reaching agreement on a decision rule can lead to conflict and confusion, and there may be slippage between the formal rule and its implementation (Gastil 2010, 101).

[67] Gastil 1993; Mansbridge 1983.

[68] Gastil 1993.

sion. Since the minority faces difficulty in persuading the majority in small groups (Moscovici 1980; 1985), a rule that includes minorities can substantially alter group dynamics. A seminal experimental study of mock juries reports that people shift their views during discussion more under unanimous than majority rule (Hastie, Penrod, and Pennington 1983). Such shifts are testament to the strength of the consensus norm that a rule can produce. The norm of cooperation can be seen in Nemeth's finding that mock juries instructed to use unanimous rule produced more expressions of agreement than those instructed to use majority rule (1977).[69] Unanimous rule also leads to a fuller sharing of information by deliberators (Mathis 2011). Perhaps because it creates a dynamic of mutual information exchange, engagement, and inclusion, unanimous rule can increase a sense that the decision was legitimate and appropriate and renders it more widely and deeply acceptable.[70]

That satisfaction is all the more telling when it extends to the preference minority, and in fact, preference minorities are also more satisfied with the group decision under unanimous than majority rule (Kerr et al. 1976). Under some conditions, groups distribute resources less equitably and form factions more often under majority than unanimous rule (Thompson, Mannix, and Bazerman 1988). As further indication that the process by which people interact shapes their views of the group, group consensus generated through talk can lead to increased cooperative behavior (Bouas and Komorita 1996). Thus unanimous rule leads to consensus-oriented norms of inclusion. These norms can protect numerical minorities beyond the direct veto power of the rule itself (Mendelberg 2002).

To be sure, under conditions of grave conflict, a group governed by the requirement to reach agreement may end up pressuring the minority.[71] The requirement to reach agreement may end up cultivating a norm that suppresses disagreement.[72] In that sense, unanimous rule does not benefit the numerical minority under all conditions.[73]

Regardless of whether unanimity empowers the preference minority or muzzles it, no one has considered whether the protective effect that the rule can carry for *preference* minorities holds for social *identity* minorities. Even as scholars devote attention to the effects of rules and group processes on preference minorities, we know almost nothing about the effects on social identity minorities. We argue that unanimous rule, and the consensus process it tends

[69] Although the results are muddied by the fact that these juries engaged more frequently in various forms of speech.

[70] Frolich and Oppenheimer 1992; Kameda 1991; Kaplan and Miller 1987; Nemeth 1977.

[71] Some studies qualify these positive effects, finding that majority rule better neutralizes the power of a dominant member (Falk 1981), perhaps only when that member is selfish (Ten Velden, Beersma, and De Dreu 2007).

[72] Falk 1982; Gero 1985.

[73] See, for example, Gastil 1993, 50–53.

to prompt, elevates the participation and influence of social identity groups when they are few. The most important claim we make is that norms of inclusion and cooperation tend to benefit women when they are the minority.

There are several reasons to expect that what unanimous rule does for preference minorities, it will do for gender minorities. In either case, the rule places an emphasis on inclusion and cooperation. As studies reviewed above show, the norm that unanimous rule creates is the expectation that everyone should be included in the decision making. As Mansbridge explains, "a consensual rule can actually create unity" (1983, 256). While unanimous rule may also pressure minorities to go along with the group's central tendency at the end of the day, nevertheless, unanimous rule produces the expectation that each voice should be heard.[74] This may help those in the minority by elevating their level of participation—and influence. As Gastil hypothesizes, "consensus assumes that the minority viewpoint is crucial, so members may go out of their way to draw out quieter group members. Listening may also be enhanced, since consensus relies upon members understanding and considering what each other says. Without such listening it becomes far more difficult to arrive at a decision acceptable to all group members" (1993, 52).

Unanimous rule also signals that the group should orient to its members' commonalities, and may create the expectation that the group is a social unit, and that decisions should be based on equal respect (Mansbridge 1983, 14). As Gastil argues, "it is more likely that consensus groups will direct energy toward maintaining a healthy relational atmosphere" (1993, 52). Under unanimity, no voice can be overlooked because every vote is pivotal. And we argue that this veto power generates an overarching emphasis on common bonds, strengthening the identification with the group as a social category and the view of the members as brethren. As Aristotle put it, "unanimity [homonoia] . . . seems akin to friendship" (quoted in Mansbridge 1983, 14), and as Mansbridge argues, "the rule of consensus seems not only to reflect empathy but to create it" (1983, 256).

Conversely, majority rule signals that conflict is acceptable and that some perspectives may not be included in the group's final decision. Majority rule sets a norm whereby decisions are based on a contest of interests, and on numerical power. With this norm, majorities are less likely to indicate inclusiveness, and minorities are less likely to assume that their voices matter and that they should speak. As Gastil puts it, under majority rule, "majorities have no short term need to hear minority opinions" (2010, 99). Under majority rule the power of numbers matters most, and minorities are ultimately at a disadvantage.

The packaging of majority rule with other adversarial aspects of the polity is most clearly seen in Mansbridge's foundational work, *Beyond Adversary Democracy*, which also draws a clear contrast between the norms of unanimity

[74] On the former claim, see Miller 1989; Mendelberg 2002; Devine et al. 2001.

and majority rule.[75] "Majority rule" is "the classic adversary method" (1983, 265). Indeed, the formal adoption of majority rule developed in response to strong conflict. For example, the ancient Greeks may have used it to head off civil violence (1983, 13). As Mansbridge puts it, "a formal vote is the crucial mark of the legitimacy of conflict" (1983, 13). The English parliament adopted a formal majority vote as it became increasingly riven by deep cleavages, and by the mid-seventeenth century it "had departed enough from its traditional informal practice of unanimity to begin making decisions more than half the time by majority vote" (1983, 16). By instituting majority rule, the group acknowledges the legitimacy of conflict.[76] If the group sets out to use majority rule, and especially if it does so without the expectation of repeated unanimous votes, then it will lack a norm of developing consensus. The group is shaped by this expectation from majority rule, and the process of discussion will reflect the norm of explicit conflict. Rather than expecting to accommodate nearly everyone as much as possible, as a norm of unanimity demands, the group will assume that there will be winners and losers. Rather than banishing the very notion of faction, which the unanimity model of friendship requires, groups that rely on majority rule will tend to accept them as natural or inevitable. And instead of downplaying the role of self-interest, as the unanimity model does, the majority rule model takes it for granted that self-interest is the primary motive of the members. In groups where majority rule is common, interests are assumed to be more in opposition than reconcilable, the ground divided more than common.

The implied rule of unanimity generates a group priority on equal respect. By contrast, the implied rule of majority produces a priority on only the basic guarantee of equal individual voting power. Unanimous rule gives all the power to the unified collective; majority rule gives all the power to the more numerous faction and none to the minority.[77] Coupled with minority rights, majority rule can serve its main function of preventing the Hobbesian nightmare of a "war of all against all."[78] But that is all it can do—it cannot encourage the listening and mutual exchange of a consensus process.

[75] This discussion draws heavily on the ideas in Mansbridge (1983).

[76] As Mansbridge writes, "By accepting some conflict as legitimate and by instituting the formal procedures of one citizen/one vote and majority rule, Athens became the first society to move away from unitary democracy" (1983, 15).

[77] On the notion of faction, consider Aristotle's view that in the consensus-oriented group, members "will not tolerate faction at any cost" (quoted in Mansbridge 1983, 14).

[78] Mansbridge and Gastil tend to distinguish between a consensus process versus a formal unanimity voting rule (Gastil 1993, 50–53; Mansbridge 1983). However, in our view the distinctions between the formal rule and the actual process are not as important as the commonalities, and we view the two as more overlapping than distinct. We suggest that the unanimous voting rule tends to signal the need to engage in a consensus process. We grant Mansbridge's point that a formal unanimity rule is likely to signal a less consensually oriented process than the absence of any formal rule, and that a formal rule may be used at both ends of the conflict spectrum (1983, 33). The

The key is that these functions of the rule are likely to shape the view of the participants of what their interaction is all about and to alter their behavior to conform to those expectations. Because "people usually adopt [a consensus process] when they expect to agree," the person who learns that the group will use unanimous rule is likely to expect that the group will take on a cooperative orientation, then act respectfully and with the expectation of mutual respect in return.[79] In groups ruled by the imperative to include each member, norms develop that "make it difficult even to suggest that individual interests might conflict" (Mansbridge 1983, 32–33). These groups would regard bargaining, side payments, or other mechanisms that assume conflicting interests to be morally suspect (33).

And by the same token, majority rule is the best-known way of "making decisions whenever interests are both expected to conflict and do conflict on specific issues" (Mansbridge 1983, 265). In groups expecting to end their discussion with a majority vote, the members are likely to regard self-oriented acts as legitimate. Thus the presence of majority rule signals to members that the goal of discussion is to figure out what the sides are and which side will likely have its way. As Gastil puts it, "[majority rule] can lead to tense relationships among group members. Majority rule often works as a zero-sum game: one subgroup's victory is another's defeat. If the process becomes highly competitive, adversaries may begin to question one another's mutuality and competence, and group discussion can turn into hostile debates" (1993, 54).

In sum, unanimous rule signals, and is likely to generate, equal status for each person, and an inclusive, cooperative norm, whereas majority rule signals the notion that the majority is entitled to get its way and is likely to produce a more competitive norm.[80]

---

most prominent example Mansbridge notes is the UN Security Council. This body uses unanimous rule in the sense of giving a veto power to each member, but that institution does not impose a sense that it is illegitimate for a member country to act exclusively in its self-interest. Similarly, economists tend to view unanimous rule as a rule like any other, one that generates individualistic strategic behavior rather than transformative cooperative norms (Austen-Smith and Feddersen 2006). However, these claims do not materially affect our argument here, which is that adopting a unanimous rule is likely to move the group further along toward a norm of cooperation and inclusion. That claim assumes a relative movement from what may be a very low level of cooperation. Such an effect may apply to a highly contentious group whose members are constrained from developing meaningful friendship as well as to the closely bonded group whose members assume the existence of shared basic interests (Gastil 1993; Mansbridge 1983). Some of Mansbridge's writings are consistent with our argument, as when she argues that unanimity often serves the function of protecting interests from tyranny and of building bonds of amity and commonality (1983, 263).

[79]The quote is from Mansbridge (1983, 32), but the idea that rules create norms, while drawing on her discussion, is primarily our conjecture.

[80]To be sure, the mere existence of a formal vote is not as important as whether the group develops a norm of orienting to consensus. As Mansbridge puts it, "Although the [Athenian] assembly used majority rule, it may well have made most of its decisions by consensus" (1983, 14). That is, groups may use the option of taking a majority vote yet still rely on a pro forma vote for

However, on their own, the gender composition of the group and its decision rule are only partial explanations. What is needed is an account of how each conditions the effects of the other. And that is what we aim to provide. We theorize, then, that decision rule and gender composition will interact to shape patterns of participation and influence within the group. This is our *interaction hypothesis* (see table 3.1).

The interaction hypothesis claims, first, that unanimous rule produces a group dynamic in which various types of numerical minorities—social identity as well as preference minorities—are included more than they would be otherwise. Compared to majority rule, unanimous rule benefits both genders when they are in the numerical minority of the group. But the effects of unanimity are best understood in contrast to the speech participation of each gender minority under majority rule. When women are the minority under majority rule, the gender effects we have documented will kick in, and they will speak and influence less than men in the group. But when men are the minority under majority rule, the same gender effects will restrain women from completely dominating men, so women will leverage the power of their majority only so far as equality with men in the group. Thus minority women will be included more under unanimous than majority rule, and this will shrink the gender gap in the group, rendering women more equal to men. Minority men will be also be included more under unanimous than under majority rule, and this will neutralize the potential power of women's large numbers. Under unanimous rule the gender gap may remain unaffected as women's numbers increase, or even grow. Unanimity will elevate both genders when they are in the minority, but women go from underrepresentation to equality, while men go from equality to overparticipation.

One possible explanation for why the elevating effect of unanimous rule produces different gender gaps is that each gender minority increases its participation under unanimous rule for a different reason. As noted earlier, in small group discussion, on average men tend toward individual agency, women toward cooperation (Miller 1985; Smith-Lovin and Brody 1989). Therefore, women in a numerical minority may interpret unanimous rule to mean that they should make at least a minimal contribution, more than in majority rule, but avoid dominating the discussion. Minority men may interpret unanimous rule as a signal that they should maximize their individual participation. That is, gender may create a bifurcated interpretation of the meaning of a consensus requirement. The reason it does so is that consensus contains within it two opposing elements. As Gastil puts it, "[consensus] radically empowers group

nearly all decisions, with the expectation of unanimity in general. In that case, the actual decision-making procedure is unanimity rather than majority rule. In such a group, for any given discussion the likely expectation is of a unanimous vote, if a formal vote is to be bothered with at all. In such groups, the de facto rule becomes unanimous rule.

members, often making them aware of both their autonomy and their responsibility to the group" (1993, 52). Individual autonomy exists in tension to its direct opposite, the responsibility of the individual to the collective. We argue that social identity shapes which of these two elements of unanimous rule the individual member tends to internalize. Furthermore, this effect of social identity may come into play when that social identity is made salient by the group's gender composition. Consequently, men may view minority status as requiring maximum individual input from the minority and act on this view when they are the minority under unanimous rule. Relative to majority rule, we expect that unanimous rule elevates the participation of both gender minorities, men and women. By extension, unanimous rule helps female minorities, closing the gender gap in those groups, but it also helps male minorities, and that exacerbates the gender gap there.

Our attention to the interaction of gender composition and decision rule thus significantly qualifies the gender role hypothesis about the effect of women's numbers, leading to our second major prediction: Women should increase their participation with greater numbers only under majority rule. That is, under majority rule, the implicit norm is that of numerical agency, and this benefits women when they are the gender majority. But under unanimous rule, greater numbers do not benefit women in the same way, because this rule aids minority men to the detriment of majority women. Succinctly stated, our interaction hypothesis is as follows. A significant interaction between gender composition and decision rule exists: the gender gap in speech and influence favoring men *decreases* as the number of women increases under majority rule, but remains the same or *increases* as the number of women increases under unanimous rule.

No interactive effect of decision rule and gender has been taken into consideration in the literatures on gender or decision rule. Yet an interaction is plausible in light of what we know about each variable in isolation. Attention to this interaction represents our theoretical contribution to these literatures.

Conclusion

We have laid out the general framework that guides us in the remainder of the book. Numbers matter, but their effects depend on the decision rule. For a number of reasons, women on average tend to have lower confidence and to be more affected by that lower confidence, to dislike conflict and seek cooperation, and to seek a sense of connection to others. These differences between men and women, which can be small, may become consequential when individuals assemble in groups. We identified two possible reasons why groups matter in this way. First, the fewer women are present, the more the interaction takes on a masculine character. In addition, the fewer women, the more confident participants the women encounter and the lower their sense of capacity to function as a valued member of the group. We have called this the "minority status" hypothesis. A corollary is the "enclave" hypothesis: all-female groups provide a special boost to women.

However, these effects of gender composition are qualified by the nature of the institution—specifically, the rules and procedures of interaction. Unanimous decision rule sets a norm of inclusion. That norm can be based on social bonds and mutual affinity, or alternatively, on the protection of the veto. The dynamic of affinity will help elevate women's participation. That is because women more than men may need an interaction style that emphasizes social solidarity and cooperation, and because their lower confidence may make them especially sensitive to a dearth of, and thus especially responsive to the presence of, positive reinforcement from the group. So when women are few, they will benefit from the generally protective dynamic of consensual norms that are more likely to develop under unanimity rules. But unanimity empowers any minority group, so men, who tend to be more oriented toward individual agency, may leverage the power of the veto when they are the gender minority to maximize their participation. Consensual norms can, therefore, be a double-edged sword for women, helping them when they are the minority but not when they are the majority.

Gender is not merely a demographic characteristic of individual men or women. Gender also produces more feminine or more masculine ways of thinking, acting, and interacting. Gendered expectations in society build up lower reserves of authority for women than for men. Gender socialization leads women, on average, to have lower confidence during formal discussions, to orient more toward cooperation than conflict, and to react more sensitively to social bonds, relative to men. However, a person's degree of masculinity or femininity is shaped by the situation. A man, or a woman, may behave in ways that are more or less masculine or feminine as the environment shifts. The expectations, norms, and habits of interaction that apply to men or to women, with their implicit codes of thought and action, nudge a person toward masculinity or femininity, but the setting can shift those expectations, norms, and habits. In that sense, settings and institutions are gendered. That is, gender is a characteristic of processes and institutions that does not necessarily refer to individual men or women at all (Winter 2008).

We identified two characteristics of the setting that help to determine whether women will experience lower authority: the number of women present and the rules and procedures that govern the discussion. The number of women is gendered in that it sets in motion signals about women's authority and can shape the interaction to be more or less masculine or feminine. A decision rule is also gendered in that unanimous rule better matches the interaction style of women than of men, and produces more influence for women than for men. Gender is actively produced, defined, and reinforced (Scott 1986) and perhaps most powerfully when it is not noticed as such. Our contribution to this theoretical framework is to show how two gendered features of the setting or the institution—numbers and rules—jointly produce a new set of gendered dynamics.

In the following chapter we present our own study and offer methodological considerations on how to best go about testing the implications we have derived here.

CHAPTER 4

The Deliberative Justice Experiment

THERE IS NO SHORTAGE OF commentary about women's presence in decision-making groups. And given the many studies that have accumulated on that topic, readers may wonder whether in fact they need this one. Surely by now we know that the presence of more women results in more participation and representation?

Well, actually, no. As we reviewed in chapter 1, studies of gender composition have come to an inconclusive end. For example, the most comprehensive study of women's participation in meetings, Frank Bryan's mammoth study of Vermont town meetings, found that the higher the percentage of women attenders, the *lower* is women's share of speakers. Bryan left no rock unturned in Vermont; he examined every variable under the sun, including the most venerable variables known to cause political participation.[1] Yet the explanation for women's relative quiescence remains elusive. Studies in an entirely different continent yield similarly puzzling findings. As noted in chapter 1, the variables that typically elevate disadvantaged groups' speech in Indian village meetings fail to elevate women's speech. And so it goes with other studies—and whole literatures—on the topic of women's participation and representation. There is still much to learn about women's speech, and in particular when, and why, women's numbers matter, and how institutions shape women's voice and representation.

Part of the challenge of answering the lingering questions about women's voice and authority is methodological. For example, many of the studies that take up the question of gender do not disentangle group gender composition from individual gender or do not involve sufficient variation in gender composition to allow for a full understanding of group-level factors. In particular, there are many ways that gender composition and decision rule could be correlated with other possible causes of women's participation and substantive

[1] He examined the town's Democratic vote share, its vote for Vermont's ERA, its turnout levels, other measures of town's liberalism/conservatism, the town's size, its political economy and women's place in it, and so on.

representation at a meeting. An observational study that tries to control on all these factors is likely to fail. Certain types of places or certain types of groups may, for example, be more or less likely to draw in women—or certain types of women—as participants and to shape the extent to which women exercise voice and authority. These tendencies complicate our ability to understand the effects of gender composition on its own. Similarly, certain types of groups may be more likely to choose unanimous decision rules, and this endogeneity will complicate any attempt to isolate the independent effects of institutional processes. In addition, the vast majority of attempts to study the characteristics of groups that matter for equality end up either with too few groups or inadequate measures of the causes, outcomes, discussions, or social interactions we are studying. In the chapter appendix we take up these issues in detail by cataloging a number of methodological gaps in existing studies.

What We Do in Our Experiment

We designed an experiment to remedy the shortcomings of previous studies. We wished to include a larger number of groups than the typical study has done. We wanted to assemble a dataset with many groups in each of several different gender compositions. Without enough variance on one of our key variables, we could not study its effects properly. We also wanted to avoid conflating gender composition, or decision rule, with other factors that may be correlated with them and that may also affect the outcomes we examine. Those factors include group size, the political context (more liberal or conservative), the level of women's mobilization, the attitudes correlated with gender but not an essential part of gender itself, and more (as we elaborate below). In addition, we wanted to examine a wider range of outcomes from women's presence and from decision rule than those we found in existing studies. Among those outcomes are measures of what actually goes on during deliberation, and what happens as a consequence of the conditions of discussion and the content of discussion. Therefore, we wanted to record in minute detail every utterance by every speaker and link it to the speaker's attitudes and preferences before and after the discussion. A laboratory experiment offered a means to achieve these research aims.

This design would allow us to ask questions such as: how much do women and men speak? How much do women and men talk about issues of distinctive concern to women? Do men use interruptions to establish their status in the group? Do women use them to create a warmer tone of interaction in the group? Do women express their preferences during discussion? And how does what happens during the discussion affect the decisions the group ultimately makes? Finally, we needed postdeliberation measures to ask questions such as: How does all this affect women's and men's sense of their own worth, and sense of other members' worth, after deliberation? Is women's authority affected by gender composition and decision rule?

Finally, we wanted to be able to say that it is gender, and not something correlated with gender, that produces the results of gender composition. And that it is gender, and not something that women just happen to have more than, or less than, men, that is doing the work. To that end we needed a way to measure the person's views before deliberation starts and see if the effects we observe really do fall out by the person's gender and not by the person's preferences. (In addition, measuring views before deliberation can tell us if women express these views as much as men.) We needed to assess the person's political views and hold those constant when examining differences between men and women.

Since our goal is to home in on the individual's gender and not end up spuriously studying the effects of factors that tend to go hand in hand with the person's gender, we pause here to spell out the difference between these concepts. Gender is a constellation of factors that is not reducible to the substance of political attitudes or to incidental demographic characteristics that men may have more of, such as income, or that women may have more of, such as education or age. By political attitudes we mean a person's level of liberalism or conservatism, and the kinds of attitudes that tend to feed into this political ideology, especially the person's level of egalitarianism. A general adherence to, or rejection of, egalitarian values is particularly pertinent for our study, since our respondents were asked to consider such matters as what is fair in redistributing income in society (and among themselves), how much the well off should be taxed in order to help the poor, and what are the respective obligations of the individual to get along on their own and of the society to help those who cannot help themselves. These are all questions that are intimately linked to the opinions that our groups will discuss—the appropriate level of government spending, how much to tax and who should be taxed, and how much income inequality is acceptable or desirable (Bartels 2008; Feldman and Steenbergen 2001). For that reason, when we construct multivariate models, we add statistical controls for egalitarian attitudes in order to get at pure gender effects from being a woman versus a man. Where it makes sense to do so, we also control on the person's predeliberation preferences about the specific principles of income redistribution that groups were instructed to discuss and decide, and whether this preference was in the majority for that group.[2] Adding these controls helps us to separate out political attitudes and ideologies that are not core aspects of gender. As we elaborate in the next chapter, we will call these alternative hypotheses, respectively, *Preferences* and *Efficiency*.

In addition, we investigate whether demographic characteristics such as age, education, or income drive the results. As we will note throughout, we find that they do not, either at the individual or the group level. While these factors have not been experimentally manipulated, when we substitute the number of group members above the median income or age, or the number of college graduates,

[2]The online appendix (http://press.princeton.edu/titles/10402.html) provides the question wording and response options we used to measure egalitarian attitudes.

for our indicator of gender composition, we find that these demographic characteristics have no effect.[3] With few exceptions, these indicators rarely even come close to statistical significance, either as additional controls or as substitutes for our measures of gender, so we have generally chosen to leave them out of our standard model in order to conserve statistical power. Most importantly, the results lead away from the conclusion that gender is a mere proxy for other demographic characteristics.

What that leaves us with is gender itself. At the level of the individual, and when it comes to stable characteristics of the person, we take gender to be a combination of the traits and attitudes that arise from gender socialization, such as the level of a person's confidence, the person's sensitivity to situations that send signals about one's competence, aversion to conflict, the level of priority one places on social ties, and the effect of signals about the level of warmth and social connection in the group.

There is some overlap between what we consider correlated political attitudes on the one hand and the core aspects of gender on the other hand. Socialization into gender roles in part explains why women tend to seek a higher level of equality, to endorse more economically liberal policy, and to believe that it is government's role to provide for those least well off in society. However, many men also adhere to these beliefs and pursue these preferences, and gender role socialization is not the main reason that people hold these beliefs. So while the total effects of gender do extend to political ideology and preferences, we will conduct a hard test of the effects of gender by bracketing the effects that work through these political attitudes and leaving only the remaining effects of gender socialization and gender roles.

In addition to ensuring that we are getting at the effects of gender per se, we want to be sure that the effects we attribute to gender composition, and to decision rule, could only be due to these and no others. That is the main reason we use a controlled experiment. Although our study requires an artificial setting to allow us to create controlled circumstances, its high internal validity is valuable despite the trade-off with external validity (McDermott 2011). Once we can be confident of the effects of gender composition under controlled conditions, we can then ask whether the results apply in more natural settings, as we do in the penultimate chapter.

The reader by now may be asking a simple but devastating question: how can you assign people to gender composition if you cannot assign gender to a person? Put differently, does this count as an experiment?[4] Our general response to these questions is that yes, the design in this study incorporates the defining features of experimentation. In their classic discussion of experimentation,

[3]Neither demographic characteristics nor political preferences have been experimentally manipulated, the implications of which we discuss in the online appendix.

[4]An extended discussion of this question can be found in the online appendix section on methodology.

Kinder and Palfrey (1993) argue that experiments share an "interventionist spirit" in which researchers "*intrude* upon nature" in order to "provide answers to causal questions" (6). Morton and Williams (2010) agree, arguing that an experiment occurs "when a researcher intervenes in the data generating process (DGP) by purposely manipulating elements of the DGP," where manipulating means "varies the elements of" (42). We varied the elements of the data generating process—specifically, the gender composition and decision rule for all groups in our sample. In addition, we use the hallmark of experiments as traditionally conceived: random assignment.[5] However, because gender is not randomly assigned, we cannot treat gender composition as a purely randomized variable, and we must control on variables potentially correlated with it, as we explained above.

Finally, because ours is a study of gender inequality, we must decide how to measure that inequality. In most of what follows, we have in mind not the *total* participation or influence of men or women in the group, but participation or influence *per capita*. In other words, we examine the participation or influence of the *average* man or woman in the group. The problem with looking at the total (or in other words, combined or summed) female percentage of talk or influence is that rising numbers of women could increase women's total proportion of talk or influence even if the average woman speaks far less than the average man.

For example, consider a hypothetical group containing four women and one man—that is, with 80% women—and imagine that the women collectively speak for 70% of the discussion. If we rely on women's *total* percentage of discussion, then women appear to dominate the discussion, since together they take up a large majority of it. We would then conclude that the conditions that produced this percentage have created a large advantage for women over men. But when we look at the *average* woman's percent of discussion, we come to the opposite conclusion. In the same hypothetical group, the average woman takes 17.5% of the conversation (that is, 70% divided by 4), while the man takes almost double that (30%). These rates yield a female/male ratio of 58%, indicating a high degree of gender inequality. In other words, the average in this example shows us that women actually participated much less than their share of members, and that their relative participation is actually far less than men's. This is the definition of equality that we have in mind when we hypothesize about a gender gap in participation or influence.

Focusing on the average participation of men and women, respectively, also gives us a standard metric that allows us to see how the patterns of participation, including the gender gaps, change across different gender compositions.

[5]Specifically, our approach uses what Cynthia Farrar, Don Green, and their colleagues call a "passive" experimental design—one that randomly assigns individuals to the discussion group based on their demographic, ideological, or other preexisting characteristics, and observes the outcomes (Farrar et al. 2009, 617–18). While individual gender cannot be manipulated, a group's gender composition can be. So, too, can other features of the group, such as the decision rule.

We can easily compare what women do in groups where women comprise 20% of the group to what they do in groups where women are 40%, 60%, or 80% of the discussants because we are adjusting for the random chance that more individuals produce more activity.

A focus on average or per capita participation is the approach we will pursue for most of the book. But this is not to say that patterns of total participation are meaningless or unhelpful, either normatively or empirically. When we turn to the question of group decision making in chapter 9, we will bring total participation back in as we explore the relationship between participation patterns, the content of discussions, and the group's eventual choices. In explaining those choices, we will want to know whether average gender gap, the total gender gap, or both matter most.

To be clear, when we analyze participation or influence, whether total or average, our definition of equality is when participation or influence of a given gender is proportional to its numbers in the group. When it is not—and especially when the patterns of advantage or disadvantage are systematic, as we will show—then we will conclude that the standard of equality has been violated.

In sum, we designed our study to do the following: (1) generate a sufficient number of groups in various gender compositions to create adequate variance in this independent variable;[6] (2) test for the predicted interactive effects of gender composition with decision rule; (3) use random assignment to create exogenous gender composition and decision rule variables so as to gauge their unbiased effects; (4) measure the actual level of speech participation of individuals and match it to their individual characteristics, including their gender; (5) measure, and control for, egalitarianism and other aspects of political ideology, both of the person and of the group; and (6) assess the effects for different types of women, and the effects on various types of outcomes (speech patterns, speech content, agenda setting, and influence), accurately measured.

The Deliberative Justice Experiment

Our experiment followed the basic procedure of a previous study by Frohlich and colleagues (Frohlich, Oppenheimer, and Eavy 1987; Frohlich and Oppenheimer 1990 and 1992). We told participants that they would be performing tasks to earn money and that the money received would be based on a group decision about redistribution, with the decision based on unanimous rule or majority rule.[7] Prior to group deliberation they were not told the nature of the work.[8] This uncertainty about the work task meant that participants did not

[6] We stratified by gender to avoid a balanced gender mix in most groups.

[7] A control condition of no deliberation was included for other purposes.

[8] In the Frohlich and Oppenheimer study, this was meant to simulate the Rawlsian veil of ignorance, designed to prompt people to consider principles of justice.

know whether they were likely to earn a great deal of money or only a little, and therefore what their individual interests would be in a decision about income redistribution. Following Frohlich and colleagues, we instructed participants to make a collective decision that would apply not only concretely and immediately to themselves and their group but also hypothetically to society at large, so we could generalize beyond the lab situation to the decisions people make about redistribution in politics.

Between August 2007 and February 2009, students and community members were recruited, randomly assigned to one of the decision rule and gender composition conditions, and brought together for two hours. Potential participants were asked to take part in a two-hour experiment investigating "how people make decisions about important issues." Recruitment was conducted through a wide variety of methods including e-mails to students,[9] postcards to purchased random lists of community members, online advertisements, flyers posted on and off campus, and direct contact to local community groups.

The experiment occurred in three parts. In the first part, participants answered a pretreatment questionnaire about their social and political attitudes. (Question wording for key survey measures can be found in the chapter appendix.) After completing this initial questionnaire, participants were given a brief handbook that introduced them to some basic principles of redistribution that would be the focus of their group discussion later. The principles were as follows:

1. Maximize the Floor: *The lowest income in the group is raised to 80% of the group's average.* We told participants that maximizing the floor meant "giving those who have the least the most help possible."
2. No Taxes or Redistribution: *Everyone gets exactly what they earn.* Participants were told that this principle gives "everyone the greatest incentive to work hard and produce more" because with this principle, no redistribution would occur at all.
3. Set a Floor Constraint: *The group decides on an exact dollar amount to which the lowest incomes will be raised.* The instructions for this principle emphasized the creation of a safety net "ensuring [that] everyone has enough to get by" and that the exact level of the safety net could be decided by the group.
4. Set a Range Constraint: *The group decides on an exact dollar amount that is the highest allowable difference between the highest income and the lowest income.* With this principle, the instructions emphasized the goal of "reducing the extremes between rich and poor."

For each principle, the participant handbook explained the values and purposes that motivate some people to prefer it as a method of redistribution.

[9] At the northeastern university, student e-mails were those of volunteers for previous experiments in their lab, and later to the entire student body. At the western university, several random samples of the entire student body were obtained and used.

(See the online appendix for a full description of these principles and other instructions.) As they considered each principle, participants were instructed to "think about values that you hold. For example, think about how to promote equality of opportunity, how to reduce the gap between rich and poor, how best to provide for the poor, or how to reward talent and hard work." They were also asked to think about how the principles would affect them, depending on the income they might ultimately earn: "Will you be happy keeping only what you earned in a low income situation? Will you be happy with a guaranteed minimum income? Will you be happy giving up your wages in a high income situation? Which principle is most fair or just for the group as a whole?"

During this initial period of instruction, we also gave participants examples of how the principle could be applied in the context of the experiment. For example, we explained that if a group were to choose a range constraint of $0, the group would be choosing to distribute the money earned by the group such that each member would earn the exact same amount. We also showed participants several different sample distributions of income and how choosing different principles would affect the way income was redistributed. After reading the material, each participant completed an eleven-question quiz to test their basic understanding of the principles. Participants who missed questions were given another opportunity to respond and were told the correct answer. This was to assure that all group members began the discussion with a roughly equal minimal level of understanding of the principles. Finally, participants were asked to privately disclose their preferences about how best to redistribute income or whether redistribution was an important goal at all.

In the second part of the experiment, participants were brought together in groups of five and were instructed to conduct a "full and open discussion" and to choose the "most just" principle of redistribution. They were asked to choose a principle that would be applied to money they and their group members earned during the experiment but that could also function as a principle for society at large. The only requirement was that they deliberate for at least five minutes; on average, the groups we analyzed spent just over twenty-five minutes (SD = 11) in discussion. All instructions, other than those pertaining to the specific decision rule to be used by the group, were exactly the same across conditions. During deliberation, each participant was recorded on a separate audio track, and the full conversation was also recorded on a master track that included all participants.[10] This allowed us a precise and detailed account of what each person in the group said during group discussion. To avoid self-clustering in the deliberative area, participants were seated randomly around the table.

[10]Our software measures the participation of each member precisely; see the online appendix for further details.

The experimenter opened discussion by asking, "Would someone like to start by explaining which principle they believe to be most just and why?" The experimenter then remained in the room during the deliberation to manage the recording equipment and answer clarification questions about the distribution principles or other aspects of the process, but did not otherwise moderate or direct the discussion.

Participants appeared to take their deliberations seriously. Group deliberations typically extended well beyond the five-minute minimum, sometimes lasting as long as an hour or more. Consistent with the instructions, group discussions nearly always explored how group members' choices about principles would work outside the experimental setting. The discussions touched on meaningful topics related to the redistribution, including the nature of equality, the needs of the poor, the importance of incentivizing work, the possibility of economic mobility, the fairness of various systems of taxation, and the value of charity. (A sample transcript is in the online appendix.)

For example, in a discussion on the East Coast, a female participant describes why she thinks a generous floor amount for the poor is important:

> From my experience in American society though, the problem comes in that we—there are so many things you can't predict, like you can't predict how much money a family needs to survive. And if that's the case, then there are people who are still living within pretty minimal surroundings, and other people who are living quite extravagantly, and they're saying "well, this is a living income here." But the living income so often doesn't seem to be a living income for a family.

Later in the discussion, another participant explores the possibility of a range constraint and wonders out loud about the work ethic of the very rich:

> The range constraint appeals to me because there's such a disparity between the richest and the poorest, but it might flatten things too much in terms of giving people an incentive to work really hard, who are already up there. . . . I mean the implication might be that people who are poor don't work really hard, and that's just not true, or at least not in a lot of cases, and a lot of rich people don't work hard. I mean it's like you can't assume that because somebody has a lot of money that they work hard, and because they don't, they don't work hard.

In a Western discussion, the group members similarly explore the balance between providing an incentive to work and meeting the needs of the poor. One participant expresses concern about "loopholes" that would allow the poor to receive income without sufficient effort:

> But I just, I see a lot of loopholes, and with, like, other systems and things like when, when the poor are, like, blaming their situation in life that they're born in, like, oh I'm poor and this, I'm not going to do much because I'm poor. If, you know, I just—I don't know. I just have an issue with that kind of thing.

Another participant agrees that work is important, but reminds the group that in the larger society, it is also sometimes the case that individuals work hard but still face hardships:

> No, I kind of agree. I think that there—like you said, there's strong incentive, but . . . if there's no floor or if there isn't anything, . . . then if they don't make enough to actually support themselves, that's an issue too. And we've seen that today just with our society.

At this point, a third group member chimes in that many poor people work very hard, and a fourth explores whether the circumstances of one's birth should have such a significant effect on one's life chances:

> I grew up in a family where we were taught that, you know, how hard you work is how much you get, but what I've learned is that's not always the case. Like, depending on what circumstances you're born into, like, it affects a ton of your life . . . I've just learned that, like, you can't help where you're born and that has such a huge effect on the rest of your life. And so it's really not fair that . . . how hard you work should determine how much you get paid, like, some people just can't help it.

As these examples show, the groups did much more than wonder about how they could maximize their pay in the context of the experiment. Often they explored the various principles of redistribution in great detail, thinking together about the concept of justice, the meaning of poverty, and how best to encourage self-sufficiency and also care for others. The conversations moved back and forth between the various principles they were considering, their own experiences in life, and the principles they wanted to encourage in society at large. As they worked through these issues, they expressed preferences for different principles and different levels of generosity for the safety net (poverty line), frequently exploring the implications of choosing different levels of support for the poor.

When the group members indicated they were ready to stop the conversation and vote on a preferred principle, the experimenter stepped in to conduct the formal vote, which occurred by secret ballot.[11] If no principle of redistribution received sufficient support (either majority or unanimous, depending on the decision rule to which the group had been assigned), participants were told to return to discussion until they felt ready to vote again. Participants were instructed that if they were not able to agree on a principle of redistribution after four votes, the experimenters would assign a principle to the group. Groups were not told what the assigned principle would be, and no groups asked what principle would be chosen for them. Most importantly, all groups reached agreement, so experimenters never assigned a principle.

[11] All group members had to agree that they were ready to end the conversation.

If the group chose either a range constraint or a floor constraint, they had one additional decision to make: what would the constraint be? Groups choosing these principles had to specify an exact dollar amount for those constraints and had to agree on these amounts according to their assigned decision rule. For example, if the group chose a floor constraint, they were asked to specify the income level below which no one would be allowed to fall. Because we asked them to think not only about the specific income they would be earning in the context of the experiment but also about rules that could be applied to society at large, we asked them to interpret the floor as "the minimum income a household is guaranteed each year." In other words, groups choosing a floor amount had to specify what the poverty line in terms of an annual salary should be. In the instructions for deliberation, we asked groups to think about dollar amounts that could actually be used in society at large.

After deliberation came the third and final part of the experiment. Participants returned to private computer terminals and answered a set of questions about their assessments of the discussion, the group, its members, and their own experience. (Question wording for key survey measures is available in the chapter appendix.) They again had an opportunity to express their private preferences about principles. Participants then performed several rounds of "work"—correcting as many spelling errors in a block of difficult text as they could find within a two-minute time limit (replicating Frohlich and colleagues' choice of procedure). Participants earned money according to their performance on the spelling task, and these earnings were distributed to group members according to their chosen distribution scheme. During the work period, earned incomes were given on a scale of annual incomes. At the end of the experiment, these were converted to a payment scale that ranged between \$10 and \$70. At the end of the task period, participants responded to a series of questions on attitudes and beliefs and were debriefed.

We use a 6×2 between-subjects experimental design, randomly assigning individuals to one of six gender compositions (that is, to a group that ranged from zero to five women) and one of two decision-rule conditions, unanimous rule or majority rule.[12] Gender composition was randomly assigned to dates on the schedule of experimental sessions, and subjects who signed up to attend on that date were assigned to the corresponding gender composition condition. This ensured that group types did not cluster on particular days of the week and that participants had a roughly equal probability of being assigned to each group type. Thus each man or woman had the same probability of being

[12] Because experimental sessions were run over an extended period of time, there is no correlation between gender composition type and the day of the week or the time of the session. Typically, we conducted one experimental session at each site per day, and sessions started at similar times of the day. If fewer than five participants showed up, the session was canceled and participants could sign up for subsequent sessions. See the online appendix for additional details.

assigned to a given gender composition. This satisfies the random assignment assumption, which is *not* that each treatment is equally likely to be assigned to a given person, but rather that each person is equally likely to be assigned to a treatment (Morton and Williams 2010). We recruited more than five participants for each session, and the alternates helped ensure that we could fill the day's assigned type of gender composition. Randomization of decision rule was achieved by the roll of dice prior to each session. Randomization checks and propensity score analyses find that individuals were assigned by a random process and groups are equivalent on relevant covariates.[13] In other words, we find that our groups are comparable in terms of their basic attitudes about politics and their demographic characteristics, such as income or education. Further details on the procedure, subjects, and other methodological matters are in the online appendix.

We have data on 470 individuals in ninety-four deliberating groups. Table 4.1 summarizes our experimental conditions and the number of groups and individuals in each condition. Although our statistical power is still somewhat limited, our research design includes a much larger sample of groups than typical in group research.

The experiment was conducted at two different sites—a small town near the mid-Atlantic coast and a medium-sized city in the Mountain West. Both locations include universities that recruit students from all different parts of the country. In the regressions we control on site because subjects are assigned randomly within but not across sites. As is common in controlled experiments, our goal was not a nationally representative sample but one with sufficient variance, and the sample did vary on relevant characteristics such as socioeconomic status and political attitudes, though our participants tend to be relatively highly educated, with most having at least some college experience (online appendix table B1).

Because our interest is in individuals and groups, we account for both, and we examine the data at the individual level and at the group level. We employ individual-level analysis in order to control on the characteristics of men and women that are correlated with gender but not core aspects of gender. As discussed earlier, those tend to be the person's level of egalitarianism, and as needed, their liberalism, their prediscussion preferences over the group decision, and whether they are with the preference majority in their group. We also control on group-level characteristics, typically, the number of egalitarians. Because we can rely on the virtues of random assignment to condition, we

[13] Demographics such as education, income, age, partisanship, and student status had no significant relationship with gender composition and rule. We performed three tests on each set of propensity scores: a two-sample t-test, a Wilcoxon-Mann-Whitney test, and a Kolmogorov-Smirnov test. Full details of our randomization checks are available in the online appendix.

Table 4.1: Experimental Conditions and Sample Size

	Unanimous # groups	Majority # groups	Total Groups	Total Individuals
0 Women	8	7	15	75
1 Woman	10	9	19	95
2 Women	6	7	13	65
3 Women	9	7	16	80
4 Women	8	8	16	80
5 Women	7	8	15	75
Total Groups	48	46	94	—
Total Individuals	240	230	—	470

sometimes report the raw experimental means without any controls, to give a basic sense of the effects. When we add individual- or group-level controls, we generally employ standard OLS regression, or probit with limited dependent variables, though we have also checked our results with other models, including, for example, both random- and fixed-effects models. Those alternative approaches yield results that are almost always identical to the results we report here, so we have opted for the most easily interpretable methods whenever possible. When we examine individuals rather than groups as the unit, we use robust standard errors clustered by the group. This sets the bar for finding statistically significant effects higher, but it has the virtue of adjusting for the fact that individuals share the experience of being in the same group and are therefore not fully independent of each other. We chose cluster robust standard errors over other approaches, such as hierarchical linear models, because clustering allows us to achieve roughly the same ends with fewer strong modeling assumptions. When we use group-level data—discussing what groups do or what a variable characterizing the group does—we use the number of groups to test for significance.[14] Otherwise we use the number of individuals. When we report predicted values to show the effect of a causal variable, we estimate the values of the dependent variable from the model in each of our experimental conditions and allow the other variables in the model to take on their observed values.[15] Descriptive statistics, scaling and wording for all variables, are in table

[14] When we have a clear directional hypothesis, we often employ one-tailed tests of statistical significance. In other cases, where our expectations are less clear or our hypotheses are more speculative, we employ a two-tailed test.

[15] This procedure yields very similar results to alternative approaches in which we hold the other values in the model constant at their means or medians.

B2 in the online appendix.[16] Question wording for key survey measures can also be found in the appendix for this chapter.

External Validity

The strength of experiments, of course, is their strong internal validity (Kinder and Palfrey 1993). But what about external validity? What does a lab study have to do with the natural world? We address a number of subsidiary questions on this theme.[17]

A fair question is whether it is worth the bother of studying gender compositions that do not occur much in the real world. For example, perhaps in today's America, most groups that discuss matters of common concern have fairly balanced numbers of men and women. If most discussion groups are fairly balanced we do not need to know what happens in nonbalanced compositions. Perhaps we especially do not need to study homogenous gender groups. A different version of this question is whether there are too few groups where women are a majority to bother looking at fine distinctions between 60% female, 80% female, and 100% female. Our first answer is that we saw in chapters 2 and 3 that women *and* men are actively involved in organizations that hold meetings, and that the most common setting is one in which women make up about 20% of the participants. Still, groups vary widely in their gender composition, and there are even enough groups where men encounter only men, and women only women.

To further address this question, we can look at several additional sources. First, Bryan's study of recent New England town meetings finds that the percentage of women ranged from approximately 18% to 70% of attenders.[18] Second, a survey of American city councils provides some useful information. The average number of women on a city council is one. In addition, 24% of councils

[16]For the sake of completeness, we report the sample means for all our variables, but many of these variables are affected by the experimental conditions themselves, as predicted. So the overall sample mean is not substantively meaningful. For example, the overall gender gap in talk time is the mean across very different experimental conditions, and large gender gaps in some conditions are canceled out by small or nonexistent gaps in others. In addition, some of these experimental conditions—such as majority-rule groups with a minority of women—are far more common outside the lab setting than others, and the means for those more common settings should be used if one wishes to generalize from our sample to the population at large.

[17]How far and exactly to which types of people and situations we can generalize is a question addressed in the conclusion chapter. Here we address the question of whether our experiment is sufficiently realistic to apply to natural settings.

[18]The distribution of percentage of women attenders is normal with a center at 47% (Plot 1); this average percentage has held steady over the course of the 1990s (figure 2). This tells us that at least in New England town halls, most meetings are evenly balanced, but that there are enough groups both under and over this balance point that they are worth studying. Figure X-E at http://www.uvm.edu/~fbryan/newfig%20X-E.pdf; http://www.uvm.edu/~fbryan/Chap_IX_links.html.

are all male (Nelson 2002). So in at least some settings of interest to us, the typical group is not evenly balanced and women are a small minority. Moreover, male enclaves are common enough to study. Third, further evidence comes from Hannagan and Larimer, who studied a random sample of appointed commissions in Iowa (2011a). In their sample, evenly balanced groups were a minority, and enough groups lay at the extremes of the gender composition distribution to make it worth our while to study the full distribution.[19] As these numbers show, official committees range across the entire spectrum of gender composition. The real world contains enough groups with balanced numbers, with high or low gender compositions, and with male and female enclaves.

We can also see if the groups we studied under controlled conditions share some important features with natural groups. For one, we might ask about the length of deliberation. Our groups deliberated on average for about half an hour. In juries Gastil and colleagues studied, the median juror spent about one hour deliberating (2010). Similarly, state legislative hearings in Kathlene's study lasted just over an hour (1994). The school board meetings we study in chapter 10 lasted on average about two and one-half hours. This is longer than our study's median deliberation time, but not a qualitatively different experience such as one might find in, say, a full-day meeting.

A key feature of the group is size. We assembled groups of five members. The average size of US city councils is six members (Nelson 2002, 2–3). The average size of school boards is five to seven, as we document in chapter 10. Jury size is similar, as is the size of local boards Hannagan and Larimer (2011a) studied. We conclude that size is not a problem for external validity in our study.

Our experiment examined the behavior of non-Latino whites. We made this choice with difficulty. We do not intend to imply that studying nonwhites is less important. In fact, nonwhites do take an active part in civic groups. Black politics in particular is characterized by vibrant organizations, especially churches.[20] Among the significant experiences that African Americans encounter in churches is activity in church committees (Brown and Brown 2003). The gender composition of these groups is well worth studying, especially since some findings suggest that women may not derive the same political participation boost as men do from church involvement (Robnett and Bany 2011). However, we have reason to believe that the gender dynamics in predominantly nonwhite

[19] See Hannagan and Larimer 2011a, table 1. They found roughly the following (with a membership from four to eleven):

- All-male: three groups (10%)
- Small minority female (under 33%): seven groups (23%)
- Even split: five groups (17%)
- Large minority female (around 40%): six groups (20%)
- Majority female: eight groups (27%)
- All-female: one group (3%)

[20] Calhoun-Brown 1996; Harris-Lacewell 2004; Harris 1999; McClerking and McDaniel 2005; Patillo-McCoy 1998.

groups may be sufficiently different that a rigorous study requires full attention to these groups. In other words, the research question as applied to nonwhites requires a full replicate of nonwhite groups, something we cannot do with our existing resources.

Moreover, we find that many official boards and other groups are not as integrated along lines of race or ethnicity as we would prefer. This is an unfortunate but real consequence of the continued high levels of segregation and underrepresentation of people of color in official decision-making situations. There are very few nonwhites on official deliberating groups. Town council members are overwhelmingly white (as well as either lawyers or business people) (Nelson 2002). To be exact, approximately 6% of council members are nonwhite (calculated from Nelson 2002, 3, table 4). School board members are also overwhelmingly white (see chapter 10). We will be in a position to comment on the dynamics of school boards with some nonwhite members, and on racial dialogue groups that contain nonwhites, but since these samples of nonwhites are extremely small, our conclusions about gender composition cannot be applied with enough confidence to nonwhite members.

Our experimental sample is varied in age and education. We made substantial efforts to recruit from the towns at large. But nevertheless, our sample is heavily laden with young people and college students, and the lowest levels of educational achievement (those with less than a high school education) are not well represented.[21] We take seriously the concerns about relying on students (Sears 1986; but see Druckman and Kam 2011). We are reassured, however, by several considerations. As we noted in chapter 2, the problem of women's underparticipation affects young women and college students no less than others. The gender gap is not going away. In fact, the college setting is a revealing place in which to look at why young women are not leveraging their greater educational achievements. And as we indicated above, we also replicate our main findings with a control for age, education, and income. Furthermore, we will address head on the concern that our findings may not apply to people at middle age or beyond when we analyze school boards.

An additional possible concern about our experiment is its procedure. We are asking people to make a decision about redistributing resources that they earn in a study. What does that have to do with politics? Our answer is that the decision was explicitly framed as one that would apply to society. And our attempt is to go beyond the typical survey questions about preferences on political issues to understand how citizens puzzle through these issues in a collective setting. In this sense, our experimental approach was closer to the sorts of actual decisions people make in public meetings than an individual-level survey can achieve. At real-world meetings, people are often speaking to decisions that directly affect them. At local council or town meetings the decisions

[21] Fifty-two percent of our sample are students.

have a direct bearing on the well-being of those who show up to comment. The town council decides which neighborhood's garbage gets picked up and how often. The zoning council decides if the local land developer can build ten stories or three, netting more or less profit for him and obscuring the views of the neighbors to a greater or lesser degree. Not all these decisions involve concrete resources, but many do.

School boards, whose meetings we study in chapter 10, make just such decisions. How much to tax the population of our school district? How much do we spend on the needs of disabled or poor children in our district? Or, take the case of civic associations and their meetings. Again, these meetings are likely to revolve around issues such as how much to ask different church members to contribute to the church and whether there should be a sliding scale for these fees. The PTA must decide whether to fund the eighth grade trip to Washington, DC, or staff the playground before school hours to help care for kids whose parents work (Eliasoph 1998). These are the types of decisions we wish to analyze. Asking people abstract questions about their support or opposition to assisting the poor seems a more remote way to assess the types of decisions that people make in their meetings. At the same time, we want the decision to reflect more than the immediate and relatively trivial matter of the study's take-home pay; this is why we asked them to make the decision as if it applied to society at large. Again, we can lay possible concerns to rest in our chapter on school boards, by replicating the core results with a sample of actual groups making real decisions.

In addition, we are reassured that some of our basic findings are replicated elsewhere. As we mentioned earlier, Bryan found that despite nearly equal attendance rates, women speak less than men. To be exact, Bryan found that the percentage of female attenders who speak at least once (34%) is about two-thirds the percentage of male attenders who speak at least once (52%). This is similar to the findings we shall report in the next chapter. It is also similar to the results we report in our replication chapter on school boards. (We shall have more to say about external validity in the concluding chapter.)

As we are about to detail, our experimental evidence reveals pervasive gender gaps in various dimensions of women's voice. We present these results with some reassurance that they are not merely products of an odd setting, unusual participants, or strange procedures. The control we can exercise with our experiment is thus useful in its payoff and not too demanding in its cost. And just as importantly, our experimental approach allows us real insight into how the gender gaps can change by altering the institutional features of the group.

CHAPTER 5

Speech as a Form of Participation: Floor Time and Perceived Influence

Only one thing is more frightening than speaking your truth. And that is not speaking.

—AUDRE LORDE

DO GENDER INEQUALITIES EXIST in deliberating groups? Are they significant? What conditions exacerbate or mitigate these disparities? To answer these questions we measure the amount of talk. But we do not stop there. To understand why talk matters, we examine its effects on the perceptions of influence.

While talk is only one measure of participation in deliberation, and not as informative as the content of speech, it is a crucial measure for the theoretical debates we are addressing. As Sanders writes, "If it's demonstrable that some kinds of people routinely speak more than others in deliberative settings, as it is, then participation isn't equal, and one democratic standard has fallen" (1997, 365). Sunstein concurs: "in some deliberative processes, members of lower status groups speak less and are given less respectful attention. If people are not heard, and if they do not speak, both democracy and deliberation are at risk. And if members of certain groups receive less respectful attention, both liberty and equality are at risk" (2002a, 155). And Thompson argues along similar lines that "equal opportunity, random selection, proportional representation, representative sampling, and *equal time* are among the versions of the standard that may be applied to assess equality" (2008, 506, emphasis added). Equal talk time features specifically as a good measure of equality in Thompson's critique of an empirical study of deliberation: "A measure of speaking time (by gender, race, education) might be a more useful test of equal participation" (2008, 507). Furthermore, Knight and Johnson define equality in deliberation not merely in terms of the equal formal right to join the meeting but also as the effective opportunity to influence the deliberation (1997). Talk and the influence it begets are thus important measures of equal effective participation.

Despite this importance, quantitative studies of citizen deliberation that analyze the speaking behavior of deliberators are extremely rare (Bryan's *Real*

Democracy being the main exception). Yet as the theorists cited above argue, and as Mansbridge (1983) has emphasized, speech is a crucial type of political act in a democracy, and all the more so in deliberative settings. Specifically, the more a person speaks, the more authority they may carry, so inequalities in voice may translate into inequalities in the dynamic of deliberation. And as we discussed in chapter 1, it is just this inequality that theorists who critique deliberation claim exists in deliberation.

A critic of this standard of equal talk time might respond that chattiness is not only produced by inequality but may also be a randomly distributed personality dimension. If the amount of talk is mostly determined by the vagaries of individual idiosyncrasies, then a person's proportional floor time is irrelevant to normative criteria of equality. Our response is that if a person's share of the group's discussion rests in significant measure on the status of the person's social membership, then talk is not mere chattiness. And then the principle of equal deliberation comes under significant threat.

Another counterargument is that authority produces less talk, not more. When an individual has a great deal of authority, they have no need to say much—the mere indication of the person's preference winds down the debate. A variation of this argument is that a quiet person may carry a great deal of influence by adopting a concise style and allowing the power of their incisive ideas to do the work. Many people have experienced groups in which the most influential person in the room affects the group's decisions with a few well-chosen or well-timed words. However, the evidence we present will show that this dynamic is the exception, not the rule.

Instead, we find that in a formal discussion, the proportion of talk is a robust indicator of authority. This evidence is consistent with other studies. For example, when an individual is arbitrarily assigned to be in a formal position of authority in a group, they talk more. This elegant finding is demonstrated in an experiment in which investigators assigned a randomly selected member to be the group's spokesperson; even though the selection was random, and the selected were no better leaders, they talked much longer than the other members (Shelly et al. 1999; see also Cappella 1988; Johnson 1993). That is, when a person believes they have authority, they talk more. Talk becomes an indicator of an objective measure of power.

Furthermore, because talk is shaped by status, it in turn signals status (Fiske 2010).[1] For example, in one experiment, talk participation was more correlated than the speaker's actual expertise with the perceived influence of the speaker, even though the group's task required expertise and had a correct objective solution (Bottger 1984; Dubrovksy, Kiesler, and Sethna 1991). And as we reviewed in chapter 3, various studies find that when the interaction involves

[1] For more on this point, see chapters 3 and 8. Studies of talk time and number of turns taken often cite the early work of Bales (1970) and Zimmerman and West (1975) and include Aries, Gold, and Weigel 1983; Carli 1989; and Karakowsky and Siegel 1999.

people in a position of unequal status, the member with higher status speaks more. Put differently, if men tend to be "loquacious" and women tend to be "timid" during discussions of matters of common concern, and talk begets power, then women are disadvantaged by their quiescence.[2] Consequently, if men speak more than women in settings where speaking is the mechanism for deciding matters of common concern, then speaking becomes an indicator of illegitimate inequality in deliberation. Deliberative design may thus need to concern itself with equal opportunity to speak and with the equal use of that opportunity, much as democracies concern themselves with the formal right to political expression and with ameliorating socially based inequalities in who actually engages in such expression (Burns, Schlozman, and Verba 2001).

In order to characterize the extent and conditions that give rise to inequality in deliberation, we need to examine the volume of voice and the patterns of silence. To fully understand gender inequalities, in other words, we need to look inside the black box of deliberation.

In this chapter we ask whether the critics are correct that women participate less than men during deliberation and thus have less perceived influence in it. We also ask whether the pervasive effort to increase descriptive representation—that is, the proportion of women—raises women's deliberative voice (speech participation) and authority (perceived influence). We provide the first rigorous test of these claims with a large data set of deliberating groups randomly assigned to treatments, and we link individuals' speech with pre- and postdeliberation preferences and attitudes. Moreover, we find support for our own interaction hypothesis: the number of women matters, but it interacts with the group's decision rule. Institutional rules governing deliberating groups affect equality.

How Will Gender Composition and Decision Rule Affect Talk Time?

As we elaborated in chapter 3, we begin with gender role theory. This theory argues that in groups where women discuss matters of common concern with men, women tend to defer to the assumed expertise or displayed confidence of men. Men tend to be perceived as more competent and to enjoy a higher status than women in discussions of what are perceived to be masculine subjects, including politics (Ridgeway and Smith-Lovin 1999; Sanbonmatsu 2003). Consequently, when women discuss political or legal issues in mixed-gender groups, they may speak less, feel less confident, and exercise less influence than men do, and the more men there are, the more this gender gap grows.[3] In addi-

[2] We borrow here the terms used by Hibbing and Theiss-Morse (2002, 203).

[3] See Aries 1998; Bowers, Steiner, and Sandys 2001; Croson and Gneezy 2009; Eagly 1987; Giles et al. 1987; Hastie, Penrod, and Pennington 1983; Huckfeldt and Sprague 1995; Karakowsky and Siegel 1999; Ridgeway 1982; Strodtbeck, James, and Hawkins 1957.

tion, as chapter 3 detailed, gendered dynamics of interaction shift with gender composition. Groups with many women tend to adopt communication characteristics associated with femininity, while groups with many men tend to adopt masculine norms of interaction. Gender role theory provides two specific subhypotheses, which we introduced in chapter 3 and now briefly review again.

The first and most general is *minority status*: numerical minority status affects women's status in the group and thus their participation and authority in group discussion.[4] We might expect a gender gap in participation and authority in groups where women are a minority, where there are more active, confident participants to which the women defer, or where masculine norms of interaction might depress women's participation.[5] Both the explanation grounded in confidence and the explanation grounded in group norms lead to the same prediction: the gender gap will shrink as the number of women in the group increases.[6]

Minority status holds, then, that women are worse off when they are few and that men do not experience these difficulties to the same extent. This perspective thus implies a corollary that addresses the most highly imbalanced gender compositions and that we label as *token*. Women may be especially disadvantaged when they are the lone female member of their group (Johnson and Schulman 1989; Taps and Martin 1990). Men will not suffer the same disadvantage when they are the gender token (Craig and Sherif 1986). Therefore, "token" women's participation and authority will be lower than "token" men's.

Two alternatives to gender role theory contradict the token corollary. First, *equal disadvantage* argues that extreme minority status affects men and women similarly because it emphasizes the salience of the individual's gender, leading to more negative stereotypical judgments (Kanter 1977a and 1977c). Thus token men and women participate at equally low levels. Second, *violated entitlement* asserts that men may be *more* negatively affected than women by numerical minority status because they are less familiar with it. When men are in a small minority, their expectation that they be more influential than women is violated and their sense of confidence may lessen. Women may be more familiar with being less influential than men and may not be affected as much by their token status (Chatman and O'Reilly 2004; van Knippenberg and Schippers 2007). Thus token men will participate less than token women.

The second hypothesis from gender role theory is the *enclave* hypothesis: women flourish in all-female settings. Because women are disadvantaged in political discussions with men, they may do best without any interactions with

[4]Throughout the book, "minority" and "majority" refer to numerical minority status in the group, not to race.

[5]Support for the "minority status" hypothesis can be found in Aries 1998; Johnson 1994; Piliavin and Martin 1978; Smith-Lovin and Brody 1989; see also Mendelberg and Karpowitz 2007.

[6]No specific functional form is expected and nonlinear effects are not considered disconfirming evidence.

men and may benefit most from their own discussion space (see also Karpowitz, Raphael, and Hammond 2009 on theorists' advocacy of protected settings for disempowered minorities). Thus women's participation and authority will be higher in all-female than in gender-mixed deliberating groups.

In summary, gender role theory produces two hypotheses—minority-status and enclave—and a corollary to the minority-status hypothesis, token. They share the premise that women in more masculine situations will do more poorly than men in their group or men in the minority, all the more so the fewer women there are.

The gender role hypothesis is the reigning theory in the literature on gender and discussion. It has received much attention and support. However, we argue that it is incomplete and only partially accurate. Institutions and norms can erase the inequalities that low numbers produce or interfere with the potential advantages of high numbers. Specifically, we focus on the group's decision rule, and the ways it acts in combination with women's numbers. As explained in chapter 3, we call this the *interaction hypothesis*.

The interaction hypothesis begins with the claim that unanimous rule produces a group dynamic in which various types of numerical minorities—including social identity minorities—are included. Conversely, majority rule may signal that the group will operate on the principle of power in numbers. Consequently, minority women do better under unanimous than majority rule. Unanimous rule requires the minority for a decision and thus brings all voices into the conversation, while majority rule means that majorities can make decisions without the minority, and thus excludes them. As a result, when women are a minority the gender gap within the group will be smaller under unanimous than majority rule. But minority men also do better under unanimous than majority rule. Because unanimous rule causes majority women to attempt to be more inclusive of men, these women do not increase their participation. That is, under unanimous rule, majority women do not leverage the advantage of numerical majority status and they participate no more than minority women who use that rule. The inclusiveness effect of unanimous rule also explains why majority women are worse off under unanimous than majority rule, where women are not encumbered to the same extent by the norm of inclusiveness.[7]

In sum, our interaction hypothesis makes the following predictions: Women underparticipate compared to men in the group either as minorities under majority rule or as majorities under unanimous rule. Minority women participate more under unanimous than majority rule, while majority women do the reverse. Minority men will also do better in groups deciding unanimously than by majority rule. Thus our interaction hypothesis significantly qualifies the minority status and token hypotheses of gender role theory. Our hypothesis makes the same prediction that gender role theory does about the

[7] See chapters 3 and 4 for details on the hypotheses.

benefits of increasing numbers of women, but only under majority rule. It contradicts gender role theory by arguing that minority women are not inevitably unequal when they are a minority, because unanimous rule protects them. Finally, it adds predictions about the advantages of minority men and the disadvantages of majority women under unanimous rule.

Controlling for Other Explanations

One virtue of our research design is that it allows us to test other explanations for the participatory dynamics of groups. Opposing both gender role theory and our interaction hypothesis are two alternative possibilities. One is *preferences*: differences due to gender are spuriously caused by preferences or attitudes correlated with individual gender. We discussed this possibility in chapter 4, but recap it here briefly. We are examining deliberation about redistribution, so preferences over the principles of redistribution or attitudes about egalitarianism are relevant. Simply put, a person may speak more, or less, because they have a more liberal, or more conservative, general view about redistribution, and not because the person is a man or a woman or is surrounded by more men or women. Controlling for these preferences is important because they are correlated with gender (Crowder-Meyer 2007; Shapiro and Mahajan 1986). The other alternative hypothesis, *efficiency*, is that women are quiet not because of gender disadvantage or gendered communication but because others are articulating their preferences. If one's preferences are already voiced, efficiency dictates that there is no need to waste time or effort on repetition. This would happen if women are members of the preference majority in the group, when the discussion is likely to proceed in their preferred direction. For that reason, to get at the more "pure" effects of gender and gender composition, we control on whether the individual shares the same preferences as the majority in the group. These controls thus help us to isolate the effects of gender, as opposed to other elements of an individual's relationship to the group.

The Effects of Composition and Rule on Speech Participation

Advocates of deliberation argue that they "create an environment in which [gender or class] inequalities in the broader society do not distort the deliberative process" (Fishkin et al. 2010, 8–9). Critics argue that deliberation entails the "the systematic disregard of ascriptively defined groups such as women" (Sanders 1997, 353). Which is more accurate? Specifically, does deliberation produce gender equality or inequality? To answer these questions, we divide the number of seconds each individual spoke by the group's total number of seconds to construct an individual's *Proportion Talk* (scaled 0–1). This allows contrasts across groups with varying total talk times. (Descriptive statistics,

Table 5.1: Average Individual *Proportion Talk* by Gender and Experimental Condition

	Unanimous			Majority		
Gender Composition	**Men**	**Women**	***Gender Gap***	**Men**	**Women**	***Gender Gap***
0 Women	0.200	—	—	0.200	—	—
1 Woman	0.205	0.179	*0.026*	0.218	0.130	*0.088****
2 Women	0.216	0.176	*0.040*	0.222	0.166	*0.056***
3 Women	0.240	0.173	*0.067***	0.255	0.163	*0.092****
4 Women	0.289	0.178	*0.111***	0.183	0.204	*-0.021*
5 Women	—	0.200	—	—	0.200	—

Note: Gender gap is the average male *Proportion Talk* minus average female *Proportion Talk* in each condition. Positive numbers indicate male advantage. Stars indicate gender gaps significantly different from 0. *** $p < 0.01$, ** $p < 0.05$, * $p < 0.10$, one-tailed unpaired difference of means test, group-level analysis.

question and response wordings, and scaling information for all variables are in the online appendix.)

Table 5.1 shows, for each condition, the average male *Proportion Talk*, the average female *Proportion Talk*, and the difference between them (with associated group-level t-tests). If men and women participated at equal rates in a five-person group, the average individual *Proportion Talk* for each gender would be 0.20 (in other words, the average male and the average female would each take 20% of the conversation), resulting in a gender gap of 0.[8] But in five of the eight conditions, the t-test indicates a nonzero gender gap (always favoring men), confirming the critics and disconfirming the advocates.

Figure 5.1 shows the magnitude of the gender gap more clearly, displaying the ratio of the average female to the average male *Proportion Talk* in each condition. In most of the conditions women's participation is less than 75% of men's; in three of the eight conditions it is less than two-thirds of men's. This is consistent with the broader literature on women's participation we reviewed in the opening chapters. The critics of deliberation have cause for concern—women often participate less than men, sometimes substantially so. Of particular concern is that the high gender gap obtains in the most common configuration in political settings—minority women under majority rule.

But these results also show that the inequality varies with the group's decision rule and gender composition, consistent with the interaction hypothesis. Table 5.1 largely disconfirms gender role theory's minority status hypothesis, which predicts equality in the four conditions where women are a majority and inequality in the four conditions where they are a minority; only three of these eight predictions are confirmed. But table 5.1 confirms seven of the eight

[8] For a graphical representation of these patterns, see chapter appendix figure A5.1.

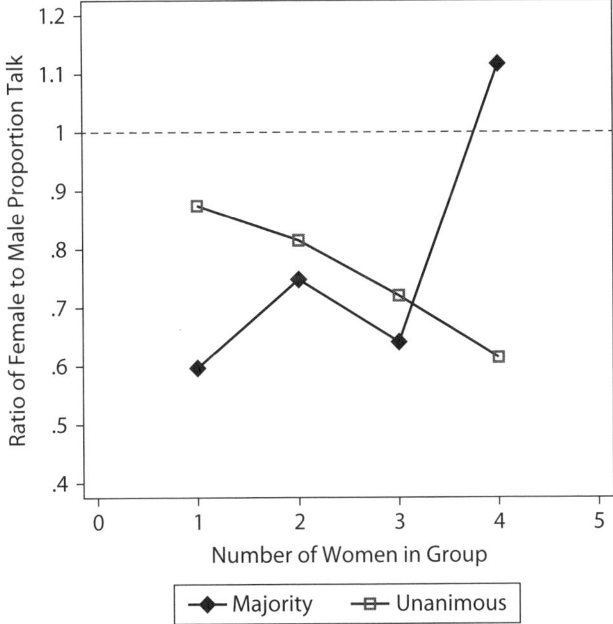

Figure 5.1. Ratio of average female to average male *Proportion Talk*. Note: A ratio of 1 means equality of speech participation.

predictions of the interaction hypothesis. Under majority rule, there is a large and significant gender gap in the one- and two-female conditions but not in the four-female condition. Under unanimous rule, we see the reverse: a large and significant gender gap in the three- or four-female conditions but not in the one- and two-female conditions. Larger numbers help women under majority rule but not unanimous rule.

Observing how the behavior of women changes within each decision rule also bolsters this conclusion. Table 5.1 shows that under unanimity, the average woman accounts for a little less than 18% of the conversation no matter what the gender composition of the group. Under majority rule, the average woman's *Proportion Talk* moves from a mere 13% of the conversation in groups with only one woman to over 20% in groups with four women—a substantial and statistically significant difference (p = 0.02, one-tailed). This contingent effect of gender composition is not anticipated by gender role theory, but is predicted by the interaction hypothesis.

A small anomaly is the disconfirmation of one of the eight predictions of the interaction hypothesis: under majority rule, women underparticipate men in the three-female groups.[9] Our interaction hypothesis does not predict an

[9]Specifically, under majority rule, the three-female condition is not statistically different from the one-female or two-female conditions.

exact functional form for the relationship between gender composition and speech participation, leaving open the possibility that women's disadvantage is sufficiently powerful that it requires a supermajority to overcome. It is also quite possible that the result for the three-female groups is simply noise. We are reassured that the movement toward equality in the four-female groups is large and statistically meaningful. In our view, the unexpected result for the three-female groups qualifies, but does not undermine, our interaction hypothesis. The main conclusion remains: gender composition matters largely as expected by the interaction hypothesis.

Having shown a pervasive but contingent gender gap, we directly test the minority status and interaction predictions about what increases or decreases the gap, using OLS with group-level data (table 5.2).[10] The dependent variable is the *Gender Gap in Speech Participation* (scaled –1 to 1), which is the difference between the group's average female and average male *Proportion Talk*.[11] There is no statistically significant effect of gender composition in Model 1, which includes no interaction terms, disconfirming gender role theory's *minority status* prediction. Model 2 confirms the interaction hypothesis: the coefficient on the number of women and the interaction term of number of women and majority rule are each in the expected direction, statistically significant, and substantively large. As the interaction hypothesis predicts, only under majority rule does the gender gap shrink as the number of women increases; the reverse effect obtains under unanimous rule. Furthermore, consistent with the interaction hypothesis, unanimous rule mutes the gender gap in the group when women are few. We see this in part from the coefficient on the majority rule variable, which is large, significant, and positive. When we combine that with the effect of gender composition, we find that in groups with one woman, a larger gender gap is present under majority rule than unanimous rule.[12] Small numbers are not destiny for numerical minority women.

[10] All regressions also control for one outlier group in the one-female, majority-rule condition. This outlier is well over 2 standard deviations away from all other groups in that condition (as well as all groups in the experiment). No other majority-rule group is that far from the other groups in its condition. We follow Choi (2009) and control for the outlier (see also Bollen and Jackman 1985) rather than discard it. The key interaction terms are statistically significant regardless of the presence of this control or the control for experimental location.

[11] This variable is created by subtracting the average male *Proportion Talk* from the average female *Proportion Talk* for each group. The empirical range of *Gender Gap in Speech Participation* is -0.27 to 0.48. We employ this difference measure as our dependent variable in the regressions because the interpretation of the coefficients is easier. With the ratio measure, the predicted values from the model exceed the bounds of the dependent variable. Patterns of significance are the same.

[12] Technically, the coefficient for majority rule represents the effect of decision rule at the gender composition intercept. The effect of majority rule varies with the gender composition of the group, so when we take the gender composition into account, predicted values from all models in table 5.2 indicate that the difference in the gender gap between decision rules is significant in groups with one woman ($p = 0.02$, one-tailed). The difference between decision rules is not significant in groups with two women.

Table 5.2: Determinants of the *Gender Gap in Speech Participation* in Mixed-Gender Groups (Group-Level Analysis)

	(1)	(2)	(3)	(4)	(5)
Majority Rule	0.002	0.174**	0.190**	0.165**	0.142
	(0.034)	(0.078)	(0.081)	(0.098)	(0.126)
Number of Women	-0.004	0.028*	0.026	0.028*	0.021
	(0.015)	(0.019)	(0.021)	(0.021)	(0.023)
Majority × Number of Women		-0.069***	-0.076***	-0.081**	-0.076**
		(0.028)	(0.030)	(0.032)	(0.033)
Number of Egalitarians			0.011	0.003	0.011
			(0.018)	(0.025)	(0.028)
# Favoring Max. Redistribution			0.012	0.014	-0.026
			(0.027)	(0.028)	(0.051)
# Favoring No Redistribution			-0.006	-0.008	-0.014
			(0.025)	(0.025)	(0.043)
Majority × # of Egalitarians				0.014	0.005
				(0.030)	(0.034)
Majority × # Max Redistribution					0.057
					(0.061)
Majority × # No Redistribution					0.009
					(0.054)
Constant	0.077	-0.002	-0.019	-0.003	0.014
	(0.047)	(0.056)	(0.073)	(0.082)	(0.101)
Observations	64	64	64	64	64
R-squared	0.057	0.144	0.160	0.164	0.178
Control for Outlier	Yes	Yes	Yes	Yes	Yes
Control for Experimental Location	Yes	Yes	Yes	Yes	Yes

Note: Dependent variable for all models is *Gender Gap in Speech Participation*. Standard errors in parentheses. *** $p < 0.01$, ** $p < 0.05$, * $p < 0.1$, one-tailed test.

The results hold when controls for the *preferences* hypothesis, an alternative explanation to the interaction hypothesis, are included (Model 3, table 5.2). The *preferences* hypothesis predicts that the effect of gender composition is the spurious result of the group's redistribution preferences or general egalitarian attitudes that are correlated with the group's gender composition.[13] To test this

[13] Results do not change when we substitute a measure of the number of liberals in the group for our measure of the number of egalitarians in the group (see online appendix table C5.2).

possibility, we added to our interactive model three variables measured prior to deliberation: the number of group members who scored above the scale midpoint (nearly identical to the mean) on general egalitarianism, the number who favored no redistribution, and the number who favored very high levels of redistribution from rich to poor (see the online appendix for details of all measures). The effect of the interaction between decision rule and gender composition remains strong and statistically significant in the presence of these controls, disconfirming the notion that the gender gap is primarily explained by the preferences or attitudes of group members.[14] Patterns of participation are tied to the interaction of rule and gender composition, even when we take the attitudes of the group members into account. This strong effect for the interaction between gender composition and decision rule continues to hold even when we examine fully saturated models that interact controls for egalitarianism or for preference about redistribution with decision rule (see Models 4 and 5). The protective effect of unanimous rule for minority women also holds with controls, evidenced in part by the positive and (nearly always) significant majority rule coefficient and confirmed by predicted values from the models. No matter what set of controls we employ, the gender gap is significantly larger under majority rule than under unanimity in groups with one woman.[15] Gender composition and decision rule are thus the keys to the dynamics of speech participation in our deliberating groups.

Table 5.3 conducts an individual-level test of *preferences* and of the other alternative to our interaction hypothesis, *efficiency*. As we detailed in chapter 4, we use OLS regression with cluster robust standard errors since individuals are nested within groups.[16] The dependent variable is individual *Proportion Talk* (scaled 0–1). Model 1 is the individual-level test of our interaction hypothesis and includes individual gender, gender composition, decision rule, and interactions between those variables in mixed-gender groups.[17] Model 2 adds control variables to test *efficiency* and *preferences*. According to the *preferences* hypothesis, women speak less regarding redistribution not because they are women affected by reason of their gender's numerical status, but because they have more generous attitudes about redistribution, and what appear to be gender differences may be due to differences in these attitudes instead. Therefore, we include

[14] Alternative measures of group preferences, including measures of the gender gaps in predeliberation egalitarianism and preferences for redistribution, produce similar results. We find no relationship between gender composition and the gender gap in predeliberation egalitarianism under either rule.

[15] For groups with one woman, the difference in the predicted gender gap is significant at $p < 0.02$ (Models 3 and 4) and at $p < 0.03$ (Model 5). All tests one-tailed.

[16] This method achieves the same end as multilevel analysis, without requiring such strong assumptions. Other regression approaches, including random-effects regression (with a random effect for each group), produce nearly identical results.

[17] The interactions are also significant in models that include gender homogeneous groups.

Table 5.3: Determinants of Speech Participation in Mixed-Gender Groups (Individual-Level Analysis)

	(1)	(2)
Female	–0.001	0.000
	(0.049)	(0.049)
Majority Rule	0.045**	0.043**
	(0.024)	(0.024)
Female × Majority	-0.112**	–0.112**
	(0.064)	(0.063)
Number of Women	0.023**	0.024**
	(0.012)	(0.012)
Female × Number of Women	–0.023	-0.023
	(0.020)	(0.020)
Majority × Number of Women	–0.024*	-0.023*
	(0.015)	(0.015)
Female × Majority × Number of Women	0.046**	0.046**
	(0.025)	(0.025)
Egalitarianism		–0.034
		(0.035)
Match Group's Predeliberation Preferences		0.002
		(0.011)
Constant	0.178***	0.191***
	(0.019)	(0.025)
Observations	320	320
R-squared	0.067	0.070
Control for Outlier	Yes	Yes
Control for Experimental Location	Yes	Yes

Note: Dependent variable for both models is individual *Proportion Talk*. Cluster robust standard errors in parentheses. *** $p < 0.01$, ** $p < 0.05$, * $p < 0.1$, one-tailed test.

a measure of the individual's predeliberation level of egalitarianism.[18] Table 5.3 also tests the *efficiency* hypothesis—that women speak less because they are part of the group's predeliberation preference majority, when they are satisfied with the direction of discussion, not because of the group's gender composition and decision rule. We thus include a dummy variable tapping whether the individual's predeliberation preferences about redistribution matched the group's predeliberation majority preference.

[18] The size and statistical significance of all key terms in the model remain the same if a control for the number of egalitarians in the group is included (model not shown).

Both models confirm the interaction we expect: under majority rule, women talk more, relative to men, as the number of women increases (seen in part in the positive and strongly significant *Female x Majority x Number of Women* term). Predicted values from the model with controls confirm that the findings from basic t-tests persist in the presence of controls: women's average *Proportion Talk* increases from a low of about 13% of the conversation in majority-rule groups with only one woman to over 20% of the conversation in groups with four women. In majority-rule groups, the estimated difference between the *Proportion Talk* of men and women is large (9 percentage points) and significant ($p < 0.01$) in groups with a token woman, but small (2 percentage points, favoring women) and not significant ($p = 0.26$) in groups with a token man.

Also consistent with the interaction hypothesis, when women are few, unanimous rule elevates their volume of speech relative to majority rule.[19] In addition, under unanimous rule, women's participation holds steady as the number of women increases, but men's participation increases, creating a widening gender gap (for a visual representation see chapter appendix figure A5.1). Predicted values from the model show that the size of the predicted gender gap in speaking behavior increases nearly fivefold as the number of women increases under unanimous rule, even when controls are included.[20] *Efficiency* and *preferences* predict that these effects of gender composition and rule will disappear when controls are added in Model 2, but these predictions are disconfirmed.[21] This evidence thus undermines the alternative explanations that women are speaking less than men only because (1) they have different preferences than men or (2) they do not take the trouble to speak because others already articulate their ideas, as may occur when they are the preference majority. The gender gap is due to the difference between women and men in responses to the gendered dynamics in the group, as the interaction hypothesis predicts.[22]

These findings—that decision rule and gender composition depend on each other—are supported by a second measure of how the talk time within each

[19] For groups with one woman, a test of predicted values from the models indicates that the difference between decision rules in women's *Proportion Talk* is significant at $p < 0.05$.

[20] Specifically, the gender gap in predicted *Proportion Talk* is only 2.3 percentage points (p-value of the difference = 0.49) in unanimous groups with one woman. The gap in groups with four women is 9.3 percentage points ($p = 0.04$).

[21] Results are identical if we substitute controls for liberalism for our measure of egalitarianism. Substituting controls for the number of group members above the median age or income or the number of group members who are college graduates also makes no difference.

[22] As a robustness check, we replicated the results with an alternative measure of deliberative participation, *Percent Speaking Turns*. See Figure C5.1 in the online appendix for a graphical depiction of the means for men and women in each condition. Results hold when we substitute controls for liberalism in place of the control for egalitarianism (see table C5.3 in the online appendix), and adding controls for age, income, and education do not change the basic patterns either (not shown). In no model do age, education, or income come close to statistical significance, so we do not include them in our standard model.

group is distributed. For each group, we computed a Gini coefficient, which is a well-known measure of inequality—in this case, inequality in the talk time within each group. Lower Gini coefficients represent less inequality. Participants noticed when the group's talk was distributed more equally. In groups with lower Gini coefficients, participants were significantly less likely to agree that "a few people dominated the discussion."[23] Using this second measure, we find the same pattern: under majority rule, group talk times are more equally distributed as the number of women in the group grows (see chapter appendix table A5.1, Model 1). Under unanimous rule, the effect runs in the opposite direction (though the increase in inequality does not reach significance), with the highest levels of inequality to be found in groups with four women, so that again, unanimous rule alleviates the gender gap when women are few but not when they are many.

The same pattern can be found if we separate the genders and focus on how *women's* talk time is distributed among the women in groups with at least two women (chapter appendix table A5.1, Model 2).[24] We find that under majority rule, as the number of women grows, the Gini coefficient for women falls, meaning that talk time among the women in the group is more equally distributed. The most equal distributions of women's talk time—those with the lowest Gini coefficients—are found among majority-rule groups with many women.[25] Put differently, this analysis shows that not only are women accounting for more of the conversation as their numbers grow, they are also sharing the floor time more equally among themselves. Under unanimous rule, the effect of women's numbers is the reverse.

Whether the dependent variable is the gap in average talk time or the Gini coefficient, the results are the same. Women speak more and share the floor in more egalitarian ways as their numbers increase under majority rule. This increased willingness to share the floor equally applies to the women in the group and to the group as a whole. Under unanimous rule, women achieve equality of floor time (and a more equal sharing of the floor among themselves) when women are few, and the greatest inequalities occur in mixed-gender groups with many women. Groups where the combination of numbers and rule has equalized women's status produce a more egalitarian discussion process.

The *token* corollary from gender role theory also makes specific predictions about women who are the lone females in their groups: that they will be uniquely disadvantaged compared to token men. By contrast, the *equal disadvantage* and *violated entitlement* hypotheses predict that token men participate

[23]The two measures are correlated at 0.46 ($p < 0.001$) and the relationship remains large in a regression with a control for location ($p < 0.001$).

[24]The dependent variable here is the Gini coefficient computed only for the women in the group.

[25]Predicted values from the model estimate a Gini coefficient of 30.4 for majority-rule groups with four women. This is lower than the predicted value for any other mixed-gender experimental condition.

Table 5.4: Effects of Gender and Decision Rule on Token Speech Participation (Group-Level Analysis)

	(1) Majority Rule Only	(2) Unanimous Rule Only	(3) All Tokens	(4) All Tokens
Female	−0.075**	−0.116**	−0.091***	−0.111**
	(0.035)	(0.062)	(0.036)	(0.051)
Majority			−0.097***	−0.106**
			(0.037)	(0.054)
Majority × Female				0.029
				(0.074)
Constant	0.206***	0.259***	0.276***	0.284***
	(0.030)	(0.055)	(0.037)	(0.042)
Observations	17	18	35	35
R-squared	0.550	0.217	0.330	0.334
Control for Outlier	Yes	Yes	Yes	Yes
Control for Experimental Location	Yes	Yes	Yes	Yes

Note: Dependent variable for all models is *Proportion Talk*. Standard errors in parentheses. *** $p < 0.01$, ** $p < 0.05$, * $p < 0.1$, one-tailed test.

equally or less than token women. Table 5.4 tests these three competing hypotheses by analyzing the *Proportion Talk* of tokens. As the results in the table show, violated entitlement and equal disadvantage are disconfirmed, and gender role theory's *token* is supported: the "female" term is negative in Models 1, 2, and 3. Female tokens talk less than male tokens, whether the decision rules are analyzed separately or pooled. On average, the difference is about 9 percentage points. However, as the interaction hypothesis predicts, Model 3 shows that token males and females each perform better under unanimous rule than under majority rule (see the negative, significant coefficient on the "majority" term). The difference-in-differences in the effect of decision rule on the two gender tokens, represented by the interaction term in Model 4, is not statistically significant; in other words, the effect of unanimity is roughly the same for men and women. This equal effect, combined with unequal starting points under majority rule, means that unanimous rule elevates the token male above his female group members while it equalizes the token female with her male group members. As the interaction hypothesis predicts, unanimous rule helps minority women but hurts majority women.

Figure 5.2 explores the *enclave*, the final expectation from gender role theory: that women do best in their own all-female discussions, away from the forces that produce gender inequality, while men do not benefit in this way.

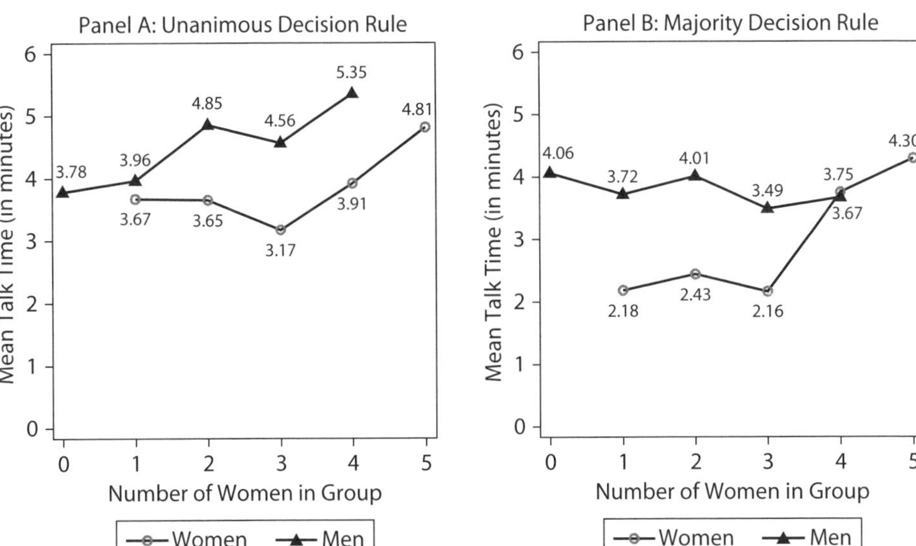

Figure 5.2. Mean *Talk Time* for men and women, by experimental condition.

Here we use *Talk Time*, men's and women's average talk time in the group in minutes, since it allows us to examine the gender-homogeneous groups.[26] Consistent with the *enclave* thesis, female participants do tend to talk longer when surrounded only by other women.[27] The average woman talks more in enclaves than in the pooled majority-female groups (significant at $p < 0.04$, one-tailed, group-level test and at $p < 0.01$ in a one-tailed test with individual-level data). This test is not significant for men. Further evidence in favor of the *enclave* thesis comes from the Gini coefficient: women in enclave groups also distribute their talk quite equally—under majority rule, about as well as groups with four women, and under unanimous rule, much more equally than groups with four women. Enclaves seem to provide some benefit to women, and not to men, as the enclave hypothesis predicts.

The final evidence regarding enclaves comes from the group's overall length of discussion. When we explore the group's total talk time, we also find evidence that groups composed entirely of women speak longer than all other groups. The average discussion time for female enclaves is about 22% greater than the average for all other groups (pooled). This difference is marginally significant at $p < 0.10$ (one-tailed group-level t-test), and average talk times

[26] In mixed gender groups, there is no effect of the rule-gender composition interaction on the group's total talk time.

[27] This finding also argues against the alternative that gender homogeneity spuriously represents preference homogeneity; preference homogeneity would produce shorter rather than longer talk times.

are longer in women's enclaves across both decision rules.[28] Results hold in regression models that also control for decision rule and experimental location. Group talk times for all-male groups are indistinguishable from the length of mixed-gender discussions (pooled). Clearly, women's quiescence in mixed-gender groups is not because they have nothing to say; under the right conditions, they are willing to talk for much longer than they do with men.

The evidence shows that rules and numbers both significantly affect women's relative contribution to the group's central activity—its talk. Why is that? It is not because the number of women happens to stand in for what really matters—the number of individuals who prefer that the group make the more egalitarian decision. Rather, it is because the rule and the numbers create norms of interaction. We shall have more to say about that in later chapters, but for now, we can point to one piece of evidence that rules beget norms. If unanimous rule works in part by signaling the need for more inclusion, as we contend, then we should observe longer talk times in groups told to use that rule. And that is what we find—unanimous rule prompts mixed-gender groups to talk somewhat longer.[29] Putting all these findings together, we can conclude that rules and gender composition work because they set in motion interaction norms, not merely because they affect an individual's strategic behavior regardless of gender.

The Consequences for Perceived Influence

As we have argued, speech participation matters because it may produce authority, specifically, perceived influence. We have two measures of influence: self-assessments and the assessments of the other group members.[30] For self-assessments, immediately after the discussion we asked each participant to gauge the extent to which his or her "voice was heard during the group discussion" and the extent to which his or her "opinions were influential in shaping the group discussion and final decision." The response options were: strongly disagree (coded 0), disagree (coded 0.25), neutral (coded 0.5), agree (0.75), or

[28] Mean talk times in female enclaves are longer than the average for all other groups regardless of decision rule, though when we disaggregate by rule, the limited number of enclave groups (eight majority rule and seven unanimous) means that the statistical tests fall short of standard levels of significance ($p < 0.20$, one-tailed test).

[29] In a regression model with a control for location, unanimous rule groups talk about three minutes longer than majority rule groups ($p = 0.06$, one-tailed), and this effect is similar without the location control, though when we look separately at each location, the effect is slightly stronger in the eastern site. Figure 5.2 shows that unanimous rule boosts each gender's average individual talk time in nearly every condition.

[30] In chapter 9, we will add a third measure: the relationship between talk and the group's decisions about redistribution.

Table 5.5: The Effect of *Proportion Talk* on Self-Efficacy, Mixed-Gender Groups Only (Individual-Level Analysis)

	Women		Men	
	Opinions Influential	**Voice Heard**	**Opinions Influential**	**Voice Heard**
Proportion Talk	0.66*** (0.18)	0.42*** (0.13)	0.36*** (0.11)	0.31*** (0.09)
Egalitarianism	0.06 (0.10)	0.10* (0.07)	–0.07 (0.11)	–0.08 (0.07)
Number of Egalitarians	–0.00 (0.01)	–0.01 (0.01)	0.00 (0.02)	0.01 (0.01)
Predeliberation Confidence	0.21*** (0.08)	0.18*** (0.07)	0.09 (0.09)	–0.04 (0.07)
Group Choice Matched Preferences	0.09*** (0.04)	0.06* (0.03)	0.02 (0.03)	0.03 (0.02)
Constant	0.34*** (0.08)	0.55*** (0.06)	0.58*** (0.07)	0.79*** (0.05)
Observations	157	157	163	163
R-squared	0.25	0.19	0.07	0.11
Control for Outlier	Yes	Yes	Yes	Yes
Control for Experimental Location	Yes	Yes	Yes	Yes

Note: Cluster robust standard errors in parentheses. *** $p < 0.01$, ** $p < 0.05$, * $p < 0.1$, one-tailed test.

strongly agree (coded 1). Table 5.5 presents the effect of *Proportion Talk* on these two measures, separately for men and women. We control for the number of egalitarians in the group, for individual egalitarianism, for the respondent's predeliberation sense of confidence in his or her ability (to try to isolate the effect of speech during discussion) and for whether the respondent's preferred principle was chosen by the group (to distinguish the effect of speaking from the group's decision).[31]

Men as well as women build their self-efficacy on their quantity of talk, but women do so more than men. Figure 5.3 displays the predicted values for the "opinions were influential" question, which are restricted to the maximum and minimum value of *Proportion Talk* for each gender. As the figure illustrates, women are more strongly affected than men, a result confirmed by the

[31] The details of the confidence measure are discussed further in the next chapter. Findings are similar if these controls are not included and if we use an ordered probit model instead of OLS.

coefficients in table 5.5 for the influence question.[32] Women's coefficients are about double the size of men's, with the difference-in-differences between the genders significant at $p < 0.05$ (one-tailed test). The gender differences in the effects of speaking behavior on the "voice was heard" variable are also large and in the expected direction but fall short of statistical significance ($p < 0.12$, one-tailed).[33] The key point is that those who speak more are much more likely to feel that others listened and that they made a difference in the group, and some evidence indicates that speaking more is especially beneficial to women.[34]

Moreover, we also find evidence of a direct relationship between the experimental conditions and self-efficacy. In the conditions in which women are more empowered—majority rule with many women and unanimous rule with few women—women are more likely to feel that their "voice was heard" during

[32] Results are identical when we substitute controls for liberalism in place of egalitarianism (not shown). Substituting controls for other characteristics, such as the number of group members above the median in age or education and the number of college graduates, does not change the findings in any way. Age, education, and income do not drive the results, either in individual models or in group-level models.

[33] Talk time is also related to women's overall sense of satisfaction with the discussion (online appendix table C5.1). For men, overall satisfaction is not related to talk time.

[34] We also asked participants whether or not they were satisfied with the group's discussion. But given the lack of deep acrimony in the discussions, this question yields very little variation: 90% of participants said they were "somewhat" or "very" satisfied with the discussion. Even so, women in mixed-gender groups whose *Proportion Talk* was above the median for their gender were far more likely than women below that median to say they were "very satisfied" with the discussion (63% versus 47%, $z = 1.97$, $p = 0.02$, one-tailed difference of proportions test). When we combine the satisfaction variable with other similar questions, we find a greater level of variation (half of participants scored above 0.74 on a scale from 0 for least positive to 1 for most positive about the discussion). These questions included levels of agreement or disagreement with whether the discussion was fair, whether group members shared "the same basic values," whether group work led the respondent to feel like he or she "accomplished more" or "made everything slower and harder to accomplish," whether group members treated each other with "respect and courtesy," whether "all different perspectives were welcome" in the discussion and whether disagreement made the discussion "difficult." Two items were reverse coded to avoid response set bias (group work made everything "slower and harder to accomplish," and disagreement made discussion "difficult"). These variables scale together well ($\alpha = 0.77$) and load highly on a single factor. Women in mixed-gender groups whose *Proportion Talk* was above the median for their gender scored approximately 4 percentage points higher on the satisfaction index than those who were below the median ($p = 0.06$, one-tailed test). There is no significant effect on men's satisfaction from scoring above the median of male *Proportion Talk* ($p = 0.20$, one-tailed). In addition, we find some evidence that men are more satisfied in the experimental conditions where men are empowered. That is, predicted values from a linear, interactive model regressing the satisfaction index on the experimental conditions show that men's satisfaction is highest in majority-rule groups with only one woman or unanimous groups with four women. Women's satisfaction is not affected by the conditions—in a linear model, there is no significant interactive effect of the experimental conditions on women's index of satisfaction. However, we do find that women who speak the most in majority-rule groups with few women are *less* satisfied than women who speak the least in these groups ($b = -0.49$, $SE = 0.22$, $p < 0.01$, one-tailed). In all other conditions (pooled), the relationship between women's *Proportion Talk* and their satisfaction index is positive ($b = 0.165$, $SE = 0.11$, $p < 0.08$, one-tailed).

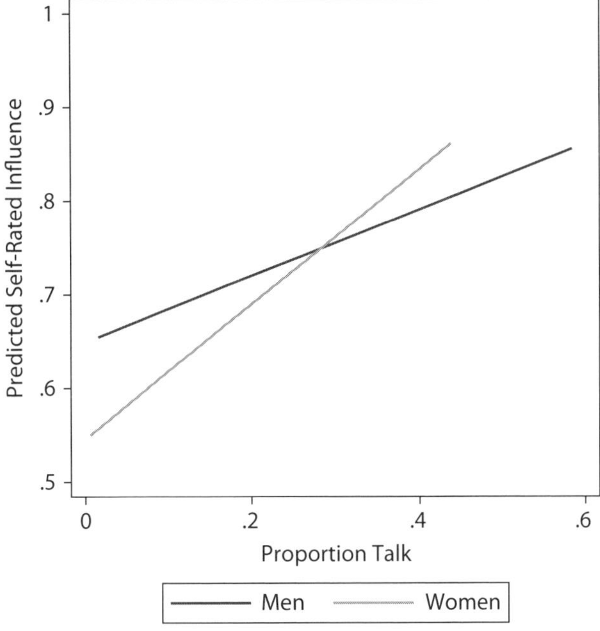

Figure 5.3. Effect of *Proportion Talk* on self-rated influence.

group discussion (see chapter appendix table A5.2). Although the effects are not huge—few participants walked away from the lab discussions feeling deeply alienated or upset—we again see the familiar interaction pattern.[35] When women are numerous, they provide more positive assessments under majority than unanimous rule. The reverse happens when women are few, where unanimous rule makes women more likely to strongly agree that "my voice was heard." More empowering conditions grant women a higher sense of efficacy as deliberators. Among men in mixed-gender groups, for assessments of "my voice was heard," we see the mirror image of the effects of the conditions on women. Just as minority women are more likely to feel heard under unanimous than majority rule, the same is true for minority men. In sum, when it comes to feeling heard, both men and women are more likely to feel efficacious when the conditions empower their gender.

If speaking up during the discussion can build standing and authority, we should see those effects not only in the participants' own self-assessments but also in the way others in the group saw each member. We measured *Influence* after discussion by asking each group member to indicate the (one) person who

[35] With respect to the "opinions were influential" question, the expected interaction effects from the conditions obtain for both men and women, but the effects are smaller than effects for "voice was heard" and not statistically significant.

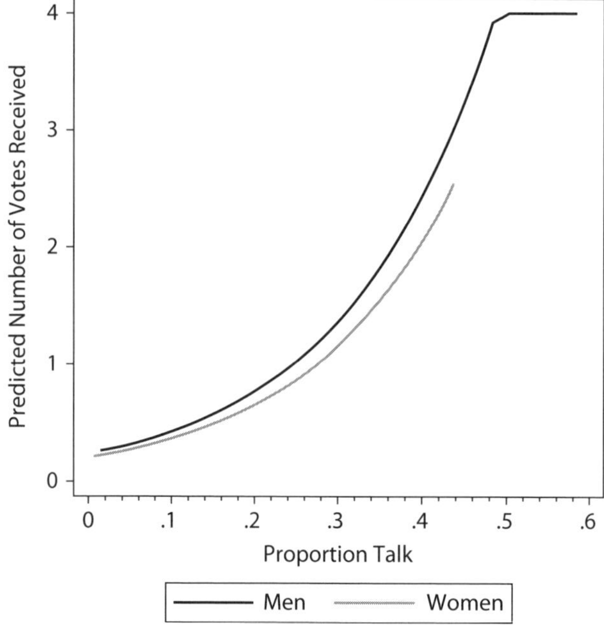

Figure 5.4. *Proportion Talk*'s effect on perceived influence. Note: Figure represents the predicted values generated from a negative binomial regression. The results are as follows: *Influence* (0–4) = -1.86 + 5.80 (*Proportion Talk*, SE = 0.49) + 0.33 (*Predeliberation speaking confidence*, SE = 0.24) + 0.40 (*Predeliberation preference matched group outcome*, SE = 0.11) + 0.17 (*Female*, SE = 0.11) + 0.17 (*Experimental Site*, SE = 0.06) + 0.10 (*Outlier*, SE = 0.05). N = 470. Log Pseudolikelihood = -515.49. Cluster robust standard errors. Own votes are excluded from the dependent variable.

was "most influential" in the group's discussion and decisions.[36] We tallied the number of votes each individual received from other group members, a measure that runs from 0 to 4. *Influence* is thus our measure of how other members of the group saw each individual.

Figure 5.4 shows the effects of deliberative participation on *Influence*. As in the previous figure, the lines for men and women only extend as far as the maximum value of *Proportion Talk* found in the data for each gender. The figures derive from the model whose coefficients are provided with the figure.[37] The unit of analysis is the individual, with cluster robust standard errors. We include controls for predeliberation confidence in one's own speaking ability (see the online appendix for wording) and whether or not the individual's predeliberation preferences matched the group's eventual decision as controls on

[36] Self-votes are eliminated. Results are essentially identical if own votes are included.

[37] We employ a negative binomial regression for *Influence* since the dependent variable skews toward 0. Just over 60% of the sample, and nearly 70% of women, received 0 votes. Predicted probabilities were constrained at the limit of possible votes.

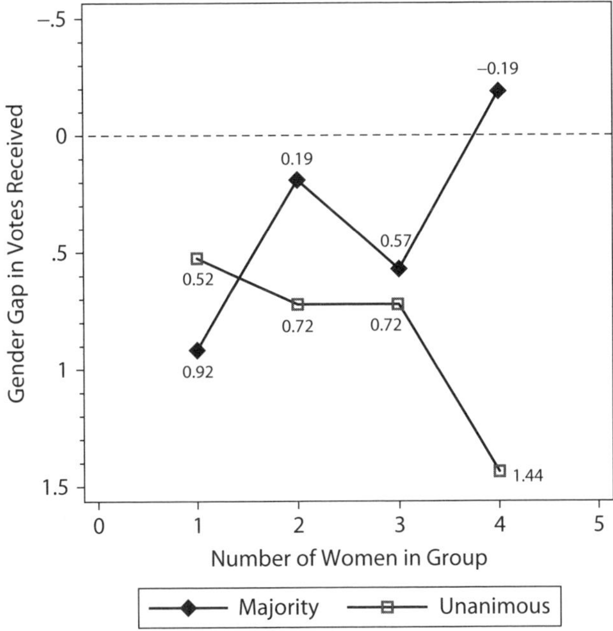

Figure 5.5. *Gender Gap in Perceived Influence,* by experimental condition. Note: The Gender Gap in Votes Received is the average number of influence votes in the group for men minus the average number of votes in the group for women. Positive numbers thus indicate an advantage for men; negative numbers indicate an advantage for women. The *y*-axis is reversed so that women's disadvantage appears as numbers below the dashed line of equality.

individual gender.[38] Participants who held the floor for a greater percentage of the group's deliberation were more likely to be seen as influential by the other members of the group. The active use of voice translates into greater perceived influence for men and women, as we expect.

And again, the experimental conditions help to produce these effects. Figure 5.5 illustrates the predicted interactive effect of rule and composition on the *Gender Gap in Influence.*[39] In table 5.6, we test our interaction hypothesis using the same group-level OLS models we used to test the *Gender Gap in Speech Participation*, this time with the *Gender Gap in Influence* as the dependent variable (the average number of influence votes in the group for men minus the average number of votes in the group for women, scaled –4 to 4). Model 1 tests the minority status hypothesis, and just as in our analyses of speech participation, we again find no significant effect of the number of women in models that do

[38]The results are similar without these controls or when additional demographic controls are added, including income and party preference.

[39]See online appendix figure C5.2 for the average influence votes received by men and women in each condition.

Table 5.6: Determinants of *Gender Gap in Influence* (Group-Level Analysis)

	(1)	(2)	(3)	(4)
Majority Rule	−0.400	1.141*	1.095*	0.044
	(0.320)	(0.732)	(0.768)	(0.661)
Number of Women	−0.035	0.257*	0.260*	0.116
	(0.139)	(0.184)	(0.197)	(0.164)
Majority × Number of Women		−0.621**	−0.590**	−0.170
		(0.267)	(0.282)	(0.244)
# of Egalitarians			−0.003	−0.066
			(0.170)	(0.140)
# Favoring Maximum Redistribution			−0.076	−0.143
			(0.257)	(0.211)
# Favoring No Redistribution			0.122	0.157
			(0.237)	(0.194)
Gender Gap in Speech Participation				5.531***
				(1.050)
Constant	1.155**	0.445	0.348	0.453
	(0.446)	(0.527)	(0.694)	(0.570)
Observations	64	64	64	64
R-squared	0.067	0.146	0.153	0.441
Control for Outlier	Yes	Yes	Yes	Yes
Control for Experimental Location	Yes	Yes	Yes	Yes

Note: Dependent variable for all models is *Gender Gap in Influence*. Standard errors in parentheses. *** $p < 0.01$, ** $p < 0.05$, * $p < 0.1$, one-tailed test.

not include an interaction term. Model 2 adds the interaction effect and yields strong evidence that the gap in influence narrows as the number of women increases under majority rule, but expands significantly in groups with more women under unanimous rule. Model 3 adds the familiar controls from the alternative hypotheses, *efficiency* and *preferences*, which again receive no support.[40] As the interaction hypothesis predicts, the interaction term is significant whether or not the controls are included.

To better illustrate the magnitude of the interactive effect, consider who wins the influence vote count; when women are the majority, a woman is much more likely to win under majority rule (73%) than unanimity (53%), but as

[40] Again, the same conclusions are reached with a fully saturated model that includes interactions with decision rule and controls for preferences (see chapter appendix table A5.3) and if we substitute controls for liberalism for our measures of egalitarianism (online appendix table C5.2).

the minority, women win more often under unanimous (25%) than majority rule (13%).[41] Women's low influence ratings in the groups with few women and majority rule are striking. In majority groups, no token woman ever wins. Influence within the group is thus structured by the interaction of gender composition and decision rule, as the interaction hypothesis predicts; the same conditions that create disproportionate silence by women also create disproportionate authority for men.

The remaining question is whether speaking behavior mediates the effect of the conditions on influence, as the interaction hypothesis leads us to expect. Baron and Kenny (1986) suggest that a test of mediation includes three models: one that shows a relationship between the conditions and the *Gender Gap in Speech Participation*, another that shows a relationship between the conditions and the *Gender Gap in Influence*, and a third that shows a smaller or nonexistent relationship between the conditions and the *Gender Gap in Influence* when the *Gender Gap in Speech Participation* is included in the model. We have already reviewed the results of the first two models. The remaining model is Model 4 in table 5.6, which shows that the interaction in Model 2 disappears once the *Gender Gap in Speech Participation* is included. Thus the effect of the conditions on influence is mediated by speech participation. The conditions affect how much men and women speak, which in turn shapes their influence within the group.

We employ the formal test of mediation of Imai, Keele, and Tingley (2010). Table 5.7 shows that a significant percentage of the effect of our interacted experimental conditions on the *Gender Gap in Influence*—59%—is mediated by the *Gender Gap in Speech Participation*.[42] A Sobel test yields similar results. Together, the regressions and mediation tests show that speech matters—it affects influence.[43] Conditions that increase speech increase influence and thus authority, and they do so in interaction, as the interaction hypothesis predicts.

Summary

Our analyses provide mixed support for gender role theory. Our first supportive finding is that women are often disadvantaged in speech participation, while men are never disadvantaged. Second, women participate less than their

[41] Winning is receiving the highest number of votes in the group, ties included.

[42] The results are a partial estimate because Imai, Keele, and Tingley (2010) have not yet extended their method to include the interaction + main effect when the model includes an interaction between experimental conditions. For the same reason we cannot run a sensitivity analysis of the mediation using the method of Imai, Keele, and Tingley; correspondence with these authors tells us that this test is not yet extended to interactions between experimental treatments (e-mail, Dustin Tingley, December 15, 2011).

[43] A similar test shows evidence that *Proportion Talk* mediates the relationship between the experimental conditions and self-efficacy. The average causal mediation effect is significant at $p < 0.10$, two-tailed.

Table 5.7: Results of Mediation Analysis

	Sobel Test		Imai et al. Test
Indirect Effect	0.37**	Average Causal Mediation Effect	1.49**
Direct Effect	0.25	Direct Effect	1.02
Total Effect	0.62	Total Effect	2.51
Proportion of Total Effect That Is Mediated	0.59	Proportion of Total Effect That Is Mediated	0.59
Ratio of Indirect to Direct Effect	1.47	Ratio of Indirect to Direct Effect	1.46

Note: The analysis shows how much of the effect of the interaction between gender composition and decision rule (*Unanimous*Number of women*) on the *Gender Gap in Influence* is mediated by the *Gender Gap in Speech Participation*. Analyses are group level; models include main effects for group gender composition and for decision rule, controls for outlier group and experimental location. Asterisks indicate a statistically significant mediation effect. ** $p < 0.05$, two-tailed test.

equal share when they are a minority and at equal rates when in a large majority (at least under majority rule). Third, women tend to do best in enclave groups. Fourth, female tokens participate less than male tokens. Finally, women's influence gap shrinks as their numbers grow (under majority rule). Further support for gender role theory comes from disconfirmation of the competing hypotheses to the *token* corollary, *equal disadvantage* and *violated entitlement*, and from its ability to withstand the effects of controls on predeliberation attitudes and preferences.

However, opposite to the expectations prompted by gender role theory, in groups assigned to unanimous rule, women approach equality in voice and authority when in the minority. Unanimity substantially boosts the speech participation of minority women, relative to majority rule. Finally, and most troublesome for the gender role hypothesis, under unanimous rule, the gender gap in voice and authority is biggest when women are a majority, not a minority.

The interaction of decision rule and group gender composition best explains this pattern of results; the gender role hypotheses about gender composition are largely correct under majority rule but largely incorrect under unanimous rule. Unanimous rule protects minority women, and under this decision rule they take up their equal share of the conversation, but it is a double-edged sword because it also protects minority men. Minority women leverage unanimous rule to reach equality, while minority men leverage it to exacerbate inequality. These conclusions about rule would not be possible without interacting it with gender composition. Rule protects or hinders numerical minorities depending on who these minorities are.

Conclusion

Advocates and critics of deliberative democracy posit equal meaningful participation as a necessary requirement of deliberation. Our results show how far actual discussion deviates from that ideal standard, at least in this study, where women speak substantially less than men in most mixed-gender combinations. Further, speech is a crucial form of participation that meaningfully shapes perceptions of authority. As critics of deliberation contend, deliberation can produce inequalities of participation that affect deliberators' influence.

Unequal time used, not merely unequal speaking opportunities given, is problematic for democratic deliberation especially when it is associated with lower authority. Even if men and women enter deliberation with the same preferences and equal formal rights, the disproportionate exercise of these rights by men erodes the political and civic standing of women, a group not yet equal in society. The evidence that less speech leads to less efficacy and authority lends further weight to the importance of speech as a criterion of equal participation. In deliberative settings, speech is not mere "chattiness"—it is the heart of the group's purpose and thus represents a meaningful opportunity to build standing and influence with the other members of the group. Our results show that the critics of deliberation are right to worry; inequalities of voice have a strong tendency to translate into inequalities of authority.

The philosopher Miranda Fricker explains why and how deliberation that devalues women matters. According to Fricker, when a speaker's credibility is given less weight simply because of the social identity of the speaker, this is a form of "epistemic injustice" that wrongs the speaker as a subject of knowledge (2007, 4). Social injustice tends to cause epistemic injustice; the hearer perceives the speaker to be less credible because of stereotypes about the speaker's identity that create shared, distorted prejudgments about who is credible. Credibility in turn shapes who can exercise power and influence in the dissemination of knowledge and information. The capacity to be a "subject of knowledge," to be a source of information and wisdom, is "essential to human value," argues Fricker (2007, 5). The hearer wrongs the speaker by devaluing her as a "giver of knowledge." This is an important meaning of standing, worth, and authority.

But our point is that this inequality, and injustice, must be understood in light of the gender context and institutional rules within which men and women deliberate, because the effect of gender is contingent on the structure of the group setting. This has direct implications for the debate among political theorists about whether deliberation is a positive force for democracy and its precept of equality or instead undermines the voices of subordinate group members. We suggest that a way to resolve this debate is to focus on the conditions that give rise to one or the other. Both views are empirically correct but contingent on circumstances. The fact that gender inequality disappears under some conditions means that deliberation can in fact meet the standard of equality, as its advocates contend.

Our results allow us to address several alternative explanations. First, one might argue that low talk time is not a problem if it is caused by efficiency—if it occurs when there is no need to repeat what others already say because one is in the preference majority. In response, we showed that women speak less than men whether their preference is widely shared or not. In addition, if women are silent because they are the preference majority, that does not explain the interactive effects.[44] Thus less voice is an indicator of less influence, not the product of desire to avoid redundancy with preference allies. Neither is it the result of the judicious exercise of subtle power. Quiet neither reflects nor begets power, but powerlessness.

Second, the controls reassure us that the differences between women and men are not due to a correlated difference in attitudes about redistribution, but to the divergent responses of men and women to the interaction taking place. Third, the rule shapes talk and influence in part by shaping the norm of interaction—unanimous rule does not matter merely because it sets individual strategy, but because it produces a more inclusive exchange. Finally, while randomly distributed chattiness may partially explain why some people talk more than others, it does not explain the gender gap or why it changes as it does. There are likely considerable differences among men and among women, but there is also a difference between the sexes.

One might raise the argument that social equality must be traded off against another important purpose of deliberation—reason and the search for truth. Deliberative advocates rely on public discussion as a path to public enlightenment, or less grandly, as a means to aid the collective search for valid and accurate knowledge that serves group goals. Our response is that in addition to the question of justice, the analysis of talk time sheds light on the question of collective reason. Available evidence suggests that justice does not compromise reason, but that justice serves reason. In a recent study of group problem solving, researchers found that the number of women in the group substantially affects the group's ability to solve problems collectively—even when accounting for the capacity of the individuals in the group (Woolley et al. 2010).[45] The gender composition affects group ability through the members' average empathic ability. These effects held even after controlling on the members' intelligence. That is, some groups were "stupider" than the sum of their parts, and that is partly due to the dearth of women, because the presence of more women was correlated with equal talk and with the presence of empathetic people. Neither the group's average intelligence nor the intelligence of a few brilliant members

[44] Furthermore, if women talk less when the group has homogenous preferences, and gender simply stands in for preference, that does not explain why women talk most in all-female groups.

[45] The problem solving included a wide variety of cognitive, social, and values-oriented tasks.

affected the group's problem-solving ability; what did affect it was equally distributed talk and a high average ability to empathize, both of which were produced by having lots of women. The implication of these results is that gender inequality matters not only for justice but also for the group's ability to solve problems accurately. Deliberative theorists often argue that an important mission of discussion is to uncover truth, hence their emphasis on reason and rationality. Gender inequality may undermine that mission, aside from violating the deliberative precept of equal voice.

We will return to the question of external validity later, when we analyze patterns of talk on school boards and in our concluding chapter, but our results so far lead us to some preliminary conclusions about practical implications for policy making to enhance democratic participation.[46] It is possible to produce equal voice in citizen deliberation by adopting specific decision rules and assigning deliberators to particular gender compositions. Many government and nongovernmental organizations that run discussions can do so since they control the conditions of deliberation. The results provide some simple guidelines for promoting gender equality of participation and influence. When women are outnumbered by men, use unanimous rule; when women are a large majority, decide by majority rule. To avoid the maximum inequality, avoid groups with few women and majority rule. To minimize male advantage, assemble groups with a supermajority of women and use majority rule. To maximize women's individual participation, gender homogenous groups are best.[47]

More generally, the results so far yield important implications. Perhaps most importantly, political science has something unique to add to the study of gender relations: the notion that the institutional rules under which men and women participate in collective decision making have a significant effect on gender dynamics. Studies of women's representation in legislatures recognize the importance of institutional rules and norms, as we noted in chapter 1. Our results suggest that rules and norms also shape interactions among citizens.

The results also reinforce the notion in several recent studies of political behavior that gender matters but does so contingent on the environment. As we reviewed in chapter 3, Burns, Schlozman, and Verba (2001) find that the gender composition of civic groups can increase women's level of political information, interest, efficacy, and participation (see also Crowder-Meyer 2010). Our study seconds this finding. Together, these studies' results imply a conceptual

[46] Government units at the local, state, and federal levels are increasingly turning to group discussions for input into policy making or for conflict resolution, and many citizens actually participate in these deliberations when invited to do so (Neblo et al. 2010). Small group discussions are also common in civic life, in voluntary organizations, workplaces, and educational settings (Walsh 2007; Fung 2007; Macedo et al. 2005; Merelman Streich, and Martin 1998; Jacobs, Cook, and Delli Carpini 2009; Ryfe 2005).

[47] In addition, to maximize women's individual average talk time, unanimous rule is always better than majority rule, as figure 5.2 shows.

distinction between individual gender and gender composition and other gendered aspects of the setting (see Sapiro 2003). Studies of political behavior or of political decision making may not capture all that gender does if they only account for individual-level gender and omit gender composition and gendered interaction.

In addition, the results add to our understanding of decision rules. Unanimous rule helps not only preference minorities but also identity groups that find themselves a numerical minority in a deliberation. However, there is an asymmetry to the influence of rules on identity groups' participation. Unanimous rule helps women and men equally, but given men's advantaged default, it exacerbates the gender gap within the group when men are the minority, even as it shrinks the gap in the group when women are the minority. We also found that while majority rule helps women when they are the majority, it takes a supermajority for the benefit to materialize to women, but a small majority for the benefit to accrue to men. In this sense, the results here underscore the notion that rules work differently for different types of people. To predict the effect of a rule on a group, we must first know who is in it and what are the members' relative proclivities to speak.

But while the results are in line with some existing hypotheses about gender composition or about institutional rules, our chief result goes beyond the existing literatures. The interdependent effects of gender composition and decision rule in small group interaction have not been a focus of any literature. We find that these effects matter for both men and women, and for the ability of democratic institutions to reach normative goals of equality.

Finally, our results have implications for the debate over substantive or descriptive representation. As Mansbridge (1999) notes, "In theory, deliberation seems to require only a single representative, or a 'threshold' presence, in the deliberation to contribute to the larger understanding . . . in practice, however, disadvantaged groups often need the full representation that proportionality allows in order to achieve several goals: deliberative synergy, critical mass, dispersion of influence, and a range of views within the group" (636). We argue that the same logic applies to the volume of voice. Mansbridge is correct that "getting the relevant facts, insights, and perspectives into the deliberation" is not enough for substantive representation; it is also necessary that many members of the disadvantaged group air those facts, insights, and perspectives, and that they do so more than once.

CHAPTER 6

What Makes Women the "Silent Sex" When Their Status Is Low?

Early in my career, I went to numerous meetings where I was the only woman present. I would want to contribute to the conversation but would think, if I say that, everybody will think it's really stupid.

—MADELEINE ALBRIGHT[1]

MADELEINE ALBRIGHT IS one of the most accomplished women in recent US history. She holds a doctorate from Columbia University, speaks multiple languages fluently, served as the US ambassador to the United Nations, and was the first female secretary of state. Recently, she was awarded the Presidential Medal of Freedom, the highest civilian honor in the country, granted to individuals who have made "an especially meritorious contribution to the security or national interests of the United States." Clearly, she is not defined by some want of insights or knowledge or some inability to express herself. And yet, as the epigraph indicates, even the most ambitious and accomplished women can feel less confident and speak up less often when women are scarce and the group follows a masculine norm of discussion. Describing her experiences in these early-career meetings, Dr. Albright goes on to say, "And then a man would say exactly what I had in mind and the other participants would find it brilliant." In other words, what women have to contribute but choose not to articulate may be of great value to the group, and there is no good reason for women to hold back.

Yet in the previous chapter, we showed that women do in fact speak less than men, sometimes dramatically less. However, the size of the gender gap depends upon the nature of the group—specifically, its gender composition and its decision rule. We also showed that inequalities in speaking behavior are closely related to inequalities in authority within the group. Speech participation affects how others in the group assess their fellow group members. These key findings

[1] http://www.realsimple.com/work-life/life-strategies/inspiration-motivation/how-to-tactfully-speak-your-mind-00100000081879/index.html.

highlight a major theme of our book: group-level factors can profoundly alter the way men and women participate in deliberating groups and the influence they amass from their participation.

However, we want to know not only how much women and men are speaking, but also *which* women and men talk and which do not, and whether the answers to those questions change as the group-level context changes. We are especially interested in whether we can account for some of the mechanisms through which this inequality of speaking behavior emerges in the conditions that are especially damaging to women. To that end we turn now to exploring how the characteristics, beliefs, and preferences of men and women differ and how those characteristics, beliefs, and preferences are associated with their speaking behavior across the different conditions.

The Trinity of Gendered Attitudes

In chapter 3, we asked what might hold women back from exercising their voice in political discourse. There we noted that existing literature raises three possible individual-level explanations for women's lower levels of participation: they may have less confidence than men; they may dislike conflict and competition; and they may be more empathetic and sensitive to social bonds, thus frustrated by situations where such bonds are weak or absent.

The most likely suspect is a constellation of beliefs, attitudes, and scripts related to confidence. To briefly recap our extensive discussion from chapter 3: society creates expectations based on gender, teaching its denizens that women are naturally suited to feminine roles—namely, physical attractiveness and nurturance; that women thus have less competence in areas not clearly marked as their domain; and that women who overstep these bounds deserve condemnation or at least dislike when they take overt leadership actions, assert themselves, or otherwise violate the dictates of nurturance. As a consequence, women tend to have less confidence than men, to assert themselves to a lesser, and less overt, degree, and to engage in leadership actions gingerly and with compensating behaviors that signal nurturance and connection. These are not necessarily conscious beliefs, but they tend to be well internalized and pervasive.

For example, even very accomplished women tend to have lower self-perceptions about their abilities than men, rating themselves lower on measures of competence than comparable groups of men (Beyer and Bowden 1997). In a meta-analysis of a large number of studies, Kling and colleagues (1999) find that men tend to adopt a more "self-congratulatory" view of themselves and have persistently greater levels of self-esteem than women. Women are less likely than men to view themselves as capable and efficacious in the political arena. In Mansbridge's interviews in Selby, Vermont, women were much less likely than men to believe that "the town pays any attention to what people like you think" or to believe that they have "any say about what the town does" (1983, 311). As Fox and Lawless (2011) summarize, this tendency for women to undervalue their skills and abilities can persist even among women who have already achieved high levels of success.

Not only are women more likely to rate themselves lower on measures of confidence, self-esteem, or self-efficacy, their confidence in group settings also tends to be more sensitive to social cues, including group context. As Linda Babcock and Sara Laschever put it, "women's feelings of self-confidence fluctuate more than men's in response to the specifics of a situation" (2003, 142). Susan Hansen (1997) argues that settings in which politics is discussed can be especially alienating contexts for women, with the "content and style of political discourse" being off-putting. When describing deliberative settings more generally, Hibbing and Theiss-Morse (2002) assert, "The chorus in the interest-group pluralism heaven may sing with a decidedly upper-class accent, but in direct deliberation heaven it sings with a decidedly white, male, educated, confident, blowhard accent" (203). Therefore, we expect that women will not only tend to express lower levels of confidence and self-efficacy prior to deliberation, but they will also be especially sensitive to group-level cues—how does the group discussion proceed, what are the norms of interaction, how do others in the group respond to women's initial comments? Are the speakers mostly confident "blowhards" or not? Such group-level features may have a profound effect on women, especially those who come into the conversation harboring worries about their ability to participate successfully. As the female doctor we quoted in chapter 3 described her experiences on charity committees, "You get your cues right away. I will make comments about things, but it seems that no one hears me or no one agrees with me. And then I clam up."

Related to both confidence and increased sensitivity to the social context is women's tendency to have greater difficulty than men rebounding from negative feedback. As we summarized in chapter 3, previous work finds that men are more likely than women to disregard negative cues, while women are strongly influenced by them (see Roberts 1991). In our earlier review of the literature, for example, we mentioned the study by Horvath, Beaudin, and Wright (1992), which found that men were much more likely to persist as economics majors when they received grades lower than B in an introductory economics course. And fMRI studies show that women are less likely than men to show resilience to negative feedback about their performance (Montague et al. 2012).

Jane Mansbridge's interviews with residents of Selby, Vermont, show that even the *prospect* of negative feedback can cause women to withdraw from participation. For example, Edith Hurley describes her concerns that others will judge her negatively at the town meeting: "I don't like to get up in town meeting and say, well, this and that . . . well, everybody's looking, or doing something, and they'll say [whisper], 'She's a fool!'" Florence Johnson, who has never attended a town meeting, cites similar worries when explaining why she and others don't attend: "If you go there, and you speak up, they make fun of you for speaking up and so on, and I guess people just don't want to go and be made fun of" (Mansbridge 1983, 61).

In chapter 3 we also raised a second possibility: perhaps women's relative silence has less to do with confidence and resilience and more to do with the level of conflict in the group. In a study of deliberative groups discussing health care reform, Esterling, Fung, and Lee (2010) find that moderate levels of disagreement can be productive for participants and result in a rich, healthy exchange of views. High levels of disagreement, however, result in participants viewing the group as dysfunctional. The research we summarized in chapter 3 suggests that men and women may have differing preferences for conflict and that women prefer more consensual, less competitive forms of group interaction. Jane Mansbridge's in-depth interviews in Selby, Vermont, again illustrate the point. Edith Hurley stays away from the Selby town meeting not only because she is worried about criticism, but also in part because of the disagreements she expects to face. "You get in a lot of hubbub . . . people get quarreling," Hurley confides, and an older woman concurs: "I just don't like disagreeable situations" (Mansbridge 1983, 65). Altogether, Mansbridge reports, nearly one-quarter of the residents she interviewed expressed some concern about the conflictual nature of face-to-face interactions in town hall meetings (65).[2] Perhaps, then, it is the conflict-averse women who withdraw from the conversation when they confront more competitive, conflict-heavy norms of discussion and interaction, the sorts of norms the gender literature tells us are especially likely to be found in groups where men outnumber women.

Our third pillar of the trinity of gendered attitudes involves the social bonds among group members. As we discussed in chapter 3, Susan Beck's (2001) study of gender and municipal councils concludes that women are especially attuned to the level of collegiality and fellow-feeling among council members, and Lyn Kathlene's (2001) study of Colorado state legislators finds that women were much more likely to use words that emphasized social-connectedness instead of autonomy. Similarly, Karpowitz and Frost (2007) present evidence that women are more likely than men to make communitarian arguments when giving testimony before the town council. Once again, Mansbridge's Selby interviews illustrate the point well. One of the larger concerns she identifies is how friendships and other such close personal connections will be affected by the arguments and debates found at the town council meeting. As Phyllis Gunn laments, "They get so darned *personal* at town meeting!" (Mansbridge 1983, 63). Put differently, Phyllis Gunn is concerned about how the sometimes-conflictual norms of interaction at the town meeting will intrude upon the social bonds

[2]Mansbridge does not report whether there are gender differences in her sample with respect to conflict avoidance.

among the townspeople. Such a reaction could be the result of conflict aversion alone, but it could also be tied to a desire for a more empathetic form of communication in which emotional connections are more carefully cultivated. Thus this line of research suggests that empathy may be a key explanatory variable. Women who are oriented toward greater prosociality will withdraw from conversations, this approach predicts, when the norms of interaction neglect social bonds and the connections among deliberators.

Our review of previous work thus highlights three distinct mechanisms for women's verbal participation: confidence and resilience to negative feedback, aversion to conflict, and feelings of empathy or prosociality. Each of these is tied to the cues women receive through group norms. Does the group welcome all views, or is it a competitive environment where only the most confident may want to venture into the fray? How much conflict is present in the group? How sensitive is the group to social bonds, and do the group members send cues that they care about their personal connections with each other?

The existing literature leads us to expect that these mechanisms will make a difference even when controlling for other factors that are commonly thought to be associated with increased participation, such as income, age, or education. Women's lower level of confidence and increased sensitivity to social signals within the group is not merely a function of education or income. Even well-compensated, well-educated women can experience these effects. In other words, we have reason to expect that factors like confidence, comfort with disagreement, or empathy can affect the level of women's participation in discussion even when we have controlled for women's socioeconomic status. In this chapter, our aim is to understand the extent to which confidence, conflict aversion, and empathy help to explain gender disparities across different conditions. That is, we want to know not only what mechanisms help to explain the participation of men and women but also how those mechanisms are affected by the experimental conditions.

Prior to deliberation, we asked each participant a number of questions about their beliefs and preferences. As we saw in the previous chapter, this allows us to explore how individuals with differing predeliberation attitudes behave during group deliberation. Participants privately indicated their level of agreement or disagreement with several different statements on a 5-point Likert scale ranging from strongly disagree to strongly agree. We presented participants with statements designed to tap precisely the mechanisms we discussed in the earlier chapters. For example, our measure of confidence includes two traditional measures of internal political efficacy—"I feel that I have a pretty good understanding of the important political issues facing us today" and "Sometimes politics and the government seem so complicated that a person like me can't really understand what is going on" (reverse coded). In addition, we asked participants to respond to statements designed to measure their sense of confidence in articulating themselves to others—"I am frequently frustrated by my inability to express my opinions to others" (reverse coded)—and their ability to effectively take part in group deliberations—"I am capable of participating effectively in group discussions about important political issues." To these we also add two statements tapping a general sense of self-assurance—"In general, I do better on most things than most people" and "I am confident in my abilities, even when confronting tasks I haven't done before." These questions scale together well ($\alpha = 0.71$), and factor analysis shows that they load highly on a single factor. Together, they comprise a scale designed to measure predeliberation confidence, especially confidence in one's ability to talk with others about politics.[3] For ease of analysis, we recode the scale to run from 0 to 1, with high scores indicating greater confidence.

We measure comfort with disagreement using an item inspired by Goldstein's (1999) conflict communication scale (see also Mutz and Reeves 2005). Participants indicated their level of agreement or disagreement with the statement, "I feel uneasy and uncomfortable when people argue about politics." Similarly, our measure of empathy is an item drawn from Caprara and colleagues' (2005) "prosocialness" scale. This item—"I easily put myself in the shoes of those who are in discomfort"—captures the concern for the feelings and thoughts of others in the group, and the tendency to tune in, and accommodate, to their needs. Caprara and colleagues (2005) show that this item tends to produce significant differences in empathy between men and women, thus making it especially helpful for our purposes.[4] Our empathy measure also captures well the general differences in prosocial behavior between men and women identified by other researchers (Eagly and Crowley 1986).

Participants also spent part of the time prior to deliberation reviewing information about various principles of redistribution provided to them in the participant handbook. We wanted to be sure that all members of the group shared at least a minimal understanding of the purposes and values behind different approaches to redistribution and how those different approaches might work in the context of the experiment. To test their understanding, we administered a brief, eleven-item quiz designed to review the four main principles of redistribution that were discussed in the participant handbook. As respondents completed the quiz, we gave them feedback about whether each answer was correct or not. For those who answered incorrectly, we offered an additional opportunity to respond, and then we provided the correct answer, along with an explanation of why it was correct (and why other options were wrong). Thus the quiz gave each respondent clear cues about their understanding of the principles to be discussed by the group. By the end of the quiz, all respondents

[3] Full question wording and descriptive statistics are available in the online appendix.

[4] Ideally, we would have included the full conflict avoidance and empathy scales, but because of concerns about completion time for the full experiment, we only had space for a limited number of items.

should have achieved roughly equal knowledge of the definitions and purposes of the principles as well as how each principle would work if the group were to choose it during deliberation. In this sense the quiz score is not a pure measure of knowledge held during discussion, as all participants either answered correctly or were provided the correct answers.

The quiz does, however, give us a measure of how often respondents received negative cues about their understanding of the topic to be discussed by the group. We constructed a "negative quiz feedback score" variable that shows the proportion of questions for which participants received negative feedback. The fact that we provided feedback along the way means that those who answered incorrectly on the first try received negative signals about their performance. Higher negative quiz feedback scores thus indicate not only lower initial levels of performance (a fact we hoped to remedy by providing the correct answer and explanations) but also—and more importantly for our purposes—more negative cues about their understanding of the topic of group discussion. Those who answered most quiz questions correctly on the first try received very little negative feedback, and those who made more mistakes during the quiz received considerably more negative feedback. Our review of the gender literature tells us that women might be especially sensitive to these sorts of negative cues about their performance. The variable is scaled from 0 to 1, with the value representing the proportion of quiz questions for which the participant received negative cues. The lowest score thus means the participant received no negative cues, and higher scores indicate higher doses of negative cues about competence.

So far we have described the factors that we treat as the core aspects of gender. In addition, however, we want to control on related factors that are less centrally part and parcel of gender. Included among these is the now-familiar variable of egalitarianism (see the chapter 4 appendix for question wording and the online appendix for additional details). In addition, prior to debriefing, respondents indicated their age, income, education level, partisanship, and liberal-conservative ideology. The partisanship and ideology questions are standard questions asked in many political surveys, and full descriptions are available in the online appendix.[5]

Our analysis shows some differences between men and women with respect to many of the attitudes and characteristics we asked our participants to report. In table 6.1, each of the variables of interest other than age has been recoded from 0 to 1 for ease of comparison and interpretation.[6] As can be seen in the table, the mean differences are statistically significant but tend to be small to

[5]We placed the party and ideology variables at the end of the session in an effort to avoid priming partisan identities prior to deliberation.

[6]The table shows predicted values from an OLS model that includes gender and controls for experimental location.

Table 6.1: Mean Differences between Men and Women

	Men	Women	Difference	p-Value of difference
Confidence Index	0.63	0.52	0.11	0.001
Negative Quiz Feedback	0.13	0.20	−0.07	0.001
Comfort with Disagreement	0.70	0.59	0.11	0.001
Empathy	0.64	0.72	−0.08	0.001
Egalitarianism	0.48	0.55	−0.07	0.001
Liberalism	0.44	0.51	−0.07	0.030
Education	0.65	0.68	−0.03	0.070
Income	0.34	0.28	0.06	0.001
Age	25.9	29.4	−3.5	0.001

Note: Cell entries are predicted values from the regression of each variable on a dummy variable for women and a control for experimental location. N = 470.

moderate in size, ranging from a difference of 3 percentage points to as many as 11—results that are fully consistent with larger studies of individual-level gender differences (Sapiro 2003). For example, the female advantage in education is small (and does not quite achieve traditional levels of statistical significance), with both the average man and average woman in the sample having experienced some college, though having not yet completed their degrees. Similarly, the male advantage in quiz scores amounts to little more than three-fourths of a question on an eleven-point quiz, and the vast majority of both men and women score at least nine out of eleven. In general, we find the expected gender differences in basic demographic characteristics (income, education, age), social-psychological characteristics (confidence in discussion contexts, comfort with disagreement, and empathy), and political attitudes (egalitarianism and liberalism). While small to moderate in size, all of these differences run in the directions previous work on gender differences would lead us to anticipate. In this sense, our sample appears to reflect well the larger tendencies of men and women in the population.

Nonetheless, sometimes even moderate average differences can mark substantial gender disparities in the way the variables are distributed. Most important for our purposes, only 32% of women score above the sample median on our confidence measure. If we use the overall sample's median score as a divider between high and low levels of confidence, more than 60% of men qualify as "highly confident." That is, *men are twice as likely as women to score above the median of confidence.* These differences are also found at the extremes of the distribution. More than 16% of men in our sample score in the 90th percentile or higher on our confidence measure, while less than 4% of women reach the top decile: a fourfold difference. Conversely, nearly 16% of women score in the bottom decile on the confidence measure, while less than 5% of men qualify as having such very low levels of confidence. All of these results converge on a clear conclusion: male participants in our experiment are much more likely to be found at the high end of the confidence measure, while women are found disproportionately at the low end of the scale.

We found meaningful differences between men and women in the three key factors we expect may be implicated in women's lower participation levels. In addition, although we found small differences in negative feedback received (the quiz score), we expect that men and women will react differently to the presence of such negative responses. The key question, moreover, is whether the conditions of deliberation activate these gendered differences or suppress them.

A Note about Method

Given this set of differences between men and women, our question is how these attributes are related to women's speaking behavior and, more importantly, how those relationships change across the experimental conditions. At the outset, we want to make clear that our analysis here is different from the experimental approach we have adopted to this point (and to which we will return in subsequent chapters). The attributes and mechanisms we will discuss in this chapter have not been experimentally manipulated. However, random assignment means they should be roughly equally distributed across the conditions (a fact that chapter appendix table A6.1 confirms). Thus our experimental research design allows us to investigate how the relationship between an attribute of the person and their talk time *changes* across the experimental conditions. As we explore how the connections between individual characteristics and talk time vary across different types of groups, we can gain insights into the mechanisms through which the gender dynamics we discovered in the previous chapter are produced. For example, if the relationship between confidence and talk time is the same across the experimental conditions, then confidence cannot be a key mechanism through which the differences in speaking behavior are produced. If, however, confidence becomes a more important predictor of talk in the group-level conditions where women talk least, then we have evidence that the group-level factors are affecting talk time in part by moderating the relationship between confidence and speaking behavior.[7]

The set of mechanisms we explore in this chapter also allows us to tease out differences between those factors that are, we argue, related to gender but

[7] Of course, the causal story would be even stronger with an experimental manipulation of confidence, something that could be undertaken in future work.

distinct, such as demographic characteristics like income, education, or age, and characteristics that get at deeper differences between men and women. Although gender differences exist with respect to the demographic characteristics (women have lower incomes, and in our sample they are slightly older and better educated), we do not assume that such differences capture core distinctions between the genders, and we want to be sure that they are not spuriously driving the gender differences we have presented to this point. In the previous chapter, we showed that gender gaps in authority and speaking behavior were not spuriously related to preferences for principles of redistribution, agreement with the group's predeliberation preferences, or egalitarianism. In the present analysis, we will continue to control for these differences in political preferences, but we will train our attention more directly on attributes like confidence, comfort with disagreement, and empathy. These variables capture a constellation of concepts that go beyond socioeconomic status or issue attitudes. Thus our primary focus will be on attributes that are, as we have laid out in the opening chapters, more centrally associated with gender identities.

Our estimation strategy is to regress *Proportion Talk*, the main variable from the previous chapter, on these attributes, while also controlling for demographic characteristics and relevant attitudes, particularly liberalism and egalitarianism. We then compare the coefficients across the experimental conditions. Because we have a limited number of men and women in the conditions with gender tokens, we pool together the conditions in which women are a minority (one-woman and two-women conditions) as well as those conditions where women are a majority (three-women and four-women conditions). While we expect the most meaningful differences among mixed-gender groups to be between the one-woman and four-women conditions, our sample size is too limited to run regressions with a full set of controls on gender tokens only. Pooling the conditions yields a sufficiently large sample size to run the models with a full set of controls. This approach allows us to test the conditions where women are more disadvantaged, relative to men—majority rule with one to two women and unanimous rule in groups where women predominate—against the other groups. Because we do not expect differences across decision rules among gender homogenous groups, and again to maximize our statistical power, we pool majority and unanimous conditions for groups composed exclusively of men or women. Thus our analysis includes five separate regressions for each gender—majority rule with a majority of women, majority rule with a minority of women, unanimous rule with a majority of women, unanimous rule with a minority of women, and gender homogeneous groups (male or female enclaves). As in the previous chapter, we also control for experimental location, given that participants were randomly assigned within, but not across, locations.

Tables 6.2 and 6.3 present the results of these OLS regressions and show how each of our key variables of interest—confidence, comfort with disagreement,

Table 6.2: Mechanisms Explaining *Proportion Talk* across Experimental Conditions, Women Only

	(1) 1–2 Women Majority Rule	(2) 3–4 Women Majority Rule	(3) 1–2 Women Unanimous Rule	(4) 3–4 Women Unanimous Rule	(5) 5 Women Both Rules Combined
Confidence	0.386**	0.104	0.029	0.213**	0.095
	(0.153)	(0.061)	(0.140)	(0.076)	(0.079)
Negative Quiz Feedback	−0.444**	−0.167	−0.063	−0.041	−0.112
	(0.186)	(0.095)	(0.185)	(0.066)	(0.073)
Comfort with Disagreement	−0.062	−0.062	0.156	0.033	0.014
	(0.089)	(0.043)	(0.156)	(0.055)	(0.052)
Empathy	0.039	−0.007	0.093	0.086	−0.050
	(0.079)	(0.079)	(0.164)	(0.053)	(0.056)
Liberalism	−0.318***	0.083*	0.144	−0.106***	0.039
	(0.090)	(0.039)	(0.167)	(0.032)	(0.044)
Income	−0.133*	0.029	−0.071	0.066	−0.008
	(0.076)	(0.057)	(0.170)	(0.069)	(0.039)
Education	−0.358***	0.160	0.112	0.109**	0.026
	(0.117)	(0.108)	(0.222)	(0.039)	(0.044)
Age	−0.000	0.001	0.001	−0.000	0.001
	(0.002)	(0.002)	(0.002)	(0.001)	(0.001)
Constant	0.359**	0.033	−0.185	−0.025	0.146**
	(0.132)	(0.077)	(0.318)	(0.072)	(0.061)
Observations	23	52	21	59	75
R-squared	0.685	0.318	0.381	0.285	0.129
Control for Experimental Location	Yes	Yes	Yes	Yes	Yes

Note: Dependent variable in all models is *Proportion Talk*. Individual-level analysis. Cluster robust standard errors in parentheses. *** p < 0.01, ** p < 0.05, * p < 0.1, two-tailed.

empathy, and negative quiz feedback—is related to *Proportion Talk* in each condition. Table 6.2 includes results for women, and table 6.3 shows results for men. Controls for demographic characteristics and for liberalism are included. We employ liberalism instead of egalitarianism in these models because our measure of empathy is significantly correlated with egalitarianism (p = 0.02), but not with liberalism (p = 0.50).[8] For the sake of parsimony in presentation,

[8] Findings are very similar if we control for egalitarianism instead, but reducing the correlation allows for a cleaner test of the role of empathy.

Table 6.3: Mechanisms Explaining *Proportion Talk* across Experimental Conditions, Men Only

	(1) 1–2 Women Majority Rule	(2) 3–4 Women Majority Rule	(3) 1–2 Women Unanimous Rule	(4) 3–4 Women Unanimous Rule	(5) 5 Men Both Rules Combined
Confidence	0.228** (0.096)	0.326* (0.182)	0.048 (0.124)	0.006 (0.176)	0.187*** (0.062)
Negative Quiz Feedback	-0.085 (0.226)	−0.538** (0.220)	−0.187 (0.137)	−0.292** (0.132)	−0.181** (0.070)
Comfort with Disagreement	0.022 (0.120)	−0.099 (0.103)	-0.001 (0.071)	0.203 (0.123)	0.093* (0.047)
Empathy	-0.125* (0.060)	0.001 (0.102)	-0.035 (0.095)	−0.247* (0.140)	0.038 (0.077)
Liberalism	-0.019 (0.076)	0.260 (0.166)	−0.038 (0.075)	0.009 (0.131)	−0.023 (0.068)
Income	−0.054 (0.076)	−0.099 (0.070)	0.019 (0.045)	−0.343*** (0.109)	−0.012 (0.043)
Education	−0.001 (0.093)	−0.115 (0.098)	−0.061 (0.078)	0.137 (0.261)	0.058 (0.085)
Age	0.002 (0.002)	0.001 (0.011)	0.006*** (0.002)	0.003 (0.002)	0.002 (0.001)
Constant	0.113 (0.090)	0.106 (0.194)	0.101 (0.109)	0.124 (0.161)	−0.051 (0.090)
Observations	57	21	58	25	75
R-squared	0.122	0.479	0.163	0.412	0.210
Control for Experimental Location	Yes	Yes	Yes	Yes	Yes

Note: Dependent variable in all models is *Proportion Talk*. Individual-level analysis. Cluster robust standard errors in parentheses. *** $p < 0.01$, ** $p < 0.05$, * $p < 0.1$, two-tailed.

these regressions include all of our main variables of interest together, but the results are very similar if we analyze confidence, quiz score, comfort with disagreement, or empathy separately, adding only controls for the demographic characteristics and liberalism to the models.

The Shifting Effects of Women's Confidence

We begin with the effects of confidence, displayed in the first row of table 6.2. Confirming our expectation, table 6.2 shows that women's confidence in their ability to articulate opinions and participate in group discussion is strongly re-

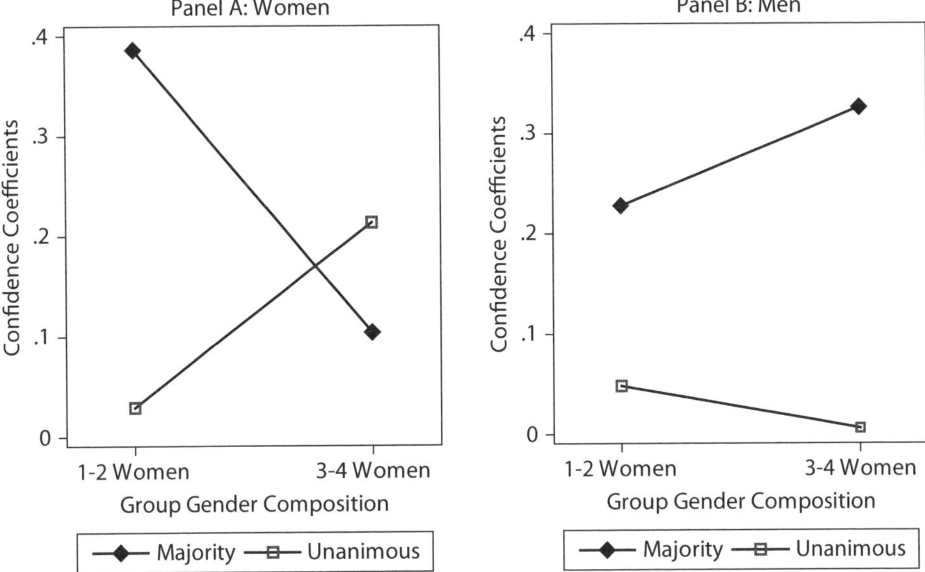

Figure 6.1. Effect of confidence on *Proportion Talk*, by condition, mixed-gender groups only.

lated to women's proportion of the group's talk time. But as expected, the table shows that the magnitude of the confidence effect varies across the conditions. For example, for women, the magnitude of the confidence coefficient is more than 3.5 times larger in majority-rule groups with few women than in majority-rule groups with many women. And the coefficient in the majority-rule groups with few women is over 13 times larger than in the unanimous-rule groups with few women. When the circumstances of discussion shortchange women's authority, and women are severely disempowered in terms of talk time, confidence matters much more.[9]

Figure 6.1 illustrates our findings by showing the confidence coefficient point estimates for women and men across the mixed-gender experimental conditions. For women, we see a pattern of strong interaction between gender composition and decision rule: the effect of confidence is large and statistically significant ($p < 0.03$) in majority-rule groups with few women, but much

[9]Importantly, the confidence results replicate when the individual items in the confidence scale are substituted for the full scale, and the sizes of the confidence coefficients are always larger than the items tapping empathy and comfort with disagreement. The relationships between confidence and talk time are strongest for the following two items: "I am frequently frustrated by my ability to express my opinions to others" (reverse coded, $p < 0.01$) and "I am capable of participating effectively in group discussions about important political issues" ($p < 0.01$). So it is not the case that the findings are driven by the fact that confidence is measured with a scale and the others with a single item. In addition, of the two items with the strongest connection to talk time, one has a direct reference to politics, while the other does not.

smaller and not close to statistical significance in unanimous groups with few women. In groups with many women, the pattern is reversed: confidence matters more in groups with many women, with a statistically significant coefficient that is nearly twice the size of the coefficients for majority-rule groups. For women, confidence matters most in the conditions where women's status is lowest, and the effect of confidence is greatest in those groups where women tend to face the greatest inequalities in speaking behavior—majority rule with few women and unanimous rule with many women.

As the figure shows, confidence is important for men too, but the pattern highlights large differences across decision rules and no prominent interaction between decision rule and gender composition. Although high-confidence men speak more than low-confidence men under majority rule, figure 6.1 makes clear that gender composition makes no difference to this effect. Confidence differentiates among men under majority rule, regardless of their proportion. And by the same token, it has no effect under unanimous rule, whether women are the majority or minority. For example, confidence coefficients for men in the unanimous groups are extremely small and never statistically different from 0. While confidence affects women strongly where their status is lowest, and not at all where their status is highest, it does nothing like this for men.[10] Confidence does not affect men's participation more where men have low status (or where they have high status, for that matter). That is, for women (but not for men) the effect of confidence is highly sensitive to the interaction of decision rule and gender composition.

The formal test of significant difference between the coefficients often achieves or comes close to statistical significance, despite the fact that the sample size in some of our regressions is limited (see online appendix, table C6.1). Take, for example, the difference between the role of confidence when minority women operate under majority rule rather than unanimous rule. The coefficients differ by well over 30 percentage points, and the difference is significant at the 90% confidence level ($p < 0.07$, two-tailed test).[11] The difference in the effect of confidence between minority and majority women under majority rule is smaller and not significant, but is in the expected direction. And in a simplified model in which we compare only the one-woman condition with the four-women conditions under majority rule, the difference in the effect of confidence increases by 43% from the coefficient that compares minority and majority women. These results are evidence that confidence matters more for

[10]One could argue that men's status is "lowest" in the one condition where women achieve equality—majority rule with many women, particularly in groups with four women. For men, the largest confidence coefficient is in majority-rule groups with a majority of women, but this coefficient is not significantly larger than the effect under majority-rule groups with few women. For men, the more profound pattern is that confidence matters for talk time under majority rule, but not under unanimity.

[11]See online appendix table C6.1 for the regressions from which these formal tests were drawn.

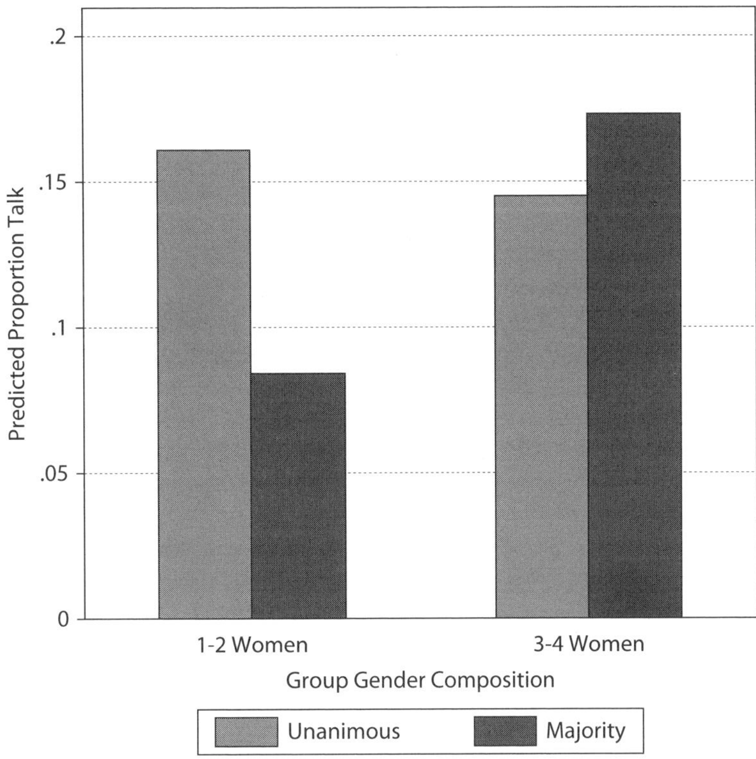

Figure 6.2. Predicted *Proportion Talk* among extremely low-confidence women.

women when women's status is low and their *Proportion Talk* lags behind that of men. When the group context leaves women at a disadvantage, those who score lower on the confidence scale tend to talk far less than those who feel more self-assured about their ability to participate in the group.

These differences across conditions can be seen even more clearly in figure 6.2, which shows the predicted *Proportion Talk* among extremely low-confidence women, defined as those who score in the bottom decile in confidence, in each of our experimental conditions. The figure shows that in the most disempowering condition for women (majority rule with very few women in the group), the least confident women are predicted to take up only 8% of the conversation—less than half of the 20% standard of equality—and much less than low-confidence women in all the other conditions. The differences between the predicted values for the lowest-confidence women in the one-woman to two-women/majority-rule condition and the estimates for all the other conditions are significant at $p < 0.05$ (two-tailed). Low-confidence women rarely reach equality under any condition, but they are especially unlikely to do so when they are outnumbered by men in groups deciding by majority rule. When

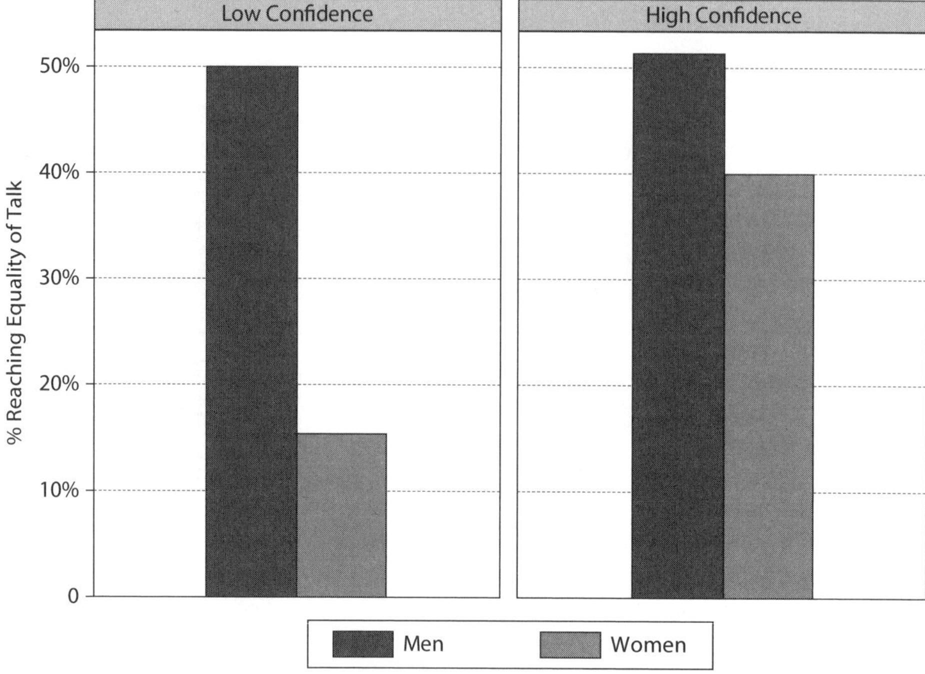

Figure 6.3. Percentage of participants reaching equality of talk, majority rule/1–2 women condition. Note: Equality of talk is defined as *Proportion Talk* of 0.20 or higher.

women's status is lower, low-confidence women tend to drop out of the discussion. They do not leave the room, but they account for less than half of their "fair share" of the conversation.

To sharpen the point, we compare low-confidence women with high-confidence women and with low-confidence men, in the setting where women's authority is lowest: majority-rule, minority-female groups. Figure 6.3 shows the raw percentage of men or women reaching the 20% standard of equality of talk. Where men have high status—under majority rule and high numbers—even low-confidence men reach equality of talk about half the time, which is about the same percentage as high-confidence men. Thus, although high-confidence men speak more than low-confidence men in this condition (as figure 6.1 showed), even low-confidence men regularly achieve equality of talk in the group. For women, the pattern is very different. Only 15% of low-confidence women reach equality, compared to 40% of their more confident counterparts.[12] In other words, confident women are dramatically more

[12] As a further point of comparison, low-confidence women in groups with few women reach equality close to 30% of the time when the group decides by unanimity—still a relatively low number, but nearly double the percentage of low-confidence women who reach equality under majority rule.

likely to reach the standard of equal participation we have been using. Even these more confident women reach equality less than half of the time, however. Figure 6.3 shows that high-confidence women reach equality less often than *low-confidence men*. When gender is a marker of status, the power of gender is strong enough that it overcomes one of our model's strongest predictors of individuals' speech. Where women's status is low, confidence matters not at all to men's ability to achieve equality in the group but makes a large difference to women's ability.

To this point we have shown that confidence matters for women's participation, but the size of the effect varies substantially across the different conditions. The level of authority, instantiated by the interaction of decision rule and gender composition, affects the speaking behavior of women in part by magnifying or muting the effect of confidence. The same is not true for men.

Importantly, these results are not a function of differences across the conditions in the distribution of confidence among women. Random assignment assures that confidence is roughly equally distributed across the conditions, and chapter appendix table A6.1 provides evidence that confidence and other characteristics are roughly equally distributed within the experiment. Thus our experimental research design reassures us in our explanation for why the behavior of women changes across the conditions; the effects of confidence also vary with the treatments.

Confidence and Resilience

Related to confidence is the effect of negative feedback about the predeliberation quiz. Recall that prior to deliberation, all participants took a quiz designed to test their understanding of the basic principles of redistribution that the group would discuss. If participants missed a quiz question, they were told that their answer was incorrect (and were ultimately given the correct answer). Figure 6.4 shows the effects of this negative feedback to the respondents about their answers on the quiz, as drawn from table 6.2 and table 6.3.

The figure makes clear that as predicted, women's patterns of resilience to negative feedback differ across the experimental conditions. Unanimous rule protects women regardless of their number, while under majority rule, women require large numbers to avoid quiescence from negative feedback. Specifically, women are not affected by learning that they gave incorrect answers under unanimous rule, regardless of gender composition. Put differently, unanimous rule mutes the effects of negative feedback on women, so that the effect of the feedback does not achieve statistical significance whether few or many women are in the group. Women benefit from unanimous rule in part because it makes them more resilient to negative inferences about their competence.

Under majority rule, however, women's numbers do matter. Negative feedback depresses the average woman's talk substantially ($p < 0.04$) when women

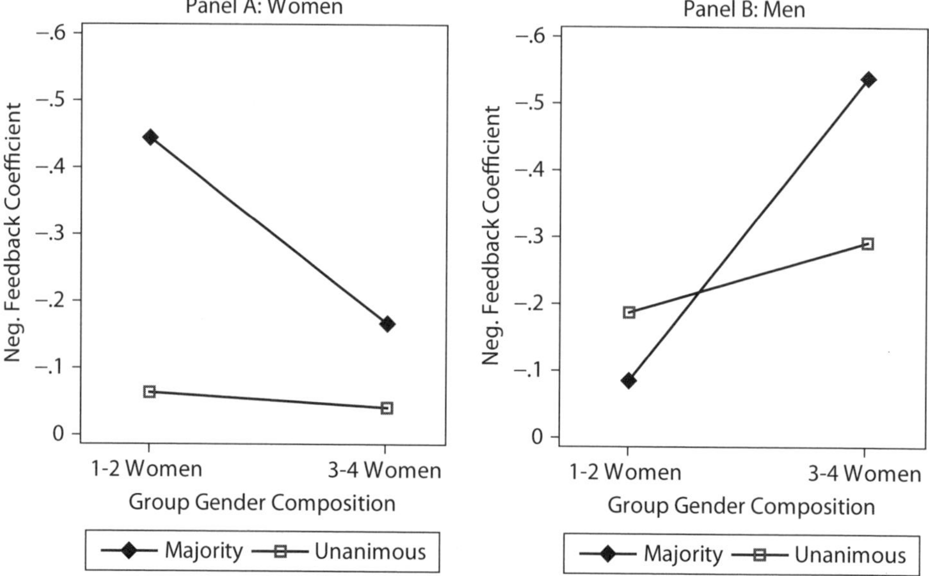

Figure 6.4. Effect of negative quiz feedback on *Proportion Talk*, by condition, mixed-gender groups only.

are the gender minority. In fact, that is by far the worst condition for women. However, the effect of negative feedback is much smaller and no longer statistically significant when women comprise the majority.[13] Although not shown in the figure, the effect of negative feedback is also small and not significant in female enclaves (table 6.2). In sum, the interaction hypothesis receives partial support—being many empowers women, but unanimous rule helps them even when they are few.

Unlike the expectations of gender role theory, men also experience adverse effects from negative feedback about their performance. Under majority rule, the effects on a man of learning that he made mistakes is the mirror image of the effect on the average woman. Negative feedback has a large and strongly significant effect on men in groups with many women.[14] Negative feedback also affects men under unanimous rule, regardless of the gender composition of the

[13]The difference in the coefficients does not reach statistical significance, however. Formal tests of the differences in the coefficients are shown in the online appendix table C6.2.

[14]We can compare more directly the relative size of the effects on women and on men in a formal test of the differences in the coefficients (see online appendix table C6.2). In groups where women's status is lowest, women, but not men, are adversely affected by negative feedback. As table C6.2 shows, the gender difference in the size of the negative feedback coefficients is marginally significant, but only using a more generous one-tailed test ($p < 0.10$). When women's status is highest, under majority rule and a preponderance of women, negative feedback depresses men's participation to a much greater extent than women ($p = 0.03$, two-tailed).

group. Unanimous rule does not protect men from the adverse effects of negative performance as it does women. In sum, men are most sensitive to negative implications about their competence when women are most empowered and not sensitive when women are least empowered. They react in between these extremes under unanimous rule, regardless of numbers.

The key finding about resilience in the face of negative feedback about one's performance is that receiving negative messages about competence can reduce the verbal participation of either men or women in groups where they are the gender minority under majority rule. Under that decision rule, being a member of the lower-status gender can powerfully enhance the negative effect of bad performance on speech. Unanimous rule helps women but not men, though men are better off there than as the gender minority under majority rule.

Having shown that negative feedback *and* confidence are especially important for women in majority-rule groups with few women, we now ask how the two mechanisms work together. By virtue of random assignment, the experimental conditions include women at both high and low confidence levels who received high, average, or low levels of negative feedback on the quiz. Those with high levels of negative feedback are defined as those who scored in the lowest quartile on the quiz; they received negative feedback on five or more questions on the eleven-item quiz. Average levels of negative feedback include participants who scored in the middle quartiles on the quiz, receiving negative feedback between one and four times. Low levels of negative feedback are defined as receiving no negative feedback. These are participants who received perfect scores on the quiz.

Figure 6.5 presents raw average *Proportion Talk* for women in the condition where they are least empowered: majority-rule groups with one to two women. It shows that among low-confidence women, only those who score at the highest levels on the quiz (the top quartile of participants) exhibit a *Proportion Talk* even close to the 20% line of equality, and even among that group, average talk does not quite reach equality. Among the larger group of women who receive average or above average levels of negative feedback, talk time drops to half the line of equality or lower. For high-confidence women, negative feedback can also matter, but it takes a great deal of it—five or more incorrect questions on the quiz—before talk time drops well below the standard of equality. High-confidence women who score at average levels on the quiz do slightly less well than low-confidence women who received little negative feedback, and high-confidence women who scored very well on the quiz tend to participate well above the standard of equality.[15] Thus high levels of negative feedback can depress the verbal participation of both high- and low-confidence women, and even low-confidence women who score moderately well on the quiz, receiving

[15]This high average is important but only suggestive because only two participants were in this category—one is from our outlier group, and she takes up 43% of the conversation. The other woman in this category takes up 21% of the group talk time.

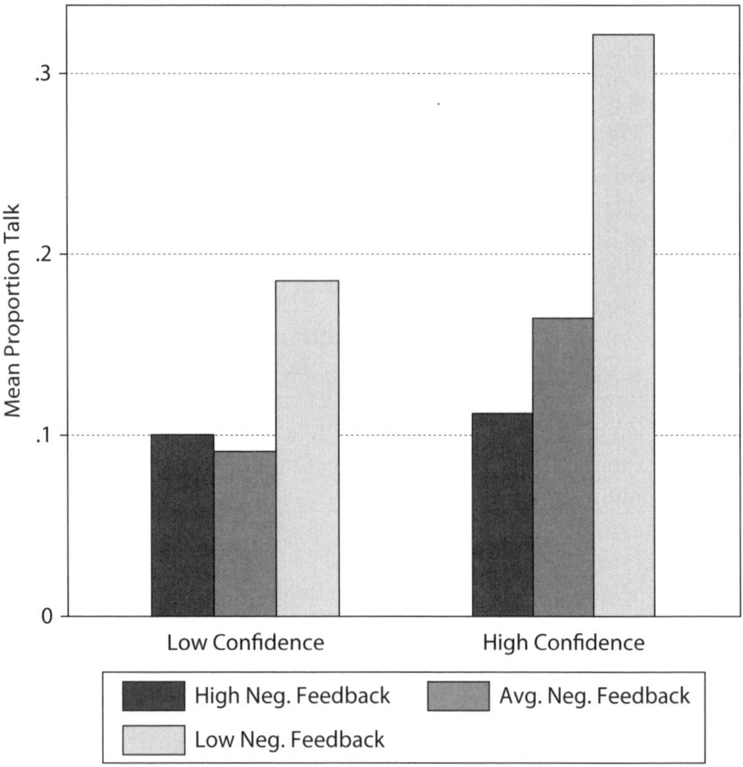

Figure 6.5. The interaction of negative quiz feedback and confidence, majority-rule/1–2 women condition.

negative feedback between one and four times, tend to remain quiet during the group discussion. The key to increased participation for women in groups where they are most disadvantaged is a combination of confidence and the absence of negative signals about their competence. The most talkative women are highly confident and received positive reassurance during the quiz. And these women not only achieved equality of participation but also asserted themselves at levels well beyond the standard of equality.

How Other Effects Shift across the Conditions of Deliberation

Two other variables that we identified in chapter 3 as potential explanations for women's reluctance to speak up—comfort with disagreement and empathy—have very little effect on women's level of participation in the discussion. Neither variable is significant in any model of women's *Proportion Talk*, nor are there substantial disparities in the effects of these variables across the experimental conditions.[16] Women who are more comfortable with disagreement are as likely to speak as women who are less so. Similarly, women who are more empathetic are neither more nor less likely to speak, though the lack of effect may simply be the result of comparatively little variation among women on our empathy measure.[17] We hesitate to draw definitive conclusions from these null results given that each concept is measured by only one item. In addition, our tests here only address the possibility that gender matters as an individual difference in levels or effects of the person's stable level of empathy or of conflict aversion. We do not intend here to ask whether the group dynamic of empathy, or the level of conflict in the discussion, matter to gender inequality. We reserve those questions for later chapters. However, our results pinpoint the source of the difference between men and women in conditions that disadvantage women in women's lower levels of confidence and resilience and not in their aversion to conflict or empathy.

The results so far have dealt with core gendered concepts, but it is worth pausing to see if the regressions in table 6.2 turned up any other interesting patterns. Because our models include a control for the participant's liberalism, we can also explore how the relationship between issue attitudes and speaking behavior changes across conditions. We know from the last chapter that the participant's commitment to egalitarianism does not make the effect of the conditions evaporate, but it may be that liberalism is more closely connected to speaking behavior in some conditions than in others. In chapter appendix figure A6.1, we see the familiar interaction between gender composition and decision rule for women's (but not men's) liberalism. When women's status is low and their verbal participation lags behind that of men, more liberal women are the ones who are less likely to speak up.[18] This effect is strongest in majority-rule groups with very few women. In the conditions where women's status is greater, liberal women speak *more* than other women, though the coefficient is not statistically significant in unanimous groups with minority women or in gender homogeneous groups. For men, the effect of liberalism is typically very small and never statistically significant. To the extent that liberalism matters for men, it appears that liberal men also speak more in conditions where women's status is greater, though this effect falls somewhat short of statistical significance.[19]

[16] Among men, we find in the two conditions where men significantly outparticipate women—majority rule with few women or unanimous rule with many women—more empathetic men speak less. The more talkative men are those who are less likely to express prosocial attitudes.

[17] More than 75% of women agree or strongly agree that they "easily put themselves in the shoes of others."

[18] The trends are similar, though somewhat smaller in magnitude, in models that control for egalitarianism.

[19] In majority rule groups with many women, the coefficient for liberal men is positive (0.26) but does not reach significance ($p < 0.14$, two-tailed test). Because the number of men in this condition is small, the large coefficient is still informative. See table 6.2 for details.

What can we glean from this? In our view, ideological self-placement, like the demographic characteristics we have included in our models, is distinct from attributes like confidence or empathy. Nonetheless, women do tend to be slightly more liberal than men, and in the conditions where women suffer the greatest inequalities of status and participation, women whose ideological commitments lean in this comparatively more "feminine" direction take up much less of the conversation. We will return to this issue in greater depth in the next chapter, when we explore the content of what women and men have to say, but for now, it does appear that groups dominated by men are less welcoming to at least some of women's preferences.

Finally, the regressions in tables 6.2 and 6.3 also show that participation in the group discussion is not primarily driven by the socioeconomic variables. In the condition in which the gender disparity in talk time is the most profound—majority-rule groups with few women—women's education is *negatively* related to voice. The best-educated women take up less of the group's conversation than the least educated women. In all other conditions, the relationship is positive but small. In no conditions are income or age significantly related to talk time. Similarly, table 6.3 shows that in general, these demographic characteristics tend to have small effects that do not reach significance for male participation either.

In the political science literature on participation, socioeconomic factors have long been shown to be closely related to political participation, especially political acts that are more demanding than voting (Brady, Verba, and Schlozman 1995; Rosenstone and Hansen 1993; Verba and Nie 1972). No doubt such factors contribute to having the resources to attend meetings or other deliberative activities. But the choice to attend may be different from the patterns of talk once the meeting has begun, and within our deliberating groups, the participation of men and women is not primarily driven by socioeconomic status. Of course, our sample is quite well educated, relative to the population as a whole, so the full range of educational achievements found in nationally representative samples is not included. The vast majority of our respondents have at least some college education, and only one woman (and no men) had less than a high school education. In this sense, our results should not be seen as a refutation of the well-established socioeconomic status model. By the same token, however, our sample is more like the men and women who, previous research tells us, actually do show up at meetings or are more likely to take part in other political events—those with higher levels of education and civic skills. Our data show that within this particular deliberative setting, it is not the case that women are talking less in some conditions because they are less educated, have fewer economic resources, or are younger. In general, we find that these factors make very little difference, and when they do matter, such as in the conditions where women are most disadvantaged, the best-educated women withdraw from the conversation—just the opposite of what the socioeconomic status model would have predicted.

Our findings support the notion that norms of participation in majority-rule groups with few women are detrimental to women because women are more deterred by lack of confidence. Women who start out with lower levels of confidence and those who receive negative cues about their competence before deliberation are most adversely affected by circumstances in which women are minorities under majority rule. In addition, we also found that women whose ideologies lean in a more liberal direction speak less in these groups. While confidence also affects men, the pattern is quite different for them. Among men, confidence matters on the other side of the distribution—rather than depressing the participation of low-confidence men, predominantly male groups under majority rule elevate the participation of the more confident men. In addition, this condition prompts a masculine pattern in which less-empathetic men are especially likely to speak. Further evidence that the same circumstances prompt quite different patterns among men and women is the finding that negative feedback on the quiz has little effect on men's speaking behavior.

These trends are not found in majority-rule groups with many women or in unanimous groups with few women. Male-dominated groups deciding by majority rule are groups where floor time goes to the confident, the less empathetic, the less liberal, and those who are best able to overcome negative feedback. All of those mechanisms favor men over women.

Conclusion

The last chapter showed that women are the "silent sex," in a manner of speaking. In the settings that characterize most arenas of politics and public affairs, and in many other formal discussions that take place in civic organizations, work teams, and other common venues, women are not a majority, and the norm of interaction has masculine characteristics. Numbers and norms of interaction combine to deter women from fully expressing their thoughts. In this chapter, we took off from this point of departure, asking why women speak less than men in such settings. Just as importantly, we looked for clues to tell us why women overcome the difficulties when they are placed in other circumstances. Specifically, we asked what it is about being a woman that makes participation less likely.

The evidence we presented points toward several aspects of gender as culprits. Most importantly, confidence has much to do with women's relative quiescence. Many more women fall into the low-confidence than the high-confidence category. Women are less likely than men to be confident in their abilities to participate effectively in group discussion, and when the group-level factors are stacked against them—such as when they are outnumbered under majority rule—such women reach equality only rarely. Women behave consistently with society's expectation that it is not proper for women to take actions of overt agency and assertion, particularly vis-à-vis men. Women are assigned particular roles, and those roles carry less power and authority than the roles of men. Gender not only divides people into biological categories, it also ranks the social worth of these categories. As the sociologist Cecelia Ridgeway put it, "The signature of status beliefs . . . is that they continue to link the higher status group with greater overall competence and with whatever specific skills are most valued by the society at that time. The evaluative content of gender stereotypes has changed in recent years, with perceptions of women becoming more positive, but the essential hierarchical element has remained: Men are still evaluated more favorably in the socially important area of instrumental competence" (Ridgeway 2001, 639).

By implication, situations where women interact with men cue these expectations—unless the dynamic of interaction actively addresses women's sense of inferiority. And indeed, we found that conditions that position women in a lower status by virtue of the combination of small numbers and a rule that disempowers those small numbers are especially bad for women with low confidence.

But this stable trait can also be affected by negative cues about women's authority or competence. Even minor negative signals, such as one or two incorrect answers on an eleven-item quiz, can lower women's average contribution from near equality to half that rate (as we showed in figure 6.5). However, these trait and signal effects only kick in where women's status is at its ebb—under majority rule, when women are few in number. This apparent lack of resiliency, however, is not particular to women. Men experience the same, in a mirror image. Men are unaffected by negative feedback when women's status is lowest, and they are most strongly affected in groups where women's status is highest—majority rule with majority women. That is, for both genders the effect of negative quiz feedback in groups deciding by majority rule is greatest when participants are part of the gender minority under a decision rule that empowers the majority. Furthermore, unanimous rule helps both sexes, but women more. In the case of negative feedback about performance, women are no more disadvantaged than men. By implication, it is the stable trait of low confidence, more than the effects of mild levels of negative performance feedback, that accounts for women's lower speech participation under conditions of low status.

Confidence and resilience are not the whole story, however. Even in conditions of high status, most confident women do not reach equal participation. Also important is the ideology of the person. In the conditions where women's status is lowest, women with more liberal ideologies seem more hesitant to speak up. Given that women's issue preferences tend to be comparatively more liberal than men's, this finding suggests that some types of groups may be less hospitable to women's views. To explore that possibility more directly, we must analyze what men and women actually say during the group discussion. It is to the issue content of speech that we now turn.

CHAPTER 7

Does Descriptive Representation Facilitate Women's Distinctive Voice?

Who is she, what does she want, and what sort of action shall she undertake? Is she a human being who can give a spoken account of herself? If so, what language does she speak?

—JEAN BETHKE ELSHTAIN[1]

IN A STRIKING ILLUSTRATION OF COOPERATION, psychologists studying one of our cousin species have found that lab rats engage in a persistent effort to liberate their caged fellow rats. They do so even when they gain no reward, are denied the company of the liberated compatriot, and despite giving up a portion of a favorite treat. The rats had to overcome their fear of the situation and to learn to open a door to a cage, a highly challenging task. The lesson for humans—that we too may be hardwired to help each other—might end there, but for one more wrinkle. Among rats equally adept at opening the door, the females freed the trapped compatriot much more speedily and consistently than the males (Bartal, Decetey, and Mason 2011). This gender gap in compassion is no surprise to students of the human species. Back in the human world, women, too, tend to be more other-regarding and prosocial than men, whether by nature, nurture, or both.[2]

[1]Quoted in Hansen (1997, 73).

[2]That is not to say that sex differences are immutable, or that environment plays a lesser role than genes. Rather, contemporary research underscores that genes find expression in large measure depending on environmental factors. As the biologist Arthur Arnold writes: "Although sex may be considered to be determined primarily biologically, our gender (i.e., the social perception and implications of our sex) is arguably equally or more important for our lives. Sex and gender differences are created by an intricate reciprocal interaction of numerous biological and environmental forces" (Arnold 2010). He further states: "Because sex-specific environmental forces correlate so strongly with sex-specific biological factors, it is often impossible to separate their effects, especially in humans. Environmental factors causing sex differences are often routinely excluded or ignored by biologists because they have been considered to be outside of the realm of biology. Nevertheless, such forces interact strongly with biological factors" (Arnold 2010).

But humans, unlike rats, have developed organizations and institutions. In these complex forms of social organization women are not always able to act on their prosocial inclinations. Some institutions facilitate the impulse to help those in need, while others stand in the way. What are these institutions, and how do they inhibit or empower women's voice of care and compassion? In particular, we ask: does increasing the descriptive representation of women increase their substantive representation—specifically, their chances of voicing women's distinctive concerns? Put differently, does increasing the proportion of women in a deliberating body also affect the content of the discussion, and how do institutions moderate the effect of numbers on the words uttered in the conversation?

One of the virtues of our experiment is that it allows us to examine what people say in their own words, and to connect those words with their attitudes and actions. A known virtue of the controlled experiment is "internal validity"—in this case, confidence that the decision rule and gender composition are the only possible causes of the effects we observe. But a controlled study provides an additional opportunity—careful measurement. It allows us to carefully track individuals' speech and link it with pre- and postdeliberation preferences, attitudes, and behavior. That way we can systematically analyze who says what under what conditions. This tells us if women mention more issues of distinctive concern to women when they occupy a more equal position with men in the group, holding constant the attitudes they carry with them when they arrive to deliberate. It can also tell us how their speech affects the decisions they reach after they speak.

There are important consequences to women's representation. As we will detail, women far more than men prioritize the protection of vulnerable and poor populations and support government intervention on "compassion" issues (Hutchings et al. 2004). Were women to gain more equal standing and authority, deliberations in public settings may well come to reflect a different set of priorities.

Is There a Different Voice?

Our question is whether conditions that promote equal participation in deliberation also produce more speech about women's distinctive priorities. But before we can address that question, we first explore whether women have distinctive concerns and what those might be.[3] In earlier chapters, we have al-

[3]Before we start, we want to note that defining "women's distinctive issues" is by no means a straightforward task, and we do not wish to naturalize, essentialize, or reify gender stereotypes. Certainly, women's concerns consist of vastly different things in different places, times, and for different subgroups. To take a particularly apt example, in one Indian province the provision of roads is deemed an issue of particular importance to men, while in another it is of much more concern

ready hinted at some fairly robust though small- to moderately sized general differences between the views of American men and women. Women tend to be more empathetic and prosocial than men. Now, what does this mean for women's and men's distinctive political priorities?

Women currently hold a number of political perspectives and priorities that differ from men's. In advanced industrialized countries, women now tend to vote more left wing than men by about ten points, and their ideological position lies to the left of men's (Inglehart and Norris 2010, 130). In the most recent review of the US gender gap in public opinion, conducted on two large national samples with extensive political assessments (American National Election Study and National Annenberg Election Study), political scientist Melody Crowder-Meyer (2007) finds that even after controlling on variables such as party identification, women are more likely than men to believe that "it is problematic that not everyone in the U.S. has an equal chance in life," are considerably more supportive of government's role in addressing economic distress and social needs such as health care, prefer less room for the free market, and are more concerned about economic inequality. Women are more eager for government spending on the poor, elderly, and children. Women are also more racially egalitarian (Hutchings et al. 2004).[4]

Even more relevant to what people will say in a deliberation than their stands on issues are their issue *priorities*—the issues they believe are most important for the country and those on which they rely the most in choosing among parties or candidates. Especially pertinent are responses to open-ended formats, where people speak in their own words about the nation's pressing needs. The largest gender gaps are in these priorities, with women much more likely than men to view poverty and economic inequality as an important problem. As Crowder-Meyer summarizes, women are "eighty percent more likely than men to mention poverty or homelessness" (2007, 13).

Women's priorities differ most from men's on the topic of children. Women are "two and a half times more likely than men to mention children's issues as a most important problem" (Crowder-Meyer 2007, 14). Perhaps most strikingly, "the least commonly mentioned most important problem for men is children's issues, while women are more likely to mention these as a problem than illegal

---

for women (Chattopadhyay and Duflo 2004). We do not mean to minimize the importance of these definition problems. But we do think that we can learn a great deal by asking what concerns, perspectives, and priorities women, on average, would bring to the table, in a given place and time, if they could (see Carroll 2001, viii–xiv). We do not minimize the variety within women, which is indeed so large that it often dwarfs the difference between the sexes (Sapiro 2003). But we wish to see if there are central tendencies to women's and men's priorities and note places of difference between them. Everything we say here is intended to apply to the particular place and time at hand, and with the implicit understanding that much variety lurks within a gender category.

[4] Women are also less supportive of military means and aggressive or coercive government policy (Conover and Sapiro 1993; Gilens 1988). Concurring results are found in Washington (2008, 312).

immigration, taxes, outsourcing, and energy and gas prices" (Crowder-Meyer 2007, 14).

Additional evidence about women's distinctive priorities comes from their contemporary behavior. College majors that serve populations in need are overwhelmingly female—health (85%), education (77%), and psychology and social work (74%) (Carnevale, Strohl, and Melton 2011). Women are more likely than men to spend on children in the household (Lundberg et al. 1997). When women's income increases, measures of their daughters' well-being rise (Duflo 2003; Thomas 1990). The same holds for political behavior. Female activists and officials tend to prioritize issues of children and family and are more likely to work to pass measures that benefit them (Burns, Schlozman, and Verba 2001; Carroll 2001). Among people driven to action on a specific issue, by far the biggest chunk of women is active on the issue of education—no matter if they are advantaged, disadvantaged, married, single, or whatever. The biggest chunk of men is active on the issue of taxes—no matter if they are advantaged, disadvantaged, and so on; in fact, even fathers are more likely to participate on taxes than on education (Burns, Schlozman, and Verba 2001, 128–29). The biggest difference in the type of organization that women and men join is in educational associations (Burns, Schlozman, and Verba 2001, 78). This priority has a long history. For many decades before the law guaranteed woman's suffrage, women were active in education (Burns, Schlozman, and Verba 2001).[5] The needs of children thus take a position front and center for women, far less so for men.

Further evidence about priorities, and people's willingness to act on them, comes from a very different setting, and one that generalizes well to the discussions we studied. When men and women are asked to render a verdict in a simulated trial of first-degree sexual assault on a six-year-old child, women tend to convict and men to exonerate (Golding et al. 2007). So in small group deliberations, as in survey and real world settings, women tend to place a high priority on the needs of vulnerable people, and significantly more than men.

Some issues emerge as distinctive priorities for men. Men are more concerned than women about financial issues—outsourced jobs, energy and gas prices, and taxes (Crowder-Meyer 2007). We will make use of these issues as a basis for contrast with the issues that women tend to emphasize.

[5] Legislatures are another arena where we see different priorities by gender. As women's numbers grow, Swedish municipalities increased expenditure on child care (Svaleryd 2002). Comparative studies of legislatures across countries or across states in the United States find that as the number of women increases, women introduce more bills dealing with issues of women, children, and families relative to their male counterparts and to other women, accounting for the member's party (Poggione 2004; Thomas 1991). Even accounting for party membership or the party in control of government, higher numbers of women lead to a rise in adoption and scope of maternity and child care leave policies (Kittilson 2008). Female US state house members place a higher priority than men do on these issues (Thomas and Welch 1991; Thomas 1994). Female legislators work to increase family assistance and strengthen child support enforcement (Besley and Case 2003).

In all, women are more concerned with children and the needy than they are with taxes or prices. Men's priorities are the reverse.

How Gender Composition May Matter

As we said in chapter 1, meetings mean discussion in a small group setting, and discussions in small groups in turn typically mean that women interact with men. Gender role theory provides a good starting point for thinking about what happens in the course of this interaction. To recap our earlier discussion: this theory posits that the greater the number of women in the group, the more that women will be inclined to express their views. Women are probably reluctant to speak to their distinctive concerns when surrounded by many men and when the task is a collective decision on a matter that is not defined as a domain of competence for women. Women continue to be less likely than men to view themselves as qualified to deal with politics, to talk about it, to tell others what to think or do about it, and to decide it. That is, women view themselves in a way that gives them lower status as members of a group discussing politics. And men may view women accordingly and act to reinforce and further depress women's low status in their group. The more men in the group, the stronger these effects are likely to grow.

In addition, women are socialized to engage in cooperative discussion, while men tend to engage in more competitive and assertive forms of exchange. The more men in the group, the more the discussion is likely to reflect a norm of assertion. A balance of members tilted toward men may create stereotypically masculine characteristics for the exchange. The discussion dynamic may take on the characteristics of individual agency rather than mutual assistance.

For these reasons, gender role theory predicts that when women are the gender minority in discussions of politics, they not only speak less, feel less confident, and exercise less influence than men, they will also be less likely to bring up views that society deems women's concern, and that men may not share. The fewer women in the group, the less we will hear women's distinctive concerns.

We also revisit the enclave hypothesis from gender role theory. We ask whether all-female groups act as a protected space that fosters women's full participation. Here we investigate specifically whether gender homogeneity produces a stronger voice for women's distinctive issues.

However, as we have emphasized, all this is subject to a big fat "it depends." And what it depends on is the decision rule. Scholars have long known that unanimous rule creates norms of consensus and inclusion. If you want people to cooperate, yoke them to each other, up the stakes, and don't give them a way out. That is, in a nutshell, what unanimous rule can do. What it can do for women specifically is to bring their distinctive concerns into the discussion. Unanimous rule can compensate for the disadvantages of status in the group.

But as we noted in earlier chapters, unanimous rule is a double-edged sword; it can help women in the minority but hurt women in the majority. It may prevent women from leveraging the power of numbers when they are the majority. For the same reason that minority women do better under unanimous than majority rule, majority women may do better with majority rule than with unanimous rule.

We expect that the frequency of women's references to issues of distinctive concern to women will shift with the circumstances of women's representation in deliberation. When women are a numerical minority under majority rule, they speak up less often and carry less influence in the group, as we detailed in chapter 5. But our argument is that the loss of authority and standing also affects what women *say* when they do contribute to the group discussion. Lacking empowerment, they may feel not only less qualified to speak but also specifically more reluctant to speak about their distinctive priorities as women, unless protected by unanimous rule. These settings may make salient women's tendency to view themselves as less expert and competent in politics. The norms created by unanimous rule may help women by signaling to them that their distinctive concerns are a legitimate topic of conversation. This effect can be seen in contrast to circumstances where women participate less than men.

Specifically, our interaction hypothesis predicts the following: (1) Women will mention care issues the least, and succeed the least in aligning the group's decision with those issues, as minorities under majority rule, because their low numbers disadvantage them. (2) Women will mention care issues most, shifting the outcome accordingly, as majorities under majority rule, where they benefit from high numbers without the encumbrance of a consensus norm empowering minority men. (3) Minority women will mention care issues, with corresponding outcomes, more under unanimous than majority rule, while (4) majority women will do the reverse.

Thus our interaction hypothesis is a departure from the hypothesis of gender role theory. Our hypothesis makes the same prediction that gender role theory does about the benefits of increasing numbers of women, but only under majority rule. It contradicts gender role theory by arguing that minority women are not inevitably quiescent about women's distinctive issues when they are a minority, because unanimous rule protects them. Finally, it adds predictions about the disadvantages majority women under unanimous rule experience.[6]

A final caveat is in order: as in our earlier analysis, we need to address the possibility that differences apparently due to gender are spuriously caused by preferences or attitudes correlated with individual gender. We examine deliberation about redistribution, so political attitudes, especially regarding egalitarianism, are a possible confounding factor (Crowder-Meyer 2007; Shapiro and Mahajan 1986). We control for the individual's egalitarianism and for the

[6] We do not expect substantial differences by rule among the all-female groups because there we expect norms of inclusion regardless of rule.

number of egalitarians in the group. We also replicate the results with controls on the person's predeliberation redistribution preferences and their membership in the predeliberation preference majority.

Data and Methods

As we noted in chapter 4, participants in our experiment were told that they would be performing tasks to earn money and that the money they actually received would be based on a group decision about how much, if any, income redistribution to undertake, using unanimous or majority rule. We provided an explanation of several principles of redistribution and instructed participants to reach a group decision that would not only apply concretely and immediately to themselves but also could apply hypothetically to society, in order to generalize beyond the lab to the decisions people make about redistribution in politics. And as we explained in chapter 4, groups followed these instructions by exploring together how the principles would work outside the experimental setting.

Here we focus on the issue content of the group discussions by examining the specific words participants used. Our word categories correspond to the issue priorities we identified above as of distinctive concern to women: (1) children, (2) family (as a related concept to care for children), (3) poor, and (4) needy. For contrast, we chose three other categories for the purpose of discriminant validity: (1) rich, (2) salary, and (3) taxes. "Rich" resembles children, families, and the poor in referencing a social group, but it is not a social group that women prioritize. It serves as a placebo for references to social groups. The remaining two categories ("salary" and "taxes") reflect the distinctive priorities we identified above for men. We expect that references to issues of distinctive concern to women will rise in the conditions that give rise to gender equality, while references to the remaining categories will not.

We chose not to define women's distinctive priorities based on the most frequently used words uttered by women and those uttered by men in our discussions, because that would be tautological. That is, we want to see how the conditions alter the frequencies of topics that women care more about, and thus we cannot use that same frequency to define the topics that women care more about. Instead, we rely on the variety of settings listed above to reveal women's, and men's distinctive priorities, including their choice of occupations, their budget priorities, their responses to questions about the nation's most important problems in one-on-one survey interviews, and so on. That way we are not contaminating our measure of women's distinctive priorities with the effects of women's status in the measurement situation. We can get a clean measure of the concept of issue priorities by defining it a priori and see if it moves up or down with the conditions in our study.

We defined the categories using standard dictionaries for words associated with the topics of children, family, needy, and poor, and for rich, taxes, and salary, following the synonyms of each word in turn to their synonyms, and ruling out false positives by human checking. We also checked this list against related category lists in the Linguistic Inquiry and Word Count software (LIWC), a widely used program for linguistic analysis in the behavioral sciences, to ensure that we did not miss any relevant words (Newman et al. 2008). We use the LIWC software to conduct the word counts and calculate the percentage of the person's total words for each category, though we do not use LIWC's predefined categories since they are neither as comprehensive nor as relevant for our needs as our custom-constructed and human-verified categories.[7] See chapter appendix B for the list of words.

We replicated our results with another method, using the TM module in the R statistical package. This method differs from the other in using only the most-frequent words the speakers in our sample uttered. This method first identifies the words most frequently used by our sample as a whole, regardless of their relevance to any topic. It then produces for each word its proportion of each person's total words. We classified these most-frequent words based on their relevance to the topics we identified a priori above. Thus this method guards against the possibility that we are missing some frequently used, relevant words.[8]

We compute two versions of the dependent variable: (1) a dummy variable indicating whether or not the person mentioned any words in that category at least once (*Mention*), and (2) the number of the person's words falling into the category (*Frequency*) per one thousand words spoken.[9] When multiplied by the total number of women in the group, even small individual increases in *Frequency* can mean dramatic changes in the number of times the concept is raised overall during the group's deliberation. In a twenty- to thirty-minute conversation, for example, raising a topic an additional nine to ten times represents a significant shift in the focus of the discussion.

When Do Women Talk about Issues of Distinctive Concern to Women?

As we saw in chapter 5, descriptive representation elevates women's participation and perceived influence, but the decision rule fundamentally alters this effect. When women are assigned to be the numerical minority in groups in-

[7] We tried other more elaborate computer-based techniques that scale text, but LIWC most fully suited our aims for these analyses.

[8] The words identified by the two methods overlap, suggesting that the words we chose a priori are among the most often used, but they differ enough that the similar results provide somewhat independent replication.

[9] On average, women spoke approximately 700 words over 3.5 minutes, while men spoke approximately 800 words over 4 minutes, but as shown in chapter 5, averages vary significantly across the experimental conditions.

structed to decide by majority rule, they are significantly less likely to speak than anyone else. In other words, minority women under majority rule speak less than men in their groups, men in the same minority status, and women in other groups. Unanimous rule seems to protect minority women's deliberative participation from the inequalities that arise when women are a minority, though unanimous rule also empowers men when they are the numerical minority, leading them to participate at disproportionately high rates. Increasing the descriptive representation—that is, women's proportions—under majority rule increases not only speech participation but other forms of substantive representation as well. The less any person spoke (woman or man), the less influential they were rated by other members of their group, so that low descriptive representation depresses perceptions of influence in the discussion in part by affecting quiescence.

With those findings in mind, we now turn to the effects of experimentally induced descriptive representation and decision rule on the issue content of deliberation. Our main interest is how often women discuss the topics we identified as distinctive to women—namely, children, family, the poor, and the needy. We will refer to these issues as "Care" issues, and the issues of salary and taxes as "Financial" issues.

Such references can be found throughout the transcripts. For example, in the midst of a discussion about how much is needed to survive in today's society, a woman asks, "Let's say there's one person who's bringing the income and then a spouse and a child or something like that, or you could even spend it as a single, like, mother who's working with two kids. How much do they need to get by or something like that?" To this question, another female participant replies, "Oh, goodness, I'd say a single person raising two children? At least 50 [$50,000], I mean because if you figure you're keeping a roof over their head, food on the table, clothes, electricity, plumbing, I mean just paying the minimum bills. You know what I mean you've got kids growing, they're going to need clothes and food." Another group of women discussed their personal experiences with poverty. One female participant volunteers, "[I'd] consider a hand-out because I'm poor. My husband is college educated. I'm trying to go to school, and I have two children, nursing one of them." These are two typical examples of how themes of children, family, poverty, and the needs of vulnerable populations emerged in the deliberation.

To make clear how we coded the discussions systematically, and to illustrate how the conditions shaped these word counts, consider the following two contrasting examples, one from the relatively gender-egalitarian condition of majority-female, majority rule, and one from the gender-inegalitarian condition of minority-female, majority rule. In the first example, the group consists of four women and one man and uses majority rule. A woman introduces the topic of children, using it to highlight the needs of children and the difficulties of those who care for them. A man then takes up the topic sympathetically.

In the second example, the group is composed of two women and three men and uses majority rule. A woman tries to initiate a discussion of her brother who has Down syndrome (where "brother" indicates the topic of family) and is twice interrupted by a man, who brings the discussion back to a more abstract topic. In this way, such groups give women's distinctive topics much less attention. We have highlighted the words that our method counts as belonging to one of women's distinctive topics:

Gender-egalitarian condition: Majority women, majority rule

0:09:01	Woman A: Well you just have a little **baby** that's one thing. Try getting you know a single mom and two **teenagers** or [crosstalk] high and my fees are almost a thousand dollars a year to send my **kids** to school. You know what I mean it's like—
0:09:15	Woman B: I honestly have no idea.
0:09:17	Man D: But, but we're just saying like one **child** and let's say he's you know eighteen or sixteen or something so we're in high school, one **kid**—
0:09:24	Woman B: [interposing] And driving—
0:09:26	Man D: —sixteen driving sure and I think that takes a lot more money than like one **baby** would or something 'cause that's true it changes everything.

In the previous exchange, issues of children and family take center stage, with both men and women contributing their views and personal experiences about the challenges of raising kids on limited income. In the next conversation, though, the special needs some families might face are completely marginalized, and the woman who attempts to raise them is interrupted, then ignored. She cannot even finish her sentence about her special needs brother.

Gender-inegalitarian condition: Minority women, majority rule

0:19:49	Woman C: [interposing] Like my **brother** has Down syndrome—
0:19:49	Man E: [interposing] But what is our goal? Our goal is the overall—
0:19:51	Woman C: [interposing] —he's never going to make—
0:19:51	Man E: —group's effectiveness right?
0:19:54	Woman A: We're also still going for society, though.

0:19:54 Man B: [interposing] Our group is to find an idea that we feel is most just for—
0:19:56 Man D: is most just.
0:19:57 Man B: —for society.
0:19:59 Man E: So it's not to maximize our efforts.
0:20:00 Man B: No. It's just to find a thing that we feel that is most just for society.
0:20:04 Man D: You know, to find a balance between well we want to maximize but we also want to help. I mean there's got to be a balance. We just find the best.
0:20:09 Woman C: Right.
0:20:09 Man B: Yeah.

A third example also illustrates this point that men are more likely to discuss and validate the concerns of women when women have higher status in the group. In the example below, men outnumber the female speaker, but the group decides by unanimity. The woman introduces concerns about the welfare of parents and children, and a man in the group adopts similar language and validates her concerns.

Gender-egalitarian condition: Minority women, unanimous rule

0:18:42 Woman B: Well if we're going to talk about the single **mom** with two **kids** again I worry about if, if there's—we're just getting by and getting by means not having the cable or something like that I agree with that statement. I can't argue that, but I think getting by eliminates no incentive again if you were a single and you have two little **kids** and you have a lot more expenses than some—a single person would with the same amount of income so I still think that we're leaving that group behind, but I'm not sure it's the right choice.
0:19:23 Man C: You're [crosstalk] the single **parent** with the **children**?
0:19:25 Woman B: Single **parent** with the **children** and also just maybe someone with a **handicap**. They're going to have more medical expenses, they're going to have more, and what do we do with these people? I mean if, if you can't give them some kind of hope at the end of the day and they're just getting by that's when I think people turn to extremes.
0:19:50 Man C: So you're, you're concerned that setting a certain specific dollar amount might not be adequate to a certain **person's needs** so I mean to people who are at the certain

dollar amount one of them might actually have more needs than that—Interesting, okay.

0:20:04 Woman B: [interposing] Correct.

These examples illustrate three notable exchanges, but our effort in counting words is to identify more systematic trends that occur across the experimental conditions. While our word count method has the virtues of simplicity and ease of systematic analysis, it cannot tell us what is being said *about* these categories. The biggest threat to the validity of our scheme is the possibility that a person mentions the category in order to articulate a position against assisting people in it. To rule out the possibility that speakers mention women's distinctive topics unsympathetically, we classified each mention as sympathetic, neutral, or negative. The unit of analysis is the speaking turn containing a reference to a topic of distinctive concern to women (N = 1,926, which contains the entire set of "care" words we analyze below). For example, negative mentions include: "rob from the rich to give to the poor." Examples of sympathetic phrases are: "whether the poor ever get help by anyone, that is not even raised here"; "if like the range is like 50,000 or whatever . . . then the poorer they don't get anything. It's kind of risky"; "I thought maximize the floor income was, that was my number one, help those who have the least." We found that only 5.0% are negative. That is, mentions of the vulnerable or needy are rarely unsympathetic.[10]

Do the conditions that affect the quantity of women's participation in the group discussion also affect the content of their participation? The bottom line is "yes." Women's average *Frequency* of words referencing care issues varies considerably across these conditions. In chapter 5 we found that the condition that most disadvantages women's floor time and influence is majority rule and minority women. Consistent with this finding, we now see that women's average *Frequency* of care issues in this setting is 6.3 words per 1,000—about half the *Frequency* in any of the other settings.[11] Conversely, the setting that stands out for producing the greatest *Frequency* of women's references to care issues is the same setting where women's influence and speaking are highest (nearly 15 per 1,000)—majority rule with majority women.[12] *Frequency* is in between these

[10]Neutral, 79.8%, and positive, 11.7%. The remaining 3.5% are false positives (word usages that did not turn out to be relevant to "care" issues; example: "that is a *poor* choice of words"). Also, among the entire sample, children, family, poor, and needy are more often mentioned by women than by men; salary is the reverse. Taxes, which groups are explicitly asked to discuss, are mentioned equally. The difference by gender (clustering by group) is significant for children, poor, and salary. However, these global gender differences are much less important to our argument than the changes across conditions.

[11]These are raw means for all care issues summed, in mixed-gender groups. In all-female groups, *Frequency* is high across both rules (13.2 in unanimous and 14.6 in majority).

[12]The difference from groups with minority women is significant at $p < 0.01$, two-tailed t-test. This result is very similar using *Mention*, which also shows a large, statistically significant difference across these conditions ($p < 0.01$). "Combined" for *Mention* means averages of *Mention* for the four topics.

two extremes for unanimous rule groups with minority or majority women (11 words per 1,000 in each of these two conditions).

These percentages represent substantial changes in the emphasis of the discussion. And when multiplied by the total number of women in the group, even small individual increases can significantly affect the number of times the concept is raised overall. We will see more clearly how meaningful this number of references is a bit further on, when we contrast it against the percentage of references devoted to topics that are not women's distinctive concern.

We now turn to regression analysis, with the individual as the unit of analysis. We employ probit for *Mention* (since it is coded either 0 for no references or 1 for one or more references) and OLS for *Frequency*, with cluster robust standard errors.[13] (Descriptives and coding for all variables are in the online appendix.) We use two models: a dummy variable model, containing a set of dummy variables representing each condition, and the same linear model we used in earlier chapters, containing a dummy variable for majority (1) versus unanimous (0) rule, a variable counting the number of women, and a variable that multiplies the two. We control on number of egalitarians in the group (as a count from 0 to 5), a dummy variable for experimental site, the person's predeliberation egalitarianism, and (for *Mention)* the log of the person's overall word count (see chapter appendix table A7.1 for details).[14]

Figure 7.1 displays the predicted values for the topics we identified as of distinctive concern to women: the poor, children, family, and the "needy," depicting the overall *Frequency* summed over the four care topics (see chapter appendix tables A7.1 and A7.2 for the models used to predict these results; *Mention* is presented in chapter appendix figure A7.1). If descriptive representation enhances substantive representation, then it will increase talk on women's distinctive concerns. And that is what we find, but, as predicted, only under majority rule. As the number of women increases, so too does the percentage of women who reference care topics. The effect is quite large. As the number of women in the group increases from one to four, *Frequency* for the care topics increases by more than sevenfold, moving from 2.3 to 16.1 words per 1,000; for *Mention*, the average probability of referencing one of the care topics increases from 16% to 54%.[15] This same upward trend can be seen for the summary measure of all care issues, and also each of its constituent parts is examined separately (see figure

[13] We also employed OLS on *Mention*, finding similar results.

[14] Women in our sample as in others are somewhat more egalitarian. We do not include an explicit control for word count when the DV is *Frequency*, as this measure already controls for overall verbosity in its denominator. Figure 7.1 displays the sum of the predicted values for the individual elements of the content categories from chapter appendix table A7.1. See chapter appendix table A7.2 for models in which the dependent variable is a summary measure of all care or financial categories. Both approaches yield essentially identical results.

[15] Female enclaves are essentially the same as groups with four women. Chapter appendix figure A7.2 shows that the pattern of results described above is not limited to only one topic.

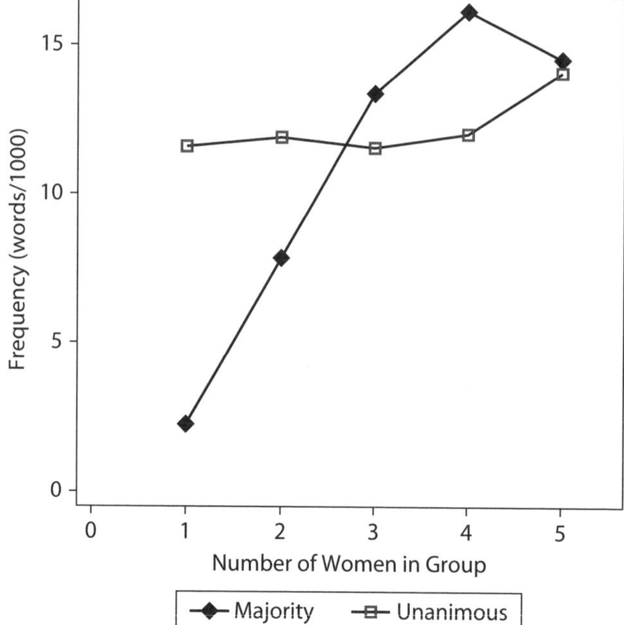

Figure 7.1. Frequency of care words used among women, by rule (predicted values).

A7.2 in the appendix to this chapter). Moreover, there is no effect under unanimous rule on either *Mention* or *Frequency*. However, when women are the minority in their group, they are much more likely to mention care issues and to use them with greater frequency under unanimity rule than under majority rule.[16]

Notably, figure 7.2 shows that the increasing talk of care issues in figure 7.1 is not found for financial issues (panel A) or for the placebo category of "rich" (panel B). In fact, if anything, talk of financial issues declines as the number of women increases, though nearly all the decline occurs between groups with one woman and groups with two women; in groups with more than one woman, women's talk of financial issues remains relatively constant and low.[17]

Recall that a second hypothesis from gender role theory predicts that women flourish in all-female settings. However, here, enclaves do not substantially increase care issue references above groups in which women predominate. Women

[16]These differences are tested using raw data and a difference of proportions test for *Mention* ($z = 3.12$, $p < 0.01$, two-tailed) and a difference of means test for *Frequency* ($t = 2.49$, $p = 0.02$, two-tailed). Tests of predicted probabilities from linear models with controls (table 7.1 or table A7.1) confirm these results.

[17]As seen in figure 7.2, and verified with TM. The effect of number of women (one to four) on financial issues using TM is -0.196, SE = 0.066, p = 0.004, controlling on site, including a majority rule dummy and rule × number of women, excluding all-female groups.

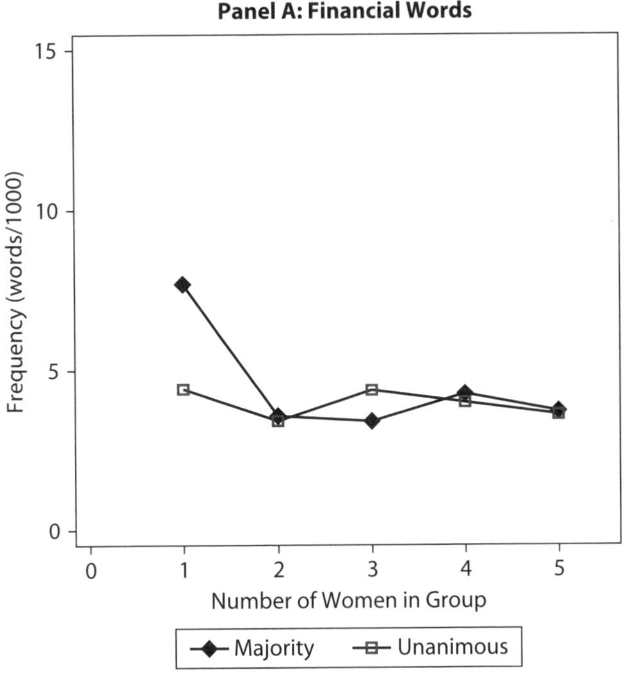

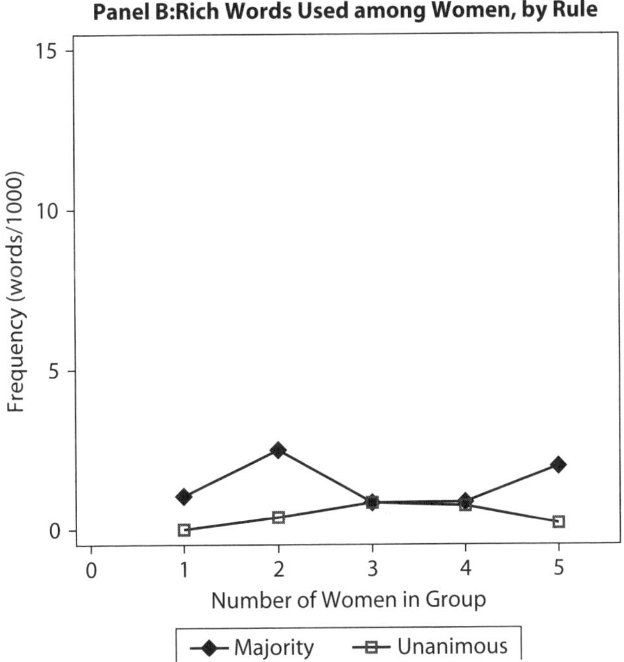

Figure 7.2. Frequency of financial and rich words used among women, by rule (predicted values). *Top*: Financial words; *Bottom*: Rich words.

raise care issues frequently in all-female groups under both decision rules, but not at a greater rate than in three-female or four-female groups.

As a further test of our predicted interaction of rule and gender composition, we estimated our familiar linear model for the mixed-gender groups. Table 7.1 shows that the interaction term is significant, confirming that the effect of descriptive representation differs under the two rules. In addition to controlling for group and individual egalitarianism in all these models, we also ran each analysis omitting these controls, or replacing them with controls for predeliberation preferences and/or subjects' age in a variety of different configurations, including a fully saturated model in which we interact the number of egalitarians in the group with the decision rule. The inclusion or exclusion of age, egalitarianism, or predeliberation preference controls has no effect on any of our key findings with respect to the use of care topics.[18] The magnitude and standard error of the key interaction term is virtually unchanged no matter what set of controls we use.[19] In addition, when we remove the individual-level controls and explore our interactive model at the group-level only (Models 5 and 6 of table 7.1), we again find the same, strong evidence of an interaction between decision rules and gender composition.[20]

When women are outnumbered, the paucity of care topics can be quite striking. Under majority rule, lone women *never* mention family, and only 11% mention children. Only 13% of minority women mention children at least once. In the unanimous condition, however, 46% of minority women mention children (with similar findings for family; $p < 0.01$ for children and family; all from raw means). When in the majority, 42% of women mention children in the majority-rule condition, compared with 47% under the unanimous condition. Women's quiescence can reach the level of complete silence, making unanimous rule all the more important in protecting minority women's voice.

We replicated these results using the TM method, which selects only the most frequently used words in the study. Among the most frequently used words are two that reference education ("school" and "education"). We reviewed the studies

[18]The overall correlation between gender and egalitarianism is moderate (0.36 for the group-level relationship between number of women and number of egalitarians). Our regression results for women are nearly identical if we control for liberalism instead of egalitarianism (see Mendelberg, Karpowitz, and Goedert forthcoming.).

[19]For a graphical representation of the small difference made by including controls, see online appendix figure C7.1, which presents the predicted values for women in the majority-rule condition from models with and without controls. In addition, adding controls for age, education, or income (not shown) make no difference to the individual-level results in any of the models reported in the chapter.

[20]The dependent variable in the group-level models is the average *Frequency* of care issues for women in the group. Adding controls to the group-level models for the number of participants above the median for age or income shows that those indicators have no effect. Adding a control for the number of college graduates also does not alter the effect of gender composition, but there is an additional effect of the number of college graduates on women's references to care issues. Women who are college graduates tend to reference care issues more often than those who have not yet graduated from college in settings where women are empowered.

Table 7.1: *Frequency* of Care Issue Mentions among Women: Egalitarianism Controls vs. Preference Controls

	(1) Egalitarianism Controls	(2) Saturated Egalitarianism Controls	(3) Preference Controls 1	(4) Preference Controls 2	(5) Group-Level Analysis	(6) Group-Level Analysis
Majority Rule	−1.091 **	−0.820	−0.959**	−1.015**	−1.196***	−1.009*
	(0.451)	(0.527)	(0.448)	(0.443)	(0.434)	(0.515)
Number of Women	0.013	−0.003	0.044	0.017	0.004	−0.009
	(0.090)	(0.088)	(0.088)	(0.086)	(0.112)	(0.114)
Majority Rule × Number of Women	0.389**	0.443**	0.344**	0.366**	0.427***	0.467***
	(0.158)	(0.177)	(0.154)	(0.155)	(0.160)	(0.171)
Individual Egalitarianism	−1.005**	−1.014**	—	—	—	—
	(0.488)	(0.478)				
Number of Egalitarians	−0.006	0.072	—	—	−0.055	0.001
	(0.144)	(0.111)			(0.091)	(0.123)
Majority Rule × Number of Egalitar-ians	—	−0.148	—	—	—	−0.108
		(0.191)				(0.159)
PrPredeliberation Preference for Floor Principle	—	—	−0.215*	—	—	—
			(0.109)			
Predeliberation Preference for Maxi-mum Redistribution Principle	—	—	—	−0.182	—	—
				(0.221)		
PredeliberationPreference for No Redistribution	—	—	—	−0.212	—	—
				(0.305)		
Preferred Principle Matched Pref. Majority	—	—	−0.234	−0.092	—	—
			(0.149)	(0.179)		
Constant	1.433***	1.278***	1.257***	0.991***	1.096***	0.989**
	(0.382)	(0.372)	(0.330)	(0.326)	(0.341)	(0.376)
Observations	157	157	156	157	64	64
R-squared	0.131	0.138	0.123	0.111	0.211	0.218
Control for Experimental Location	Yes	Yes	Yes	Yes	Yes	Yes

Note: Standard errors in parentheses (cluster robust standard errors for individual-level analysis). Groups composed of five women excluded. *** $p < 0.01$, ** $p < 0.05$, * $p < 0.10$, two-tailed test.

we noted above and education is in fact among the issues that women tend to emphasize in various settings, including choice of college majors (Carnevale, Strohl, and Melton 2011); as Crowder-Meyer found that women are "about seventy-five percent more likely than men to believe education is the most important problem facing the U.S." (2007, 13). We grouped "school" and "education" with the care category, and find the same interaction pattern with these new words and with the overall care category generated by TM (see chapter appendix A for words and see chapter appendix table A7.3 for the linear interaction model using this alternate construction of care). Thus these two separate approaches—LIWC and TM—produce the same result. Women mention topics of distinctive concern to them less often in group settings where they are disempowered.

When Do Women Introduce Topics of Distinctive Concern to Women?

How do care issues get on the agenda in the first place? An important measure of women's exercise of voice is whether they introduce the topics of distinctive concern to them into the deliberation. Figure 7.3 depicts how often a woman was

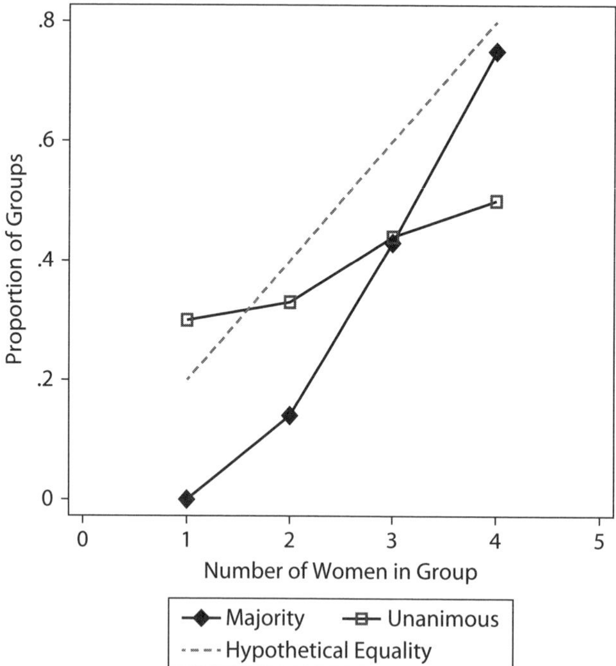

Figure 7.3. First mention of care topic by women (raw means, by group). Note: The y-axis represents the portion of groups in which women mentioned care topics first.

the first one within the group to mention a topic of specific concern to women, coded at the group level. The dotted line in figure 7.3 shows how often women would mention care topics first if there were no difference between men and women (for example, women would be first mentioners 40% of the time when they composed 40% of the group). When women are in the minority, the first mention of a care topic was made by a woman in only 6% of groups under majority rule, but in 31% of groups under unanimity rule ($p < 0.04$, one-tailed, raw means). The difference between rules disappears when women are the majority (53% under majority versus 47% under unanimity rule, n.s.).

Table 7.2 examines the effect of the conditions on the probability of first mention of care in an individual-level probit model with controls for individuals'

Table 7.2: Probability of First Mention of Care Category among Women

	(1) Egalitarianism Controls	(2) Saturated Egalitarianism Controls
Majority Rule	−1.620**	−1.262
	(0.761)	(0.821)
Number of Women	−0.199	−0.223
	(0.150)	(0.155)
Majority Rule × Number of Women	0.478**	0.570**
	(0.223)	(0.241)
Percent of Care Mentions	0.053	0.047
	(0.103)	(0.112)
Speaker's Percent Talk	1.610	1.555
	(1.015)	(0.994)
Individual Egalitarianism	−0.449	−0.517
	(0.865)	(0.864)
Number of Egalitarians	0.101	0.216
	(0.109)	(0.144)
Majority Rule × Number of Egalitarians	—	−0.217
	—	(0.182)
Constant	−0.820	−1.005
	(0.659)	(0.660)
Observations	157	157
Pseudo R2	0.053	0.060
Control for Experimental Location	Yes	Yes

Note: Entries are probit coefficients. The dependent variable is the probability that an individual woman will make the first mention of a word in one of the four care categories. Individual-level analysis. Cluster robust standard errors in parentheses. Women in all-female groups excluded. *** $p < 0.01$, ** $p < 0.05$, * $p < 0.10$, two-tailed test.

"care" *Frequency*, verbosity, egalitarianism, and on location and the number of egalitarians in the model.[21] The interaction of rule and composition remains strong and significant. Thus both group- and individual-level analyses lead to the same conclusion: women talk more about the topics they prioritize and are more likely to introduce those topics in the first place in conditions that empower them by the combination of numbers and rule.

The pattern is familiar. Under majority rule, the average woman in the majority is the first to mention care issues much more often than the average minority woman; there is no such effect of gender composition under unanimity. The magnitudes are again striking: for example, *no* lone woman is the first to mention care issues under majority rule, but a lone woman produces the *highest* chance of mentions under unanimous rule, underscoring the importance of decision rule.

How Do Women's Distinctive Issues Compare to Men's Distinctive Issues?

We can get a clearer picture of women's substantive representation by examining the relative balance of care and financial topics across the conditions. We do this by computing the ratio of average *Frequency* of care topics to average *Frequency* of financial topics for each individual in the experiment.[22] The ratios are shown in figure 7.4 (raw means by condition) and support our interaction hypothesis.[23] Majority status matters under majority but not unanimous rule:

[21] The DV is coded 1 if the person was the first to mention any of the care issues, 0 otherwise. This variable is always 1 for one member of each group, and 0 for all other members; some groups have no mentions of one or more care categories, but every group includes at least one mention of *some* care category. The results become stronger when controls for a person's percent of care mentions and their overall percentage of group speech are omitted. Results are similar when excluding the controls for location/egalitarianism/number of egalitarians, and they remain robust when controls for age, education, and income are included.

[22] This ratio is computed by dividing the individual's average *Frequency* per care topic by his or her average *Frequency* per financial topic. We adjust for the number of topics in order to avoid the artificial inflation that could result from the fact that there are more care topics (four—children, family, poor, and needy) than financial topics (two—salary and taxes). Even with that adjustment, the magnitude of this ratio is largely a function of the unequal number of possible words in the care and financial categories. Thus its absolute magnitude does not imply a general female advantage or disadvantage. If an individual made no references to financial topics, the ratio is undefined and not included in the analysis. When we include these individuals by assigning them a very low financial *Frequency* and imputing the ratio, the results are very similar to the patterns we see in the figures. We do not include these imputed values in our analyses, however, because of the inherent uncertainty about exactly what the assigned financial *Frequency* should be. Small differences in the assigned value can make a large difference in the ratio.

[23] We combine groups in which women are a minority (one- and two-women groups) and groups with a majority of women (three- and four-women groups) to simplify the presentation of results and avoid the problem of small N in groups with a single woman.

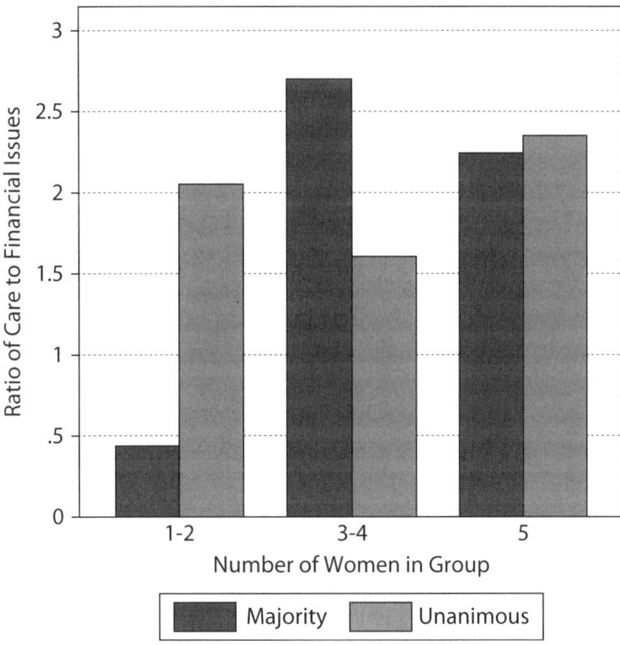

Figure 7.4. Ratio of care words to financial words among women (raw means).

the average woman's ratio of care to financial topics increases under majority rule, from 0.44 as a minority to 2.7 as a majority ($p < 0.01$), but declines slightly and not significantly under unanimous rule (from 2.05 as a minority to 1.61 as a majority, $p = 0.29$). These numbers also show that unanimous rule helps women who are outnumbered by men (0.44 under majority rule and 2.05 under unanimous rule, $p = 0.02$). Finally, the interaction between gender composition and decision rule is significant, meaning that the effect of increased numbers is different under majority rule than under unanimity ($p < 0.01$).[24] Numbers benefit women only under majority rule, while unanimous rule protects minority women's voice.

We have focused primarily on women since it is women's voice that is at issue in the theoretical and political debates that prompt this study. Figure 7.5 displays predicted values for men (using the same model as above) and shows that the average man is also affected by women's descriptive representation

[24] All tests are two-tailed and are computed using predicted values from a regression model with controls. We regress the ratio of care to financial topics on a dummy variable for majority rule, a dummy variable for whether the group had a majority of women, and the interaction between the two; models include controls for egalitarianism, the number of egalitarians in the group, the interaction between rule and the number of egalitarians, and experimental location. We predict values from the model and conduct a formal Wald test of the difference between the predicted values.

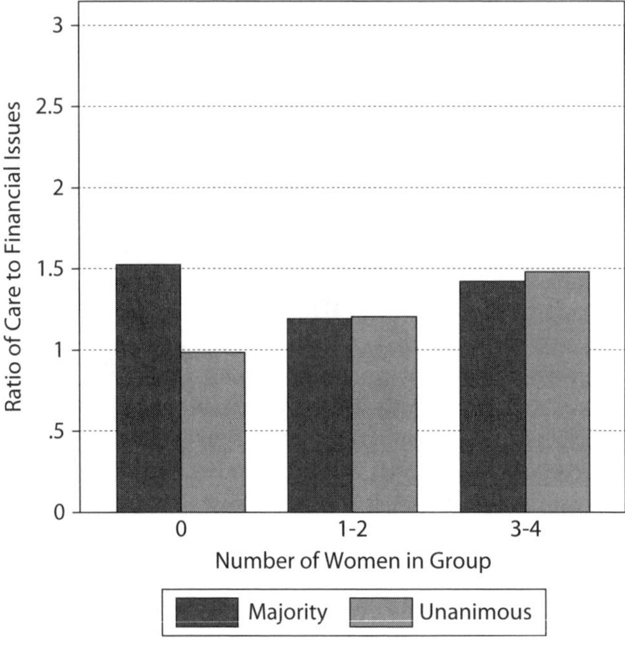

Figure 7.5. Ratio of care words to financial words among men (raw means).

under majority rule, but by a more modest magnitude than the average woman: the ratio of care to financial *Frequency* increases from 1.19 (with female minorities) to 1.42 (with female majorities). Under unanimous rule, the ratio increase is similar, from 1.20 to 1.48. In addition, unanimous rule does not substantially elevate the average man's relative emphasis on women's priorities when women are a minority—unanimous rule protects minority *women's* voice but does not empower women to influence *men's* speech.[25]

Men are, however, affected by the experimental conditions with respect to the topic that is most distinctively women's concern: children. Under majority rule with one woman present, only 19% of men raise the topic of children, versus 69% who mention salary-related issues. However, surrounded by four women, men's focus reverses: 62% now mention children as compared to 50% who discuss salary.[26] But the effects of gender composition do not extend to

[25] The figure also appears to show a difference across rule for male enclaves, but this difference is driven entirely by two men in one group whose ratio measures are more than three standard deviations above the mean for the sample. In the absence of those two outliers, the ratio for male enclaves is identical across rule and low.

[26] These are raw means; from the model with controls (*Mention*, chapter appendix table A7.1), we can see that the increase in men's propensity to mention children is statistically significant ($p = 0.01$), but it is only when women are a supermajority under majority rule that men mention this most stereotypically feminine topic more often.

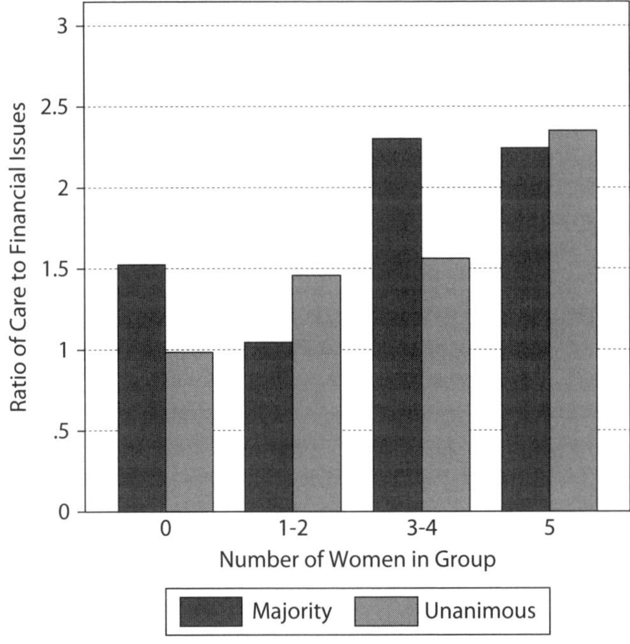

Figure 7.6. Ratio of care words to financial words, all participants (raw means).

discussions of the poor or the needy (predicted probabilities from the dummy model using *Mention*, chapter appendix table A7.1). Overall, figure 7.5 shows evidence of movement in the direction of a higher ratio of care to financial issues, but the movement is modest and not statistically robust.

Finally, the overall substantive representation of women's distinctive issues can also be measured by the average ratio for all participants, including both women and men. Figure 7.6 shows that when they are empowered by the combination of the rule and their numbers, women can move the overall focus of the group discussion. The ratio of care to financial *Frequency* goes up substantially—more than doubling—as women go from minority to majority, but only under majority rule, where it increases from 1.04 to 2.30 (p = 0.01, two-tailed).[27] For unanimous rule the effect of gender composition on the group is much smaller, from 1.45 to 1.52, and not statistically significant.[28] Women need the joint power of large numbers and a rule that favors large numbers to have the biggest effect on the terms of the group discussion. Unlike the finding on women's talk and consistent with men's talk, unanimous rule confers no statistically discernible benefits over majority rule in minority-female

[27] The formal test of significance is the same as described above, but the models include all participants in the sample.

[28] The difference-in-differences in the effect of gender composition under majority, as opposed to unanimous, rule is significant at p = 0.03 (two-tailed).

groups (the ratios increase from 1.04 under majority rule to 1.45 under unanimous rule).[29] Despite their increased attention to issues of care, women's small numbers make it difficult for them to affect the overall tenor of the discussion.

Are Women's Voices Disadvantaged Relative to Men's?

So far we have not asked if women's voices are disadvantaged relative to men's—that is, if a gender gap in voice exists, or how it changes with the conditions. We do so using the *Mention* measure, which can be interpreted as the chance that a given person refers to the issue and allows us to move the question from how much a person talks to how many people talk. We ask whether women are less likely to raise their distinctive concerns than men are to raise theirs in the conditions prevalent in the real world—majority rule and minority women. The answer is yes. In these conditions, women's probability of mentioning care issues is 57%; men's probability of mentioning financial issues is 81% ($p < 0.03$). Thus in most political settings there is a gender gap in voice. When women compose a majority under majority rule, the percentages reverse: 89% for women and care, versus 68% for men and financial, respectively (they differ at $p < 0.04$; see figure A7.3 in the appendix to this chapter for a graphical representation of the percentages in this paragraph).[30] But that is not the only way to remedy women's disadvantage. Leaving women as a minority but changing the decision rule from majority to unanimous also helps, raising women's probability of mentioning care issues to 91% and lowering men's probability of mentioning financial issues to 72% (in these groups, these percentages differ at $p < 0.05$). That is, women are severely disadvantaged relative to men as a minority under majority rule and heavily advantaged as a majority under majority rule or as a minority under unanimous rule.[31] (As a majority under unanimous rule, there is virtually no gender gap and nearly each individual mentions their gender's distinctive issues.)

We can see these patterns in the following example where a female participant introduces feminine issues, but the others do not take up the topic though they give them passing attention. The topic quickly shifts to the potential benefits of taxing the highest earners. The man shifts the topic from issues important to women (bold, underlined) with words connected to financial issues (bold, italicized).

[29] Under unanimity, the group's *overall* ratio of care to financial *Frequency* rises slightly as the number of women in the group increases. This increase does not contradict our hypotheses, however, because the *average female* frequency does not rise under unanimous rule.

[30] These are raw means; the same relative effects obtain from predicted probabilities for *Mention* using controls for locations, egalitarianism, and log word count.

[31] The advantage minority women receive from unanimous rule does not mean that the overall ratio of care to financial issues changes dramatically, in part because where women are outnumbered they receive a much lower weight in the group average.

Gender-inegalitarian condition: Minority women, majority rule

0:04:45	Woman D: It would be easy for you to think that way 'cause that's probably how it's been for you but there's a lot of people that don't have the opportunities and so even though they may have had the ability if given opportunities they'll never know and just **get by**.
0:05:01	Man C: I mean I look at it more as we should let the top pull us up than **the bottom** pull us down.—
0:05:05	Woman D: Hm.
0:05:06	Man C: [interposing] And if you let people with the top keep doing their thing and doing what they can actually do and then, you know,—
0:05:08	Woman D: Hm.
0:05:09	Man C: [interposing] Yeah, give a little bit at **the bottom** but the more that they get unless they would take 10% if they're ***earning*** say a million dollars that 10%—
0:05:19	Woman D: Hm.
0:05:20	Man C: [interposing] is a lot more than a hundred thousand's 10% and whereas if it's just like okay, you know, then if we set a range then why would I want to work 'cause if I'm making 50—and that's the minimum, well cool—
0:05:32	Woman, D: Uhuh. Yeah, I could see how that could happen.

The regressions confirm the effect we can illustrate with qualitative examples. Both types of analysis show that in conditions of gender equality, women introduce women's distinctive topics; when these topics are introduced, subsequent speakers take them up; and women tend to mention these topics to argue for generosity, help, or meeting a need. In conditions with high gender inequality these are less likely, and when a women's distinctive topic is mentioned, it tends to die in the conversation.

Does Talk of Women's Distinctive Issues Decrease Women's Satisfaction and Perceived Influence?

We can also ask how talk of women's distinctive issues affects the way men and women think about their experience during discussion and about their influence in the group. How does the content of the discussion affect deliberators' evaluations of the discussion and of each other? Recall that after the discussion, we asked a variety of questions about how each participant felt about their experiences. These questions include whether the participant felt his or her voice was heard and whether different perspectives were welcome. Response options

Table 7.3: Effects of Person's *Frequency* of Care Issues on Evaluations of Group Functioning

	My Voice Heard		Different Perspectives Welcome	
	Women	Men	Women	Men
Frequency of Care Issues	0.027**	0.019	0.027***	0.037**
	(0.012)	(0.017)	(0.009)	(0.014)
Egalitarianism	0.054	−0.075	0.120	−0.160*
	(0.064)	(0.078)	(0.091)	(0.084)
Number of Egalitarians	−0.009	0.016	−0.011	0.008
	(0.013)	(0.011)	(0.013)	(0.011)
Constant	0.742***	0.828***	0.701***	0.788***
	(0.040)	(0.039)	(0.052)	(0.038)
Observations	157	163	157	163
R-squared	0.033	0.048	0.032	0.061
Control for Experimental Location	Yes	Yes	Yes	Yes

Note: Individual-level analysis. Cluster robust standard errors in parentheses. The coefficient for *Frequency* of Care Issues shows the effect of a 1 percentage point increase in care issues as a percentage of all words spoken. Dependent variables are coded to span from 0 to 1. *** $p < 0.01$, ** $p < 0.05$, * $p < 0.1$, two-tailed test.

were on a five-point scale ranging from "Strongly Disagree" (0) to "Strongly Agree" (1). Table 7.3 shows the effects of the person's frequency of care issues on the person's assessments, for men and women, respectively.

Although the effects are not large—no one left feeling extremely angry or upset—the results in table 7.3 show a number of meaningful consequences from the exercise of women's voice. First, the experiences women have during discussion affect women's perceptions that their voice was heard. The more they mention care issues, the more women felt that what they had to say had been heard during the deliberation.[32] Mentioning care issues does not have this effect on men; though the coefficient is positive for men, it is smaller and not statistically significant.[33] As we might expect from our discussion in chapter 3, men are less likely than women to rest their sense of efficacy on the substance or the dynamics of the conversation.

[32] Results are robust to a variety of different controls, including liberalism, age, education, and income (not shown).

[33] Nor do we find that mentioning financial issues has any effect on men's efficacy. Substituting financial issues for care issues into the results for men in the second column of table 7.3, we find no statistically significant relationship ($p = 0.58$, two-tailed).

Furthermore, the more they talk about care issues, the more women tend to view discussion as airing different perspectives. And in this, they are joined by men. We did not expect men to react to their own focus on care issues, but they do. If anything, men shift even more than women with respect to the assessment that the discussion aired diverse views when care issues are an increased part of their own talk. When they speak to care issues, both genders feel better about the discussion as a whole, but only women's sense of efficacy is clearly affected.[34] We take this as evidence that women's sense of confidence, competence, and efficacy in deliberation is more sensitive than men's, and that it responds to women's ability to articulate their distinctive issues.

One potential caveat about the results is that while mentioning women's distinctive issues benefits women's representation, it may also decrease women's perceived influence in the eyes of other members of the group. If this were true, increasing women's substantive representation by changing the agenda would not be as beneficial overall for women's authority and thus their representation. However, we find that there is no association between a woman's *Frequency* of care issues and her perceived influence after deliberation.[35] Women's overall substantive representation does not suffer from women's voice.

The Dog That Didn't Bark

We have been completely silent on one matter. We have said nothing about women's own distinctive needs and interests as women. While we have spilled much printer ink (clicked many keyboard keys?) in the service of documenting and explaining women's other-regarding motives and actions, what women want for themselves remains a mystery. In the discussions in our experiment,

[34] Using the satisfaction index we introduced in chapter 5, we also find that in mixed-gender groups, women's average group-level satisfaction increases as the group devotes more attention to care issues: $b = 0.07$, $SE = 0.04$, $p = 0.05$, one-tailed. The regression includes controls for the experimental conditions, the interaction of decision rule and gender composition, the number of egalitarians in the group, the interaction of egalitarians and rule and experimental location. Men's satisfaction falls short of significance ($b = 0.03$, $SE = 0.04$, $p = 0.25$, one-tailed). When we examine the relationship between satisfaction and the ratio of care to financial issues, we find that both women and men feel more satisfied with the discussion as the ratio increases: for women, $b = 0.014$, $SE = 0.006$, $p < 0.02$, one-tailed; for men, $b = 0.011$, $SE = 0.006$, $p < 0.03$, one-tailed (average group-level satisfaction computed separately for each gender within each group). Again, regressions include the same controls listed above. As the ratio increases, both men and women are also more likely to feel that no one individual dominated the discussion. Across multiple measures we find that talk of care issues prompts women (and sometimes men, too) to feel satisfied with the discussion.

[35] Subjects were asked postdeliberation to vote on which group member was most influential in their deliberation, and we tabulated the votes, as summarized in the online appendix and described in chapter 5. With respect to all subjects, women only, and only minority women in majority-rule groups, the effect of care issue references on others' ratings of one's influence is not significant, with and without controls for individual and group egalitarianism.

neither women nor men tended to raise the issue of gender directly. Specifically, our counts yield few references to "women" or "woman," nor did we hear much talk of "men" or "man." More importantly, the talk that did refer to these terms did not shift according to any meaningful pattern across our conditions. Settings that shift women's status and influence, and that elicit more or less talk of issues of distinctive concern to women, do not produce more discussion of women themselves. At least not when the task at hand is not explicitly tied to women or to gender. It seems that when the decision is not about women specifically, women are not mentioned specifically.

When the topic is redistribution, women may not think readily about the needs of women, simply because that is not how redistribution is usually discussed in public discourse. However, that does not make it any less meaningful to discover that women do not regard themselves as a relevant group when considering who needs assistance or generosity. After all, households headed by single women are twice as likely as those headed by single men and over five times more likely than those headed by a couple to live in poverty.[36] And yet despite the difficulties that these single women face in supporting their households, the word "women" is extremely scarce in our discussions of poverty, inequality, and redistribution. This absence is all the more striking considering that in some forums of public discourse, women's well-being and economic conditions have been noted as highly relevant to general inequality and well-being.[37]

A likely reason for the silence on this topic is that the women of America seldom articulate their own interests or needs as women as part of the public agenda. Few women call themselves feminist, and women have little warmth for feminists (Huddy, Neely, and Lafay 2000). If one wants to predict support for abortion rights, either in the populace at large or among citizens active on a political issue, the last variable one should reach for is the person's gender, and if one does select this predictor, prepare to encounter the opposite sign (Burns, Schlozman, and Verba 2001, 123–24). Burns and her colleagues, who took thorough stock of women's participation on women's issues, "were struck at how little activity—pro or con, by women or by men—is animated by concern about women's issues" (Burns, Schlozman, and Verba 2001, 127). Under the ordinary circumstances of day-to-day political life, women bear little resemblance to the compatriots of Betty Friedan, Shirley Chisholm, or Gloria Steinem. Many of today's young women might be hard-pressed to tell you who

[36] According to the National Poverty Center at the University of Michigan, US census data show that "poverty rates are highest for families headed by single women, particularly if they are black or Hispanic. In 2010, 31.6 percent of households headed by single women were poor, while 15.8 percent of households headed by single men and 6.2 percent of married-couple households lived in poverty." http://www.npc.umich.edu/poverty/#4.

[37] For example, the Nobel laureate Amartya Sen wrote in the Indian magazine *Frontline*: "An enhancement of women's active agency can, in many circumstances, contribute substantially to the lives of all people—men as well as women, children as well as adults." http://www.frontlineonnet.com/fl1822/18220040.htm.

Gloria Steinem is, and bra burning may be viewed as a quaint, vaguely funny, ancient ritual their grandmothers might have practiced. But age aside, women young and old prioritize the needs of others, of the collective, of the vulnerable, over their own—or so it is in politics.

Conclusion

In chapter 5, we saw that when we vary the number of women and the decision rule of deliberating groups we either produce a gender gap in participation during discussion and in ratings of a member's influence, or we close that gap. Our starting point thus was the notion that composition and rule interact to shape women's status in the group.

In this chapter we found that in the same conditions where women speak more and carry more perceived influence, women are also more likely to speak to their distinctive concerns. Not only do women speak less when they are minorities under majority rule, they also speak less to the concerns women tend to raise and act upon. In other words, a valuable set of perspectives and considerations is nearly entirely lost to the group in the setting where women's standing is lowest. What is true of talk time is also true of the content of the talk: women are worst off in groups with few women and majority rule. To avoid the single most deleterious setting for women, avoid majority rule with few women.

Unanimous rule dampens, eliminates, and even reverses this deleterious effect of minority status for women. As we found with participation and influence, so it is with the agenda—when women are numerical minorities they are better off with unanimous rule, and as majorities, better off with majority rule.[38] When women interact with men, large numbers tend to help women when they operate under norms that advantage large numbers.[39]

However, while unanimous rule provides a much-needed boost to women in the minority, the most effective setting for women's agenda setting in interactions with men is majority rule with many women. That setting is where many aspects of women's substantive representation come to fruition. That is, there are different types of substantive representation, and our findings indicate that the same setting that elevates one type tends to elevate the others. Majority rule with a large majority of women tends to:

- free women to introduce women's distinctive issues into the agenda;
- maximize the average woman's and women's collective voice on women's distinctive issues, including on the ratio of women's to men's issues;

[38] Under unanimous rule, large numbers help women's substantive representation in shaping the content of discussion only in all-female groups, where the rule makes little difference.

[39] However, we note that in this chapter, the major difference between the rules for the average woman in majority female groups is found in the ratio of care to financial words, and not found in every measure of agenda setting we examined.

- prompt men to adopt some aspects of the care agenda, but primarily with respect to discussion of children, and only when women form a supermajority; and
- increase the overall group voice for women's distinctive issues and its emphasis on care over financial issues.

If one had to pick the one setting that yields the most forms of substantive representation for women, one should pick majority rule with many women.

But women's enclaves emerge as another space that provides a high degree of substantive representation for women. Although these settings are not dramatically different from the empowering settings where women interact with men, they are worth noting as one more way that women can publicly speak to their distinctive concerns. Across both decision rules, these groups function much like the majority-rule groups with many women to elevate women's talk of care.

Raising issues and topics that do not come up much otherwise is a crucial form of power, as theories of the second face of power have long noted (Bachrach and Baratz 1962; Gaventa 1982). Our findings shed light on one neglected reason why this form of power matters. It matters in particular by elevating the sense of empowerment that disadvantaged groups feel. We found that the more that women speak to women's distinctive concerns, the more they tend to report that their voice was heard.

But the results here do not imply that women's empowerment comes at a cost for the quality of deliberation. In fact, we found that both women and men tend to evaluate the overall discussion as more inclusive the more they speak to issues of care. The more one speaks about the needs of vulnerable populations, the more one tends to report that the discussion aired a variety of perspectives, and this holds as much or more for men as for women.

Beyond the impressions of the deliberators themselves, deliberation is better when all sides raise their distinctive perspectives more fully. For some theorists (Sanders 1997), a more complete telling of one's side of the story means that deliberators voice their views *in their own words*. Our results show that women choose different words—words that are more closely tied to their set of distinctive concerns—when they are empowered. In the settings where their standing is greatest, the terms of discussion and debate shift—literally—in ways that are more friendly to considerations that tend to be important to women. This change in the content of the discourse, this increased ability for women to make their arguments on their own terms, is a meaningful mark of substantive representation as well as deliberative inclusion.

Our measures have important limits. One potential weakness of our analysis is that mention of a topic does not indicate a particular position on the left-right policy spectrum. We have three responses to this valid criticism. First, studies we reviewed suggest that women are both more likely to mention these topics when asked about their concerns and priorities, and likely to take a liberal position on these topics. Thus women tend to indicate that these populations are on their mind and to take a sympathetic position toward them—talking about them and sympathizing with them seem to go hand in hand. Second, we provided evidence that the mentions in our study are almost never negative. Third, the salience of a topic is itself an important type of substantive representation; in fact, as we noted above, some theorists argue that the presence of an issue on the agenda is the most important measure of political power (Bachrach and Baratz 1962; Gaventa 1982). The disagreement cannot come to light and no view on the issue can be aired if the topic remains off the agenda. To be sure, in groups where people mention women's issues but women lack power, the outcome may not conform to women's general preference for generosity to the vulnerable. Nevertheless, chapter 9 will show that the conditions where women speak to their distinctive topics on the whole tend to foster group decisions in line with women's preference for generous aid to the needy. All this tells us that the way we have counted words is a useful way to analyze representation, especially since we accounted for the direction toward which these words lead.

Validation of these results comes from an experiment on "mock-jury" deliberation in a simulated sexual assault legal case featuring an adult who sexually assaults a six-year-old child (Golding et al. 2007). In keeping with the notion that women place a higher priority on protecting children than men do, women's initial preference was to convict, men's was to exonerate. However, this priority was much more likely to find expression in the deliberations of the majority-female groups than in the other groups. And in these same groups where women's priority found greater voice, the individual votes and group verdict were much more likely to tilt toward that priority. Thus, as in our study, the groups where women articulated their priorities were the groups where the outcome was more in line with women's preferences and women had more influence.

However, the key point of the study is that women's voice in deliberative settings varies a great deal with the institutional setting. Studies of women's representation in legislatures recognize the importance of institutional rules and norms among political elites (Carroll 2001; Grünenfelder and Bächtiger 2007). Our results suggest that rules and norms also shape interactions among citizens. These norms of communication affect men as well as women. They also produce quite different levels of conversational salience for the topics that tend to concern women. In these ways institutional settings can contribute to or detract from equal substantive representation, for as Mansbridge (1999) notes, descriptive representation can affect the quality of deliberation in political institutions by bringing in the commonly shared perspectives of the disadvantaged group. We have taken a step toward unpacking the black box of deliberation to show how, and when, descriptive representation matters for substantive representation.

The analysis in this chapter makes a number of contributions to the larger scholarly literature on gender and substantive representation. Although studies have documented that female representatives act on a distinctive set of concerns (for example, Carroll 2001; Kathlene 2001; Swers 2002), we are not aware of studies showing that women articulate different topics or words from similar men in public discussions (for excellent small-N studies, see Kathlene 1994 and Mattei 1998). That women tend to articulate a "different voice" is suggested by a number of studies of women in office; for example, Beck found that on the issue of local leaf collection, men tended to focus in their interview with her on financial implications and women on the needs of the vulnerable population in the town (Beck 2001, 57). Our results confirm but extend such findings to the world of ordinary citizens and do so in a way that makes clear that group-level factors are key determinants of the content of group discussion. Linking speech to predeliberation preferences also allows us to control on predeliberation egalitarianism and preferences over the group decision and thus isolate the effects of gender from the effects of these attitudes and preferences. Thus we can conclude that conditions that increase women's talk of women's distinctive topics do so by altering the gender dynamic specifically and not because they shift people regardless of gender. Our placebo tests further indicate that the shift occurs on women's distinctive issues only and is not caused by nongendered conformity or general majority-induced dynamics. In addition, we are not aware of studies documenting that men adopt speech similar to women's and do so as women's influence rises.

We end with a note about why it matters that women bring their distinctive concerns to the group's agenda. We have been discussing women's agenda setting at a practical and concrete level, and for justifiable reasons. But women's agenda setting matters at a more abstract level too. As the philosopher Fricker (2007) argues, a fundamental injustice is the disadvantage that social identity groups experience in defining the terms of discussion. For example, Fricker notes that a woman who experiences rape in a community that does not recognize the meaning of that term experiences a profound disempowerment because the injustice of the experience has no name, and without a name, there is no recognition and no understanding of the harm (2007, 6). Such a woman cannot possibly articulate her needs or perspectives in a discussion when she herself does not know that these are needs and perspectives, what they are, and how to describe them to others. Less dramatically, we can think of the needs of children, the homeless, the sick, the destitute, the victimized, and the infirm in similar terms. If no one names their problems, afflictions, needs, or perspectives, they do not exist. A community or a society cannot begin to address a problem that has no name or help a group viewed as irrelevant to the collective. What women do by raising their distinctive concerns is more than naming a problem; they are including marginalized or disadvantaged groups in the conception of "us." To raise women's distinctive issues is to situate vulnerable populations as a legitimate subject in the community as well as in the discussion.

To do so is to participate equally in the practices through which shared social meanings are created, and this may be the highest form of influence.

We have been arguing that women's probability of talking about women's distinctive topics is shaped by conditions of gender equality. A missing piece in this argument is evidence that women talk in ways that reflect their lower status and influence in the group, and that men talk in ways that help them instantiate power. We next tackle this question.

CHAPTER 8

Unpacking the Black Box of Interaction

Powerlessness and silence go together.

—MARGARET ATWOOD[1]

PEOPLE DELIBERATE IN ORDER TO exchange words, and the words they choose tell us what the discussion is about and in what direction people's preferences are heading. But speech is also a fundamental form of action. And so, the form that speech takes matters too. We already examined one form of speech—how much, and how often, people speak. We found that women speak less than men in the conditions that simulate most settings of public discussions. In these settings, women are a numerical minority, and there is no unanimous rule, and thus, nothing to elevate their participation in the discussion. As we saw, the more a person speaks, the more influence others attribute to him or her. Speaking provides an opportunity to establish authority—that is, it elevates one's standing as a valuable member of the group. One of the functions of the act of speech is to instantiate power or status.

Here we explore one more way that a person can instantiate power through speech. We examine interruptions of other speakers and the responses to those interruptions. The way in which participants interact while speaking may enhance or undermine women's status in deliberation. Gendered roles and expectations construct women's speech as less authoritative to begin with. But the way that women's speech is received can reinforce women's lower status in the group and their authority deficit in the deliberation (Kathlene 1994; Mattei 1998). Our argument throughout the book is that the rules of interaction and the gender composition of the deliberating body jointly affect the degree to which speech elevates or depresses women's authority. In this chapter we home in on the nature of interaction between speakers to illuminate how gender affects women's relative authority—that is, their symbolic representation in discussion. As ever, we ask how the group's rule and gender composition shape the nature of interaction and ultimately, women's representation.

[1]Quoted in Weekes (2007, 404).

However, women's authority may derive not only from power but also from warmth. Speech is not only a means to power, it can also establish social connection and solidarity (Tannen 1993).[2] Social interaction is a crucial means for creating a sense of warmth and personal acceptance. Talk can communicate approval of the other person's speech and positive regard for that person. Thus speech can be a form not only of instrumental cooperation but also of personal affirmation. The more one interrupts another in a positive way, the more support one is expressing for the speaker. The more supportive interruptions members provide for each other, the stronger the norm of "niceness" in the group (see Lawler 2003). It is a norm that could create a more inclusive dynamic that invites women's participation. An important condition for women's full participation and representation, we argue, is the group's culture of warmth and affirmation.

Here we examine interruptions as a means of achieving each of these functions of speech, in turn. We ask whether women's descriptive representation and the decision rule influence women's relative power and the level of social solidarity in the group by shaping the use of interruptions.

A key distinction we pursue is between negative and positive interruptions (following Smith-Lovin and Brody 1989; see Li 2001). Negative interruptions are a power play. They represent one member's attempt to seize the floor from another to express opposition or deprecation. We can see examples of how these negative dynamics operate in Beck's (2001) case study of a suburban town council, where female council members experienced meetings in a more negative way than men, sometimes finding themselves "publicly demeaned" by male colleagues when they tried to express their views (Beck 2001, 59). Beck finds a common pattern in which women are more likely than men to "hold back" from expressing their views in response to the hostility they receive. As a female town council member told Beck during an interview: "Nobody hears me" (2001, 59). Negative interruptions are a way of asserting power and conflict—and even disrespect. In this sense, they may negatively affect women in particular.

Positive interruptions also represent power, but not of the negative kind. They are a way of collaborating, cooperating, and supporting the original speaker without detracting from that speaker's effectiveness. In fact, positive interruptions can be a way to enhance the power and authority of both speakers.

Positive interruptions also play a crucial role in prompting speakers to believe that the audience is listening to them. When a speaker receives many positive interruptions they have instantaneous reinforcement in the form of agreement. The positive attention of other members may thus be important, perhaps especially to women's choice to exercise their voice. One way that speakers can communicate this attention is to offer positive interjections.

[2] A long tradition of research on group discussion going back at least to the foundational work of Bales establishes that the two basic dimensions of speech are instrumental or task orientation and social (Bales 1970).

Positive interruptions are also a way to establish rapport and bonds of fellow feeling. At the group level, many negative interruptions create an atmosphere of conflict and negativity; many positive interruptions create one of consensus and solidarity. If women are sensitive to the level of warmth and connection around them, then groups that exhibit more positive interjections may elevate that connection, and therefore increase women's participation in discussion.

We ask whether the conditions that promote more gender equality in speech participation also exhibit a pattern of high power for women and high solidarity in the group. We ask a set of questions about power. In settings where we expect gender equality, do we see women receiving fewer negative interruptions? Do we see women receiving more positive interruptions? Do women who receive negative interruptions lose authority? We also ask a set of questions about solidarity. Are women more likely to use positive interruptions when there are many women—that is, are positive interruptions one of the consequences of creating predominantly female settings? Put differently, do predominantly female settings create higher levels of group warmth and affirmation?

The Meaning of Interruptions

Status

The act of speaking provides an opportunity to establish authority and status as a valuable member of the group, but the group's reaction is what affords the speaker this status. Interruptions are a communication signal. People signal their own and others' status through their use of such communication cues, and they glean status from others' signals (Ridgeway et al. 1985). Individuals independently verified as, or made to be, the more dominant or confident members of a conversation use a constellation of verbal forms that signal their higher status: they speak more; they speak earlier; they may initiate and complete more negative interruptions during a discussion, especially regarding a conflict; and they may issue fewer positive interruptions to their subordinates than subordinates issue to them (Dovidio et al. 1988; Johnson 1994; Kollock, Blumstein, and Schwartz 1985; Ng et al. 1995). Interruptions are correlated with volubility but carry a clearer signal of individual agency than volubility, which may indicate pure sociability (but see Tannen 1993). And they may have a particularly negative, silencing effect on lower-status groups, since those groups' authority is fragile, and disagreements they may direct at high-status members tend to be countered with aggressive reactions or backlash (Ridgeway and Johnson 1990; Rudman and Glick 2001). Differences in patterns of interruptions are thus an indicator of, and reinforce, status inequality in conversation.

Because men have more authority than women do in society, they tend to use communication acts that symbolize high status, while women tend to employ those that mark low status (Dovidio et al. 1988; Lakoff 1975; Wood and Karten 1986; Ridgeway and Smith-Lovin 1999). A meta-analysis of forty-three studies confirms that interruptions conform to a pattern of gender hierarchy (Anderson and Leaper 1998); men tend to negatively interrupt more than women, especially in groups. Other studies confirm that men issue negative interruptions more often and positive interruptions less often than women, and talk longer (Aries 1976; Carli 1990; Kathlene 1994; Mulac et al. 1986; Mulac et al. 1988; Zimmerman and West 1975; but see James and Clarke 1993). Moreover, because women lose influence when they act too assertively, and may intuit this fact, women may be more likely than men to interpret disagreements they receive as a negative signal of their authority (Ridgeway 1982). Anderson and Leaper also found that women are three times more likely than men to yield when negatively interrupted in a group discussion on a gender-neutral task (1998; see also Smith-Lovin and Brody 1989). Gender differences of this kind are sharpest when the task involves a domain considered masculine (Karakowsky and Siegel 1999; Leaper and Ayers 2007). Politics is such a domain; women are viewed, and view themselves, as less confident and expert about politics, regardless of their actual level of expertise (Fox and Lawless 2011; Kanthak and Krause 2010; Mendez and Osborn 2010). Because women are more likely to enter a formal discussion of politics with a lower sense of authority, they may be more subject to and more affected by interruptions.

Social Rapport

Positive interjections can be a form not only of instrumental cooperation and agreement but also of warm affirmation of and rapport with others. Because they enter with less authority, women may be especially affected by a lack of affirmation, and thus by an absence of positive interruptions. Women sometimes complain that when they do speak, people don't listen. As a woman who participated in a grassroots deliberative reform said to one scholar: "I went to three or four meetings . . . No one ever listened to my suggestions. They were uninterested" (Britt 1993, cited in Agarwal 1997, cited in Cornwall 2003). The same refrain is clear in a quote from a middle-aged female doctor interviewed by a journalist about her service on charitable committees. The doctor summed it up this way: "*You get your cues right away.* I will make comments about things, but it seems that no one hears me or *no one agrees with me. And then I clam up*" (emphasis ours).[3] The absence of positive acknowledgment may signal to the speaker that their speech lacks value. As one interviewee told Mansbridge after a town meeting, "if you don't say what they want to hear you're not even

[3]Quoted in Bernstein 2012. "Speaking Up Is Hard to Do: Researchers Explain Why," *Wall Street Journal*, February 7, 2012, http://online.wsj.com/article/SB10001424052970204136404577207020525853492.html.

acknowledged" (1983, 69); that is, lack of acknowledgement may be taken as indirect negativity toward the speaker as a group member, not just toward the specific content of their speech, and have a depressive effect. The positive attention of other members may thus be important, perhaps especially to women. One way that speakers can communicate this attention is to offer positive interjections, and these may have a stronger effect on women's perceived influence than on men's.

The Effect of Numbers on Interruptions

Only a handful of studies have examined the effect of group gender composition on interruptions, and they are limited by small group N and inconsistent findings. One study assigned university students to a six-member work group and found that majority-male groups engaged in more negative interruptions than other groups (Karakowsky, McBey, and Miller 2004). Similarly, Aries, Gold, and Weigel (1983) found that dominant-personality women interrupt negatively when interacting in all-female groups but not in mixed-gender groups. Another controlled study, however, found only limited composition effects (Smith-Lovin and Brody 1989). These studies use only between twenty and thirty-six groups.

Observational studies of political settings are also few and also involve a very small number of groups, lacking the ability to contrast across compositions. They do, however, tend to find that men use negative interruptions especially against women and that this correlates with other indicators of women's lower status in the discussion setting (see especially the pioneering work of Kathlene 1994). Laura Mattei (1998) conducted the most in-depth analysis of language patterns in her study of female and male witnesses testifying before the all-male Senate Judiciary Committee on the nomination of David Souter to the Supreme Court. She found that relative to male witnesses, women were given less speaking time, experienced proportionately more hostile interruptions, were asked more challenging questions, were asked to bolster their testimony with more evidence, and were denied the floor when they attempted to interrupt. This pattern obtained for Democratic and Republican senators (all male). Female witnesses interrupted the senators back, but at a rate of one given to three received, while male witnesses, by contrast, responded at a rate of approximately one to one (Mattei 1998, 451). Finally, when men interrupted senators, they were given the floor to continue more often than women. In other words, in heavily masculine settings, men may use negative interruptions to assert their authority and to detract from women's. Again, however, these conclusions are highly uncertain, because they are based on very small samples.

As we noted, interruptions fulfill two distinct functions, and power is only one of them; the other is social solidarity and interpersonal support (Bales 1970;

Tannen 1993). Women tend to perform this function more than men, but gender composition matters, as women do so especially in interacting with other women. As we discussed extensively in chapter 3, women are more likely to express emotion when talking to other women than to men. Men are least likely to do so when interacting with men (Aries 1976; Carli 1989, 1990; Piliavin and Martin 1978). Mixed-gender groups pull each gender toward the middle. Thus descriptive representation may elevate the rate of positive and depress the rate of negative interruptions of female speakers.

The general theory revolves around the notion that gender roles produce gendered subcultures of talk and interaction (Tannen 1990). These subcultures are learned in grade school and developed in sex-segregated playgroups. Girls' groups entail actions that grease the social wheels and emphasize cooperation and solidarity; hence, they are more expressive, less directive, and less overtly conflictual. Boys' groups entail actions that signal individual agency, including issuing directives and joking at others' expense (Maltz and Borker 1982). Consequently, as Cathryn Johnson puts it, "women nurture conversation to keep it going by obeying the rules of polite interaction, while men more often dominate the conversation and violate the rules of turn-taking without repercussion" (1994, 124). Groups composed predominantly of women implicitly follow the feminine style of interaction; those with many men tend to follow the masculine style.

Decision Rule and Interruptions

As we noted in chapter 3, however, the extent to which gender inequality exists in speech acts, whether that act involves speaking at length or issuing interruptions, depends on the group's procedures. Yet none of the studies we have just reviewed investigated a group's rules or process norms. No study examined the effect of rules on the authoritative use of particular speech acts such as interruptions. As we argued in earlier chapters, the level of gender inequality in speech acts depends on the group's procedures, specifically, the group's decision rule, which operates jointly with gender composition.

Decision rules can create norms of decision making that apply to the deliberation preceding the decision. These norms may either override or boost the effects of gender on authority. Specifically, under unanimous rule, everyone must agree, and this expectation in turn creates norms of consensus, cooperation, and mutual respect. By implication, when each person matters, every voice is given adequate respect, even when that voice comes from women. The consensual norm created by unanimous rule may override the expectation of deference with which women tend to enter the discussion, and this benefits women when they are few. Consistent with this notion, in chapter 5 we reported that women's floor time equals men's when women are few and the group is instructed to use unanimous rule. Consequently, when women are few, we should see that the number of negative interruptions directed at women declines, and positive interruptions increase, under unanimous rule relative to majority rule.

However, unanimous rule does not create inviting dynamics across the board. As we reported in chapter 5, when women predominate, men are more talkative and are perceived as more influential relative to groups with few women and unanimous rule and to groups with many women and majority rule. We may find that the inclusive dynamic that women experience under unanimous rule applies only when women are the minority. We hypothesize that unanimous rule decreases negative interjections and increases positive interruptions toward women only when women are few.

Finally, as we argued in chapter 5, majority rule can create a dynamic of conflict and individual agency. We hypothesize that majority rule creates a high level of gender inequality in interruptions when women are few and thus occupy a low status. This may produce conditions where men engage in assertive speech acts, and where women have difficulty in taking and retaining the floor. Specifically, under majority rule with few women, relative to the other combinations of numbers and rule, we may see high levels of negative interruptions directed by men at women, and women may receive fewer positive interruptions.

Measuring Interruptions

We operationalize an interruption as an overlap in two speakers' words that lasts at least 0.5 seconds, in which the first speaker spoke for at least 1.5 seconds, and the interrupting speaker spoke for at least one second.[4] That is, the speaker must clearly hold the floor, and a second speaker clearly attempts to take the floor. Our software classified each speaking turn as an interruption turn based on these criteria. We then checked these interruptions by human coding.[5]

We defined interruptions as positive, negative, or neutral, following established definitions and building on Stromer-Galley's coding (Johnson 1994; Leaper and Ayers 2007; Stromer-Galley 2007).[6] These scholars define a posi-

[4]These thresholds maximized the joint distribution of the number of interruptions and the minimal clarity of the speech, i.e., they gave the most interruptions that were words rather than coughing or other such sounds.

[5]We in turn check-coded the human verifier who classified a turn as an interruption with a second human coder, on a sample of 101 interruptions from two randomly chosen groups. The alpha between the two coders is 0.90. Our data set has 4,376 verified interruptions. Multiple interruptions of the same turn that begin at the same time are coded separately. For example, if A is interrupted by C and D at essentially the same time, we created separate entries for C's and D's interruptions. In the analysis we account for this and other issues in analyzing the dyad, as we explain later.

[6]We also coded each interrupted turn as complete or incomplete, but the conditions did not affect these consistently.

tive interruption as supporting, agreeing with, or adding to the first speaker's comment. Positive interruptions are a way of supporting the original speaker without detracting from that speaker's effectiveness. Accordingly, we defined a positive interruption as either: (a) expressing solidarity with, affection, or support for the speaker or the speech, or (b) an interruption that completes the prior speaker's thought in the same direction without disagreement or contradiction. Positive interruptions often begin with "I agree," "yeah," and so on. See online appendix E for coding details.

Negative interruptions are a power play. They represent one member's attempt to seize the floor from another to express opposition or deprecation. A negative interruption disagrees, raises an objection, or completely changes the topic. A negative interruption may begin with phrases such as "well," "but," "however," "not," "I sort of disagree," "I'm not sure about that," or "I don't know." Not all negative starts are a negative comment, however. It is negative if it changes the topic without expressing understanding of the previous turn; does not use acknowledgment cues; or does not refer to the prior turn in any way, implicit or explicit.[7]

We also coded the interruption as elaborated or unelaborated. We defined elaboration as explaining one's meaning. For positive interruptions, this entails adding content rather than simply echoing what the current speaker is saying. For negative interruptions, this means giving reasons for one's disagreement. This is a measure of direct engagement by one speaker of another and reflects a measure of quality of deliberation. But it is also a measure of power. A negative interruption that is not elaborated represents a form of dominance behavior; conversely, a positive interruption that is not elaborated represents pure support for the speaker, and thus anchors the other end of the conflict-support continuum.[8]

For reliability, one coder coded all the discussions, and another coder independently coded 248 interruptions, 10% of the total. The percent agreements and Krippendorff's alphas (in parentheses) are as follows: for positive, negative, and neutral interruptions: 83% (0.65), 79% (0.53), and 88% (0.43). For elaborations: 75% (0.50). The alphas are lower than desirable, but the standards in the

[7] A neutral interruption does neither. It provides insufficient content to indicate a positive or negative direction, or comments or asks for information without evaluating the first speaker's comment, or complies with an interruptee's request to provide input, or answers a nonrhetorical question the interruptee posed. Examples include "what do you mean?"; "what do we think?"; "what is the vote on?" We used this code sparingly, and all analyses we attempted with this variable proved substantively and statistically insignificant, perhaps given the very few instances of such interruptions. A statement might include an apparent agreement but move quickly to disagreement, by saying something like: "I agree with that, but . . ." Because this has both positive and negative elements, this counts as a positive and also counts as a negative. The turn is coded as a "1" on each of those two categories.

[8] Positive and negative elaborated interruptions are in between those extremes, with positive elaboration closer to support than to dominance, and negative elaboration the reverse.

literature come from text that is much more orderly and clear, such as interviews, speeches, or structured forums where speakers take clearly delineated turns and attend to grammar, which makes positive or negative content much easier to discern (Fay et al. 2000). We view these alphas as satisfactory considering the challenges of coding five-member informal interactions where turns are sometimes not clear and grammar is often murky. We note that the effects on these measures are no less trustworthy as a consequence of lower alphas; in fact, the effects must be powerful in order to cut through the noise of these measures.

For the whole sample, the average group's positive interruptions are the most numerous, negative ones less so, and neutral interruptions are very few (see chapter appendix figure A8.1). Elaborations are much more likely for negative than positive interruptions, but summed across the valences they are fairly common in the average group (when pooling positive, negative, and neutral, the average number of elaborations per group is 19.5). However, we are concerned with variations across conditions and by gender, as we will explain.

We create two measures of interruptions. One is the negative proportion of all interruptions received.[9] This measure holds constant the act of interrupting to focus on the balance of negativity and positivity of the interruption. It has the virtue of not conflating the likelihood of speaking or even of interrupting with the tenor of the interruption. Also, neutral interruptions are very few and have a lower coding reliability, and this measure sets them aside. As a second measure, we use the proportion of the person's total speaking turns that were interrupted.[10] We use separate measures for the negatively and positively interrupted proportion of the speaker's speaking turns.[11] This measure is not as clean as our first measure, but it includes individuals with zero interruptions received, while the first measure omits them.

We must guard against the possibility that the interrupting behavior of men (or of women) changes as the number of men (or women) changes simply because there are more men (or women) who could issue interruptions. To

[9]This is the average dyadic proportion received by each person, excluding neutral interruptions. For example, we divide the number of negative interruptions given by B to A by the sum of negative and positive interruptions given by B to A; we do the same for those given to A from the others. Then we sum these dyadic proportions and divide the sum by the number of participants who gave a positive or negative interruption to A. We repeat this procedure to calculate the average dyadic proportion given to B and so on for each member who received a positive or negative interruption. When we look at gender subgroups, this measure adjusts for the shifting gender proportion.

[10]We separately examine the proportion of a person's speaking turns that issued an interruption.

[11]For the speaker's negatively interrupted proportion of speaking turns, we sum the negative interruptions given to A from each other member; we divide that sum by the number of members in the group minus the speaker (or when examining interruptions given only by one gender, by the number of members of that gender). Then we divide this average by A's speaking turns. We repeat for interruptions given to the rest. We follow the same process for the positively interrupted proportion of the speaker's turns.

account for this spuriousness, we constructed our interruption measures by calculating the average behavior of the interrupters of each interrupted person. Thus when we ask if men increase the interruptions they issue to women across the conditions, for example, we are looking at the average interruptions males issued to each female.

Consistent with the previous chapters, our statistical strategy is to use OLS regression with robust clustered standard errors to account for the interdependence of observations within the deliberating group. We control on location, the interrupted person's egalitarianism, and the number of egalitarians in the group, so that we can get at the pure effect of gender and gender composition rather than of political attitudes that correlate with gender but that are more peripheral to it (Huddy, Cassese, and Lizotte 2008; Sidanius and Pratto 1999). As needed we add controls for the quantity of the person's speech—typically, the speaker's number of speaking turns. Where the dependent variable is skewed and concentrated at zero, we replicate the main results with alternative estimators, typically Tobit (see online appendix C8.iii). We also replicate the main results with a fully saturated control model that includes a term for the interaction of decision rule and number of egalitarians (see online appendix C8.iv). That interaction term is never close to statistically significant, while the main and interactive effects of number of women remain fairly steady. We also find similar results when we replace egalitarianism and number of egalitarians with liberalism and number of liberals (see online appendix C8.v). Finally, demographic controls for age, education, and income never change our basic findings, either when we control for individual-level attributes or how those attributes are aggregated within the group.

The Balance of Negativity

We begin with our first measure of authority in speech, the negative proportion of interruptions received.

Table 8.1 displays the results of an OLS regression with the controls listed above as well as a control for the interruptee's number of speaking turns, for mixed-gender groups, since we expect rule to matter more consistently when women interact with men. We estimate the effects of the conditions separately for each gender combination in the interruption dyad: women interrupted by men, women by women, men by men, and men by women. The first column shows that women are more likely to be negatively interrupted by men as a minority under majority rule than as a minority under unanimous rule. The coefficient on majority rule is positive, and predicted values from the model show that the difference across rules is significant at $p < 0.05$, two-tailed, for groups with one woman. Unanimous rule thus protects women when they are few, but this effect of rule erodes as women's numbers increase (the negative interaction

Table 8.1: Negative Proportion of Men's and Women's Interruptions Received, Separately by Male and Female Interrupters, Mixed-Gender Groups Only

	(1) Women from Men	(2) Women from Women	(3) Men from Men	(4) Men from Women
Majority Rule	0.470**	0.066	0.078	−0.041
	(0.205)	(0.373)	(0.159)	(0.124)
Number of Women	−0.018	−0.109*	0.050	0.002
	(0.052)	(0.060)	(0.060)	(0.036)
Majority Rule × Number of Women	−0.185***	−0.038	−0.118	0.045
	(0.068)	(0.105)	(0.093)	(0.055)
Number of Speaking Turns	0.004***	0.003**	0.003**	0.003***
	(0.001)	(0.001)	(0.001)	(0.001)
Egalitarianism	0.040	−0.556**	−0.277	0.021
	(0.244)	(0.223)	(0.229)	(0.167)
Number of Egalitarians	0.089**	0.106***	0.008	−0.078*
	(0.042)	(0.038)	(0.038)	(0.040)
Constant	−0.068	0.729**	0.246*	0.277**
	(0.190)	(0.277)	(0.137)	(0.125)
Observations	102	94	107	111
R-squared	0.24	0.17	0.13	0.12
Control for Experimental Location	Yes	Yes	Yes	Yes

Note: Dependent variable for all models is the proportion of received interruptions that were negative. Individual-level analysis. Cluster robust standard errors in parentheses. *** $p < 0.01$, ** $p < 0.05$, * $p < 0.10$, two-tailed test.

term for majority rule and gender composition). Put differently, numbers help women only under majority rule, and rule helps women only when they are few.

Figure 8.1 displays predicted values from this regression (holding all other variables at their observed values). When women receive an interruption from men, that interruption is much less likely to be negative than positive as their numbers grow, but only under majority rule. The magnitude of the effect of composition under majority rule is quite large: negative comments make up anywhere from approximately 70% (at worst) to just over 10% (at best) of the interruptions women receive from men. Gender composition shifts the tone of men's direct engagement with women from clearly negative to highly positive. But it does so only under majority rule. Women do not enjoy the power of numbers under unanimous rule; under that rule, composition makes no difference. Finally, unanimous rule does help women in the minority relative to majority rule.

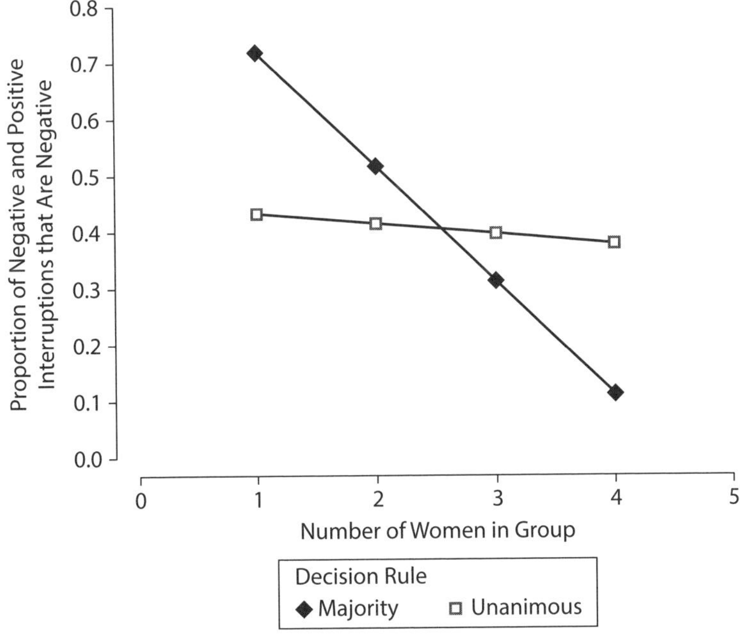

Figure 8.1. Negative proportion of negative and positive interruptions received by women from men, mixed groups only.

Some illustrative examples can give a flavor for how these patterns of interaction play out. In a majority-rule group with only two women, for example, one participant begins by acknowledging that he has spoken too much and tries to offer the floor to a woman. But almost immediately, he jumps back in, interrupting the woman repeatedly.

Gender-inegalitarian condition: Minority women, majority rule

00:04:44	Man E: Yeah, go ahead, I talk too much.
00:04:46	Woman D: [interposing] Maybe it doesn't make a point to talk about an option we don't have, but it still seems that, as a version—
00:04:54	Man E: That's a good point. My only problem with one is, you generate a big group of people with almost the same income.
00:05:02	Woman D: Yeah, which isn't necessarily good because you never—
00:05:04	Man E: [interposing] That's my only problem.
00:05:05	Woman D: Yeah there's no—

00:05:07	Man E: [interposing] Then you also somehow also eliminate the idea of the competition as well, right?
00:05:12	Man, C: With setting a floor constraint, my problem with that is . . .

Participant C goes on to speak for nearly a minute without interruption. Thus Participant D's repeated, polite attempts to gain the floor—and to offer positive reinforcement to her conversation partner—are ultimately unsuccessful. She cannot utter a full sentence without interruptions from the men in the room, who are focused on "their problems" with the principles they are considering.

Contrast the dynamic in that majority-rule group with what happens in a unanimous-rule group with only one woman. In this group, the group members engage in a series of positive interruptions, each of which reinforces what the previous person has said.

Gender-egalitarian condition: Minority women, unanimous rule

00:12:21	Man D: Yeah. That's what—I agree with whoever said—I can't remember who said it, but to choose between the four is kind of hard, because it's somewhat like—from what we're talking about, we need, like, a middle between no taxes and then some kind of floor constraint, but with some provision of saying, like, there'd be a way to decide who—
00:12:41	Woman E: Who gets the aid and who doesn't.
00:12:41	Man D: [interposing] Who gets—yeah, exactly. Depending upon—
00:12:42	Woman E: [interposing] That's what we need.
00:12:43	Man B: [interposing] Yeah.
00:12:45	Man D: We could make that. Can we?
00:12:47	Woman E: [to moderator] Are we allowed to make our own options?

[Laughter]

The dynamic could not be more different from what occurred in the majority-rule condition. The group laughs and jokes together, and the lone woman in the group repeatedly receives positive reinforcement about the points she is attempting to make. The sense of group solidarity is palpable, and Participant E is a full participant, sometimes finishing the thoughts of the men in the room and even ending this exchange by asking a question on behalf of the other group members.

So in conditions that give women the power of numbers or that protect them when they are few, women fare better. These settings serve to protect women by curtailing men's dominant speech forms. This protection is clearly needed, as can be seen by the high level of men's negativity toward women in the condition where women's status is lowest—when women are a small numerical minority under majority rule. Unanimous rule protects minority women from this high negativity, though women do best as a majority under majority rule.

The effects apply only to men's interruptions of women. Women direct a somewhat lower negative proportion of interruptions at other women as their numbers in mixed-gender groups grow, but this is unaffected by rule (table 8.1, column 2).[12] Finally, the negativity men experienced is unaffected by the conditions (columns 3 and 4).[13] Neither men nor women alter their behavior toward men as men's proportion shrinks. (Figure A8.2 in this chapter's appendix shows the same patterns with the raw proportions.)

These results represent an important validation of our argument that the mechanism accounting for women's participation and representation in group discussion is women's status. And that status is driven by men's behavior toward women—not their behavior toward people, and not people's behavior toward women, but specifically, men's behavior toward women. Men take a dominant posture toward women in the conditions where we expect women to have low status, and by the same token, men undergo a drastic change when women's status improves—they become far less aggressive toward them.

The composition and the procedures of deliberation jointly shape women's authority during deliberation. Where women's status is lowest—under majority rule and few women—over two-thirds of the interruptions women receive from men are negative. Where women's status is likely to be highest—as majorities under majority rule—that proportion more than reverses, and over 80% of the interruptions they experience from men are positive. Men's experience does not shift; only women's does. And only men's interruptions of women undergo this shift. What the conditions of deliberation do, then, is to shift men's displays of power toward an affirmation of women. That is, interruptions appear to function as an indicator of women's shifting status in the group, and men significantly affect that status.

Positive or Negative?

Are these patterns a result of a wave of negative interruptions, or of a steep decline in the number of positive interruptions, or both? We examine the proportion of the person's speaking turns that received an interruption, separately for negative and positive interjections.[14]

[12] We are cautious about contrasting this effect of male and female interrupters against each other because they consist of somewhat different composition conditions.

[13] The effects undifferentiated by the gender of the issuer are found in online appendix table C8.ii.1, which confirms the basic results.

[14] Here we do not control on the interrupted speaker's number of speaking turns since they are already present in the denominator of the dependent variable. We do control on the average number of speaking turns of the interrupters.

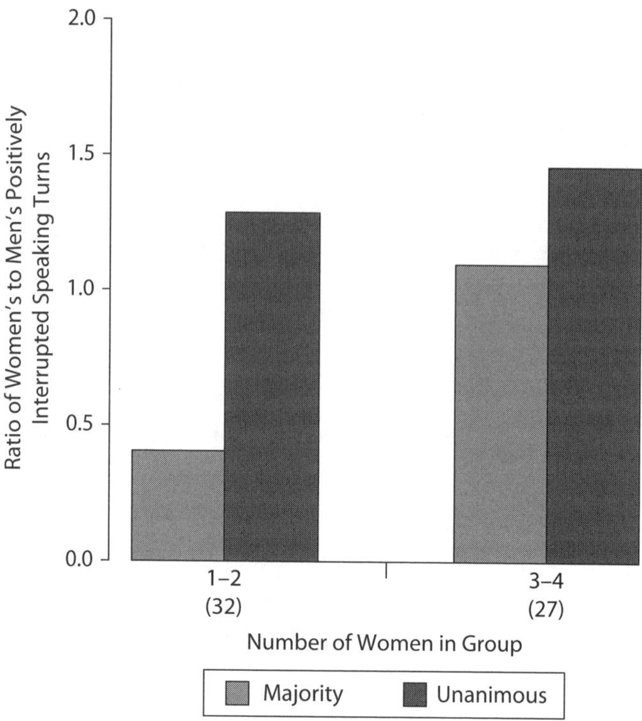

Figure 8.2. Ratio of women's to men's positively interrupted speaking turns, mixed groups (raw).

We begin by comparing women to men. We take the proportion of a person's speaking turns that received a positive interruption and calculate a gender ratio—the group's average for women divided by its average for men, for mixed gender groups. Figure 8.2 shows the raw percentages, grouping the minority conditions together and the majority conditions together, to increase the statistical power to detect differences between them. One on the *y*-axis of figure 8.2 indicates gender parity; numbers below one indicate women are receiving fewer positive interruptions on average than men.

Figure 8.2 makes a number of points. First, the conditions shift the likelihood that women will receive a positive interruption. Second, minority women under majority rule are much worse off than other women or men. These women receive positive affirmations at less than half the rate enjoyed by men in their group: 40% of men's, to be exact. Third, this visual impression is confirmed by statistical significance tests, for the most part.[15] The effect of rule on groups with minority women is statistically significant; minority women are

[15] Results are similar when we subtract women's from men's average instead of taking the ratio of women's to men's. The gender ratio of the negatively interrupted proportion of the person's speaking turns does not change in a statistically discernible way (results not shown). Neither does the

far more disadvantaged than men in their group under majority than unanimous rule ($p = 0.01$, two-tailed, group-level). Also, as expected, the effect of composition on groups with majority rule is significant; under majority rule, majority women do much better than minority women, as compared to men in their group ($p = 0.005$, two-tailed). Fourth, as expected, composition does not have this effect with unanimous rule—increasing numbers of women does not matter under unanimous rule ($p = 0.73$). The final test fails: the effect of rule on majority-female groups is not statistically significant, contrary to our expectation, indicating that majority rule is no better than unanimous rule for majority-female groups.

One other finding (seen in chapter appendix figure A8.3) also underscores the unusually bad situation women face when they are a small minority under majority rule. Lone women under that rule issue one of the highest rates of positive reinforcement of any gender group under any condition. Yet they receive the lowest rate of affirmation in turn. These women receive only about one-fourth of the affirmations that lone women get with unanimous rule, and about half of the affirmations that lone men receive under majority rule. The majority-rule example above shows precisely this dynamic.

These tests largely support our basic argument: what the conditions do for gender equality is to correct the high level of inequality that minority women experience under majority rule. This can be achieved either by introducing unanimous rule in groups with few women or by increasing the number of women and keeping majority rule. Majority rule is good for majority women, while unanimous rule is good for minority women, relative to the men in their group.

In sum, women's inequality relative to men in the group is marked, but only where their status is lowest—as a minority under majority rule. It manifests especially in the gap in affirmations one experiences when one is speaking. Unanimous rule reverses the inequality in the experience of warmth and support regardless of women's numbers. So do numbers.

To test these hypotheses more rigorously, table 8.2 presents regressions of the proportion of speaking turns that are positively interrupted, and those that are negatively interrupted, separately for interrupted men and women.[16] The only significant coefficients are for women's positively interrupted proportion of speaking turns (column 1), and they show the expected pattern: women do worst as a minority under majority rule, and improve their situation as their numbers rise under that rule. Figure 8.3 displays these results.

Figure 8.3 shows, as expected, that women's positively interrupted proportion of speaking turns increases as the number of women rises under majority rule. Again, we see the difference that rule makes to the effect of numbers—

---

gender ratio of the interruption proportion of the issuer's speaking turns, for either positive or negative interruptions (results not shown).

[16] We do not control on the interrupter's number of speaking turns since that would only be needed if we looked at dyads by gender subgroup (e.g., men interrupting women).

Table 8.2: Proportion of Turns Receiving Positive and Negative Interruptions, Mixed-Gender Groups Only

	Women		Men	
	(1) Positive	(2) Negative	(3) Positive	(4) Negative
Majority Rule	−0.025** (0.011)	0.003 (0.008)	0.005 (0.007)	−0.004 (0.005)
Number of Women	−0.002 (0.003)	−0.001 (0.002)	0.000 (0.003)	−0.001 (0.001)
Majority Rule × Number of Women	0.007* (0.004)	−0.003 (0.003)	−0.003 (0.003)	0.001 (0.002)
Egalitarianism	−0.020** (0.010)	−0.011 (0.007)	0.013 (0.009)	−0.000 (0.007)
Number of Egalitarians	−0.001 (0.002)	0.005*** (0.001)	0.001 (0.002)	0.001 (0.001)
Constant	0.041*** (0.011)	0.012* (0.006)	0.018*** (0.005)	0.014*** (0.004)
Observations	157	157	163	163
R-squared	0.07	0.11	0.04	0.03
Control for Experimental Location	Yes	Yes	Yes	Yes

Note: Individual-level analysis. Cluster robust standard errors in parentheses. *** $p < 0.01$, ** $p < 0.05$, * $p < 0.10$, two-tailed test.

composition does not have an effect under unanimous rule. There are no significant effects on the negative interruptions women received (table 8.2, column 2). The rule and rule-composition interaction coefficients for negative interruptions do run in the opposite direction from those in the positive column, but those changes are not significant. Men's experience of interruptions is unaffected (columns 3, 4).[17] In sum, composition helps women receive increased positive reassurance, but only under majority rule, and unanimous rule protects minority women.[18] Men are not affected, further indicating that the pattern of interruptions acts on women's authority but not on men's.

The raw data on positive and negative interruptions also allows us to shed some light on a question we posed in our earlier chapter on floor time. There we saw that token men under unanimous rule take up an unusually high proportion of the group's time. We did not know whether this was the result of

[17] We find no effects on the giver's interrupting proportion of speaking turns.

[18] A Wald test of predicted values from the model shows that in groups with one or two women, women receive more positive interruptions under unanimous rule than under majority rule ($p = 0.03$, two-tailed).

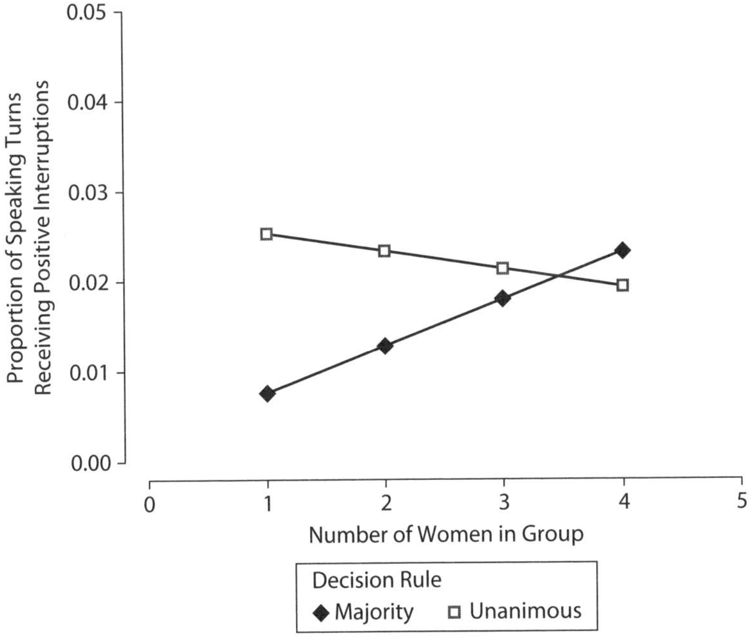

Figure 8.3. Proportion of women's speaking turns receiving a positive interruption, mixed groups only.

dominant behavior by the man or by deferential or friendly behavior on the part of the women in the group. Now, in figure A8.3, we can see that this token male is not engaging in power plays to obtain disproportionate floor time. His rate of issuing negative interruptions is no higher than that of other men or women. Neither is there evidence that women in these groups are attempting to wrest control from the token male—the rate of negatively interrupted turns that men receive from women does not move across the conditions (regression not shown).[19] Instead, we see that the token man in these unanimous rule groups receives a high rate of positive interruptions (chapter appendix figure A8.3). It seems that token men take unusually high floor times with the encouragement of the women around them, rather than by using dominant forms of speech. In these groups, women forego the power of numbers voluntarily and actively encourage the man among them to take a position of leadership.

Overall, we have now seen that settings that empower women do so by increasing the positive encouragement they receive.[20] Relative to other women,

[19]This result comes from the coefficient of zero for Number of Women in a regression of the negatively interrupted proportion of men's speaking turns received from women, where the specification is the same as in table 8.2.

[20]However, the number of negative interruptions is smaller, making shifts more difficult to detect with certainty.

and to men in their own group and in other conditions, women receive far fewer encouragements when in the minority under majority rule. In this sense, unanimous rule protects minority women. There, women receive concrete evidence that they are indeed being listened to. Similarly, we now understand why majority rule is bad for minority women—they seldom hear encouragement when they speak. And as we saw in earlier chapters, women's proclivity to speak in the masculine setting of group political discussion is more fragile than men's when their status is low. The combination of a few negative feedback and sparse positive feedback, deceptively neutral and inconsequential, represents a powerful dose of invalidation for women—and not for men.

Elaborated Interjections

Next we examine whether the interjections come with elaboration on the current speaker's comments. Elaboration is an indicator of the quality of discussion—more elaboration enriches the discussion by adding content that is not currently articulated. In addition, more relevant to our study, elaboration added to a negative interruption softens the interruption; conversely, a negative interruption without elaboration tilts more toward pure hostility rather than toward conflictual engagement. However, elaboration of a positive comment works (moderately) the other way—elaboration allows the interjector to add their own thoughts and thus detract attention from the speaker, while unelaborated positive interjections simply support the speaker. So elaboration on the positive means a moderate loss of power by the original speaker, while elaboration on the negative protects the speaker's authority. Consistent with this interpretation, our initial look in chapter appendix figure A8.1 revealed that negative interruptions are more likely to be elaborated than are positive interruptions. This tells us that negative interruptions that are not elaborated are probably perceived as hostile, and the elaboration is meant to soften them. We assume that elaborating on the negative is an attempt to soften the hostility of the interruption and is an indicator of respect to the interruptee.

Unelaborated positive interruption

0:01:58.8	Man C: [The floor income] should be high enough to support a person, but low enough that it's uncomfortable—
0:02:12.8	Woman D: [interposing] I agree.
0:02:12.3	Man C: —so that they don't feel content to sit there and not do anything and mooch off of society.

Elaborated positive interruption

0:06:59 Man E: I guess it depends on where you set it. I think the problem you run into, I just think that whenever you cap what someone can do, like, this destroys incentive. You do not want to push things.

0:07:09 Woman D: [interposing] If you know anything about economics, then you know that that is totally every principle of it.

Unelaborated negative interruption

00:04:38 Woman E: I would say like the set range, that way everybody gets approximately the same amount. Say you work a little harder . . . you get a little bit more, but then nobody is screwed. That's a good goal.

00:04:42 Man A: It's not the most ideal.

Elaborated negative interruption

00:24:23 Man D: Yeah, the floor one. It's just not—I don't really—I mean, it may not have—I just don't see too many negatives of it—

00:24:39 Woman C: [interposing] You're almost doubling the low class.

00:24:40 Man D: —as compared to the no redistribution.

Accordingly, we divide elaborations into negative and positive and examine them separately. We want to see if a rise in women's status from rule and numbers increases the elaborated proportion of negative interruptions issued to women and decreases the elaborated proportion of positive interruptions women receive.

The familiar interaction pattern comes through cleanly in figure 8.4, which shows the elaborated proportion of negative interruptions women received from either men or women. The figure shows predicted values from a regression in chapter appendix table A8.1 (column 1).[21] Women receive more respect from those around them as their status rises. As we saw in the earlier analysis of talk time, rising numbers alone are no guarantee of greater respect; women's numbers only help when numbers carry an advantage, that is, under majority rule.

[21] The high level of random error in elaborations makes statistical significance less likely even for real effects, and that is why we report an effect that only approaches significance.

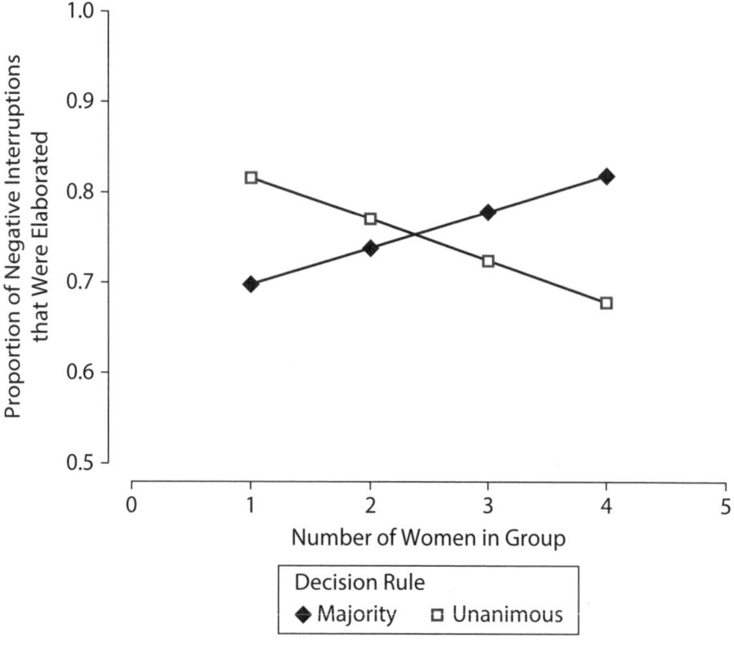

Figure 8.4. Elaborated proportion of negative interruptions received by women from men and women, mixed groups only. Note: Based on predicted values from chapter appendix table A8.1, column 1.

When we examine these effects separately by each gender combination in the dyad, we find one model with effects even approaching significance—and that is for men positively interrupting women. Table 8.3 shows that the positive interruptions women receive from men are much less likely to be elaborated in conditions where women have higher status—the familiar interaction effect we find throughout our analyses shows up here and is highly significant. We also see the protective effect of unanimous rule for minority women.[22] Figure 8.5 shows the predicted values from the model in table 8.3 and clearly illustrates how men change their elaboration behavior as women's status increases. Under majority rule when women's status is the lowest, nearly 63% of the positive interruptions they receive from men are elaborated; this decreases to about 19% when women are at their strongest. Similarly, women receive more positive elaborations from men as the unanimous rule's protective effect weakens.

[22] A Wald test of the predicted values from the model provides evidence that in groups with one woman, women receive more elaborated positive interruptions under majority rule than under unanimity (p = 0.057, two-tailed). The difference in decision rules is not significant for groups with two women (p = 0.39, two-tailed).

Table 8.3: Elaborated Proportion of Positive Interruptions to Women from Men, Mixed-Gender Groups Only

Majority Rule	0.545**
	(0.239)
Number of Women	0.077
	(0.058)
Majority Rule × Number of Women	–0.225***
	(0.079)
Egalitarianism	0.022
	(0.284)
Number of Egalitarians	–0.003
	(0.047)
Constant	0.232
	(0.208)
Observations	83
R-squared	0.11
Control for Experimental Location	Yes

Note: Individual-level analysis. Cluster robust standard errors in parentheses. *** $p < 0.01$, ** $p < 0.05$, * $p < 0.10$, two-tailed test.

Women receive a more polite form of disagreement when their status is high (though this effect only approaches significance), and in such settings they also receive considerably more unambiguous support when interrupted, specifically from men. Using a positively worded statement when interrupting a speaker is a standard form of politeness that saves face and preempts conflict. But it can be a means to achieving an instrumental end. A polite maneuver designed to take the floor for oneself serves the goal of articulating one's own view. Men are much less likely to use such polite means to assert their thoughts during women's floor time as women's status rises. Put differently, men are more likely to simply affirm women rather than to affirm them while taking the floor for their own thoughts. That only women experience this rise in simple support, while men do not, suggests that women's shifting status is at work. Furthermore, men are the ones shifting their behavior, and they do so only in addressing women. This again supports the notion that the explanation lies in men's recognition of women's status. Men are the ones instantiating women's rise in status in the group.

Overall, we found a number of ways in which women's numbers and the group's rules—our indicators of women's status—shape women's experience of authority. First, women receive fewer positive interruptions when their status is low, and thus experience a high negative-to-positive balance of interjections,

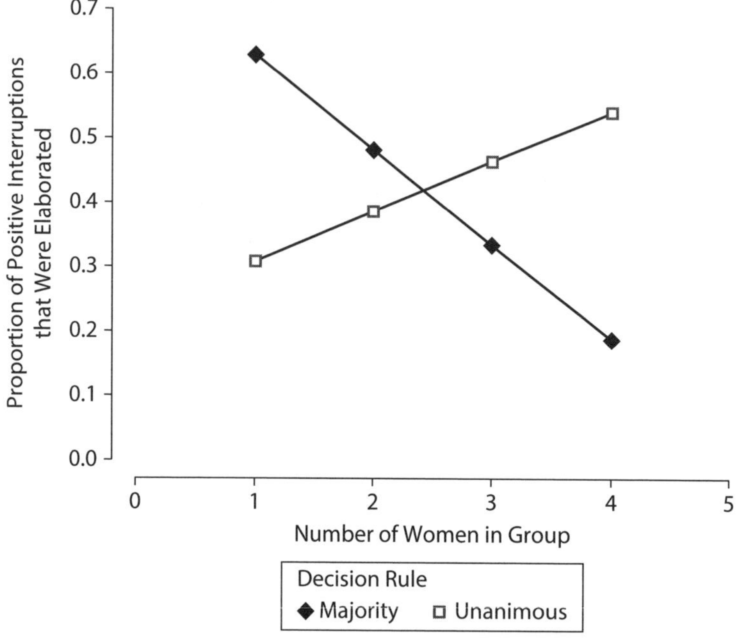

Figure 8.5. Elaborated proportion of positive interruptions received by women from men, mixed groups only.

particularly from men. Second, what positive interruptions they do receive are more likely to include elaborations that involve intrusions upon their floor time, again particularly from men. Third, the negative signals directed toward women are more likely to be hostile—raw expressions of disagreement not accompanied by any attempt to soften the comment with further elaboration, from both men and women. It is not just that women are receiving fewer positive interruptions in conditions where they have low status (though that's important), it is also that the positives are less affirming and the negative signals are more negative.

The Effects of Interruptions

Next we ask whether the balance of positivity and negativity is associated with other indicators of authority, measured after discussion. Do interruptions have an effect on perceived influence in the eyes of others? Recall from chapter 5 that the conditions of deliberation affect the influence of deliberators as measured by the number of other members who chose a given member as "the most influential member of your group during the group discussion" (ranging from 0 to

4). We found there that the more women, the more likely is the average woman to be chosen as most influential—but only under majority rule. The effect of composition reverses under unanimous rule, where the average woman is more likely to be seen as influential when women are few than when they are many. Now we can see if interruptions help explain these patterns of influence.[23]

Figure 8.6 displays the effects from panel A of table 8.4. That table shows the negative binomial regression estimates of the effect of the person's negative balance of interruptions received on others' ratings of that person's influence in the group, controlling on talkativeness, for both mixed-gender and enclave groups. The figure and table show that for women especially, the higher their balance of negative interruptions, the fewer the influence votes they receive. The figure shows that as the proportion of negative interruptions moves across its range, the perceived influence of women in mixed-gender groups drops by over two-thirds. The effect is similar in all-female groups, but much smaller for men, whether in mixed or all-male groups.

It seems that women's authority is especially affected by the experience of affirmation rather than hostility in conversation. The conditions of deliberation that cause male members to negatively interrupt women without providing significant positive feedback also cause women to lose standing as deliberators. What groups do while interacting can lower or raise women's ability to make valued contributions to the collective.

And what about participants' sense of their own influence? The results in panel B of table 8.4 show that on the key measure of "my opinions were influential," the negative balance of interruptions again matters. A higher balance of negative interruptions is associated with lower perceptions of women's self-efficacy in discussion (column 1), but not with men's (columns 3 and 4). Furthermore, the effect on women applies only when they interact with men; when we examine all-female enclaves separately, the effect decreases

[23] We also explored the relationship between the negative balance of interruptions and our individual-level index of satisfaction with the discussion. We find that both genders feel less satisfied with the discussion when the interruptions they experience are more negative, though the source of the interruption and the group-level conditions also appear to matter. For women, satisfaction decreases only when they are negatively interrupted *by men* in the condition where women's standing tends to be lowest: majority-rule groups in which women are the minority ($b = -0.12$, $SE = 0.09$, $p < 0.06$, one-tailed; regression includes controls for *Proportion Talk* and experimental location). Negative interruptions are not related to satisfaction under other conditions or when the interruptions come from women. Men tend to be less satisfied when they experience negative interruptions across a variety of contexts, but for men, the biggest decrease in satisfaction comes when they are negatively interrupted *by women* in unanimous groups with many women ($b = -0.30$, $SE = 0.15$, $p < 0.04$, one-tailed; controls for *Proportion Talk* and location included). Thus for women, satisfaction may decrease when interruptions come from men in conditions where women experience less power; for men, satisfaction may decrease the most when interruptions come from women in the condition where unanimous rule should empower men. We do not put much weight on these results since they are not strong deductions from our core hypotheses.

Table 8.4: Panel A: Effect of Negative Proportion of Interruptions Received on Others' Ratings of Speaker's Influence, All Groups

	Women		Men	
	(1) Mixed	(2) Enclave	(3) Mixed	(4) Enclave
Neg / (Pos + Neg)	–1.315***	–1.098**	–0.541*	–0.631
	(0.388)	(0.537)	(0.318)	(0.715)
Egalitarianism	–0.181	–1.474*	–0.552	–1.357*
	(0.933)	(0.820)	(0.488)	(0.754)
Number of Speaking Turns	0.019***	0.011***	0.011***	0.024***
	(0.005)	(0.004)	(0.002)	(0.007)
Constant	–0.947**	0.083	0.035	–1.156**
	(0.472)	(0.561)	(0.231)	(0.585)
Alpha	0.646	0.516	0.138	0.371
	(0.319)	(0.315)	(0.119)	(0.349)
Observations	128	65	141	59
Control for Experimental Location	Yes	Yes	Yes	Yes

Note: Coefficients from a negative binomial model. Individual-level analysis. Cluster robust standard errors in parentheses. *** $p < 0.01$, ** $p < 0.05$, * $p < 0.10$, two-tailed test.

Panel B: Effect of Negative Proportion of Interruptions Received on Self-Rating of Speaker's Influence, All Groups

	Women		Men	
	(1) Mixed	(2) Enclave	(3) Mixed	(4) Enclave
Neg / (Neg + Pos)	–0.132**	0.084	–0.039	–0.036
	(0.053)	(0.156)	(0.052)	(0.063)
Egalitarianism	–0.018	0.039	–0.035	0.006
	(0.088)	(0.170)	(0.112)	(0.109)
Number of Speaking Turns	0.001	0.002	0.001	0.003***
	(0.001)	(0.001)	(0.001)	(0.001)
Constant	0.688***	0.471***	0.690***	0.580***
	(0.059)	(0.131)	(0.055)	(0.051)
Observations	128	65	141	59
R-squared	0.07	0.05	0.02	0.27
Control for Experimental Location	Yes	Yes	Yes	Yes

Note: Individual-level analysis. Cluster robust standard errors in parentheses. *** $p < 0.01$, ** $p < 0.05$, * $p < 0.10$, two-tailed test.

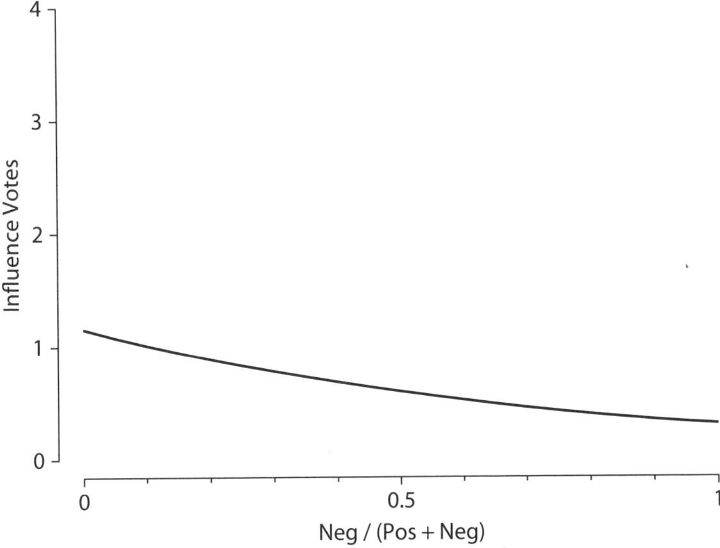

Figure 8.6. Effect of negative interruptions on perceptions of women's influence, mixed groups. Note: Predicted values from table 8.4, panel A, column 1.

and loses statistical significance (column 2). Women's sense of their contribution to the group depends on the balance of interjections they receive, but not when they are in all-female groups. One of the functions of women's enclaves is to take the sting out of other people's responses to one's opinions. Men do not need male enclaves to be able to brush off hostility or the absence of approval.

Finally, the effect on women's rating of their own influence holds when we replace the negative balance with the positively interrupted proportion of speaking turns (b = 2.6, SE = 0.85) but not with the negative proportion of turns (the effect is 0.71, SE = 1.26, the wrong sign and not significant).[24] A few negative comments do not deter women as long as they also receive a good number of positive reinforcements. Women need positive validation while they speak in order to feel that they matter; men do not. The importance of the positive in communication is underscored by the fact that if the message is positive frequently enough, the negative becomes irrelevant.

A formal test of mediation (Imai, Keele, and Tingley 2010) confirms the basic result. The mixed-group conditions affect women's influence—in their own eyes and in the eyes of others—in part through their effect on the negative

[24]Men are unaffected, except that in enclaves, when men have more positively interrupted turns, they rate their influence the "wrong direction"—lower. b = -1.05**, SE = 0.42 for positive proportion of speaking turns for men in groups with only men.

proportion of interruptions received (see online appendix table C8.ii.2). The conditions substantially affect the balance of negativity directed toward women, and it, in turn, affects women's authority. In sum, the relative negativity one receives is a crucial factor in women's—and others'—sense of their influence. The conditions of discussion shape the kinds of social interactions women experience, and those interactions can elevate or depress women's authority.

Positive interruptions play a particularly helpful role for women who entered the discussion with low levels of confidence in their ability to participate. In chapter 6 we presented evidence that confidence enables women's increased participation, especially in conditions where they are disempowered. Now we can ask how the dynamics of discussion affect women with varying levels of confidence. Pooling across all mixed-gender conditions, we find that for both low- and high-confidence women, a higher proportion of positive interruptions is correlated with increased talk time during the discussion and more influence votes from other members of the group afterward (online appendix table C8.ii.3). But positive interruptions also yield a unique benefit to low-confidence women, increasing their self-rated sense of efficacy at a higher rate than that of high-confidence women (the difference-in-differences is significant at $p < 0.09$, two-tailed test; online appendix table C8.ii.4).[25] Put differently, confidence moderates the effect of positive interruptions on feeling that one's opinions influenced the group's discussion and eventual decision.[26] When they receive few positive interruptions, women with low predeliberation confidence report lower levels of postdiscussion efficacy than those who entered the discussion with more confidence. But when they receive more encouraging feedback in the form of a higher rate of positive interruptions, low-confidence women equal and even surpass high-confidence women in feeling that their opinions helped to shape the group (online appendix figure C8.ii.1).[27] This effect holds only for mixed-gender groups. In all-female enclaves, efficacy is unaffected by positive interruptions.

[25] In addition, Panel B of online appendix table C8.ii.3 presents suggestive evidence that low-confidence women who receive a higher proportion of positive interruptions may also benefit disproportionately in terms of influence votes (difference-in-differences is significant at $p < 0.15$).

[26] The dependent variable is a self-report that "my opinions were influential in shaping the group discussion and final decision." We do not find an interaction between confidence and positive interruptions with respect to our other measure of efficacy: "I feel like my voice was heard during the group discussion." High-confidence women are always more likely than low-confidence women to agree that their "voice was heard," no matter what the pattern of positive interruptions.

[27] A difference of means test shows that high-confidence women are also more likely than low-confidence women to receive positive interruptions ($t = 2.25$, $p = 0.025$). Women of lower confidence experience fewer positive interruptions and also seem to have lower self-efficacy when they receive fewer positives. This fact underscores that our data here are only correlational; we cannot tell if the former causes the latter or vice versa.

Positive interruptions are thus especially important for women who entered the discussion harboring some concerns about their ability to participate effectively, and only when they interact with men. Strong positive signals during the discussion provide a substantial boost to the postdiscussion efficacy of those women, which they appear to need more than others do. By comparison, positive interruptions have no effect on the efficacy of men, regardless of their level of prediscussion confidence.[28]

Another way to examine the encouraging effects of interruptions is to ask if positive interruptions elevate the speaker's percentage of talk in the group. In table 8.5 we find that for female speakers, the answer is yes, but only when the encouragement is issued by the gender empowered in that condition. That is, women accelerate their talk the more they are encouraged either by men in conditions where women are least empowered (majority rule, few women), or by women when women are empowered (majority rule, majority women). That is, women speak more when they get more positive interruptions from men, but not from women, when women are disempowered, and they speak more when they get positive encouragement from women but not from men when women are the dominant gender. Female speakers thus calibrate the volume of their speech to the more powerful gender in the group. Men are not affected in this way.[29]

We have seen that the experience of interruptions carries crucial consequences for deliberators. In particular, the relative negativity one receives when other members engage with one's speech is a crucial factor in women's sense of their influence and in others' perception of women's influence. The heart of the matter is whether women receive positive signals; when they do, they can withstand the occasional negative response.

And again we see that the same experience can elicit very different responses by men and women. Women need frequent positive validation while they speak in order to feel that they matter; men do not.[30]

[28] In addition, we find no evidence that confidence moderates the relationship between *negative* interruptions and self-efficacy, self-rated influence, or other-rated influence votes among men or women. This lack of moderating relationship holds for both measures of negativity—the negative proportion of interruptions received and the proportion of speaking turns that receive negative interruptions.

[29] The equivalent table (online appendix table C8.ii.5) for male speakers does not show this pattern. Men accelerate their speech only under unanimous rule with majority women. But even there, they only respond to encouragement from men, not from women. So women seem to decide how much to speak based on how much the dominant gender encourages them; men decide how much to speak based on how much men encourage them where women are neither disempowered nor dominant. The negative proportion of positive or negative interruptions the speaker receives does not affect either women's or men's *Proportion Talk*.

[30] Of course, it may be that if men never hear any positive validation over a long period, they would be affected.

Table 8.5: Effect of the Proportion of Speaking Turns Receiving Positive Interruptions on Women's *Proportion Talk*

	Women in Enclaves		Minority Female (1–2 women)				Majority Female (3–4 women)			
			Majority Rule		Unanimous Rule		Majority Rule		Unanimous Rule	
	(1) Majority Rule	(2) Unanimous Rule	(3) From Women	(4) From Men	(5) From Women	(6) From Men	(7) From Women	(8) From Men	(9) From Women	(10) From Men
Prop. w/ Positive	0.960	0.202	–0.701	3.157**	0.779	–0.465	2.453***	–0.085	0.838	0.624
	(0.664)	(0.502)	(0.744)	(1.257)	(0.901)	(0.922)	(0.358)	(0.587)	(0.584)	(0.419)
Constant	0.176***	0.193***	0.174***	0.115***	0.157***	0.190***	0.140***	0.190***	0.159***	0.162***
	(0.017)	(0.017)	(0.029)	(0.024)	(0.014)	(0.037)	(0.011)	(0.017)	(0.016)	(0.018)
Observations	40	35	14	23	12	22	53	53	59	59
R-squared	0.05	0.00	0.02	0.16	0.06	0.01	0.34	0.00	0.04	0.05
Prop. w/ Positive	1.025	0.216	–0.368	2.143**	0.620	–0.103	2.481***	–0.077	0.751	0.528
	(0.759)	(0.650)	(0.853)	(0.854)	(0.886)	(0.854)	(0.325)	(0.644)	(0.540)	(0.420)
Egalitarianism	–0.033	–0.002	–0.194**	–0.224**	0.167	0.210	0.042	0.017	–0.074	–0.072
	(0.043)	(0.179)	(0.068)	(0.098)	(0.370)	(0.158)	(0.047)	(0.076)	(0.073)	(0.073)
Constant	0.187***	0.193	0.223***	0.208***	0.034	0.048	0.118***	0.171***	0.211***	0.211***
	(0.032)	(0.105)	(0.047)	(0.055)	(0.184)	(0.084)	(0.025)	(0.045)	(0.039)	(0.041)
Observations	40	35	14	23	12	22	53	53	59	59
R-squared	0.05	0.00	0.12	0.26	0.43	0.14	0.35	0.01	0.07	0.07
Control for Experimental Location	Yes	Yes	Yes	Yes	Yes	Yes	Yes	Yes	Yes	Yes

Note: Dependent variable in all models is *Proportion Talk*. Individual-level analysis. Cluster robust standard errors in parentheses. *** $p < 0.01$, ** $p < 0.05$, * $p < 0.10$, two-tailed test.

The Rapport of Enclaves

Finally, we argued that the level of rapport in the group not only matters to women, but also that a preponderance of women may elevate it, and particularly so in female enclaves. So now we pose our final question: when does the group take on an affirming, friendly, and inviting character? For this analysis we examine the group as a whole without differentiating women and men. We control on location, the number of egalitarians, and the group's average number of speaking turns.

Table 8.6 shows that the number of women matters to the tenor of interaction in the group—but only with enclave groups included. As the number of women increases, the number of positive interjections in the group rises (without regard to rule).[31] In addition, when we look only at positive interruptions that elaborated on the content of the initial speaker's thought, we find the same result—the more women, the more positive elaborated interruptions in the group. That is, the positive tone is accompanied by meaningful content. The interrupter offers some substance that goes beyond what the speaker articulated. Not only are predominantly female groups warmer and friendlier, they also use this rapport and friendliness to advance the discussion and provide a meaningful exchange of views.[32]

This interpretation rests on the assumption that women elevate the positive—and not the negative. To test this hypothesis, we look at negative interruptions. These results are displayed next to the positive interruptions results in table 8.6. Unlike positive interjections, negative interruptions remain flat across the conditions. Neither do the conditions affect the number of negative interruptions with elaboration.[33]

Finally, table 8.6 shows that when we omit the enclave groups and examine only mixed-gender groups, the only significant effect is for gender composition on neutral interruptions with elaboration. Positive interruptions do not rise with the number of women when women interact with men. They increase only among female enclave groups. That is, the warmth effect from greater numbers of women is located specifically in gender-homogeneous groups.[34]

These results tell us that the chief effect on groups as a whole is located with women's enclaves. These settings are exceptionally supportive. Further, these

[31] The dependent variables in table 8.6 are the sum of each type of interruption occurring in a group.

[32] Online appendix table C8.ii.6 shows that the number of women also increases the chance that women complete their thoughts in the face of negative interruptions while prompting the interrupter to stop before finishing the interruption (column 1), regardless of rule. For interrupted men the effect is not significant (column 2).

[33] Interestingly, the number of women also elevates the group's neutral interruptions.

[34] We do not wish to make much of the effect on neutral or on elaborated neutral interruptions because they are so few.

Table 8.6: Group-Level Effects on Total Number of Interruptions, Mixed-Gender and Enclave Groups

	Positive		Negative		Neutral	
	(1) All	(2) Elaborated	(3) All	(4) Elaborated	(5) All	(6) Elaborated
Mixed-Gender Groups Only						
Majority Rule	1.34 (6.58)	2.30 (4.18)	3.20 (4.18)	1.64 (3.39)	−0.53 (1.87)	−0.42 (1.19)
Number of Women	1.10 (1.68)	0.85 (1.07)	0.10 (1.07)	−0.29 (0.86)	0.79 (0.48)	0.59* (0.30)
Majority Rule × Number of Women	−0.81 (2.39)	−1.33 (1.52)	−1.27 (1.52)	−0.71 (1.23)	−0.09 (0.68)	−0.04 (0.43)
# of Speaking Turns	0.09*** (0.02)	0.05*** (0.01)	0.09*** (0.01)	0.07*** (0.01)	0.03*** (0.00)	0.02*** (0.00)
# of Egalitarians	−0.23 (1.43)	−0.75 (0.91)	0.50 (0.91)	0.44 (0.74)	−0.76* (0.41)	−0.42 (0.26)
Constant	0.28 (6.22)	−1.23 (3.95)	−9.15** (3.95)	−6.43** (3.20)	−1.50 (1.76)	−1.28 (1.13)
Observations	64	64	64	64	64	64
R-squared	0.47	0.37	0.65	0.64	0.54	0.46
Control for Experimental Location	Yes	Yes	Yes	Yes	Yes	Yes
Mixed-Gender Groups and Enclaves						
Majority Rule	1.66 (4.36)	0.68 (2.39)	−0.47 (2.48)	−1.07 (2.05)	0.13 (1.26)	−0.34 (0.83)
Number of Women	2.41** (1.01)	1.14** (0.55)	0.08 (0.58)	−0.28 (0.47)	0.53* (0.29)	0.27 (0.19)
Majority Rule × Number of Women	−0.76 (1.43)	−0.43 (0.78)	0.47 (0.81)	0.53 (0.67)	−0.05 (0.41)	0.14 (0.27)
# of Speaking Turns	0.12*** (0.01)	0.06*** (0.01)	0.09*** (0.01)	0.07*** (0.01)	0.03*** (0.00)	0.02*** (0.00)
# of Egalitarians	−2.47** (1.18)	−1.57** (0.65)	−0.63 (0.67)	−0.42 (0.55)	−0.97*** (0.34)	−0.57** (0.22)
Constant	−3.05 (4.91)	−1.85 (2.69)	−7.62*** (2.80)	−5.20** (2.30)	−1.57 (1.42)	−0.97 (0.93)
Observations	94	94	94	94	94	94
R-squared	0.60	0.53	0.69	0.68	0.57	0.48
Control for Experimental Location	Yes	Yes	Yes	Yes	Yes	Yes

Note: Group-level analysis. Standard errors in parentheses. *** $p < 0.01$, ** $p < 0.05$, * $p < 0.10$, two-tailed test.

results imply that this affirmation is the main way that elaboration is conveyed when one speaker directly engages another. In female enclaves, elaboration is achieved primarily through positive rather than negative or neutral interruptions. The warm tone of the group's exchange directly affects the group's success in providing new thoughts that add meaningful content to what is being said. Women's enclaves create an inclusive discussion tone, and this affirming tone, unlike a hostile or conflictual tone, carries with it the contribution of one speaker to another's thoughts.

Conclusion

We began this chapter with a question. Do women's numbers affect the nature of the interaction and thus women's ability to express their voice? Our results suggest that the answer is yes, but the rule moderates the effect. In mixed-gender conditions, groups with more women and majority rule, and groups with few women and unanimous rule, produce a more positive interaction style among the members. Moreover, women are the main beneficiaries of this style. It goes hand in hand with greater perceived influence, self-efficacy, and their active participation in discussion.

Some highlights of our detailed findings reveal the basic dynamics at work. More women make the balance of interruptions more positive under majority (but not unanimous) rule. This mainly occurs through more positive interruptions. Positive interruptions from men are less likely to be elaborated as women's status rises, providing women with a more pure form of support and attention. Negative interruptions from men and women are (marginally) more likely to be elaborated, softening the disagreement women encounter while speaking.

Especially badly off are women in the gender minority under majority rule. For these women, deliberation is a negative experience in which their speech is interrupted in a dismissive manner and their words rarely affirmed. Lone women, for example, issue a higher rate of positive interjections than any other gender subgroup but receive the least in return (in each case, relative to their speaking turns). At 20% or 40% of the group, women are less than half as likely as men in their group to experience approval while speaking.

In an earlier chapter we saw that in this majority-rule minority-female situation, low-confidence women are particularly quiet. It may be that the pattern of interruptions we documented partly explains why these women react so strongly to those conditions. The absence of positive affirmation in these conditions would likely affect women with low confidence especially badly. Evidence presented here is consistent with this notion.[35] Although we found

[35] Because the number of women in majority-rule groups with few women is limited, we do not have the statistical power to further parse the differences between high and low levels of confidence

an association for all women between receiving positive interruptions and elevated levels of talk and of influence votes, the association between positive interruptions and efficacy is especially strong for low-confidence women.

The results fit a broader pattern of gender inequality in deliberation. In the usual circumstances of political discussion, women are a numerical minority, and the group uses a norm of majority rule, whether it is officially stated or implied; thus, the expected style of interaction is one of individual agency and conflict. There, behavior tends to conform to a gendered pattern of differential power. Men tend to assert themselves through actions that society associates with higher power or status; women tend to behave in the opposite.[36]

Our large-N findings replicate those from legislatures, such as the confirmation hearings for Justice David Souter or the Colorado state legislature. There, women encounter more hostile speech patterns than men (Kathlene 1994). These cases also illustrate our findings that the ability of women to be heard in deliberation depends on the forms of speech. The pattern of interruptions one receives is a significant indicator of and instantiation of one's authority. Most importantly, Mattei's narrative fits well with our results from minority-female, majority-rule conditions: women constituted 40% of the witnesses, yet "the average male witness had a higher proportion of floor time," and (the all-male) senators "*interrupted women more frequently than men*." That this is a gender effect is driven home by her finding that "senators from both parties were more likely to undermine the authority of female witnesses than that of males, particularly through higher rates of empirical questions, disagreements, challenges, and the citation of other authorities to contradict women's testimony, and the characterization of women's words as unreasonable" (1998, 459 for all quotes; emphasis ours).

That is, we see in the lab what we see in the most consequential settings of power: when the procedure does not account for the default inequalities between men and women, even near-equal levels descriptive representation do not lead to equal substantive representation. Substantive representation, whether in the most official or the most casual public settings, depends on the social structure—namely, gender composition—and on institutional norms and procedures that are neutral on their face but carry profound consequences for social inequality. Finally, these real-world cases illustrate our own findings in the sense that the ability of women to be heard depends on the forms of speech. The pattern of interruptions one receives is a significant indicator of and instantiation of one's authority and goes hand in hand with other such indicators, such as floor time. Not only the logical and evidentiary content of speech matters, its social content and meaning also matter a great deal, and perhaps matter most of all.

---

across the experimental conditions. The findings about the relationship between positive interruptions and efficacy are based on analysis that pools all mixed-gender conditions.

[36]However, men in mixed groups who gave more interruptions to other participants were not perceived as more influential by the other participants, regardless of disposition (results not shown).

Similar patterns obtain in two other, very different settings. High-performing work teams exhibit a ratio of six positive to one negative comments, while poor performers have a ratio of about 1 positive comment for every 3 negative (Losada and Heaphy 2004). In our study, the most negatively interrupted members—minority women under majority rule—experience a ratio similar to that of the poorly functioning work teams. The implication is that the typical setting for political discussion, where women are a numerical minority under majority rule, is a dysfunctional one for women.

This turns out to be a common pattern in an altogether different realm—marriage. Studies of married couples by the psychologist John Gottman find that what predicts marital longevity and satisfaction is not the negativity but the positivity of the couple's interaction (Gottman 1994). A couple may exchange a large number of negative comments, but these are irrelevant as long as the couple also exchanges a far larger number of positive comments (five to one, to be exact). The results in this chapter point in a similar direction. The positive percentage of interruptions is a crucial indicator of successful interaction in a variety of settings.

Our key point, however, is not found in previous studies; when the procedure does not account for the default inequalities between men and women, increasing descriptive representation does not increase other forms of representation. Representation depends not only on gender composition but also on institutional norms and procedures that are neutral on their face but carry profound consequences for social inequality. While our results paint a dark portrait of gender inequality, the effects of unanimous rule are heartening for advocates of deliberation and for the goal of social justice. The dismal situation of minority women under majority rule improves dramatically under unanimous rule. The decision rule is a simple yet powerful element of institutional design. It restrains the disrespect that men sometimes direct toward women where women have low status, and raises their affirmations of women's speech. In these ways, it creates a norm of interaction that actively includes women. Simple institutional procedures can create equality and justice in the process and outcome of representation.

When we alter the conditions of discussion, the ones to change their behavior are, mostly, men. Men become nicer to women as the conditions elevate women's status. Some might say something like this: "well, why don't women just talk more? It's women's responsibility to speak—no rule prevents them from doing so, and no one stands in their way." Our reply is our finding that men change their behavior in such a way as to make women's participation less rewarding and more difficult. The process is subtle and, by any formal measure, legitimate, but it ends up carrying particularly negative consequences for women.

The assumption that women are not valuable in discussions that decide the fate of the collective produces gender inequality. If women are not needed for making decisions, then they will not be much included. Conversely, our findings about rule imply that when women are needed, women are included. Women are needed when they are a majority under rules that give a majority power and when they are a minority under rules that give the minority power. The rule can elegantly set in motion a whole set of conversational practices that increase the warmth and affirmation that in turn elevate women's representation. Simple institutional procedures can equalize representation.

In addition, we now know the secret to women's enclaves: they are nice! Women's distinctive ways of interacting—supporting one another with considerable positive feedback—come to the fore in these all-female groups. This dynamic takes the sting off negative interruptions, making women more resilient in the face of engaged opposition. To be sure, the average woman's experience is not qualitatively different in enclaves than in the best of the majority-female conditions; however, when we look at the group as a whole, all-female groups emerge as the most mutually supportive environments, and only there is women's sense of efficacy in the group impervious to the effects of negative interjections.

We also argued that interruptions are a means to establish a norm of rapport. Centuries ago the French observer Tocqueville was impressed by what he viewed as Americans' zeal to form civic associations. One of the remarkable characteristics of these associations, he maintained, is the face-to-face meeting: "the power of meeting," he noted, lies in part in its "warmth and energy" ([1835] 2006, book 1, chapter 12). We saw that female enclaves are the most mutually affirming groups. In this sense, political philosophers are right to endorse the notion that disadvantaged groups can benefit from spaces of their own. Now we can say why this insight may be on the mark. These groups are distinguished from others specifically on the dimension of mutual support and rapport. Interestingly, these groups are no different from other groups in their negative interruptions. What they do instead is supply more positive interjections. This changes the balance of negative to positive.

The results fit a broader pattern of gender inequality during interactions between men and women. In the usual circumstances of political discussion in the United States, women are reluctant to participate in the exchange as fully as men do. In these settings, not only are women a minority, but there is also a norm of majority rule, whether it is officially stated or implied by the political context. There, where women tend to be less numerous than men and where the expected style of interaction is one of individual agency and conflict, behavior tends to conform to a gendered pattern of differential power. Men tend to assert themselves through actions that society associates with higher power or status; women tend in turn to behave in ways that signal lower status or power. [37]

Our results also speak to the ideal of civility in deliberation (Kingwell 1995). For some liberal theorists, such as Gutmann and Thompson (1996), reciprocity

[37] People may not be using interruptions to establish power consciously.

is the foundation of deliberative democracy, and civility is an integral part of reciprocity (Macedo 1999). On this view, civility is a fundamental civic virtue in a liberal democracy (see Herbst 2010, 13; White 2006). For other theorists, civility is also necessary, though in the specific form of a display of respect in the face of morally abhorrent actions (Calhoun 2005).

We view civility as inadequate for deliberation on two grounds. First, theories of dialogue or deliberation that advocate civility as a virtue tend to ignore the social stratification function of civility. Sociological and historical accounts emphasize that civility entails "markers of politeness, decorum, courtesy or good manners that enabled one to distinguish oneself from others" who are more "savage" (White 2006, 447). Civil behavior was appropriate to members of the upper classes in European and European-dominated societies; other social classes were deemed incapable of civility because they were incapable of self-regulation and thus of regulating others (Sapiro 1999). That is, civility creates a social distinction between privileged, high-status groups, whose civil manner marks them as socially superior and capable of governance, and their inferiors. The flip side of the same coin is that charges of incivility could be used to enforce political conformity and silence the numerical minority, in the view of John Stuart Mill (Herbst 2010, 16). "'Invective, sarcasm,' and other forms of rudeness were only denounced when they were used 'against the prevailing opinion'" (Mill quoted in Herbst 2010, 16). A more contemporary twist on the uses of the accusation of incivility is that when groups such as women attempt to challenge the political or social hierarchy, they may be accused of uncivil behavior (Sapiro 1999; Hertz and Reverby 1995).[38] A final variation on this theme is that dominant groups' dominant behavior toward subordinate groups may too often be unconstrained by norms of civility; as Calhoun puts it, "social norms of civility may fail to condemn the contemptuous treatment of socially disesteemed groups, because they interpret such contempt as civilly displaying the appropriate measure of respect" (2005, 266).[39] Thus the concept

[38] As Lynn Sanders (1997) argues, certain standards of public talk can have "pernicious consequences" that distract "from more basic problems of inclusion and mutual recognition," ultimately making it more likely that "the talk of an identifiable and privileged sector of the American public will dominate public dialogue" (370).

[39] However, Calhoun (2005) eloquently defends the concept of civility as benefiting marginalized groups: "Members of disesteemed social groups are more likely to experience displays of contempt, intrusions on their privacy, intolerance of their conceptions of the good, and the discounting of their feelings and aims as less important. The last thing they need is for the privileged to be acting out, without restraint, their personal views about homosexuals, or independent women, or Jews, or blacks. What they need is precisely for the privileged to feel constrained to control their hostile, contemptuous, disapproving, and dismissive attitudes. Those constraints will be supplied, if they are supplied at all, by norms of civility, since civility just is the display of respect, tolerance, and consideration toward others no matter what we might privately think of them. What the disesteemed also need is for there to be shared social understandings about the intolerability of prejudiced and oppressive behavior. Those shared social understandings, if they exist, will define the bounds of

of civility has intellectual and historical roots in a hierarchical and time-bound meaning that we reject.

Second, civility is a social code of politeness (Brown and Levinson 1987), and politeness can be quite cold and indifferent in its emotional tone. Civility merely dictates that the listener get out of the speaker's way by avoiding negative interruptions and hostility. Witness the emphasis in the historical concept of civility on self-restraint, quiet (Kingwell 1995), and other forms of self-control (Herbst 2010, 13–16; White 2006). Avoiding action that gives offense is an important criterion, but it is not sufficient.[40] A narrow focus on civility can lead to a cold and formal proceduralism or politeness that is insufficient for the inclusion of women. Real inclusion requires something more than the absence of rudeness or a recursion to overly formal ways of managing potential disagreements.

We view the key concept for gender equality as rapport rather than civility. To be sure, many women may require that listeners avoid expressions of hostility, contempt, and arrogance. However, at least in this time and place, and given the gendered experiences that shape women before they enter deliberation, women also tend to require something more positive and proactive —affirmation and support, not merely the absence of negative attacks. In fact, our enclave result shows that disagreement per se is not deflating to women at all—as long as it occurs in an environment that is socially supportive. Thus what deliberating groups should strive to achieve is something close to friendship (Mansbridge 1983). As sociolinguists put it, friendship is characterized by speech patterns that demonstrate a high level of supportive engagement, a "talking along" that creates solidarity and affirmation (Tannen 2009), camaraderie, and rapport (Lakoff 1975). This is the concept we attempted to measure here, and it differs from the more minimal requirement of politeness, and from the hierarchically inflected concept of civility.

The results also speak to Mansbridge's work on deliberative democracy, specifically her distinction between adversarial and consensual styles (1983). Mansbridge distinguishes between adversarial modes of decision making, involving voting, majority rule, and the aggregation of individual preferences; and unitary modes, typically associated with small, intimate groups, where the focus is on consensus building.[41] In an adversary system, the assumption is that conflict

---

civility. While it is true that in morally imperfect social worlds civility norms fail to protect the disesteemed, the problem is not that civility is overvalued; and the solution is not to care less about being civil. The problem is in the shared understandings embedded in our norms of civility. These need to be contested, not the value of civility in general" (274–75).

[40] Self-regulation is also a distinctly conservative moral value in the United States today (McAdams et al. 2013). Another criticism of civility is that it is inauthentic—it is the "appearance" of "esteem" that hides the lack of true esteem (Tönnies [1887] 1988, 78), a veil that obscures how one genuinely feels (Tocqueville [1835] 2006, book 3, chapter 14).

[41] Or with the need to avoid the nuclear option that would destroy the group.

exists and the issue is how to deal with it while preserving individual autonomy and rights, and how to aggregate the preferences that exist in an appropriate way. In a unitary system, the assumption is that members share basic interests, that conflict is resolvable, and that the main task of the group is to function as a unified whole. In unitary groups, the work of politics involves extended discussion of common interests. In adversary groups, the work of politics involves negotiation of competing interests. The distinctions follow from one key question—does the group have deep conflict? Groups with conflict do, and should, use adversarial means. Groups with less conflict and a high level of shared interests and understandings do, and should, use more unitary means. Or so goes the argument.

Our notion of what happens in discussion is close to Mansbridge's, but we place the emphasis a bit differently. Where Mansbridge sees the prediscussion level of conflicting interests and understandings as the key to whether a group is unitary or adversary, we see a key to the group's unitary or adversary nature as lying in the dynamics of interaction during discussion. Where Mansbridge tends to see adversary democracy as a characteristic of larger systems, and unitary democracy as a driving force of small groups, we see that the small group can have either adversary or unitary characteristics. Small does not mean unitary; small can be highly adversary. And where Mansbridge classifies the meeting as unitary or adversary based on the use or avoidance of procedures such as majority rule, we classify it as unitary or adversary based on the social aspects of exchange.[42]

According to our modified concept of adversary versus unitary democracy, some groups are characterized by a highly unitary mode of discussion even though they use the structures of adversary democracy. These are the majority-female groups under majority rule. And by the same token, the same lengthy, face-to-face discussion assuming common interests can be a place where gender inequality is reinforced, as with many women and unanimous rule, or instead a place where women are empowered and men are content with their empowerment—namely, unanimous rule with minority women.

So we view the interaction style at the meeting as a key distinction between unitary and adversary systems. In unitary discussions, members take equal floor time, issue lots of mutual affirmations, and invite marginalized social groups to articulate their distinctive concerns. In adversary discussions, members take unequal floor time, issue more negative than positive interjections, and focus on their own gendered agenda to the exclusion of the other's. The same small group size can produce dramatically different styles. In producing these styles, the group can set itself on an adversary or unitary course—regardless of its starting assumptions about its level of conflict and how to

[42] See also Gastil 1993 for a discussion of variations on adversarial and unitary processes in small groups.

handle that conflict. What shapes the style is the interaction of decision rule and gender composition.

The results here also address the assumptions behind Habermasian theories of deliberation. A group may set out to deliberate with open-mindedness and mutual respect and to exchange reasons and appropriate evidence, as a Habermasian would like (Chambers 2003). But the socioemotional tenor of the discussion matters to its success. The logical and evidentiary content of speech is not the only dimension of speech that matters; its social meaning matters too, by shaping a speaker's authority. If members offer criticisms without affirmations, the group dynamic will turn *socially* adversarial. And this, in turn, undermines social equality, a mainstay of the Habermasian preconditions of discussion. As Anderson and Honneth argue, deliberation rests on "relationships of mutual recognition," and "empathic engagement" (2005, 113). Our study contributes to the deliberation literature by spelling out the meaning of "mutual recognition" and "empathic engagement" in discussion. In this chapter, we showed that deliberators perform a crucial aspect of empathic engagement and mutual recognition by using specific forms of speech that are widely perceived to convey exactly those messages. We further demonstrated that these validating forms of speech in turn lead to more equal social authority. Ten years ago, Chambers asked what conditions give voice to the socially disadvantaged (2003, 322). Our answer is: conditions that fit of the discussion rules to the numbers, because that fit creates the rapport that marginalized voices require.

But we provide an additional piece of the puzzle of deliberation and equality by showing how the latter directly aids the former. The rapport that facilitates women's full representation in discussion is a conduit for the very engagement that deliberation seeks. We found that women's enclaves elevate elaborated positives, not just thoughtless support. And the conditions that empower women prompt men to elevate the elaborated proportion of their positive interruptions of women—again, evidence that men become not just more respectful of women, but that this respect carries men's own thoughts in response to women's words.

We have spent quite a bit of our efforts, and of the reader's patience, analyzing the floor time, issue content, and interruption patterns of group discussion—without commenting much on what the members say they want the group to do. We now turn to this final component of the study and analyze the concrete preferences people express about the course of action they wish the group to take.

CHAPTER 9

When Women Speak, Groups Listen—Sometimes: How and When Women's Voice Shapes the Group's Generosity

When Bill Gates was on his way to becoming the world's richest man, he rejected advice to set up a charitable foundation. . . . Just three years later, Mr. Gates ranked third on Fortune's list of the most generous philanthropists in America. In between he welcomed his first child: a daughter. Mr. Gates has reflected that two female family members—his mother, Mary, and his wife, Melinda—were major catalysts for his philanthropic surge. Mary "never stopped pressing me to do more for others," Mr. Gates said . . ." "We should help everyone have a decent life."[1]

WHEN WOMEN SPEAK, do men listen? Do women speak up for more generosity and cooperation? More generally, under what conditions do women influence others to the same extent as men, and do women create more generosity by frequently "pressing" men—and other women—to "do more for others"?[2]

[1]The first quote is from Adam Grant, "Why Men Need Women: It's Not What You Think," *New York Times Sunday Review*, July 21, 2013, 6. The last sentence comes from Bill Gates's interview with *60 Minutes*, May 12, 2013, http://www.cbsnews.com/video/watch/?id=50146683n.

[2]Several studies find an effect from a rising number of female relatives on men's policy preferences. Of particular note is Ebonya Washington's finding of a daughter's effect on male congress members' liberal votes, especially but not exclusively for reproductive rights (2008). The number of women in the household matters, and not just becoming the father of a daughter; among fathers of two children (either sons or daughters), there is a bigger effect of having two daughters over one daughter than in having one daughter over no daughters. Similarly, among fathers of three children (sons or daughters), we see a bigger effect from having three over two daughters than from having two daughters over one daughter. The results are specific to daughters—they are not caused by having sons. The effects do not apply to female congress members, but those null results may be due to these women holding more liberal attitudes already. They do apply to male members of either party. Other studies confirm the pattern. Parents who have only daughters are more likely to support profemale policies than those with daughters and sons, and fathers of mixed-gender offspring are more so than fathers who only parent sons (Warner and Steel 1999). For example, in an experiment using an allocation game, men who gave more generously to anonymous partners

In previous chapters, we have explored how group features affect the dynamics of the discussion, including speaking time for men and women, the content of the discussion, and patterns of interruptions. We now turn to the question of group decision making. Normative justifications for deliberation include its ability to consider principles of justice. As Thompson writes, "all [deliberative theorists] agree that to some extent the nature of justice should itself be the subject of deliberation" (2008, 508). In our research design, groups were asked to do exactly that—to discuss principles of just income distribution. Moreover, they were also instructed to reach a collective decision on the level of the minimum guaranteed income—one they would apply as a rule for society but that would also affect their own interests, specifically, the amount they would earn at the end of the experiment.[3] In this chapter we explore how the conditions of deliberation affect the definition of justice adopted by both individuals and groups, and how these concepts of justice influence their concrete policy decisions about income redistribution.

As we documented in chapter 7, the preferences of women and men tend to differ with respect to redistributive policies.[4] For example, women are more likely than men to be concerned about economic inequality in the United States; to be more supportive of government's role in addressing economic distress and social needs such as health care; to prefer less room for the free market; and to embrace government spending on the poor, elderly, and children.

These gender differences in policy preferences are directly relevant to the subject of deliberation and decision making in our research design. At the beginning of the experiment, participants were told that they would be asked to discuss and arrive at a group decision about how to redistribute the money earned by group members during the study. Before they came together for the discussion, participants were introduced to four basic principles of income redistribution.[5] They did not know the nature of the task they would be doing to

---

were 40% more likely to have had sisters (but not brothers) than men who did not allocate generously (Van Lange et al. 1997).

[3] We sometimes call this minimum guaranteed income the group's "safety net" or "poverty line" or "floor amount." For stylistic purposes, we use all four terms interchangeably.

[4] The most recent survey data confirm these conclusions. For example, a 2012 Pew Research Center survey found large differences between men and women in support for more social services. This result is consistent with a gender gap in views of the role of government in Pew Center surveys over the last decade: women are much more likely than men to favor increased government intervention focused on more services for those who might be struggling. Specifically, the most recent Pew Center survey finds that women favor more government help for the elderly, children, and poor people at much higher rates than men, with the gender gaps ranging between 9 and 11 percentage points. And in terms of government priorities, close to 60% of women cited helping the poor and needy as a top priority for government, compared to less than half of men. For an overview of all findings, see http://www.people-press.org/2012/03/29/the-gender-gap-three-decades-old-as-wide-as-ever/.

[5] For details, see chapter 4 and the online appendix.

earn income, to encourage them to think about the principles from the perspective of all different income levels.[6] They were encouraged to think about the values they most prized and to consider the question of what is most fair or just. Moreover, they were instructed to make a decision that would apply to their group and to the society at large.

The handbook participants received prior to deliberation summarized each principle as follows:

1. *Maximize The Floor Income: "Help Those Who Have The Least"*
   Value Statement: The most just distribution of income is most concerned with the poorest among us. Application: The higher incomes are taxed so that everyone receives at least 80% of the group's average income.
2. *Set A Floor Constraint: "Ensure Everyone Has Enough To Get By"*
   Value Statement: The most just distribution of income provides a safety net of guaranteed income no one can fall below. Application: The group must set a dollar amount for the floor, and all incomes above the floor will be taxed enough to raise everyone to that floor. If your group does not happen to produce enough to achieve the floor you set, we will reset the floor to be 80% of the average.
3. *Set A Range Constraint: "Reduce The Extremes Of Rich And Poor"*
   Value Statement: The most just distribution of income increases equality by reducing the differences between the rich and the poor. Application: The group sets a dollar amount for the range. Money is redistributed from high incomes to low incomes until they fall within the set range. If incomes are already within the set range, no action is taken, even if the low income is below average, and as low as zero.
4. *No Taxes Or Redistribution: "I Keep What I Earn"*
   Value Statement: The most just distribution of income best rewards those who produce the most. Application: Everyone keeps exactly what they earn, no more and no less.

Groups were asked to set a dollar amount for the floor or range, unless they chose no redistribution.

Each principle represents a different way of thinking about inequality and a different way of addressing it. The handbook offered participants some helpful information about the values associated with each principle, about how the principles would be applied to their earning from the income-earning work tasks they would perform during experiment, and about the concrete

[6] In the original experiment designed by Frohlich and Oppenheimer (1992), this uncertainty about the work task at the time of deliberation was meant to simulate the Rawlsian "veil of ignorance," that is, participants could not be sure whether they were likely to earn a lot or a little, to encourage them to consider the most just principle. The principle of maximizing the floor was meant to parallel Rawls's notion of justice as providing the greatest benefit to the least well off. These connections to Rawls are not important for our purposes.

implications of each principle for those at all different income levels in society. After reading the handbook and walking through some examples of how each principle would be applied, participants were given a brief quiz to be sure they understood each principle thoroughly. Finally, each participant was asked to rank the principles in order of their private, individual preferences.

Prior to deliberation, there is a gender gap in preferences consistent in nature and size with the gap documented in other studies.[7] For one, women are much less likely than men to favor the least generous principle: no taxes or redistribution. Second, although the most popular principle among both men and women is setting a floor, women favor this at significantly higher rates than men.[8] The gender differences in support for the other two principles—maximizing the floor and setting a range—are small and not statistically significant. Deliberation does not change this pattern (as the bottom half of chapter appendix table A9.1 shows).

Aside from replicating the typical gender gap among national samples and on issues of public policy, these results also replicate the "real world" in another important sense. They show that before and after deliberation, the most commonly preferred principle was setting a floor. This is also the principle ultimately chosen by nearly 90% of the groups.[9] That nearly every decision ultimately settled on the actual system of redistribution in capitalist systems is further testament that our participants were thinking the same way that citizens do about how the political system should approach redistribution. That is, they were guided by the principle that the worst-off should get some protection from utter destitution, but that otherwise, individuals keep what they earn.

An example from a majority-rule group with four women illustrates these patterns well. In this exchange, which occurs early in the discussion, several group members chime in to state their views about the principles. Two women in the group begin by arguing for setting a floor, comparing it to the minimum wage and adding that they like the principle because they want to preserve some role for "personal incentive." A man responds that he favors no redistribution because it rewards merit and gives an incentive to "do something great in society." The first woman pushes back, though, to point out that equality

[7]The top half of table A9.1 shows the individual-level distribution of preferences before discussion.

[8]The size of the predeliberation gender gap in preferences for no redistribution and for setting a floor is similar to the gap in other studies of redistribution preferences: 10–15 percentage points for each of the two principles (each difference is significant at $p < 0.02$ in a regression model that includes controls for experimental location).

[9]The principle of setting a floor had the highest average predeliberation ranking in 84% of groups. (Predeliberation preferences include ties in which two principles were equally highly ranked by group members. Ties occurred in four groups.) Given the small number of groups choosing a principle other than the one they preferred prior to deliberation, it is difficult to draw any firm conclusions about the conditions under which such change occurs. We find some evidence, however, that such change is more likely to occur in majority male groups than in majority female groups, but again, such conclusions are only tentative.

of opportunity is not yet a reality and that this fact needs to play a role in the group's choices.

0:07:14.8 Woman A: I like the floor constraint because it's just like the minimum wage, but yeah, still. As long as, as long as it's not high, it still has personal incentive.

0:07:28.0 Woman D: Yeah, I agree with that. I thought the setting a range constraint can be a little bit too extreme sometimes and I thought the same about the maximizing the range income. And I really like the floor constraints. I didn't like no tax redistribution. Didn't think that was fair—

0:07:48.1 Man C: My opinion was actually for no redistribution because that's what I consider to be fair. 'Cause you're getting money based on your performance. If you perform well then somebody's taking money away from you. I mean even if I were in the lowest income bracket I don't want to be taking money away from someone else who's actually earned it. 'Cause the difference between being rich because your dad was rich and being rich because you've actually done something great in society. And I don't believe we should be taxing the people who just make the most money because they're actually doing something useful. It's something that's been happening in our society. We see them as needing to help the poor.

0:08:26.6 Woman A: You know, I think the only problem with that is that that's assuming that our society is completely just and it's completely based on capitalism. Which if we've lived in a completely capitalist system and everyone were given an equal opportunity thing, then yes I would be all for it. But, I mean I think—go all the way and say that it's completely determined by chance or it's completely determined by ability.

Discussions like these can be found throughout our transcripts. The participants state their preferences, explore the reasons for and against each alternative, and ultimately converge on a principle that they consider to be "most just." In what follows, we analyze the patterns of these deliberations and collective choices.

When Are Women the First to Articulate a Preference?

We begin by asking who sets the agenda—that is, who weighs in first to articulate a preference about the principles under discussion. Previous studies have shown that agenda setters can have a strong effect on group choices—especially when those agenda settings are high-status members of the group (Dubrovsky, Kiesler, and Sethna 1991; Hoffman 1978; McGuire, Kiesler, and Siegel 1987). Given its potential influence, this agenda setting represents an important form of power (Bachrach and Baratz 1962). So one measure of women's standing in the group is their willingness to speak up first and communicate what they wish the group to choose. We created a variable indicating who set the agenda for the group by being the first to publicly advocate for a principle. We asked coders to read each transcript and find the first moment when any member of the group indicated his or her support for one of the principles of redistribution.[10] If our interaction hypothesis is correct, then we should find that women are more willing to articulate the first preference and thus attempt to set the agenda where the combination of decision rule and gender composition gives them increased authority.

The results confirm this expectation about the women's attempts to set the agenda. Where women's status is lowest—as the gender minority under majority rule—they articulate the first preference in the discussion in only 12.5% of the groups; the same minority under unanimous rule articulates the first preference in 37.5% of the groups. As the gender majority, however, women set the agenda in approximately 60% of the groups, regardless of rule. But rule does matter even when women are the large majority: in four-female groups, women set the agenda 75% of the time under majority rule, but only 50% of the time under unanimity. Chapter appendix table A9.2 shows that the strong interaction effect between gender composition and decision rule persists in the presence of controls.[11] The likelihood of having a female agenda setter increases under unanimity as the number of women in the group increases (see the positive and significant coefficient for Number of Women in chapter appendix table

[10] Of the participants who were the first to speak up, only 22% did not advocate the same principle they preferred privately. While small, this slippage could have a variety of causes, including uncertainty or ambivalence about the initial preference, strategic action, or social pressure. Women are slightly more likely than men to express the same preference both privately and publicly (83% of women and 73% of men, though this difference falls short of statistical significance, $p = 0.23$, two-tailed difference of proportions test). The conditions did not affect the slippage among men or women. A probit regression of a dummy variable indicating whether the participant's private preference matched his or her public expression on our linear, interactive model yields no effect for decision rule ($p = 0.67$), for gender composition ($p = 0.68$), or for the interaction between the two ($p = 0.60$).

[11] In some groups, participants were somewhat reluctant to begin talking, and if this was the case, the moderator was instructed to ask participant A to begin the conversation. (Because the participants were randomly assigned to a letter for the purposes of seating around the table, the choice to begin with participant A was essentially random.) If participant A articulated his or her preference in response to the researcher's question, this could muddy our measure of agenda setting. However, even if we remove all groups in which participant A spoke first and was the first to articulate his or her preferences, the same strong interaction between decision rule and gender composition is present (for the interaction term of this model, $p < 0.03$, one-tailed test).

A9.2).[12] Under both decision rules, women are more likely to be agenda setters as the number of women in the group increases, but the interaction term shows that the difference-in-differences is significant; in other words, the effect is larger under majority rule than under unanimity.

If our argument about empowerment is correct, the conditions that elevate women's status in the group should also increase the likelihood of the group actually choosing the agenda setter's preference.[13] The number of gender-mixed groups where a woman was the first to express her preferences is limited in some of the conditions, preempting a definitive statistical test, but the data suggest that women are more successful at persuading the group to support the principle they first espoused in the conditions where they are most empowered. When women are the majority, female agenda setters are more successful under majority rule (78%, N = 9) than under unanimity (50%, N = 10), and this difference is marginally significant.[14] In addition, as the interaction hypothesis predicts, when minority women are empowered by unanimity rule, the group chooses the female agenda setter's preference every time (100%, N = 6), as compared to only half the time under majority rule (50%, N = 2). Put differently, the power of numbers helps women under a rule that favors numbers (78% of majority-female groups versus 50% of minority-female groups), while it does not help when the rule favors minorities (50% of majority-female groups versus 100% of minority-female groups under unanimity). The results thus suggest not only that women are more likely to set the agenda but may also be more successful in doing so in conditions where the combination of rule and gender composition favors them.

When Is Women's Confidence in Their Views Enhanced?

Another way to analyze the empowering effect of a discussion on women is to see whether it increases their confidence in their own mind. As we explained in chapters 2 and 3, one of the difficulties women experience in the world of public affairs is that they are not confident that they are competent enough to influence others. And in chapter 6, we saw that women's predeliberation confidence

[12] Results do not change if we substitute controls for liberalism and the interaction of liberalism and rule for egalitarianism and the interaction of egalitarianism and rule (not shown).

[13] Later we will take up our more central, and general, prediction—that whether they are agenda setters or not, women are more likely to move the group decision in the conditions where women are empowered.

[14] Comparing the effect of rule in groups where women are a majority, $z = 1.25$, $p = 0.10$, one-tailed difference of proportions test. Our argument does not require that women be agenda setters to be empowered, and our point here is narrow: women are more likely to be agenda setters when they are empowered, and those agenda setters are more successful when women's standing increases.

influenced their patterns of participation. In addition, we reported in chapter 8 that negative feedback during discussion affects women particularly negatively. A discussion can be deemed equalizing in part if it succeeds in increasing women's certainty that their opinions are valid. To the extent that women encounter a respectful and engaged response during discussion, they may become more certain that their views have merit. That in turn could create a felicitous feedback loop in the future, where women may be more ready to put their views forward for others to consider.

In the predeliberation survey, immediately after asking participants to rank the principles, we also asked them how sure they felt about their rankings. Five response options were provided, ranging from "very unsure" (coded 1) to "very sure" (coded 5).[15] We then asked the exact same question, this time about their opinion after deliberation. We expect that conditions that empower women during discussion will increase their certainty about their own preferences (which, for the most part, do not change). These expectations are borne out in the data: the settings where women are more empowered are the settings that increase women's certainty after discussion. Table 9.1 presents the OLS regression coefficients from our familiar model interacting decision rule and gender composition, with controls for experimental location, egalitarianism, number of egalitarians in the group, the interaction of egalitarians and rule, and predeliberation certainty over one's preference ranking of the four principles, separately for women and men. Predicted values from Models 1 and 3 are in figure 9.1.

Before describing the results, we note that the conditions have no effect on predeliberation certainty. That means that any effect of the conditions on post-discussion certainty occurred because the conditions produced different types of discussion.[16] After deliberation, women exhibit a pattern fully consistent with our interaction hypothesis. Under majority rule, women are *more* certain of their views in groups with many women than in groups with few women. But under unanimous rule, a woman in the gender majority is *less* certain than a woman in the gender minority.[17] In line with our expectations about the pro-

[15] Both men and women were more certain of their preferences after discussion, with both genders' levels of certainty increasing by more than half a point on the 5-point scale. Women increase from an average of 3.37 before deliberation to 3.90 afterward ($p < 0.01$), and men moving from 3.53 to 4.09 ($p < 0.01$). Both prior to and after deliberation, men expressed somewhat more certainty about their preferences than women. The gender differences are significant at $p = 0.10$ prior to deliberation and $p = 0.01$ afterward (two-sample unpaired difference of means tests).

[16] A regression of predeliberation certainty on our linear interactive model shows that none of the coefficients in our interactive model are significant at conventional levels, and the direction of the point estimates is often different from what we find in the postdeliberation models.

[17] These patterns are identical in models that use the participant's change in certainty as the dependent variable. In addition, as seen in Models 2 and 4 of table 9.1, the results for a fully saturated model that includes interactions between majority rule and the number of egalitarians in the group are also nearly identical. Controls for age, education, and income make no difference in the model

Table 9.1: Effects of Experimental Conditions on Male and Female Certainty about Postdeliberation Preferences, Mixed-Gender Groups Only

	(1) Women	(2) Women	(3) Men	(4) Men
Majority Rule	−0.93**	−0.82*	0.28	0.23
	(0.40)	(0.44)	(0.23)	(0.24)
Number of Women	−0.12*	−0.13*	0.00	0.01
	(0.07)	(0.07)	(0.07)	(0.07)
Majority Rule × Number of Women	0.24*	0.27*	−0.06	−0.07
	(0.13)	(0.14)	(0.10)	(0.11)
Predeliberation Certainty	0.32***	0.32***	0.19**	0.18**
	(0.08)	(0.08)	(0.07)	(0.07)
Egalitarianism	−0.21	−0.20	−0.75***	−0.75***
	(0.35)	(0.35)	(0.27)	(0.27)
Number of Egalitarians	−0.17**	−0.14*	0.00	−0.01
	(0.08)	(0.08)	(0.07)	(0.08)
Majority Rule × Number of Egalitarians		−0.06		0.03
		(0.11)		(0.09)
Constant	3.69***	3.61***	3.59***	3.63***
	(0.32)	(0.33)	(0.32)	(0.33)
Observations	157	157	163	163
R-squared	0.20	0.21	0.12	0.12
Control for Experimental Location	Yes	Yes	Yes	Yes

Note: Individual-level analysis. Cluster robust standard errors in parentheses. *** $p < 0.01$, ** $p < 0.05$, * $p < 0.1$, two-tailed test.

tective effect of unanimity, women in groups with few women are significantly more certain of their postdeliberation views under unanimity than minority women in groups using majority rule.[18]

In other words, the more equal women's status in the group, the more standing and authority women have, the more that group discussion boosts women's confidence in their postdeliberation preference. As further evidence that this result comes from women's position of authority, men's sense of certainty after the discussion has little relation to the experimental conditions. We note, too,

---

(not shown). Substituting liberalism for egalitarianism, the general trends are similar, though the change in certainty under majority rule is smaller when liberalism is the control (see online appendix table C9.6).

[18] Predicted values from the model show that the difference in certainty across decision rules is significant at $p < 0.02$ (two-tailed) for groups with one woman or groups with two women. These differences in predicted values hold in models that control for liberalism instead of egalitarianism.

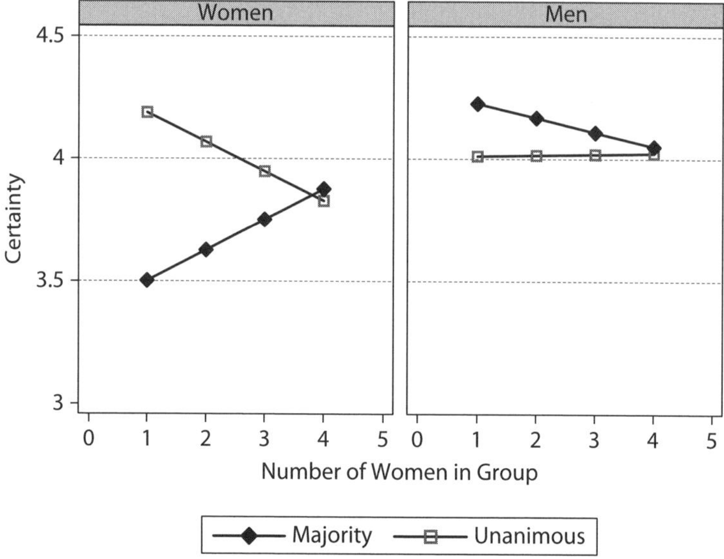

Figure 9.1. Certainty about postdeliberation redistribution preferences, by gender and condition. Note: Predicted values from Models 1 and 3 of table 9.1.

that in the case of certainty, women are best off with unanimous rule and few women. That condition produces the most certainty of all, and moreover, it is the only mixed-gender condition where women's certainty equals men's (comparing the two panels in figure 9.1).[19]

As we saw in earlier chapters, women are more likely than men to respond to the group's signals about the worth of their views. Consistent with that notion, women are more likely than men to rely on group discussion—and specifically, their authority within it—to draw conclusions about the legitimacy of their preferences.

How Numbers and Rules Affect the Expression of Preferences

To this point, we know that the experimental conditions affect women's confidence in their opinions in ways that are consistent with our expectations about empowerment or inclusion. With respect to the actual decisions made, we know that most groups implement most women's preferred principle, but this

[19] In female enclaves, levels of postdeliberation certainty are slightly higher than women's certainty in mixed-gender groups with many women, but pooling both decision rules, those small differences are not significant. As table 9.1 indicates, male certainty is not affected by the experimental conditions.

does not tell us that women are empowered to affect the outcome because men tend to prefer the same principle. We know, too, that women are more likely to set the agenda by being the first to articulate a principle for the group to choose in the conditions where women are more empowered. But the groups quickly agreed on a principle, and it was very often one that both men and women initially tended to favor. This leaves us with additional questions about how often and with what effect women articulate preferences for generosity toward the poor.

Fortunately, we have a second outcome to examine. When groups chose to set a guaranteed minimum income, or poverty line, below which no one would be allowed to fall, they had to make an additional decision: what, exactly, would that minimum income be? Groups had complete freedom to set the floor at a level as generous, or stingy, as they wished.[20]

Unfortunately, we did not privately ask each individual's preferred floor amount prior to deliberation, but we do have data on the individual's expressed preference for the floor. We asked coders to comb through each transcript and to identify every expression of endorsement for a specific guaranteed income.[21] While some participants kept their preferences very close to the vest and never publicly commented on any floor amount, a majority of our participants (237 out of 470) did make one or more explicit endorsements.[22] This is clearly not a perfect substitute for the privately expressed preferences of each participant before discussion. It tells us nothing about the preferences of those who never declared their preferred minimum incomes, for example, and it may be affected by the discussion that preceded the statement. But this measure does give us a sense of what those participants who did speak up were willing to publicly champion. And in that sense, it is a good reflection of how the groups collectively explored the issue of assistance to the poor. Moreover, our interest is in the conditions that foster, or inhibit, this precise type of action—the willingness to take a public position. So while we cannot use this variable to assess

[20] Indeed, perhaps the principle's attractiveness to so many groups can partly be attributed to its ability to allow this considerable flexibility.

[21] Intercoder reliability analysis shows that in the set of statements that both coders agreed were preference statements, agreement about the nature of the statements (that is, which principle it supported, and the amount) was nearly perfect: Support for Maximum Redistribution, 100% agreement, Krippendorff Alpha = 1.00; Support for No Taxes, 100% agreement, Krippendorff's Alpha = 1.00; Support for a Range Constraint, 98.6% agreement, Krippendorff's Alpha = 0.92; Support for a Floor Constraint, 94% agreement, Krippendorff's Alpha = 0.87; Amount of Floor Constraint, 94% agreement, Krippendorff's Alpha = 0.85. Given the difficulty of determining whether a statement is an expression of a preference from the group transcripts, coders did not always agree with each other about whether a statement was a preference expression, but of all coding judgments made, coders achieved agreement about preference expression and the content of the expression about 93% of the time.

[22] Some participants did not endorse floor amounts because the group chose a different principle and did not need to discuss guaranteed incomes. Other participants endorsed principles, but not specific poverty thresholds. In the sample as a whole, only 9% of the sample never endorsed either a principle or floor amount at any time during the group discussion.

women's private preferences, we can use it to measure the effects of empowering conditions on women's willingness to advocate for generous assistance to the poor for the purpose of affecting the group decision.

Before we address the issue of women's empowerment, we pause to note the general effect of the rule. We have reason to believe that the conditions may affect how much participants speak about their preferences. Specifically, we began by arguing that rules are more than the means to aggregate preferences. Rules breed norms of interaction, and unanimous rule in particular holds out the promise of inclusion and cooperation. Evidence for this proposition was presented in chapter 5, where we found that unanimous rule elevates the group's talk time. If the rule elevates individual participation, we would observe not only more talk, but also that more people express their preferences under that rule.

And that is what we find. Under unanimous rule, participants in mixed-gender groups speak up more often for their preferred principle or their preferred poverty line, by a statistically significant margin.[23] Relatedly, a basic difference of proportions test reveals that more individuals express at least one preference about the floor under unanimity than under majority rule.[24] In sum, individuals are not only more likely to speak but also to express preferences for or against a principle under unanimity than under majority rule. The rule draws individuals into the conversation in a substantive way, where they disclose their preferences about the issue under discussion—and tend to do so more often. And all of these patterns apply to women, specifically, as well as men.[25]

[23] Counting the number of times a participant advocated a principle of any kind, we find for all groups an average of 2.6 times for unanimous rule and 2.3 times under majority rule, $t = 1.73$, $p < 0.05$, one-tailed; for mixed-gender groups: Unanimity: 2.7, Majority 2.1, $t = 2.70$, $p < 0.01$, one-tailed. These results are similar for the total number of statements a participant made either *for* or *against* any principle. For all groups: Unanimity: 3.18, Majority, 2.68, $t = 2.45$, $p < 0.01$, one-tailed. For mixed-gender groups: Unanimity: 3.18, Majority, 2.46, $t = 2.93$, $p < 0.01$, one-tailed. These relationships remain strongly significant in an OLS regression model that includes controls for *Proportion Talk* (to control for overall talkativeness) and experimental location. These same patterns hold when we examine men and women separately. These results apply only to decision rule; we find no evidence of an interaction between decision rule and gender composition.

[24] With all groups, the percentages are: Unanimity: 54.2%, Majority: 46.5%, $z = 1.66$, $p < 0.05$, one-tailed. These numbers are very similar when we examine mixed-gender groups only: Unanimity: 50.9%, Majority 41.9%, $z = 1.60$, $p < 0.06$, one-tailed. When we control for overall talkativeness by adding *Proportion Talk* to the regression model; however, these patterns are still in the same direction, but fall short of significance ($p = 0.15$, one-tailed test). Both male and female enclaves seem to function similarly to unanimous rule in generating widespread preference expression in the group, so that participants in enclaves are more likely to express preferences than those in mixed-gender groups ($z = 2.45$, $p < 0.01$, one-tailed) across both decision rules.

[25] Across the sample as a whole, women are no more or less likely than men to make a statement of any kind (online appendix table C9.2, Models 1 and 2), and among participants who made any statements about their preferences, women made the same number of statements as men (online appendix table C9.2, Models 3 and 4).

Of course, we are interested not only in whether a preference was expressed but also what those preferences are. Our hypothesis is that the experimental conditions affect the generosity of public endorsements. Consistent with our interaction hypothesis, we find that in mixed-gender groups, the experimental conditions have a substantial effect on the magnitude of the floor preferences expressed by both men and women (analyzed separately).[26] Table 9.2 presents the familiar interaction model. The dependent variable is the maximum floor amount endorsed—that is, the deliberator's most generous preference.[27] Data are analyzed at the level of the individual and include controls for individual-level and group-level egalitarianism.[28] As the table shows, the basic interaction is large, strongly significant, and in the same direction for both men and women. Both genders expressed support for less generous minimum incomes in groups where women held less power because of the combination of rule and gender composition—majority-rule groups with few women or unanimous rule with many women—and supported comparatively more generous minimum incomes in majority-rule groups with many women or unanimous groups with fewer women.[29]

Figure 9.2 shows the predicted values that emerge from Models 1 and 3 of table 9.2. As the figure shows, the effects of women's status on women's public generosity are substantial. Under majority rule, for example, a woman's largest endorsed floor is predicted to rise by almost $10,000 as the number of women in the group increases from one to four, moving from just under $21,000 to almost $31,000—nearly a 50% increase. To put this in perspective, $21,000

[26] When we pool all conditions, women tend to endorse much more generous floor amounts than men. Whether we examine the individual's first stated preference, their maximum stated preference, their minimum stated preference, or their last stated preference, women on average favor more generous redistribution of income to the poor than men. These gender differences are strongly significant and amount to guaranteed minimum incomes that are between $3,000 and $3,400 per year higher than those endorsed by men, or a 13% increase from the average amount endorsed by men (online appendix table C9.3). Controls for experimental location are needed because participants in the East Coast location tended to choose higher floor amounts than those in the Mountain West location.

[27] Results are essentially the same if we use other measures, such as the first endorsed preference or the minimum endorsed preference. We chose maximum floor amount endorsed because this gives us a sense of exactly how generous toward the poor men and women were willing to be. Results do not change if we substitute controls for liberalism and number of liberals in the place of egalitarianism and number of egalitarians (see online appendix table C9.7), nor do they change when we add controls for age, education, or income (not shown).

[28] The key interaction term remains similar in magnitude and in significance in a fully saturated model that also interacts decision rule with the number of egalitarians in the group (see Models 2 and 4 of table 9.2). In addition, controlling for the number of college grads or the number of group members above the median in age or education makes no difference to the findings, either on their own or in interaction with decision rule (not shown).

[29] In enclaves, women's expressed preferences also diverge markedly from men's, averaging between $5,700 and $6,900 more ($p < 0.05$, two-tailed; see online appendix table C9.3).

Table 9.2: Effect of Experimental Conditions on Maximum Endorsed Floor Amount by Gender, Mixed-Gender Groups Only

	(1) Women	(2) Women	(3) Men	(4) Men
Majority Rule	−11.85**	−5.75	−13.29***	−7.09
	(4.67)	(4.83)	(4.85)	(5.86)
Number of Women	−0.72	−1.19	−2.86**	−2.76*
	(1.11)	(1.08)	(1.41)	(1.42)
Majority Rule × Number of Women	4.02**	5.88***	4.75**	5.11***
	(1.94)	(1.84)	(1.79)	(1.81)
Egalitarianism	1.66	0.40	7.64	7.30
	(4.23)	(4.13)	(6.39)	(6.34)
Number of Egalitarians	0.53	1.95	1.03	1.90
	(1.32)	(1.32)	(1.37)	(1.58)
Majority Rule × Number of Egalitarians		−3.73***		−2.67*
		(1.36)		(1.53)
Constant	24.58***	22.79***	25.61***	23.15***
	(3.25)	(3.38)	(5.26)	(5.46)
Observations	78	78	71	71
R-squared	0.28	0.34	0.26	0.28
Control for Experimental Location	Yes	Yes	Yes	Yes

Note: Dependent variable is maximum endorsed floor amount in thousands of dollars. Individual-level analysis. Cluster robust standard errors in parentheses. *** $p < 0.01$, ** $p < 0.05$, * $p < 0.1$, two-tailed test.

was the poverty line set by the federal government for a family of four at the time of the study, so $31,000 represents an increase of nearly half the actual income guaranteed to poor families by the federal government. Group-level averages provide further support for these results: in mixed-gender, majority-rule groups with few women, women's average maximum floor endorsement exceeds $25,000 in only one group. In mixed-gender, majority-rule groups with many women, by contrast, women's average endorsed floor exceeds $25,000 in 60% of groups. The conditions thus have a profound effect on the floor amounts groups debate.

The predicted effect of numbers on men under majority rule is not quite as steep, but is still substantial. Under majority rule, a man's generosity moves from about $22,000 in groups with only one woman to nearly $28,000 in groups with four women—an increase of nearly 30% over the federal government's poverty line. At the group level, the average man's floor endorsement is $22,000 or less in over half of the groups in which men predominate, but never less than $22,000 when women are more numerous. Thus both women and men advocate for meaningfully increased support for the poor when they deliber-

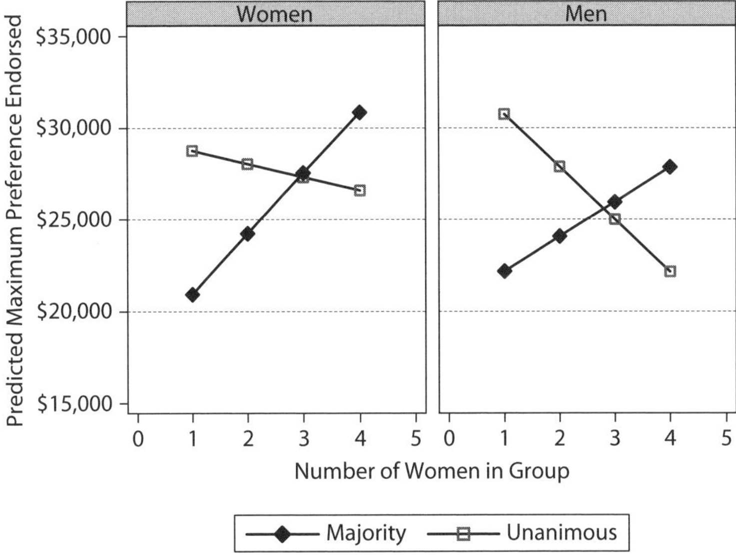

Figure 9.2: Maximum endorsed safety net, by gender, mixed-gender groups only. Note: Predicted values from Models 1 and 3 of table 9.2.

ate in majority-rule groups populated predominantly by women rather than men.[30]

Under unanimous rule, the effects of gender composition run in the opposite direction, as our interaction hypothesis predicts. With that rule, the average woman's generosity *decreases* by $2,000 as the number of women increases from one to four. The negative effect of women's numbers on men is even more dramatic: nearly $8,000. Taken together, these results show that where women have more equal status—unanimous rule with few women, or majority rule with many women—both men and women tend to endorse more generous floor amounts.[31]

[30]The federal poverty line is technically known as the "poverty guidelines," and it is set yearly by the federal government to determine eligibility for various federal programs that assist the poor. In 2007, the year of the study, the level for a family of three was $17,170, and the poverty guideline for a family of four was $20,650. See http://aspe.hhs.gov/poverty/07poverty.shtml regarding the facts in this note. We did not inform the participants of the actual poverty guidelines because we wanted to observe their own decisions without bias toward the status quo.

[31]Online appendix table C9.5 shows the effect of the conditions when we pool male and female members of the group. The effects hold not just for the individual's most generous expressed preference, but also the first floor amount endorsed by the individual, the minimum floor amount endorsed, or the last floor amount endorsed. The differences across the conditions are substantial. In majority-rule groups with one woman, the predicted maximum floor amount endorsed by individuals is approximately $21,797 (from Model 3 of table A9.5). But in majority-rule groups with four women, the predicted maximum floor amount endorsed by the deliberators is $29,815—a

The interaction continues to hold at the group level, where the dependent variable is the average poverty line endorsed by women in the group, including in the presence of a variety of additional controls. Those include the number of egalitarians in the group, the interaction of egalitarians and rule, the group's median predeliberation warmth of feeling toward the poor, the number of group members preferring maximum redistribution, and the number of members preferring no redistribution prior to discussion.[32]

Thus across multiple models with many different potential controls, the result is the same: the conditions where deliberators endorse more generous floor amounts are the same conditions in which we earlier found other indicators of women's empowerment. That is, groups where women are empowered by rule or numbers, and where women took up more floor time, talked about vulnerable populations, were more warmly received, and were seen and saw themselves as more influential, are also groups where women and men advocate explicitly for more generous policy for the poor.[33]

We can further parse these relationships by bringing speaking time into the equation, asking what preferences the most talkative men and women advocate and how those differ from the statements of those who talk less. One implication of our interaction hypothesis is that when women are empowered, they should use their greater floor time to express more generosity toward the vulnerable populations they tend to favor. To explore this possibility, we used a slightly different analytic strategy: we regressed the person's expressions of generosity on their proportion of talk, on an indicator of their gender, and on the interaction between the two, separately in each of the experimental conditions. We present the results for majority-rule conditions in chapter appendix table A9.4. Under unanimous rule (not shown), the relationships we discuss below for majority rule are muted for both men and women.[34]

---

difference of about $8,000. That is a nearly 40% increase. In unanimous-rule groups, the number of women has the opposite effect. Using group-level data instead of individual-level data (pooling men and women in each group), with the group's average maximum floor as the dependent variable, the interaction between decision rule and group gender composition is significant at $p < 0.05$ (one-tailed).

[32] The results are found in chapter appendix table A9.3. Results persist when we use controls for the number of liberals and the interaction between rule and the number of liberals or between rule and demographic characteristics such as age, education, or income (not shown). When we explore the group-level patterns for men (not shown), the interaction between decision rule and gender composition remains marginally significant, except when controls for the number of deliberators favoring no redistribution is included.

[33] These findings are especially noteworthy because of our experimental approach, with random assignment to group conditions. Recall that our randomization checks showed that the groups were essentially equivalent in terms of multiple different demographic characteristics. We can be confident that the differences in expressed preferences across the conditions are not the result of selection bias, with some groups having very different types of deliberators than others.

[34] Under unanimous rule, interactions between talk time and the experimental conditions are not statistically significant.

Matching our expectations, we find that under majority rule the relationship between the average woman's talk time and her generous expressions is larger in groups with many women than in groups with few women.[35] Figure 9.3 presents the model's predicted values for men and women in majority-rule groups, with the x-axis in the figure representing participants' *Proportion Talk*. It shows that in groups with few women, women at all levels of talkativeness endorse similar—and low—levels of generosity. That is, when women have little authority, the relationship between their talk time and preferred floor amount is small and not statistically different from zero or from the pattern we see for men.

In groups with a majority of women, however, the relationship is positive and large; women who talk more advocate for much more generous policies toward the poor. To be sure, even those women who talk least in this condition tend to advocate floor amounts that are at least the equal of those advocated by the most talkative women in majority-rule groups with few women. But as the right-hand panel of the figure shows, the most talkative women advocate minimum incomes that are nearly $10,000 higher than that.[36] In other words, when they are empowered, nearly all women use their floor time to endorse a relatively generous safety net, but those who talk the most leverage their standing to advocate for dramatically increased levels of financial assistance for the poor.

Now we come to a possible dark spot in what so far has been a sunny story of women's empowerment. Women's elevated status in the group does not mean that men simply parrot women's preferences, especially *among those men who hold the floor the longest*. In fact, in majority-rule groups where women are empowered by their numbers, the most talkative men are estimated to endorse guaranteed minimum incomes that are about $6,000 *lower* than those endorsed by the least talkative men.[37] Although these predicted values still tend to be slightly higher than what talkative men advocate in majority-rule groups with few women, the key point is that the relationship between talk time and generosity is not the same for men and women when women are empowered. Evidence for this conclusion is the statistically significant interaction term in Models 3 and 4 of chapter appendix table A9.4.[38] Thus the increase in generosity among men that we saw in figure 9.2 must be somewhat qualified. While some men do match women's generosity to the poor in majority-rule groups with many women, the most talkative men in these groups push back against the much higher guaranteed incomes advocated by the most talkative women.

[35] Figure 9.3 shows the predicted values that emerge from Models 2 and 4 in table A9.4.

[36] The difference in the predicted values for the low and the high ends of the scale is significant at $p < 0.01$, two-tailed.

[37] There is some uncertainty around the point estimates, however. For men, the difference between the predicted values at each end of the scale is significant at $p < 0.12$, one-tailed test.

[38] Results are identical if we include controls for liberalism and the number of liberals or if we control for the participant's age, education, and income (not shown).

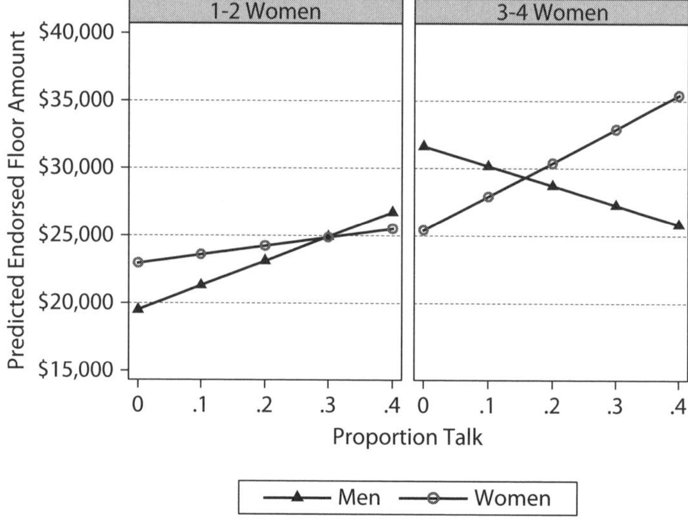

Figure 9.3. Relationship between speaking time and expression of safety net generosity, majority rule/mixed gender groups only. Note: Predicted values from Models 2 and 4 of chapter appendix table A9.4.

When the decision rule gives women more overt power because of numbers, the main message from men in these groups is one of resistance to women's preferences.[39]

While this is bad news for women's empowerment, it is potentially good news for deliberative democracy. In conditions that empower women, women's voice rises, but that sound does not drown out men. To the contrary, the debate is sharpened. Deliberators take the floor to define the alternatives clearly and to make their preferences known on more of the key choices before the group.

A more precise test of how the conditions might empower women's expression of preferences is the extent to which women publicly express support for principles other than their privately disclosed first choice (or the extent to which they publicly oppose those same principles). A woman who is more em-

[39] Male resistance to women's preferences in ways that are not moderated by speaking time can also be seen under unanimous rule with respect to a different aspect of the discussion: advocacy of no taxes or redistribution. In the sample as a whole, men are more likely than women to favor this principle: nearly 17% of men expressed support for no redistribution at least once during the conversation, compared to less than 7% of women. But again, the experimental conditions matter. Under unanimous rule, women express the least support for this principle in groups with few women—the groups where their standing is greatest with that decision rule. But for men, the effect works in the opposite direction: they are *most* likely to endorse no redistribution in unanimous groups with few women. Evidence for these patterns can be found in table C9.1 in the online appendix. Men press their desire for the least generous principle in the unanimous-rule groups where women's standing is greatest.

powered would be less likely to endorse a principle other than her favorite, and more likely to publicly oppose it. And that is exactly what we find in table 9.3.[40] The interaction between the number of women and majority rule decreases the number of times women publicly support principles other than their first preference. That is, women's empowerment reduces women's preference falsification. Women's empowering conditions also increase women's frequency of opposing their disfavored principles. The example at the beginning of the chapter highlights how such empowerment looks in practice: a woman in a majority-rule group with many women pushes back when a man articulates his preference for no taxes or redistribution.

Figure 9.4 shows the predicted values from Model 1 of table 9.3. Under majority rule, the least empowered women endorse disfavored principles nearly 1.5 times, on average, while the most empowered women do so only rarely. When women are not empowered, the rate of endorsing principles other than their most preferred is nearly six times greater than when they are empowered. That is, figure 9.4 underscores, again, just how disempowered women are when they are few under majority rule. They are far more likely than other women to endorse principles they did not prefer. It is not simply a matter of women remaining quiet because their voices are not needed. Instead, when women do speak up, they are more likely to express a viewpoint with which they privately disagreed prior to the discussion.

The effect of the conditions on men is quite different. While majority rule prompts minority women to speak up in *favor* of principles they did not prefer, it prompts minority men to speak up *against* principles they did not prefer. Specifically, men are most likely to *oppose* their disfavored alternatives under majority rule with many women. In that sense, minority status disempowers women but empowers men. Turning to the majority-rule groups with many women, both genders more freely express opposition to principles that do not rank as their most preferred. Again we see that conditions that most empower women do not detract from men's voice, to the benefit of a deliberative airing of opinions.

To sum up, women's public expression of generosity toward the poor is substantially affected by the conditions of deliberation at the heart of our experiment. In conditions that prompt women to speak more and to discuss women's distinctive issues more often, and where women come to be seen as more influential members of the group and receive more positive interjections, they also advocate more generosity to the down and out. They are more likely to express support for higher minimum guaranteed incomes, are less likely to speak

[40] As the table shows, patterns remain the same—and if anything become slightly stronger—in fully saturated models. Results are identical with controls for liberalism (see online appendix table C9.8), and adding controls for age, education, and income or for group-level measures of the number of group members who are college graduates or the number of group members above the median in income or education makes no difference to our key gender interaction (not shown).

Table 9.3: Endorsement of or Opposition to Principles Other Than Most Preferred

	Endorsements of Principles Other Than Most Preferred				Opposition to Principles Other Than Most Preferred			
	(1) Women	(2) Women	(3) Men	(4) Men	(5) Women	(6) Women	(7) Men	(8) Men
Majority Rule	2.73***	2.53**	−1.11*	−0.70	−3.64*	−3.45	−2.32**	−1.63
	(0.98)	(1.05)	(0.67)	(0.77)	(2.00)	(2.24)	(1.15)	(1.45)
Number of Women	0.43*	0.44*	0.06	0.05	−0.54	−0.55	−0.10	−0.15
	(0.25)	(0.25)	(0.22)	(0.23)	(0.34)	(0.35)	(0.22)	(0.24)
Majority × Number of Women	−0.87***	−0.92***	0.24	0.29	1.10*	1.16*	0.80**	0.98***
	(0.28)	(0.27)	(0.28)	(0.30)	(0.58)	(0.59)	(0.36)	(0.35)
Egalitarianism	1.16	1.22	−0.73	−0.78	−2.00	−2.01	0.38	0.48
	(0.97)	(0.98)	(0.61)	(0.62)	(1.99)	(2.03)	(1.00)	(0.99)
Number of Egalitarians	0.28**	0.22	0.08	0.19	0.12	0.17	0.02	0.19
	(0.12)	(0.14)	(0.16)	(0.21)	(0.24)	(0.33)	(0.21)	(0.31)
Majority × Number of Egalitarians		0.11		−0.19		−0.12		−0.43
		(0.17)		(0.28)		(0.45)		(0.36)
Proportion Talk	1.29	1.31	1.84	1.82	4.47*	4.44*	1.32	1.45
	(1.46)	(1.47)	(1.25)	(1.24)	(2.30)	(2.28)	(1.73)	(1.85)
Constant	−3.28***	−3.19***	−0.41	−0.64	−1.18	−1.28	−2.12**	−2.53**
	(1.00)	(1.01)	(0.58)	(0.59)	(1.52)	(1.50)	(0.88)	(1.12)
Alpha	−0.08	−0.07	0.46*	0.45	0.16	0.15	−2.35	−2.64
	(0.33)	(0.32)	(0.27)	(0.28)	(0.91)	(0.90)	(7.97)	(10.26)
Observations	156	156	162	162	156	156	162	162
Control for Experimental Location	Yes	Yes	Yes	Yes	Yes	Yes	Yes	Yes

Note: Entries are negative binomial regression coefficients. Individual–level analysis. Cluster robust standard errors in parentheses. *** $p < 0.01$, ** $p < 0.05$, * $p < 0.1$, two-tailed test.

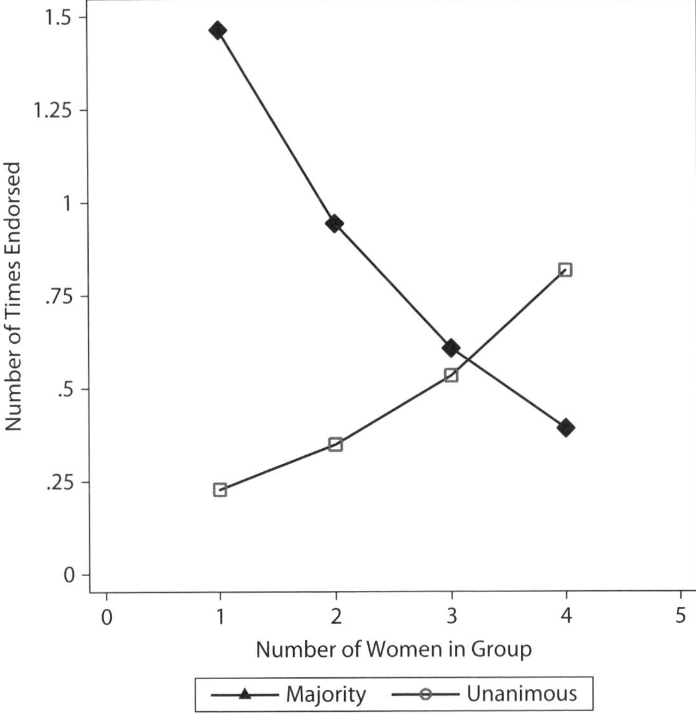

Figure 9.4. Endorsement of redistribution principles other than their most preferred, women only. Note: Predicted values from Model 1 of table 9.3.

on behalf of principles that are not their first preference, and are more likely to oppose those disfavored principles. In other words, in the conditions when women are more empowered, women influence the conversation, turning it more frequently to women's distinctive issues, endorsing more generous approaches to redistribution, and aligning their public expressions of generosity with their private preferences.

Men are less profoundly affected by the interaction of decision rule and gender composition, but they are not wholly insensitive to it. Under unanimous rule, men support *lower* minimum guaranteed incomes as the number of women in the group increases; men are more generous when surrounded by few rather than by many women. Under majority rule, increasing the number of women leads to *more* expressions of generosity among both men and women. However, the most talkative men in these majority female groups resist the extremely generous safety net that the most talkative women in those same groups advocate. In addition, even when controlling for talkativeness, men in these groups are more likely to articulate their own views—they express opposition to principles they dislike and embrace the principle of no redistribution.

Stepping back to consider both genders and across the experimental conditions, we find that empowering conditions increase women's advocacy for the poor, with some mixed effects on men, including evidence that some men resist the call for increased generosity when women are empowered.

When Do Women Influence Group Decisions?

Although what women say is an important indicator of their attempt to influence, what the group chooses to do after hearing women's voices is the ultimate measure of women's actual influence. Full representation entails not only speaking for a view but also seeing that view through to implementation. We thus turn to the final outcome: the group's decision. Our question is whether the measures of women's empowerment, documented in earlier chapters, in turn have an effect on what the group decides. Do women's elevated talk time, their more frequent talk of care issues, their experience of more positive engagement while speaking, and their expressions of preferred generosity translate into different group decisions? Specifically, did the conditions that empower women in these ways affect the group's generosity toward the poor?[41]

Figure 9.5 presents the predicted minimum guaranteed income for each experimental condition (with dummy variables for each condition and a control for site).[42] The figure shows, first, that among mixed-gender groups, increasing women's descriptive representation under majority rule moves group decisions in the direction of more generous redistribution of income to the poor. All-female groups tend to be much more generous than all-male groups, with the average difference exceeding $7,000. A simple regression model of all majority-rule groups confirms that the guaranteed minimum income is significantly higher—more than $4,000 higher—in majority female than minority female

[41] One challenge of this analysis is how to translate the differing principles into a single, comparable metric of generosity. For groups that selected the principle of setting a floor, this is simply the dollar amount the group chose as an acceptable minimum standard of living. Similarly, the single group that chose no taxes or redistribution was assigned a dollar amount of $0, consistent with that principle. We assigned groups that chose to "maximize the floor" (N = 5) a minimum income of $35,000, which is the 90th percentile of the amounts chosen by the "set a floor" groups. Finally, the six groups that chose to "set a range" were assigned imputed floor amounts in proportion to the gap they preferred between rich and poor. For example, groups that chose a very low gap ($0) were assigned high floor amounts ($35,000), again using the 90th percentile rule. The patterns we report below are similar whether we use only those groups that actually set a floor or whether we add the groups that chose other principles.

[42] According to the US Census Bureau's Cost of Living Index for 2010, our East Coast site had the highest state-level cost of living in the nation, while our Mountain West site was slightly below the national average. Consistent with these differences, East Coast participants tended to set minimum guaranteed incomes that were approximately $6,500 higher than those chosen by participants in the Mountain West. For this reason, our controls for experimental site are especially important for this analysis. When we analyze the effect of the conditions on the two sites separately, however, the patterns are very similar (see chapter appendix, figure A9.1).

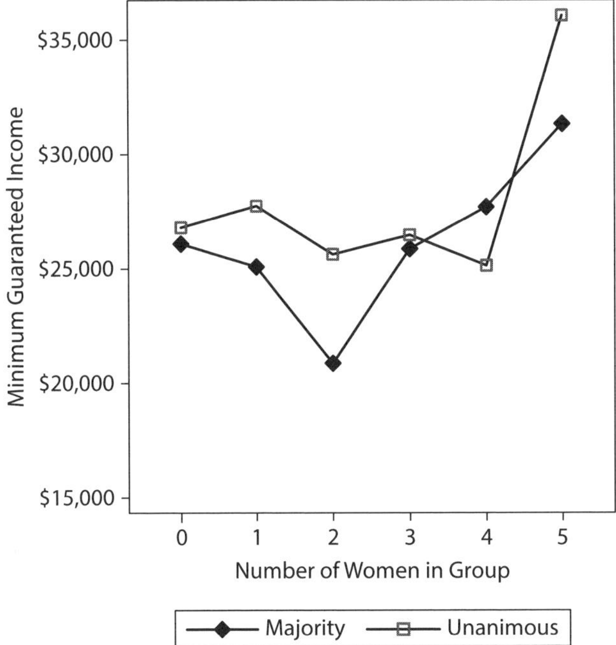

Figure 9.5. Group's chosen minimum guaranteed income for safety net, by experimental conditions. Note: Estimated values include controls for experimental location.

groups ($p < 0.05$, one-tailed test, chapter appendix table A9.5).[43] This substantial effect of numbers persists when controls for the number of egalitarians in the group are included. In groups deciding by unanimous rule, however, there is no statistically significant difference in generosity between majority- and minority-female groups, though female enclaves were much more generous than any mixed-gender condition (chapter appendix table A9.5). When we restrict the analysis to mixed-gender groups only, we find modest evidence of our predicted interaction between gender composition and decision rule. The interaction of rule and the number of women is marginally significant at $p < 0.10$ (one-tailed test; chapter appendix table A9.6, Model 1) and remains positive and marginally significant ($p < 0.07$) with controls for the number of egalitarians and the interaction of decision rule and the number of egalitarians (chapter appendix table A9.6, Model 2).[44]

[43] This result holds if we substitute the number of liberals in the group for the number of egalitarians. See online appendix table C9.9. In addition, the effect of gender composition is strong and significant if we add group-level controls for the number of college graduates or the number of group members above the median in income or age (not shown).

[44] Substituting a control for the number of liberals and the interaction between rule and number of liberals dampens the results slightly. The basic pattern of results is very similar (as can be seen in online appendix figure C9.1), but the interaction term is not significant ($p = 0.12$, one-tailed).

While figure 9.5 has the virtue of displaying the actual amounts in each specific combination of numbers and rule, figure 9.6 paints a clearer picture of the conditions' effects by fitting a regression line through each trend. That figure also shows the effect of the conditions after controlling on the number of egalitarians and the interaction of egalitarians and rule (predicted from the linear, interactive model in chapter appendix table A9.6, Model 2).[45] The figure shows that while the effect is modest, there is in fact a clear interaction between rule and composition among mixed-gender groups. Groups choose a more generous safety net under majority rule as the number of women rises. Under unanimity, the effect of numbers reverses. Thus, as anticipated by our interaction hypothesis, women interacting with men do best as a numerical majority only under majority rule, and unanimous rule is the better rule for minority women but not for majority women.

By what mechanism do the conditions affect the generosity of the group's chosen safety net? We saw earlier that the conditions affect the generosity women express, and now we ask whether that generosity affects the group's decision, holding constant men's expressed generosity.[46] Chapter appendix table A9.7 (panel A) shows that indeed, the more generous are women's stated preferences for the safety net, the higher is the group's safety net, even after we account for the effect of experimental location, of egalitarians, of predeliberation preferences for principles, of predeliberation attitudes toward the poor, and of the direct effect of the conditions.[47] Specifically, in mixed-gender groups, as the average woman's endorsed poverty line increases by $1,000, the group's chosen safety net rises by approximately $400–500 (with a similar effect from the average man's endorsement). Thus when we consider simultaneously the effects of the average woman's and the average man's stated preferences for the safety net, we find that in general, women have a substantial effect regardless of what men

---

However, tests of the predicted values show that just as in models with controls for egalitarianism, the difference across decision rules is marginally significant when the number of women is low. In addition, the interaction is significant with controls for the number of liberals if we use a dummy variable for majority women in the group instead of the linear indicator of the number of women (see online appendix table C9.9). In general, we can say that the results for the group's decision are slightly less statistically robust when we control for liberalism instead of egalitarianism, but the general pattern is unchanged. Results are also similar if we add controls for the number of college graduates and the number of participants above the median age or income (not shown).

[45] Predictions hold constant the number of egalitarians in the group at the sample median (three).

[46] The clearest explanation for the group's eventual decision is what preferences are actually expressed during the group deliberation period; for all groups, the correlation between the group's decision and the maximum endorsed poverty threshold by men and women is 0.83 for women and 0.85 for men.

[47] This analysis is limited to groups where both women and men endorsed a safety net preference. Because of those data limitations, we cannot reliably disaggregate by experimental condition. We have already shown, however, that the conditions profoundly affect the level of safety net endorsements. Thus even if the relationship between endorsements and group decisions is positive across all conditions, the overall effect is likely to vary with condition. Results are essentially identical if we substitute controls for the number of liberals in the group (not shown).

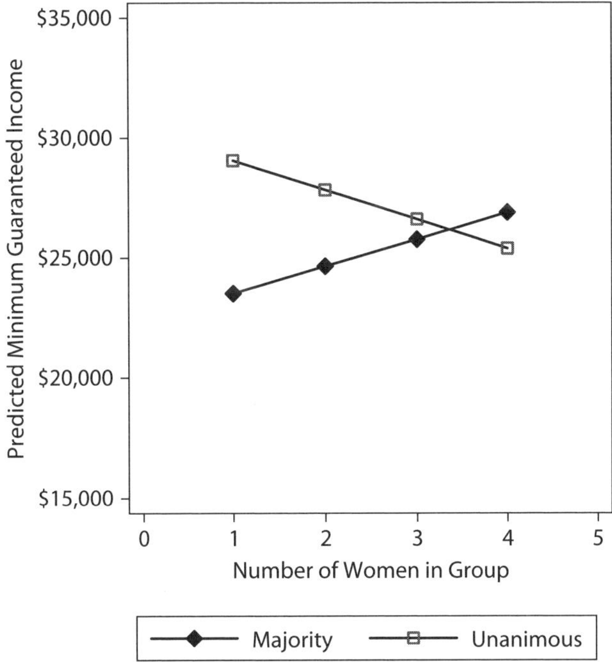

Figure 9.6. The interaction of decision rule and group gender composition on group's safety net, mixed-gender groups only.

say.[48] This is a significant indicator of the power of women's voice, and a main avenue for women's instrumental influence over the group decision.

Most of our analyses to this point have focused on the effect of the average woman or man in the group, for reasons outlined in earlier chapters. But when it comes to group decisions, we also want to know about the total effect of men and women. A group decision may rest not only on the average but also on the collective, or the aggregate. One way to account for this aggregated women's voice is to weight the average woman's expressed preference by a measure of women's total proportion of the conversation. By doing so, we can see how much influence women (or men) have as a whole on the ultimate group decision. Relying on this measure makes sense in particular given that as chapter 5 demonstrated, the conditions have a large effect on women's talk. We thus computed a measure of the total "volume" of women's (or men's) expressed preferences by multiplying the average woman's maximum endorsed safety net (or the average man's) by the total proportion of the conversation taken by *all* women (or men) in the group.

[48] We cannot draw a causal inference here, of course, since expressed generosity is endogenous and we have not controlled on all the possible correlated predictors.

Regression analysis shows that this measure is strongly associated with the group's safety net, including in the presence of controls (see panel B of chapter appendix table A9.7).[49] The greater the total volume of generous endorsements, the greater is the group's chosen floor amount, even after controlling for the effects of the experimental conditions.[50] In fact, in the presence of the most stringent controls (Model 5), women's volume of generosity matters while men's has no effect. When women take up more of the discussion in order to express a generous preference, they shift the group's eventual decision toward generosity. Thus, by some estimates women have more influence than men—but only if they take up a good deal of floor time and speak for generosity. This finding refutes any doubt about the meaning of our earlier finding about women's tendency to speak less than men: women's relative quiescence matters.

The most direct test of women's influence, however, is what happens when men's and women's endorsed preferences diverge. Specifically, the question is what effect women have when they advocate for a more generous safety net than men do. To find out, we defined generous support as a poverty line above the median endorsement for all participants in the study and created variables indicating whether or not men and women in each group were, on average, above or below that median, and whether they expressed any preference for a floor. We then created dummy variables indicating every possible combination of men's and women's average preferences—women endorse generous floor amounts but men endorse low floor amounts, women endorse low floor amounts but men endorse high floor amounts, both men and women endorse high floor amounts, men endorse low floor amounts and women say nothing, and so forth. The excluded category in the model thus captures groups where both men and women endorse low floor amounts.

Do women have their way when they publically disagree with men's low generosity? The answer is no. Table 9.4 shows that the coefficient on this dummy, while positive, is far from significant.[51] The other notable finding in table 9.4 is

[49] Results are robust to using controls for the number of liberals instead of the number of egalitarians and to controls for the number of group members above the median in age or education and the number of college graduates (not shown).

[50] Groups where women or men did not endorse a safety net preference were assigned a volume of 0. We also computed a second measure of the total "volume" of women's preference expressions by multiplying each woman's (or man's) maximum endorsed safety net amount by the total number of preference expressions made by that woman (or man), then summing for all women (or men) in the group. We find that this measure has no significant relationship to the group's chosen floor amount, though the coefficients are in the expected direction.

[51] The other effects are not much relevant to the main questions. Also, when men do not take a position but women do, the group is likely to set a more generous safety net, indicating that men lose influence when they are silent and women are expressive, just as women do when they are silent and men are expressive. In addition, controls for the number of liberals instead of the number of egalitarians make no difference to the findings reported above, nor do controls for other group-level demographic characteristics, such as the number of group members above the median in age or income or the number of college graduates (not shown).

Table 9.4: Women's Preference Expression and Group Generosity toward the Poor, Mixed-Gender Groups Only

	(1)	(2)	(3)
Men Low/Women High	2,456.59	2,353.77	2,421.56
	(4,092.53)	(4,148.22)	(4,297.57)
Men High/Women High	7,964.39***	7,980.79***	7,591.43***
	(2,155.60)	(2,175.19)	(2,421.19)
Men High/Women Low	764.21	655.90	1,227.08
	(2,996.20)	(3,052.86)	(3,239.14)
Men High/Women No Endorsement	9,495.00***	9,419.19***	8,342.60**
	(3,396.20)	(3,438.87)	(4,121.52)
Men Low/Women No Endorsement	−3,559.88	−3,463.96	−3,811.05
	(2,354.42)	(2,405.43)	(2,561.02)
Men No Endorsement/Women Low	1,571.84	1,550.03	2,826.21
	(4,151.67)	(4,188.41)	(4,763.50)
Men No Endorsement/Women High	8,487.44***	8,152.00**	8,141.19**
	(2,756.74)	(3,086.36)	(3,325.47)
Majority Rule			1,083.08
			(4,385.45)
Number of Women			−665.55
			(1,172.94)
Majority × Number of Women			618.18
			(1,603.72)
Number of Egalitarians		184.02	813.06
		(734.83)	(1,090.41)
Majority × Number of Egalitarians			−973.43
			(1,353.22)
Constant	20,928.16***	20,581.94***	20,709.87***
	(1,227.98)	(1,856.23)	(3,658.34)
Observations	64	64	64
R-squared	0.52	0.52	0.52
Control for Experimental Location	Yes	Yes	Yes

Note: Group-level analysis. Dependent variable is the group's chosen minimum guaranteed income, in dollars. Standard errors in parentheses. *** $p < 0.01$, ** $p < 0.05$, * $p < 0.1$, two-tailed test.

the effect when men speak for low generosity and women articulate no preference; that coefficient is no different from 0, indicating that when men advocate low generosity, women's silence is equivalent to their agreement. Thus silence is a risky strategy for women who prefer more generous support for the poor; it is unlikely they will find themselves in groups where men, on average, take up the banner of a more generous safety net. If women prefer to increase support for the poor, then they will often need to speak up.

These results provide insight into the effects of disagreement ignoring women's status, but more relevant is whether that status moderates those effects. Because female-empowering conditions move men's expressions toward women's, and male-empowering conditions move women's toward men's, we do not have sufficient groups where women and men disagree to allow us to separate out the effect of disagreement within each of the experimental conditions. However, we can approximate such an analysis by again incorporating total speaking time. Our core argument is that women carry more influence when they have more authority. One indicator of that authority, as we showed in chapter 5, is speaking time. Therefore, we can examine whether women's high or low speaking time changes the effect of women's disagreement on the group's safety net. To do so, we restrict the analysis to groups in which men and women disagreed. For this analysis we cannot use the dummy defined previously because we run out of groups. Therefore, we define disagreement as groups where women's average endorsed safety net was at least $2,000 higher than men's. We also categorize the groups as high or low in women's speech by dividing them at the median of women's total share of the group's talk time in mixed-gender groups (the median of women's share of the group talk is 40%). We find that this disagreement between men and women translates into more generous group decisions only when women take up 40% or more of the total group conversation.[52] In other words, women can leverage their preference for a more generous safety net into a more generous group decision, but only when they are active deliberators, accounting for a large portion of the total conversation. When women and men disagree, quiescent women carry no influence.

By implication, we can now see the full negative impact of women's quiescence, documented in chapter 5. There we found that a token woman under majority rule takes less than 20% of the group talk. That rate clearly falls in our "low" speech category, since it is less than half of the median speaking rate for women. Recall too that in these same groups, men are almost invariably likely to endorse low generosity. Putting these findings together, we arrive at a stark picture of women's powerlessness: in majority-rule groups where women typically account for much less than 20% of the conversation, any expression of generosity women might articulate will have no influence.

[52] In groups with preference disagreement where women take less than 40% of the conversation, the average floor amount is $21,833. In groups where women collectively account for more than 40% of the conversation, the average floor amount is $28,375, a difference that is significant at $p = 0.057$, one-tailed. These results hold in regression models that control for the experimental location and the number of egalitarians in the group. The opposite trend occurs when men prefer more generous floors and women do not, though the difference in the generosity of the group decision is not statistically significant ($p = 0.167$, one-tailed).

Together, the multiple results we have reviewed here lead us to suspect that the effect of the conditions on the group's eventual outcome is mediated by the preferences expressed during deliberation. The interaction of women's numbers and the rule affects the generosity of expressed preferences, the extent of the gender disagreement in that generosity, and the group's eventual generosity. Furthermore, we found that when we include expressed floor preferences in the model, the effect of the conditions on the floor decision is dramatically muted, and the effect of endorsed preferences is strong and significant, whether we include the average preferences or the total volume of preferences (see chapter appendix tables A9.4 and A9.8). A formal mediation model confirms a significant indirect effect of the experimental conditions on the group's floor, working through the preferences expressed during discussion.[53] In sum, women's status in the group, as set by the experimental conditions, substantially affects what participants advocate for, including the extent to which men's and women's distinct perspectives are fully articulated, and those statements in turn drive the group's eventual decision.

Does Talk of Care Issues Change the Group's Decision?

If women's endorsements of more generous poverty thresholds can affect the group's outcome in conditions where women are empowered, do other aspects of the conversation influence the decision as well? In previous chapters, we explored the effect of the conditions on talk of care issues. Now we ask whether talk of care issues also affects the group decision about generosity toward the poor.

There is reason to think so. For one, children are far more likely to live in poverty than adults.[54] Thus to the extent that poverty policy is more generous to the poor, children will especially benefit. So people concerned with the needs of children, as women tend to be, may well be more interested in a generous minimum income for the poor, which allows a higher standard of living, and the more that the discussion focuses on the needs of children and their care, the higher the poverty line will move. In addition, all the referents on which care issues focus—children, families, the vulnerable, and the poor—tend to be viewed

[53]Whether the mediator is the average expressed preferences for the group as a whole, for women only, mediation models (Imai, Keele, and Tingley 2010) show a large and significant average causal mediation effect ($p < 0.05$), with the interaction of decision rule and gender composition affecting average preferences, which in turn affect generosity. For the "total volume" of preferences measure, the pattern is slightly different, but we still find evidence of mediation. For that measure, the direct effect of gender composition is more important than the interaction of composition and rule, but we still find evidence of mediation, with gender composition affecting volume, which in turn affects generosity (average causal mediation effect is significant at $p < 0.05$). For the measure of preference divergence, the formal test of mediation is not significant, however.

[54]http://www.census.gov/hhes/www/poverty/data/incpovhlth/2009/pov09fig05.pdf and http://www.census.gov/prod/2011pubs/p60-241.pdf.

favorably or sympathetically (Gilens 1999); so the more they are discussed as beneficiaries of assistance, the more generous the assistance is likely to be.[55]

To explore these issues, we follow an approach similar to our earlier analysis of preference endorsements, this time looking to the measure we employed in chapter 7 as our key indicator of women's voice on issues of distinctive concern to them: the ratio of care to financial issues. As we explained there, care issues are references to children, family, the needy, or the poor, and financial issues refer to words like salary or taxes. For each mixed-gender group, we computed a ratio for the average woman and the average man in the group.[56] We then created a dummy variable indicating whether or not each ratio was above or below the overall median ratio for all groups in the sample. Then we created an indicator for all four of the possible combinations of the ratios—women with a high ratio of care to financial issues and men with a low ratio of care to financial issues, women with a low ratio and men with a high ratio, both men and women with a high ratio, and both men and women with a low ratio.

Our chief interest is whether women's focus on care issues affects the group's decision about floor amounts when men voice a different priority. And as in our earlier discussion of preference expressions, we also want to know whether this effect is moderated by the amount of time women hold the floor. For this reason, we add an interaction between the dummy variables and women's total *Proportion Talk* during the discussion. The excluded category in the model is groups where both genders had a low ratio of care to financial issues. The results can be found in table A9.9, and control on the effects of egalitarian composition and its interaction with rule, and on whatever other effects are produced by the conditions. Chapter appendix table A9.9 shows that even when men fail to focus on care issues, women can move the group toward greater generosity by speaking more about the poor, children, and families and less about taxes and other financial issues. But this effect is conditional: it only occurs when women's voices account for more of the conversation. Predicted values from Model 2 of the table clarify the effect of women's total *Proportion Talk* in groups where women's ratio is high but men's is low. Where women take up only 20% of the conversation, the group's chosen floor amount is about $18,170, but when they hold the floor for 80% of the group's discussion, the predicted floor rises to $28,270, an increase of nearly 56%.[57] The total volume of women's speech is

[55]See chapter 7 for documentation and explanation of our claims about care and financial issues.

[56]Groups in which the ratios are undefined are excluded from this analysis, but as we indicated in chapter 7, imputing values for those groups does not change the basic pattern of results.

[57]A Wald test shows that this difference is significant at $p = 0.05$ (one-tailed). Predicted values from Model 1 yield very similar results. In addition, the model shows that these effects obtain no matter what the behavior of men. And when both men's and women's ratio of care to financial issues is low and women take 80% of the conversation, the predicted floor is $20,280 (predicted from Model 2 in table A9.9.) Additional analysis (not shown) demonstrates that the patterns are unchanged when controls for men's and women's preference expression (the same variables seen in

critical to whether or not the content of speech has a liberalizing effect on group decisions.[58] For their distinctive concerns to affect the group's outcome in the direction of greater generosity, women must do the very thing they tend not to do when their standing is low: they must speak up.[59]

The evidence thus leads us to conclude that the content of discussion affects group outcomes in two ways: through the safety net amounts endorsed by group members and through the group's focus on care issues instead of financial issues. But women's overall willingness to speak up matters, too. When women do not hold the floor sufficiently, talk of generous safety nets, of the poor, of children, or of families has little effect.

We pause here for a caveat. Because women's volume of care talk and volume of expressed generosity are each caused by the conditions, and are intercorrelated with each other (and with other features of discussion explored in previous chapters), identifying which measure contributes most to the outcome effect is challenging. The experimental conditions have multiple, simultaneous effects on a host of variables, all of which are connected to each other, so we are not arguing that one of our measures of discussion content necessarily carries a bigger causal effect than the other.

Nonetheless, our experimental design allows us to say that the interaction of decision rule and gender composition affects many aspects of the group's dynamic and the content of discussion, and that ultimately—whether directly or through the mediators we presented—these conditions causally affect the group's decision. When the conditions equalize women's status, the gender gap in floor time and influence decreases, positive reinforcement to female speakers increases, the group talks more about issues of distinctive concern to women, and women articulate more generous preferences and preferences that are more distinct from those of men. Group-level factors affect group norms of how group members interact and what they say. Both the norms of interaction and the substance of the conversation thus move in directions that are favorable to women. And in the experimental conditions where these dynamics are more

---

table 9.4) are included in the models or when we substitute the number of liberals for the number of egalitarians or when we substitute group-level demographic controls for age, education, and income.

[58] We also find similar results by using women's average *Proportion Talk* instead of their total talk in the model. When we use the average measure, predicted values from the model show that when women have a high ratio of care to financial issues but men do not, an increase from *Proportion Talk* of 0.10 (severe underrepresentation) to 0.20 (equality) moves the group's floor decision from $17,150 to $29,790 (this difference is significant at p = 0.02, one-tailed, predicted from model with controls for experimental conditions).

[59] Coefficients from the model may at first glance indicate that, paradoxically, when women's ratio is low and men's is high, more talk by women leads to more generosity. However, predicted values from the model show that the rise in the generosity of group floor decisions as women's *Proportion Talk* increases is small, and the difference between groups with low and high *Proportion Talk* is not statistically significant (p = 0.23, one-tailed).

likely to occur, groups make decisions that involve more substantial support for the vulnerable populations that women tend to want to benefit.

Conclusion: How the Conditions of Deliberation Shape Its Outcomes

In this chapter, we have shown that discussion under conditions that elevate women's status affects who sets the agenda, shapes the expression of women's and men's preferences, helps women to become more certain of their views about the proper ways to redistribute income, and, ultimately, affects the group's eventual decision. Our deliberating groups tended to agree on the basic principle that should guide redistribution, and the large majority chose to guarantee a minimum standard of living—a system much like the safety net now in place in their country and around the world.[60] Yet among these many groups, we find considerable disagreement about the magnitude of that minimum income. This is no surprise when we consider that in politics, the fundamental principles are set and rarely discussed, with broad agreement on the basic notion that government should help the poor in some way and that government should tax citizens at least to some extent. The real disagreement occurs on how much government should help.

And women's status in the group affects their engagement in that disagreement, and the consequences of that engagement for the group choice. We find that the conditions that empower women profoundly influence deliberators' public endorsements of generosity. When women are empowered—and especially in majority-rule groups with many women—they are more likely to endorse a higher amount of minimum guaranteed income. This preference is consistent with women's more general inclination toward generous government intervention on behalf of the poor and the vulnerable. In addition, when women's standing is higher, women's preference falsification decreases and their willingness to argue against less preferred alternatives increases. In those female-empowering groups, women's expressed preferences for a generous safety net, and their increased talk of women's distinctive issues, ultimately translate into group decisions that set a higher guaranteed income for the poor, even though in those settings the most talkative men raise their voice for less generosity in turn.

Settings that empower women also increase women's confidence in their own opinions. As we saw in previous chapters, confidence is a key barrier to women's equal participation. Now we can see that conditions that raise women's

[60]There are gender gaps in preferences about principles, but they mostly boil down to the fact that a minority of men wish for no taxes and no redistribution, while very few women prefer this principle.

status in the group alleviate the problem of confidence in part by strengthening women's internal compass about the proper course to follow. Consistent with the interaction hypothesis, unanimous groups with few women and majority groups with many women are much more certain than women who find themselves in the least empowered condition—majority rule with few women.[61]

Finally, the results have implications for our finding from chapter 5, that status equalizes women's talk time with men in the group. There, we saw that women's relative quiescence is associated with lower perceived influence. Now we can see that women's quiescence also carries a concrete, instrumental penalty for women, and for the groups that women tend to want to assist. In groups where women are least likely to speak, they are also most likely to express no preference and least likely to focus on vulnerable populations such as children, and this in turn has independent effects on group decisions, rendering them far less generous.

Thus we see that the interaction of gender composition and decision rule affects multiple aspects of the group's functioning. We cannot understand group deliberation or women's empowerment by focusing only on one of those aspects at the exclusion of the others. If we only examined preferences and group outcomes, we would fail to understand how the preferences convert to the outcome. If we only examined the group decision, we would fail to understand *how* the setting empowers women. It is only by exploring the combination of the volume of speech, the content of comments, the mismatch between the person's views and what they say, and the group's ultimate decision that a more complete picture of the influence of group-level conditions emerges. And in order to understand how authority shapes discussion and group decisions, all of this must be done by comparing the behavior of groups who walk in with more authority to those who come with less authority.

The results have implications not only for women's empowerment but also for deliberation. From the perspective of designing good deliberation, majority rule where women are few functions badly. This conclusion may not be immediately obvious, because of a potentially misleading finding. We found that in this condition, women speak up for principles of redistribution that they disfavored before discussion. At first glance, this might appear to indicate open-mindedness, and thus, a desirable deliberation. However, the problem with this interpretation is that this seeming open-mindedness occurs only among women, and then, only where their status is lowest. It does not occur among men where they are the minority (or anywhere else). If a discussion prompts support for disfavored views only among disempowered social groups under conditions that also exhibit various markers of their disadvantage, then that

[61] See figure 9.1. Certainty is highest under unanimous rule with few women, lowest under majority rule with few women. Among groups with many women, certainty is the same no matter the decision rule.

type of open-mindedness is not a feature of good deliberation but of disempowerment. The implication is that expressions of open-mindedness cannot be taken as features of good deliberation universally, or even frequently. If they are not reciprocal between empowered and disempowered groups, then they are a red flag for inequality and for its corrupting influence over deliberation.

In addition, the conditions that most empower women—majority rule with many women—also produce a good deliberative exchange. There, not only are women most likely to articulate preferences, and to articulate generous preferences, men are also most likely to articulate their own, less generous preferences. The result is a fuller, more robust engagement of deliberators with each other. Discussion includes more elements of debate, with the felicitous side effects—diverse alternatives receive a hearing and the group can then make more informed choices.

As previous chapters demonstrated, when deliberation is not structured with the explicit goal of addressing social inequality, it produces significant social inequality. Although the goal of deliberation is to create equality within discussion, the way that deliberation is conducted has a good deal to do with its ability to achieve that goal. As the theorist Dennis Thompson writes, "For many deliberative theorists, one of the main points of deliberative democracy is to expose inequalities to public criticism and create less unjust conditions in the future" (Thompson 2008, 509). Deliberative democracy in practice, however, not only fails to expose inequalities and injustices but also worsens them, on multiple dimensions. When women are not set up to have equal influence in discussion, not only do they emerge with less authority but also other groups, such as the poor and vulnerable, are worse off as a result. Gender inequality within discussion produces a cascade of inequalities for many vulnerable groups in society.

We have now seen that conditions that empower women produce a whole set of consistent effects. Women speak more, discuss issues of distinctive concern to women more often, receive more positive affirmations while speaking, are viewed as more influential and view themselves as more efficacious, express their more generous preferences more often, and ultimately shift the group decision. But all this happens in an artificial setting. We now turn to a very different setting to see what we can learn there.

CHAPTER 10

Gender Inequality in School Boards

ON JANUARY 5, 2012, the school board of Londonderry, New Hampshire, gathered for its first meeting of the new year. Founded in 1722, Londonderry is a small town in the southern part of the state that boasts of its high quality of life, considerable open space, and excellent schools. The January school board meeting was attended by five board members—four men and Nancy Hendricks. Over the course of the two-hour and ten-minute meeting, Nancy made three comments, no motions, and offered one second to a motion made by another board member. The four men at the meeting accounted for all the other actions the board secretary recorded. Although Nancy Hendricks was 20% of the board, her motions and comments accounted for less than 9% of the speaking turns that evening.

Just a few days earlier, on December 21, the school board of Wakefield, New Hampshire, held one of its last meetings of 2011. Wakefield, like Londonderry, can boast of its long history. Founded in 1774, it advertises its "New England Town Charm" and high quality of life. Its school board is also made up of five members, but unlike Londonderry, four of the elected officials are women. Over the course of the three-and-one-half-hour meeting, the women together accounted for 84% of the speaking turns and 88% of the motions made—both numbers slightly higher than their proportions at the meeting.

Our aim in this chapter is to explore the experiences of men and women in Londonderry, Wakefield, and many other towns and cities across the country. To this point, our focus has been almost entirely on our experimental data. We have done so for good reason: with their random assignment to group conditions and carefully controlled lab setting, the experimental data give us high levels of internal validity about the causes of women's and men's behavior. They also allow us to explore systematically what transpires during discussion and to measure the perceptions and views of the participants before and afterward. We explored a large number of variables, and did so with high confidence that we are tapping into causal relationships in a meaningful way. But we also care about external validity. That is, we want to be sure that the patterns we found in the lab can also be seen in the real world of deliberating groups, including groups discussing issues other than the redistribution of income.

We have reason to believe that the gender gaps we found in our experimental groups are likely to be found outside the lab. First, natural settings vary in women's level of speech, one of our key dependent variables. In his study of New England town meetings, for example, Frank Bryan found that the percentage of female speakers ranges from 5% to 68% and that the ratio of women's percentage of speaking turns at the meeting to male percentage of turns ranges from 0.23 to 3.37. Second, many natural settings seem to produce a significant participatory disadvantage for women. On average, in Bryan's study, women comprise 47% of meeting attenders, but only 36% of the speakers and only 28% of the speaking turns.

This chapter thus has several goals. First, it seeks to show that the findings we obtained in the lab, under controlled but artificial conditions, replicate with actual deliberators and in the real world, where some groups meet many times and the members get to know one another, and where people make statements and reach decisions free of the obtrusive gaze of an experimenter. Second, we wish to see if women obtain more substantive representation when the agenda deals with a women's issue. Women have long been active in education institutions, and their levels of engagement and knowledge on school board matters equal men's, as we detail. Therefore, examining the effect of gender composition within school boards constitutes a hard test for our hypothesis that women need particular circumstances to participate and influence as effectively as men do. In addition, our experiment examined groups without a formal leader. But in the real world, many groups assign formal leadership positions to their members. Our school board data allow us to examine whether women's formal leadership position improves women's participation and influence, either directly or in combination with their descriptive representation. Our school boards study thus introduces a factor we did not vary in our experiment—the gender of the group's formal leadership—and allows us to test the limits of our findings by examining settings focused on children's education, a topic of distinctive concern to women.

There are two things that this chapter does not do. First, it does not directly compare the effect of the decision rule within our sample of school boards because all the boards use majority rule. We thus test our hypothesis about numbers under majority rule only, though we turn to the question of unanimous rule with a second data set of community meetings. Second, we cannot provide a rigorous causal analysis of these meetings. This chapter aims at external validity; strong causal inference and high internal validity was the aim of the experimental chapters.

Strikingly, these new data sets reveal precisely the same trends we found in the lab. Women who serve on a school board where men outnumber them participate far less than their already low proportion of board members. When women comprise a majority of the board, their participation comes close to equality, though it takes a supermajority of women before the voices of men and women are balanced. Thus even among an arguably elite sample of women who were elected *in order to speak up* for their constituents, we find that when women's authority is low, women are the silent sex.

School Boards in America

We have argued from the outset that the sorts of small group discussions that were at the heart of our experimental work are ubiquitous and important in American political life, from the local to the national level. Perhaps nowhere is that better evident than in the regular meetings of school boards held all over the United States. At these meetings, Americans gather, discuss issues of importance to the local educational system, and make collective decisions that are binding for those within the school district.

School boards are notable for our purpose for several reasons. First, there are lots of them. To be more specific, there are over 14,000 in the United States. This large number means that boards are a common venue for local decision making. It also provides us with many potential cases. The plethora of boards helps with our particular purpose, which is to study what happens inside boards that differ in their gender composition. With so many boards, we are likely to find enough variation all the way from 0 to 100% female.[1] Then we can say what difference composition makes. As Reingold notes in her review of the literature on women in office, few studies of women's representation examine variation across decision-making bodies that vary in gender composition (2008, 140). The variation that 14,000 potential units afford is far higher than the variation afforded by the fifty state legislatures, the most commonly studied setting by scholars interested in gender composition (Reingold 2008, 140). While we cannot analyze the contents of 14,000 board meetings, we can leverage this high number for a sample with adequate variance in the independent variable.

Second, school boards are among the most important public institutions in a community. Boards are authorized to and in fact direct and oversee the main educational institutions in the community. Their budgets are often substantial by local standards. And they are quite powerful. They have the ability to enact

[1]By contrast with the average 40% female composition of school boards, corporate boards are far less diverse, composed on average of 15% women. In addition, 87% of the Fortune 500 companies have at least one female board director but less than 20% had three or more women (Pande and Ford 2011, 27, citing Catalyst Census: Fortune 500 Women Board Directors, available at http://www.catalyst.org/file/320/2009_fortune_500_census_women_board_directors.pdf). Female percentages in European boards are also very low, only improving recently as a consequence of laws mandating minimum quotas. See, for instance, http://www.nytimes.com/2011/01/27/world/europe/27iht-women27.html?_r=1&pagewanted=all.

budgets, enter into contracts, issue and campaign for bond issues, handle all manner of constituent needs and complaints, and generally provide leadership on educating the young (NSBA).[2] In other words, the decisions they make involve real power, with important implications for children, parents, and the larger community. Boards are active and meet often; over 90% of boards meet once or twice a month (NSBA table 48).

Third, a large majority of boards have either five or seven seats (NSBA table 39), making boards a good place to see if our five-member lab group findings apply in real settings. Board meetings are one example of the sort of group deliberation we had in mind when designing our experiment, and the number of board members parallels well the lab setting we constructed.

Do Women Participate More When Women's Issues Are on the Agenda?

Our board study also differs from our lab investigation in one important way: the subject of discussion is always, in some sense, the welfare of children in the community. Whereas our lab groups could choose whether to frame redistribution as about children, families, the poor, and the needy, or instead about taxes and the work ethic, board members are nearly always dealing with what might broadly be considered issues of distinctive concern to women: education and the needs of children. As we have presented our lab findings to other political scientists around the United States, one frequent response is to assert that the dynamics we found in the lab would have been different if we had picked a different topic, one that was more centrally focused on the issues women care most about. A focus on school boards allows us to examine this proposition.

The education of children has long been viewed as women's purview. Women were allowed to teach Sunday school in churches even as they were barred from voting or even discussing church matters (Burns, Schlozman, and Verba 2001). Women compose the majority of PTA groups.[3] Women thus are likely to view the topic as a close fit with their traditional gender role. They may feel qualified and confident in speaking up in school board meetings.

Consistent with this notion, there is no place where women find higher representation: about 40% of board members are women (Burns, Schlozman, and Verba 2001, 104; Donahue 1997; NSBA). That is about double the female per-

[2]Superintendents report that boards have a substantial degree of autonomous authority and are not required to seek approval for their most important actions. For example, city or county councils have to approve school board budgets in only 9% of districts (NSBA table 49). Nearly two-thirds of boards have the authority to levy taxes, although such levies frequently require voter approval (NSBA tables 50–51). In 79% of cases, boards are solely authorized to call bond elections (table 52).

[3]It is one of the organizations listed as gender segregated in Burns, Schlozman, and Verba (2001).

centage in city councils, state legislatures, or Congress (Crowder-Meyer 2010). Thus women may view themselves, and may be viewed by voters, as qualified to serve on boards, to judge by their relatively greater numbers there. Furthermore, board members are well educated and possess financial means, so the women who serve on boards are not likely to suffer from a deficit of participatory resources (NSBA). If women participate equally, and have equal authority and influence, anywhere in elected office in the United States, we will see it here.

Women may engage in public discussion when it deals with the spheres implicating women's role as women. Consistent with the notion that women engage when the issues speak to them, Delli Carpini and Keeter found that the sizable and consistent gender gap in political knowledge shrinks considerably or disappears—and even reverses—for some issues. These are issues that reflect women's "special concerns" (2005, 40). And perhaps for the same reasons that women are far more likely to serve on school boards than in any other legislative setting, women are more likely than men to know who their school superintendent is (Burns, Schlozman, and Verba 2001). Women close the knowledge gap with men on issues of local politics (Delli Carpini and Keeter 2005). When discussion is more focused on women's distinctive issues, then women may accelerate their participation in it.

Will the fact that the board is always talking about one giant women's issue —education—mean that gender differences on school boards are muted? Some argue exactly that. On this view, local politics is different because the topics of discussion and decision making tend to consist of some of the issues that women often prioritize, such as education. This in turn means that women and men are equally likely to care, to feel qualified, and to participate. Tolleson-Rinehart finds in her study of mayors that at the local level gender differences are in fact muted (in Carroll 2001). Similarly, Donahue studied school committees and came to that same conclusion (Donahue 1997).

Others claim that gender differences at the local government level will be apparent, but in women's favor. Janet Boles found that among county and municipal legislators, women were more likely to take leadership roles than men on women's issues and establish new programs on these issues. Susan Beck studied women and men in local town councils and found that women tend to be more responsive to constituents and more persistent in their questioning.[4] But no one has looked at, or reported, the effect of gender composition in local settings (see Hannagan and Larimer 2011a, 2011b).

If gender differences are minor when the agenda is fixed on a women's issue, then by implication gender composition may matter little. Do women participate equally to men regardless of their numbers when the agenda is permanently fixed on a women's issue? We don't think so. Bryan finds that women's speech participation in Vermont town meetings is no greater when the meeting

[4] Both the Boles and Beck studies are referenced in Carroll (2001).

agenda includes school issues (Bryan 2004, 220). Not surprisingly, there are some conflicting studies. Rosner found more women's participation in kibbutz meetings when the topic is education (Bryan 2004, 220, note 11). And Bryan suggests that women may participate more in discussions of education when it is not formally on the agenda. However, the evidence is nuanced and mixed (Bryan 2004, 250–52), and the evidentiary base is thin.[5]

In any case, training our analytic focus on the ways in which the gender composition of school boards affects the participation of women allows us to examine this question directly. Perhaps more importantly, the analysis of school boards is, we assert, a tough test for our theory. Not only is the topic of discussion women's issues, but also the women who comprise the school boards are elected officials. They have put themselves forward as representatives of their communities and are, presumably, willing to speak up when issues of importance to them are on the agenda. These women are well educated and above the median income (NSBA). If we continue to find a relationship between women's participation in group discussion and group gender composition, even among a group of elected officials discussing issues of special importance to women, then we will count this as important evidence on behalf of our theory.

Politics as a Man's Game—or a Woman's

Burns, Schlozman, and Verba's *PROPA* offers another compelling hypothesis that we could not test in our experiment but can test on school boards. *PROPA* provides a terrific analysis of the mobilizing, enlightening, and empowering effect that female leaders have on ordinary women. Other studies second this finding and extend it: the more women run for a high-visibility office, the more that women voters in that election learn about their leaders, the more that they feel efficacious, and the more that they attempt to converse with and persuade others (Hansen 1997). There is something empowering for women about other women playing what is widely still perceived as a "man's game" (Burns, Schlozman, and Verba 2001, 334). What happens when women find themselves in a situation with visible, powerful women—that is, when politics becomes more of a woman's game?[6]

One thing that does *not* happen is a simple role model effect. It is not the case that any woman on the ballot moves women. The females running for office have to be visible and viable. This can happen because they get a lot of publicity, or because the office they seek to obtain is visible. Either of these

[5] He also suggests, with anecdotal evidence, that men participate more when discussion is focused on road machinery (Bryan 2004, 249).

[6] A similar effect obtains in seventeen Latin American countries—the presence of women among a country's elected officeholders increases women's political involvement (Desposato and Norrander 2009).

may be needed before the election can send a signal that politics *is* a woman's game. When women run for office in a widely hailed "year of the woman," as they did in 1992, they have a big impact on other women. But when they run in other years for lower-visibility offices, such as the US House of Representatives, their effect on women's engagement, such as women's attempt to "politically proselytize"—that is, to persuade someone about politics—is null (Hansen 1997).[7] As Atkeson summarizes, "Viable symbolic representation enhances political engagement and may increase substantive representation, but token symbolic representation does not" (Atkeson 2003, 1053).[8]

In other words, what women may be doing by running for or holding important offices is resetting the norm about who is entitled and qualified to lead the polity. This is a lesson that women take in and act on. We may find a similar effect in small groups. When a woman occupies a visible powerful position in the group, such as chair or president, she may be implicitly signaling to other women that the meeting is not a man's game.

Just such evidence comes from village meetings in India. A study by Beaman and colleagues (2010) takes advantage of the fact that some local leadership positions are reserved for women on a random basis.[9] The study finds that a woman attending the meeting is 25% more likely to speak at the meeting when the local leader position is reserved for a woman. Whether this effect obtains because women see female leaders at the meeting or because of broader or indirect changes brought about by instituting quotas for female leadership is unclear. Regardless, this finding supports the notion that a visible female leader elevates women's participation.

Further support for the notion that authoritative female figures affect women's engagement comes from Atkeson and Rapoport's study of women's opinionation (2003). As we noted in chapter 2, they found that women are less likely than men to respond with an opinion, or to respond with as many opinions, when asked what they liked or disliked about the parties and candidates of the day. But the gender gap is smaller for women whose *mothers* were more interested in politics (at least, as best as they could recall, though recall is not a great measure). No such effect obtains for men or from fathers. In other words, politically interested women may confer on their daughters a socialization effect—perhaps, a sense that they can, and are expected to, be politically active (see also Delli Carpini and Keeter 2005). Again, this finding prompts us to ask

[7]Based on the NES question: "During the campaign, did you talk to any people and try to show them why they should vote for or against one of the parties or candidates?"

[8]"Women are more internally efficacious, more likely to discuss politics, discuss politics often, convince others, and comment on the political parties and less likely to say 'don't know.' The fact that this finding holds true across multiple dependent variables, with controls for psychological, situational, and structural factors as well as the power gained from multiple election years makes these results robust and powerful" (Atkeson 2003, 1053)

[9]We note as a caveat the criticism of this natural experiment, discussed in chapter 4.

what expectations and sense of entitlement to participate may be set for women by authoritative women around them.

The School Board Study

We sampled board meetings widely in order to minimize a correlation between gender composition and other variables. For example, in a recent national survey of members, small districts are more likely to have male members (two-thirds of members in small districts are men), while other districts are as likely to have men as women (NSBA table 1). Small districts are also more likely to have conservative members, white members, and slightly less wealthy members (though the central tendency is the same as in other districts—members in all districts are likely to be nonconservative, white, and wealthy). So it is important for us to look at equal numbers of small, medium, and large districts within each gender composition to avoid confounding gender composition with these other characteristics of boards.[10]

In addition to size and rural character of the district, gender composition may be correlated with the general conservatism of the district. Also, the effects of gender, and of gender composition, may differ in conservative and liberal settings. For example, Dolan and Ford (1995) found that female state legislators in the South were less "feminist" but more devoted to the issues traditionally viewed as women's province and those we have identified as "women's issues" in an earlier chapter—children and family.

Our sampling strategy is based on access to minutes from board meetings. To that end we first searched all fifty states, using the National Association of School Boards and the state Departments of Education to produce a comprehensive list of districts within each state. We then focused on states that provided links to district web pages. We found that thirty-nine of the fifty states offered such links.[11] To further supplement our population of available boards, we contacted BoardDocs, a private company that provides website and document hosting services for government entities and school boards all over the country. BoardDocs provided us with a list of all school boards who use their service. Using both the state school board information and the BoardDocs list, we undertook a search for school boards that post their minutes online.[12]

[10] In small districts 43% are conservative; in large districts, 27% are liberals and 22% conservatives. African Americans constitute 21.8% and Latinos 6% in the large districts. Small districts include only 6% African Americans and 1% Latinos (table 2 in the NSBA report). Large districts report somewhat higher incomes but even in small districts, 42% have incomes over $100,000 (NSBA).

[11] States without web directories included Arkansas, California, Georgia, Indiana, Kansas, Montana, Nebraska, New York, North Carolina, Tennessee, and Vermont.

[12] Between these sources we located electronic minutes for boards in forty-eight states.

We then identified school boards whose electronic minutes included sufficient detail and information on our key variables.[13] We sought boards with meeting notes that were detailed enough to record the presence of board members; the speaking turns for each board member; and the motions, seconds, and votes that occurred during the meeting. Fortunately, most boards do post minutes online, though there is considerable variation in the level of detail of the meeting minutes. Our data set includes only meetings with sufficiently detailed official minutes. All told, we have eighty-seven meetings from twenty different states. Nearly all boards in the sample are elected, not appointed (97%), and nearly all of those elections are nonpartisan (95%), meaning that candidates for office did not label themselves as Republicans or Democrats. Full descriptive statistics for the boards in our sample can be found in the online appendix table C10.1. Our sample of meetings contains school boards located in all different regions of the country, including the South. However, because our aim was to find sufficient variation in the gender composition of the boards we analyzed, we are mindful that our sample is not randomly drawn and may not be representative.

Our data collection efforts involved careful attention to the gender composition of the meetings. As we identified school boards with useable minutes, we sorted them into gender composition categories—0% female, 1–20% female, 21–40% female, 41–60% female, 61–80% female, 81–99% female, and 100% female. Within each category, we randomly sampled meetings with minutes that were sufficiently detailed to code. Our procedure resulted in at least eight meetings in every category, with a larger number of boards in the middle categories of the distribution.[14] In the analysis that follows, we use the exact percentage of women attending the board meeting; our five categories were only for purposes of collecting a diverse sample.

As Reingold notes, scholars of women's representation have been especially interested in settings where women are a small minority. For some, that is operationalized as less than 15%. In some studies, token women are actually more likely to actively pursue women's interests and carry more influence in doing so than are more numerous women (Bratton 2005; Crowley 2004). Bratton argues that in legislative settings, unlike other settings, women may be viewed as experts on women's issues and gain authority as such. Our own lab findings suggest that women's influence will depend on their percentages in ways that are not necessarily monotonic. The 50% mark is important for some measures

[13]The NSBA survey finds that 56.2% post board minutes and supporting documents online. Almost all large districts post minutes online; most other types of districts do too, but less uniformly. Eighty-four percent of large districts do so; 54 percent of the smallest districts do. We also found that school boards in some states were less likely to post minutes online; these were often in the South.

[14]Chapter appendix figure A10.1 presents the distribution of our sample by the gender composition of the board members attending the meeting.

of substantive representation. A supermajority is needed for yet others. Our sample includes forty-two boards where women are a minority, thirty-nine boards where they comprise a majority, and six boards that are evenly divided. And finally, we need enough enclave groups to gauge the effects of gender-homogenous dynamics. To that end, we sampled enough groups to fill finely sliced categories of gender composition, including nine all-male and nine all-female groups.

Existing studies also show that token women may have a higher level of perceived responsibility for acting on women's issues and think that if they don't, no one else will do so, while more numerous women have a more diffused and weaker sense of personal responsibility (Carroll 2002; Reingold 2000). We are specifically interested in a subset of this "small minority" category—tokens. As we found in our lab study, being the lone member of one's gender can affect a person even more than being a small minority with company. Our sample includes twenty-seven boards with gender tokens—fifteen males and twelve females. Another threshold may be around a quarter. Reingold puts it this way: women will "avoid acting for women until they are surrounded by a critical mass of female colleagues," and the "transformation" of the institution and its politics will be "unlikely until women constitute at least a substantial minority (20–30%) of officeholders" (Reingold 2008, 140).

Along with numbers, we examine the official role or position within the board—something that was not possible with our experimental data, where no group members were given a formal leadership position of any sort. As scholars of women's representation note, women's power within the institution depends on occupying the formal roles that grant that power. Cindy Rosenthal, for example, finds that as women's numbers increase in state legislatures, male committee chairs become "less inclined toward such integrative behaviors of leadership as collaboration, inclusiveness, and accommodation," while women chairs become "more likely to embrace these integrative strategies" (in Reingold 2008, 141). Rosenthal's online survey of state legislators found that most women believed that men in leadership positions "forget to include women" and "discount women's advice" (2005, 211, cited in Reingold 2008, 141). In other words, when it comes to school board meetings, women's increasing numbers may make the dynamic less friendly to women if men run the meeting and more friendly to women if women are chairing it. In any case, we want to attend carefully to how the dynamics of participation change when women run the meeting, as compared to boards where men are in charge.

For each board meeting in our sample, coders recorded the presence or absence of each board member, the board member serving as chair or president, and each speaking turn, including motions, seconds, and other recorded comments, identified in the official minutes. Our focus is on the participation of elected board members, not any other speakers, including school superintendent, staff, or citizens. Clearly, our data set is not the same as the careful recording of every single utterance that occurred in our lab setting. We expect that board clerks or secretaries tend to focus on major interventions from board members, not small asides or comments that our recording equipment caught in the lab. But we do find that a sufficiently large number of boards record a great deal of detail in their minutes, and a few boards make full transcripts of their meetings available. Thus for every board meeting, we know the gender composition of the meeting attenders, the identity of formal board leaders, and several types of verbal participation. For most boards meetings, the length of the meeting was also recorded. A sample of such detailed minutes is included in online appendix H.

The official minutes typically reference three forms of verbal participation: motions, seconds, and recorded comments. Motions are formal interventions that move the board members to a vote or propose some other official action. In one sense, these are the most authoritative forms of verbal participation, as they are the first step needed for the board to make a collective decision. They are also easy for those keeping the meeting minutes to record, which means that this measure is likely to be the most reliable. Recorded comments are general speaking turns about a topic under discussion by the board. Because our data are culled from the official board minutes and we have only a small number of full transcripts, we rely on the board clerk or secretary for this measure, and we are unable to tie the clerk's record of the comment to the length of each speaking turn. And comments during executive sessions—portions of the meeting that are not open to the public—are not recorded in any of our boards. Nonetheless, these are verbal interventions in the public portions of the meeting rising to a level of prominence that the clerk felt merited inclusion in the official minutes. The final measure is seconds to a board member's motion. Like motions, these are easy to identify and record, but they are less authoritative than motions in that they simply express agreement or endorsement of what another board member has done. Two of our three measures—motions and comments—thus represent more authoritative and demanding forms of verbal participation, with seconds scoring substantially lower on both counts.

The Effects of Gender Composition

We expect that the gender composition of the meetings will matter in ways that are largely consistent with the patterns we saw in the majority-rule groups in the lab. This means that women's participation should increase as the percentage of female board members present at the meeting increases. But our argument in the preceding chapters is not simply that women participate more, on aggregate, when there are more women in the group. Instead, we have argued that women's voices are *disadvantaged* when they are the gender minority in a deliberating group that makes decisions by majority rule. That is, in such contexts, women's voices will be underrepresented relative to their presence at the meeting. When women comprise only 20% of the group, they are significantly less likely to take up even 20% of the conversation in groups deciding by majority rule. Equality, on this understanding, is defined as voice proportional to representation in the group.

To test our expectations about the relationship between equality and gender composition, we develop a new measure: the ratio of women's proportion of speaking turns to their proportion of attendees. A score of one on this "equality ratio" measure would mean that women spoke in exact proportion to their presence in the group: in a group comprised of 20% women, women would account for 20% of the speaking turns; if women were 40% of the group, they would take 40% of the speaking turns, and so on. Scores less than one signify underrepresentation for women, relative to their presence in the group; scores above one mean overrepresentation.

In our experimental data, all groups had five members, so we could always use a 20% standard to measure equal participation. Our school board data, however, include a greater variety of group sizes. While about half the boards in our sample are comprised of five members, another third of the sample includes six or seven members, and a few have as little as three or as many as twelve members. Thus the ratio of proportion of speaking turns to proportion of attendees who are women allows us to standardize across board size and is ultimately analogous to the approach we used in chapter 5. The models we report below also add a control for board size in case the overall number of people at the meeting matters.

Table 10.1 shows the relationship between the proportion of women at the meeting and the equality ratio in mixed-gender groups. The dependent variables include the two most demanding sorts of verbal interventions, motions and recorded comments. Bivariate relationships are shown in columns one and three, and full models with a variety of controls for various attributes of the board or meeting can be found in columns two and four. All models include cluster robust standard errors, with the clustering accounting for differences across states.[15] As in our experimental data set, we have one significant outlier in our data set, and we control for this outlier in our models, just as we did in their earlier analyses of speaking time.[16]

With both dependent variables, motions and recorded comments, we find a significant relationship between the board's gender composition and the extent

[15]Because education is primarily a state-level responsibility, clustering by state in the group-level data sets is warranted.

[16]This outlier is over four standard deviations away from all other groups in the sample with respect to the equality ratio for motions and nearly three standard deviations above groups in the 95th percentile of our sample.

Table 10.1: Ratio of Proportion of Turns Taken by Women to Proportion of Women Attending, Mixed-Gender Groups Only

	(1) Motions	(2) Motions	(3) Recorded Comments	(4) Recorded Comments
Proportion Women	0.64***	1.01**	0.49***	0.48**
	(0.19)	(0.43)	(0.17)	(0.21)
Size of Board		−0.04		−0.07
		(0.10)		(0.06)
Board Experience (median years)		−0.03		0.02
		(0.02)		(0.02)
No. of College Graduates on Board		0.05		0.09*
		(0.06)		(0.06)
Public Comment at Meeting		0.08		0.09
		(0.14)		(0.17)
Urban		0.26*		−0.16*
		(0.17)		(0.12)
Superintendent is Female		−0.18*		0.05
		(0.12)		(0.15)
No. of Students Enrolled (log)		−0.12**		0.02
		(0.05)		(0.07)
Budget per Student (log)		−0.23		0.07
		(0.22)		(0.23)
Length of Meeting		0.03		0.08
		(0.05)		(0.07)
South		−0.14		−0.01
		(0.36)		(0.13)
West		0.16		0.14
		(0.12)		(0.15)
Midwest		−0.08		0.11
		(0.12)		(0.15)
Constant	0.55***	3.38	0.57***	−0.67
	(0.14)	(2.01)	(0.09)	(2.30)
Observations	69	63	69	63
R-squared	0.30	0.45	0.07	0.22
Control for Outlier	Yes	Yes	Yes	Yes

Note: Group-level analysis. Cluster robust standard errors in parentheses (cluster by state). *** $p < 0.01$, ** $p < 0.05$, * $p < 0.1$, one-tailed test.

to which women's voices are equal to their numbers.[17] When women are the minority in the group, they are much less likely to take speaking turns equal to their presence in the group. Put differently, women on boards with few women are disadvantaged, even relative to their minority status in the group.[18] As the percentage of women in the group rises, however, so too does women's participation, and as women come to outnumber men, women's voice comes much closer to or even exceeds equality. These relationships hold in the presence of controls for district size, budget, location, or other attributes, such as the length of the meeting, whether the superintendent is female, or whether the meeting included public comment from citizens.[19]

The magnitude of the effect can be dramatic. Figure 10.1 shows the predicted values that emerge from the models with controls (Models 2 and 4 in table 10.1). Notably, the point estimates only rise to the level of full equality for motions when the board is composed of at least 60% women, and boards only approach equality for the recorded comments when at least 70% of the members are women.[20] When the dependent variable includes motions only, predicted values for the equality ratio move from 0.48 in boards with only 10% women to 1.29 in boards with 90% women, and in the model that includes recorded comments, the estimates run from 0.60 to 0.99. The confidence intervals that surround these point estimates (not shown) only overlap one when women form a large portion of the group—again above 60%. As in the experimental data, a supermajority of women is required before women reach equality of participation.

A somewhat different look at the results, using raw data and collapsing the gender compositions into minority or majority female, shows the same pattern. The mean equality ratio for recorded comments when women are the gender minority is 0.72—that is, women participate at a little less than three-fourths of their presence in the group. When women are the gender majority, the average equality ratio rises to 0.92. Average equality ratios for men, by contrast, never dip below 1, whether they are the gender minority or the gender majority.

In addition, we can combine the measures of comments and motions and calculate the percentage of groups in which women face a severe disadvantage, defined as an equality ratio of less than 0.5 (that is, when women contribute less than half of the motions and speaking turns that their proportion in the group would predict). We find a severe disadvantage in equality ratios for 24%

[17] The relationship is also statistically significant if we combine motions and recorded comments together (not shown).

[18] We only have one board with seven or more women that has a majority of women, so we cannot test the interaction of gender composition and board size.

[19] Six mixed-gender groups did not record the length of their meetings, but the patterns are identical if we exclude the meeting length variable to allow the inclusion of those groups.

[20] Those are the points at which the 95% confidence intervals for the point estimates in figure 10.1 cross the line of equality (a ratio of 1).

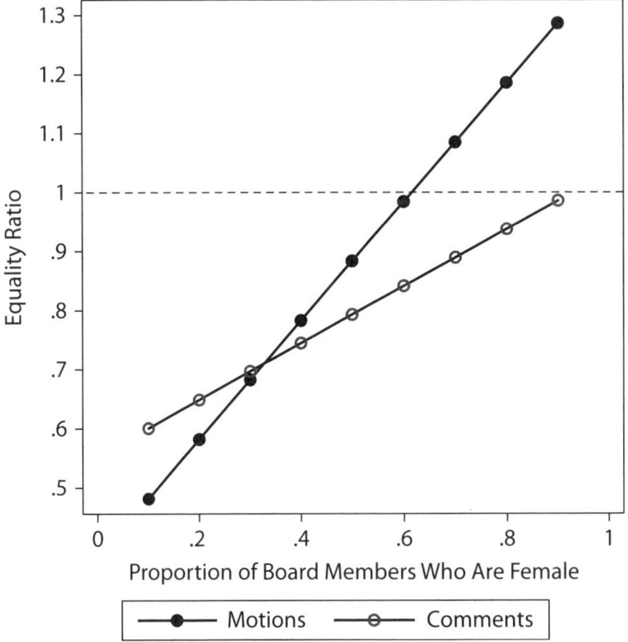

Figure 10.1. Ratio of women's proportion speaking turns to proportion present at meeting, mixed-gender groups only.

of the groups in which women are the gender minority. When they are the gender majority, women experience a severe disadvantage in only 2% of boards. Men face a severe disadvantage relative to their numbers in only two groups in our entire sample, and in only eleven of the sixty-nine mixed-gender boards do men have an equality ratio for motions and comments of less than 0.9. In other words, women face a persistent deficit in verbal participation relative to their presence in the group when they are in the minority, rarely coming close to levels of participation that match their numbers, and it takes more than a majority before women come close to equality. Men routinely participate at levels equal to or much higher than their numbers in the group might anticipate. Only when women are a supermajority are the equality ratios of men and women roughly comparable.

Our analysis to this point reflects exactly the same patterns we saw in our majority-rule experimental groups, providing helpful validation of the results we found in the lab. But the school boards are different from our lab groups in at least one important respect. In our experimental groups, no member of the group was given any sort of formal power to lead the meeting or guide the decision making. Unlike our lab experiment, however, most school boards choose a formal leader or board chair who might have special responsibilities to conduct the meeting or otherwise speak up. What happens when we account for this formal position of leadership in our models?

Table 10.2 highlights these results by adding to the models in table 10.1 a control for whether or not the board chair is a woman. Model 1 of the table shows that this formal leadership position makes no difference to the pattern for motions. Women's equality ratio is still strongly influenced by the proportion of women attending the board meeting, even in the presence of controls for women's leadership responsibilities. In the vast majority of meetings in our sample, the board chair does not make any motions whatsoever, so this increase in the likelihood of making motions comes primarily from the other, nonchair women in the group.

Model 2 of Table 10.2 shows, though, that formal female leadership makes an important difference to the equality ratio for recorded *comments*. Formal authority exerts a large and positive effect, swamping the effect of the board's gender composition. Closer examination shows that this effect holds for boards with few women and boards with many women.[21] This is good news for minority women: the equality ratio for comments is 0.57 without a female chair—about half of what we would expect given their numbers on the board—but 1.20 with a female chair.[22] In groups with a majority of women, the equality ratio is 0.71 in boards without a female chair and grows to above the line of equality (1.08) with a female chair (see chapter appendix table A10.1).[23] Regardless of the gender composition of the board, women are much more likely to reach our standard of equality, and even exceed it, if the board chair is a woman.[24] We interpret this finding as evidence that formal authority in the form of a leadership position in the meeting can be a critical factor for women's equality of voice.

Does this result mean that formal authority is all that matters for women's speaking turns and that gender composition is unimportant? Our answer to that question is no, for two distinct reasons. First, gender composition is strongly related to the likelihood of having a female chair. It is rare for a woman to occupy a position of leadership when the gender composition of the board tilts toward men. Only 19% of mixed-gender groups with a majority of men in our sample have a female chair, while 67% of groups with a majority of women have a female leader. This strong relationship holds up in models that control for a variety of other important board-level factors, as shown in chapter appendix

[21] If we separate meetings where a high proportion of the attending board members were women from meetings with a low percentage of women, the effect of having a female chair on the equality ratio for recorded comments is positive and statistically significant (not shown).

[22] This difference is significant at $p < 0.01$, one-tailed t-test ($t = 3.39$).

[23] This difference is significant at $p < 0.01$, one-tailed t-test ($t = 2.95$).

[24] The effect of gender composition is the wrong sign and is not significant for boards with a majority of women or for boards with a minority of women (analyzed separately).

Table 10.2: Effect of Female Board Chairs on the Ratio of Proportion of Turns Taken by Women to Proportion of Women, Mixed-Gender Groups Only

	(1) Motions	(2) Recorded Comments
Proportion Women	1.08***	0.02
	(0.40)	(0.21)
Female Chair	−0.08	0.51***
	(0.15)	(0.13)
Size of Board	−0.05	−0.03
	(0.10)	(0.04)
Board Experience (median years)	−0.03	0.01
	(0.02)	(0.02)
No. of College Graduates on Board	0.06	0.08**
	(0.05)	(0.04)
Public Comment at Meeting	0.08	0.09
	(0.14)	(0.19)
Urban Area	0.26*	−0.16*
	(0.18)	(0.10)
Superintendent is Female	−0.16*	−0.05
	(0.12)	(0.14)
No. of Students Enrolled	−0.12**	0.00
	(0.05)	(0.05)
Budget per Student	−0.24	0.12
	(0.23)	(0.15)
Length of Meeting	0.03	0.07
	(0.05)	(0.06)
South	−0.15	0.05
	(0.33)	(0.29)
West	0.17*	0.10
	(0.12)	(0.12)
Midwest	−0.07	0.08
	(0.13)	(0.15)
Constant	3.43	−0.97
	(2.09)	(1.54)
Observations	63	63
R-squared	0.46	0.40
Control for Outlier	Yes	Yes

Note: Group-level analysis. Cluster robust standard errors in parentheses (cluster by state). *** $p < 0.01$, ** $p < 0.05$, * $p < 0.1$, one-tailed test.

table A10.2.[25] The predicted probability of having a female chair is less than 13% in boards comprised of 20% women, but rises to 65% for boards where 80% of the attending members are women.[26] In other words, gender composition still matters for verbal participation in part because it is strongly correlated with the likelihood of having a board chair who is a woman, and female board chairs—like all board chairs—tend to participate actively in the meeting. Put differently, the effect of gender composition on equality of speaking behavior is mediated by the gender of the official leader of the group. Formal tests of mediation yield strong evidence for just such a relationship.[27]

But gender composition matters for a second reason as well: it may also affect the remaining board members who do not hold leadership positions. To explore their behavior, we turn from the board-level data to an individual-level analysis. This move allows us to separate the board members who are chairs from those who are not and to control for other individual-level attributes, such as the member's education or length of tenure on the board, that may affect a willingness to make comments during the meeting.[28] In this analysis, we subtract all comments the board chair made and look closely at how all other comments were distributed among the remaining board members. The dependent variable is the proportion of all nonchair comments the individual board member made. In table 10.3, we examine women only, and we find that as the proportion of women among the nonchair members of the board rises, so too does the proportion of speaking turns made by the average woman. The effect holds in the face of controls for the number of years served on the board as well as for a variety of other attributes of the board, including its size, location, and even whether the chair is a woman (see Models 2 and 3 of table 10.3).[29]

The effect of gender composition on nonchair women is substantial, as can be seen in figure 10.2. Where 20% of the nonchair members are women, the average nonchair woman accounts for a little less than 15% of the nonchair recorded comments. For boards where 80% of the nonchair members are women,

[25] We note, for example, that boards with a female superintendent are also more likely to choose a female chair, even after controlling for the gender composition of the board.

[26] These predicted probabilities are computed from Model 2 of chapter appendix table A10.2.

[27] Both a Sobel test and the approach of Imai, Keele, and Tingley (2010) yield statistically significant evidence of an indirect relationship between gender composition and the equality ratio for recorded comments ($p < 0.01$).

[28] We were also able to collect demographic data on 420 of our 510 board members, and not surprisingly, the board members are a well-educated group. Only 8% of the board members for whom we could find information stopped at a high school education, and another 18% had some college or technical training, while nearly 40% had completed some form of postgraduate education. We control for education with a dichotomous variable indicating whether or not the member was part of the 74% of the sample that had graduated from college. The patterns we report below are very similar if we drop this control and use the full data set. The primary difference in the full data set is that the effect of gender composition on men is even smaller.

[29] In this individual-level analysis, standard errors are clustered by board.

Table 10.3: Effect of Gender Composition on the Proportion Recorded Comments among Nonchair Women, Mixed-Gender Boards Only (Individual-Level Analysis)

	(1)	(2)	(3)
Proportion Women (among Nonchairs)	0.10**	0.11**	0.10**
	(0.05)	(0.05)	(0.05)
# of Nonchair Board Members	-0.01	-0.01*	-0.02*
	(0.01)	(0.01)	(0.01)
Years Served on the Board	0.01*	0.01*	0.01*
	(0.00)	(0.01)	(0.01)
Board Member Education	0.01	0.02	0.01
	(0.04)	(0.05)	(0.05)
Board Has Female Chair			-0.02
			(0.03)
Public Comment at Meeting		0.02	0.02
		(0.03)	(0.03)
Urban Area		0.00	-0.00
		(0.03)	(0.03)
Superintendent is Female		0.01	0.01
		(0.02)	(0.02)
# of Students Enrolled		-0.00	0.00
		(0.01)	(0.01)
Budget per Student		0.08*	0.08*
		(0.06)	(0.06)
Length of Meeting		0.01	0.01
		(0.01)	(0.01)
South		-0.06*	-0.07
		(0.04)	(0.05)
West		0.02	0.02
		(0.04)	(0.04)
Midwest		0.01	0.01
		(0.04)	(0.04)
Constant	0.16**	-0.59	-0.58
	(0.07)	(0.55)	(0.55)
Observations	143	133	133
R-squared	0.06	0.08	0.08
Control for Outlier	Yes	Yes	Yes

Note: Dependent variable is the proportion of comments made by nonchair board members; cluster robust standard errors in parentheses (cluster by board). *** $p < 0.01$, ** $p < 0.05$, * $p < 0.1$, one-tailed test.

the average woman accounts for about 21% of the conversation.[30] This six-point change in average participation may at first glance seem small, but it is not. The ratio between the predicted value for women and the prediction for men when women comprise 20% of the group is 0.65, meaning that women are speaking at a rate of about two-thirds that of men. When women comprise 80% of the group, the ratio rises to 1.13—a little higher than the rate for men. Nonchair women's voices thus move from severe underrepresentation to slight overrepresentation relative to men as the gender composition of the nonchair board members changes.

Restricting the analysis to boards that have a female chair only, we find that the patterns are exactly the same as with the full sample: gender composition is a powerful determinant of the participation of nonchair women ($p < 0.05$, one-tailed for the Proportion of Nonchair Women coefficient). More to the point, we can directly test the effect of a female board chair on women who do not hold this formal leadership position by regressing the proportion of comments from nonchair women on a dummy variable for whether the board has a female chair. This analysis shows that on boards where women are the minority, the presence of a female chair has no significant effect on the participation of the other women at the meeting.[31] Thus having a female chair does not dramatically elevate the talk of nonchair women on boards with few women; among the women who do not occupy formal positions of leadership, we continue to see that participation is strongly influenced by the gender composition of the group, not by the presence of a woman in a position of power. These results put the findings from table 10.2 in context. They show that female chairs affect women's average comments because female chairs speak a great deal, not because the other nonchair women change their patterns of participation in groups with female leaders.

Figure 10.2 also shows that the participation of nonchair males appears to fall as the gender composition changes—the more women, the lower the proportion of comments made by the average man—but these trends fall short of statistical significance in models with controls (online appendix table C10.3).[32] In addition, even when women heavily outnumber them, men's participation

[30] These are predicted values computed from Model 3 of table 10.3.

[31] The coefficient indicating the presence of a female chair is small and does not come close to significance ($p = 0.42$, one-tailed). This result comes from analysis in which we restrict the sample to boards with less than 50% women. The model includes the same set of controls used in table 10.3, though results are the same without controls. In addition, the presence of a female chair has no effect on the participation of nonchair women when women comprise 50% or more of the board.

[32] Readers may wonder why the decrease for men is not commensurate with the increase we see for women. If we were analyzing the total proportion of comments by men and the proportion of comments by women, these two would move in tandem and always sum to 1. But here, the predicted values from the regression are essentially showing the average proportion of comments made by men and the average proportion for women, similar to the individual-level analysis of verbal behavior found in chapter 5. These averages are sensitive to the overall number of board

never sinks to the exceptionally low levels we find among women in groups with many men. In groups where men are heavily outnumbered (80% women and 20% men), for example, men still account for more than 19% of the conversation. By contrast, when men similarly outnumber women, they account for only 14.7% of the conversation. In other words, the same gender imbalance affects female board members more deeply than male board members. Finally, just as we saw above, figure 10.2 shows that nonchair women do not reach or exceed equality of voice—in the sense of equal participation by the average man and the average woman—until the board's gender composition moves heavily in favor of women. Men's advantage continues until they find themselves in groups where more than 60% of nonchair board members are women.

As in chapter 5, we also examined how equally the board members distributed their speaking turns by computing a Gini coefficient for the comments board members offered. In part because chairs, both male and female, tend to offer many more comments than most other members of the board, we do not find any relationship between the Gini coefficient and the percentage of women present at the meeting when board chairs are included in the analysis. However, when board chairs are removed from the analysis and we look at how speaking turns are distributed among the nonchair members only, we again find a strong relationship between the number of women present at the meeting and speaking turns. When more women are present in mixed-gender groups, speaking turns among nonchair board members are distributed more equally.[33]

In sum, when female chairs are present, the board's overall equality ratio—the relationship between the speaking turns of the average man and the average woman on the board—improves because the chairs themselves make a large number of comments. This mutes the relationship between the equality ratio and the board's gender composition. But when we examine women who do not hold these leadership positions, we continue to find evidence of a relationship between gender composition and verbal participation. Nonchair women speak less and comments from board members are distributed less equally when women's numbers are low; women speak more and speaking turns are more equally distributed when women's numbers increase. While female chairs take an especially active role in the meeting, the mere presence of a female leader does not shield the nonchair women on the board from the influence of the board's gender composition.

members and the number of men or women on the board, and the movement we see in the predicted values may not be perfectly parallel.

[33] In a board-level regression analysis in which the dependent variable is the Gini coefficient for speaking turns, the relationship between the percentage of nonchair women present and the Gini coefficient is strongly significant ($b = -19.7$, $SE = 6.5$, $p < 0.01$, one-tailed). Analysis is restricted to mixed-gender groups only. The Gini coefficient runs from 0 to 100, so this means the level of inequality in the distribution of speaking turns declines by about 20 percentage points as gender composition moves from its minimum to its maximum.

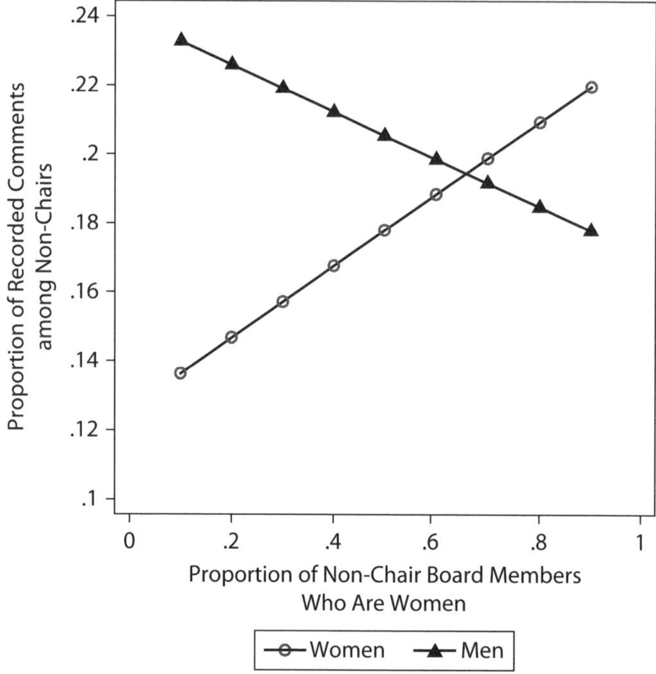

Figure 10.2. Proportion of recorded comments among nonchair board members, mixed-gender groups only.

Of course, a more complete test of these findings awaits a larger sample of school boards (including a larger sample with female leaders) and a more detailed list of comments made during the meeting. The latter is probably only available with full transcripts of meetings where we could also explore for the length of speaking time for each board member. As we indicated already, the measure of comments from detailed meeting minutes is the most subject to the preferences of the board clerk in terms of what to record in the official report of the meeting. Perhaps, for example, we find such a powerful effect of board chairs in part because clerks are especially attentive to the ways in which the formal leaders manage the meetings and move through the agenda items.

Those caveats aside, our results for both motions and comments are quite consistent in both direction and magnitude with our findings from the lab. The fact that motions—a form of power leading to actual decision making in formal groups—depend so heavily on women's numbers in the group is especially important evidence, in our view. Women are simply much less likely to attempt to influence the group with formal proposals when their numbers are few. They do offer such interventions when they gain additional power in the form of increased presence in the group.[34] With respect to comments, we find a similar story, though this is complicated somewhat by the effects of alternative sources of power such as a formal leadership position in the group.

In our experimental data, we paid special attention to the speaking behavior of gender tokens—lone men or women surrounded by the opposite gender. This condition, we found, brought significant disadvantage to women, as compared to men in similar circumstances. Our sampling strategy with the school boards, designed to ensure equal representation across different gender compositions, allows us to explore gender tokens in these groups as well. We have fifteen token men and twelve token women in our sample. Figure 10.3 shows the mean equality ratio for tokens of both genders. The figure includes the equality ratio for recorded comments and for motions. In both cases, we find a dramatic disparity between the speaking behavior of token men and token women. Token men still average at or above the equality ratio of one; they average 1.00 for comments and 1.07 for motions. Token women, on the other hand, have predicted equality ratios of about 0.6 (0.61 for comments and 0.59 for motions).[35] Women's equality ratios hover well below our standard of equality, and they represent significant underrepresentation of women's speech relative to their already-small position in the group. Once again, these patterns mirror our findings from the experimental data quite closely, with the possible exception of the fact that token men on school boards were, if anything, less disadvantaged than those in our experimental groups. Token men in our sample of school boards simply do not speak less than their proportion in the group, while token women often do—and often substantially less.

Our data set also includes one additional form of verbal participation: board members speaking up to second a motion made by another member. These are expressions of agreement with the proposal put on the table by the motion, and they do not contain any additional content or substance beyond the desire that the proposal should move to a vote or some other form of action. When it comes to this form of participation, the board's gender composition has essentially no effect (see online appendix figure C10.1, which shows the relationship between the equality ratio for seconds and the proportion of women attending the meeting). Even when women make up a small portion of the board, many are willing to speak up to offer seconds. In one group comprised of 20% women, for example, the equality ratio nearly reaches three, a rate that well exceeds any result for comments or motions. It seems that women participate by

[34] We do not analyze the relationship between motions and passage rates because in our sample, very few of the issues being debated were highly controversial. We do not find enough variation in passage rates of motions to analyze this relationship fully.

[35] These equality ratios are predicted from OLS regressions of the equality ratio for comments and motions on an indicator for token women, with a control for our outlier group. In both regressions, token women are significantly different from token men ($p < 0.01$, one-tailed). Raw means tell an essentially identical story.

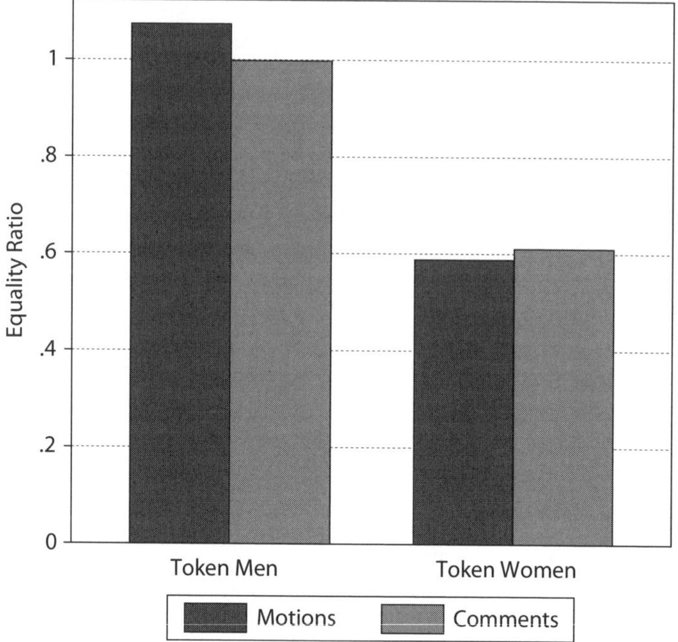

Figure 10.3. Equality ratio for gender tokens.

seconding even when their numbers are low, though they do not offer more demanding and authoritative forms of comment. This pattern fits what we saw in chapter 2 of women's participation in American society more generally; women volunteer, and act, when the act is viewed as a form of help to the group, but shy away from acts viewed as more assertive or opinionated.

While we want to tread carefully, given that our measure of comments is simply a summary from the board clerk or secretary, we find this pattern to be substantively meaningful in addition to providing reassurance about the wider applicability of our lab results for the majority decision rule. In conditions in which women are less empowered because of the group's gender composition, women are less likely to engage in the more authoritative and substantive forms of speech, but such reticence does not apply to the less authoritative seconding of others' motions.

Our analysis so far has focused almost entirely on the behavior of men and women in mixed-gender groups. We have explored the extent to which both genders intervene in board meetings at rates consistent with their proportions in the group. Such measures do not apply to gender enclaves, where by definition women will always take 100% of the conversation in all-female groups, and the same applies to men in all-male groups. What can we say about the nature of conversation in gender homogeneous groups? Unlike with the experimental data, where we have a rich set of variables to examine, the indicators from the board minutes are more limited. Nonetheless, the school board minutes do allow us to explore at least one aspect of gender homogeneous meetings: the duration of the meeting.

In our analysis of the experimental data, we found that women's average talk time was longest in gender enclave groups. While we do not have an individual-level measure of talk time, we do have data on the overall length of nearly every board meeting.[36] And here we find that meetings in which the board members are exclusively women last more than an hour longer than meetings in which board members are exclusively men. All-female meetings take, on average, about three hours ten minutes, while all-male meetings in our sample last about an hour less (p-value of the difference = 0.06, one-tailed t-test).[37] That is, all-female meetings last about 50% longer than all-male meetings. As figure 10.4 shows, meetings of all-male boards are, on average, shortest; all-female board meetings tend to be longest; and mixed-gender groups are between these two extremes (2.5 hours).[38] These results are only suggestive, however, because our sample of enclave groups is relatively low—only seventeen total. In regression models that include controls for other board-level factors, the coefficient indicating the difference between male and female enclaves is large and in the expected directions, but falls short of statistical significance.

Notably, we also find no statistically meaningful difference between men and women in their respective enclaves in the number of turns (motions, comments, or seconds) taken. Total meeting time can be affected by many factors, including the issues under consideration, the level of public input, the size and location of the school district, or even the region of the country. Given these potential confounds, we are hesitant to draw any firm conclusions about the relationship between overall length of meeting and group gender composition. Nonetheless, the rough trends in our school board data are consistent with our lab findings of increased talk time in all-female groups. While much remains to be learned about the determinants of meeting length, our findings—however preliminary—point to the possibility that all-female boards have a different style of public meeting, one that is more inclusive or at least more willing to gather and discuss issues for longer periods of time. It is certainly not the case that female board members have less to say. In fact, they may have more to say than men do. But the conditions of deliberation dramatically affect their likelihood of saying it.

[36] Six mixed-gender boards and one gender homogenous board did not record total meeting time in their minutes.

[37] Both averages are inflated by one outlier meeting—a six-hour meeting in the case of women and a five-hour meeting for men, but if those outliers are removed, the difference is still substantial and statistically significant: all-female meetings last 2.7 hours and all-male meetings last 1.8 hours (p-value of the difference = 0.03, one-tailed t-test).

[38] If we exclude the outlier meetings that last more than five hours, all-male meetings last 1.8 hours, mixed-gender groups last 2.3 hours, and all-female groups last 2.7 hours.

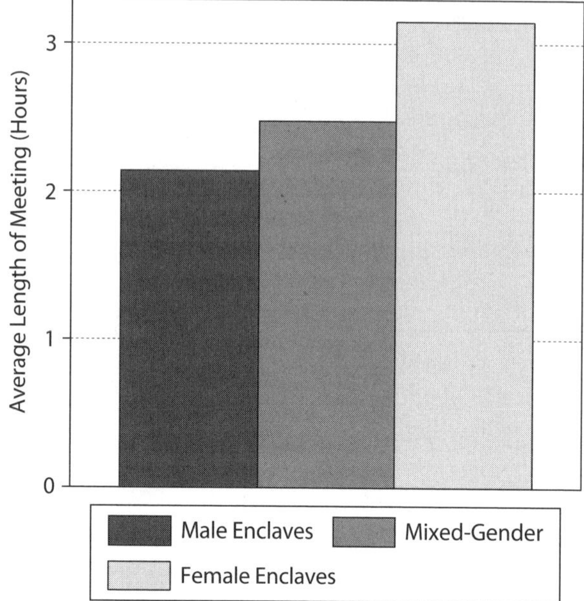

Figure 10.4. Length of meeting, by gender composition (raw).

Our analysis in this chapter has focused primarily on whether women reach our standard of equality, which we define as a proportion of speaking turns equal to women's proportion on the board. But when do men and women achieve a balance in terms of total participation? To answer that question, we examine the gap between the proportion of total turns taken by all men and those taken by all women on the board. Figure 10.5 presents this gap when the two most important forms of verbal participation in our data set, motions and comments, are combined. The *y*-axis in the figure is the gender gap at the meeting, defined as the proportion of motions or comments taken by women minus the proportion for men. Thus a meeting at which only women spoke and made motions would be at 1 on the scale and a meeting completely dominated by men would be at -1. The horizontal dashed line indicates a perfectly even balance in verbal participation, and the vertical dashed line indicates a meeting in which half the board members are men and half are women. Because of our sampling strategy, exactly half of mixed-gender boards in our sample have more men than women, and exactly half are evenly split or have more women than men.

The figure shows that the board's gender composition profoundly influences the overall balance of voices found at the meeting. When women are the gender minority, their voices are heard less often than men's about 88% of the time, and when women are the gender majority, female voices are less prominent than men's only 27% of the time. In other words, descriptive representation

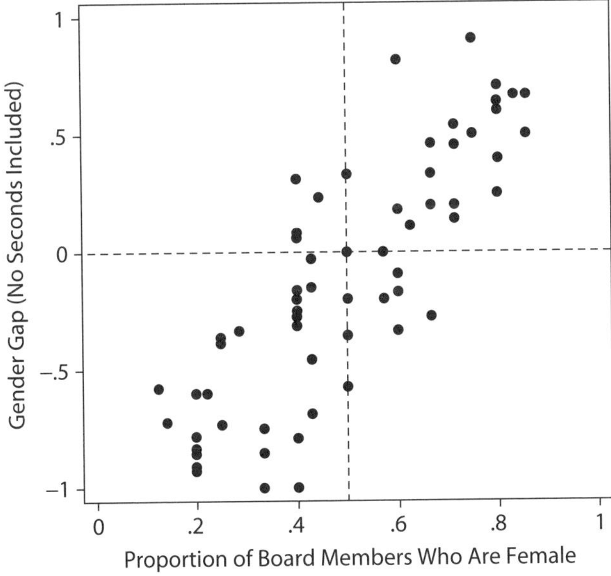

Figure 10.5. Gender gap in speaking behavior, mixed-gender groups only.

helps women's total participation. However, descriptive representation does not translate into total participation in a commensurate way; it takes boards that are heavily populated by women before women achieve an equal balance or better of total participation. Of the fifteen boards in our sample where women comprise 50 to 65% of board members, women's total participation lags behind men's in over half of them. These can be seen in the lower right quadrant of figure 10.5. Only when women's descriptive representation exceeds 65% do they regularly attain or exceed equality of total participation. That is because even where women are a majority, men tend to speak more than their numbers. We can see this by comparing minority women and minority men. While women speak less than men in 88% of the boards where women are the minority, men speak less than women in only 73% of the boards when they are the minority.

And what about the size of the gender gap in total participation? As figure 10.5 indicates, the size of the gap changes with the gender composition of the board, but on the mixed-gender boards where women are the minority, the average gap is -0.48 on the -1 to 1 scale. Men outnumber women on these boards, but even so, men take an average of 50% *more* turns than their already large proportion of the board membership would predict.[39] When women are the majority, any overrepresentation of participation relative to their numbers

[39] On average, the gap between men and women's proportion of the board when women are the minority is 0.32. The gap of 0.48 in total speaking time is thus 50% greater than the gap in seats on the board.

on the board is much smaller than what we find among men.[40] Put simply, the measure of total participation is a second indicator that men talk more than one might expect even accounting for their overrepresentation on the board.

Thus when women are the minority on the board, men's comments and motions heavily outnumber women's, and they do so far beyond the imbalance in numbers. When women are in the majority, their voices predominate, though their dominance is not as dramatic as that of the male majority. These findings hold in a more rigorous analysis that includes the long list of controls we have used in previous models (see online appendix table C10.4). In sum, the measure of total participation confirms the problems we saw when focusing on average participation: when women are outnumbered, boards have a deep imbalance of voices—deeper even than gender imbalance in board membership would predict—and it takes a supermajority of women before women's voices achieve balance or better.

What about Groups That Do Not Decide by Majority Rule?

To this point, we have focused exclusively on settings in which school boards make decisions by majority rule, which is the rule typically employed by elected bodies throughout the country. Yet our interaction hypothesis holds that the dynamic will be very different in groups that use unanimous rule. Accessing a sufficiently large data set of verbal participation in nonlab groups using that rule is difficult. For example, juries often decide by unanimous rule, but their deliberations are private, making systematic analysis of the dynamics impossible.

Our solution is to look to the world of deliberation and civic forums, where there has been a concerted effort to provide new opportunities for public dialogue and discussion. Often, deliberative groups ask participants to achieve consensus or pursue other forms of decision making than simple reliance on majority rule (Walsh 2007). Still other groups eschew formal group decision making altogether, preferring to focus on community building through public discussion. The civic dialogue groups studied by Katherine Cramer Walsh (2007) are a good example of groups brought together to explore issues of public concern in an atmosphere of inclusion. As the Everyday Democracy website puts it, the goal is "to help create communities that work better for everyone because all voices are included in public problem solving."[41] The groups Walsh studied were convened specifically to discuss the potentially thorny issue of

[40] Only when we restrict the analysis to boards comprised of more than two-thirds women do women's voices exceed their proportion of the board. In boards where women heavily outnumber men, the gap in total speaking time is, on average, 15% greater than the gap in seats on the board.

[41] This was one of the organizations involved with the dialogue groups; it was formerly known as the Study Circles Resource Center. http://www.everyday-democracy.org/en/Page.WhatWeDo.aspx.

race relations. But the important aspect of these groups from our perspective is that they set as their explicit goal a high level of unity through explicit instruction that participants should involve everyone and attend to "all voices."

If these intergroup civic dialogues do not make collective decisions, how are they relevant to our interaction hypothesis? In our view, our argument about group dynamics is not necessarily about the need for a formal rule of unanimity, but rather about creating a norm of inclusion, solidarity, and support—a place where all members of the group are valued and encouraged to participate. These are precisely the goals of the civic dialogue groups Walsh studied. The instructions to participants in these dialogue groups include, for example, an encouragement to "speak your mind freely, but don't monopolize the conversation," to "really try to understand what others are saying and respond to their ideas, especially when their thinking is different from yours," and to "listen carefully" (quoted in Walsh 2007, 42–43). The idea is to create a "safe space" where all can be heard, where inclusiveness is explicitly valued, and where the group focuses on the goals of discovering a common good (Walsh 2007, 40).

Intergroup civic dialogue thus attempts to generate many of the group dynamics that, we have argued, are fostered by unanimous rule. In this sense, it offers us a unique opportunity to explore patterns of participation in groups organized around norms of inclusion as they naturally occur. The focus of Walsh's study were twenty-two meetings held by five groups in various parts of Illinois and Wisconsin, each of which met multiple times to discuss issues of race and ethnicity in their communities. Group sessions included as few as six participants and as many as sixteen, with the average group numbering about nine participants. All groups included both men and women. Happily for our purposes, Walsh carefully documented the number of speaking turns and the gender of each participant at each meeting (2007, 187–91). We analyze these data to explore how the gender composition at the session is related to patterns of verbal participation for men and women.

Just as we did with our school board data, we compute an equality ratio for each civic dialogue session. This is the proportion of speaking turns from women divided by the proportion of participants who are women. If we are correct in our assumption that these civic dialogue groups were likely to develop the same norms of inclusion we would expect from a formal rule of unanimity, then the relationship between the equality ratio and the group's gender composition should be very different from what we found among school boards. Our interaction hypothesis predicts that unlike in the majority-rule school boards, the equality ratio should *decrease* as the percentage of women at the session increases.

And that is exactly what we find. Figure 10.6 presents the relationship between the equality ratio and each session's gender composition for each of the five dialogue groups in Walsh's data set, along with the fitted regression line for all sessions combined. The pattern is distinctly downward. Although the group

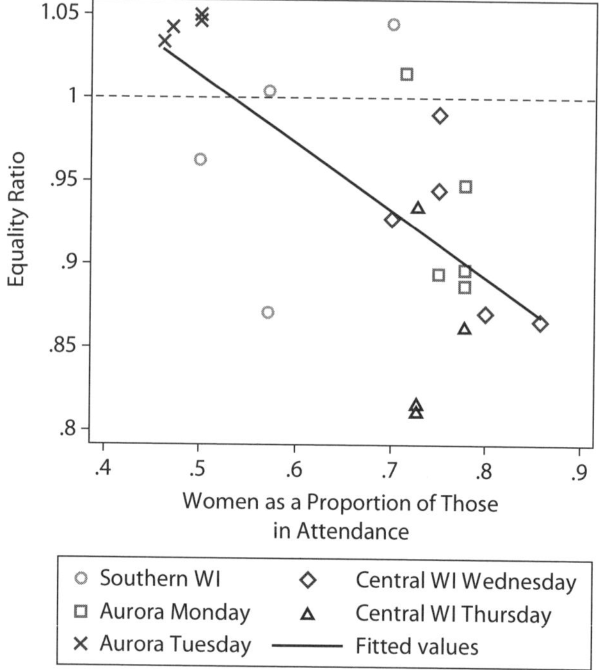

Figure 10.6. Ratio of women's proportion speaking turns to proportion present at meeting, mixed-gender civic dialogue groups.

gender composition is limited—most groups included a majority of women—the equality ratio is highest in sessions with a minority of women and declines as the proportion of women attending the session increases. When women are a minority, the equality ratio slightly exceeds the line of equality (1.04), and when women comprise 80% or more of the group, the ratio falls to 0.89. The magnitude of this change is not large, but dramatic inequalities are probably not to be expected when the group makes inclusion such an explicit goal. Moreover, this negative effect of gender composition is strongly significant ($p < 0.001$), even when we control for the total number of speaking turns in the session and whether or not the group facilitator was a male (see chapter appendix table A10.3). In fact, that analysis shows that male facilitators are correlated with a small but statistically significant decrease in the equality ratio. This is further evidence that facilitators trained in general dialogue techniques that do not specifically account for gender are not a panacea for the gender dynamics we have described throughout the book.

While a limited data set cannot ultimately be a definitive test of our hypothesis, these findings are fully consistent with our interaction hypothesis. Walsh's data were collected for different purposes and without our interaction hypothesis, or gender dynamics, in mind. Unlike our experiment, the groups met repeatedly, not just once. The topic was race, not economic redistribution. Nonetheless, the patterns echo those we found in the lab. The results tell us that when groups develop a norm of inclusion and mutual support, the dynamics can be wholly different from what we find under majority rule. That pattern works to the benefit of women when they are fewer and to the detriment of women when they are many.

Conclusion

In her review of the literature on gender and office holding, Reingold concludes:

> It is at the level of institutions . . . that some of our most challenging and creative efforts could be directed. We could capitalize on the most recent critiques of critical mass theory and consider the numerous ways in which the gender—and racial and ethnic—diversity of a political institution night (or might not) affect individual and collective behavior on behalf of women and women's interests. Beyond questions of numbers . . . we should be open to considering the gender dynamics of . . . procedural rules." (2008, 145)

We have attempted to engage in just such a "challenging and creative" effort. Our focus here, as it has been throughout the book, is on the intersection of numbers and procedural rules. While we cannot look at variation in formal rules, we were able to examine variation across numbers within a rule—the most common rule in politics, and the defining institutional feature of democracy: majority rule. We were also able to examine a different type of institutional feature—the official leadership of the board. And we explored the other side of our interaction hypothesis in naturally occurring midwestern groups that met on repeated occasions.

While our school boards data set is culled from official meeting minutes and thus has some limitations, we regard the findings we have reviewed here as a tough test of our expectations for majority-rule meetings. Not only are these settings ostensibly (though perhaps not always in actuality) focused on the needs of children—an issue highly important to women—but they are also comprised of women who are elected representatives. These are women with sufficient efficacy and confidence to have successfully run for elected office in the places where they live, women whose official position involves speaking up on behalf of their constituents. In that sense, these women are among the more privileged and powerful people in the country.

And yet even with this group of citizens successful and ambitious enough to become local officials, and even when the discussion deals with matters of importance to women, we find evidence of disparities of voice. While women in minority female groups tend to participate substantially less than their proportion on the board, minority men never face this participatory deficit. Token women are especially disadvantaged, and in our sample, minority women face severe disadvantage (verbal participation at rates of less than half of their proportion in the group) about one-quarter of the time. Women come closer to equality of participation—defined as voice in proportion to attendance—as the proportion of women on the board increases, but it typically takes a supermajority of women before they reach our definition of equality. These findings are most robust with respect to motions, the most assertive form of speech, and disappear as we might expect on seconds, the least opinionated and proactive form of participation. With respect to comments recorded by the board clerk, the trend is in the direction we expect.

We also find that women's disadvantage can be somewhat offset when women occupy the formal positions of power, such as board chair, but these leaders are the only women who benefit from their formal role. Although female leaders themselves talk more, their presence does not appear to help the remaining women who do not serve as board chairs. Absent the responsibility of formal authority or the power that comes from increased numbers, women's voices are, quite simply, more silent.

Conclusion

'Tis woman's strongest vindication for speaking that the world needs to hear her voice.

—ANNA JULIA COOPER[1]

THE MEETING HAS LONG BEEN VIEWED as an essential practice of democracy. Centuries ago the French observer Tocqueville wrote: "Town-meetings are to liberty what primary schools are to science; they bring it within the people's reach, they teach men how to use and how to enjoy it" ([1835] 2006, book 1, chapter 5). Tocqueville's words apply today, not only to town meetings, but also to formal settings of all kinds where people talk about matters of common concern. Public talk is the lifeblood of democracy and of community. And meetings remain an essential way for people to make collective decisions that matter.

This faith in public talk has prompted impassioned arguments in favor of deliberation in civic and political life (Gutmann and Thompson 1996). Some supporters of deliberation ground their advocacy in part in the notion that the people of a democracy have an obligation to become adequate citizens of it, so they can fulfill their function in the political system and thus sustain that system. An adequate citizen, on this view, has the basic knowledge needed to hold officials accountable and to decide matters of common concern (Converse 1964; Delli Carpini and Keeter 1996). Deliberation properly constructed can allow people to arrive at more considered, authentic views free of manipulation (Fishkin 2009). In addition, the adequate citizen is one who is willing to engage respectfully with views opposed to their own (Mutz 2006). Thus, some observers are excited about the potential of deliberation to raise the public's level of information and reasoning about politics and its willingness to listen to "the other side" (Walsh 2007; Fishkin 2009; Mutz 2006; Myers and Mendelberg 2013; Rosenberg 2007a). Deliberation also has the potential to lay bonds of mutual trust and cooperation, and even enlarge citizens' interests beyond their selfish confines, to the benefit of the communal enterprise (Walsh 2007; Gastil et al. 2010; Macedo et al. 2005; Myers and Mendelberg 2013). As a bonus, deliberation can boost the legitimacy of the system, strengthening it not only by

[1]Quoted in Weekes (2007, 403).

creating strong citizen building blocks but also by granting it an aura of integrity (see, for example, Gastil et al. 2010, 19–21; Myers and Mendelberg 2013). All these are ways in which deliberation could serve the needs of the political community.[2] Put simply, deliberation can lay the foundation of citizenship and thereby secure the health of democracy.

But to participate in deliberation about matters of common concern is more than an opportunity for learning, competence, and enlightenment. The reason that meetings are so important to democracy goes beyond their ability to educate the masses in the skills and knowledge they need to be competent, as some might be tempted to interpret Tocqueville's "school for democracy" passage. That phrase is about education, to be sure, but it also serves as a ringing endorsement of liberty. Meetings are good because they allow the people to "use" and "enjoy" liberty—that is, agency. Discussion in meetings is a basic necessity and a fundamental right of the citizen because it reflects, and shapes, the citizen's agency. And when it comes to agency over public affairs, citizens can only carry influence if their authority is as high as others'. The democratic citizen, by our definition, is not merely an individual in need of education and enlightenment, or a cog in the machinery of government, she is first and foremost an equally authoritative member of a political community. Therefore, exercising equal participation and influence is a crucial way for people to reap the benefits of citizenship, to achieve the same high standing in the self-governing community that the highest governor enjoys. Meetings are not merely medicine for the body politic, taken to fix its ills and get it to do its proper work. They enable status in the community of self-rulers and authority in society at large.

Put differently, meetings matter because meetings grant the citizen equal standing in the political community. As a British juror remarked after serving for the first time, "I've been approached after 35 years and this has now made me feel that I've been treated like a British citizen" (quoted in Gastil et al. 2010, 22). It is this sense of worth, or value in a community—including how individuals see themselves and the authority and respect given by others—that this book has sought to understand.[3] As Supreme Court justice Anthony Kennedy has argued, the Fourteenth Amendment protects "equal participation in civic life" and thus the right to jury service because to be a juror is not only a "duty" but also an "honor" (*Holland v. Illinois* 1990, 488–89). We agree, but take a still broader view, beyond the jury setting. Basic honor, which we call worth, standing, and status, is essential to any person, because it is the currency of society and a fundamental social need.

We have shown that standing, worth, and status are heavily shaped by the interaction among people at the public meeting. The meeting is thus not only

[2]Normative advocates and their arguments are reviewed in chapter 1.

[3]The Supreme Court specified and affirmed this worth in rulings on jury service (Gastil et al. 2010, 7–10).

necessary for the empowerment of the people to govern but also can create equality among the people as they attempt to self-govern. That is the promise of the public meeting. But the dark side of the public meeting is that equality is too rare and the reality too distant from it. We have documented just how far discussion lies from the standard of equality, in the common circumstances of politics. The conditions of deliberation in many political settings produce a marked disadvantage for one-half of the human species.

Women are no longer officially restricted from full participation in public gatherings. On paper, they have equal access to juries, university seminars, voluntary association boards, government committees, and even work teams. And so, in theory, we would expect to find that they participate and exercise power at the same rate as men do at the meetings that govern our society in these influential spaces. Yet women are still underrepresented in the ranks of active and influential participants in many of these settings. Consequently, women do not benefit as men do from meetings as a school for democracy. Nor do they gain the recognition and standing that men do as valued members of the community. Writing about class differences, Tocqueville wrote, "The humblest individual who is called upon to co-operate in the government of society acquires a certain degree of self-respect; and as he possesses authority, he can command the services of minds much more enlightened than his own" ([1835] 2006, chapter 14). In most political settings, ordinary women do not reap these rewards of self-respect, authority, liberty, and influence as much as their male counterparts.

In turn, women's continued lower overall position in politics, and their continued disadvantages in many areas of society, may be reinforced by their continued devaluation as persons of equal worth in the consequential setting of the public meeting. Despite gaining resources and making enormous advances toward equality in American society, women are frequently still expected to be less suited to the exercise of authority. Politics continues to be a "man's game" that generates continued gender gaps in participation and influence. As Nannerl Keohane has written, "Very few women have exercised authority in institutional settings over men and women of comparable social and economic status" (2010, 125). Wielding power is still deemed an activity that is not fully appropriate for women's feminine gender roles. To sum it up, gender continues to be a dimension of political underrepresentation today, all the more so when authority is at stake. And meetings are a site of authority.

While some women may respond that they are content with this state of affairs, and they choose not to participate in public discussion in the ways that men do, there are real problems with this response. To be sure, women do tend to provide worthwhile contributions via their traditional feminine role, by working behind the scenes. Often women function quietly as the backbone of an organization, the mainstay of the community, and they may be appreciated for the important service they provide. While there is value in serving in this sort of understated way, when women disproportionately occupy this role, they are unlikely to be given their due in important modes of collective decision making. As we found, by speaking less, women exercise less influence, are viewed as less authoritative, and their distinctive priorities and perspectives are less likely to be aired and heard. As William Lloyd Garrison Jr. said in the nineteenth century of the abolitionist movement, women are an "army of silent workers, unknown to fame" (quoted in Jeffrey 1998, i). If women restrict themselves primarily to these behind-the-scenes roles and forego opportunities to discuss their interests or concerns more openly, they deny themselves the full standing as members of the community. No matter how much they are valued as workers, they are not valued as citizens.

Another counterargument posits that women accomplish as much, or more, by speaking seldom. The power of the quiet, restrained, and judicious approach may be understated by our findings. Or so the argument goes. However, the findings here, and in other studies, are clear: people who speak little are perceived as less influential, tend to perceive themselves that way, and in fact *are* less influential. Women incur this penalty from relative quiescence even more than men do.

A related counterargument is that by lamenting women's underparticipation relative to men, we have set up the talkative masculine style as the desirable normative standard and devalued a quieter style perhaps more typical of women. On this view, women tend to talk less than men, and it is men's tendency to talk too much that is the problem. Rather than find ways to elevate women's talk time, we should find ways to depress men's volubility. To that we respond that our baseline for comparison is not only men's volume, but also women's own volume when men are not around. Our findings show that women talk less with men than they do with women. In other words, women in fact talk more than men do when they do not face the deleterious interactions of the typical mixed-gender group. By implication, the quiescence we have found among women is not what women do when free of constraints and is not a desirable normative standard for women.[4]

Granted, speaking a great deal, and doing so with a great deal of assertiveness, is not always advantageous. The masculine style can backfire on the speaker and surely is maladaptive to the group if exercised too aggressively. Dominance can turn into clueless failure to read the subtle cues of other members and slide into norm-violation that triggers social sanctions.[5] Extremely hypertalkative men may lose influence if they deviate radically from the social script of the give-and-take and forego the codes of minimal politeness that discussion presumes.

[4]The fact that women also get their way more, and are rated more influential, when they speak less, is further evidence that women's relative quiescence is bad for women.

[5]For example, see Ridgeway and Diekema 1989.

However, there is little evidence that many highly engaged, talkative people, men included, use overly dominant styles that carry a large net cost. In the most common settings of public meetings, women speak at two-thirds the rate of men, and in doing so, they are not exercising influence by virtue of avoiding the pitfall of assertion run amok. Instead, they are doing themselves, the meeting, their gender, and their society a disservice by holding back too much.

Summary of the Findings

If public meetings are crucial to democracy, and are in fact widely practiced and attended, then we need to know what goes on in them. Do women exercise their voice where all voices should be heard? Under what conditions do they do so equally, and as effectively as men?

To generate expectations about circumstances that help or prevent women from speaking and carrying influence, we began with the dominant framework in social science—gender role theory. This theory predicts that the more women in the group, the more the average woman participates and gains substantive and symbolic representation in it. That is, the power of numbers will cause women to speak more; to do so with fewer negative interruptions and with more positive affirmations; to articulate the issues of distinctive importance to women; to state their individual prediscussion preferences about the group decision; to be perceived, and perceive themselves, as efficacious and influential; and to have confidence in their own opinion. In this view, it is difficult for women to gain authority and power when they are few. Conversely, they have all they want when they are many.

We found that this view is partially true, but very incomplete. The effect of women's numbers depends on the group's procedures. Low numbers do not doom women to powerlessness, and that is the good news. But high numbers do not always solve women's problems, and there lies some unexpected bad news.

The procedure we examined in depth is the decision rule. We picked the decision rule because theories of behavior directed our attention to its power to set group norms of interaction. And in our study, too, we found evidence that the decision rule affects how members converse with each other. When we assigned a unanimous rule rather than a majority rule, we found several indicators of an inclusive, consensual norm. The group talked longer. More members articulated their preference over the group decision. The members expressed their preferences more often. Unanimous rule tends to create a more inclusive norm of discussion.[6] To be sure, level of inclusion varies tremendously, as we explain below. But still, there is sufficient evidence that the rule in fact begets norms of interaction, as we claim.

[6] See chapters 5 and 9.

There are other reasons to study the effect of procedural rules such as the decision rule. The decision rule is a feature of the group that is easy to control and simple to implement. That means that groups are likely to adopt it once they understand its benefits, and it can effectively serve the goal of reform. Finally, the rule is a clean experimental treatment in the study of groups and allows us to draw clear conclusions about the effects of procedure. Yet unanimous rule is often not practical. We will address this problem, and others, later in this chapter. For now, the point is that unanimous rule can have dramatic democratic effects, and that it—and more practical procedures that set in motion the same equalizing norms—can be leveraged into a major force for social equality. However, our key argument is that the rule does not operate alone, and neither do women's numbers. Unanimous rule helps women when they are few, while majority rule helps women when they are many.

Many studies have suggested that unanimous rule helps the minority, but they focus on preference minorities.[7] We went a step further and generated hypotheses about how unanimous rule could help a very different kind of minority—a social identity minority. We reasoned that unanimous rule creates norms of inclusion, and that these norms raise the participation and influence of both men and women when they are the numerical minority in the group. And that is generally what we found, but with some important wrinkles.

Because women start at a lower level of participation than men, the elevating effect of unanimous rule carries a paradoxical consequence for gender equality. When women are the numerical minority, the unanimous process raises their voice and authority. Unanimous rule is an aid to democracy, giving more authority to a social identity group whose status remains low in society and politics. But the rule's equal effect means that when men are the numerical minority, men participate and influence even more than they do otherwise. That in turn increases the gender gap in participation within the group. So unanimous rule is good for women when women are the minority, as the gender gap in their group shrinks, but it is bad for women when they are the majority, when the gender gap in the group grows as men—the numerical minority—increase their participation.

We found consistent support for the notion that unanimous rule protects women in the minority, on a variety of measures of participation and representation. We also found that unanimous rule elevates the participation of numerical minority men, and this means that women in the majority do not benefit under unanimous rule. However, unanimous rule does not consistently affect other forms of men's representation, such as talk of issues of distinctive concern to men. Unanimous rule also does not appear to make minority men more "masculine" or assertive—they do not engage in unusually high levels of

[7] In addition, as we reviewed in chapters 3 and 4, some studies contradict this conclusion for preference minorities, and the literature on rules tends to suffer from various methodological problems.

negative interruptions, for example. In fact, unanimous rule with any gender composition prompts members to provide women with a higher ratio of positive to negative engagement while they speak than does majority rule with few women. Thus on the whole, relative to majority rule, unanimous rule acts to include not only preference minorities but also identity groups who find themselves a numerical minority in a deliberation. That boost helps minority women considerably. The same boost for minority men carries negative consequences for majority women's participation, but not consistently so for their substantive representation. Thus the rule matters a great deal, in combination with the gender composition of the group. Women's numbers alone do not tell the story of women's equal representation.

Where gender role theory wins strong vindication is under conditions of majority rule. Here we found that the more women, the more the average woman participates and obtains substantive and symbolic representation. That representation consists of several elements: women gain perceived influence, raise their self-assessment of efficacy in the group, are more likely to introduce into the conversation issues of distinctive concern to women and to mention these issues more frequently, are more likely to experience a warm reception while they speak, are more likely to articulate their own predeliberation preferences, and are better able to enact their preferences in the group's decision. Why does majority rule boost a woman's authority when she is surrounded by many women? Because majority rule signals that the more numerous groups—whether it is the preference majority or the social identity majority—are entitled to exercise power. Women benefit from this signal to exercise power.[8]

But again, there are some wrinkles to the happy story of majority rule. Women require a supermajority for some of the benefits of increasing descriptive representation to materialize. By contrast, men benefit from their majority status at a bare majority. In addition, when these majority women advocate for their positions during the discussion, they encounter more resistance from men in the group. These findings qualify the gender role hypothesis somewhat. Majority status is good for women but not in a simple or unqualified way. Put differently, majority rule is good for women when women are the majority, but not as good as it is for men when they are the majority.

We also explored several subsidiary hypotheses of gender role theory. Most important is the enclave hypothesis. We found that all-female groups operate

[8]We were able to find some of the breakpoints in the effects of descriptive representation under majority rule. In chapter 5, the breakpoint for the ratio of female to male *Proportion Talk* lies at 80% women. In chapter 7, women's frequency of care words increases dramatically above 20%, and again after 40% (and the first mention breakpoint is at 40%). From that point, we mostly run linear models in subsequent chapters after the raw data suggest that the breakpoint is between minority and majority female groups. In addition, in chapter 9 we see that endorsement of nonpreferred principles decreases dramatically above 40% women. Finally, we found that enclaves set dramatically higher floors than all other groups.

largely as gender role theory expects—as environments that nurture women. These environments allow them more full expression as individuals, they generate longer talk times, they prompt women to engage in mutually supportive interjections, and in these groups women reach more generous decisions that help the worst off. Female enclaves, that is, generally create warm, cooperative, and nurturing interactions and outcomes. However, rarely do these groups display a qualitative difference from majority-female groups (especially compared with largely female groups under majority rule). Enclaves are the best setting for women's full participation and representation, but not because the absence of men makes them an alternate universe. Rather, they help for the same reason that a large increase in women's numbers helps. All-female groups, for the most part, merely represent the final increment in women's rising numbers.

All these effects are relative, so we should be clear about what they are relative to. The central comparison point for the conditions of deliberation is the setting that is most prevalent in the world of politics—majority rule with few women. Recall from chapter 1 that women often tend to compose about a fifth of the members of a deliberating body. That number is found around the world, across the American states, and at nearly all levels of American government. Moreover, even in the instances when women exceed this percentage, they are very rarely anything but a small numerical minority.

In these common settings with conflictual norms and few women, we found a litany of ills. Women speak far less than men, they are almost never viewed as the most influential member of the discussion group; they view themselves as powerless; they very rarely introduce topics of distinctive concern to women or dwell on them; their references are rarely picked up in the conversational thread; they receive little positive reinforcement while speaking; men interrupt their speech with hostile remarks, which in turn depress women's chances of discussing children and lower their sense of efficacy in the discussion; and finally, women are less likely to advocate for generous measures of redistribution for the group and for society at large. It is little surprise that these settings produce an outcome far out of line with these women's specific preferences about redistribution, and with the general orientation of most women to help those in need.[9]

Especially badly off in our experiments are women who enter the deliberation with low levels of confidence. In general, women tend to walk into deliberative settings with lower levels of confidence than men, and this confidence disparity is especially harmful in the common setting of majority rule with few women. There, confidence plays a large role in women's willingness to participate actively, and those with the least confidence rarely speak up at a rate anywhere close to women's proportion of the group. The combination of low confidence and negative feedback about competence is especially damag-

[9]See also the detailed summary of effects on page 334, the section on elite women.

ing to women's participation, and women who experience both in majority-rule groups with few women barely join the conversation at all. These results apply to women of all different backgrounds—if anything, the best-educated women participate the least in the conditions where women's standing is lowest, suggesting that they may be the most sensitive to the signals of women's disempowerment.

These confidence patterns are not immutable, however. Where women have greater standing—either because of rule or numbers—the effects of confidence on women's participation evaporate. In those settings, women are also likely to be bolstered by more positive interruptions, and such affirming feedback is uniquely important in building the efficacy of low-confidence women. Women's predeliberation confidence disparity is not destiny, therefore; when women's standing increases and when the conversational dynamic is more supportive, both low- and high-confidence women speak up.

Because these findings come from experiments, we provided validation from real world settings. We chose school boards, with their traditionally feminine mission of educating children, and their higher-than-average female representation. This was a hard test for our hypotheses. But we expected that because these are public meetings dealing with matters of common concern to the community, and because they use majority rule, we would find the same pattern as in the experiments—the average woman would only speak equally to the average man when women composed a significant majority of the members. And that is exactly what we found. In addition, when women hold official positions of leadership, those women become a more active part of the conversation, though this beneficial effect does not alter the participatory patterns of the other women on the board.

Gender, and not alternative factors, is at work in these results. The evidence is indirect, because the experiments only took us so far—while we created gender composition and assigned rules, we cannot experiment with the individual's gender. But the available methods of analysis nevertheless suggest that the differences we observed between men and women are due to being a man or a woman—that is, to gender itself. We ruled out the main alternatives to gender—the person's and the group's egalitarianism, liberalism, and predeliberation preferences about income redistribution.[10] We also rule out other possible confounding variables that may be correlated with gender, especially income (more on that below). When it comes to talk time, we located much of women's quiescence in conditions in which they are disempowered in attributes that are closely connected to gender, such as their confidence in their speaking ability and in their adverse reactions to negative feedback about their expertise. A general discomfort with disagreement had little effect, however. Women appear to

[10] We used statistical controls to test these alternative explanations; future work could also experimentally manipulate these aspects of groups.

be affected by conflict not because it carries disagreement, but because it signals their low relative value in the group.

Furthermore, these differences are produced specifically by gendered norms of social exchange, which affect women and men differently, and not by pure, gender-free strategic considerations that people pursue regardless of their own sex and of the gendered norm around them. Being a woman rather than a man means not only being more egalitarian, liberal, and favoring generous income redistribution to assist the vulnerable, on average. It means something beyond the orientations to politics that characterize many men as well as many women. It means the tendency to be less confident about one's competence (often unrealistically) and thus one's lower authority in society (often realistically), to be more sensitive to negative engagement with one's speech, to avoid conflict or competition, and to be affected by the lack of warm social bonds in the group. We directly examined the extent to which the effects of gender composition and decision rule depend on these core features of the person's gender and found that they do indeed. And so we can point to gender itself, and not its more peripheral attachments or confounding correlates.

In addition, we can point to the gendered norms, and their differential effects on the average man and woman, rather than merely gender-free strategic motivations as an important cause of the patterns we observed. If people were simply operating as strategic actors, they would seek a group decision matching their prior preference and change their behavior according to the preferences prevalent in the group. But that does not square with a number of the results we found.

Put differently, the strategic model yields predictions that do not find support and cannot explain our results. In the strategic model, gender does not matter in itself, only preferences over outcomes do. For example, it predicts "cheap talk"—the average man, because he is likely more economically conservative, accelerates his talk of women's distinctive concerns in majority-female groups simply because he wishes to convince the female majority to choose the low amount of a minimum guaranteed income he most prefers. It also predicts that the average woman speaks less in groups with many women and unanimous rule because there, the majority shares her views, and she need not take the trouble to talk. And by the same token, it predicts that the average woman does not divulge her prediscussion preference over the group's decision simply because she figures out that the majority-male group, being also majority conservative, will never consent to it. Could these strategic motivations to accommodate to the preference majority, or to free ride on its coattails, or to capitulate to it, explain the results?[11]

[11] Here we are addressing some stylized predictions from a game theory literature on information exchange by strategic actors motivated to implement their preferences over a group decision, such as Ban, Jha, and Rao (2012), who predict that in Indian village meetings with diverse prefer-

The evidence clearly answers in the negative. First, the analyses control on the member's attitudes toward equality between groups in society, on their liberal or conservative political orientation, and on their preference for a group decision for more rather than less redistribution. Furthermore, the analyses also control on the number of members with these views and on the match between the member and the group's preferences regarding income redistribution. So the results cannot be accounted for by the notion that the average man or woman changes what they say simply to adapt to the change in the preference majority. Neither can the model account for the interaction of rule and gender composition, or the further interaction of these factors with individual gender. That is, this gender-free strategic model cannot explain why women speak, agenda-set, and influence less than men in their group—and less than minority men do in other groups—but do so only under majority rule. Neither can it explain why female majorities are more powerful under majority rather than unanimous rule, or why majority women are less powerful than majority men. Only a model that accounts for the different tendencies of individual men and women to respond to gendered norms can do so.

Thus the bottom line is that who is present matters, and the norms governing the interaction matter—but most of all, the two matter together. Equal representation for people defined by their social identity comes from either a critical mass where the mass matters or on inclusive norms actively applied to women. These findings shed light not only on gender composition but also on how rules work; the rule depends on who the people are. Rules are not universal in their effect despite being neutral on their face. To know what a rule will do to a group, we must understand the identities of the members.

Implications for Women's Participation and Representation

Gender Norms and Gendered Institutions

The fact that women underparticipate men in public meetings is at odds with women's strides in American society and politics. Women now have more education and have made significant advances in employment and the resources it provides—resources that prompt and enable participation in politics, including *attendance* at meetings. And so, women's dearth of participation and influence *in* meetings presents a puzzle.

---

ences, the meeting focuses most on the median voter's top priorities; that is, the person most likely to decide the vote is the person whose preferences are discussed the most and who then influences the decision the most. We control on preferences in order to address this model. These and related predictions are based on theoretical models such as Austen-Smith and Feddersen (2006) and Meirowitz (2006).

The solution to this puzzle is that women continue to be socialized into subordinate positions of authority in society. Women only equal (or exceed) men in modes of participation that follow their traditional gender roles, such as dutiful community member. Women continue to underparticipate men in modes of participation that are not primarily duty driven and that entail leadership over men (see chapter 2). And so, just as women are less likely to run for elected office than comparable men, to follow news about politics, and to develop into opinionated citizens, so are they less likely to speak up on matters of common concern when interacting with men. Even though the gender gap in political participation and engagement tends to be modest relative to the inequalities produced by age, race, and class, in some areas it rivals them (see chapter 2). Even when women have high qualifications, they are much less likely than men to put themselves forward in ways that appear to violate gender roles. Women still earn less personal income, train in less prestigious occupations, and are out of the labor force for longer periods than men. But the continued gender gap in the structural causes of participation, such as full-time employment, occupational status, and income, only accounts for part of the continued gender gap in political participation and engagement. Something besides women's continued material or concrete disadvantages is at play. That something is gender itself—the same things that constitute people as women also constitute them as unequal participants in politics.

An important component of gender is found in norms, and forms, of interaction. Norms of interaction can be inclusive of women, or exclusive of them. In addition, they can signal a cooperating group or a conflictual group. Women are more likely to attempt to participate in groups where the norm is inclusive and cooperative. In this sense, gender works as a characteristic of interaction.

One implication of our argument that gender works as a feature of social interaction is that gender is more than a trait of the individual. As West and Zimmerman stated succinctly: "a person's gender is not simply an aspect of what one is, but, more fundamentally, it is something that one does, and does recurrently, in interaction with others" (West and Zimmerman 1987, 140). The context has much to do with whether, and how, gender is manifested; as Bohan argued, "in particular contexts, people do feminine; in others, they do masculine" (quoted in Aries 1998, 77). While we do not view gendered traits as quite so variable as that, our findings confirm that context shapes levels of inequality between people defined by gender categories. We spell out one neglected aspect of that context—procedures. And we show that the group context and composition can build particular gendered interactions, or undermine them.

Our findings are also inspired by and support the theoretical concept of gendered institutions (Thomas in Tolleson-Rinehart and Josephson 2005, 253; see also Duerst-Lahti 2002a, 2002b; Duerst-Lahti and Kelly 1995; Kathlene 1994, 1998; Kenney 1996, cited in Thomas 2005; Ridgeway 2001). If gender is not just an individual difference, a quality of individuals, then it can also be a characteristic of settings, procedures, and norms. Gender composition is exactly such a characteristic. As the sociologist Cecilia Ridgeway put it:

> More than a trait of individuals, gender is an institutionalized system of social practices. The gender system is deeply entwined with social hierarchy and leadership because gender stereotypes contain status beliefs that associate greater status worthiness and competence with men than women. Gender status beliefs create a network of constraining expectations and interpersonal reactions that is a major cause of the "glass ceiling." In mixed-sex or gender-relevant contexts, gender status beliefs shape men's and women's assertiveness, the attention and evaluation their performances receive, ability attributed to them on the basis of performance, the influence they achieve, and the likelihood that they emerge as leaders. Gender status beliefs also create legitimacy reactions that penalize assertive women leaders for violating the expected status order and reduce their ability to gain compliance with directives. (Ridgeway 2001, 637)

In this sense the decision rule is itself gendered, meaning that it creates modes of interaction that are associated with feminine or masculine norms of behavior, and that it can produce or mute gender differences and inequalities. That is, a decision rule can implicitly signal to participants the expectation that they engage in modes of behavior that society defines as feminine or masculine. Most importantly, unanimous rule signals the more "feminine" norm of inclusion—all voices should be part of the conversation and the decision-making process. Our finding that unanimous rule aids numerical-minority women makes sense in light of this notion.

A final implication of our findings is for the concept of representation. Scholars have established the utility of different types of representation for disadvantaged groups (for example, Mansbridge 1998). Descriptive representation refers to the physical presence of a social group in the setting of decision making. Substantive representation occurs when the concerns, values, sensibilities, or interests of that group are expressed, acted upon, and ultimately influence the outcome in some way. Symbolic representation is defined as the notion that the group is capable of governing, that its exercise of power is legitimate. Our findings suggest an additional type of representation. In order to obtain substantive and symbolic representation, a subordinate group requires that the conditions of discussion provide the group with *authoritative representation*. That is, the setting, structure, and interaction norms of decision making must grant group members equal status during the decision-making process. In our view, such authoritative representation is a key aspect of deliberative equality.

Descriptive representation can build substantive and symbolic representation for women, but only if it grants women authoritative representation, that is, equal status in the group. Similarly, procedures grant women the capacity to produce substantive and symbolic representation but only if they equalize women's status in the group, that is, build authoritative representation. To obtain substantive and symbolic representation—the outputs of the process of representation—representatives must operate with authoritative representation. That type of representation is only loosely connected to descriptive representation, but can build upon it.

The Effects on Men

While we have focused on the representation of women, that is not to deny the legitimate contributions of men, or the value of differences between men and women.[12] Discussion groups may benefit from both masculine and feminine perspectives and modes of action, and in our view, deliberation functions best when both genders contribute fully. However, the problem is that groups are commonly structured in ways that privilege the voices, perspectives, and interaction styles of men, to the detriment of women.

The loss is not only women's. First, some men share the views that tend to be distinctive to women. Not all men prioritize financial issues above care for human beings, for example. Men are moving partway into traditional feminine roles in society, whether by significantly investing time and effort in the care of their children, taking more responsibility for domestic chores, or even holding traditionally feminine jobs. Economically developed societies are becoming a bit less rigid about gender roles, and if that trend accelerates, views and preferences about politics may follow. Importantly, there is variance within each gender, in the content of people's views and in their interaction styles. Some women are masculine; some men are feminine. If women are included in the conversation, men may feel freer to express their individual preferences, or to adopt the interaction style they personally find the most comfortable, less constrained by the straitjacket of the masculine gender role. Some studies are already finding that larger numbers of women may shift men's actions in legislatures, including men's willingness to advocate legislation related to issues of care (Bratton 2005).

In fact, we find that men behave in less stereotypically masculine ways in the conditions where women are more empowered. When women have greater standing, men share the floor more equally, adopt the language of care for children more often, endorse more generous safety net support for the poor, are less likely to interrupt women in hostile ways, and provide more positive forms of support and encouragement to female speakers. At the same time, men do not give up on their own distinctive preferences when women are empowered—they become more likely to oppose ideas or principles that they did not favor prior to deliberation, and the most talkative men resist women's more generous preferences. Still, women's voice may free or encourage men to articulate per-

[12] We focus on women because they are the group that suffers most often and most acutely from participatory deficits.

spectives that would be viewed as not gender normative and thus stigmatizing for them to voice when women play a smaller role in the group discussion.

Second, the loss of women's voice is not only women's loss, because that voice can benefit the group. Of course, there is a great deal of variability within each gender. And in political institutions, women often tend to conform to the expectations of the roles they occupy within an organization, which can wash out much of what is distinctive about women's preferences. However, because women tend to arrive at the table with some perspectives, values, and vocabularies that are distinct from men's, when they are silent and those perspectives are not articulated, the group as a whole is disadvantaged. When one gender is disproportionately silent and ultimately regarded as less authoritative, then the group is less than the sum of its parts; moreover, it pays the opportunity cost of failing to become more than the sum of its parts. In other words, the role of gender in group discussion is worthy of study because the voices of both women and men are equally valuable to the common good.

What Do Women's Voices Say?

What do women's voices say when they speak? In our experimental data and more broadly, what many of women's priorities have in common is an orientation toward community. A community is a society of mutual assistance, a stable entity of cooperation. The stability of cooperation depends on a standing decision to cooperate—a norm. The norm is a widely shared standard of behavior by which a person's eligibility to belong to the group is judged.[13] Women tend to lean toward this norm in all its permutations. This explains why women are more likely than men to be "civic specialists" even though they are less likely than men to be "electoral specialists," to use the labels of Zukin and colleagues (2006). Women in American state legislatures tend to use a more consensual legislative style (Thomas 2005). On average, women are more oriented than men toward connection and social responsibility.

The orientation toward community takes various forms. Some forms are geared toward helping others. This help may extend to various vulnerable populations, as we saw in our analysis of the issues that women tend to prioritize more than men. Other forms are geared toward upholding moral standards of conduct. Concerns about slavery in the early nineteenth century, the squalid lives of immigrants in the late nineteenth century, alcohol abuse in the 1920s, and more recently, abortion, share in common not only the needs of the vulnerable but also the notion that people are obligated to act morally. Women were at

[13] Definitions of norm tend to miss this part but it is crucial. A norm is not merely a widely shared standard of behavior, it is the standard by which membership is conferred, or withdrawn. This judgment can operate in degrees; membership grows stronger, and the person is deemed more and more a group member, the more they conform to and in turn uphold the norm with respect to others' behavior.

the forefront of the effort to abolish slavery and the settlement movement to aid the poor concentrated in cities, both movements with strong moral claims about proper behavior (Jeffrey 1998; Sklar 1985). Women's long-standing involvement with education in and outside the home is a reflection in part of their desire to inculcate standards of behavior in others that foster the health of the community. For these women, education was not only a means to personal achievement or enlightenment, as we tend to regard it today, but a method of cultivation that feeds the common good (Kelly 2006).[14] In addition, women's efforts to help themselves have often been wrapped up with their quest for moral uplift, justified in terms that appealed to women's needs and to their obligations to reject moral "vice" (Pascoe 1993, 32). Women have been "key contributors" in efforts to reform government so that it ceases to serve personal, narrow ends and orients to the collective as a whole (Norton et al. 2012, 509). What do prostitution, government, and sewers have in common? All are causes that women took up in the broader mission to clean up the moral standards of the community. In fact, woman suffrage campaigns made explicit rhetorical statements about women's distinctive inclinations in this direction (Pascoe 1993). Thus over the course of American history, women have taken on causes that not only help others but also tie more tightly the fabric of community around each of its members, including themselves. These ties may bind and constrain, but women are less bothered by this than men, because for women, bindings enable community.[15]

Because women are more likely to be communitarians, the groups that include them produce communitarian decisions. Groups where women speak up

[14]That is not to downplay other motives, such as the agency of entry into civil society and participating in the public sphere (Kelly 2006). But part of the motive and the rhetorical justification to the entry of women into the public sphere was their responsibility for "superintending the physical energies of children, the development of their moral habits . . . and the forming of their religious character," in the words of a prominent supporter of female education, George Emerson (quoted in Kelly 2006, 27).

[15]Women are more moralistic and religious perhaps because they are more communitarian. Women are far more likely to be formally affiliated with a religious institution, to attend services frequently, and to participate in other activities in it (Burns, Schlozman, and Verba 2001, 89). A large majority of women say "religion is very important" and support prayer in schools (106). Women and men join religious associations in equal rates, but among the members, women are far more likely to attend a meeting of these groups (78, table 3.3; also 84–85). Even when women were excluded from deliberations of their congregation and denied a vote in its affairs, they were active as moral agents in it, teaching Sunday school during the nineteenth century and later on serving as missionaries (88). Women's religiosity is a facet of their general orientation to upholding the community, which to them means upholding its moral standards. Among those active in a religious institution, the most common reasons mentioned for their activity, other than affirming their religious faith (80%), are to "lend a hand to people in need" (77%), and "make the nation better" (67%) (106). Even at a young age and in the most recent decade, girls are more likely to indicate that religion plays a "very important role" in their lives (see http://www.childtrendsdatabank.org/?q=node/302).

as much as or more than men are more likely to protect the needs of everyone in the community, including the most vulnerable. As part of their tendency toward communitarianism, women are comparatively cool to the free market and have an affinity for strong centralized government. Even our youngest cohort exhibits a gender gap on the basic notion of government regulation. Women ages fifteen to twenty-five are more likely than men in this cohort to indicate that "government regulation of business is necessary to protect the public interest." Women are far more averse than men to a hands-off approach that allows each person to keep what they earn without regard for the needs of others. Women are not averse to the notion that people need incentives for hard work—in a community, everyone should do their fair share—but they do not believe that hard work is incompatible with support for the vulnerable or concern for the broader public good. A purely individualistic or libertarian approach to freedom undermines community in ways that are less likely to be embraced by many women.

Women's Communication Styles

The same orientation to community that shapes women's views in a communitarian direction explains why women use more prosocial cues in communication, and why they are affected by these signals. A desire to function as an integrated, mutually interdependent unit shapes how people behave as they interact with others. It leads to interaction styles that invite others to participate and to exchange. It is a style that can accommodate differences but works hard to avoid hostility and destructive conflict—the kind of conflict that could distance the members of the group from one another. It emphasizes inclusion and rapport. Women are socialized to be the grease that allows the gears of the group to turn. Because women tend to be communitarian, they tend to do best in communitarian settings. A group where members function as an integrated unit is a group in which women are likely to feel comfortable and content. This is why women tend to participate more, and more freely, in groups where people act "nice."

Our finding that the level of rapport in the group affects women's participation and representation in deliberation squares with other studies of political discussion. Political scientist Diana Mutz studied what happens when people talk to a friend, relative, or acquaintance about a political subject on which they disagree (Mutz 2006). Two key ingredients emerge in predicting whether exposure to this political disagreement translates into the benefits deliberation advocates seek. One is the extent to which the person is aware of the rationales for the other's position. The other ingredient is a focus on social connection. But importantly for our argument, the cognitive side—the awareness of rationales for the conversation partner's political views—depends on the social side. A person comes to know the other's reasons primarily by having a "civil orientation" to conflict. What exactly does that mean? It means combining "an acknowledgment of the importance of expressing dissenting views with an emphasis on social harmony" (Mutz 2006, 75). That is, people exposed to uncongenial arguments defensively forget those arguments unless they not only believe in dissent but also care about social harmony. These results are consistent with our conclusion that deliberation is fed by rapport.

Not only do citizens need social rapport in order to learn, but also they need it in order to tolerate. An important benefit that deliberation advocates envision for deliberation between people who disagree is that exposure to disagreement will produce tolerance of that disagreement. Mutz finds, though, that those exposed to disagreement become more politically tolerant in general *only* if the social connection is there. That social connection can happen if the person is aware of the rationales of their disagreeing discussant—which we have just noted is in turn rooted in a civil orientation to conflict. Or it can happen if the person is oriented toward intimacy with the conversation partner (Mutz 2006, 76, 78). In other words, if people prioritize social harmony or care about maintaining a personally close relationship, then they can develop the kinds of attitudes that liberal democracy wishes to see among its citizenry—an exchange of views in a general atmosphere of respectful toleration. Democracy rests on social connection.

All of this tells us that social factors are crucial in determining the meaning of political conversation. Many people who are protective of their social ties are likely to shy away from disagreement, and this is a tough problem for deliberation.[16] Nevertheless, desiring social harmony does not shut down the exchange of reasons and evidence; in fact, a sense that harmony and disagreement can coexist may represent the most beneficial combination of all.

Most important for our argument, it is a combination that affects women more than men. Settings that promote social ties are especially helpful to women. In these settings, the bonds of community welcome women into full participation in the conversation, enabling both men and women to articulate their views fully, and thus to exchange perspectives fruitfully.

However, gender is not only, or even primarily, about differences in the level of communitarian orientation between men and women. It is also about status and authority. Settings that equalize participation and representation do so in part by elevating women's status in the group. Because women occupy a lower status in society by virtue of their gender, women tend to enter into discussion with less confidence than men and to be more affected by low confidence. Even more important, they are more sensitive to discussion dynamics that fail to provide positive reinforcement and to negative feedback about their competence. Women's lower confidence comes into play more powerfully when they interact with men, and all the more so when there are many men.

[16] And as Mutz (2006) argues, for political participation more generally.

Is Gender Inequality Bad If It Reflects Differences in Relevant Expertise?

We have been arguing that the gendered patterns of participation and representation in common types of public discussion are problematic for the democratic standard of equality. However, democratic theories often leave room for legitimate inequalities based, say, in relevant expertise, knowledge, or experience. More precisely, liberal theories tend to emphasize expertise over strict equality, because they are more concerned with the true value and rationality of collective decision making. So if women were on average less educated, less knowledgeable about politics, or less expert at the issue under discussion, then liberal theories may not find it so troubling that women speak less.

Such are not the only democratic theories, of course. Group-rights theories hold the reverse order of priorities. For this type of democratic theory, equality is more important to achieve than rational decision making. The good of the average person is a less relevant marker of the good of society than is the good of the average disadvantaged member of the society. In addition, postmodern theories tend to argue that what counts as expertise is itself shaped by societal structures and ideologies that privilege the knowledge and beliefs of the dominant groups. If women are less expert than men, postmodern theories would question why women's expertise is not considered general expertise and given equitable weight as such. What do we make of these theories, and how do they apply to our findings?

The most problematic theory for our argument is liberal theory, so we address it directly.[17] In our experiment, there is no meaningful difference between men and women on the expertise specific to the issue under discussion. We provided each person with the same detailed, relevant information about the decision they were charged with making—that is, on principles of income distribution. We gave each person this information before they began deliberating. We then gave each person a quiz to measure how well he or she had learned the material (see chapter 4). Men and women scored at nearly the same high level on the quiz. We then gave each person the correct answer to any quiz questions they got wrong, further ensuring that each person began with the same information and was able to draw the same valid inferences from that information. Thus men and women came to the discussion with training that should have generated a level playing field. And yet women underparticipated relative to men.

In addition, the problem of women's quiescence is not a felicitous result of poorly educated people getting out of the way of their more competent fellow

[17]In national samples there is a statistically significant but small gender gap in knowledge (see chapter 2). Not only is the gender gap small, but also the gap in political knowledge is shaped by motivation that, as we showed in chapter 2, is deeply rooted in gendered practices. By implication, changing the gender dynamic can completely equalize political expertise, neutralizing this potential justification for gender inequality.

deliberators. Overall in our experiment, education had no meaningful effect on talk time, for men or for women. Perhaps that is because nearly everyone in our experiment had some college education. And that renders most of our deliberators, men as well as women, minimally qualified to talk. And crucially for our argument, in the condition in which women are least empowered—majority rule with numerical minority women—the more educated women actually speak less than women with lower education (see chapter 6). In our sample of school boards, too, a woman's expertise (in the form of years of service on the board) and formal education had little effect; women do not speak more when they have served longer or are more educated. By contrast, board gender composition played a very large role in women's patterns of verbal participation, even after controlling for that board's experience and education. In sum, women's quiescence does not come predictably from more educated men speaking more than less educated women, and it therefore does not function as the price we must pay for the active involvement of the well educated.

It is not the case that the gender inequalities we observed are produced by their coincidence with competence. The gender gap in participation and influence is not an expertise gap. Men are not the more educated sex, either in our sample or in the nation. Inequality is not a necessary price groups must pay for the rule of knowledge, education, and expertise. There is no good defense of gender inequality in meetings.

How Does Our Research Design Affect the Interpretation of Our Findings?

Our study draws much of its evidence from our controlled randomized experiment. That choice of research design provides advantages but predictable disadvantages. While we undertook an extensive discussion of these issues in our method chapter, we summarize the main points here in order to review them and address the primary criticisms of our choice. The experiment at the core of our study has some important advantages that go beyond the existing scholarship on public deliberation. It used a larger number of groups than is typical. It recorded individual participants and linked each participant's utterances to that person's attitudes and characteristics, allowing us to control on predeliberation opinions and to examine postdeliberation perceptions. We examine situations that we create and over which we have a much higher level of control than other existing studies of political discussion. This allows us to examine the pure effect of gender composition and of institutional rules, something that is very tough to do with observational studies. We can have high confidence in the causes of the effects we observed because we exercised a high level of control over the conditions of deliberation and randomly assigned individuals to these conditions without the possibility that they would choose to select either into or out of their assigned condition. We have created conditions that vary across the full range of descriptive representation, from 0 all the way to 100% women. This also allowed us to see if there are specific breakpoints or thresholds for the effects of gender composition and to locate them precisely. Finally, we have created conditions that simulate a variety of real world situations and examined several types of designs that can be used in structuring actual deliberations.

While the experiment we used allows us much greater control than usual, it is far from perfect. As we discussed in chapter 4 and in further detail in the online appendix, we can control the number of women, but obviously we cannot assign a person to a gender. In addition, when we draw conclusions about the mechanisms responsible for the effect of the conditions, we lack the strong causal inference that we have for the direct effects of the conditions. For some experimentalists, any attempt to explore mechanisms outside of an experimental framework in which our preferred mechanisms are experimentally manipulated is probably misguided (Bullock, Green, and Ha 2010). We agree that the only definitive test of a mechanism is to manipulate it exogenously. However, that does not mean that we must abandon any attempt to say anything about mediators or mechanisms. Our strategy has been to look at different measures of mechanisms that are produced by the experimental treatment. Together, those variables make the case about the likely mechanisms even if we cannot experimentally manipulate those mechanisms. We see that speaking time, influence, conversational dynamics (interruptions and such), and content (words and expressions of preferences) are all affected by our experimental manipulations in ways that are consistent with our theory about status (and not with other potential stories). We see this as good, if not definite, evidence for the mechanism we propose. It is an advance over the existing state of scholarship in the field, and we regard it as valuable for that reason.

While the control afforded by our experimental design is an important advantage, there are predictable and well-known shortcomings from that design as well. Our study has the virtues and liabilities of high control and thus strong internal but weaker external validity. Most importantly, the results come from artificial settings and populations. However, we have taken large steps toward addressing these deficiencies.

A number of similarities between our experiment and actual settings are important to note. The task resembled the task in many deliberative settings in that the members were making decisions about the distribution of resources to themselves and, simultaneously, to others in society. Examples include: town planning (Karpowitz and Mansbridge 2005); school budgeting (Myers 2011); designing a new electoral system for a state or a province, as in British Columbia (Warren and Pearse 2008); reforming the country's resource allocation (Humphreys, Masters, and Sandbu 2006); allocating local services (Fung 2004; Fung and Wright 2003); and so on. In that sense the task facing our participants is not dissimilar from what real world deliberating citizens may do. While our group decisions were nonbinding outside of the experimental setting, so are the recommendations of many actual citizens' deliberative bodies. Neither is our degree of control unusual; in many real world settings deliberations are structured and directed by officials or authorities. They take place in formal settings that are not always familiar, much as ours did. In addition, while we assembled people unfamiliar with each other to avoid the confounding effects from familiarity, so do many real world settings. As Jacobs, Cook, and Delli Carpini find, in general, meeting attendees are unlikely to know each other (2009, 72). In sum, our experiment resembled the "real world" in several important ways.

In addition, most importantly, we reported a replication of some key results in actual school board meetings. There we find that the average woman on boards with very few women is disadvantaged, especially with respect to authoritative moves like making motions. This disadvantage dissipates as women make up a larger percentage of the board. To find this effect even among accomplished women who have been elected to speak for others in the town is substantial reassurance that our lab findings are picking up dynamics that can also be found in the real world.

Nevertheless, below we take some pains to think through how various conditions of actual deliberation probably do, or don't, change the main findings.

How Real World Conditions, and Additional Variables, May Alter the Findings

Our group size is not uncharacteristic in real world deliberations (for example, Esterling, Fung, and Lee [2009]), but worth further study as a possible contingent factor. A small group size may be more inclusive of women, which may make the rules and composition less influential. But it may also make little difference if the key factor is a formal setting where women's act of speaking takes on an association with leadership. Because the expectations of it are ambiguous, and yet it holds the potential to play an important role in muting women's disadvantage, group size is a candidate for further study.[18]

A similar question arises about the size of the community in which the discussion takes place. Our results may apply in most community sizes except perhaps the very smallest. We conclude this from Bryan's finding that women's participation is much higher in communities of 250 registered voters or less.[19]

[18] In Vermont town meetings, women's share of speakers and of speaking turns moves up with a decrease in the meeting's size, though the effect is small (Bryan 2004, 223).

[19] Versus those of 250–500 registered voters (Bryan 2004, 227). See online supplementary figures at http://www.uvm.edu/~fbryan/newfig%20X-N.pdf. In the smallest towns (250 registered voters or less), women's share of speakers and turns is 80–90%; in the biggest towns (above 2,500 registered voters), the share is 59% and 73% respectively (Bryan 2004, 227). Bryan (2004) finds almost no association between community size and percentage of women attending town meetings

This suggests that the character of the community as a place where people know each other and, perhaps, interact in more sociable ways, matters to women's equal participation. That is, the high level of women's share of participation may be caused by the change from an impersonal to a personal community. This is in line with our interpretation of decision rules. Perhaps the same mechanism we believe is created by a unanimous decision rule is at work in small communities, and in both cases, helps women participate more. More study of the sociable nature of interaction, and specifically an exploration of whether sociability rises predictably with particular characteristic of the community whose members are invited to deliberate, would be a fruitful direction for future research.

Would the dynamics change over repeated opportunities for the same individuals to interact? In other words, do women have more influence and standing when they are part of a group that meets repeatedly? There is no reason to think the results go away with repetition, and if anything, norms grow stronger with more interaction (Cialdini and Trost 1998, 158). Evidence from Bryan's study of town meetings helps: there is almost no correlation in women's speaking participation across back-to-back meetings within a town;[20] the first meeting may have a high level of female participation while the next one will have a low level, and vice versa (2004, 218–19).[21] And as we have already indicated, in our school boards data set length of service on the school board had little effect on women's patterns of participation. All this suggests that repeated interactions with the same group does not increase or decrease women's equality in participation.

The groups we study make decisions, but not all discussion groups do so. Women's inequality may be muted when the stakes of the group interaction are low, when the group goal is exploratory rather than decisive or directive, and thus when a member's authority is less implicated in the interaction.

Some groups are charged with discussing matters that involve opinion or values, while others deal merely with the determination of fact. Groups are

---

from 1970 to 1998. That is, small communities elevate women's discussion participation without elevating their numbers. http://www.uvm.edu/~fbryan/newfig%20IX-E.pdf. It is also possible that town size generally decreases participation; it decreases the overall rate of attendance at town meetings measured as a percentage of the registered voters, as discovered by Zimmerman for meetings taking place in the 1990s, in a study of six New England states (Zimmerman 1999, 165). Town's socioeconomic status or diversity have either a negative or, when controls are included, no relationship with overall rate of meeting attendance, and the same is true of individual-level socioeconomic status (Bryan 2004, 114–22). When both town and meeting size are examined simultaneously, it is town and not meeting size that matters for women's share of participation (Bryan 2004, 227–28). In our school boards data set we do not have a good measure of town size, in part because school districts are often not identical to town boundaries; some districts span across multiple towns, while others include only parts of cities or towns. In our sample of school boards, female board members speak somewhat more in rural districts.

[20] See figure IX-C, plot 1: http://www.uvm.edu/~fbryan/newfig%20IX-C.pdf.

[21] Bryan also found that length of residency by the town's residents also matters little.

prone to various kinds of cognitive biases and suboptimal sharing of information even when the mission is to reach an objectively accurate decision. Socially informed expectations and stereotypes are not held at bay merely because values are bracketed off in the group's mission. So there is no strong reason to expect our findings, or gender inequality, to differ depending on this aspect of the group's mission.

Would gender gaps mute online? It is possible that online discussions may mute gender differences, if they mute cues to gender or gender roles. There are too few studies yet to be able to draw conclusions, and very few Americans participate in deliberations online (4% of a weighted national sample, according to Jacobs, Cook, and Delli Carpini [2007, 40]). Contrast this low percentage to the 25% who report participating in a face-to-face forum in that study. Nonetheless, as online communities become more prevalent, online deliberation may be a promising venue for gender equality, and worth further exploration.

Applying the Results across Lines of Class, Race, and Age

Education and Class

Our sample is highly educated, and we found that the women most affected by women's low status in the group are highly educated. We also found that all the key results held even when we controlled on the person's education and income and measures of the group's class or educational composition. We found that these demographic variables do not account for the results—that is, they are not responsible for the effects of gender, and controlling on them does not alter the effects of gender or rule.[22] So in all, the evidence implies that class does not explain away the effects of gender, and that while educated women are more vulnerable, all women are negatively affected.

Still, it is appropriate to ask if the findings from our experiment apply where participants are less educated. One possibility is that we found that women underparticipate relative to men because we examined middle-class women who tend to be socialized to especially feminine norms of behavior. Perhaps working-class women are less deferential to working-class men than middle-class women are to middle-class men. While this is a plausible hypothesis, there is no evidence for it. In fact, existing studies pull in the opposite direction.[23]

[22] See results of models that include income and education in chapter 6, tables 1–3 and discussion section, and in chapters 5 and 7–9 we indicate in footnotes that key models are unchanged when education and income are controlled. In chapter 10 we do not have a measure of age for a sufficient number of board members to include it as a control, but we do control for their education and years of experience on the board and find these do not change the effect of board gender composition.

[23] Bryan finds very little association between a town's education or educational diversity (or any of several other measures of socioeconomic status, or of diversity of socioeconomic status, or of

For example, in Bryan's study of New England meetings, the share of women's participation was often far from equal regardless of the town's occupational, income, or educational profile (Bryan 2004, 217, figure 9.1). Neither does the town's percentage of working women associate with women's share of participation at the meeting (Bryan 2004, 224). In other words, there is no evidence that working-class settings produce different patterns of gender inequality.[24]

Race

Our sample consisted entirely of non-Hispanic whites, for a reason. We expected that nonwhite women and nonwhite men behave differently from white women and men. We mean this in the sense of the overall gender gap, which we expect is smaller among African Americans in particular, and in the sense of the reactions of each gender to gender composition. African American women may be less deferential to African American men than is the case for white women and men. Gimpel, Lay, and Schuknecht (2003, 87, 92) found that teen girls are actually more politically knowledgeable and internally efficacious than teen boys—among African Americans.

Our analysis of Walsh's data on race dialogue groups supports the findings from our lab study. Although her groups were racially diverse, they behaved very similarly to our unanimous-rule groups, and we found the same pattern of declining average female speech participation there as we did with our experiment.

A more thorough and systematic study, however, is warranted. Unfortunately, even our school board data is very short on nonwhite members. How segregation shapes racial composition and thus the discussion dynamics is a worthy question for future research.

Age

A final demographic of possible relevance for the results is age. The mean age in our experiment was twenty-eight (SD 12). Several implications follow. First, the results tell us that younger women do not escape the ill effects of gender inequality. Gender inequality is not a problem confined to older cohorts. It will not automatically disappear with the passage of time. We saw this when we reviewed the general

economic situation) and its women's share of meeting attendance or share of speakers or of speaking turns (2004, 205). This is despite a strong association between the town's percentage of college graduates and the vote for Vermont's Equal Rights Amendment, controlling for the Democratic voters in the town (Bryan 2004, 204). See also http://www.uvm.edu/~fbryan/newfig%20IX-H.pdf.

[24] A cross-country analysis found that as levels of women's education rise, and as the community's overall level of education rises, so does women's status in politics (Fish 2002). Electoral support for the Equal Rights Amendment granting women equal status in the United States increased with the community's level of education (Bryan 2004). Relatedly, in a study of city councils, the evidence suggests there is little relationship between a city's socioeconomic status and the share of female council members (Welch and Karnig 1979; the cities all had populations over 25,000).

problem of women's continued lower participation in politics, in chapter 2. Similar findings from mock jury studies also suggest that the gendered dynamics we found apply to younger people (for example, Golding et al. 2007, who studied college students). So our findings about younger women are no surprise.

Second, it is not the case that the women in our experiment were easily cowed or silenced because they are young. Our standard deviation is 12, which means that a considerable minority of participants were well into their adult lives.

Third, when we control on age in our analysis, the findings hold. That is, the results are not restricted to young women or to groups with a preponderance of young women.

Mistaking Average Female Representation for the Representation of All Women

We have, for the sake of economy, been talking about women as a whole. Yet women are far from monolithic in their perspectives, opinions, and interests. In no way do we mean to discuss women as if they are unvarying and unified. In fact, doing so carries the risk that the representation of more privileged women will serve as a mistaken signal that underprivileged women are adequately represented (Cornwall 2003). Clearly, raising the number of women as women risks short-changing the representation of women from disadvantaged groups (Dunning and Nilekani 2013; see also Strolovitch 2008). Future work should prioritize the question of how demographic and ideological diversity among women shapes the patterns we have documented here. If women with lower socioeconomic status or members of racial and ethnic minority groups are especially badly off in conditions where women are underrepresented, for example, then remedies may need to take these dimensions of inequality into consideration. Or if measures that aid women as a whole also aid more privileged women disproportionately, then additional or different remedies may be needed.

Do the Results Apply in Other Countries, Cultures, and Places?

Culture

Do norms of discussion vary with culture? How? How would that affect the effects of decision rule and gender composition? How might these effects vary when we move to societies that are more gender egalitarian than the United States? That are less?

First, we begin by noting again that we conducted our experiment in two very different cultural milieus in the United States—one a socially conservative, highly religious community in Utah, and the other a liberal, secular, and wealthy community in New Jersey. We controlled for this variable in all our analyses, and the results we reported thus are not peculiar to one place. That is, the effects of rule and composition are not unique to a particular type of cultural milieu. In places with more and with less gender equality, the same factors shape women's relative participation and representation.

In addition, our analysis of school board meetings took place in a set of highly varied communities across the United States and replicated the findings from our experiment. This supports our ability to generalize widely within the country about the factors that shape women's authority in discussion.

Nevertheless, it is worth thinking further about the role of culture, with its behavioral scripts and expectations, when it comes to gender inequality. Let us move for the moment to a very different setting from the United States: the slums of Nairobi, Kenya. There, government services are minimal; the large majority of the population lives without electricity, running water, or other basic necessities; and unemployment is extremely high. But many people, especially women, are members of civic associations that attempt to fill this gap (Kilavuka 2003, cited in Greig and Bohnet 2009).

The behavioral economists Greig and Bohnet conducted an economic "game" style experiment with residents of these Nairobi neighborhoods, gauging their willingness to cooperate with others by the extent to which they choose to contribute private resources for the benefit of everyone in the game. In the study, participants are instructed to decide how much to contribute of the private resource given to them by the investigators, and their sacrifice is rewarded to the extent that other players also contribute their own private resource for the mutual benefit of the players. The researchers randomly assigned women to mixed-gender groups or to all-female groups. They found that in general, women tend to view other women as far more likely than men to cooperate in donating private resources for the common good of the players. Consequently, the women in all-female groups are more likely than women in mixed-gender groups to (1) believe that the people with whom they are making joint decisions will behave more cooperatively, and (2) behave more cooperatively themselves (Greig and Bohnet 2009). In other words, this study replicates our finding that relative to mixed-gender groups, female enclaves are more focused on women's issues, more generous to the disadvantaged, and more cooperative in their interaction dynamics.[25]

[25] Further replication in Africa comes from an experiment conducted by Humphreys, Fearson, and Weinstein in Liberia. There, each person had to decide how much of their personal earnings from the study they would contribute to a project to aid their local community (Humphreys, Fearson, and Weinstein 2011). Individuals made the decision independently, but if enough members of the group individually decided to contribute their private resource toward a common good, then the investigators would add a reward, and the whole group—and its village—would benefit. The investigators introduced two treatments: gender composition (individuals were assigned to all-female or mixed-gender groups) and democratic leadership (instituting elected democratic councils for the village). The councils' treatment strengthens the capacity of village leaders to hold meetings and otherwise coordinate the members' actions so they choose to contribute their private resource. The study found that in groups not assigned to the democratic leadership condition,

This and similar replications suggest that the United States is not the only country where women are less likely to participate in deliberation, where women and men have distinct preferences in politics, where women articulate a different voice in deliberation, and where voice matters to the outcome only when women are numerous. Replication in countries with a lower level of social, economic, and political development suggests that the patterns we found are not restricted to highly developed countries.[26]

Does Gender Inequality in Discussion Vary across Places?

While we have reason to believe that women's participation and representation respond similarly to the conditions we identify as important regardless of the place, a related but separate question is whether some places are better than others.

We can get a systematic look at the effect of the community's level of development on women's participation by looking at Bryan's analysis of Vermont towns (2004). Women's level of participation during Vermont town meetings is not affected by the degree to which the town is "modernized" or follows a traditional pattern of social and economic relations. To measure the level of development of the town, Bryan constructed variables such as population growth, percentage of native Vermonters in the population, loss of agricultural lifestyle, isolation from larger towns, and sense of the community as bounded. It turns out that none of these indicators of a traditional community matter for

---

all-female groups generated nearly 10% higher collective income for their group and donated 12% more of their private income than did mixed-gender groups. As in our study, there is no effect of individual gender; women contribute more than men only when their group consists of other women. In addition, the democratic reform lifts the mixed-gender groups up to the level of public goods contribution shown by the all-female groups. Mixed gender groups *can* make high contributions to the public good, but they rely on mechanisms of coordination from elected leaders. By contrast, women's groups are more generous without the top-down efforts of leaders. These results parallel ours in highlighting the role of gender composition, in finding that all-female groups are particularly prosocial and cooperative, and in drawing attention to the way institutional procedures and leadership, broadly conceived, can overcome the problems of gender composition and lead to positive outcomes.

[26]Our results are also consistent with some patterns of women's participation in Indian village meetings (Ban and Rao 2009). Ban and Rao's study found that in villages where women's representation quotas are mandated and where women thus have higher descriptive representation in meetings, "within women's talk the preferences of women take up more time." In addition, the Ban and Rao study replicates our finding regarding the importance of talk for power over group decisions; the more that land-owning, privileged villagers talk, the more the outcome matches their preferences. That is, powerful groups—in this case, the landed—dominated meetings, and did so mostly through voice. A similar study of villages found that women and illiterate men are "less likely to both hear of and attend these meetings" (Besley et al. 2005a, 652). See the chapter 4 appendix for more details.

women's level of participation during discussion.[27] This suggests that towns that are more traditional in their politics and economics will not necessarily display higher levels of gender inequality. In our study, too, the political milieu of the town made no difference. We already noted that the factors we varied had similar effects in both liberal and conservative locations. Women on the whole participated no more in Princeton (a more gender-egalitarian place) than Provo (a more gender-traditional place). Conversely, more developed communities and perhaps societies do not automatically leave gender inequality behind. As one review of women's presence and influence in government and corporate boards concludes, "economic development does not beget female leadership" (Pande and Ford 2011, 5).

What does seem to matter for the level of women's participation is the general standing of women in the society. Among Bryan's most powerful findings is that the passage of time, from 1970 to 1998, substantially increased women's share of attendance, speakers, and speaking turns (2004, 226–27). While the passage of time could indicate many disparate causes, women's general status in society is among the plausible ones.

More evidence in line with this notion that women's general status in society affects women's participation is found in a clever study using a controlled experiment in two societies with significant differences in women's status. The Masai in Tanzania represent a highly patriarchal society, while the Khasi in India are matrilineal. In the patriarchal society, men choose to enter a competition twice as often as women. In the matrilineal society, the gender gap reverses, and women are more likely to choose to compete than men (Gneezy, Leonard, and List 2009). While this study does not look at discussion, it does suggest the possibility that women's status in a society has profound consequences for women's proclivity to participate in situations where status is on the line, perhaps including meetings.[28]

More generally, what these studies suggest is that the society's fundamental norms about gender matter. In places and times where women are granted more authority, women participate more. Perhaps they matter because they

[27] When all of these measures are included simultaneously, only out-of-town employment has an effect, but not a large one (Bryan 2004, 225).

[28] We do not wish to overstate the case, and there is a dearth of evidence. Furthermore, attitudes about women's place in society, and indicators of women's integration (such as women's labor force participation and education), are only weakly related to each other and to women's level of descriptive representation in government. See Pande and Ford 2011, 5, and http://www.pewglobal.org/2007/12/05/how-the-world-rates-women-as-leaders/. Women may be educated and employed, and the society generally approves of equal gender roles, and yet women's leadership status may remain far behind unless women's authority in society becomes nearly equal to men's. An additional factor is gender quotas; to circumvent the dearth of women in leadership positions in order to comply with international pressure and norms, even countries with traditional gender arrangements may adopt gender quotas (Pande and Ford 2011).

permeate within the society broadly and trickle down to the interactions that take place between the genders.

Do the Results Apply to Elites?

We have designed our study to comment on discussion among ordinary people, which raises the question: do the results apply in all levels of government, including the highest?

For example, Senator Patty Murray was the only woman among the twelve members of the so-called supercommittee charged with deficit reduction in fall 2011. The committee used majority rule, the common decision rule in governmental settings. As we noted in the introductory chapter, women are a small minority in the vast majority of legislative settings, and majority rule is the common rule (with variations, such as a supermajority rule). Thus female senators often face the circumstances that we identify as especially deleterious to women's voice. Does it matter if Senator Murray is alone or with other women on a committee? Does the heralded historic rise of women to 20% of the US Senate matter? More generally, do elites differ from citizens in how they react to gender composition or to procedures and rules?

At first it may seem that the answer is yes—elites are different. Especially at the higher levels, it takes an unusual woman to seek the office in the first place, given the paucity of women in that arena, and an even more unusual woman to do what it takes to obtain it. The women who seek leadership—an activity viewed as masculine—may be highly masculine individuals. They may be interested in the issues men are socialized to prioritize, such as finances or hardware. For example, while a barrister, Margaret Thatcher specialized in taxation—a traditionally male priority. Such pathbreaking women may be comfortable with conflict at the start and relish engaging in it and winning. They may be inclined to use an assertive communication style. Thatcher, for example, tended to use the "language of conflict and confrontation" (Campbell, quoted in Keohane 2010, 133). When pressed to do a "U-turn" on policy, she once famously responded: "You turn if you want to. The lady's not for turning!" These ambitious women appear to know their mind and stick to it. And they may value their agency as individuals and their ambition to govern above cooperation with others. After all, the vagaries of personality, the idiosyncrasies of personal experience, and the tendencies built in by genetic codes all generate significant individual variation within women, and within men. In other words, some women may be inclined toward views and interaction styles that characterize the male central tendency. Accounts of Thatcher, Indira Gandhi, Golda Meir, and Angela Merkel sustain this view. In that sense, not all women fit our story.

Moreover, once this tough-as-nails, superconfident, highly qualified woman achieves a leadership role, she may not be much influenced by what the men around her do—because she already acts in traditionally masculine ways. These rare women must have talked a fair amount and been perceived as highly influential to get where they did, and they did so in a nearly all-male environment. So in this sense, clearly we can say that there are outliers among women who are not deterred by gender roles, or shaped much by them.

However, in a number of ways even women in the high positions of government may exhibit the patterns we have documented. First, the fact that these women adopt a highly masculine style is consistent with one of our claims. These women behaved in a masculine way in a heavily masculine environment. As we have shown, in conflictual settings in which women are few, those women who do speak tend to articulate masculine issue priorities and views. Relative to women in any other circumstance, women in groups with majority rule and only 20% females speak to the care of others only once for every four times, and speak to financial topics about half again as often as other women. Unlike other women, these women never initiate a discussion of children, families, or the vulnerable.[29] They are about 50% more likely than other women to advocate for principles of redistribution that they did not prefer—an indicator of conformity to the masculine group environment.[30] And they speak for the same ungenerous safety net that the men in these groups do.[31] In fact, these women are so eager to conform that they become hypermasculine in their terms of speech; their ratio of care to financial words is about half—or less—of men's ratio in any condition. Because of these women's hypermasculine emphasis, the overall ratio of care to financial references in these groups is no higher than in male enclaves; that is, in highly masculine settings, women's presence has no feminizing effect at all.[32]

Consistent with this notion that predominantly male, conflictual environments prompt women to talk in masculine ways and to align their public speech with men's, elite women in those settings seem aware that their unusual gender is an inescapable part of their public persona. They behave as if they must operate in a masculine fashion, and they attach masculine traits and styles to that persona.[33] The nicknames by which they are known testify to the salience of

[29] Specifically, see chapter 7, figures 1, 2, and 3.

[30] Chapter 9, figure 4.

[31] Chapter 9, figure 2.

[32] Chapter 7, figures 4, 5, and 6.

[33] Salient exceptions such as Sarah Palin may prove the rule—while some commented favorably on her feminine self-presentation, Palin was subjected to a high degree of negative coverage that highlighted her self-presented feminine traits and roles in a negative way (Carlin and Winfrey 2009, e.g., 338; see also the case of France's Segolene Royale, discussed by Campus 2013, 6). However, some women, such as Hillary Clinton, also include cues to the mother stereotype to soften the

their female sex and to the juxtaposition of masculine traits. These monikers include phrases such as "Iron Lady" (Thatcher), "Iron Frau" (Merkel), "Ellen-she's our man" (Ellen Johnson Sirleaf), and "the only man in the Cabinet" (Golda Meir).[34] Similarly, Sarah Palin, the 2008 Republican candidate for US vice president, came to be called—and described herself as—a "pitbull with lipstick" (Carlin and Winfrey 2009, 338).[35] These examples are consistent with our argument that when women are few and men many, women tend to adopt masculine styles as an adaptation to the predominantly male, masculine environment (see also Dodson 2006; Lovenduski 2005). These pathbreaking women behaved as if their very political survival dictated that they shun femininity, at least in style—do not give in, do not show weakness, do not compromise, do not appear to fail.[36] Each one conforms to our story about the effects of gender composition on the contents of women's issue agenda and policy goals.

Interview evidence specifically supports our argument that many women at the highest levels of politics believe that they cannot get far with a feminine style. Interviews of members of the US Congress reveal a pervasive sense by women that they operate in a man's world and must conform to its expectations in order to succeed: "The women most admired by congressmen were those who had adjusted most effectively to the workways [*sic*] and habits of the House" (Gertzog 1995, 65, quoted in Dodson 2006). In her interviews with most of the new members in the burgeoning ranks of female MPs of Britain's Labour Party, Childs found that feminine styles were perceived as illegitimate in the predominantly masculine environment of the House of Commons. She concludes:

> Many of the Labour women MPs considered that the House of Commons was not conducive to women acting in a feminised way. They talked about their perceptions of how their style of politics was considered less legitimate and less effective and they

---

perception that they are hypermasculine and thus overly "calculating" or cold, as with the famous "3 a.m." ad (Carlin and Winfrey 2009, 335–37). Media commentators were not entirely persuaded; as one remarked, "Hillary Clinton didn't figure it out. She didn't put a skirt on!" (quoted in Carlin and Winfrey 2009, 338). See the discussion of the "double bind" in Jamieson (1995).

[34] Some terms opponents used are not flattering or are meant to evoke derision or hostility, such as "Attila the Hen" for Thatcher or "Old Witch" for Indira Gandhi. For nicknames, see Keohane 2010, 133 and 137–38. Many of these names conform to the "iron maiden" category in Kanter's typology of sexist stereotypes of corporate women (1977a). Media coverage can feed these perceptions, which sometimes reflect fears of female domination. For example, MSNBC's Tucker Carlson remarked about Hillary Clinton that "when she comes on television, I involuntarily cross my legs"; Chris Matthews referred to her male supporters as "castratos in the eunuch chorus" (quoted in Carlin and Winfrey 2009, 338).

[35] The masculine terms ("iron," "man") are contrasted in these nicknames with the feminine ("lady," "frau," "she").

[36] To be sure, many also used feminine tropes and appealed to feminine icons, when it served them. Some of these are stereotypically feminine: the nurturing mother (Gandhi, Sirleaf); the moral person untainted by masculine corruption or infighting (Thatcher, Merkel). Some are feminine versions of otherwise masculine traits of valor and fierceness (a mythical Warrior Queen or goddess, in the case of Gandhi or Thatcher). See Keohane 2010, chapter 4 for a concise discussion.

> discussed the pressures they experienced to conform to the traditional norms of the House. There was also an acknowledgement of the costs associated with acting like (and for) women. (Childs 2004a, 14)

That is, even highly ambitious and successful women are shaped by the gender dynamics around them.

Furthermore, even high-achieving political women may initially experience such masculine settings as more difficult or hostile than their male counterparts do. That too conforms to our argument—masculine settings are tougher for women, even women inclined in a masculine direction. When two women joined the formerly all-male Senate Judiciary Committee after the Senate election of 1992, widely hailed as the "year of the woman" in American electoral politics for electing unprecedented numbers of women to the Senate, they asked not a single question of the witnesses in the Supreme Court confirmation hearings that this committee held (Mattei 1998, 446–47, note 6). Similarly, as we noted in an earlier chapter, US Secretary of State Madeline Albright wrote that at the beginning of her career, as the only woman in many committee meetings, she was reluctant to speak for lack of confidence. It took time for her to realize that what she had to say was in fact quite valued by the group, and to determine how to "interrupt at the right moment." Albright says that she "*learned* that you shouldn't wait to speak" (emphasis added).[37] That is, even at the very highest levels of government, at least some women must go through a process of adapting to masculine environments before they feel equally able to participate and assert their authority. Similarly, Angela Merkel "*learned* to use 'hard power' to consolidate her political position" (emphasis added; Thompson and Lennartz 2006).[38] Eleanor Roosevelt put it this way: "all women in public life needed to develop skin as tough as rhinoceros hide" (quoted in Keohane 2010, 144). The process is one of learning—learning how to interrupt, when to take the floor, to brush off hostile reactions, and generally, learning the specific forms of masculine speech acts that instantiate influence when people interact. That even tough, otherwise masculine women at the highest level of achievement and ability feel that they must learn to adapt to masculine environments suggests that some of the patterns we identified here may apply in a variety of settings, from the lowest to the most rarefied levels of public life.

Although women in elite masculine settings may adapt to masculine styles of interaction and decision making, and may shift their agenda toward the issues of

[37] http://www.realsimple.com/work-life/life-strategies/inspiration-motivation/how-to-tactfully-speak-your-mind-00100000081879/index.html.

[38] Powerful women outside official positions of government testify to a similar evolution. The publisher of the *Washington Post* during its Watergate heyday, Katharine Graham, wrote that she had to "outgrow" her habit of breaking into tears at work. She "outgrew" a debilitating lack of self-confidence and "deep feeling of uncertainty and inferiority and a need to please" rooted in the assumption that "we [women] were not capable of governing, leading, managing" (quoted in Keohane 2010, 136).

priority to men, some may seize whatever small opportunity comes their way to articulate or act on a somewhat more care-oriented perspective than their male counterparts. Socialization into care may exert a sufficiently powerful force on most women's values that it could set women on a higher level of cooperative or nurturing preferences and priorities, relative to otherwise comparable men.

For example, female senators on the Armed Services Committee appear to place a higher priority on issues of care than male counterparts. The first woman to serve on the committee, Senator Margaret Chase Smith, "crusaded during her House career for sexual equality in the military" and "continued that path when she joined the Senate committee in 1953."[39] In 2013, many of the women on the committee focused on eliminating sexual assault against female soldiers, more so than their fellow males.[40] Although these women are in a predominantly masculine setting (composing 29% of that committee as of 2013),[41] and even though the committee is defined by the highly masculine task of overseeing the military, they tend to bring a more care-oriented set of priorities than do their male colleagues. As Senator Kirsten E. Gillibrand said to the *New York Times*, "The men asked all the questions about ships, hardware, that sort of thing. We asked why divorce and suicide rates were so high."[42] This is not an artifact of the preponderance of Democrats among the female senators. Republicans have prioritized care issues too: Senator Kay Bailey Hutchison of Texas "focused on military family issues," and Senator Susan Collins was "an early voice on the sexual assault issue," a point validated by Carroll (2001).[43] Women may not be articulating that agenda as consistently and influentially as they would in a majority-female or in a unanimous-rule setting; for example, Senator Gillibrand's bill, intended to crack down on sexual violence against military women, was replaced by the male chairman of the committee, who crafted a weaker version supported by three of the seven female senators.[44] But women may still on average demonstrate a higher level of commitment to

[39] *New York Times*, June 2, 2013.

[40] Jennifer Steinhauer, "Women in the Senate Confront the Military on Sex Assaults," *New York Times*, June 2, 2013, A1. That women prioritized the issue more than the men on the committee was highlighted by Senator Bill Nelson: "When I raised the issue of rape in the military seven years ago, there was dead silence. Clearly they [that is, the female senators] are changing things around here" (ibid).

[41] http://www.nytimes.com/2013/06/03/us/women-in-the-senate-gain-strength-in-rising-numbers.html?pagewanted=2&partner=rss&emc=rss&utm_source=feedly&pagewanted=all&_r=0. Accessed June 21, 2013.

[42] The senator was referring to her experience on the House Armed Services Committee, but drew the same conclusion about the Senate committee (*New York Times*, June 2, 2013).

[43] http://www.nytimes.com/2013/06/03/us/women-in-the-senate-gain-strength-in-rising-numbers.html?pagewanted=2&partner=rss&emc=rss&utm_source=feedly&pagewanted=all&_r=0.

[44] http://www.armed-services.senate.gov/press/releases/upload/SASC-RCVs-ON-FY-2014-NDAA-MARKUP.pdf. The committee did not hold a roll call vote on Gillibrand's proposal, but instead on a weaker rival proposal, with the female vote breakdown as follows: In favor: McCaskill (D), Ayotte (R), Fischer (R); Opposed: Hagan (D), Shaheen (D), Gillibrand (D), Hirono (D). See also

care issues than their male counterparts.[45] These are merely anecdotes, but they are consistent with our systematic findings. Women are usually socialized to care for others, and even comparatively "masculine" women, if to a small extent, may tend to act on this agenda more than comparable men do, when the opportunity to do so opens up.

In addition, when more women enter the political setting, women may act in somewhat more feminine ways, at least with one another. This pattern parallels the behavior of women in our enclave groups. For example, after the number of women in the British Labour Party increased in the House of Commons, women reported a sense of sisterhood and solidarity with one another as women. They tended to provide the supports of friendship to one another. In language that fits our findings well, one MP said that "it does help to have other women who will sympathize with you and understand the predicament you are facing" (Childs 2013, 137). These women tended to regard their interactions with female colleagues as different from the parliamentary culture, which they view as "tough and hard." Some women said they could "reveal" themselves "emotionally" when interacting with other women and not with men, and felt that the men but not the women regarded them as a "threat" (136). Finally, when women reach very large numbers in committees, the tenor of interaction can change, as we found in our study. A study of German and Swiss parliamentary discourse found that "it is mainly groups with female dominance that are conducive to higher respect levels" (Grünenfelder and Bächtiger 2007, 16). That is, women tend to behave in women's enclaves within masculine institutions along the lines we found in our experiments—in a more mutually supportive and warm way.

Findings from the realm of the judiciary are also consistent with our argument about the effect of procedural norms on women's representation. The findings come from rigorous, large-scale studies of US Court of Appeals panels, which consist of three judges.[46] The vast majority of these panels—68%—are all male.[47] However, when a female judge is assigned to sit on a panel, the panel

---

http://www.politico.com/story/2013/06/senate-armed-services-committee-sexual-assault-prosecutor-amendment-92674.html. Accessed June 21, 2013.

[45] Swers's recent book-length study of the US Senate validates this conclusion (2013). Additional anecdotes abound. Even Thatcher herself took some care-oriented positions at odds with many in her party: she voted for an early bill to decriminalize homosexuality (Thatcher 1995). Similarly, when one of the first female presidents of elite universities, Judith Rodin of the University of Pennsylvania, explained her decision to help a local neighborhood in trouble, she said, "Perhaps I was more determined to fix the neighborhood because I was a woman and a mother" (quoted in Keohane 2010, 132).

[46] The findings in this section come from Massie, Johnson, and Gubala 2002; Boyd, Epstein, and Martin 2010; Farhang and Wawro 2010; and Peresie 2005.

[47] This figure was calculated based on the descriptive statistics reported in table 1 in Farhang and Wawro's 2010 working paper. Of the 881 cases in Farhang and Wawro's sample, only 278, or approximately 32%, included female judges.

issues more pro-plaintiff decisions, even after accounting for the judge's liberal or conservative ideology.[48] The effects are not due to logrolling across cases, that is, they are not produced by a bargaining process in which the male judges acquiesce to the female judge in order to gain her vote elsewhere. Further evidence that the effects are due to gender differences between male and female judges is that these decisions occur only in particular cases—criminal procedure, civil rights, employment discrimination, or sexual harassment. The specific nature of these cases is telling—they focus on vulnerable populations with whom women tend to concern themselves. That is, women carry influence, and do so as women, in areas of distinctive concern to women.

This is what we would predict under a unanimous process. Sean Farhang and Gregory Wawro, who helped to pioneer this literature, speculate as much, pointing to the norm of unanimity on courts of appeals. About 95% of cases before these courts are decided unanimously, despite the official majority rule. But how can we know if the unanimous process is at work? While we have no majority-process equivalent in hand, we do know one other fact. Recall that under unanimity, increasing the number of women does little, nothing, or even backfires, because unanimity enhances the power of women when women are few. Importantly for our argument, these studies find that adding a second woman does nothing more. If the norm on these panels were one of de facto majority rule, we would not see this influence by lone women, but we would see women's influence when they are the two-thirds majority. Again, consistent with our argument, unanimity helps women when they are few but does not allow women to leverage the power of large numbers.[49]

Women in high positions of power may be an exception to our general pattern, but in some ways their actions and experiences confirm our findings. Not all women are feminine—there is much variety within gender. The rare women we have considered here—women who are unusually confident and masculine in their general leaning—are a testament to the variation surrounding averages. In addition, women tend to conform to the role requirements of leadership positions in political and formal settings, which tend to be masculine. Here, their performance is often judged based on masculine criteria of achievement, such as financial prosperity, efficiency, status, or victory over enemies. How-

[48] These effects extend not only to the panel's decision, but also specifically to male judges' votes, indicating that the female judge's influence extends to both male judges, not just to one male judge who votes with her and against the remaining male judge. The assignment process simulates random assignment conditional on judge and case factors, according to Boyd, Epstein, and Martin (2010).

[49] As in our experimental findings, elite women may benefit from particular procedures and rules. For example, Pearson and Dancey (2011) analyzed floor speeches in the US House and found that women actually spoke much more often than men. We interpret this finding in light of the specific rules that govern speeches on the floor of the US House of Representatives. Turn taking in this setting is highly regulated and controlled. When men do not have the opportunity to interrupt women, and when access to the floor is not determined by the individual's proclivity to initiate speech, then we see that women may actually out-participate men.

ever, even if these elite women are inclined toward masculinity as a general matter, and even more so when occupying roles judged by masculine criteria, they are also affected by the forces we identified as powerful: gender composition and norms of interaction. As the women in our study did, elite women also seem to adopt more masculine ways of acting and interacting when they travel in predominantly male, highly conflictual, and agentic masculine settings.[50] In that sense their cases support our argument about the power of the setting and its gender signals to influence individuals' gendered behavior and the gendered nature of interaction. The institution's norms of interaction, and its social composition, partly determine whether women face barriers, participate, articulate distinctive priorities and views rooted in care for others, and ultimately, govern.

Implications for Change

What Does Not Help

As we have argued throughout, simply adding a few women to primarily male groups is not the answer. There are other, less obvious implications of our work about what does not work, and we take them up here.

It is clear that broad democratic procedures or reforms do not suffice. In Indian villages as in Vermont town meetings, women's participation remains unequal even as other measures of democracy improve. For example, villages with higher literacy rates pull up the participation rates of some disadvantaged social groups, as one study concludes: "Illiterate, landless and [Scheduled Caste or Tribe] individuals . . . are more likely to participate in higher literacy villages"—"but not women" (Besley et al. 2005a, 654). These disadvantaged groups not only attend meetings at higher rates than do other groups, but they reap the rewards of doing so—they are more likely to be the beneficiaries of public policy at villages that use these meetings than at villages that do not hold them (Besley et al. 2005a, 655).[51] By contrast with the beneficial effects of democratic meetings on illiterate, landless, and Scheduled Caste members, "it is clear that Gram Sabhas are not a forum for women in their current form" (Besley et al. 2005a, 656). That is, merely holding meetings may not suffice.

In addition, simply increasing the proportion of female local leaders does not increase the level of participation by female residents in local meetings. These already abysmally low rates of participation do move up a bit, but remain

[50] A telling testimony is Keohane's, which emphasizes her stereotypically feminine mode of decision making while in a women's enclave setting and her shift to a masculine mode only slightly distinguishable from her male counterparts when she was the chief executive of a university (2010, 153).

[51] It is not clear if the decision to hold the meeting is the causal factor or if instead there are other correlated factors that are the real cause; these results are suggestive but not definitive about the causal effect of holding the meetings (Besley et al. 2005a, 656).

extremely low. In West Bengal, for example, they move from 7% to 10% of meeting attendees when villages are randomly assigned to have female quotas for local leaders (Chattopadhyay and Duflo 2004, 982).[52] Our findings from the school boards underscore this conclusion. Having a female chair of the meeting increases the overall participation rate of women because female chairs, like all chairs, tend to talk more as they lead the meeting. In that sense, female chairs make a significant difference. But the mere presence of a female chair does not transform the participatory patterns of the other, nonchair women, and the likelihood of having a female chair changes substantially with the overall gender composition of the group. While the presence of a female chair enables the participation of the chair herself and is, no doubt, symbolically important, having a woman in a position of leadership does not, by itself, solve the problem among the other women at the meeting or render moot the need to attend to the larger gender composition and decision rules of the group.[53]

Unanimous Rule

Our results do have two clear implications for remedies. One is to raise the number of women, which we address below. The other is to adopt unanimous rule—or procedures that achieve the inclusion that this rule produces—in situations where women constitute a minority of members. However, there are some difficulties in doing so, which we address here.

One difficulty with our suggestion to adopt unanimous rule is the perception that unanimous rule is uncommon. And this perception raises the question of whether it is practical and desirable. If it were so, then wouldn't many more instances of it show up? Our response is that the dearth of unanimous rule is exaggerated, and that in any case, its dearth would not necessarily mean that it could not be fruitfully used, in some variation or other. The setting we examine is one where groups are sufficiently small to allow an exchange between individuals. While unanimous rule is obviously impractical in large democracies, it becomes much more realistic where groups are sufficiently small to allow interaction among the members. The jury system is the best-known setting for official unanimous rule. But there are other settings where unanimous rule is used, and/or where it is a good rule to use.

Unanimous rule has been used in a variety of official settings. Prominent international organizations, such as NATO, WTO, and Mercosur, make rules

[52] The danger of assuming that descriptive representation equals substantive representation is high. As Mohanty writes, "'the mere presence of women in the decision making committees without a voice can be counter-productive in the sense that it can be used to legitimize a decision which is taken by the male members'" (2002, 1, quoted in Cornwall 2003, 1330).

[53] As we explained above, simply using the general techniques of facilitation is inadequate. Majority-female groups, which are frequently found in situations where the group attempts to use a norm of inclusion, tend to respond to such norms by producing gender inequality.

for their members by unanimity rule (Maggi and Morelli 2006). The European Union and the International Standards Organization did so for a time as well, with the EU deciding by unanimity on "sensitive" issues, and by majority rule on "technical" issues (Maggi and Morelli 2006, 1138). In these settings, unanimous rule actually makes more sense than majority rule, because the organization lacks effective enforcement capacity. A recent formal model of voting by the economists Maggi and Morelli "yields unanimity as the optimal system for a wide range of parameters" when the members interact repeatedly and when they cannot be forced to go along with a majority decision (2006, 1138). Many groups hold discussions in which the group outcome is not enforceable, or perhaps enforceable on paper but in reality quite difficult or costly or sensitive to carry out. In fact, some scholars suggest that unanimity is the typical rule in a common type of situation: discussion groups populated by representatives of organizations. While majority rule is typical in committees populated by individual members of the same organization, it may be rare in many cases where members represent diverse organized interests (Scharpf 1989, 154). In addition, rational choice scholarship suggests that in single-shot exchanges where the members have no expectation of future interaction, unanimous rule is the optimal one. That rule is "likely to maximize individual liberty and to increase allocative efficiency" (Scharpf 1989).

The biggest problem with unanimous rule is that it is sensitive to the "reversion point" or "default condition" (Ostrom 1986). The default condition is what ends up happening if the group fails to reach a decision. Some members may like the default condition and thus have little incentive to reach an agreement that leaves them worse off than the default.[54] Olson (1982) argued that in many cases, unanimity protects entrenched interests, and no decision ends up benefiting them at the expense of the common good. In other words, unanimity rule is biased toward the status quo, even if that status quo is dysfunctional or disproportionately benefits certain interests.

Let us take a closer look at the objections. They can be decomposed into two parts. First, the objection to unanimous rule is that it is a bad rule because it is prone to deadlock. Second, a member or a faction of members who are willing to cause deadlock can essentially use a veto by threatening to deadlock the group, preventing it from reaching a decision, and leading the group to revert to their preference, the status quo. If these minority members prefer the status quo to the majority's preferred outcome, then the minority can get significant concessions by threatening to refuse to reach agreement. That is, unanimous rule may be better for minority women, but it may be worse for the

[54] An example from the criminal jury system in the United States may help. If I serve on a jury whose majority wishes to convict, and I wish not to convict, all I have to do is refuse to reach agreement and I get my wish—the jury is deadlocked, the trial is over, and the probability of a retrial in which the accused is found guilty is small. That default outcome is almost as good as the jury voting to acquit.

preference majority, which is subject to the hijacking power of the preference minority.

However, we have no evidence that people operate this way. First, in our experiment, we had no deadlocked groups, although one might argue that the stakes were not high enough that we can learn much about deadlock. Second, an instructive place to look is the place where unanimous rule is used widely—the American jury system. While there are infamous cases of jury deadlock, in fact, juries hardly ever deadlock. And those that do, do not show evidence of hijacking by a preference minority.

The most systematic and rigorous study of hung juries is by Hannaford-Agor and colleagues (2002). These scholars examined official records from nearly two decades, starting in the 1980s, and determined that the rate of deadlocked juries in federal cases was between 1% and 2% per year (Hannaford-Agor et al. 2002, 22). The yearly rates are extremely stable over time and consistent across circuits. Most relevant to the type of discussion we are interested in are civil cases. Rather than determining the narrow question of what the relevant facts are and what objective conclusion about truth they support, as in criminal cases, the jury's task in civil cases, particularly in applying punitive damages, is closely related to the kinds of discussions about values and political priorities that we are most interested in. In federal civil cases, the hung jury rate is only 1% to 1.5% per year.[55] One might wonder if these results are unusual because they come from the federal criminal justice system. The authors were able to obtain good data in only thirty jurisdictions for state criminal trials. They found that the rate in these state criminal trials was higher than in federal cases, but still only 6% (Hannaford-Agor et al. 2002, 25, 83). That figure is very close to the estimated 5% provided by the classic study of Kalven and Zeisel, who studied an earlier period yet came up with a nearly identical estimate (1966). Even when we look for the jurisdiction with the highest rate, we find that it peaks at 15% (Los Angeles County).[56] The "hung" jury, that is, is a rare—and in many places extremely rare—occurrence.[57]

In addition, the fear that a preference minority will hijack the group is also unfounded in the American jury system. Hannaford-Agor and colleagues found that the large majority of hung juries are evenly split at the start of deliberations, while the large majority of nonhung juries had a clear leaning toward one side or the other side (2002, 66). In addition, the rate of hung jury is much

[55] We do not wish to make too much of the contrast, because there are other important differences between civil and criminal cases, such as six rather than twelve jurors, and lower standards of evidence in civil cases (Hannaford-Agor et al. 2002, 23). However, Mendelberg (2012) finds a similarly low rate of hung juries in a large set of experimental mock juries using civil cases.

[56] In addition, data for all sixty-two counties in New York for an eighteen-month period in the late 1990s shows a statewide deadlock rate of 2.8% (Hannaford-Agor et al. 2002, 26).

[57] There is no relationship between the gender or other composition of the jury and its likelihood of deadlock (Hannaford-Agor et al. 2002, 57).

higher among evenly split or small-majority straw poll cases than among large majority cases (2002, 66). That is, when a jury has a majority preference, it almost never hangs, which means that the minority rarely hangs a jury. What hangs a jury is the lack of a majority, not the obstinate behavior of a small minority.

We see little evidence that leads us to worry that preference minorities sabotage the group or exert disproportionate influence over it as a result of unanimous rule. It may be that the ability to walk away and prevent the group from making an official decision is easier under unanimous rule, but it does not seem to pose significant problems for the group or for the majority opinion, at least in a jury system.

We did find that unanimous rule is better for minority men than for minority women. That is because when they are the gender majority, women defer to men under unanimous rule—and not because minority men aggressively dominate the conversation. At least, we found no evidence of hijacking attempts by minority men under unanimous rule, either in our analysis of interruption patterns or in the preferences that people articulated for the group decision.[58] We have been cautious throughout the book to explain that unanimous rule is not a panacea, specifically because it does not always help majority women. However, minority men are evidencing no power plays, and the disadvantages majority women experience with unanimous rule are self-imposed.[59] Finally, unanimity on the whole helps women without exacerbating male dominance because women are in the minority in so many political settings.

The last point of objection is that unanimous rule is inefficient—it takes too many evenings, to paraphrase Oscar Wilde's comment about socialism. Efficiency may well be a trade-off with unanimous rule, as the classic work of Buchanan and Tullock (1962) argued. Unanimous rule is less efficient in the general sense—it requires more work to negotiate a decision that everyone can endorse. But Buchanan and Tullock argued that this cost is worthwhile if the members have a need to protect themselves from adverse decisions. When the group could reach a decision highly adverse to members, the members may reasonably choose to use unanimous rule. A loss of efficiency thus is (narrowly) rational under these circumstances.

It is up to each group to decide whether gender equality is worth an increase in tedium. Deliberative democracy certainly prioritizes the former above the

[58] What evidence we have appears to be consistent with a pattern of women being more deferential to men (including a willingness to endorse principles other than their most preferred) in unanimous groups with many women. But of course, this could also be women deferring to other women.

[59] As we noted in earlier chapters, what is most likely happening in this condition is that women read the meaning of unanimous rule to be: do not take too much of the conversation or impose your will. Men may be likely to read it as: each person should maximize their individual agency—note that this is not "dominate the group" but rather "express yourself."

latter.[60] We would argue that any model of robust democracy should attempt to reduce social inequality in participation and representation even if it leads to longer meetings.

However, our argument is not so much about the power of, and need to adopt, a formal rule of unanimous vote. Rather, an official rule is merely one way to achieve the desired process: a conversation based on inclusion. That process is what we are fundamentally concerned with. As Scharpf puts it, aside from formal decision rules, there are "decision styles": "cognitive and normative patterns characterizing the way in which interests are defined and issues framed and resolved" (1989, 159). The styles Scharpf defines includes the following:

> *Confrontation* refers to competitive interactions in which winning, or the defeat of the other side, has become the paramount goal, and in which the battle can typically be decided only by superior prowess or force. *Problem-solving* . . . implies the pursuit of common goals and the cooperative search for solutions that are optimal for the group as a whole. (Scharpf 1989, 159)

While confrontation maximizes the individual's payoff, problem solving focuses on the collective good. We have argued that decision rules can signal the expectation that a particular decision style is appropriate or will be used by the members. Unanimous rule is likely to signal that members should all cooperate in the outcome and thus generate a cooperative conversational dynamic. A majority rule carries the implicit expectation that the exchange is about who has more votes, and thus those with more power will win.[61]

[60] Is use of rule endogenous to number women at the meeting? In other words, are groups consisting predominantly of women more likely to adopt unanimous rule, either formally or by using informal procedures that mimic it? Are women less likely to attend meetings with majority rule and secret ballot? That is, it may be that gender composition shapes the rule. If women tend to prefer consensus in order to avoid conflict, then groups composed predominantly of women may be more likely to adopt unanimous rule. Hannagan and Larimer (2010) suggest as much when they argue that female groups are more likely than male groups to converge on the median. Inconclusive evidence comes from Bryan's study of town meetings (2004). He found that there is no association between the percentage of women attending and the meeting's use of ballots (a more adversarial procedure than voice vote). The question remains open to investigation.

[61] Some procedures or practices are likely to produce the kind of inclusion that we have identified as a key beneficial process of unanimous rule. One nonobvious way that groups use procedures resembling unanimous rule is the voice vote. The rules that govern Vermont meetings allow decisions by voice vote, standing vote, or Australian (secret) ballot (Bryan 2004). By law most elections of officers must take place by ballot, but most of the decisions the town meetings make are not the election of officers, leaving considerable room to use voice vote. The decision to use a voice vote indicates the expectation that the gathering is largely in agreement and thus approximates the expectation of consensus. The decision to use a ballot may be an indicator of conflict, and its use may thus be associated with the kinds of majoritarian dynamics that go hand in hand with majority rule (Mansbridge 1983). So here we have an approximation of our rule variable—procedures that either resemble unanimous rule in signaling the expectation that broad agreement is afoot,

However, in some cases, a style can come about even without an explicit rule as a way of solving problems that would be difficult to solve otherwise. In line with this reasoning, in a number of settings majority rule is the official voting rule, but in practice the group has developed an unofficial norm that comes closer to consensus. In these cases, the decision is reached with the votes of many more than the necessary "minimum winning coalition," and even with complete unanimity.[62] As we pointed out earlier, American courts of appeals operate on a strong norm of consensus even though their official rule is majority vote (Farhang and Wawro 2004; 2010). The variety and number of settings where consensus operates implicitly under the shadow of majority rule—US congressional committees and appeals courts, within and among European countries, and some international governing bodies—suggests that our recommendation to institutionalize norms of consensus is not unrealistic or overly onerous. While in many cases the consensus comes about because of a "bargaining" decision style, it is possible that in some cases the underlying decision style is more like "problem solving." It is this problem-solving style that we are interested in, because it characterizes the kind of interaction process that we believe aids gender equality in deliberating groups.

Why Discussion Facilitators Sometimes Get It Wrong, and How to Get It Right

An objection to our basic finding that women are often disadvantaged in common settings is that deliberations are often moderated by experienced facilitators. A good moderator will pursue fairness rather than passive neutrality (Walsh 2007, 303). As Siu and Stanisevski put it, moderators are "important to umpiring the deliberative process and maintaining equal opportunity for the involvement of all participants" (2012, 92). In other words, the objection goes, the presence of discussion moderators may mitigate deep gender inequalities of the sort we have documented.[63]

---

versus procedures that signal the opposite—conflict rather than cooperation. Consistent with our notion that women do not do well under majority rule unless they are a clear majority of the participants, Bryan found that "women did significantly better on verbal participation when the Australian ballot was not in use," although this result is far from definite given that it goes away when other controls are included (Bryan 2004, 219). We take it as a possibility consistent with our findings that the use of the secret ballot indicates a meeting norm of conflict as opposed to consensus, and the use of voice vote indicates a meeting norm of cooperation and inclusion. As Mansbridge found, the less formal the voting procedure, the more the group operates with a norm of consensus (1983).

[62] See Shepsle and Weingast (1981) for US congressional committees, the "consociational democracies" studied by Lijphart (1969), and federalism in Germany (Scharpf 1989).

[63] Indeed, moderators can exercise a big influence over members' attitudes in general (Humphreys, Masters, and Sandbu 2006).

We have several responses to this view. First, our findings are meant to apply most directly to groups that tend to lack facilitators trained in inclusivity. This is the type of group that predominates in virtually all political settings. The local school board, the town or neighborhood council, the PTA committee, the legislative committee, the party caucus meeting, the church council, the jury, or even the Supreme Court—none of these deliberative bodies are facilitated by trained moderators. Even when these groups have a formal leader, the leader's role often does not extend to actively managing the discussion, and certainly not with participatory equality in mind, and the leader is typically not trained in the use of inclusive facilitation.

Second, even trained moderators and highly facilitated discussions can fall prey to gender inequality. Some doubt that there is much of a problem to preempt in the first place. As Collingwood and Reedy put it in their sanguine review of deliberative practices, "critiques of power imbalances [between groups in society] caused by deliberation have little empirical support" (2012, 234).

But mostly, the problem is a widespread sense among advocates of facilitated deliberation that their standard procedures already preempt social inequalities. While many trained moderators believe that they already prevent the deleterious effects of gender without the need to pay explicit attention to gender, there is reason to question this complacency. It is unlikely that most moderators in fact equalize discussion by gender. As Mansbridge and colleagues found, moderators are often not focused on assuring equal floor time for disadvantaged populations, and are not focused at all on gender equality; they are focused on airing various perspectives, but they may not tune in to inequalities by social identity (Mansbridge et al. 2006).

Our findings from dialogue groups second this conclusion. Our reanalysis in chapter 10 of the speech patterns of racial dialogue groups Walsh studied suggests that even when groups are moderated by a trained facilitator, and even if the groups signal their aim to be inclusive while airing differences and making a safe place for all perspectives to be heard, women will speak proportionately less than men if they are a majority. While the gender gap in the dialogue groups we reanalyzed is not large, it is not trivial either, with some majority-female groups exhibiting an inequality ratio of 80%.[64] That is, instructing participants to air all views and listen respectfully solves the problem of gender inequality only when women are not a clear majority of the group. Thus trained facilitators do not solve the problem with their standard instructions and procedures.[65]

[64]That is, the average woman's speech is 80% of the average man's speech.

[65]This discussion also applies to the findings of Jacobs and colleagues, who report that most of their deliberating respondents indicate that their moderator attempted to ensure that all opinions were heard, and that the goal of the meeting was to reach agreement (2009, 75–77). Attempting to air all views and to reach consensus are characteristic of settings where we find a disadvantage for women when they are the gender majority.

Paradoxically, it is precisely in forums that emphasize cooperation and inclusion that women may experience gender disadvantage from high numbers. Unlike many of the settings in politics, which are characterized by the conflictual dynamic captured by majority rule, dialogues, civic forums, and other settings that emphasize civic duty, inclusion of various views, or cooperation among individuals may attract large numbers of women. After all, as we discussed repeatedly, women tend to prioritize these considerations or interaction styles more than men do. If women speak less than men in majority-female groups that stress inclusion and the need for individuals to be civic-minded during discussion, as our results suggest, then gender inequality is likely a problem in many settings that emphasize this theme.

To illustrate the difference between our argument and the conventional wisdom among practitioners, consider the *Journal of Public Deliberation*. This journal is a prominent outlet for academic-minded writings on how to conduct deliberations. We searched the journal for any article that focused on the topic of social inequalities within deliberation. We found only one (Kadlec and Friedman 2007). It seems that social inequality is not a problem that the world of applied deliberation spends much effort thinking through. Moreover, in that article, the practitioner-authors write a rebuttal of Young, Sanders, and other theorists who criticize deliberation for neglecting social inequality. They argue that experienced moderators are already able to avoid the problem of social inequality in deliberation through their standard procedures. Their way of neutralizing this problem is to use the approach they have developed to deal with conflict in general. That approach consists of working with existing organizations to set up the list of participants in order to ensure adequate representation of the various perspectives, providing nonpartisan guidebooks that present multiple views on an issue, and conducting the meeting with an orientation of "confluence." Confluence means to "explore multiple perspectives by focusing together on the examination of an issue from as many vantage points as possible . . . [it] seeks ongoing input and insight from the range of possible stakeholders in a process that clarifies serious differences as well as potential common ground" (Kadlec and Friedman 2007, 13–14). Thus the approach common to practitioners of facilitated deliberation is focused on airing and encouraging the process of listening to various views by all relevant stakeholders for a given issue or conflict.[66]

[66] A concrete case of well-meaning but insufficient instructions is the "Friendly Advices on the Conduct of Quaker Meetings for Business" (Gastil 1993, 51). Quakers are exhorted to practice humility and refrain from dominance. "Let not certain Friends be known for their much speaking. Brevity is desirable in meetings for business as in meetings for worship." "If thou art tempted to speak much and often, exercise restraint . . . having spoken on a matter of business, it is well for thee to refrain from speaking again till after others have had full opportunity to voice their concerns . . . should thy concern not meet with the general approval of the meeting, in common courtesy and in true humility withdraw thy concern that the meeting may act in some measure of unity" (quoted in

The problem with this approach is that it conflates a stakeholder, or a deliberator, with a gender. Airing a variety of perspectives relevant to a given issue will not in itself air the distinctive perspectives of women if the issue does not explicitly deal with women. A group may articulate a variety of views yet still not focus on the needs that women tend to prioritize. For example, groups may articulate both liberal and conservative positions on an issue, thus appearing to satisfy the "various views" criterion, yet spend little time on the issues that women may care more about, thus failing the agenda-setting criterion of equal gender representation. When women are not stakeholders, focusing on including and airing the views of stakeholders will not solve the problem of gender inequality. Nor will that procedure lead to equal rates of speech participation and influence by men and women when women are the majority. In ignoring the gender basis of women's tendency to speak less and to avoid asserting their views, this approach allows the gender inequalities we documented to flourish. Moderators would need to be trained specifically to address issues of equal social participation and influence.

Our recommendations can thus be useful even for moderators who believe that they already know how to avoid the problems of social inequality. Unanimous rule and the elements of a general inclusive, cooperative process help women when they are a gender minority. But otherwise, it is not enough for moderators to attempt to get a variety of *views* on the table. Moderators should thus not only monitor the assembly on their "various views" radar but also through the lens of gender inequality (and by extension, other salient social inequalities). They should ask themselves whether women are speaking at rates similar to men, in terms of floor time and speaking turns. They should attend to agenda setting—whether the issues, topics, and populations that women tend to prioritize have received as much focus as those that men tend to prioritize. They should attend to the "warmth" of the group dynamic, and they can monitor the patterns of active support granted to female speakers while they are speaking—avoiding hostility is necessary but not sufficient. And they need to ask themselves whether women articulated the preferences that they walked in with as much as men did (this requires findings out individuals' private, prediscussion views).

Gastil 1993, 51). These are classic elements in the consensus process. And the typical assumption is that a group that follows these precepts will automatically protect any type of minority, because it protects any given individual. Our results give a resounding endorsement to that assumption—but only when women are few. Our findings imply that when the members are predominantly female, the female members may hold back far more than male members. Consequently, men are likely to be "much speaking," "tempted to speak much and often" and not exercise much "restraint" or "refrain" from speaking again," thereby denying the women "full opportunity to voice their concerns." Whether this inequality in fact obtains in Quaker meetings, we do not know, but our results from moderated dialogue groups point to the need to closely examine the effects of procedures on social identity minorities.

We have not tested these specific practices, but our expectation, based on the effects of unanimous rule and the processes it sets in motion, is that they can help. We summarize them as follows:

1. Do not rely on random selection, or allow self-selection, into discussion groups. A virtue of deliberative polls and similar events is that they randomly draw from the population, creating a microcosm within the room of the broader society outside. But while random selection at this phase is beneficial for adequate representation of various social groups, the process should not stop there. And using random assignment into discussion groups, or alternatively, allowing people to choose their group, means that gender composition cannot be managed. It is just such management that designers need in order to avoid the deleterious effects on gender inequality. We recommend that discussion groups be assembled with the purpose of fitting the gender composition to the procedures: majority-female groups for majority-rule and its related process of agency, and minority-female groups for a consensus process.[67]
2. Make access to the floor easy. Do not put it on a speaker to take the floor. The more assertive a person has to be to take or keep the floor, the higher the level of gender inequality that develops in a mixed-gender group. However, this procedure is not sufficient, because merely removing obstacles will likely not be powerful enough to overcome the strong patterns we documented.
3. Require each person to speak some minimum number of times. One can invite this type of participation with a ritualized going around the room to hear what each member thinks the discussion should be focusing on, or to articulate what concerns they currently have, or simply to say what's on their mind at the moment. This has the side benefit of providing a check of the agenda and focusing the meeting on the concerns that will need to be articulated at some point in the process. This "go around the room" can be instituted repeatedly in a given meeting, say, at the beginning, middle, and end.
4. Enforce turn taking. A moderator's basic role is to ensure that once a person has the floor, there are no interruptions. Negative interruptions tend to be directed by men at women under conditions of majority rule and few women, and they carry especially harsh consequences for women.
5. To ensure that no one person monopolizes the floor, the moderator can set an upper time limit on any turn, and a cumulative bound on number of turns. Men are more prone to monopolize in conditions of majority

[67] Although majority women with majority rule is the combination most likely to achieve gender equality across the various forms of representation we examined, minority women in a unanimous group have trouble moving the full group in the direction of women's preferences (see chapter 7).

rule with many women or unanimous rule with few women. This technique may alleviate this problem.

6. Invite members to indicate explicitly when they agree with a statement immediately after a relatively quiet person talks, and why they do so. We found that positive interruptions matter to women in particular. Women benefit from hearing others supporting them while they speak. However, if a moderator prohibits interruptions, this supportive function can be met in other ways. One such way is to build in support immediately after a speaking turn by a woman, especially if she has not spoken much yet, and especially early in the discussion. Of course, members should not be invited to express agreement when they do not actually agree, and establishing group rapport does not mean ignoring or discouraging authentic differences of opinion. The invitation to articulate support for a quiet speaker must not overtake the expression of legitimate disagreement. But asking whether anyone agrees with the statement is a way to invite the expression of agreement where it exists without implying that it should exist. Furthermore, specifically inviting agreement that elaborates on the prior speaker is a way to further the dialogue. Elaborated agreement functions to support women in particular without interfering with meaningful dissent and disagreement, which are crucial elements of high-quality deliberative exchange.
7. Monitor women's speaking time, number of turns, and participation early and at decisive moments in the discussion, even if the topic has nothing to do with gender on its face.
8. Assess each individual's perception of what the main issues are, what are the more urgent problems for the group to discuss, and what their preferences and attitudes are on these issues and problems. Do so *before the group assembles*. Then monitor that women are as likely as men to express their predeliberation views.

Raising the Number of Women

Given that many official settings use majority rule, the most obvious remedy is to increase the number of women in decision-making positions. However, for the same reasons that women don't speak, women also "don't run" (Lawless and Fox 2010). We reviewed the relevant literature in earlier chapters, and it is clear that women are less likely to choose to run for office despite having identical qualifications to men. Women now make up almost 60% of college graduates and receive slightly more than half of the advanced professional degrees in the United States, yet approximately one-third of that number makes it to the US House of Representatives and to American state legislatures (Crowder-Meyer 2010). The problem is a closed circle—women do not participate because they do not feel capable and valued, and the discussion does not center on issues they care about, but they do not feel capable and valued, and their issues are absent, when they do not participate. How can we break this closed circle? Can the percentage of women running be raised?

Studies of candidate recruitment suggest that there are some negative practices that decrease women's chances of running and winning, and which could potentially be reformed. An important place to examine is the local level, because people who hold higher office often begin their career at the local level. That is, the local level is a feeder for higher levels. In her large survey of local parties in the United States, Crowder-Meyer found that female party chairs are more likely than male chairs to recruit female candidates for local offices. Local parties could therefore increase the number of women in local leadership positions by appointing more female party leaders who in turn are more likely to select female candidates. In addition, the party leaders' own *social* networks tend to be composed of more women than their *party* networks; by turning more often to their own social network, male party leaders can elevate the proportion of women running and winning office (Crowder-Meyer 2010).[68]

One fact working in favor of the increase in the number of women in leadership positions is that voters are no longer much biased against them, at least not in any direct way. Unfortunately, local party leaders still tend to believe that women are less electable than men, even though that belief is largely erroneous (Crowder-Meyer 2010). Perhaps some headway could be made by informing and educating party leaders about women's electability.

Finally, male party chairs recruit more female candidates when they look outside the narrow network of party officeholders, which is predominantly male, and turn to networks with high proportions of women. These networks are found in organizations that tend to be composed of many women, such as schools, teachers' unions, parents' organizations, and women's groups such as women's business or professional associations. Here again we see the potential value of women's enclaves, or groups consisting of heavy majorities of women and designed to serve the distinctive concerns of women. By implication, local party leaders can increase the number of women in local office by seeking out recruitment pools composed of many women, thereby significantly filling this crucial first section of the pipeline to higher office. Perhaps most practical would be to launch an effort to inform groups in which women predominate of their potential role in supporting and encouraging women to get involved in politics. In that way, women's groups may help foster in potential candidates the motivation to seek leadership positions, not only by running for elected office, but also in the many civic spaces where people come together for collective decision making.

In the near term, women are unlikely to occupy far more than the current 20% or so of seats in official decision-making bodies. Still, the incremental rise of women from 20% to 40% is not impractical over the next couple of decades. And our experimental findings indicate that the gender gap in participation

[68] Similarly, women's scarcity on corporate boards may be caused in part by reliance on predominantly male networks from which members are recruited (Pande and Ford 2011, 8).

narrows as the number of women moves above the 20% threshold. Although it often takes a supermajority of women to fully erase gender disparities, the biggest disadvantages can be avoided when women account for more than one-fifth of the group. Should women achieve that rise, their substantive and symbolic representation is likely to improve, even if moderately.

Additional Remedies

If more women obtain political leadership positions, they will change the balance of voices heard at meetings. We saw in our school boards chapter that when a woman chairs a board, that woman plays a meaningful role in the meeting and changes the overall balances of voices heard. Although this benefit does not extend to the participatory behavior of the other women present, women can still help to close the overall gender gap by assuming leadership positions when women are scarce. This will be difficult to achieve, to be sure. As we saw in chapter 3, even in settings where women predominate or that are associated with feminine qualities, such as teaching or clerical work, men are more likely than women to obtain leadership positions. And in our school boards data, we saw that the likelihood of a female chair is closely tied to the overall gender composition of the board. So in a world in which women are still underrepresented on many decision-making bodies, the chances that a woman will obtain a position in charge of a discussion are lower than the chances of a man doing so. Still, lower chances do not mean impossible chances.

In addition, as we saw in earlier chapters, women's engagement rises with the salience of women's issues or viable female candidates. This suggests two remedies. One is to increase the salience of powerful female role models. We saw in the earlier chapters that no simple role model theory can explain the pattern of women's participation. But women who run for visible office and are lauded as such do prompt women's engagement (Burns, Schlozman, and Verba 2001; Hansen 1997). Similarly, as we saw in chapter 2, women who recalled having politically interested mothers were more engaged. Mothers may be able to make a difference to their daughters' engagement and leadership activities.

A second possible remedy is to bring women's interests and issues into the agenda. We saw that women are more engaged and knowledgeable on issues of special concern to them. Perhaps changing the issue agenda will engage women in discussion.

A third way is to integrate enclaves into the process. Enclaves could be assembled before the mixed-gender interaction begins and operate in parallel with mixed-gender deliberations (Young 2004, 50, cited in Siu and Stanisevski 2012, 96; Sunstein 2002b; Dryzek 2000; Mansbridge 1996). Scholars of gender and development have been advocating such remedies for some time. For example, Cornwall identifies enclaves as the single most important measure in raising women's level of influence within deliberative settings: "The presence of a gender-progressive nongovernment organization (NGO) or women's organization is a major factor: membership makes women more self-confident, assertive and vocal in mixed gatherings" (2003, 1330, citing Agarwal 1997). Enclaves are not only a remedy for women in developing areas where they tend to be heavily marginalized and subordinated; these can be useful in the United States and other countries where women enjoy a far higher status (Cornwall 2003, 1330; Karpowitz et al. 2009). Enclaves could also be built into the broader setting and not only into the deliberating situation. Women's groups where women gather regularly to hold conversations where participation is active and influence is more equally distributed could be a partial solution as part of the general life of the institution where deliberation occurs. Our results suggest that enclaves can help, though they rarely make a dramatic difference beyond mixed-gender groups where women predominate.

Of course, enclaves could carry their own downside and potential pitfalls. First, there is the risk of essentializing gender by marking it as socially salient. Second, there is the potential for heightened tension or conflict between the sexes as a result from men's perception that women are developing in opposition to men. Third, women's (and girls') interactions with each other are not all supportive and cooperative. We have emphasized the norm that develops when females interact with each other, and our evidence and others' does suggest that his norm leans toward mutual support. However, that norm can also coexist with more subtle ways in which females can exercise power over other women. The argument is that because women are socialized to be nice to others, and as a result of a norm or gendered subculture of avoiding overt assertion among girls, when women do feel aggression toward others, they hide it in the guise of niceness.[69] Although there is not much systematic study of this dark side of women's relationships, we do want to flag its possibility as a factor to look for in the future. In the final analysis, however, we surmise that these potential problems can be overcome. Certainly, the benefit is worth the attempt to implement enclave-like spaces.

It is also important to carve out some remedies that individuals can undertake to help themselves. Our most important finding regarding the individual-level mechanism behind women's relative silence is that confidence matters. We found that women low in confidence tend to fare worst in the most common conditions of deliberation.[70] By implication, women can help themselves by joining programs and undertaking activities that build up their sense of confidence. The intuitive place to start is with simple measures that can increase competence in public speaking and in domain-relevant knowledge. For example, women tend to have less knowledge of politics; this can easily be remedied by occasional

[69]See Simmons 2002. The aggression then comes out in ways that are no less damaging than overt expressions, but difficult to detect and to combat. The point is not to disagree with our claim that women's interactions tend to be more mutually supportive; in fact, this alternative view endorses that claim. The point is that the norm of niceness does not mean that women are not pursuing aggression in other, more insidious ways.

[70]Also, women who received positive signals about their aptitude and had high levels of confidence actually participated at far above the rate of equality.

news consumption. Some television shows provide the kinds of entertainment that women tend to enjoy and also some informational content as a by-product (Baum and Jamison 2006). Women can raise their knowledge without putting unrealistic efforts into becoming a supercitizen. In addition, women can join organizations that empower women, by intent or as a side benefit. As we saw in chapter 3, such organizations are associated with higher meeting-relevant skills for women, especially all-female groups. Here again, enclaves can be a benefit.

However, while it can be empowering to women to know that they can affect their own circumstances, we do not wish to lose sight of the more important implication of our study: the conditions matter. As Wolbrecht concludes, "the persistent lesser influence and power of women thus draws our attention not to deficiencies of women as political actors but to the constraints of the social, economic, and political structures in which they act" (Wolbrecht 2008, 5).

Men can also do a great deal to hinder or help gender equality. We saw in the analysis of interruptions that men's behavior is the primary moving part in the dynamics of interaction. By elevating their positive reinforcement of women and decreasing their negativity, men could make a significant difference in creating egalitarian conditions. Even a few positive interjections can make a difference to women's experience. The remedy does not require an onerous change of habit.

Taking Stock of Deliberative Democracy

Long ago, Tocqueville placed civic and town meetings at the heart of American democracy. An important element of "the right of association," he wrote, "is the power of meeting" ([1835] 2006, chapter 12). By thinking about deliberation in terms of equality, we can come to see it not only as an avenue for rationality but also as an avenue for justice. Many scholars and advocates of deliberation are interested in it because they believe that deliberation can reveal correct solutions to collective problems. Put differently, they believe that deliberators should, and do, seek the truth value of language. They ask questions such as: Is the speech accurate? Is it logical? Is it well informed? Does it lead the group toward the optimal decision for its needs? These are worthy questions, but they are not the only ones we can and should pose. The social uses and meanings of language matter too. We asked not whether speech is informed, accurate, and logical, but whether it excludes or includes, whether it creates social inequality or equality, whether it privileges one gendered mode of interaction and perspective or reflects them both.

When we began our project, there was almost no large-scale study of what talk is actually like in deliberating groups. In his review of the scholarship, Ryfe summed up the situation as follows:

> Deliberation . . . can lead to decisions that not only conflict with expert opinion but also conflict with subjects' own opinions. . . . Why should this be the case? We simply

do not know. And we won't know, I think, until we learn more about how people actually deliberate with one another. Surprisingly, this issue remains something of a void in the literature. (Ryfe 2005, 54)[71]

We have set out to fill this gap, and in the process, understand why deliberation can fall so short of its ideal of equality.

In addition to a gap in our understanding of the content of deliberation, we have attempted to fill a gap in our understanding of how group-level factors operate on deliberation. Empirical scholarship on deliberation has tended to view deliberation as a collection of individuals rather than as a process shaped importantly by group characteristics such as composition. For example, Luskin, Fishkin, and Jowell argue that the composition of groups does not matter in any significant way (2002; see also Fishkin et al. 2010). And when scholars do look for the effects of group-level factors, they do not always find them. For example, Price, Cappella, and Nir (2002) find no meaningful effects on individuals randomly assigned to one of sixty heterogeneous or homogenous groups. What the findings in our book suggest is that the composition of the group does matter, but in ways that depend on other factors. The key is to understand what those factors are and how they work jointly with the characteristics of the group.

What then are we to make of exhortations to deliberate? Should a society attempt to institute and promote deliberation as a means to enhance democracy? On the one hand, as we saw in chapter 1, deliberation holds out the hope of vital, real democracy—true self-rule by the people, the transformation of narrow interests, the enlargement of civic capacity, the enlightenment of the individual, and equality of voice. On the other hand, these lofty and admittedly idealized goals are obviously impossible to achieve in the real and messy world of politics (Thompson 2008). Our findings show that in conditions resembling many of those in the real world, women do poorly in important respects. It would be plausible to conclude that the public meeting "accentuates rather than redress[es] the disadvantage of those with least power in society" (Mansbridge 1983, 277). As Mansbridge concludes, "participation in face-to-face democracies is not automatically therapeutic: it can make participants feel humiliated, frightened, and even more powerless than before" (Mansbridge 1983, 71).

Accordingly, some scholars categorically reject deliberative democracy. Hibbing and Theiss-Morse put it this way:

> Deliberation will not work in the real world of politics, where people are different, and where tough, zero-sum decisions must be made. Democracy in authentic, diverse settings is not enhanced by town-meeting-style participation; it is probably diminished. Given the predilections of the people, real deliberation is quite likely to

[71] Similarly, Laura Black recently wrote that "very few studies provide detailed descriptions and depictions of the actual communication that occurs in deliberative civic engagement events . . . studies could explore some of deliberation's social dimensions such as . . . respect, to see how these are communicated and what happens when they do no occur (2012, 77).

> make them hopping mad or encourage them to suffer silently because of a reluctance to voice their own opinions in the discussion." (Hibbing and Theiss-Morse 2002, 207)

Hibbing and Theiss-Morse conclude that in place of meetings, democracy should rest on representative assemblies: "representative democracy at least affords representation to those who shy away from the give and take of politics" (Hibbing and Theiss-Morse 2002, 207). For this reason, while they certainly have their differences, Mansbridge and Hibbing and Theiss-Morse advocate a significant role for representative institutions.

Our position is different. Our remedy to the ills of deliberation in practice is to use the power of institutions to address those ills. We have specifically argued that institutions can be used to address discursive inequality. Representative democracy does not cure the ills of deliberative democracy, because representatives themselves must deliberate. One cannot have a representative assembly without assembly. As Hibbing and Theiss-Morse recognize, "deliberation is going to have to be a part of any realistic democratic polity" (2002, 208). So we are back to the same problem we started with. If democracy entails interaction among people, whether among citizens or representatives, then the question is how to design it so that it minimizes social inequality.

One problem that deliberation does not in fact face is conflict avoidance. We found that people who tend to avoid political conflict are no more quiescent than people who seek it. This is not as surprising as it might seem. Political scientist Diana Mutz found that people seek to avoid political conflict only when it comes to the people they know and care about (2006). Many of the settings we are talking about are not restricted to interactions among intimates. Similarly, while Hibbing and Theiss-Morse identify conflict avoidance as a mainspring of Americans' willful apathy and withdrawal from politics, at the end of the day, they move away from this claim, concluding that "most people are actually drawn to conflict" and "people crave picking a side and being part of a group with a shared concern" (2002, 224). The problem is not that people hate conflict, but that they view their political system as biased or ineffective, and they do not understand the relevance of most issues and the need to attend to the details of policy, or the legitimacy of political perspectives different from their own. But if that is the problem, then the remedy is to design institutions that can teach people and motivate them to think about policy alternatives and the legitimacy of diverse points of view. Deliberative settings could become part of this solution. But again, the question is how to design these settings.

And that is our main contribution to the debate: deliberation can work extremely well—in fact, by some measures gender inequality can be completely erased—under the right institutional conditions. Our findings vindicate the most optimistic advocates of deliberation—but the conditions must be right, and creating them takes thought, and effort.

Appendixes

Chapter 4 Appendixes

Appendix A: Methodological Issues in Existing Studies

We lack conclusive results about the effects of gender composition in part because of methodological problems. Here we discuss each problem in turn.

First, many studies that examine small group situations do not disentangle gender composition from individual gender. This can be seen in the large literature on jury decision making (Devine et al. 2001), which rarely examines gender differences apart from gender composition effects.[1] While lawyers and consultants may believe that demographic characteristics strongly shape jury preferences, little systematic evidence exists to support this belief. A comprehensive assessment of the jury literature suggests, first, that "few if any juror characteristics are good predictors of juror verdict preferences," and that those few tend to have "weak and inconsistent effects" (Devine et al. 2001, 673). The recent review by Cornwell and Hans seconds this conclusion.[2] Only a handful of studies examine the effects of gender composition specifically on men and women (for example, Golding et al. 2007, on which we elaborate in chapter 7).[3]

Second, many studies examine only a few groups (Devine et al. 2001). This is a common problem in empirical studies of deliberation. Not only does the small

[1]For example, the oft-cited study of jurors by Mills and Bohannon studied individual, not group, characteristics (1980). A classic study of jury decision making found that men initiated 40% more comments than women but did not separate gender differences from gender composition (Hastie, Penrod, and Pennington 1983, 141–42; see also Kirchmeyer 1993; Diamond, Rose, and Murphy 2006). Similarly, we know that women are still less likely to be elected jury foreperson, but not if this varies with gender composition (Cornwell and Hans 2011, 671). A much-cited study, reporting that men composed about 40% of jurors but were chosen as the jury foreperson 90% of the time, rests on eighteen juries (Ellsworth 1989, 213, cited in Sanders 1997). See Hickerson and Gastil (2008) for a study that does attempt to estimate and examine the effect of the gender composition of juries.

[2]Cornwell and Hans write that "previous research on juries has been limited in its ability to contextualize jurors' participation because of a lack of variation in, or information about, case- and jury-level characteristics" (2011, 672).

[3]Of particular note is the dearth of studies investigating the impact of group composition in a controlled setting rather than in field studies where jurors are interviewed after the fact, sometimes much later, and in which the number of juries is often small (Devine et al. 2001, 673; as an example, see Cornwell and Hans 2011; Hickerson and Gastil 2008).

number of groups hamper the study of gender composition, it also prevents the study of any feature of the group, including its discussion—presumably the very process of interest in our understanding of deliberation (Myers and Mendelberg 2013).[4] Studies set in natural settings, such as legislatures, often include too few groups. For example, Kathlene's pioneering study of gendered hearings uses twelve hearings (1994), and Mattei analyzed one committee (1998).

Third, even if a study includes many groups, it may not have much variation in its gender composition. For example, the emerging literature on judicial panel effects typically includes only a few groups that are not all male (for example, 84% of the panels in Farhang and Wawro's 2010 study are all male).

Fourth, studies of officeholders examine only a few of the possible effects of gender composition, missing the chance to understand how the process of deliberation ties to outcomes. Some studies of officeholders focus on interruption patterns in hearings but not on other effects (Kathlene 1994; Mattei 1998). Many other studies examine the views of legislators (for example, Reingold 1992). Still others examine bill sponsorship, amendments, votes, and policy outcomes but not the process of communication that may shape these actions (Swers 2002). While no one study can do everything, what is needed is a holistic approach in which male and female individuals are situated within groups, and the characteristics of both the individuals and the groups are analyzed. We trace the process of interaction, showing how all this leads to various group decisions and affects individuals afterward. We need to understand the outcomes of group-level decisions and the dynamics that helped to shape those outcomes.

Fifth, existing studies are missing some types of analysis altogether. No study has rigorously examined the issue agenda as it takes shape during actual discussion. No study has examined systematically the effects of gender composition on speech participation or communication dynamics. We need to know more about the varied forms of women's participation and representation, and how gender composition and decision rule affect each in turn.[5]

Sixth, even when studies have enough groups and enough variance in gender composition, they suffer an additional problem: the gender composition in the group may be correlated with other factors. The findings on the effects of enclaves, reported in chapter 3, illustrate the problem. Groups with many

[4]This comes from the general focus on the individual and the indifference to the group level of analysis. In fact, in some studies of deliberation, we do not know how many groups are included because the unit of analysis is the individual and the number of groups deemed irrelevant (see Karpowitz and Mendelberg 2011; and Myers and Mendelberg 2013, for a review).

[5]Again, Kathlene's study illustrates the problem. This study is a wonderful, pathbreaking investigation of detailed speech acts in the Colorado state legislature. But Kathlene (1994) relies on twelve hearings that vary simultaneously in gender composition, female chair holding, whether the bill deals with women's issues, whether the bill's sponsor is female, and so on. In other words, while there are bits and pieces of analysis, some executed brilliantly with a small number of cases, some big pieces are missing, and so far we lack a complete picture of the different types of effects.

women are likely to be groups assembled to address women's issues. That is, groups with more women may have set women's topics to begin with, and this could be why they attracted more women. Our question is whether numbers lead to issues; we cannot answer this with groups whose issues lead to numbers.

There are a number of other ways that gender composition could be confounded by other causal variables. Some aspect of the locale may act as a confounding factor. For example, women's level of engagement in politics may shape the presence of women in decision-making groups and women's level of voice and influence in those groups. The activities of women's organizations and women's movements may increase the number of women present and the participation and representation by those women. Nonpolitical traits of the town or country may also confound the story of gender composition.[6] Without random assignment of individuals to gender composition, we do not know if the effects we observe for gender composition are actually due to town size, for example.[7] Similarly, groups with more women may be smaller. Smaller groups may be more inclusive of their members. Or perhaps people feel obligated to speak more when there are few other members.[8]

A case that has garnered considerable scholarly attention illustrates the value of using controlled experiments to make sure that factors that coexist with our treatment variable do not interfere with its effects. As we discussed in chapter 1, the Indian constitution empowers villages to make official, binding decisions governing themselves. Some view these remarkable meetings as "among the most widespread deliberative spaces in regular and routine use within a system of government in human History" (Ban and Rao 2008a, 20). It is no wonder that several studies have attempted to study whether these meetings succeed in producing more democratic decisions, including more egalitarian ones. And

[6]Or, take for example the finding that the more women, the less corruption. We do not know if the women decreased corruption or if less corrupt places are more likely to draw women into politics. A similar criticism applies to the effect of gender composition in countries or their subunits. Chattopadhyay and Duflo put it this way (2004, 1410): "For example, Dollar, Fisman, and Gatti (2001) find a negative correlation between representation of women in parliaments and corruption. Does this mean women are less corrupt, or that countries that are less corrupt are also more likely to elect women to parliament? Besley and Case (2000) show that worker compensation and child support enforcement policies are more likely to be introduced in states where there are more women in parliament, after controlling for state and year fixed effects. But they explicitly recognize that the fraction of women in parliament may be a proxy for women's involvement in politics, more generally."

[7]The number of women on town councils grows steadily with the city's size, from an average of one out of five or six for cities under 25,000, to an average of five out of fourteen in cities over one million (Nelson 2002, 2–3).

[8]Bryan found in Vermont that the smaller the meeting size, the higher was women's share of speech participation; while the size of this effect is small, it nevertheless raises the more general worry about a conflation of size and gender composition. Jury studies find that size can matter in various complex ways (Cornwell and Hans 2011). If gender composition correlates with group size, we cannot tell whether it is size or gender composition that drives the effects we see.

indeed, some studies find that in Indian villages constitutionally required to set aside one-third of village council seats for women, the decisions tend to be more aligned with the preferences of women and more oriented toward the common good of the village. In these villages, female leaders pursue policies more aligned with female preferences and more oriented to the common good (Chattopadhyay and Duflo 2004). But other studies find no such effect (see Ban and Rao 2008b for a summary). That is, quotas for women sometimes produce less democratic processes and outcomes. In some quota villages, women's preferences are less likely to be mentioned in the discussion than in nonquota villages (Ban and Rao 2008b, 19).

Why do these studies reach conflicting conclusions? It is difficult to know for sure, but the contradiction in these findings may be due to the inability to fully account for other features of the deliberation and its institutional context. For example, the presence of higher-level officials at the meeting may be an important moderator variable that either allows or inhibits women's distinctive voice (Ban and Rao 2009). When high officials are present at the meeting and intervene to ensure women's participation in the discussion, women's presence can shape the discussion. If other factors interact with women's descriptive representation—with the percentage of women present—then a research design has to assess these factors accurately. That is exactly why a controlled experiment such as ours is needed. Using such a design can help resolve the mystery of contradictory findings from observational studies that cannot allow investigators the control they need.

Groups with more women may draw a particular type of man, and a particular type of woman, and these types may cause the effects we attribute to gender composition. Perhaps men who are more egalitarian are repelled by settings where men predominate, especially if those settings originate in a history of male chauvinism. Perhaps feminist women are more likely to reject these settings as well. That would create a spurious correlation between gender composition and gender egalitarian conversations. The effects we might attribute to gender composition may actually be produced by the fact that the individuals have more egalitarian views about gender. This association could work in the opposite direction instead. That is, perhaps women who feel more anxious than most women do when in mixed gender groups opt out of those mixed gender groups and into safer environments composed predominantly of women. Women who join groups with few women, conversely, may be more confident than most women. That might mute the effects of increasing numbers of women on levels of women's self-assertion during discussion. That is, there are many ways in which gender composition may be correlated with factors that cause or detract from more gender egalitarian interactions and outcomes in groups.

Seventh, the findings for gender composition reported in chapter 3 rest on respondents' reports of the gender composition of their organizations and of their own behavior. However, people are notoriously bad at canvassing their memory and providing accurate reports of their experiences or behaviors (Krosnick 1999).[9] Not everyone answers these questions, and people who do reply may be different from those who do not.[10]

Two recent studies illustrate the challenge of self-reporting for even the highest quality observational work. For example, Gastil et al. 2010 found that "the frequency with which jurors speak up does *not*, in turn, reinforce their post-service sense of political efficacy" (Gastil et al. 2010, 144–45). This conclusion is not consistent with our results and may be due to different methodological choices. Gastil and colleagues studied naturally occurring juries, and their high level of external validity thus comes at the price of lower control over measurement. That study thus was not able to measure speaking directly, as our study did, but rather had to measure speaking frequency by the participants' own self-report. Similarly, Jacobs, Cook, and Delli Carpini (2009) relied on self-reports removed in time from the actual discussion to assess the experiences of deliberators. The reported features and contents of the deliberation may be colored by the positive or negative attitudes of the deliberators toward some aspect of the experience.[11] Thus our choice of research design provides an advantage in the ability to use clean, controlled measures of key aspects of the discussion and its structures, and this choice has important consequences for our ability to draw valid conclusions.[12]

[9]The respondent's thought process may be something along these lines: "Did I express an opinion at a meeting? Or did I speak but not actually offer an opinion? I'm really not sure." This type of response may be hard to provide with accuracy. Given the demands that a long survey interview imposes on the person's mental resources, the typical respondent may not be up to doing the mental work needed to sift through their memories (Schwarz and Oyserman 2001). In addition, the questions depend on respondents' own assessment of what is "mixed-gender" or "mostly" or "few" members of the same sex. It is possible that some people who belong to 60% female organizations call that "mixed gender" while others call that "mostly" female, or that many members of 25% female groups think of those as mixed gender rather than as "few" women, for example. And, perhaps women who feel included and active in their organization are more likely to categorize or call it "mostly" female, while those who feel less included or active are likely to call it "mixed gender." Thus we can see how random measurement error, or systematic error, could creep into the key variable of gender composition.

[10]For example, in a study of gender differences in jury influence, Mills and Bohannon found that women were less likely to report that they were chosen as foreperson and that they influenced the jury; however, these results could instead be produced by the possibility that the more influential women were simply less likely to reply to the survey. These difficulties with a survey based on self-report, and those we detail in chapter 4, apply to analysis of descriptive representation more generally, not just to the enclave hypothesis.

[11]For example, their finding that respondents reported satisfaction with moderators' elicitation of various opinions may be influenced by the fact that over 90% of respondents agreed with the group's outcome (Jacobs, Cook, and Delli Carpini 2009, 77 and 78, respectively). Other surveys of deliberative experiences share the problems of self-reports (Ryfe 2002).

[12]In addition, that study did not measure, and thus cannot account for, the structure of deliberation, including the group's gender composition, so that their finding of no differences by the person's gender (or race, class, or other status characteristics) does not tell us whether gender matters under the conditions that we find it does (Gastil et al. 2010, 158–59).

All this trouble with observational studies of gender and gender composition, and we have not even begun to spell out the problems with studies of decision rule.

First, there is the problem of endogeneity. For example, Mansbridge suggests that two types of groups tend to choose unanimous rule. One type is the group with a severe, long-term, and core conflict. The other type is its opposite—groups such as Quakers or small New England towns where people have strong social ties expect to interact frequently over a long future horizon and assume that everyone shares similar long-term core interests (1983). If so, then the implication is that unanimous rule is not random. It is a purposeful, deliberate choice, one meant to address particular conditions and needs. Here again we face the dangers of endogenous predictors. Is the group using a unanimous rule because it is already inclined to want to include everyone, including women? Are groups with many women more oriented to inclusion and thus likely to use unanimous decision rules? We do not know, and so we cannot be sure that we are capturing the effects of decision rule rather than the effects of gender composition, or the effects of preexisting common interests, or the effects of strong social ties in the community (if not in the group itself). Put differently, if we want to know the effects of decision rule, we need to separate it out from the many factors that could be driving it and also driving the outcomes we examine.

As with studies of gender composition, the dependent variables have problems. And so do the independent variables. Game-theoretic studies of decision rule, now numerous, are highly stylized, involving such decisions as whether the group has been assigned a jar with more red than more blue balls. It is quite a leap to infer from the tendency of players who drew blue balls to choose the red jar when operating under unanimous rule that jurors are more likely to convict the innocent in a criminal trial. Similarly, these studies attempt to study deliberation through highly stylized simulations, such as taking a straw poll electronically (for a critique see Myers 2011).[13] These problematic features can be seen in prominent studies in political science, such as Guarnaschelli, McKelvey, and Palfrey (2000).[14] There are often good reasons for this choice.

[13]In game-theory experiments, where much work has been done on decision rules, researchers typically recruit a small number of subjects and then cycle them through various groups. For example, Guarnascheli, McKelvey, and Palfrey (2000) use forty-eight subjects. This heavy use of a within-subjects design can be quite problematic (Morton and Williams 2011). For example the effect of any given condition may depend on prior exposure to other conditions and might have no effect without such exposure. Randomly varying the order of treatments cannot tell us if the order has an effect without a sufficiently large number of cases (Morton and Williams 2011).

[14]Game-theoretic experiments yield mixed results on the question of whether people behave strategically during deliberation. Contrast, for example, Guarnaschelli, McKelvey, and Palfrey (2000) against Landa, Dickson, and Hafer (2008). The latter conclude that many subjects "overspeak" when their incentives dictate silence: "While our subjects do respond to strategic incentives, they nonetheless come closer to the normative ideal of a free 'exchange of arguments' than

For example, Landa, Dickson, and Hafer (2008) set up a stylized deliberation consisting of sending or receiving numbers. This allowed the investigators to measure precisely the extent to which subjects conform to, or deviate from, a well-defined standard of Bayesian rationality. That standard yields specific predictions about the information that rational people should be sending to others and using in their decisions. This trade-off is defensible, but we choose to make it in the other direction and study more naturalistic forms of speech and interaction. We accept the sacrifice that this entails in the ability to measure deviations from rational individual behavior, since that is not our main research question.

The other way in which variables have been limited in the study of decision rule is that the outcome is almost always a decision in a criminal case (Diamond, Rose, and Murphy 2006, 209). Reaching a binary choice on guilt or innocence is far different from reaching a choice in a scale involving, say, money (Schkade, Sunstein, and Kahneman 2000). Juror's demographic characteristics, such as race but also gender, may have particular and narrow effects when the decision is focused on the fate of one person, and that person's gender or race is salient in the facts of the case. For example, a recent review of gender and juries concludes that from the pioneering studies by Hastie, Penrod, and Pennington (1983) and Davis et al. (1977) and onward, the "'safest generalization' about gender differences is that women are more likely than men to find the defendant guilty in a rape case" (Fowler 2005, 21). In addition, psychology studies tend to report robust effects of unanimous rule on length of discussion, but little else (Diamond, Rose, and Murphy 2006; Hans 2001).

In general, rare is the study that inquires about the effects of rule on equal participation or representation of social groups. No study has looked at the interaction of gender composition and decision rule. So for example, when Cornwell and Hans (2011) report finding no interaction between gender composition and individual gender in self-reported juror participation, we do not know if this is because they studied groups using unanimous rule and whether they would find differently among groups using majority rule.

Finally, both rule and composition studies are hampered by their lack of access to actual discussion. As noted above, game-theory studies tend to use a pale shadow of discussion, in the form of a straw poll. Many other studies rely on surveys of jurors, as the comprehensive review by Devine et al. noted (2001; see, for example, Mills and Bohannon 1980; Cornwell and Hans 2011). We have reason to wonder about the validity of juror's self-reports about discussion, such as their level of participation in it. Self-reported level of participation in

---

Bayesian-rational predictions would expect. It is particularly striking that this should be the case even in a highly stylized experimental environment, in which individuals' outcome-based interests can be quite clearly discerned."

jury discussion is likely to be biased in any number of ways. People are notoriously bad at accurately remembering and reporting their past behavior. A juror may not be noticing how much they are participating and thus be unable to accurately report that level later. This problem is exacerbated by question and response wordings that ask the respondent to report behavior in general terms. A question such as "how much did you participate in the jury deliberation" is not specific enough to capture the quantity of interest, which is the person's percentage of the group's floor time or of its total speaking turns. This question wording problem cumulates when using vague response options such as "a great deal" (Cornwell and Hans 2011). These wordings are likely to be plagued by a great deal of measurement error that compounds the problem of faulty recollection. Along with faulty memory, these self-reports are likely to be biased upward by social desirability. The good citizen is supposed to participate in deliberation, so that those who participate at relatively low levels are unlikely to report doing so. Furthermore, people who participate less but who do not wish to acknowledge doing so may create nonrandom measurement error in the variable. If women are more dutiful than men, they may be more prone to mis-remember and report inflated participation out of a sense that they should be participating. Finally, there is likely to be bias from selective nonresponse, or from different interpretations of the meaning of "a great deal" or of "participate." What seems to be "a great deal" of participation to one juror might be "only a little" to another and vice versa.

A seemingly appealing way to remedy the problems with observational studies of composition is to use natural experiments. In this design, the researcher notices that actual political actors have randomly introduced an increase in gender composition to some decision-making groups and not others. Or better yet, increased gender composition is imposed on one set of groups but not another. We measure the difference from before to afterward, and we contrast that prepost difference with the absence of difference among the untreated groups. If the process of assigning groups is random, then the researcher can conclude that any differences between the treated and untreated groups can only be due to the differences in gender composition. While this method has important strengths, it is often not as good as random assignment under controlled conditions. That is because in the real world, naturally occurring random assignment is often not really random (Sekhon and Titiunik 2012).[15] Sekhon and Titiunik make a point of highlighting this problem in particular in the case of gender composition. A number of studies have attempted to use the seemingly random application of gender quotas for elected

[15] Field experiments improve on natural experiments but suffer the problems of noncompliance, contamination of one condition by the effects of another, subjects dropping out before the study is done, and more. While they have important advantages over controlled studies, they are not without big trade-offs. Ideally a research program will use some controlled experiments together with an element of natural or field experimentation.

representatives to locales in India, for just the type of causal inference we have described. However, as Sekhon and Titiunik show, the real world is sufficiently messy as to call into serious question the ability to substitute natural experiments for random assignment to gender compositions under controlled conditions.

No study is likely to remedy every methodological problem, and some of the studies we have cited here are among the best, most pathbreaking works in their respective disciplines. Nonetheless, when it comes to the specific questions that animate our research—questions about the effects of group-level factors on what happens during deliberation, what outcomes emerge from group decision making, and how participants feel about it afterward—a controlled experiment with a sufficiently large number of groups offers a uniquely helpful way to find answers.

Appendix B: Question Wording for Key Pre- and Postdeliberation Survey Measures

RANKING OF PRINCIPLES OF DISTRIBUTION:

Pre- and Postdeliberation Preferences for Distributive Principle

—"Rank the following 4 principles of distributive justice according to your personal preference."

Response Options: Maximize the Floor Income, No Taxes or Redistribution, Set a Floor Constraint, Set a Range Constraint

Pre- and Postdeliberation Certainty about Ranking

—"How do you feel about your ranking of these principles?"

Response Options: Very Unsure, Unsure, No Opinion, Sure, Very Sure

Predeliberation Measures

EGALITARIANISM INDEX:

—"If people work hard they almost always get what they want." (Reverse coded)
—"Even if people try hard, they often cannot reach their goals."
—"This country would be better off if we worried less about how equal people are." (Reverse coded)
—"Relative equality of wealth is a good thing."
—"Any person who is willing to work hard has a good chance at succeeding." (Reverse coded)
—"It is not really that big of a problem if some people have more of a chance in life than others." (Reverse coded)

—"If people were treated more equally in this country we would have fewer problems."
—"Our society should do whatever is necessary to make sure that everyone has an equal opportunity to succeed."
—"Most people who fail should not blame the system; they have only themselves to blame." (Reverse coded)

Response Options: Strongly Agree, Agree, Neutral, Disagree, Strongly Disagree

CONFIDENCE INDEX:

—"I feel that I have a pretty good understanding of the important political issues facing us today."
—"Sometimes politics and the government seem so complicated that a person like me can't really understand what is going on." (Reverse coded)
—"I am capable of participating effectively in group discussions about important political issues."
—"I am frequently frustrated by my inability to express my opinions to others." (Reverse coded)
—"In general, I do better on most things than most people."
—"I am confident in my abilities, even when confronting tasks I haven't done before."

Response Options: Strongly Agree, Agree, Neutral, Disagree, Strongly Disagree

COMFORT WITH DISAGREEMENT:

—"I feel uneasy and uncomfortable when people argue about politics."

Response Options: Strongly Agree, Agree, Neutral, Disagree, Strongly Disagree

EMPATHY:

—"I easily put myself in the shoes of those who are in discomfort."

Response Options: Strongly Agree, Agree, Neutral, Disagree, Strongly Disagree

Postdeliberation Measures

INFLUENCE:

—"Who was the most influential member of your group during the group discussion? (Indicate using the letter on the nameplate in front of the group members.)"

Response Options: A, B, C, D, E

SATISFACTION WITH DISCUSSION:

—"How satisfied or dissatisfied are you with your group discussion?"

Response Options: Very Dissatisfied, Somewhat Dissatisfied, Neither, Somewhat Satisfied, Very Satisfied

MY VOICE WAS HEARD:

—"I feel like my voice was heard during the group discussion."

Response Options: Strongly Agree, Agree, Neutral, Disagree, Strongly Disagree

MY OPINIONS WERE INFLUENTIAL:

—"My opinions were influential in shaping the group discussion and final decision."

Response Options: Strongly Agree, Agree, Neutral, Disagree, Strongly Disagree

DIFFICULTY OF GROUP WORK:

—"Group work made everything slower and harder to accomplish."

Response Options: Strongly Agree, Agree, Neutral, Disagree, Strongly Disagree

DIFFERENT PERSPECTIVES WELCOME:

—"All different perspectives were welcome in our discussion."

Response Options: Strongly Agree, Agree, Neutral, Disagree, Strongly Disagree

FEW DOMINATED:

—"A few people dominated the discussion."

Response Options: Strongly Agree, Agree, Neutral, Disagree, Strongly Disagree

ACCOMPLISHMENT:

—"I feel like I accomplished more because I worked with other people."

Response Options: Strongly Agree, Agree, Neutral, Disagree, Strongly Disagree

LIBERALISM / CONSERVATISM:

—"On most political matters do you consider yourself to be . . ."

Response Options: Strongly Conservative, Moderately Conservative, Neither/Middle-of-the-Road, Moderately Liberal, Strongly Liberal

Chapter 5 Appendix

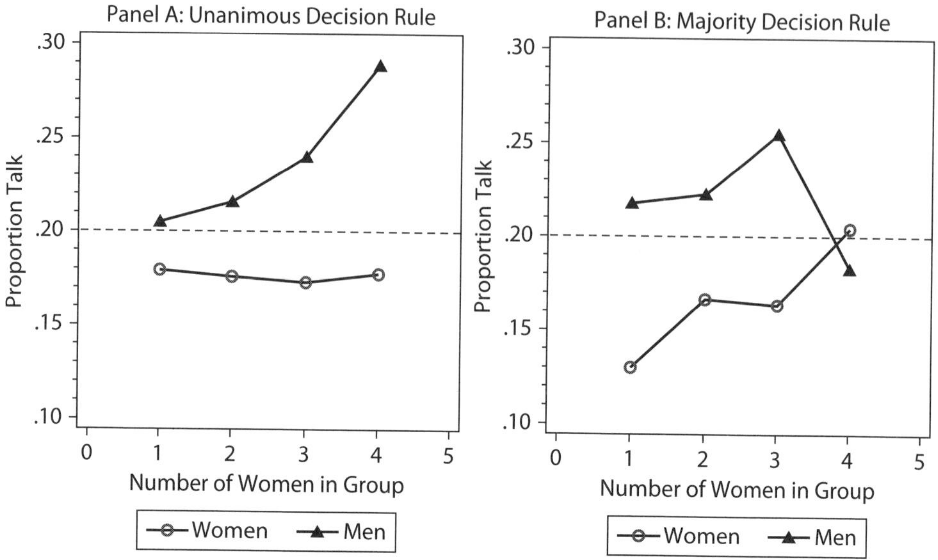

Figure A5.1. *Proportion Talk,* by gender and experimental condition.

Table A5.1: Equality of the Distribution of Proportion Talk

	(1) Group Gini Coefficient for Men and Women	(2) Gini Coefficient for Women Only
Majority Rule	12.7	70.3***
	(10.7)	(25.2)
Number of Women	0.4	11.2**
	(2.3)	(5.2)
Majority × Number of Women	–8.1**	–18.2***
	(3.5)	(7.3)
Number of Egalitarians	1.3	0.7
	(2.5)	(3.8)
Majority × Number of Egalitarians	1.7	–5.0
	(3.2)	(5.0)
Constant	40.9***	1.2
	(7.6)	(18.1)
Observations	64	45
R-squared	0.14	0.19
Control for Outlier	Yes	Yes
Control for Experimental Location	Yes	Yes

Note: Group-level analysis of mixed-gender groups only. In Model 1, all mixed gender groups are included; Model 2 is based only on groups with at least two women. Standard errors in parentheses.
*** $p < 0.01$, ** $p < 0.05$, * $p < 0.1$, one-tailed test.

Table A5.2: Effect of Rule and Composition on Feeling That "My Voice Was Heard" during Group Discussion, Mixed-Gender Groups Only

	Women	Men
Majority Rule	−0.12*	0.05
	(0.08)	(0.05)
Number of Women	−0.04***	0.03**
	(0.01)	(0.01)
Majority × Number of Women	0.06***	−0.04*
	(0.02)	(0.02)
Egalitarianism	0.02	−0.07
	(0.07)	(0.08)
Number of Egalitarians	−0.00	0.02
	(0.01)	(0.01)
Majority × Number of Egalitarians	−0.00	−0.01
	(0.02)	(0.02)
Constant	0.89***	0.81***
	(0.07)	(0.04)
Observations	157	163
R-squared	0.06	0.09
Control for Outlier	Yes	Yes
Control for Experimental Location	Yes	Yes

Note: Individual-level analysis. Cluster robust standard errors in parentheses.
*** $p < 0.01$, ** $p < 0.05$, * $p < 0.1$, one-tailed test.

Table A5.3: Determinants of the *Gender Gap in Influence* with Interactions between Decision Rule and Controls, Mixed-Gender Groups Only

	(1)	(2)
Majority Rule	0.492 (0.918)	0.738 (1.184)
Number of Women	0.309* (0.201)	0.256 (0.213)
Majority × Number of Women	–0.721*** (0.301)	–0.684** (0.310)
Number of Egalitarians	–0.197 (0.235)	–0.083 (0.264)
Majority × Number of Egalitarians	0.335 (0.282)	0.193 (0.320)
# Favoring Maximum Redistribution	–0.032 (0.258)	–0.375 (0.476)
Majority × Number Favoring Max Redistribution		0.493 (0.570)
# Favoring No Redistribution	0.080 (0.238)	0.231 (0.405)
Majority × # Favoring No Redistribution		–0.233 (0.505)
Constant	0.738 (0.766)	0.553 (0.948)
Observations	64	64
R-squared	0.175	0.190
Control for Outlier	Yes	Yes
Control for Experimental Location	Yes	Yes

Note: Dependent variable for both models is *Gender Gap in Influence*. Group-level analysis. Standard errors in parentheses. *** $p < 0.01$, ** $p < 0.05$, * $p < 0.1$, one-tailed test.

Chapter 6 Appendix

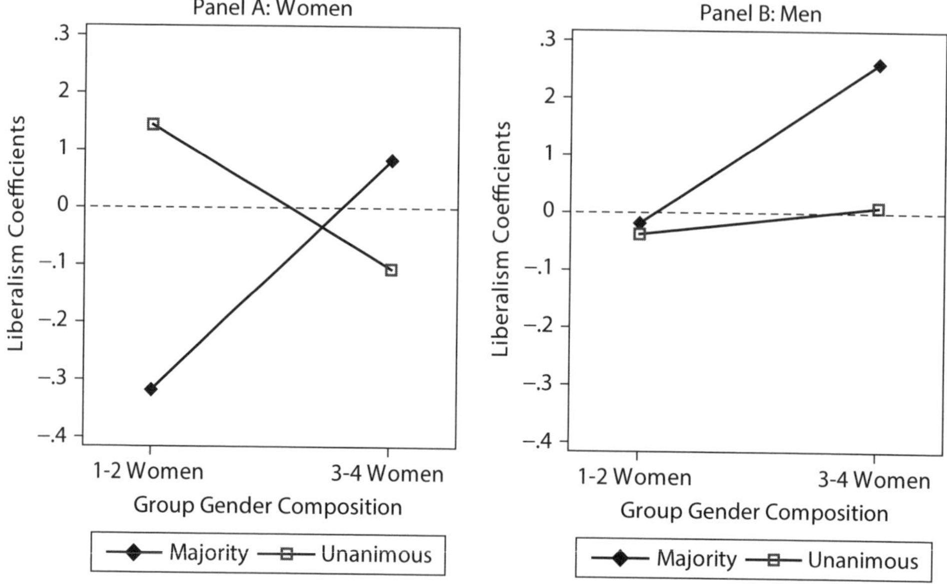

Figure A6.1. Effect of liberalism on *Proportion Talk* by condition, mixed-gender groups only.

Table A6.1: Mean Characteristics across Conditions, Women Only

	1–2 Women Majority Rule	3–4 Women Majority Rule	1–2 Women Unanimous Rule	3–4 Women Unanimous Rule	5 Women Both Rules Combined
Confidence	0.53	0.52	0.54	0.49	0.55
Negative Quiz Feedback	0.17	0.20	0.18	0.22	0.20
Comfort with Disagreement	0.54	0.60	0.65	0.56	0.60
Empathy	0.67	0.71	0.73	0.71	0.74

Chapter 7 Appendixes

Appendix A

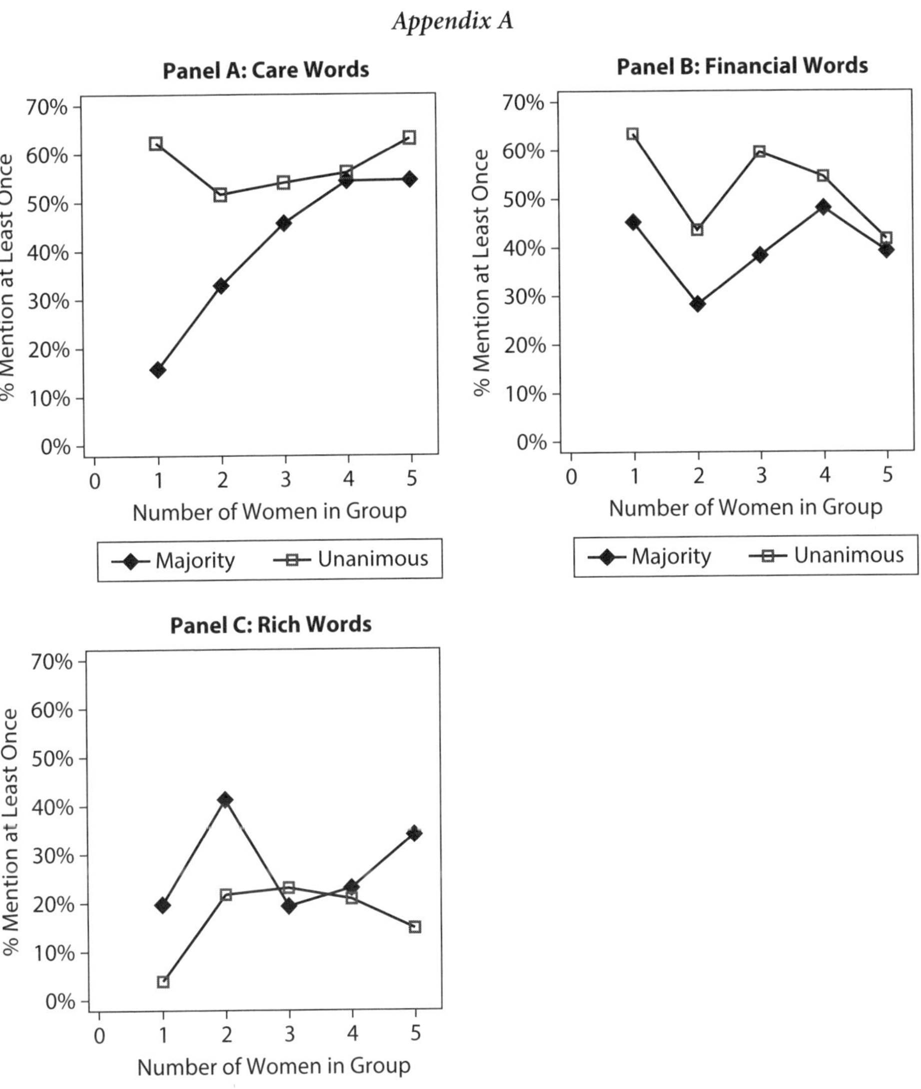

Figure A7.1. *Mention* of words among women, by rule (predicted values).

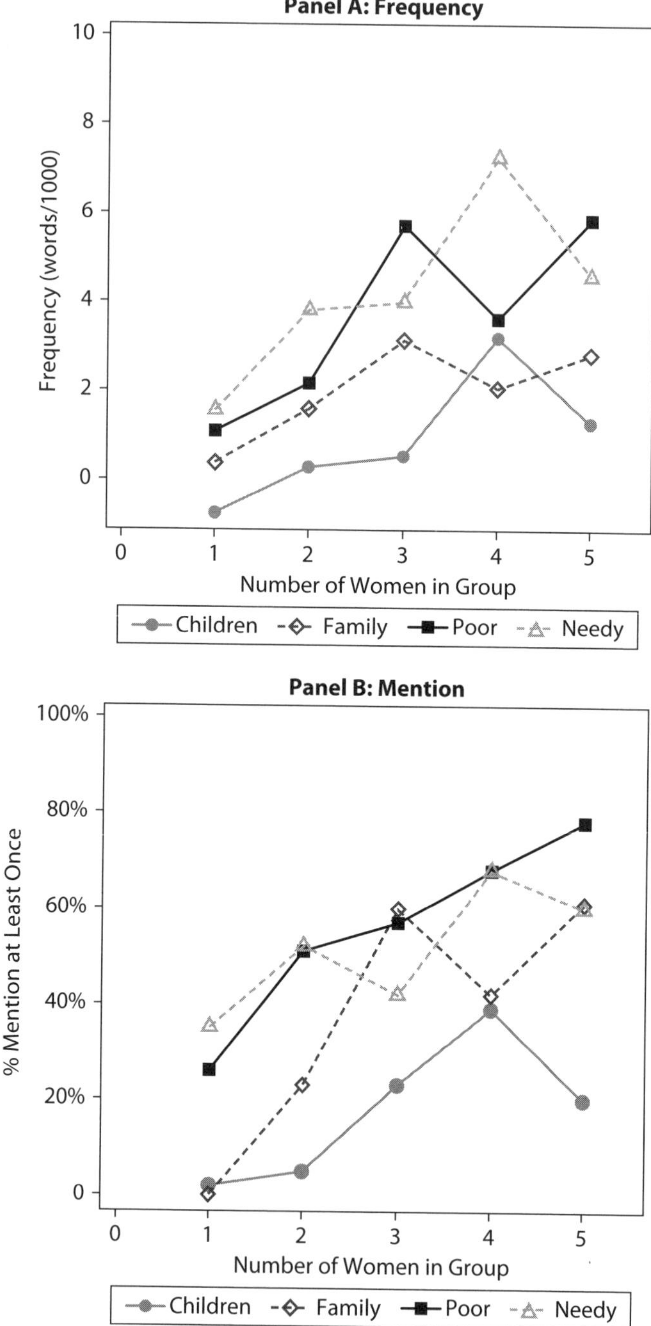

Figure A7.2. Effect of composition on individual women's *Frequency* and *Mention* of care issues, majority rule (predicted values).

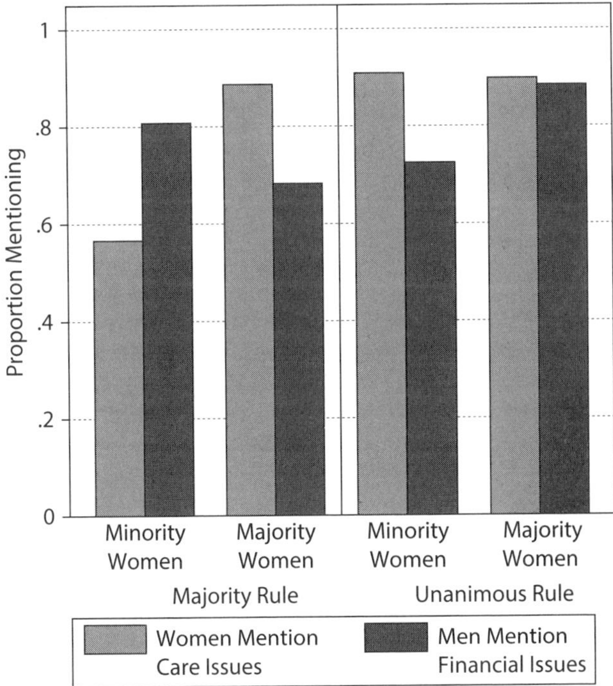

Figure A7.3. Women's *Mention* of care issues vs. men's *Mention* of financial issues.

Table A7.1: Regression Models Generating Predicted Probabilities of *Mention/Frequency* (for Figures 1, 2, 4, 5, 6, A1, A2, C7.1)

Women—Majority Rule

	(1) Children	(2) Family	(3) Poor	(4) Needy	(5) Rich	(6) Taxes	(7) Salary
				Mention (Probit)			
2 Women	0.453	5.051***	0.664	0.442	0.634	−0.368	−0.546
	(0.808)	(0.468)	(0.571)	(0.704)	(0.695)	(0.533)	(0.633)
3 Women	1.357**	6.044***	0.811	0.196	−0.014	−0.276	−0.100
	(0.549)	(0.575)	(0.569)	(0.510)	(0.662)	(0.451)	(0.500)
4 Women	1.822**	5.590***	1.098*	0.856	0.116	−0.165	0.302
	(0.736)	(0.470)	(0.609)	(0.576)	(0.627)	(0.526)	(0.517)
5 Women	1.255**	6.055***	1.387**	0.641	0.442	−0.513	0.128
	(0.631)	(0.501)	(0.599)	(0.590)	(0.644)	(0.497)	(0.578)
Individual Egalitarianism	−1.799**	0.270	−0.251	1.320	1.455*	0.425	−0.552
	(0.897)	(0.764)	(0.845)	(0.972)	(0.855)	(1.248)	(1.064)
Number of Egalitarians	−0.053	0.141	0.015	−0.148	0.166	−0.036	−0.104
	(0.197)	(0.096)	(0.161)	(0.149)	(0.109)	(0.123)	(0.121)
Log Word Count	1.794***	0.620***	0.833***	0.697***	0.584***	0.580***	1.133***
	(0.275)	(0.142)	(0.180)	(0.190)	(0.147)	(0.154)	(0.186)
Constant	−11.77***	−9.76***	−5.42***	−5.24***	−5.48***	−3.73***	−6.54***
	(1.759)	(1.078)	(1.284)	(1.372)	(1.254)	(1.144)	(1.438)
Observations	116	116	116	116	116	116	116
Pseudo R-squared	0.50	0.26	0.30	0.21	0.18	0.14	0.33
Control for Experimental Location	Yes	Yes	Yes	Yes	Yes	Yes	Yes

Table A7.1 (*cont.*)

Women—Majority Rule

	(1) Children	(2) Family	(3) Poor	(4) Needy	(5) Rich	(6) Taxes	(7) Salary
				Frequency (OLS)			
2 Women	0.104	0.121	0.108	0.226	0.144	−0.233	−0.179
	(0.067)	(0.082)	(0.164)	(0.299)	(0.123)	(0.361)	(0.238)
3 Women	0.129**	0.276**	0.463**	0.244	−0.021	−0.314	−0.115
	(0.054)	(0.118)	(0.227)	(0.333)	(0.094)	(0.351)	(0.243)
4 Women	0.396**	0.168*	0.254	0.571**	−0.019	−0.342	−0.001
	(0.160)	(0.086)	(0.197)	(0.281)	(0.095)	(0.354)	(0.259)
5 Women	0.204***	0.244***	0.477*	0.303	0.093	−0.326	−0.071
	(0.069)	(0.068)	(0.237)	(0.270)	(0.102)	(0.355)	(0.230)
Individual Egalitarianism	0.018	0.055	−0.107	−0.343	0.360**	−0.335	−0.230
	(0.144)	(0.143)	(0.333)	(0.377)	(0.170)	(0.384)	(0.194)
Number of Egalitarians	−0.068	0.029	0.044	−0.126	0.001	0.020	−0.032
	(0.041)	(0.024)	(0.095)	(0.091)	(0.021)	(0.033)	(0.039)
Constant	0.083	−0.048	0.025	0.526*	−0.059	0.599	0.480**
	(0.068)	(0.080)	(0.149)	(0.293)	(0.107)	(0.388)	(0.211)
Observations	116	116	116	116	116	116	116
R–squared	0.180	0.056	0.044	0.079	0.092	0.078	0.048
Control for Experimental Location	Yes	Yes	Yes	Yes	Yes	Yes	Yes

continued

Table A7.1 (*cont.*)

Women—Unanimity Rule

	(1) Children	(2) Family	(3) Poor	(4) Needy	(5) Rich	(6) Taxes	(7) Salary
				Mention (Probit)			
2 Women	−0.955*	−0.007	−0.337	0.230	0.986	−0.268	−1.138
	(0.520)	(0.578)	(0.578)	(0.549)	(0.628)	(0.510)	(0.694)
3 Women	−0.699	−0.281	0.761	−0.527	1.031*	0.460	−1.008
	(0.470)	(0.559)	(0.473)	(0.496)	(0.565)	(0.496)	(0.671)
4 Women	−0.970*	0.082	1.155**	−0.645	0.954	0.075	−0.865
	(0.536)	(0.476)	(0.526)	(0.491)	(0.626)	(0.512)	(0.592)
5 Women	0.102	−0.202	0.537	−0.315	0.720	0.146	−1.609**
	(0.491)	(0.543)	(0.475)	(0.494)	(0.618)	(0.466)	(0.641)
Individual Egalitarianism	0.449	−0.770	−0.244	0.611	1.838*	−0.580	0.622
	(1.098)	(1.064)	(0.888)	(0.995)	(0.939)	(1.054)	(0.851)
Number of Egalitarians	0.083	−0.027	−0.221	−0.044	0.207	−0.161	−0.171
	(0.137)	(0.154)	(0.180)	(0.145)	(0.161)	(0.124)	(0.186)
Log Word Count	0.539***	0.762***	0.751***	0.717***	0.754***	0.813***	0.773***
	(0.135)	(0.138)	(0.123)	(0.130)	(0.179)	(0.158)	(0.161)
Constant	−3.368***	−4.16***	−3.82***	−4.39***	−7.35***	−4.69***	−3.28***
	(0.945)	(1.030)	(0.942)	(0.984)	(1.359)	(1.145)	(1.208)
Observations	116	116	116	116	116	116	116
Pseudo R-squared	0.19	0.20	0.25	0.19	0.27	0.22	0.26
Control for Experimental Location	Yes	Yes	Yes	Yes	Yes	Yes	Yes

Table A7.1 *(cont.)*

Women—Unanimity Rule	(1) **Children**	(2) **Family**	(3) **Poor**	(4) **Needy**	(5) **Rich**	(6) **Taxes**	(7) **Salary**
				***Frequency* (OLS)**			
2 Women	–0.140	–0.010	0.076	0.105	0.038	–0.053	–0.047
	(0.139)	(0.105)	(0.192)	(0.190)	(0.055)	(0.084)	(0.110)
3 Women	–0.128	–0.027	0.275*	–0.124	0.084**	0.051	–0.055
	(0.103)	(0.100)	(0.146)	(0.164)	(0.040)	(0.081)	(0.113)
4 Women	–0.170*	0.018	0.311*	–0.116	0.074	0.043	–0.085
	(0.097)	(0.095)	(0.159)	(0.153)	(0.068)	(0.088)	(0.106)
5 Women	0.028	–0.073	0.175	0.120	0.019	–0.010	–0.070
	(0.124)	(0.088)	(0.157)	(0.213)	(0.035)	(0.073)	(0.117)
Individual Egalitarianism	0.228	–0.151	–0.194	–0.053	–0.043	–0.295	0.003
	(0.254)	(0.169)	(0.240)	(0.366)	(0.121)	(0.192)	(0.165)
Number of Egalitarians	–0.022	0.038	–0.032	–0.029	0.049*	0.028	–0.037
	(0.038)	(0.042)	(0.053)	(0.053)	(0.026)	(0.024)	(0.033)
Constant	0.185	0.180	0.338	0.351*	–0.009	0.261***	0.344**
	(0.147)	(0.127)	(0.202)	(0.202)	(0.045)	(0.095)	(0.139)
Observations	116	116	116	116	116	116	116
R-squared	0.101	0.036	0.061	0.082	0.097	0.104	0.023
Control for Experimental Location	Yes	Yes	Yes	Yes	Yes	Yes	Yes

continued

Table A7.1 (*cont.*)

Men—Majority Rule

	(1) Children	(2) Family	(3) Poor	(4) Needy	(5) Rich	(6) Taxes	(7) Salary
				Mention (Probit)			
0 Women	0.302	0.901***	0.126	0.386	−1.69***	0.470*	0.505
	(0.282)	(0.271)	(0.445)	(0.380)	(0.459)	(0.281)	(0.388)
2 Women	0.598	0.049	−1.03***	−0.576	−0.649	0.674*	−0.078
	(0.393)	(0.394)	(0.399)	(0.359)	(0.461)	(0.387)	(0.427)
3 Women	0.152	−0.057	−0.568	−0.322	−0.442	−0.256	−0.204
	(0.385)	(0.425)	(0.361)	(0.515)	(0.633)	(0.393)	(0.388)
4 Women	1.611**	−0.268	0.383	−0.366	−0.035	−0.110	−0.561
	(0.630)	(0.561)	(0.476)	(0.604)	(0.763)	(0.619)	(0.630)
Individual Egalitarianism	1.016	−0.084	−0.479	0.450	0.569	−0.306	−2.47***
	(1.175)	(1.021)	(0.822)	(0.768)	(0.876)	(0.905)	(0.792)
Number of Egalitarians	−0.202	0.393**	0.430**	0.239*	0.113	−0.315*	0.061
	(0.182)	(0.179)	(0.192)	(0.133)	(0.206)	(0.168)	(0.155)
Log Word Count	0.328*	0.127	0.931***	0.282*	1.161***	0.731***	0.979***
	(0.184)	(0.141)	(0.222)	(0.155)	(0.220)	(0.156)	(0.195)
Constant	−2.768*	−1.280	−5.00***	−1.712	−8.57***	−4.02***	−4.92***
	(1.451)	(1.023)	(1.403)	(1.143)	(1.629)	(1.120)	(1.165)
Observations	109	109	114	114	114	114	114
Pseudo R-squared	0.20	0.17	0.34	0.14	0.34	0.20	0.25
Control for Outlier	Yes	Yes	Yes	Yes	Yes	Yes	Yes
Control for Experimental Location	Yes	Yes	Yes	Yes	Yes	Yes	Yes

Table A7.1 *(cont.)*

Men—Majority Rule

	(1) Children	(2) Family	(3) Poor	(4) Needy	(5) Rich	(6) Taxes	(7) Salary
				Frequency (OLS)			
0 Women	0.025	0.213*	−0.210	0.101	−0.159**	0.056	0.088
	(0.032)	(0.112)	(0.151)	(0.154)	(0.060)	(0.046)	(0.099)
2 Women	0.117**	0.001	−0.305**	−0.249*	−0.065	0.057	0.032
	(0.051)	(0.074)	(0.138)	(0.147)	(0.090)	(0.050)	(0.132)
3 Women	0.019	0.056	−0.381***	0.017	−0.063	−0.024	−0.162*
	(0.034)	(0.115)	(0.099)	(0.179)	(0.087)	(0.038)	(0.084)
5 Women	0.356*	−0.058	−0.318*	−0.331*	0.104	−0.006	−0.139
	(0.207)	(0.092)	(0.181)	(0.169)	(0.173)	(0.054)	(0.135)
Individual Egalitarianism	0.212*	−0.129	0.356	0.223	0.128	−0.019	−0.156
	(0.115)	(0.272)	(0.309)	(0.284)	(0.186)	(0.124)	(0.182)
Number of Egalitarians	−0.054	0.043	0.034	0.099*	0.014	−0.031*	−0.015
	(0.036)	(0.038)	(0.076)	(0.050)	(0.030)	(0.017)	(0.036)
Constant	0.025	0.082	0.416***	0.196	0.052	0.182***	0.395***
	(0.044)	(0.086)	(0.122)	(0.143)	(0.057)	(0.041)	(0.062)
Observations	114	114	114	114	114	114	114
R-squared	0.292	0.099	0.087	0.065	0.103	0.080	0.116
Control for Experimental Location	Yes	Yes	Yes	Yes	Yes	Yes	Yes

continued

Table A7.1 (*cont.*)

Men—Unanimity Rule

	(1) Children	(2) Family	(3) Poor	(4) Needy	(5) Rich	(6) Taxes	(7) Salary
				Mention (Probit)			
0 Women	0.144	−0.165	0.649*	−0.056	0.180	−0.066	0.281
	(0.312)	(0.427)	(0.342)	(0.343)	(0.428)	(0.357)	(0.357)
2 Women	0.769**	−0.354	0.219	−0.209	−0.390	−0.195	−0.273
	(0.329)	(0.368)	(0.406)	(0.398)	(0.378)	(0.487)	(0.374)
3 Women	0.815	0.501	1.082*	0.769	0.407	0.523	−0.086
	(0.551)	(0.410)	(0.564)	(0.665)	(0.440)	(0.376)	(0.434)
4 Women	0.937*	0.476	—	−0.329	0.668	0.581	0.759
	(0.544)	(0.506)		(0.458)	(0.600)	(0.530)	(0.719)
Individual Egalitarianism	−1.887**	1.369*	−0.021	1.261*	−0.535	−0.165	0.333
	(0.833)	(0.753)	(0.857)	(0.722)	(0.749)	(0.748)	(0.600)
Number of Egalitarians	0.011	0.047	−0.182	−0.211	−0.347*	−0.45***	0.090
	(0.143)	(0.173)	(0.118)	(0.149)	(0.195)	(0.151)	(0.142)
Log Word Count	0.691***	0.835***	1.110***	0.683***	1.438***	0.659***	0.851***
	(0.237)	(0.161)	(0.217)	(0.192)	(0.229)	(0.172)	(0.192)
Constant	−3.956***	−6.01***	−7.14***	−3.89***	−9.11***	−3.17***	−5.46***
	(1.435)	(1.240)	(1.390)	(1.216)	(1.391)	(1.129)	(1.324)
Observations	124	124	116	124	124	124	124
Pseudo R-squared	0.35	0.26	0.27	0.26	0.31	0.20	0.23
Control for Experimental Location	Yes	Yes	Yes	Yes	Yes	Yes	Yes

Table A7.1 (*cont.*)

Men—Unanimity Rule

	(1) Children	(2) Family	(3) Poor	(4) Needy	(5) Rich	(6) Taxes	(7) Salary
				Frequency (OLS)			
0 Women	0.035	−0.029	0.181*	−0.103	0.013	−0.008	0.033
	(0.031)	(0.046)	(0.101)	(0.121)	(0.062)	(0.067)	(0.109)
2 Women	0.063*	−0.034	0.059	−0.109	0.004	−0.058	−0.154
	(0.035)	(0.036)	(0.090)	(0.153)	(0.058)	(0.069)	(0.107)
3 Women	0.107	0.071	0.159	0.319	0.042	0.024	−0.132
	(0.076)	(0.045)	(0.116)	(0.199)	(0.058)	(0.059)	(0.157)
4 Women	0.103	0.039	0.387**	−0.086	0.151	0.069	0.156
	(0.079)	(0.057)	(0.185)	(0.185)	(0.142)	(0.061)	(0.153)
Individual Egalitarianism	−0.123**	0.116*	−0.201	0.154	−0.008	−0.052	−0.165
	(0.061)	(0.061)	(0.172)	(0.216)	(0.083)	(0.094)	(0.159)
Number of Egalitarians	−0.020	−0.013	−0.009	−0.068	−0.019	−0.064**	0.044
	(0.019)	(0.024)	(0.033)	(0.057)	(0.023)	(0.029)	(0.035)
Constant	0.174***	0.124*	0.244**	0.579***	0.182***	0.345***	0.242**
	(0.042)	(0.065)	(0.096)	(0.187)	(0.067)	(0.081)	(0.101)
Observations	124	124	124	124	124	124	124
R-squared	0.117	0.125	0.080	0.124	0.091	0.187	0.092
Control for Experimental Location	Yes	Yes	Yes	Yes	Yes	Yes	Yes

Note: Individual-level analysis. Cluster robust standard errors in parentheses. Excluded category is 1-woman groups in all models. Empty cells in probit analyses indicate conditions under which there was no variation within a subgroup. *** $p < 0.01$, ** $p < 0.05$, * $p < 0.10$, two-tailed test.

Table A7.2: Regression Models Generating Predicted Probabilities of *Mention/Frequency* for Summary Measure of Care and Financial Issues

	Care Issues				Financial Issues			
	Mentions (probit)		Frequency (OLS)		Mentions (probit)		Frequency (OLS)	
Women Only	(1) Majority	(2) Unanimous	(3) Majority	(4) Unanimous	(5) Majority	(6) Unanimous	(7) Majority	(8) Unanimous
2 Women	1.83***	−11.70***	0.56	0.03	−0.30	−0.78	−0.41	−0.10
	(0.68)	(3.21)	(0.38)	(0.38)	(0.56)	(0.65)	(0.39)	(0.14)
3 Women	1.98***	−15.48***	1.11**	−0.00	−0.40	−0.39	−0.43	−0.00
	(0.69)	(5.48)	(0.51)	(0.29)	(0.53)	(0.71)	(0.40)	(0.13)
4 Women	2.58***	−8.47***	1.39***	0.04	0.40	−0.44	−0.34	−0.04
	(0.72)	(2.00)	(0.44)	(0.28)	(0.55)	(0.69)	(0.41)	(0.13)
5 Women	2.66***	−14.69***	1.23***	0.25	0.07	−0.63	−0.40	−0.08
	(0.72)	(5.35)	(0.43)	(0.43)	(0.56)	(0.67)	(0.39)	(0.12)
Individual Egalitarianism	1.12	−21.87**	−0.38	−0.17	−0.33	0.63	−0.56	−0.29
	(1.40)	(9.79)	(0.56)	(0.67)	(0.92)	(1.08)	(0.37)	(0.25)
Number of Egalitarians	−0.30	3.25**	−0.12	−0.05	−0.15	−0.22	−0.01	−0.01
	(0.20)	(1.62)	(0.16)	(0.11)	(0.12)	(0.18)	(0.05)	(0.04)
Log Word Count	1.27***	7.34**	—	—	1.02***	1.27***	—	—
	(0.25)	(3.44)	—	—	(0.19)	(0.22)	—	—
Constant	−8.11***	−24.09*	0.59	1.05**	−5.50***	−6.23***	1.08**	0.61***
	(1.80)	(14.20)	(0.37)	(0.40)	(1.37)	(1.36)	(0.41)	(0.16)
Observations	116	116	116	116	116	116	116	116
R-squared	0.48	0.88	0.11	0.08	0.31	0.42	0.07	0.02
Control for Experimental Location	Yes	Yes	Yes	Yes	Yes	Yes	Yes	Yes

Table A7.2 (cont.)

	Care Issues				Financial Issues			
	Mentions (probit)		Frequency (OLS)		Mentions (probit)		Frequency (OLS)	
Men Only	(1) Majority	(2) Unanimous	(3) Majority	(4) Unanimous	(5) Majority	(6) Unanimous	(7) Majority	(8) Unanimous
0 Women	2.44***	0.72	0.13	0.08	0.80**	0.65*	0.14	0.03
	(0.69)	(0.47)	(0.27)	(0.17)	(0.40)	(0.38)	(0.11)	(0.11)
2 Women	−1.48**	1.22**	−0.44*	−0.02	0.06	−0.50	0.09	−0.21
	(0.71)	(0.55)	(0.22)	(0.21)	(0.58)	(0.46)	(0.14)	(0.13)
3 Women	−0.64	1.78***	−0.29	0.66***	−0.67	0.50	−0.19*	−0.11
	(0.95)	(0.62)	(0.29)	(0.22)	(0.43)	(0.53)	(0.11)	(0.15)
4 Women	—	—	−0.35	0.44	−0.89	—	−0.14	0.22
	—	—	(0.29)	(0.30)	(0.72)	—	(0.15)	(0.16)
Individual Egalitarianism	−1.80	−0.64	0.66	−0.05	−1.09	−0.15	−0.18	−0.22
	(1.23)	(0.78)	(0.48)	(0.29)	(0.91)	(0.73)	(0.26)	(0.18)
Number of Egalitarians	1.11***	−0.30	0.12	−0.11	−0.03	−0.42***	−0.05	−0.02
	(0.34)	(0.19)	(0.10)	(0.07)	(0.21)	(0.16)	(0.04)	(0.03)
Log Word Count	1.59***	1.28***	—	—	1.52***	0.96***	—	—
	(0.45)	(0.30)	—	—	(0.28)	(0.21)	—	—
Constant	−7.98***	−6.40***	0.72***	1.12***	−8.05***	−4.37***	0.58***	0.59***
	(2.70)	(1.75)	(0.22)	(0.25)	(1.67)	(1.43)	(0.08)	(0.10)
Observations	101	116	114	124	114	116	114	124
R-squared	0.49	0.45	0.13	0.16	0.39	0.31	0.15	0.08
Control for Outlier	—	—	Yes	—	Yes	—	Yes	—
Control for Experimental Location	Yes	Yes	Yes	Yes	Yes	Yes	Yes	Yes

Note: Individual–level analysis. Cluster robust standard errors in parentheses. Excluded category is 1-woman groups in all models. Empty cells in probit analyses indicate conditions under which there was no variation within a subgroup. *** $p < 0.01$, ** $p < 0.05$, * $p < 0.10$, two-tailed test.

Table A7.3: Frequency of Care Issue Mentions among Women: Replication of Linear Model with TM

	(1) Egalitarianism Controls	(2) Saturated Egalitarianism Controls
Majority Rule	−1.474***	−1.476***
	(0.415)	(0.473)
Number of Women	−0.026	−0.026
	(0.112)	(0.113)
Majority Rule × Number of Women	0.399***	0.398**
	(0.137)	(0.152)
Egalitarianism	−0.101	−0.101
	(0.441)	(0.445)
Number of Egalitarians	0.008	0.007
	(0.090)	(0.116)
Majority Rule × Number of Egalitarians	—	0.001
	—	(0.138)
Constant	1.605***	1.606***
	(0.417)	(0.433)
Observations	157	157
R-squared	0.107	0.107
Control for Experimental Location	Yes	Yes

Note: Dependent variable for both models is *Frequency* of Care Issues. Individual-level analysis. Cluster robust standard errors in parentheses. *** $p < 0.01$, ** $p < 0.05$, * $p < 0.10$, two-tailed test.

Appendix B: Dictionaries Used for Content Analysis
Words associated with "poor" (LIWC)

*A downloadable .txt file with all words from these dictionaries is available at the authors' websites.

poor*
poverty
those in need
people in need
person in need
someone in need
somebody in need
lower class
less fortunate
homeless
hungry
hunger
have-not
have-nots
people on welfare
person on welfare
those on welfare
people who need economic assistance
those who need economic assistance
person who needs economic assistance
people who need help
those who need help
person who needs help
needy
in need
those who have less
people who have less
person who has less
beggar*
hard up
hard-up
indigent*
dead broke
penniless
poverty-stricken
in financial trouble
alms
bankrupt*
economically dependent
financially dependent
down-and-out
guttersnipe*
mendicant*
pauper*
poverty
street person
street people
suppliant*
vagrant
vagrants
ward of the state
wards of the state
indigent*
those who are lacking
low socioeconomic status
food stamps
destitute*
low earner
the bottom
low income
lower income
lowest income
don't have a home
starve*
hardship
impoverish*
indigence*
privation*
penniless*

Words associated with "needy" (LIWC)

safety net
get by
die*
eat*
starve*
survive*
in the street
in the streets
minimum standard of living
bare minimum
minimum wage
you can live
able to live
struggle*

Words associated with "salary" (LIWC)

salary*
wage
wages
paid
earn*

Words associated with "family" (LIWC)

family
families
parent*
mother*
father*
kin
relatives
household*
brother
brothers
sister
sisters

Words associated with "children" (LIWC)

child*
kid
kids
young
youth
young adult
young adults
student*
18 year old
18 year olds
18-year-old*
eighteen-year-old
adolescent*
baby
babies
youngster*
infant*
juvenile*
kiddie*
little ones
minors
newborn*

preteen*
teen*
toddler*
tot
tots
boy
girl
boys
girls

Words associated with "tax" (LIWC)

taxpayer*
tax-payer*
tax payer
tax payers
those who pay tax
people who pay tax
person who pays tax
those who pay taxes
people who pay taxes
person who pays taxes
tax
taxes
taxation

Words associated with "rich" (LIWC)

rich
elite
wealthy
CEO*
affluent
people who are loaded
those who are loaded
person who is loaded
someone who is loaded
moneyed
monied
of independent means
of substantial means
people with means
those with means
person with means
of means
rolling in it
rolling in the dough
upper class
at the very top
nouveau riche
upper crust
high earner
highest level person
at the top
doing extremely well
highest bracket
making the most

Words Used in TM Analysis Care (TM)

care
education
enough
family
food
help
kids
need
poor
poverty
school
welfare

Financial (TM)

dollar
dollars
earn
earning
incentive
job
pay
tax
taxes
work
working

Chapter 8 Appendix

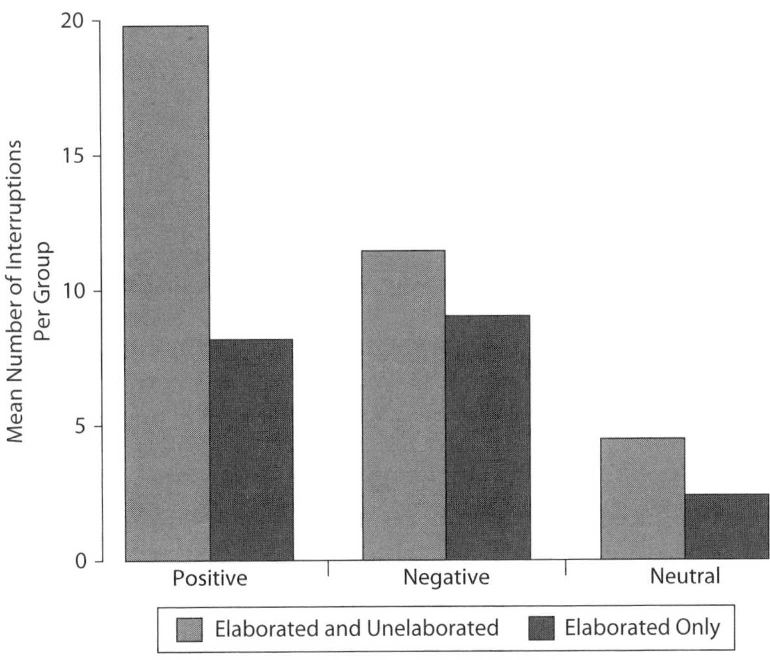

Figure A8.1. Disposition summary statistics (raw).

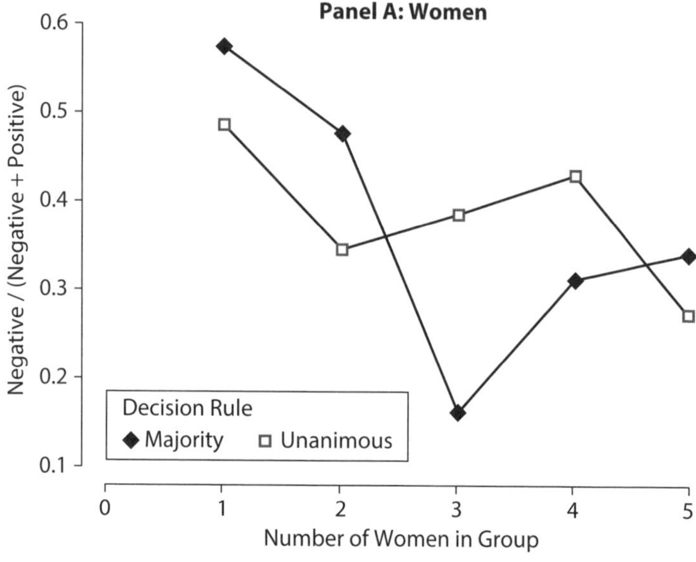

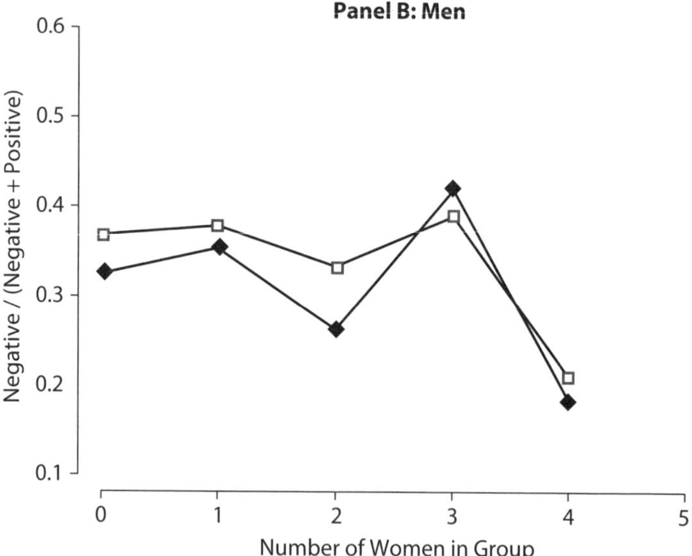

Figure A8.2. Negative proportion of interruptions received (raw). *Top*: Women, bottom: *Men*.

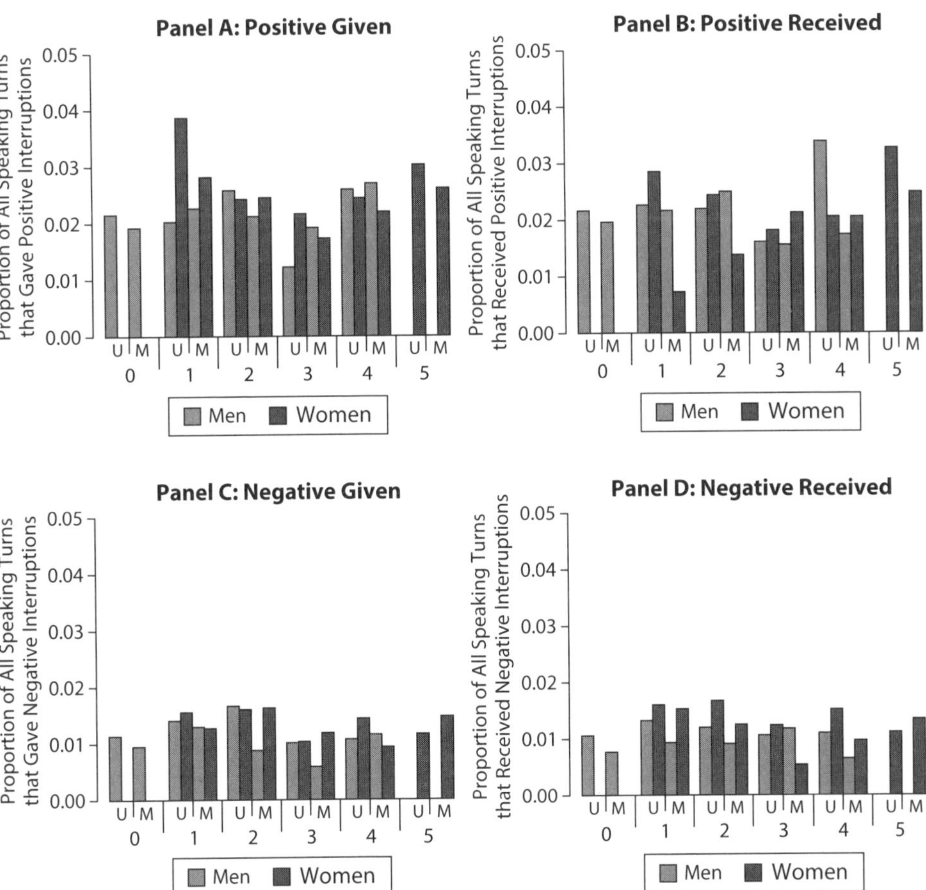

Figure A8.3. Proportion of speaking turns that gave or received positive or negative interruptions (raw). Note: Along the *x*-axis "U" represents men and women in unanimous-rule groups; "M" for majority-rule groups; stratified by number of women in the group.

Table A8.1: Elaborated Proportion of Positive or Negative Interruptions, Mixed-Gender Groups Only

	Negative		Positive	
	(1) Women by Men and Women	(2) Men by Men and Women	(3) Women by Men and Women	(4) Men by Men and Women
Majority Rule	−0.205	0.017	0.156	0.007
	(0.224)	(0.115)	(0.226)	(0.124)
Number of Women	−0.046	0.008	0.023	−0.078**
	(0.032)	(0.031)	(0.048)	(0.030)
Majority Rule × Number of Women	0.086	−0.032	−0.060	−0.015
	(0.065)	(0.053)	(0.066)	(0.052)
Egalitarianism	0.418	0.349*	−0.082	0.041
	(0.301)	(0.177)	(0.269)	(0.173)
Number of Egalitarians	−0.019	0.005	−0.068*	0.014
	(0.030)	(0.040)	(0.034)	(0.038)
Constant	0.746***	0.665***	0.526***	0.584***
	(0.195)	(0.110)	(0.179)	(0.111)
Observations	92	104	118	129
R-squared	0.10	0.06	0.06	0.07
Control for Experimental Location	Yes	Yes	Yes	Yes

Note: Individual-level analysis. Cluster robust standard errors in parentheses. *** $p < 0.01$, ** $p < 0.05$, * $p < 0.10$, two-tailed test.

Chapter 9 Appendix

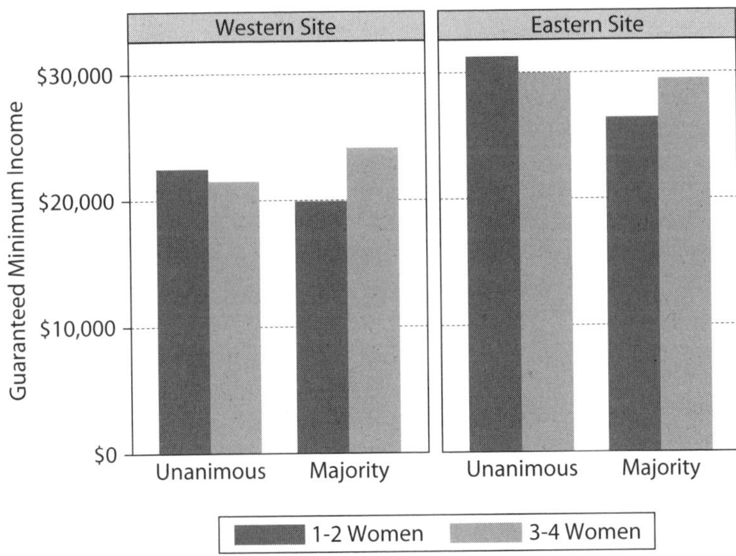

Figure A9.1. Guaranteed minimum incomes, by site, mixed-gender groups only.

Table A9.1: Individual-Level Distribution of Redistribution Preferences before and after Deliberation (%)

	Women (N = 232)	Men (N = 238)
Predeliberation Preferences		
Maximize Floor	12.5	8.8
No Redistribution	9.9	21.0
Set Floor	65.5	54.2
Set Range	11.6	15.6
Postdeliberation Preferences		
Maximize Floor	6.0	7.6
No Redistribution	4.3	14.7
Set Floor	81.9	66.0
Set Range	6.9	10.1

Note: Two respondents did not offer predeliberation preferences, and six respondents did not answer the questions about their postdeliberation preferences.

Table A9.2: Effect of Experimental Conditions on the Likelihood of Having a Female Agenda Setter, Mixed-Gender Groups Only

	(1)	(2)	(3)
Majority Rule	−2.03**	−2.31***	−2.38**
	(0.98)	(0.99)	(1.08)
Number of Women	0.21	0.30*	0.30*
	(0.19)	(0.20)	(0.21)
Majority Rule × Number of Women	0.62**	0.72**	0.70**
	(0.34)	(0.34)	(0.37)
Number of Egalitarians		−0.33**	−0.35
		(0.18)	(0.23)
Majority Rule × Number of Egalitarians			0.05
			(0.31)
Constant	−0.45	−0.01	0.03
	(0.56)	(0.61)	(0.65)
Observations	64	64	64
Control for Experimental Location	Yes	Yes	Yes

Note: Cell entries are probit coefficients. Dependent variable is a dummy variable indicating whether or not the group's agenda setter was a woman. Group-level analysis. Standard errors in parentheses. *** $p < 0.01$, ** $p < 0.05$, * $p < 0.1$, one-tailed test.

Table A9.3: Effect of Experimental Conditions on Average Maximum Endorsed Safety Net Amount by Women, Group-Level Analysis, Mixed-Gender Groups Only

	(1)	(2)	(3)	(4)	(5)
Majority Rule	–11.55**	–5.13	–8.58	–10.12**	–14.30**
	(4.87)	(5.43)	(13.14)	(4.89)	(5.68)
Number of Women	–0.45	–0.74	–0.79	–0.04	–0.66
	(1.07)	(1.02)	(1.00)	(1.01)	(1.06)
Majority Rule × Number of Women	3.92**	5.40***	3.84**	3.44**	4.21**
	(1.63)	(1.68)	(1.52)	(1.56)	(1.64)
Number of Egalitarians	0.33	1.57			
	(0.91)	(1.02)			
Majority Rule × Number of Egalitarians		–3.69**			
		(1.65)			
Average Warmth of Feeling Toward Poor			0.21*		
			(0.12)		
Majority Rule × Avg. Warmth Toward Poor			–0.04		
			(0.19)		
Number Favoring Maximum Redistribution				3.90	
				(2.41)	
Majority Rule × Number Favoring Max Redist.				–0.37	
				(3.63)	
Number Favoring No Redistribution					–2.43
					(1.97)
Majority Rule × Number Favoring No Redist.					1.80
					(2.65)
Constant	25.33***	23.16***	12.50	23.81***	29.23***
	(3.48)	(3.43)	(8.24)	(3.27)	(4.28)
Observations	40	40	33	40	40
R-squared	0.40	0.48	0.56	0.48	0.43
Control for Experimental Location	Yes	Yes	Yes	Yes	Yes

Note: Dependent variable is the average maximum endorsed safety net endorsed by women in the group. Observations for models with average feeling thermometer toward the poor are lower because some groups were not asked about their feelings toward the poor prior to deliberation. Group-level analysis. Standard errors in parentheses. *** $p < 0.01$, ** $p < 0.05$, * $p < 0.1$, two-tailed test.

Table A9.4: Effect of Speaking Time and Gender on Expressions of Safety Net Generosity, by Gender Composition, Mixed-Gender/Majority Rule Groups Only

	(1) 1–2 Women in Group	(2) 1–2 Women in Group	(3) 3–4 Women in Group	(4) 3–4 Women in Group
Proportion Talk	13.86 (14.19)	18.11 (15.15)	–18.18 (11.59)	–14.48 (12.12)
Female	4.04 (3.17)	3.44 (4.46)	–5.94** (2.13)	–6.19* (3.35)
Proportion Talk × Female	–21.13 (15.28)	–11.68 (23.08)	43.92** (16.62)	39.37** (16.10)
Egalitarianism		10.43** (3.32)		14.93* (7.16)
Number of Egalitarians		–0.57 (1.48)		–0.06 (1.79)
Constant	19.92*** (2.57)	14.77*** (2.41)	30.57*** (4.06)	23.32*** (3.11)
Observations	27	27	38	38
R-squared	0.08	0.24	0.15	0.20
Control for Experimental Location	Yes	Yes	Yes	Yes

Note: Dependent variable is maximum endorsed floor amount in thousands of dollars. Coefficients are expressed floor amounts in thousands of dollars. Individual-level analysis. Cluster robust standard errors in parentheses. *** $p < 0.01$, ** $p < 0.05$, * $p < 0.1$, two-tailed test.

Table A9.5: Effect of Majority Female Groups on Group's Safety Net Generosity, by Decision Rule, All Groups

	(1) Majority	(2) Majority	(3) Unanimous	(4) Unanimous
Majority Women in Group	4,181.46** (1,803.61)	4,118.05** (1,944.83)	1,833.62 (2,489.48)	1,679.01 (2,584.56)
Number of Egalitarians		73.40 (778.72)		348.94 (1,337.82)
Constant	22,119.23*** (1,634.19)	22,002.15*** (2,067.96)	22,419.86*** (2,097.03)	21,824.10*** (3,115.70)
Observations	46	46	48	48
R-squared	0.19	0.19	0.23	0.24
Control for Experimental Location	Yes	Yes	Yes	Yes

Note: Dependent variable is the group's chosen minimum guaranteed income, in dollars. Enclave groups included. Group-level analysis. Standard errors in parentheses. *** $p < 0.01$, ** $p < 0.05$, * $p < 0.10$, one-tailed test.

Table A9.6: Effect of Gender Composition and Rule on Group's Safety Net Generosity, Mixed-Gender Groups Only

	(1)	(2)
Majority Rule	–6,090.44*	–1,512.40
	(3,915.68)	(4,626.93)
Number of Women	–732.22	–1,223.25
	(1,005.94)	(1,021.95)
Majority Rule × Number of Women	1,908.78*	2,353.05*
	(1,443.28)	(1,539.33)
Number of Egalitarians		2,164.19**
		(1,107.80)
Majority Rule × Number of Egalitarians		–2,128.49*
		(1,427.36)
Constant	24,462.51***	20,835.46***
	(2,883.25)	(3,383.33)
Observations	64	64
R-squared	0.26	0.31
Control for Experimental Location	Yes	Yes

Note: Dependent variable is the group's chosen minimum guaranteed income, in dollars. Group-level analysis. Standard errors in parentheses. *** $p < 0.01$, ** $p < 0.05$, * $p < 0.10$, one-tailed test.

Table A9.7: Relationship between Endorsed Preferences and Group's Safety Net Generosity, Group-Level Analysis, Mixed-Gender Groups Only

Panel A: Effect of *Average* Endorsements	(1)	(2)	(3)	(4)	(5)
Average Poverty Line Endorsed by Women	459.36***	578.71***	460.89***	471.44***	358.57*
	(157.67)	(182.01)	(150.25)	(153.81)	(175.69)
Average Poverty Line Endorsed by Men	392.11***	290.24**	472.14***	409.83***	400.91***
	(121.33)	(139.46)	(126.72)	(118.49)	(118.38)
Majority Rule					4,860.35
					(4,405.61)
Number of Women					45.52
					(839.07)
Majority × Number of Women					−294.36
					(1,417.47)
Number of Egalitarians	113.76				1,642.80*
	(725.77)				(905.44)
Majority × Number of Egalitarians					−2,667.33*
					(1,526.56)
Average Warmth of Feeling toward the Poor		−67.04			
		(87.00)			
Number Favoring Maximum Redistribution			−2,217.48		
			(1,504.99)		
Number Favoring No Redistribution				912.84	
				(885.86)	
Constant	723.31	5,008.07	−354.21	−496.63	362.07
	(3,650.11)	(5,902.88)	(3,254.30)	(3,493.74)	(4,760.00)
Observations	33	27	33	33	33
R-squared	0.75	0.74	0.77	0.76	0.82
Control for Experimental Location	Yes	Yes	Yes	Yes	Yes

Note: Group-level analysis. Dependent variable is the group's chosen minimum guaranteed income, in dollars. Analysis restricted to groups in which men and women endorsed a poverty line. Some groups were not asked prior to deliberation about their feelings toward the poor. Standard errors in parentheses. *** $p < 0.01$, ** $p < 0.05$, * $p < 0.1$, two-tailed.

continued

Panel B: Effect of Total *Volume* of Endorsements	(1)	(2)	(3)	(4)	(5)
Total Volume of Women's Endorsements	180.04**	125.04	215.25***	200.44**	257.59**
	(82.66)	(95.74)	(72.31)	(80.99)	(103.64)
Total Volume of Men's Endorsements	157.52*	116.43	136.10*	154.59*	98.19
	(82.15)	(95.85)	(74.11)	(82.81)	(95.34)
Majority Rule					1,510.11
					(4,650.62)
Number of Women					−2,010.55
					(1,256.38)
Majority × Number of Women					1,727.48
					(1,501.65)
Number of Egalitarians	840.62				2,319.02**
	(740.81)				(1,060.26)
Majority × Number of Egalitarians					−2,396.93*
					(1,367.51)
Average Warmth of Feeling toward the Poor		−89.14			
		(106.22)			
Number Favoring Maximum Redistribution			4,261.02***		
			(1,092.75)		
Number Favoring No Redistribution				−584.73	
				(1,136.28)	
Constant	17,118.83***	25,138.12***	17,019.25***	19,201.25***	18,825.52***
	(2,165.43)	(6,800.62)	(1,584.97)	(2,022.84)	(4,148.27)
Observations	64	52	64	64	64
R-squared	0.34	0.28	0.46	0.32	0.39
Control for Experimental Location	Yes	Yes	Yes	Yes	Yes

Note: Group-level analysis. Dependent variable is the group's chosen minimum guaranteed income, in dollars. Groups in which no women or men endorsed a minimum income amount have a volume of 0. Some groups were not asked prior to deliberation about their feelings toward the poor. Standard errors in parentheses. *** $p < 0.01$, ** $p < 0.05$, * $p < 0.1$, two-tailed.

Table A9.8: Effect of Endorsed Preferences, Gender Composition and Rule on Group's Safety Net Generosity, Mixed-Gender Groups Only

	(1)	(2)	(3)
Majority Rule	1,500.34	4,749.58	-875.26
	(2,619.08)	(3,838.54)	(4,052.91)
Number of Women	-3.33	325.74	-809.49
	(498.45)	(749.16)	(758.75)
Majority Rule × Number of Women	-1,190.66*	-627.68	-16.69
	(893.92)	(1,209.64)	(1,419.82)
Number of Egalitarians	484.87	826.63	1,261.30*
	(557.88)	(822.26)	(777.94)
Majority Rule × Number of Egalitarians	-68.86	-2,114.86**	-587.14
	(847.85)	(1,224.04)	(1,303.88)
Group Average Maximum Endorsed Preference (All)	886.55***		
	(72.36)		
Group Average Maximum Endorsed Preference (Men Only)		721.12***	
		(89.96)	
Group Average Maximum Endorsed Preference (Women Only)			772.65***
			(128.28)
Constant	-144.77	2,065.06	3,431.51
	(2,249.33)	(3,301.62)	(3,902.39)
Observations	50	43	40
R-squared	0.86	0.77	0.77
Control for Experimental Location	Yes	Yes	Yes

Note: Dependent variable is the group's chosen minimum guaranteed income, in dollars. Group-level analysis. Standard errors in parentheses. *** $p < 0.01$, ** $p < 0.05$, * $p < 0.10$, one-tailed test.

Table A9.9: Relationship between Care Issues and Group's Safety Net Generosity

	(1)	(2)
Men Low Ratio/Women High Ratio	−12,960.90**	−17,433.66***
	(5,314.14)	(5,788.18)
Women's Total Proportion Talk	−10,959.83**	−14,961.96*
	(5,411.67)	(8,442.27)
Men Low/Women High × Women's Total Proportion Talk	25,850.63***	31,773.79***
	(9,571.47)	(10,154.88)
Men High Ratio/Women High Ratio	166.80	−3,778.57
	(5,483.41)	(5,981.58)
Men High/Women High × Women's Total Proportion Talk	7,793.34	13,716.25
	(10,852.94)	(11,530.66)
Men High Ratio/Women Low Ratio	−10,051.59**	−12,358.46**
	(4,305.76)	(4,627.25)
Men High/Women Low × Women's Total Proportion Talk	18,657.81*	21,737.39**
	(9,256.76)	(9,659.98)
Majority Rule		−7,407.16
		(5,381.98)
Number of Women		−637.89
		(1,681.74)
Majority Rule × Number of Women		2,774.47
		(1,921.29)
Number of Egalitarians	906.80	1,225.85
	(834.68)	(1,191.21)
Majority × Number of Egalitarians		−951.64
		(1,608.11)
Constant	24,232.95***	28,743.74***
	(2,818.50)	(4,207.92)
Observations	52	52
R-squared	0.45	0.50
Control for Experimental Location	Yes	Yes

Note: Dependent variable is group's chosen minimum guaranteed income, in dollars. Group-level analysis. Standard errors in parentheses. *** $p < 0.01$, ** $p < 0.05$, * $p < 0.1$, two-tailed test.

Chapter 10 Appendix

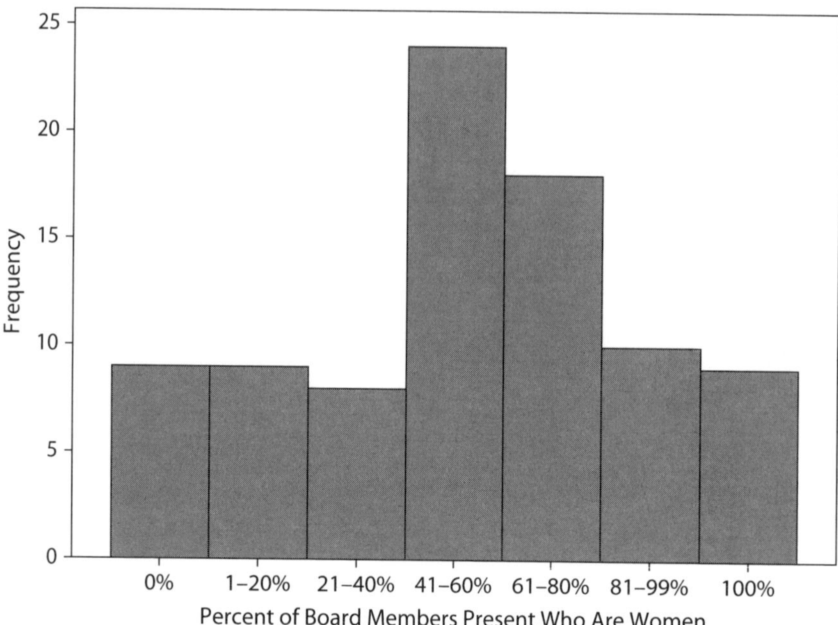

Figure A10.1. Distribution of school boards, by gender composition.

Table A10.1: Equality Ratio, by Gender Composition and Female Leadership

	Female Chair	Male Chair	Difference
Minority Women	1.20	0.57	0.63***
	(0.10)	(0.10)	(0.19)
Majority Women	1.08	0.71	0.37***
	(0.05)	(0.13)	(0.13)

Note: Boards with a minority of women are those in which fewer than 50% of attending members are women. Standard errors in parentheses. *** $p < 0.01$, ** $p < 0.05$, * $p < 0.1$, one-tailed difference of means test.

Table A10.2: Determinants of Female Chairs

	(1)	(2)
Proportion Women	3.00***	2.87***
	(0.62)	(0.57)
Size of Board		−0.25
		(0.22)
Board Experience (median years)		0.07
		(0.07)
# of College Graduates on Board		0.08
		(0.20)
Public Comment at Meeting		0.05
		(0.47)
Urban Area		0.08
		(0.31)
Superintendent Is Female		0.72***
		(0.25)
# of Students Enrolled		0.10
		(0.20)
Budget per Student		−0.35
		(0.80)
Length of Meeting		0.05
		(0.11)
South		−0.33
		(1.03)
West		0.32
		(0.39)
Midwest		0.26
		(0.49)
Constant	−1.75***	0.81
	(0.36)	(8.00)
Log pseudolikelihood	−39.71	−31.11
Observations	69	63
Control for Outlier	No	No

Note: Entries are probit coefficients. Dependent variable is dichotomous indicator of whether board chair is female. Group-level analysis. Cluster robust standard errors in parentheses (cluster by state). *** $p < 0.01$, ** $p < 0.05$, * $p < 0.1$, one-tailed test.

Table A10.3: Ratio of Proportion of Turns Taken by Women to Proportion of Women Attending, Civic Dialogue Groups

	(1)	(2)
Proportion Women	−0.40**	−0.52***
	(0.11)	(0.05)
Total # of Speaking Turns		−0.00**
		(0.00)
Male Facilitator		−0.08***
		(0.01)
Constant	1.22***	1.34***
	(0.07)	(0.04)
Observations	22	22
R-squared	0.41	0.53

Note: Dependent variable is equality ratio for women. Individual-level analysis. Cluster robust standard errors in parentheses (cluster by group location). *** $p < 0.01$, ** $p < 0.05$, * $p < 0.1$, one-tailed test.

References

AAUW Educational Foundation. 1992. *The AAUW Report: How Schools Shortchange Girls*. Washington, DC: National Education Association.

Achen, Christopher H., and Andre Blais. 2009. "Duty, Preference, and Turnout." Paper presented at the ECPR General Conference, Potsdam, September 10–12.

———. 2010. "Intention to Vote, Reported Vote, and Validated Vote." Paper presented at the annual meeting of the American Political Science Association, Washington, DC, September 2–5.

Aday, Sean, and James Devitt. 2001. "Style over Substance: Newspaper Coverage of Elizabeth Dole's Presidential Bid." *International Journal of Press/Politics* 6 (2): 52–73.

Agarwal, Bina. 1997. "Re-Sounding the Alert: Gender, Resources, and Community Action." *World Development* 25: 1373–80.

Alesina, Alberto, and Eliana La Ferrara. 2005. "Preferences for Redistribution in the Land of Opportunities." *Journal of Public Economics* 89 (5–6): 897–931.

Alexander, Amy C. 2012. "Change in Women's Descriptive Representation and the Belief in Women's Ability to Govern: A Virtuous Cycle." *Politics and Gender* 8 (4): 437–64.

Allen, Amy. 2012. "Gender, Power, and Reason: Feminism and Critical Theory." Draft for Princeton workshop on Feminist Political Theory.

Allmendinger, Jutta, and J. Richard Hackman. 1995. "The More, the Better? A Four-Nation Study of the Inclusion of Women in Symphony Orchestras." *Social Forces* 74 (2): 423–60.

Amanatullah, E. T., and M. W. Morris. 2010. "Negotiating Gender Roles: Gender Differences in Assertive Negotiating Are Mediated by Women's Fear of Backlash and Attenuated When Negotiating on Behalf of Others." *Journal of Personality Social Psychology* 98 (2): 256–67.

Andersen, Kristi. 1996. *After Suffrage: Women in Partisan and Electoral Politics before the New Deal*. Chicago: University of Chicago Press.

Anderson, Joel, and Axel Honneth. 2005. "Autonomy, Vulnerability, Recognition, and Justice." In *Autonomy and the Challenges to Liberalism: New Essays*, edited by John Christman and Joel Anderson, 127–49. New York: Cambridge University Press.

Anderson, K. J., and C. Leaper. 1998. "Meta-Analyses of Gender Effects on Conversational Interruption: Who, What, When, Where, and How." *Sex Roles* 39: 222–52.

APSA Standing Committee on Civic Education and Engagement. 2004. *Democracy at Risk: Renewing the Political Science of Citizenship*.

Aries, E. 1976. "Interaction Patterns and Themes of Male, Female, and Mixed Groups." *Small Group Behavior* 7: 7–18.

——— 1996. *Men and Women in Interaction: Reconsidering the Differences*. New York: Oxford University Press.

———. 1998. "Gender Differences in Interaction: A Reexamination." In *Sex Differences and Similarities in Communication: Critical Essays and Empirical Investigations of Sex and Gender in Interaction*, edited by Daniel J. Canary and Kathryn Dindia. Mahwah, NJ: Lawrence Erlbaum.

Aries, E., C. Gold, and R. H. Weigel. 1983. "Dispositional and Situational Influences on Dominance Behavior in Small Groups." *Journal of Personality and Social Psychology* 44: 779–86.

Arnold, Arthur. 2010. "Promoting the Understanding of Sex Differences to Enhance Equity and Excellence in Biomedical Science." *Biology of Sex Differences* 1 (1). Available online at http://www.bsd-journal.com/content/1/1/1#B27.

Aronson, J., M. J. Lustina, C. Good, K. Keough, C. M. Steele, and J. Brown. 1999. "When White Men Can't Do Math: Necessary and Sufficient Factors in Stereotype Threat." *Journal of Experimental Social Psychology* 35: 29–46.

Ashenfelter, O., T. Eisenberg, and S. J. Schwab. 1995. "Politics and the Judiciary: The Influence of Judicial Background on Case Outcomes." *Journal of Legal Studies* 24: 257–81.

Atkeson, Lonna Rae. 2003. "Not All Cues Are Created Equal: The Conditional Impact of Female Candidates on Political Engagement." *Journal of Politics* 65 (4): 1040–61.

Atkeson, Lonna Rae, and Nancy Carrillo. 2007. "More Is Better: The Influence of Collective Female Descriptive Representation on External Efficacy." *Politics and Gender* 3 (1): 79–101.

Atkeson, Lonna Rae, and Ronald B. Rapoport. 2003. "The More Things Change the More They Stay the Same: Examining Differences in Political Communication, 1952–2000." *Public Opinion Quarterly* 67: 495–521.

Austen-Smith, David, and Timothy J. Feddersen. 2006. "Deliberation, Preference Uncertainty, and Voting Rules." *American Political Science Review* 100 (2): 209–17.

Babcock, Linda, and Sara Laschever. 2003. *Women Don't Ask*. Princeton, NJ: Princeton University Press.

Babcock, Linda, Sara Laschever, Michele Gelfand, and Deborah Small. 2003. "Nice Girls Don't Ask." *Harvard Business Review* 81: 14–16.

Bachrach, Peter, and Morton S. Baratz. 1962. "Two Faces of Power." *American Political Science Review* 62 (4): 947–52.

Baer, D. L. 2003. "Women, Women's Organizations, and Political Parties." In *Women and American Politics*, edited by Susan J. Carroll, 111–45. Oxford: Oxford University Press.

Bales, R. F. 1970. *Personality and Interpersonal Behavior*. New York: Holt, Rinehart and Winston.

Ban, Radu, Saumitra Jha, and Vijayendra Rao. 2012. "Who Has Voice in a Deliberative Democracy? Evidence from Transcripts of Village Parliaments in South India." *Journal of Development Economics* 99: 428–38.

Ban, Radu, and Vijayendra Rao. 2008a. "An Empirical Analysis of the Deliberative Space: Evidence from Village Meetings in South India." Mimeograph, World Bank Development Research Group.

———. 2008b. "Tokenism or Agency? The Impact of Women's Reservations on Village Democracies in South India." *Economic Development and Cultural Change* 56 (3): 501–30.

———. 2009. "Is Deliberation Equitable? Evidence from Transcripts of Village Meetings in South India." Policy Research Working Paper 4928, World Bank, Washington, DC.

Barabas, Jason. 2004. "How Deliberation Affects Policy Opinions." *American Political Science Review* 98: 687–701.

Barber, Benjamin. 1984. *Strong Democracy: Participation Politics for a New Age*. Berkeley: University of California Press.

Barnes, Tiffany D., and Stephanie M. Burchard. 2012. "'Engendering' Politics: The Impact of Descriptive Representation on Women's Political Engagement in Sub-Saharan Africa." *Comparative Political Studies* 46 (7): 767–90.

Baron, L. A. 2003. "Ask and You Shall Receive? Gender Differences in Negotiators' Beliefs about Requests for a Higher Salary." *Human Relations* 56: 635–62.

Baron, Reuben M., and David A. Kenny. 1986. "Moderator-Mediator Variables Distinction in Social Psychological Research: Conceptual, Strategic, and Statistical Considerations." *Journal of Personality and Social Psychology* 51 (6): 1173–82.

Baron-Cohen, Simon. 2003. *The Essential Difference: Men, Women, and the Extreme Male Brain*. London: Allen Lane Science.

Barr, A. 2004. "Do Men Really Have No Shame?" Economics Working Paper Archive 0409008. Development and Comp Systems, WUSTL.

Bartal, Inbal Ben-Ami, Jean Decety, and Peggy Mason. 2011. "Empathy and Pro-Social Behavior in Rats." *Science* 334: 1427–30.

Bartels, Larry M. 2008. *Unequal Democracy: The Political Economy of the New Gilded Age*. New York: Russell Sage Foundation; Princeton, NJ: Princeton University Press.

Baum, M. A., and A. Jamison. 2006. "The Oprah Effect: How Soft News Helps Inattentive Citizens Vote Consistently." *Journal of Politics* 68: 946–59.

Beaman, Lori, Raghabendra Chattopadhyay, Esther Duflo, Rohini Pande, and Petia Topalova. 2009. "Powerful Women: Can Exposure Reduce Bias?" *Quarterly Journal of Economics* 124 (4): 1497–540.

Beaman, Lori, Esther Duflo, Raghabendra Pande, and Petia Topalova. 2010. "Political Reservation and Substantive Representation: Evidence from Indian Village Councils." In *India Policy Forum*, edited by S. Bery, B. Bosworth, and A. Panagariya. Washington, DC: Brookings Institution Press; New Delhi: National Council of Applied Economic Research.

Beaman, Lori, Rohini Pande, and Alexandra Cirone. 2012. "Politics as a Male Domain and Empowerment in India." In *The Impacts of Gender Quotas*, edited by Susan Franceschet, Mona Lena Krook, and Jennifer M. Piscopo, 208–26. New York: Oxford University Press.

Beck, Susan Abrams. 2001. "Acting as Women: The Effects and Limitations in Local Governance." In *The Impact of Women in Public Office*, edited by Susan J. Carroll, 49–67. Bloomington: Indiana University Press.

Beckwith, Karen. 2005. "A Common Language of Gender." *Politics and Gender* 1 (1): 128–36.

———. 2007. "Numbers and Newness: The Descriptive and Substantive Representation of Women." *Canadian Journal of Political Science* 40 (1): 27–49.

Beckwith, Karen, and Kimberly Cowell-Meyers. 2007. "Sheer Numbers: Critical Representation Thresholds and Women's Political Representation." *Perspectives on Politics* 5 (3): 553–65.

Behnke, Ralph R., and Chris R. Sawyer. 2000. "Anticipatory Anxiety Patterns for Male and Female Public Speakers." *Communication Education* 49: 187–95.

Belenky, Mary, Blythe Clinchy, Nancy Goldberger, and Jill Tarule. 1986. *Women's Ways of Knowing: The Development of Self, Voice, and Mind*. New York: Basic Books.

Benhabib, Seyla. 1992. *Situating the Self*. New York: Routledge.

Berdahl, Jennifer L., and Cameron Anderson. 2005. "Men, Women, and Leadership Centralization in Groups over Time." *Group Dynamics: Theory Research, and Practice* 9 (1): 45–57.

Berkman, Michael, and Robert O'Connor. 1993. "Do Women Legislators Matter? Female Legislators and State Abortion Policy." *American Politics Research* 21 (1): 102–24.

Bernstein, Elizabeth. 2012. "Speaking Up Is Hard to Do: Researchers Explain Why." *Wall Street Journal*, February 7.

Besley, Timothy, and Anne Case. 2003. "Political Institutions and Policy Choices: Evidence from the United States." *Journal of Economic Literature* 41 (1): 7–73.

Besley, Timothy, Rohini Pande, Rahman Lupin, and Vijayendra Rao. 2005a. "Participatory Democracy in Action: Survey Evidence from South India." *Journal of the European Economic Association* 3 (2–3): 648–57.

Besley, Timothy, Rohini Pande, and Vijayendra Rao. 2005b. "Political Selection and the Quality of Government: Evidence from South India." *Yale University Economic Growth Center*, Discussion Paper 921. http://ssrn.com/abstract=777507.

Beyer, Sylvia, and Edward M. Bowden. 1997. "Gender Differences in Self-Perceptions: Convergent Evidence from Three Measures of Accuracy and Bias." *Personality and Social Psychology Bulletin* 23 (2): 157–72.

Bird, S. R., and A. S. Wharton. 1996. "Stand by Your Man: Homosociality, Work Groups, and Men's Perceptions of Difference." In *Masculinities in Organizations*, edited by C. Cheng, 97–114. Thousand Oaks, CA: Sage.

Black, Laura. 2012. "How People Communicate during Deliberative Events." In *Democracy in Motion: Evaluating the Practice and Impact of Deliberative Civic Engagement*, edited by Tina Nabatchi, John Gastil, Matt Leighninger, and G. Michael Weiksner, 59–82. New York: Oxford University Press.

Bochel, Catherine, and Jacqui Briggs. 2000. "Do Women Make a Difference?" Politics 20 (2): 63–68.

Bohman, James. 1997. "Deliberative Democracy and Effective Social Freedom: Resources, Opportunities, and Capabilities." In *Deliberative Democracy: Essays on Reason and Politics*, edited by James Bohman and William Rehg. Cambridge, MA: MIT Press.

Bollen, Kenneth A., and Robert W. Jackman. 1985. "Regression Diagnostics: An Expository Treatment of Outliers and Influential Cases." *Sociological Methods Research* 13 (4): 510–42.

Bolzendahl, Catherine. 2011. "Beyond the Big Picture: Gender Influences on Disaggregated and Domain-Specific Measures of Social Spending, 1980–1999." *Politics and Gender* 7 (1): 35–70.

Bond, Red, and Peter B. Smith. 1996. "Culture and Conformity: A Meta-Analysis of Studies Using Asch's (1952b, 1956) Line Judgment Task." *Psychological Bulletin* 119: 111–37.

Bottger, Preston C. 1984. "Expertise and Air Time as Bases of Actual and Perceived Influence in Problem-Solving Groups." *Journal of Applied Psychology* 69 (2): 214–21.

Bouas, K. S., and S. S. Komorita. 1996. "Group Discussion and Cooperation in Social Dilemmas." *Personality and Social Psychology Bulletin* 22: 1144–50.

Bowers, William J., Benjamin D. Steiner, and Marla Sandys. 2001. "Death Sentencing in Black and White: An Empirical Analysis of Jurors' Race and Jury Racial Composition." *University of Pennsylvania Journal of Constitutional Law* 3: 171–275.

Boyd, Christina L., Lee Epstein, and Andrew Martin. 2010. "Untangling the Causal Effects of Sex on Judging." *American Journal of Political Science* 54 (2): 389–411.

Braden, Maria. 1996. *Women Politicians and the Media*. Lexington: University Press of Kentucky.

Brady, Henry E., Sidney Verba, and Key Lehman Schlozman. 1995. "Beyond SES: A Resource Model of Political Participation." *American Political Science Review* 89 (2): 271–94.

Bratton, Kathleen A. 2005. "Critical Mass Theory Revisited: The Behavior and Success of Token Women in State Legislatures." *Politics and Gender* 1 (1): 97–125.

Brodbeck, Felix, Rudolf Kerschreiter, Andreas Mojzisch, Dieter Frey, and Stefan Schulz-Hardt. 2002. "The Dissemination of Critical, Unshared Information in Decision-Making Groups: The Effects of Pre-Discussion Dissent." *European Journal of Social Psychology* 32: 35–56.

Brown, Penelope, and Stephen Levinson. 1987. *Politeness: Some Universals in Language Usage*. Cambridge: Cambridge University Press.

Brown, R. Khari, and Ronald E. Brown. 2003. "Faith and Works: Church-Based Social Capital Resources and African American Political Activism." *Social Forces* 82 (2): 617–41.

Bryan, Frank M. 2004. *Real Democracy: The New England Town Meeting and How It Works*. Chicago: University of Chicago Press.

Buchanan, James M., and Gordon Tullock. 1962. *The Calculus of Consent: Logical Foundations of Constitutional Democracy*. Ann Arbor: University of Michigan Press.

Buck, R. W., V. J. Savin, R. E. Miller, and W. F. Caul. 1972. "Communication of Affect through Facial Expression in Humans." *Journal of Personality and Social Psychology* 23: 362–71.

Bullock, John G., Donald P. Green, and Shang E. Ha. 2010. "Yes, But What's the Mechanism? (Don't Expect an Easy Answer)." *Journal of Personality and Social Psychology* 98 (4): 550–58.

Burke, R. J., and C. A. McKeen. 1996. "Gender Effects in Mentoring Relationships." *Journal of Social Behavior and Personality* 11: 91–104.

Burns, Nancy. 2007. "Gender in the Aggregate, Gender in the Individual, Gender and Political Action." *Politics and Gender* 3: 104–24.

Burns, Nancy, Kay Lehman Schlozman, and Sidney Verba. 2001. *The Private Roots of Public Action: Gender, Equality, and Political Participation*. Cambridge, MA: Harvard University Press.

Burrell, Barbara C. 1994. *A Woman's Place Is in the House: Campaigning for Congress in the Feminist Era*. Ann Arbor: University of Michigan Press.

Butler, Doré, and Florence L. Geis. 1990. "Nonverbal Affect Responses to Male and Female Leaders: Implications for Leadership Evaluations." *Journal of Personality and Social Psychology* 16: 358–68.

Bylsma, Wayne H., and Brenda Major. 1992. "Two Routes to Eliminating Gender Differences in Personal Entitlement: Social Comparisons and Performance Evaluations." *Psychology of Women Quarterly* 16 (2): 193–200.

Calhoun, Cheshire. 2005. "The Virtue of Civility." Philosophy and Public Affairs 29 (3): 251–75.

Calhoun-Brown, Allison. 1996. "African American Churches and Political Mobilization: The Psychological Impact of Organizational Resources." *Journal of Politics* 58 (4): 935–53.

Callahan-Levy, C. M., and L. A. Messe. 1979. "Sex Differences in Allocation of Pay." *Journal of Personality and Social Psychology* 37: 433–46.

Campbell, David E., and Christina Wolbrecht. 2006. "See Jane Run: Women Politicians as Role Models for Adolescents." *Journal of Politics* 68 (2): 233–47.

Campbell, Donald T., and D. W. Fiske. 1959. "Convergent and Discriminant Validation by the Multitrait-Multimethod Matrix." *Psychological Bulletin* 56: 81–105.

Campus, Donatella. 2013. *Women Political Leaders and the Media*. New York: Palgrave Macmillan.

Cappella, Joseph N. 1988. "Personal Relationships, Social Relationships, and Patterns of Interaction." In *Handbook of Personal Relationships: Theory, Research, and Interventions*, edited by Steve Duck, 325–42. New York: Wiley.

Caprara, Gian Vittorio, Patrizia Steca, Arnaldo Zelli, and Cristina Capanna. 2005. "A New Scale for Measuring Adults' Prosocialness." *European Journal of Psychological Assessment* 21 (2): 77–89.

Carbonell, J. L. 1984. "Sex Roles and Leadership Revisited." *Journal of Applied Psychology* 69: 44–49.

Carli, Linda. 1989. "Gender Differences in Interaction Style and Influence." *Journal of Personality and Social Psychology* 56 (4): 565–76.

———. 1990. "Gender, Language, and Influence." *Journal of Personality and Social Psychology* 59 (5): 941–51.

———. 2001. "Gender and Social Influence." *Journal of Social Issues* 57 (4): 725–41.

Carli, Linda, Suzanne J. LaFleur, and Christopher C. Loeber. 1995. "Nonverbal Behavior, Gender, and Influence." *Journal of Personality and Social Psychology* 68: 1030–41.

Carlin, Diana B., and Kelly L. Winfrey. 2009. "Have You Come a Long Way, Baby? Hillary Clinton, Sarah Palin, and Sexism in 2008 Campaign Coverage." *Communication Studies* 60 (4): 326–43.

Carlock, C. J., and P. Y. Martin. 1977. "Sex Composition and the Intensive Group Experience." *Social Work* 22: 27–32.

Carnevale, Anthony P., Jeff Strohl, and Michele Melton. 2011. "Select Findings from What's It Worth? The Value of College Majors." Georgetown University Center on Education and the Workforce. Available online at http://www9.georgetown.edu/grad/gppi/hpi/cew/pdfs/whatsitworth-select.pdf.

Carpenter, Daniel. 2011. "Gender and Recruitment by Petition: Women Canvassers in Antislavery Petitioning, 1833–1847." Paper presented at a seminar of the Princeton University Center for the Study of Democratic Politics, March 2012.

Carroll, Susan J. 2001. Introduction to *The Impact of Women in Public Office*, edited by Susan J. Carroll. Bloomington: Indiana University Press.

———. 2002. "Representing Women: Women State Legislators as Agents of Policy-Related Change." In *Women Transforming Congress*, edited by Cindy Simon Rosenthal. Norman: University of Oklahoma Press.

Case, Anne. 1998. "The Effects of Stronger Child Support Enforcement of Non-Marital Fertility." In *Fathers under Fire: The Revolution in Child Support Enforcement*, edited by Irwin Garfinkel, Sara McLanahan, Daniel Meyer, and Judith Seltzer, 191–215. New York: Russell Sage Foundation.

Case, Anne, and Timothy Besley. 2000. "Unnatural Experiments? Estimating the Incidence of Endogenous Policies." *Economic Journal* 110 (466): 781–804.

Chambers, Simone. 1995. "Discourse and Democratic Practices." In *The Cambridge Companion to Habermas*, edited by Stephen K. White. Cambridge: Cambridge University Press.

———. 1996. *Reasonable Democracy*. Ithaca, NY: Cornell University Press.

———. 2003. "Deliberative Democratic Theory." *Annual Review of Political Science* 6: 307–26.

———. 2009. "Rhetoric and the Public Sphere: Has Deliberative Democracy Abandoned Mass Democracy?" *Political Theory* 37: 323–50.

Chatman, Jennifer A., and Charles A. O'Reilly. 2004. "Asymmetric Reactions to Work Group Sex Diversity among Men and Women." *Academy of Management Journal* 47: 193–208.

Chattopadhyay, Raghabendra, and Esther Duflo. 2004. "Women as Policy Makers: Evidence from a Randomized Policy Experiment in India." *Econometrica* 72 (5): 1409–43.

Childs, Sarah. 2004a. "A Feminised Style of Politics? Women MPs in the House of Commons." *British Journal of Politics and International Relations* 6 (1): 3–19.

———. 2004b. *New Labour's Women MPs: Women Representing Women*. New York: Routledge.

———. 2013. "Negotiating Gendered Institutions: Women's Parliamentary Friendships." *Politics and Gender* 9 (2): 127–51.

Childs, Sarah, and Mona Lena Krook. 2006. "Should Feminists Give Up on Critical Mass? A Contingent Yes." *Politics and Gender* 2 (4): 522–30.

Choi, Seung-Whan. 2009. "The Effect of Outliers on Regression Analysis: Regime Type and Foreign Direct Investment." *Quarterly Journal of Political Science* 4: 153–65.

Cialdini, Robert B., and Melanie R. Trost. 1998. "Social Influence: Social Norms, Conformity and Compliance." In *Handbook of Social Psychology*, vol. 2, 4th ed., edited by Daniel T. Gilbert, Susan T. Fiske, and Gardner Lindzey. 151–92. New York and Oxford: Oxford University Press.

Clark, Janet, and Cal Clark. 1993. "The Gender Gap 1988: Compassion, Pacifism, and Indirect Feminism." In *Women in Politics: Insiders or Outsiders? A Collection of Readings*, edited by L. L. Duke, 32–45. Englewood Cliffs, NJ: Prentice-Hall.

Cohen, Joshua. 1989. "Deliberation and Democratic Legitimacy." In *Good Polity*, edited by Alan P. Hamlin and Phillip Pettit. Oxford: Blackwell.

———. 1996. "Deliberation and Democratic Legitimacy." In *Deliberative Democracy: Essays on Reason and Politics*, edited by J. Bohman and W. Rehg, 67–92. Cambridge, MA: MIT Press.

Collingwood, Loren, and Justin Reedy. 2012. "Listening and Responding to Criticisms of Deliberative Civic Engagement." In *Democracy in Motion: Evaluating the Practice and Impact of Deliberative Civic Engagement*, edited by Tina Nabatchi, John Gastil, Matt Leighninger, and G. Michael Weiksner, 233–60. New York: Oxford University Press.

Conover, Pamela Johnston, and Virginia Sapiro. 1993. "Gender, Feminist Consciousness, and War." *American Journal of Political Science* 37: 1079–99.

Conover, Pamela J., David D. Searing, and Ivor Crewe. 2002. "The Deliberative Potential of Political Discussion." *British Journal of Political Science* 32: 21–62.

Converse, P. 1964. "The Nature of Belief Systems in Mass Publics." In *Ideology and Discontent*, edited by D. Apter. New York: Free Press of Glencoe.

Cook, Fay Lomax, Michael X. Delli Carpini, and Lawrence R. Jacobs. 2007. "Who Deliberates? Discursive Participation in America." In *Deliberation, Participation, and Democracy: Can the People Govern?*, edited by Shawn Rosenberg, 25–40. New York: Macmillan.

Cooper, H. M. 1979. "Statistically Combining Independent Studies: A Meta-Analysis of Sex Differences in Conformity Research." *Journal of Personality and Social Psychology* 37: 131–46.

Cornwall, Andrea. 2003. "Whose Voices? Whose Choices? Reflections on Gender and Participatory Development." *World Development* 31 (8): 1325–42.

Cornwell, Erin York, and Valerie P. Hans. 2011. "Representation through Participation: A Multilevel Analysis of Jury Deliberations." *Law and Society Review* 45 (3): 667–98.

Craig, Jane M., and Carolyn W Sherif. 1986. "The Effectiveness of Men and Women in Problem-Solving Groups as a Function of Gender Composition." *Sex Roles* 14 (7–8): 453–66.

Croson, Rachel, and Uri Gneezy. 2009. "Gender Differences in Preferences." *Journal of Economic Literature* 47: 448–74.

Cross, S. E., and L. Madson. 1997. "Models of the Self: Self-Construals and Gender." *Psychological Bulletin* 122: 5–37.

Crowder-Meyer, Melody. 2007. "Gender Differences in Policy Preferences and Priorities." Paper presented at the annual meeting of the Midwest Political Science Association, Chicago, Illinois, April 12, 2007. Available at http://www.allacademic.com/meta/p196573_index.html. Accessed May 19, 2011.

———. 2010. "Local Parties, Local Candidates, and Women's Representation: How County Parties Affect Who Runs for and Wins Political Office." PhD diss., Princeton University.

Crowley, Jocelyn. 2004. "When Tokens Matter." *Legislative Studies Quarterly* 21: 109–35.

Dahlerup, Drude. 2006. "The Story of the Theory of Critical Mass." *Politics and Gender* 2 (4): 511–22.

———. 2012. Preface. In *The Impact of Gender Quotas*, edited by Susan Franceschet, Mona Lena Krook, and Jennifer M. Piscopo, vii–viii. New York: Oxford University Press.

Daly, John A., Pamela O. Kriesler, and L. A. Roghaar. 1994. "Question-Asking Comfort: Explorations of the Demography of Communication in the Eighth Grade Classroom." *Communication Education* 43: 27–41.

Davies, Paul G., Steven J. Spencer, and Claude M. Steele. 2005. "Clearing the Air: Identity Safety Moderates the Effects of Stereotype Threat on Women's Leadership Aspirations." *Journal of Personality and Social Psychology* 88: 276–87.

Davis, B. M., and L. A. Gilbert. 1989. "Effect of Dispositional and Situational Influences on Women's Dominance Expression in Mixed-Sex Dyads." *Journal of Personality and Social Psychology* 57 (2): 294–300.

Davis, J. H., R. M. Bray, and R. W. Holt. 1977. "The Empirical Study of Decision Processes in Juries: A Critical Review." In *Law, Justice, and the Individual in Society*, edited by J. L. Tapp and F. J. Levine. New York: Holt, Rinehart and Winston.

Davis, J. H., T. Kameda, C. Parks, M. Stasson, and S. Zimmerman. 1989. "Some Social Mechanics of Group Decision Making: The Distribution of Opinion, Polling Sequence, and Implications for Consensus." *Journal of Personality and Social Psychology* 57: 1000–1012.

Davis, J. H., M. Stasson, K. Ono, and S. Zimmerman. 1988. "Effects of Straw Polls on Group Decision Making: Sequential Voting Pattern, Timing, and Local Majorities." *Journal of Personality and Social Psychology* 55: 918–26.

Davis, J. H., et al. 1977. "Victim Consequences, Sentence Severity, and Decision Processes in Mock Juries." *Organizational Behavior and Human Performance* 18: 346–54.

Deaux, K., and B. Major. 1987. "Putting Gender into Context: An Interactive Model of Gender-Related Behavior." *Psychological Review* 94 (3): 369–89.

Delli Carpini, Michael X., and Scott Keeter. 1996. *What Americans Know about Politics and Why It Matters*. New Haven, CT: Yale University Press.

———. 2005. "Gender and Political Knowledge." In *Gender and American Politics: Women, Men, and the Political Process*, edited by Sue Tolleson-Rinehart and Jyl J. Josephon. Revised and expanded 2nd ed., 21–47. Armonk, NY: M. E. Sharpe.

Desposato, Scott, and Barbara Norrander. 2009. "The Gender Gap in Latin America: Contextual and Individual Influences on Gender and Political Participation." *British Journal of Political Science* 39 (1): 141–62.

Devine, Dennis J., Laura Clayton, Benjamin B. Dunford, Rasmy Seying, and Jennifer Price. 2001. "Jury Decision Making: 45 Years of Empirical Research on Deliberating Groups." *Psychology, Public Policy, and Law* 73 (3): 622–727.

Devitt, James. 2002. "Framing Gender on the Campaign Trail: Female Gubernatorial Candidates and the Press." *Journalism and Mass Communication Quarterly* 79 (2): 445–63.

Devlin, Claire, and Robert Elgie. 2008. "The Effect of Increased Women's Representation in Parliament: The Case of Rwanda." *Parliamentary Affairs* 61 (2): 237–54.

Diamond, Shari Seidman, Mary R. Rose, and Beth Murphy. 2006. "Revisiting the Unanimity Requirement: The Behavior of the Non-Unanimous Civil Jury Symposium." *Northwestern University Law Review* 100 (1): 201–30.

Dindia, Kathryn, and Mike Allen. 1992. "Sex Differences in Self-Disclosure: A Meta-Analysis." *Psychological Bulletin* 112: 106–24.

Djupe, Paul A., Anand E. Sokhey, and Christopher P. Gilbert. 2007. "Present but Not Accounted For? Gender Differences in Civic Resource Acquisition." *American Journal of Political Science* 51 (4): 906–20.

Djupe, Paul, Scott D. McClurg, and Anand Sokhey. 2010. "The Political Consequences of Gender in Social Networks." Working Paper, Department of Political Science, Southern Illinois University–Carbondale. Available at http://opensiuc.lib.siu.edu/pn_wp/42/?utm_source=opensiuc.lib.siu.edu%2Fpn_wp%2F42&utm_medium=PDF&utm_campaign=PDFCoverPages.

Dodson, Debra L. 2006. *Impact of Women in Congress*. New York: Oxford University Press.

Dodson, Debra L., and Susan J. Carroll. 1991. *Reshaping the Agenda: Women in State Legislatures*. New Brunswick, NJ: Eagleton Institute of Politics, Rutgers, the State University of New Jersey.

Dolan, Kathleen A. 2004. *Voting for Women: How the Public Evaluates Women Candidates*. Boulder, CO: Westview Press.

Dolan, Kathleen, and Lynne E. Ford. 1995. "Women in the State Legislatures: Feminist Identity and Legislative Behavior." *American Politics Quarterly* 23: 96–108.

Dolan, Kathleen, and Kira Sanbonmatsu. 2009. "Gender Stereotypes and Attitudes Toward Gender Balance in Government." *American Politics Research* 37 (3): 409–28.

Donahue, Jesse. 1997. "Findings about Sex and Representation from School Committee Conversations." Policy Studies Journal 25 (4): 630–47.

Dovi, Suzanne. 2008. "Theorizing Women's Representation in the United States." In *Political Women and American Democracy*, edited by Christina Wolbrecht, Karen Beckwith, and Lisa Baldez, 148–66. Cambridge: Cambridge University Press.

Dovidio, J. F., C. E. Brown, K. Heltman, S. L. Ellyson, and C. F. Keating. 1988. "Power Displays between Women and Men in Discussions of Gender-Linked Tasks: A Multi-Channel Study." *Journal of Personality and Social Psychology* 55: 580–87.

Dow, Jay K. 2009. "Gender Differences in Political Knowledge: Distinguishing Characteristics-Based and Returns-Based Differences." *Political Behavior* 31: 117–36.

Druckman, James N., and Cindy D. Kam. 2011. "Students as Experimental Participants: A Defense of the 'Narrow Data Base.'" In *Handbook of Experimental Political Science*, edited by James N. Druckman, Donald P. Green, James H. Kuklinski, and Arthur Lupia, 41–57. New York: Cambridge University Press.

Dryzek, John S. 1990. *Discursive Democracy: Politics, Policy, and Political Science*. Cambridge: Cambridge University Press.

———. 2000. *Deliberative Democracy and Beyond*. New York: Oxford University Press.

———. 2005. "Deliberative Democracy in Divided Societies: Alternatives to Agonism and Analgesia." *Political Theory* 33 (2): 218–42.

Drzyzek, John S. 2007. "Theory, Evidence, and the Tasks of Deliberation." In *Deliberation, Participation, and Democracy: Can the People Govern?*, edited by Shawn W. Rosenberg, 237–50. New York: Palgrave Macmillan.

Dubrovsky, Vitaly J., Sara Kiesler, and Beheruz N. Sethna. 1991. "The Equalization Phenomenon: Status Effects in Computer-Mediated and Face-to-Face Decision-Making Groups." *Human-Computer Interaction* 6 (2): 119–46.

Duerst-Lahti, Georgia. 2002a. "Governing Institutions, Ideologies and Gender: Toward the Possibility of Equal Political Representation." *Sex Roles* 47: 371–88.

———. 2002b. "Knowing Congress as a Gendered Institution." In *Women Transforming Congress*, edited by Cindy Simon Rosenthal, 20–49. Norman: University of Oklahoma Press.

Duerst-Lahti, Georgia, and Rita Mae Kelly. 1995. "On Governance, Leadership and Gender." In *Gender Power, Leadership, and Governance*, edited by Georgia Duerst-Lahti and Rita Mae Kelly, 11–37. Ann Arbor: University of Michigan Press.

Duflo, Esther. 2003. "Grandmothers and Granddaughters: Old Age Pension and Intra-Household Allocation in South Africa." *World Bank Economic Review* 17 (1): 1–25.

Duflo, Esther, and Petia Topalova. 2004. "Unappreciated Service: Performance, Perceptions, and Women Leaders in India." Mimeograph.

Dunning, Thad, and Janhavi Nilekani. 2013. "Ethnic Quotas and Political Mobilization: Caste, Parties, and Distribution in Indian Village Councils." *American Political Science Review* 107 (1): 35–56.

Eagly, Alice H. 1987. *Sex Differences in Social Behavior: A Social-Role Interpretation*. Hillsdale, NJ: L. Erlbaum Associates.

Eagly, Alice H., and Linda L. Carli. 1981. "Sex of Researchers and Sex-Typed Communications as Determinants of Sex Differences in Influenceability: A Meta-Analysis of Social Influence Studies." *Psychological Bulletin* 90: 1–20.

———. 2003. "The Female Leadership Advantage: An Evaluation of the Evidence." *Leadership Quarterly* 14: 807–34.

———. 2007. *Through the Labyrinth: The Truth about How Women Become Leaders*. Boston, MA: Harvard Business Press.

Eagly, Alice H., and Maureen Crowley. 1986. "Gender and Helping Behavior: A Meta-Analytic Review of the Social Psychological Literature." *Psychological Bulletin* 100 (3): 283–308.

Eagly, Alice H., Amanda B. Diekman, Mary C. Johannesen-Schmidt, and Anne M. Koenig. 2004. "Gender Gaps in Sociopolitical Attitudes: A Social Psychological Analysis." *Journal of Personality and Social Psychology* 87: 796–816.

Eagly, Alice H., and Blair T. Johnson. 1990. "Gender and Leadership Style: A Meta-Analysis." *Psychological Bulletin* 108: 233–56.

Eagly, Alice H., and S. J. Karau. 2002. "Role Congruity Theory of Prejudice toward Female Leaders." *Psychological Review* 109: 573–98.

Eagly, Alice H., Mary C. Johannesen-Schmidt, and Marloes L. van Engen. 2003. "Transformational, transactional, and laissez-faire leadership styles: A meta-analysis comparing women and men." *Psychological Bulletin* 129 (4): 569-91.

Eagly, Alice H., Mona G. Makhijani, and Bruce G. Klonsky. 1992. "Gender and the Evaluation of Leaders: A Meta-Analysis." *Psychological Bulletin* 111: 3–22.

Eagly, Alice H., and Wendy Wood. 1982. "Inferred Sex Differences in Status as a Determinant of Gender Stereotypes about Social Influence." *Journal of Personality and Social Psychology* 43: 915–28.

———. 2012. "Social Role Theory." In *Handbook of Theories of Social Psychology*, vol. 2, edited by Paul A. M. Van Lange, Arie W. Kruglanski, and E. Tory Higgins, 458–76. Thousand Oaks, CA: Sage Publications.

Eagly, Alice H., W. Wood, and A. B. Diekman. 2000. "Social Role Theory of Sex Differences and Similarities: A Current Appraisal." In *The Developmental Social Psychology of Gender*, edited by T. Eckes and H. M. Trautner. Mahwah, NJ: Lawrence Erlbaum.

Eakins, B., and R. G. Eakins. 1976. "Verbal Turn-Taking and Exchanges in Faculty Dialogue." In *The Sociology of the Languages of American Women*, edited by D. L. Dubois and I. M. Crouch. San Antonio, TX: Trinity University.

Eckel, C. C., and P. Grossman.1998. "Are Women Less Selfish Than Men? Evidence from Dictator Experiments." *Economic Journal* 108: 726–35.

Edlund, L., and R. Pande. 2002. "Why Have Women Become Left-Wing? The Political Gender Gap and the Decline in Marriage." *Quarterly Journal of Economics* 117: 917–61.

Eliasoph, Nina. 1998. *Avoiding Politics: How Americans Produce Apathy in Everyday Life*. Cambridge: Cambridge University Press.

Ellis, D. G. 1982. "Relational Stability and Change in Women's Consciousness-Raising Groups." *Women's Studies in Communication* 5: 77–87.

Ellyson, S. L., J. F. Dovidio, and C. E. Brown. 1992. "The Look of Power: Gender Differences in Visual Dominance Behavior." In *Gender, Interaction, and Inequality*, edited by C. L. Ridgeway, 50–80. New York: Springer-Verlag.

Esterling, Kevin M., Archon Fung, and Taeku Lee. 2009. "How Much Disagreement Is Good for Democratic Deliberation? The California Speaks Health Care Reform Experiment." Paper delivered at the 2nd Annual West Coast Experimental Political Science Conference, Del Mar, California, May 15.

Falk, D. 1997. "Brain Evolution in Females: An Answer to Mr. Lovejoy." In *Women in Human Evolution*, edited by L. D. Hager, 114–36. New York: Routledge.

Falk, G. 1981. “Unanimity versus Majority Rule in Problem Solving Groups: A Challenge to the Superiority of Unanimity.” *Small Group Behavior* 12: 379–99.

———. 1982. “An Empirical Study Measuring Conflict in Problem-Solving Groups Which Are Assigned Different Decision Rules.” *Human Relations* 35 (12): 1123–37.

Farhang, Sean, and Gregory Wawro. 2004. “Institutional Dynamics on the U.S. Court of Appeals: Minority Representation under Panel Decision Making.” *Journal of Law, Economics, and Organization* 20 (2): 299–330.

———. 2010. “Indirect Influences of Gender on the U.S. Courts of Appeals: Evidence from Sexual Harassment Law.” University of California–Berkeley working paper.

Farrar, C., D. P. Green, J. E. Green, D. W. Nickerson, and S. Shewfelt. 2009. “Does Discussion Group Composition Affect Policy Preferences? Results from Three Randomized Experiments.” *Political Psychology* 30: 615–47.

Fay, Nicolas, Simon Garrod, and Jean Carletta. 2000. “Group Discussion as Interactive Dialogue or as Serial Monologue: The Influence of Group Size.” *Psychological Science* 11 (6): 481–86.

Feldman, Stanley, and Marco R. Steenbergen. 2001. “The Humanitarian Foundation of Public Support for Social Welfare.” *American Journal of Political Science* 45: 658–77.

Fields, D. L., and T. C. Blum. 1997. “Employee Satisfaction in Work Groups with Different Gender Composition.” *Journal of Organizational Behavior* 18 (2): 181–96.

Fish, M. Steven. 2002. “Islam and Authoritarianism.” *World Politics* 55: 4–37.

Fishkin, James S. 1995. *The Voice of the People*. New Haven, CT: Yale University Press.

———. 2009. *When the People Speak: Deliberative Democracy and Public Consultation*. Oxford and New York: Oxford University Press.

Fishkin, James S., Baogang He, Robert C. Luskin, and Alice Siu. 2010. “Deliberative Democracy in an Unlikely Place: Deliberative Polling in China.” *British Journal of Political Science* 40 (2): 435–48.

Fishkin, James S., and Robert C. Luskin. 1999. “Bringing Deliberation to the Democratic Dialogue.” In *The Poll with a Human Face: The National Issues Convention Experiment in Political Communication*, edited by M. McCombs and A. Reynolds. Mahwah, NJ: Lawrence Erlbaum.

Fishman, Pamela. 1978. “Interaction: The Work Women Do.” *Social Problem* 24: 297–406.

Fiske, Susan T. 2010. “Venus and Mars, or Down to Earth: Stereotypes and Realities of Gender Differences.” *Perspectives on Psychological Science* 5 (6): 688–92.

Flammang, Janet. 1985. “Female Officials in the Feminist Capital: The Case of Santa Clara County.” *Western Political Quarterly* 38 (1): 94–118.

Floge, Liliane, and Deborah Merrill. 1985. “Tokenism Reconsidered: Male Nurses and Female Physicians in a Hospital Setting.” *Social Forces* 64: 925–47.

Foschi, Martha, and Sabrina Freeman. 1991. “Inferior Performance, Standards, and Influence in Same-Sex Dyads.” *Canadian Journal of Behavioural Science* 23 (1): 99–113.

Fowler, Lucy. 2005. “Gender and Jury Deliberations: The Contributions of Social Science.” *William and Mary Journal of Women and the Law* 12 (1). Available at http://scholarship.law.wm.edu/wmjowl/vol12/iss1/2.

Fox, Richard L., and Jennifer L. Lawless. 2011. “Gendered Perceptions and Political Candidacies: A Central Barrier to Women’s Equality in Electoral Politics.” *American Journal of Political Science* 55 (1): 59–73.

Fox, Richard L., and Robert A. Schuhmann. 1999. “Bringing in the Community: Gender, Representation, and City Management.” *Public Administration Review* 59: 231–42.

Franceschet, Susan, Mona Lena Krook, and Jennifer M. Piscopo. 2012. "Conceptualizing the Impact of Gender Quotas." In *The Impact of Gender Quotas*, edited by Susan Franceschet, Mona Lena Krook, and Jennifer M. Piscopo, 3–24. New York: Oxford University Press.

Fraser, Nancy. 1990. "Rethinking the Public Sphere: A Contribution to the Critique of Actually Existing Democracy." *Social Text* 25 (26): 56–80.

———. 1992. "Rethinking the Public Sphere: A Contribution to the Critique of Actually Existing Democracy." In *Habermas and the Public Sphere*, edited by Craig Calhoun. Cambridge, MA: MIT Press.

Fricker, Miranda. 2007. *Epistemic Injustice: Power and the Ethics of Knowing*. Oxford: Oxford University Press.

Frohlich, Norman, and Joe Oppenheimer. 1990. "Choosing Justice in Experimental Democracies with Production." *American Political Science Review* 84 (2): 461–77.

———. 1992. *Choosing Justice: An Experimental Approach to Ethical Theory*. Berkeley: University of California Press.

Frohlich, Norman, Joe Oppenheimer, and Cheryl Eavy. 1987. "Laboratory Results on Rawls's Distributive Justice." *British Journal of Political Science* 17: 1–21.

Fung, Archon. 2003. "Deliberation Where You Least Expect It: Citizen Participation in Government." *Connections* (Fall): 30–33.

———. 2004. *Empowered Participation: Reinventing Urban Democracy*. Princeton, NJ: Princeton University Press.

———. 2007. "Democratic Theory and Political Science: A Pragmatic Method of Constructive Engagement." *American Political Science Review* 101: 443–58.

Fung, Archon, and Erick O. Wright. 2003. *Deepening Democracy: Institutional Innovations in Empowered Participatory Governance*. New York: Verso.

Gastil, John. 1993. *Democracy in Small Groups: Participation, Decision Making, and Communication*. Philadelphia: New Society.

———. 2000. *By Popular Demand: Revitalizing Representative Democracy through Deliberative Elections*. Berkeley: University of California Press.

———. 2008. *Political Communication and Deliberation*. Thousand Oaks, CA: Sage Publications.

———. 2010. *The Group in Society*. Los Angeles: Sage Publications.

Gastil, John, Laura W. Black, E. Pierre Dees, and Jay Leighter. 2008. "From Group Member to Democratic Citizen: How Deliberating with Fellow Jurors Reshapes Civic Attitudes." *Human Communication Research* 34: 137–69.

Gastil, John, S. Burkhalter, and L. Black. 2007. "Do Juries Deliberate? A Study of Deliberation, Individual Difference, and Group Member Satisfaction at a Municipal Courthouse." *Small Group Research* 38: 337–59.

Gastil, John, E. Pierre Deess, Philip J. Weiser, and Jordan Meade. 2008. "Jury Service and Electoral Participation: A Test of the Participation Hypothesis." *Journal of Politics* 70: 1–16.

Gastil, John, E. Pierre Deess, Philip J. Weiser, and Cindy Simmons. 2010. *The Jury and Democracy: How Jury Deliberation Promotes Civic Engagement and Political Participation*. New York: Oxford University Press.

Gaventa, John. 1982. *Power and Powerlessness: Quiescence and Rebellion in an Appalachian Valley*. Urbana: University of Illinois Press.

Gero, Anne. 1985. "Conflict Avoidance in Consensual Decision Processes." *Small Group Behavior* 16 (4): 487–99.

Gilens, Martin. 1988. "Gender and Support for Reagan: A Comprehensive Model of Presidential Approval." *American Journal of Political Science* 32: 19–49.

———. 1999. *Why Americans Hate Welfare*. Chicago: University of Chicago Press.

Giles, Howard, Anthony Mulac, James J. Bradac, and Patricia Johnson. 1987. "Speech Accommodation Theory: The First Decade and Beyond." In *Communication Yearbook 10*, edited by Margaret McLaughlin, 13–48. Thousand Oaks, CA: Sage Publications.

Gilligan, Carol. 1982. *In a Different Voice: Psychological Theory and Women's Development*. Cambridge, MA: Harvard University Press.

Gimpel, James G., J. Celeste Lay, and Jason E. Schuknecht. 2003. *Cultivating Democracy: Civic Environments and Political Socialization in America*. Washington, DC: Brookings Institution Press.

Glick, P., and S. T. Fiske. 1996. "The Ambivalent Sexism Inventory: Differentiating Hostile and Benevolent Sexism." *Journal of Personality and Social Psychology* 70: 491–512.

Gneezy, Uri, Kenneth L. Leonard, and John A. List. 2009. "Gender Differences in Competition: Evidence from a Matrilineal and a Patriarchal Society." *Econometrica, Econometric Society* 77 (5): 1637–64.

Gneezy, Uri, M. Niederle, and A. Rustichini. 2003. "Performance in Competitive Environments: Gender Differences." *Quarterly Journal of Economics* 118: 1049–74.

Godsay, Surbhi, and Emily Kirby. 2010. *Voter Turnout among Young Women and Men in the 2008 Presidential Election*. College Park, MD: Center for Information and Research on Civic Learning and Engagement.

Goffman, Erving. 1967. *Interaction Ritual: Essays on Face-to-Face Interaction*. Garden City, NY: Anchor Books.

Goldin, Claudia, Lawrence F. Katz, and Ilyana Kuziemko. 2006. "The Homecoming of American College Women: The Reversal of the College Gender Gap." *Journal of Economic Perspectives* 20 (4): 133–56.

Golding, Jonathan M., Gregory S. Bradshaw, Emily E. Dunlap, and Emily C. Hodell. 2007. "The Impact of Mock Jury Gender Composition on Deliberations and Conviction Rates in a Child Sexual Assault Trial." *Child Maltreatment* 12 (2): 182–90.

Goldstein, Susan. 1999. "Construction and Validation of a Conflict Communication Scale." *Journal of Applied Social Psychology* 29 (September): 1803–32.

Gottman, John. 1994. *What Predicts Divorce?: The Relationship between Marital Processes and Marital Outcomes*. New York: Lawrence Erlbaum.

Greig, Fiona, and Iris Bohnet. 2009. "Exploring Gendered Behavior in the Field with Experiments: Why Public Goods Are Provided by Women in a Nairobi Slum." *Journal of Economic Behavior and Organization* 70 (1–2): 1–9.

Grey, Sandra. 2002. "Does Size Matter? Critical Mass and New Zealand's Women MPs." *Parliamentary Affairs* 55 (1): 19–29.

———. 2006. "Numbers and Beyond: The Relevance of Critical Mass in Gender Research." *Politics and Gender* 2 (4): 492–502.

Grünenfelder, Rita, and André Bächtiger. 2007. "Gendered Deliberation? How Men and Women Deliberate in Legislatures." Paper presented at the ECPR Joint Sessions, Helsinki, May.

Guarnaschelli, S., R. D. McKelvey, and T. R. Palfrey. 2000. "An Experimental Study of Jury Decision Rules." *American Political Science Review* 94: 407–23.

Guijt, Irene, and Meera Kaul Shah. 1998. "Waking Up to Power, Conflict, and Process." In *The Myth of Community: Gender Issues in Participatory Development*, edited by I. Guijt and M. Kaul Shah. London: Intermediate Technology Publications.

Gutmann, Amy, and Dennis Thompson. 1996. *Democracy and Disagreement*. Cambridge, MA: Harvard University Press.

———. 2004. *Why Deliberative Democracy?* Princeton, NJ: Princeton University Press.

Habermas, Jürgen. 1984. *The Theory of Communicative Action*. Vol. 1, *Reason and the Rationalization of Society*. Translated by Thomas McCarthy. Boston: Beacon Press.

———. 1989. *The Structural Transformation of the Public Sphere: An Inquiry into a Category of Bourgeois Society*. Translated by T. Burger with the assistance of F. Lawrence. Cambridge, MA: MIT Press.

———. 1996. *Between Facts and Norms: Contributions to a Discourse Theory of Law and Democracy*. Cambridge, MA: MIT Press.

Hall, J. A. 1984. *Nonverbal Sex Differences: Communication Accuracy and Expressive Style*. Baltimore: Johns Hopkins University Press.

Hannaford-Agor, Paula L., Valerie P. Hans, Nicole L. Mott, and G. Thomas Munsterman. 2002. "Are Hung Juries a Problem?" *National Center for State Courts*. Final Report to the National Institute of Justice, Department of Justice.

Hannagan, Rebecca J., and Christopher Larimer. 2010. "Does Gender Composition Affect Group Decision Outcomes? Evidence from a Laboratory Experiment." *Political Behavior* 32: 51–67.

———. 2011a. "Assessing Gender Dynamics in Local Government: Evidence from a Statewide Field Experiment." Unpublished manuscript, New Research on Gender in Political Psychology Conference. Rutgers University, New Brunswick, New Jersey.

———. 2011b. "Out-Group Threat and Gender Balance in Policymaking Groups." Presented at the 2nd European Conference on Politics and Gender, Central European University in Budapest, Hungary, January.

Hans, Valerie P. 2001. "The Power of Twelve: The Impact of Jury Size and Unanimity on Civil Jury Decision Making." *Delaware Law Review* 4 (1): 1–31.

Hansen, Susan B. 1997. "Talking about Politics: Gender and Contextual Effects on Political Proselytizing." *Journal of Politics* 59: 73–103.

Harkreader, S., and P. Y. Martin. 1993. "Multiple Gender Contexts and Employee Rewards." *Work and Occupations* 20 (3): 296–336.

Harris, Frederick. 1999. *Something Within: Religion in African-American Political Activism*. New York: Oxford University Press.

Harris-Lacewell, Melissa. 2004. *Barbershops, Bibles, and B.E.T: Everyday Talk and Black Political Thought*. Princeton, NJ: Princeton University Press.

Hartman, M. 1976. "A Descriptive Study of the Language of Men and Women Born in Maine around 1900 as It Reflects the Lakoff Hypothesis in *Language and Women's Place*." In *Conference on the Sociology of the Languages of American Women*, edited by B. L. Dubois and I. Crouch, 81–90. San Antonio, TX: Trinity University.

Hastie, R., S. D. Penrod, and N. Pennington. 1983. *Inside the Jury*. Cambridge, MA: Harvard University Press.

Heckman, James J., and Paul LaFontaine. 2007. "The American High School Graduation Rate: Trends and Levels." IZA Discussion Paper Series No. 3216.

Heilman, M. E. 1980. "The Impact of Situational Factors on Personnel Decisions concerning Women: Varying the Sex Composition of the Applicant Pool." *Organizational Behavior and Human Performance* 26: 286–95.

Heilman, M. E., C. J. Block, and R. F. Martell. 1995. "Sex Stereotypes: Do They Influence Perceptions of Managers?" *Journal of Social Behavior and Personality* 10: 237–52.

Heilman, M. E., and T. G. Okimoto. 2007. "Why Are Women Penalized for Success at Male Tasks?: The Implied Communality Deficit." *Journal of Applied Psychology* 92 (1): 81–92.

Heldman, Caroline, Susan J. Carroll, and Stephanie Olson. 2006. "'She Brought Only a Skirt': Print Media Coverage of Elizabeth Dole's Bid for the Republican Presidential Nomination." *Political Communication* 22 (3): 315–35.

Henningsen, D., and M. Henningsen. 2003. "Examining Social Influence in Information-Sharing Contexts." *Small Group Research* 34: 391–412.

Herbst, Susan. 2010. *Rude Democracy: Civility and Incivility in American Politics*. Philadelphia: Temple University Press.

Hertz, Rosanna, and Susan M. Reverby. 1995. "Gentility, Gender, and Political Protest: The Barbara Bush Controversy at Wellesley College." *Gender and Society* 9 (5): 594–611.

Hibbing, John, and Elizabeth Theiss-Morse. 2002. *Stealth Democracy: American's Beliefs about How Government Should Work*. Cambridge: Cambridge University Press.

Hickerson, Andrea, and John Gastil. 2008. "Assessing the Difference Critique of Deliberation: Gender, Emotion, and the Jury Experience." *Communication Theory* 18: 281–303.

Highton, Benjamin. 2009. "Revisiting the Relationship between Educational Attainment and Political Sophistication." *Journal of Politics* 71: 1564–76.

Hoffman, L. R. 1978. *The Network Nation: Human Communication via Computer*. Reading, MA: Addison-Wesley.

Holland v. Illinois. 1990. 493 U.S. 474.

Holtgraves, Thomas. 2002. *Language as Social Action: Social Psychology and Language Use*. Mahwah, NJ: Erlbaum.

———. 2005. "Social Psychology, Cognitive Psychology, and Linguistic Politeness." *Journal of Politeness Research, Language, Behaviour, Culture* 1 (1): 73–93.

Holtgraves, Thomas, and Joong-Nam Yang. 1990. "Politeness as Universal: Cross-Cultural Perceptions of Request Strategies and Inferences Based on Their Use." *Journal of Personality and Social Psychology* 59 (4): 719–29.

Honneth, Axel. 2005. "Reification: A Recognition-Theoretical View." Tanner Lectures on Human Values delivered at University of California, Berkeley.

Horvath, Jane, Barbara Q. Beaudin, and Sheila P. Wright. 1992. "Persisting in the Introductory Economics Course: An Exploration of Gender Differences." *Journal of Economic Education* (Spring): 101–8.

Houston, Marsha, and Cheris Kramarae. 1991. "Speaking from Silence." *Discourse and Society* 2: 387–400.

Htun, Mala, and S. Laurel Weldon. 2010. "When Do Governments Promote Women's Rights? A Framework for the Comparative Analysis of Sex Equity Policy." *Perspectives on Politics* 8 (1): 207–16.

———. 2012. "The Civic Origins of Progressive Policy Change: Combating Violence against Women in Global Perspective, 1975–2005." *American Political Science Review* 106 (3): 548–69.

Huckfeldt, Robert, and John Sprague. 1995. *Citizens, Politics, and Social Communication*. Cambridge: Cambridge University Press.

Huddy, Leonie, Erin Cassese, and Mary-Kate Lizotte. 2008. "Gender, Public Opinion, and Political Reasoning" In *Political Women and American Democracy*, edited by Christina Wolbrecht, Karen Beckwith, and Lisa Baldez, 31–49. New York: Cambridge University Press.

Huddy, Leonie, Francis Neely, and Marilyn R. Lafay. 2000. "The Polls-Trends: Support for the Women's Movement." *Public Opinion Quarterly* 64: 309–50.

Huddy, Leonie, and Nayda Terkildsen. 1993a. "The Consequences of Gender Stereotypes for Women Candidates at Different Levels and Types of Office." *Political Research Quarterly* 46 (3): 503–25.

———. 1993b. "Gender Stereotypes and the Perception of Male and Female Candidates." *American Journal of Political Science* 37 (1): 119–47.

Humphreys, M., J. Fearson, and J. Weinstein. 2011. "Democratic Institutions and Collective Action Capacity: Results from a Field Experiment in Post-Conflict Liberia." Presented at the Annual Meeting of the American Political Science Association in Seattle, Washington, September 1–4.

Humphreys, Macartan, William A. Masters, and Martin E. Sandbu. 2006. "Democratic Deliberations: Results from a Field Experiment in São Tomé and Príncipe." *World Politics* 58: 583–622.

Hutchings, Vincent, Nicholas Valentino, Tasha Philpot, and Ismail White. 2004. "The Compassion Strategy: Race and the Gender Gap in American Politics." *Public Opinion Quarterly* 68 (4): 512–41.

Imai, Kosuke, Luke Keele, and Dustin Tingley. 2010. "A General Approach to Causal Mediation Analysis." *Psychological Methods* 15 (4): 309–34.

Inglehart, Ronald, and Pippa Norris. 2000. "The Developmental Theory of the Gender Gap: Women's and Men's Voting Behavior in Global Perspective." *International Political Science Review* 21 (4): 441–62.

———. 2003. *Rising Tide: Gender Equality and Cultural Change around the World*. Cambridge: Cambridge University Press.

———. 2010 "The Developmental Theory of the Gender Gap: Women's and Men's Voting Behavior in Global Perspective." In *Women, Gender, and Politics: A Reader*, edited by Sarah Childs. New York: Oxford University Press.

Instone, Debra, Brenda Major, and Barbara Bunker. 1983. "Gender, Self-Confidence, and Social Influence Strategies: An Organization Simulation." *Journal of Personality and Social Psychology* 44 (2): 322–33.

Iowa Code §69.16A.

Jacobs, Lawrence R., Fay L. Cook, and Michael X. Delli Carpini. 2009. *Talking Together: Public Deliberation and Political Participation in America*. Chicago: University of Chicago Press.

James, Deborah, and Sandra Clarke. 1993. "Women, Men, and Interruptions: A Critical Review." In *Gender and Conversational Interaction*, edited by Deborah Tannen. New York: Oxford University Press.

James, Michael Rabinder. 2008. "Descriptive Representation in the British Columbia Citizens' Assembly." In *Designing Deliberative Democracy: The British Columbia Citizens' Assembly*, edited by Mark E. Warren and Hilary Pearse, 106–26. Cambridge: Cambridge University Press.

Jamieson, Kathleen Hall. 1995. *Beyond the Double Bind: Women and Leadership*. New York: Oxford University Press.

Jeffrey, Julie Roy. 1998. *The Great Silent Army of Abolitionism: Ordinary Women in the Antislavery Movement*. Chapel Hill: University of North Carolina Press.

Jennings, M. Kent, and Laura Stoker. 2000. "Political Similarity and Influence between Husbands and Wives." Paper presented at the annual meeting of the American Political Science Association, Washington, DC.

Jewell, Malcolm E., and Marcia Lynn Whicker. 1994. *Legislative Leadership in the American States*. Ann Arbor: University of Michigan Press.

Johnson, Cathryn. 1993. "Gender and Formal Authority." *Social Psychology Quarterly* 56: 193–210.

———. 1994. "Gender, Legitimate Authority, and Leader-Subordinate Conversations." *American Sociological Review* 59: 122–35.

Johnson, Richard A., and Gary I. Schulman. 1989. "Gender-Role Composition and Role Entrapment in Decision-Making Groups." *Gender and Society* 3: 355–72.

Josephs, R., H. Markus, and R. Tafarodi. 1992. "Gender and Self-Esteem." *Journal of Personality and Social Psychology* 63: 391–402.

Kadlec, Alison, and Will Friedman. 2007. "Deliberative Democracy and the Problem of Power." *Journal of Public Deliberation* 3 (1): article 8.

Kahn, Kim Fridkin. 1992. "Does Being Male Help? An Investigation of the Effects of Candidate Gender and Campaign Coverage on Evaluations of U.S. Senate Candidates." *Journal of Politics* 54 (2): 497–517.

———. 1994a. "The Distorted Mirror: Press Coverage of Women Candidates for Statewide Office." *Journal of Politics* 56 (1): 154–73.

———. 1994b. "Does Gender Make a Difference? An Experimental Examination of Sex Stereotypes and Press Patterns in Statewide Campaigns." *American Journal of Political Science* 38 (1): 162–95.

———. 1996. *The Political Consequences of Being a Woman*. New York: Columbia University Press.

Kahn, Kim Fridkin, and Edie N. Goldenberg. 1991. "Women Candidates in the News: An Examination of Gender Differences in U.S. Senate Campaign Coverage." *Public Opinion Quarterly* 55 (2): 180–99.

Kalleberg, A. L., D. Knoke, P. V. Marsden, and J. L. Spaeth. 1996. *Organizations in America: Analyzing Their Structures and Human Resources Practices*. Thousand Oaks, CA: Sage.

Kalven, Harry, Jr., and Hans Zeisel. 1966. *The American Jury*. Boston: Little, Brown.

Kameda, T. 1991. "Procedural Influence in Small-Group Decision Making: Deliberation Style and Assigned Decision Rule." *Journal of Personality and Social Psychology* 61: 245–56.

Kanter, Rosabeth M. 1977a. *Men and Women of the Corporation*. New York: Basic.

———. 1977b. "Some Effects of Proportions on Group Life: Skewed Sex Ratios and Responses to Token Women." *American Journal of Sociology* 82: 965–90.

———. 1977c. *Work and Family in the United States: A Critical Review and Policy Agenda*. Frontiers of Social Science. New York: Russell Sage Foundation.

Kanthak, Kristin, and George A. Krause. 2010. "Valuing Diversity in Political Organizations: Gender and Token Minorities in the U.S. House of Representatives." *American Journal of Political Science* 54 (4): 839–54.

Kanthak, Kristin, and Jonathan Woon. 2011. "Women Don't Run: Gender Differences in Candidate Entry." Paper presented at the annual meeting of the American Political Science Association in Seattle, Washington.

Kaplan, Martin F., and Charles E. Miller. 1987. "Group Decision-Making and Normative versus Informational Influence: Effects of Type of Issue and Assigned Decision Rule." *Journal of Personality and Social Psychology* 53: 306–13.

Karakowsky, L., K. McBey, and Y. Chuang. 2004. "Perceptions of Team Performance: The Impact of Group Composition and Task-Based Cues." *Journal of Managerial Psychology*. 19 (5): 506–25.

Karakowsky, Leonard, Kenneth McBey and Diane L. Miller. 2004. "Gender, Perceived Competence, and Power Displays Examining Verbal Interruptions in a Group Context." *Small Group Research* 35 (4): 407–39.

Karakowsky, L., and J. P. Siegel. 1999. "The Effects of Proportional Representation and Gender Orientation of the Task on Emergent Leadership Behavior in Mixed-Gender Work Groups." *Journal of Applied Psychology* 84 (4): 620–31.

Karp, Jeffrey A., and Susan A. Banducci. 2008. "When Politics Is Not Just a Man's Game: Women's Representation and Political Engagement." *Electoral Studies* 27 (1): 105–15.

Karpowitz, Christopher F. 2006. "Having a Say: Public Hearings, Deliberation, and Democracy in America." PhD diss., Princeton University.

Karpowitz, Chris, and Jane Mansbridge. 2005. "Disagreement and Consensus." *Journal of Public Deliberation* 1 (1): 348–64.

Karpowitz, Chris, and Daniel Frost. 2007. "We Can't Even Buy Socks in Urbana! Public Hearings, Wal-Mart, and the Quality of Local Public Deliberation." Presented at the annual meeting of the American Political Science Association, Chicago, August 30–September 2.

Karpowitz, Christopher F., Tali Mendelberg, and Lee Shaker. 2012. "Gender Inequality in Deliberative Participation." *American Political Science Review* 106 (3): 533–47.

Karpowitz, Christopher F., Chad Raphael, and Allen S. Hammond IV. 2009. "Deliberative Democracy and Inequality: Two Cheers for Enclave Deliberation among the Disempowered." *Politics and Society* 37: 576–615.

Kathlene, Lyn. 1994. "Power and Influence in State Legislative Policymaking: The Interaction of Gender and Position in Committee Hearing Debates." *American Political Science Review* 88: 560–76.

———. 1998. "(Re)Learning Gender through Expressive Writing and Critical Reflection: Electronic Discussion Groups as Idea Mediators among Students." *Language and Learning across the Disciplines* 3: 5–24.

———. 2001. "Words That Matter: Women's Voice and Institutional Bias in Public Policy Formation." In *The Impact of Women in Public Office*, edited by Susan J. Carroll. Bloomington: Indiana University Press.

Kelly, Mary. 2006. *Learning to Stand and Speak: Women, Education, and Public Life in America's Republic*. Chapel Hill: University of North Carolina Press.

Kenney, Sally J. 1996. "New Research on Gendered Political Institutions." *Political Research Quarterly* 49 (2): 445–66.

Keohane, Nannerl O. 2010. *Thinking about Leadership*. Princeton, NJ: Princeton University Press.

Kerr, Norbert L., Robert S. Atkin, Garold Stasser, David Meek, Robert W. Holt, and James H. Davis. 1976. "Guilt beyond a Reasonable Doubt: Effects of Concept Definition and Assigned Decision Rule on the Judgments of Mock Jurors." *Journal of Personality and Social Psychology* 34 (2): 282–94.

Kilavuka, J. M. 2003. "A Comparative Study of the Socio-Economic Implications of Rural Women, Men, and Mixed Self-Help Groups." *Gender Issues Research Reports Series* 20. Organization for Social Science Research in Southern Africa. Quoted in Greig, Fiona, and Iris Bohnet. 2009. "Exploring Gendered Behavior in the Field with Experiments: Why Public Goods Are Provided by Women in a Nairobi Slum." *Journal of Economic Behavior and Organization* 70 (1–2): 1–9.

Kinder, Donald R., and Thomas Palfrey. 1993. "On Behalf of an Experimental Political Science." In *Experimental Foundations of Political Science*, edited by T. Palfrey. Ann Arbor: University of Michigan Press.

Kingwell, Mark. 1995. *A Civil Tongue: Justice, Dialogue, and the Politics of Pluralism.* University Park: Pennsylvania State University Press.

Kirchmeyer, C. 1993. "Multicultural Task Groups: An Account of the Law Contribution Level of Minorities." *Small Group Research* 24 (February): 127–48.

Kishida, K. T., D. Yang, K. H. Quartz, S. R. Quartz, and P. R. Montague. 2012. "Implicit Signals in Small Group Settings and Their Impact on the Expression of Cognitive Capacity and Associated Brain Responses." *Philosophical Transactions of the Royal Society B* 367 (1589): 704–16.

Kittilson, Miki C. 2008. "Representing Women: The Adoption of Family Leave in Comparative Perspective." *Journal of Politics* 70: 323–34.

Kling, Kristen C., Janet Hyde, Carolin Showers, and Brenda N. Buswell. 1999. "Gender Differences in Self-Esteem: A Meta-Analysis." *Psychological Bulletin* 125 (4): 470–500.

Knight, G. P., and A. F. Dubro. 1984. "Cooperative, Competitive, and Individualistic Social Values: An Individualized Regression and Clustering Approach." *Journal of Personality and Social Psychology* 46: 98–105.

Knight, Jack, and James Johnson. 1997. "What Sort of Equality Does Democratic Deliberation Require?" In *Deliberative Democracy*, edited by James Bohman and William Rehg. Cambridge, MA: MIT Press.

Koenig, A. M., A. H. Eagly, A. A. Mitchell, and T. Ristikari. 2011. "Are Leader Stereotypes Masculine? A Meta-Analysis of Three Research Paradigms." *Psychological Bulletin* 137: 616–42.

Kohn, M. 2000. "Language, Power, and Persuasion: Toward a Critique of Deliberative Democracy." *Constellations* 7 (3): 408–29.

Kollock, P., P. Blumstein, and P. Schwartz. 1985. "Sex and Power in Interaction: Conversational Privileges and Duties." *American Sociological Review* 50 (1): 34–46.

Konrad, A., S. Winter, and B. A. Gutek. 1992. "Diversity in Work Group Sex Composition: Implications for Majority and Minority Members." In *Research in the Sociology of Organizations*, vol. 10, edited by P. Tolbert and S. B. Bacharach, 115–40. Greenwich, CT: JAI Press.

Kray, L. J., L. Thompson, and A. Galinsky. 2001. "Battle of the Sexes: Gender Stereotype Confirmation and Reactance in Negotiations." *Journal of Personality and Social Psychology* 80: 942–58.

Krook, Mona Lena. 2008. "Quota Laws for Women in Politics: Implications for Feminist Practice." *Social Politics* 15 (3): 345–68.

———. 2009. *Quotas for Women in Politics: Gender and Candidate Selection Reform Worldwide.* New York: Oxford University Press.

Krook, Mona Lena, Joni Lovenduski, and Judith Squires. 2009. "Gender Quotas and Models of Political Citizenship." *British Journal of Political Science* 39 (4): 781–803.

Krosnick, Jon A. 1999. "Survey Research." *Annual Review of Psychology* 50: 537–67.

LaFrance, M., M. Hecht, and E. L. Paluck. 2003. "The Contingent Smile: A Meta-Analysis of Sex Differences in Smiling." *Psychological Bulletin* 129 (2): 305–34.

Lakoff, Robin. 1973. "Language and Woman's Place." *Language in Society* 2 (1): 45–80.

———. 1975. *Language and Woman's Place*. New York: Harper and Row.

Lakoff, Robin Tolmach. 1990. *Talking Power: The Politics of Language in Our Lives*. New York: Basic Books.

Landa, D., E. Dickson, and C. Hafer. 2008. "Cognition and Strategy: A Deliberation Experiment." *Journal of Politics* 70 (4): 974–89.

Lawler, Edward E. 2003. *Treat People Right!: How Organizations and Employees Can Create a Win/Win Relationship to Achieve High Performance at All Levels*. New York: Jossey-Bass.

Lawless, Jennifer L. 2004. "Politics of Presence? Congresswomen and Symbolic Representation." *Political Research Quarterly* 57 (1): 81–99.

———. 2009. "Sexism and Gender Bias in Election 2008: A More Complex Path for Women." *Politics and Gender* 5 (1): 70–80.

Lawless, Jennifer L., and Richard L. Fox. 2010. *It Still Takes a Candidate: Why Women Don't Run for Office*. New York: Cambridge University Press.

———. 2011. "Gendered Perceptions and Political Candidacies: A Central Barrier to Women's Equality in Electoral Politics." *American Journal of Political Science* 55 (1): 59–73.

Leaper, C. 1998. "Decision-Making Processes between Friends: Speaker and Partner Gender Effects." *Sex Roles* 39: 125–33.

———. 2000. "The Social Construction and Socialization of Gender." In *Toward a Feminist Developmental Psychology*, edited by P. H. Miller and E. K. Scholnick. New York: Routledge.

Leaper, C., K. J. Anderson, and P. Sanders. 1998. "Moderators of Gender Effects on Parent's Talk to Their Children: A Meta-Analysis." *Developmental Psychology* 34: 3–27.

Leaper, C., and T. E. Smith. 2004. "A Meta-Analytic Review of Gender Variations in Children's Talk: Talkativeness, Affiliative Speech, and Assertive Speech." *Developmental Psychology* 40: 993–1027.

Leaper, Campbell, and Melanie M. Ayres. 2007. "A Meta-Analytic Review of Gender Variations in Adults' Language Use: Talkativeness, Affiliative Speech, and Assertive Speech." *Personality and Social Psychology Review* 11 (4): 328–63.

Leventhal, G. S., and D. W. Lane. 1970. "Sex, Age, and Equity Behavior." *Journal of Personality and Social Psychology* 15: 312–16.

Lewin, Kurt. 1951. In *Field Theory in Social Science; Selected Theoretical Papers*, edited by D. Cartwright. New York: Harper and Row.

Li, Han Z. 2001. "Cooperative and Intrusive Interruptions in Inter- and Intra-Cultural Dyadic Discourse." *Discourse Processes* 28 (3): 195–205.

Lijphart, A. 1969. "Consociational Democracy." *World Politics* 21 (2): 207–25.

Lloyd, Genevieve. 1993. *The Man of Reason: "Male" and "Female" in Western Philosophy*, 2nd ed. Minneapolis: University of Minnesota Press.

Lopez, Mark Hugo, Peter Levin, Deborah Both, Abby Kiesa, Emily Kirby, and Karlo Marcelo. 2006. *The 2006 Civic and Political Health of the Nation: A Detailed Look at*

How Youth Participate in Politics and Communities. College Park, MD: Center for Information and Research on Civic Learning and Engagement.

Losada, M., and E. Heaphy. 2004. "The Role of Positivity and Connectivity in the Performance of Business Teams: A Nonlinear Dynamics Model." *American Behavioral Scientist* 47 (6): 740–65.

Lott, John, and Lawrence W. Kenny. 1999. "Did Women's Suffrage Change the Size and Scope of Government?" *Journal of Political Economy* 107: 1163–98.

Lovenduski, Joni. 2005. *State Feminism and Political Representation*. New York: Cambridge University Press.

Lukes, Steven. 1974. *Power: A Radical View*. London: Macmillan.

Lundberg, Shelly J., Robert A. Pollak, and Terence J. Wales. 1997. "Do Husbands and Wives Pool Their Resources? Evidence from the United Kingdom Child Benefit." *Journal of Human Resources* 32 (3): 463–80.

Luskin, Robert C., James S. Fishkin, and Roger Jowell. 2002. "Considered Opinions: Deliberative Polling in Britain." *British Journal of Political Science* 32: 445–87.

Lustig, Myron W., and Peter A. Anderson. 1990. "Generalizing about Communication Apprehension and Avoidance: Multiple Replication and Meta-Analysis." *Journal of Social Behavior and Personality* 5: 309–40.

Maccoby, E. 1988. "Gender as a Social Category." *Developmental Psychology* 24 (6): 755–65.

———. 1998. *The Two Sexes: Growing Up Apart, Coming Together*. Cambridge, MA: Harvard University Press.

MacDonald, Jason A., and Erin E. O'Brien. 2011. "Quasi-Experimental Design, Constituency, and Advancing Women's Interests: Reexamining the Influence of Gender on Substantive Representation." *Political Research Quarterly* 64 (2): 472–86.

Macedo, Stephen. 1999. Introduction. *Deliberative Politics: Essays on Democracy and Disagreement*, edited by Stephen Macedo. New York: Oxford University Press.

Macedo, Stephen, and Yael Tamir, eds. 2002. *Moral and Political Education*. New York: New York University Press.

Macedo, Stephen, et al. 2005. *Democracy at Risk: How Political Choices Undermine Citizen Participation, and What We Can Do about It*. Washington, DC: Brookings Institution Press.

Maggi, Giovanni, and Massimo Morelli. 2006. "Self-Enforcing Voting in International Organizations." *American Economic Review* 96 (4): 1137–58.

Major, B., D. McFarlin, and D. Gagnon. 1984. "Overworked and Underpaid: On the Nature of Gender Differences in Personal Entitlement." *Journal of Personality and Social Psychology* 47: 1399–412.

Maltz, Daniel, and Ruth Borker. 1982. "A Cultural Approach to Male-Female Miscommunication." In *Language and Social Identity*, edited by John Gumperz, 281–312. New York: Cambridge University Press.

Mansbridge, Jane. 1973. "Town Hall Democracy." Working Papers for a New Society. Issue 1. Quoted in Bryan, Frank M. 2004. *Real Democracy: The New England Town Meeting and How It Works*. Chicago: University of Chicago Press.

———. 1983. *Beyond Adversary Democracy*. Chicago: University of Chicago Press.

———. 1994. "Feminism and Democratic Community." In *Feminism*, vol. 1, edited by Susan Moller Okin, and Jane Mansbridge. Brookfield, VT: Edward Elgar.

———. 1996. "Using Power/Fighting Power: The Polity." In *Democracy and Difference: Contesting Boundaries of the Political*, edited by Seyla Benhabib, 57. Princeton, NJ: Princeton University Press.

———. 1999. "Should Blacks Represent Blacks and Women Represent Women? A Contingent 'Yes.'" *Journal of Politics* 61 (3): 628–57.

———. 2006. "Quota Problems: Combating the Dangers of Essentialism." *Politics and Gender* 1 (4): 621–38.

Mansbridge, Jane, James Bohman, Simone Chambers, David Estlund, Andreas Føllesdal, Archon Fung, Cristina Lafont, Bernard Manin, and José Luis Martí. 2010. "The Place of Self-Interest and the Role of Power in Deliberative Democracy." *Journal of Political Philosophy* 18 (1): 64–100.

Mansbridge, Jane J., Janette Hartz-Karp, Matthew Amengual, and John Gastil. 2006. "Norms of Deliberation: An Inductive Study." *Journal of Public Deliberation* 2 (1): article 7.

Marcelo, Karlo Barrios, Mark Hugo Lopez, and Emily Hoban Kirby. 2007. *Civic Engagement among Young Men and Women*. College Park, MD: Center for Information and Research on Civic Learning and Engagement.

Margolis, Jane. 1992. "Piranhas, Monsters, and Jugglers: the Psychology of Gender and Academic Discourse." *On Teaching and Learning* (4): 5–26.

Massie, Tajuana, Susan W. Johnson, and Sara M. Gubala. 2002. "The Influence of Gender and Race on Judicial Decisions in the United States Courts of Appeals." Paper presented at the Midwest Political Science Association Meeting in Chicago, Illinois, April.

Mast, Marianne Schmid. 2001. "Gender Differences and Similarities in Dominance Hierarchies in Same-Gender Groups Based on Speaking Time." *Sex Roles* 44: 537–56.

Mathis, Jerome. 2011. "Deliberation with Evidence." *American Political Science Review* 105: 516–29.

Mattei, Laura R. Winsky. 1998. "Gender and Power in American Legislative Discourse." *Journal of Politics* 60 (2): 440–61.

Maynard, D. W., and A. Peräkylä. 2003. "Language and Social Interaction." In *Handbook of Social Psychology*, edited by J. Delamater, 233–58. New York: Kluwer Academic/Plenum Publishers.

Mayoux, Linda. 1995. "Beyond Naivety: Women, Gender Inequality, and Participatory Development." *Development and Change* 26 (2): 235–58.

McAdams, Dan P., Kathrin J. Hanek, and Joseph G. Dadabo. 2013. "Themes of Self-Regulation and Self-Exploration in the Life Stories of Religious American Conservatives and Liberals." *Political Psychology* 34 (2): 201–19.

McCarrick, Anne K., Ronald W. Manderscheid, and Sam Silbergeld. 1981. "Gender Differences in Competition and Dominance during Married-Couples Group Therapy." *Social Psychology Quarterly* 44: 164–77.

McCarthy, T. 1994. *The Critical Theory of Jürgen Habermas*. Cambridge, MA: MIT Press.

McClerking, Harwood K., and Eric L. McDaniel. 2005. "Belonging and Doing: Political Churches and Black Political Participation." *Political Psychology* 26 (5): 721–33.

McDermott, Rose. 2011. "Internal and External Validity." In *Cambridge Handbook of Experimental Political Science*, edited by James N. Druckman, Donald P. Green, James H. Kuklinski, and Arthur Lupia. Cambridge: Cambridge University Press.

McGuire, T. W., S. Kiesler, and J. Siegel. 1987. "Group and Computer-Mediated Discussion Effects in Risk Decision Making." *Journal of Personality and Social Psychology* 52: 917–30.

McPherson, J. Miller, and Lynn Smith-Lovin. 1982. "Women and Weak Ties: Differences by Sex in the Size of Voluntary Organizations." *American Journal of Sociology* 87 (4): 883–904.

———. 1986. "Sex Segregation in Voluntary Associations." *American Sociological Review* 51: 61–79.

———. 1987. "Homophily in Voluntary Organizations: Status Distance and the Composition of Face-to-Face Groups." *American Sociological Review* 52 (3): 370–79.

———. 1993. "You Are Who You Know: A Network Approach to Gender." In *Theory on Gender/Feminism on Theory*, edited by Paula England, 223–54. New York: A. de Gruyter.

Meirowitz, Adam. 2006. "Designing Institutions to Aggregate Preferences and Information." *Quarterly Journal of Political Science* 1 (4): 373–92.

———. 2007. "In Defense of Exclusionary Deliberation: Communication and Voting with Private Beliefs and Values." *Journal of Theoretical Politics* 19: 301–28.

Meirowitz, Adam, and Dimitri Landa. 2009. "Game Theory, Information, and Deliberative Democracy." *American Journal of Political Science* 53 (2): 427–44.

Mendelberg, Tali. 2002. "The Deliberative Citizen: Theory and Evidence." In *Political Decision Making, Deliberation, and Participation: Research in Micropolitics*, vol. 6, edited by Michael X. Delli Carpini, Leonie Huddy, and Robert Y. Shapiro. Greenwich, CT: JAI Press.

———. 2012. "Race and Gender as Context: Compositional Effects in U.S. Juries." Presented at the Canadian Political Science Association meeting, June 13, 2012, in Edmonton, Alberta, Canada.

Mendelberg, T., and C. Karpowitz. 2007. "How People Deliberate about Justice: Groups, Gender, and Decision Rules." In *Deliberation, Participation, and Democracy: Can the People Govern?*, edited by Shawn Rosenberg, 101–29. Basingstoke: Palgrave.

Mendelberg, Tali, Christopher Karpowitz, and Nicholas Goedert. Forthcoming. "Does Descriptive Representation Facilitate Women's Distinctive Voice?" *American Journal of Political Science*.

Mendez, Jeanette M., and Tracy Osborn. 2010. "Gender and the Perception of Knowledge in Political Discussion." *Political Research Quarterly* 63 (2): 269–79.

Merelman, Richard M., Greg Streich, and Paul Martin. 1998. "Unity and Diversity in American Political Culture: An Exploratory Study of the National Conversation on American Pluralism and Identity." *Political Psychology* 19: 781–807.

Miguel, Luis Felipe. 2012. "Policy Priorities and Women's Double Bind in Brazil." In *The Impact of Gender Quotas*, edited by Susan Franceschet, Mona Lena Krook, and Jennifer M. Piscopo, 103–17. New York: Oxford University Press.

Miller, C. E. 1989. "The Social Psychological Effects of Group Decision Rules." In *Psychology of Group Influence*, edited by P. B. Paulus, 327–56. Hillsdale, NJ: Lawrence Erlbaum.

Miller, J. B. 1985. "Patterns of Control in Same-Sex Conversations: Differences between Women and Men." *Women's Studies in Communication* 8: 62–69.

Miller, Patrice M., Dorothy L. Danaher, and David Forbes. 1986. "Sex-Related Strategies for Coping with Interpersonal Conflict in Children Aged Five and Seven." *Developmental Psychology* 22: 543–48.

Mills, C. J., and W. E. Bohannon. 1980. "Juror Characteristics: To What Extent Are They Related to Jury Verdicts?" *Judicature* 64: 22–31.

Mohanty, Chandra. 2003. *Feminism without Borders: Decolonizing Theory, Practicing Solidarity*. Durham, NC: Duke University Press.

Mohanty, R. 2002. "Women's Participation in JFM in Uttaranchal Villages." Mimeograph. Quoted in Cornwall, Andrea. 2003. "Whose Voices? Whose Voices? Reflections on Gender and Participatory Development." *World Development* 31 (8): 1325–42.

Morton, Rebecca M., and Kenneth C. Williams. 2010. *Experimental Political Science and the Study of Causality*. New York: Cambridge University Press.

Moscovici, S. 1980. "Toward a Theory of Conversion Behavior." In *Advances in Experimental Social Psychology*, edited by L. Berkowitz, 209–39. New York: Academic Press.

———. 1985. "Social Influence and Conformity." In *Handbook of Social Psychology*, edited by G. Lindzey and E. Aronson, 347–412. New York: McGraw-Hill.

Mosse, D. 1995. "Authority, Gender, and Knowledge: Theoretical Reflections on the Practice of Participatory Rural Appraisal." *Development and Change* 25: 497–526.

Mouffe, Chantal. 2000. "Deliberative Democracy or Agonistic Pluralism." Political Science Series 72, Institute for Advanced Studies, Vienna.

Mulac, A., T. L. Lundell, and J. J. Bradac. 1986. "Male/Female Language Differences and Attributional Consequences in a Public Speaking Situation: Toward an Explanation of the Gender-Linked Language Effect." *Communication Monographs* 53: 116–29.

Mulac, A., J. M. Wiemann, S. J. Widenmann, and T. W. Gibson. 1988. "Male/Female Language Differences and Effects in Same-Sex and Mixed-Sex Dyads: The Gender-Linked Language Effect and Mutual Influence." *Communication Monographs* 55: 315–55.

Murphy, Sheila T. 1998. "The Impact of Factual versus Fictional Media Portrayals on Cultural Stereotypes." *Annals of the American Academy of Political and Social Science* 560: 165–78.

Mutz, Diana. 2006. *Hearing the Other Side: Deliberative versus Participatory Democracy*. Cambridge: Cambridge University Press.

Mutz, Diana C., and Byron Reeves. 2005. "The New Videomalaise: Effects of Televised Incivility on Political Trust." *American Political Science Review* 99 (1): 1–15.

Myers, Charles D. 2011. "Information Use in Small Group Deliberation." PhD diss., Princeton University.

Myers, C. Daniel, and Tali Mendelberg. 2013. "Political Deliberation." In *Oxford Handbook of Political Psychology*, 2nd ed., edited by Leonie Huddy, David O. Sears, and Jack S. Levy. New York: Oxford University Press.

Neblo, Michael A., Kevin M. Esterling, Ryan P. Kennedy, David M. J. Lazer, and Anand E. Sokhey. 2010. "Who Wants to Deliberate—and Why?" *American Political Science Review* 104: 566–83.

Nelson, Kimberly L. 2002. *Elected Municipal Councils*. Special Data Issue no. 3. Washington, DC: International City/County Management Association.

Nemeth, Charlan. 1977. "Interactions between Jurors as a Function of Majority vs. Unanimity Decision Rules." *Journal of Applied Social Psychology* 7: 38–56.

Newman, Matthew L., Carla J. Groom, Lori D. Handelman, and James W. Pennebaker. 2008. "Gender Differences in Language Use: An Analysis of 14,000 Text Samples." *Discourse Processes* 45 (3): 211–36.

Ng, Sik Hung, Mark Brooke, and Michael Dunne. 1995. "Interruption and Influence in Discussion Groups." *Journal of Language and Social Psychology* 14 (4): 369–81.

Niederle, Muriel, and Lise Vesterlund. 2007. "Do Women Shy Away from Competition? Do Men Compete Too Much?" *Quarterly Journal of Economics* 122 (3): 1067–101.

Niemi, Richard G., Stephen C. Craig, and Franco Mattei. 1991. "Measuring Internal Political Efficacy in the 1988 National Election Study." *American Political Science Review* 85 (4): 1407–13.

Niemi, Richard, and Jane Junn. 1993. "Civics Courses and the Political Knowledge of High School Seniors." Paper presented at APSA annual meeting in Washington, DC.

Noelle-Neumann, E. 1993. *The Spiral of Silence: Public Opinion—Our Social Skin*. Chicago: University of Chicago Press.

Norrander, Barbara, and Scott Desposato. 2009. "The Gender Gap in Latin America: Contextual and Individual Influences on Gender and Political Participation." *British Journal of Political Science* 39: 141–62.

Norris, Pippa. 1996. "Women Politicians: Transforming Westminster?" *Parliamentary Affairs* 49 (1): 89–102.

———. 1997a. "Women Leaders Worldwide: A Splash of Color in the Photo Op." In *Women, Media, and Politics*, edited by Pippa Norris. New York: Oxford University Press.

Norris, Pippa, ed. 1997b. *Women, Media, and Politics*. New York: Oxford University Press.

Norton, Mary Beth, Carol Sheriff, David W. Blight, David M. Katzman, Howard P. Chudacoff, and Fredrik Logevall. 2012. *A People and a Nation: A History of the United States: Volume II, since 1865*. Brief edition. Boston: Wadsworth.

NSBA. 2013. "National School Boards Association." http://www.nsba.org/default.aspx. Accessed June 18, 2013.

Nyquist, L., and J. T. Spence. 1986. "Effects of Dispositional Dominance and Sex Role Expectations on Leadership Behaviors." *Journal of Personality and Social Psychology* 50 (1): 87–93.

O'Barr, William M. 1982. *Linguistic Evidence: Language, Power, and Strategy in the Courtroom*. New York: Academic Press.

O'Barr, William M., and Bowman K. Atkins. 1980. "'Women's Language' or 'Powerless Language'?" In *Women and Language in Literature and Society*, edited by S. McConnell-Ginet, R. Borker, and N. Furman. New York: Praeger.

Octigan, Mary, and Sharon Niederman. 1979. "Male Dominance in Conversations." *Frontiers* 4 (1): 50–54.

Olson, Mancur. 1982. *The Rise and Decline of Nations: Economic Growth, Stagflation, and Social Rigidities*. New Haven, CT: Yale University Press.

Ostrom, Elinor. 1986. "An Agenda for the Study of Institutions." *Public Choice* 48: 3–25.

———. 1998. "A Behavioral Approach to the Rational Choice Theory of Collective Action." *American Political Science Review* 92: 1–22.

Pajares, Frank. 2002. "Gender and Perceived Self-Efficacy in Self-Regulated Learning." *Theory into Practice* 41 (2): 116–25.

Pande, Rohini, Lena Edlund, and Laila Haider. 2005. "Unmarried Parenthood and Redistributive Politics." *Journal of the European Economic Association* 3 (1): 95–119.

Pande, Rohini, and Deanna Ford. 2011. *Gender Quotas and Female Leadership: A Review*. Washington, DC: World Bank.

Parker, Kim. 2009. "The Harried Life of the Working Mother." Washington, DC: Pew Research Center.

Pascoe, Peggy. 1993. *Relations of Rescue: The Search for Female Moral Authority in the American West, 1874–1939*. Oxford: Oxford University Press.

Pateman, Carole. 1970. *Participation and Democratic Theory*. Cambridge: Cambridge University Press.

Patillo-McCoy, Mary. 1998. "Church Culture as a Strategy of Action in the Black Community." *American Sociological Review* 63 (6): 767–84.

Pearson, Kathryn, and Logan Dancey. 2011. "Elevating Women's Voices in Congress: Speech Participation in the House of Representatives." *Political Research Quarterly* 64 (4): 910–23.

Pennebaker, J. W., M. E. Francis, and R. J. Booth. 2001. *Linguistic Inquiry and Word Count (LIWC): LIWC 2001*. Mahwah, NJ: Erlbaum.

Pennebaker, J. W., and A. Graybeal. 2001. "Patterns of Natural Language Use: Disclosure, Personality, and Social Integration." *Current Directions in Psychological Science* 10: 90–93.

Pennebaker, J. W., and L. A. King. 1999. "Linguistic Styles: Language Use as an Individual Difference." *Journal of Personality and Social Psychology* 77: 1296–312.

Penrod, S., and R. Hastie. 1980. "A Computer Simulation of Jury Decision Making." *Psychological Review* 87: 133–59.

Peresie, Jennifer L. 2005. "Female Judges Matter: Gender and Collegial Decision-Making in the Federal Appellate Courts." *Yale Law Review* 114: 1759–90.

Pfeffer, J., and A. Davis-Blake. 1987. "The Effect of the Proportion of Women on Salaries: The Case of College Administrators." *Administrative Science Quarterly* 32: 1–24.

Phillips, Anne. 1995. *The Politics of Presence*. New York: Clarendon Press.

Piliavin, Jane A., and Rachel R. Martin. 1978. "The Effects of the Sex Composition of Groups on Style of Social Interaction." *Sex Roles* 4: 281–96.

Pitkin, Hanna Fenichel. 1967. *The Concept of Representation*. Berkeley: University of California Press.

Poggione, Sarah. 2004. "Exploring Gender Differences in State Legislator's Policy Differences." *Political Research Quarterly* 57 (2): 305–14.

Postmes, T., R. Spears, and S. Cihangir. 2001. "Quality of Decision Making and Group Norms." *Journal of Personality and Social Psychology* 80: 918–30.

Powers v. Ohio. 1991. 499 U.S. 400.

Pratto, F., J. Sidanius, and S. Levin. 2006. "Social Dominance Theory and the Dynamics of Intergroup Relations: Taking Stock and Looking Forward." In *European Review of Social Psychology*, edited by W. Stroebe and M. Hewstone. New York: Psychology Press.

Price, Vincent, Joseph N. Cappella, and Lilach Nir. 2002. "Does Disagreement Contribute to More Deliberative Opinion?" *Political Communication* 19: 95–112.

Prior, Markus. 2004. "Visual Political Knowledge." Paper presented at the New York Area Political Psychology Meeting, New York.

Prince-Gibson, E., and S. H. Schwartz. 1998. "Value Priorities and Gender." *Social Psychology Quarterly* 61: 49–67.

Princeton University. 2011. *Report on Undergraduate Women's Leadership*. Princeton, NJ: Office of Communications, Princeton University.

Pugh, M. D., and Ralph Wahrman. 1985. "Neutralizing Sexism in Mixed-Sex Groups: Do Women Have to Be Better Than Men?" *American Journal of Sociology* 88 (4): 746–62.

Rapoport, Ronald B. 1981. "The Sex Gap in Political Persuading: Where the 'Structured Principle' Works." *American Journal of Political Science* 25 (1): 32–48.

———. 1982. "Sex Differences in Attitude Expression: A Generational Explanation." *Public Opinion Quarterly* 46: 86–96.

Rawls, John. 1993. *Political Liberalism*. New York: Columbia University Press.

Reingold, Beth. 1992. "Concepts of Representation among Female and Male State Legislators." *Legislative Studies Quarterly* 17 (4): 509–37.

———. 2000. *Representing Women: Sex, Gender, and Legislative Behavior in Arizona and California*. Chapel Hill: University of North Carolina Press.

———. 2008. "Women as Office Holders: Linking Descriptive and Substantive Representation." In *Political Women and American Democracy*, edited by Christina Wolbrecht, Karen Beckwith, and Lisa Baldez, 128–147. New York: Cambridge University Press.

Reingold, Beth, and Jessica Harrell. 2010. "The Impact of Descriptive Representation on Women's Political Engagement: Does Party Matter?" *Political Research Quarterly* 63 (2): 280–94.

Reskin, Barbara F., Debra B. McBrier, and Julie A. Kmec. 1999. "The Determinants and Consequences of Workplace Sex and Race Composition." *Annual Review of Sociology* 25: 335–61.

Ridgeway, Cecilia L. 1982. "Status in Groups: The Importance of Motivation." *American Sociological Review* 47: 76–88.

———. 2001. "Gender, Status, and Leadership." *Journal of Social Issues* 57: 637–55.

Ridgeway, Cecilia L., Joseph Berger, and LeRoy Smith. 1985. "Nonverbal Cues and Status: An Expectation States Approach." *American Journal of Sociology* 90 (5): 955–78.

Ridgeway, Cecilia L., and Cathryn Johnson. 1990. "What Is the Relationship between Socioemotional Behavior and Status in Task Groups?" *American Journal of Sociology* 95 (5): 1189–212.

Ridgeway, Cecilia L., K. Backor, Y. E. Li, J. E. Tinkler, and K. E. Erickson. 2009. "How Easily Does a Social Difference Become a Status Distinction? Gender Matters." *American Sociological Review* 74: 44–62.

Ridgeway, C. L., and D. Diekema. 1989. "Dominance and Collective Hierarchy Formation in Male and Female Task Groups." *American Sociological Review* 54: 79–93.

———. 1992. "Are Gender Differences Status Differences?" In *Gender, Interaction, and Inequality*, edited by Cecilia L. Ridgeway, 157–80. New York: Springer-Verlag.

Ridgeway, Cecilia L., and Lynn Smith-Lovin. 1999. "The Gender System and Interaction." *Annual Review of Sociology* 25: 191–216.

Ritter, Barbara A., and Janice Yoder. 2004. "Gender Differences in Leader Emergence." *Psychology of Women Quarterly* 28 (3): 187–93.

Ritter, Gretchen. 2008. "Gender as a Category of Analysis in American Political Development." In *Political Women and American Democracy*, edited by Christina Wolbrecht, Karen Beckwith, and Lisa Baldez, 12–30. New York: Cambridge University Press.

Roberts, T. 1991. "Gender and the Influences of Evaluation on Self-Assessment in Achievement Settings." *Psychological Bulletin* 109 (2): 297–308.

Robnett, Belinda, and James A. Bany. 2011. "Gender, Church Involvement, and African-American Political Participation." *Sociological Perspectives* 54 (4): 689–712.

Roessner, Lori Amber. 2012. "Sexism." In *Encyclopedia of Gender in Media*, edited by Mary Kosut, 328–34. Thousand Oaks, CA: Sage Publications.

Rosenberg, Shawn. 2007a. "Rethinking Democratic Deliberation: The Limits and Potential of Citizen Participation." *Polity* 39: 335–60.

———. 2007b. "Types of Discourse and the Democracy of Deliberation." In *Deliberation, Participation, and Democracy: Can the People Govern?*, edited by Shawn Rosenberg, 130–58. Basingstoke: Palgrave Macmillan.

Rosenthal, Cindy Simon. 1998. *When Women Lead: Integrative Leadership in State Legislatures.* New York: Oxford University Press.

———. 2005. "Women Leading Legislatures: Getting There and Getting Things Done." In *Women and Elective Office: Past, Present, and Future.* 2nd ed., edited by Sue Thomas and Clyde Wilcox. New York: Oxford University Press.

Rosenstone, Steven J., and John Mark Hansen. 1993. *Mobilization, Participation, and Democracy in America.* New York: Macmillan.

Rudman, L. A. 1998. "Self-Promotion as a Risk Factor for Women: The Costs and Benefits of Counterstereotypical Impression Management." *Journal of Personality and Social Psychology* 74: 629–45.

Rudman, L. A., and K. Fairchild. 2004. "Reactions to Counterstereotypic Behavior: The Role of Backlash in Cultural Stereotype Maintenance." *Journal of Personality and Social Psychology* 87: 157–76.

Rudman, L. A., and P. Glick. 2001. "Prescriptive Gender Stereotypes and Backlash toward Agentic Women." *Journal of Social Issues* 57: 743–62.

Ryfe, David. 2002. "The Practice of Deliberative Democracy: A Study of 16 Organizations." *Political Communication* 19: 359–77.

———. 2004. "Can Deliberative Democracy Work?" Paper presented at the Annual Meeting of the International Communication Association, New Orleans, May 27–31.

———. 2005. "Does Deliberative Democracy Work?" *Annual Review of Political Science* 8: 49–71.

Sackett, P. R., C. L. DuBois, L. Cathy, and A. W. Noe. 1991. "Tokenism in Performance Evaluation: The Effects of Work Group Representation on Male-Female and White-Black Differences in Performance Ratings." *Journal of Applied Psychology* 76: 263–67.

Sanbonmatsu, Kira. 2003. "Political Knowledge and Gender Stereotypes." *American Politics Research* 31: 575–94.

Sanders, Lynn M. 1997. "Against Deliberation." *Political Theory* 25 (3): 347–76.

Sapiro, Virginia. 1983. *The Political Integration of Women: Roles, Socialization, and Politics.* Champaign: University of Illinois Press.

———. 1999. "Considering Political Civility Historically: A Case Study of the United States." Paper presented at the annual meeting of the International Society for Political Psychology, 1999.

———. 2003. "Theorizing Gender in Political Psychology Research." In *Oxford Handbook of Political Psychology*, edited by David O. Sears, Leonie Huddy, and Robert Jervis. New York: Oxford University Press.

Scharpf, Fritz W. 1989. "Decision Rules, Decision Styles, and Policy Choices." *Journal of Theoretical Politics* 1 (2): 149–76.

Schkade, D., Cass Sunstein, and Daniel Kahneman. 2000. "Deliberating about Dollars: The Severity Shift." *Columbia Law Review* 100: 1139–76.

Schmitt, N., and T. E. Hill. 1977. "Sex and Race Composition of Assessment Center Groups as a Determinant of Peer and Assessor Ratings." *Journal of Applied Psychology* 65: 428–35.

Schwarz, Norbert, and Daphna Oyserman. 2001. "Asking Questions about Behavior: Cognition, Communication, and Questionnaire Construction." *American Journal of Evaluation* 22: 127.

Schwartz, S. H., and T. Rubel. 2005. "Sex Differences in Value Priorities: Cross-Cultural and Multi-Method Studies." *Journal of Personality and Social Psychology* 89: 1010–28.

Schwindt-Bayer, Leslie A., and William Mishler. 2005. "An Integrated Model of Women's Representation." *Journal of Politics* 67 (2): 407–28.

Scott, Joan. 1986. "Gender: A Useful Category of Historical Analysis." *American Historical Review* 91 (5): 1053–75.

Scott, J., R. Matland, P. Michelbach, and B. Bornstein. 2001. "Just Desserts: An Experimental Study of Distributive Justice Norms." *American Journal of Political Science* 45: 749–67.

Sears, David O. 1986. "College Sophomores in the Laboratory: Influences of a Narrow Data Base on Social Psychology's View of Human Nature." *Journal of Personality and Social Psychology* 51: 515–30.

Sears, David O., and Leonie Huddy. 1990. "On the Origins of Political Disunity among Women." In *Women, Politics, and Change*, edited by Louise A. Tilly and Patricia Gurin. New York: Russell Sage Foundation.

Segal, Jennifer. 2000. "Representative Decision Making on the Federal Bench: Clinton's District Court Appointees." *Political Research Quarterly* 53: 137–50.

Sekhon, Jasjeet S., and Rocío Titiunik. 2012. "When Natural Experiments Are Neither Natural nor Experiments." *American Political Science Review* 106 (1): 35–57.

Shani, Danielle. 2010. "On the Origins of Political Interest." PhD diss., Princeton University.

Shapiro, Robert Y., and Harpreet Mahajan. 1986. "Gender Differences in Policy Preferences: A Summary of Trends from the 1960s to the 1980s." *Public Opinion Quarterly* 50: 42–61.

Shelly, Robert K., Lisa Troyer, Paul T. Munroe, and Tina Burger. 1999. "Social Structure and the Duration of Social Acts." *Social Psychology Quarterly* 62 (1): 83–95.

Shepsle, Kenneth A., and Barry R. Weingast. 1981. "Political Preferences for the Pork Barrel: A Generalization." *American Journal of Political Science* 25: 90–111.

Sidanius, J., and F. Pratto. 1999. *Social Dominance: An Intergroup Theory of Social Hierarchy and Oppression*. New York: Cambridge University Press.

Simmons, Rachel. 2002. *Odd Girl Out: The Hidden Culture of Aggression in Girls*. New York: Houghton Mifflin Harcourt.

Simonsen, William, and Mark D. Robbins. 2000. *Citizen Participation in Resource Allocation*. Boulder, CO: Westview Press.

Siu, Alice, and Dragan Stanisevski. 2012. "Deliberation in Multicultural Societies." In *Democracy in Motion: Evaluating the Practice and Impact of Deliberative Civic Engagement*, edited by Tina Nabatchi, John Gastil, Matt Leighninger, and G. Michael Weiksner, 83–102. New York: Oxford University Press.

Sklar, Kathryn Kish. 1985. "Hull House in the 1890s: A Community of Women Reformers." *Signs* 10 (4): 658–77.

Skocpol, Theda. 1992. *Protecting Soldiers and Mothers: The Political Origins of Social Policy in the United States*. Cambridge, MA: Harvard University Press.

———. 1999. "Advocates without Members: The Recent Transformation of American Civic Life." In *Civic Engagement in American Democracy*, edited by Theda Skocpol and Morris P. Fiorina, 461–510. Washington, DC: Brookings Institution Press.

Skocpol, T., M. Ganz, and Z. Munson. 2000. "A Nation of Organizers: The Institutional Origins of Civic Voluntarism in the United States." *American Political Science Review* 94 (3): 527–46.

Smith, Adrienne R., Beth Reingold, and Michael Lee Owens. 2012. "The Political Determinants of Women's Descriptive Representation in Cities." *Political Research Quarterly* 65 (2): 315–29.

Smith, G. Daryl. 1990. "Women's Colleges and Coed Colleges: Is There a Difference for Women?" *Journal of Higher Education* 61 (2): 181–97.

Smith-Lovin, Lynn, and Charles Brody. 1989. "Interruptions in Group Discussions: The Effects of Gender and Group Composition." *American Sociological Review* 54: 424–35.

Smith-Lovin, Lynn, and Miller McPherson. 1993. "You Are Who You Know: A Network Perspective on Gender." In *Theory on Gender/Feminism on Theory*, edited by Paula England. New York: Aldine.

Songer, Donald, Sue Davis, and Susan Haire. 1994. "A Reappraisal of Diversification in the Federal Courts: Gender Effects in the Courts of Appeals." *Journal of Politics* 56: 425–39.

Spencer, S., C. Steele, and D. Quinn. 1999. "Stereotype Threat and Women's Math Performance." *Journal of Experimental Social Psychology* 35: 4–28.

Steele, C. M., and J. Aronson. 1995. "Stereotype Threat and the Intellectual Test-Performance of African-Americans." *Journal of Personality and Social Psychology* 69 (5): 797–811.

Stein, J. A., M. D. Newcomb, and P. M. Bentler. 1992. "The Effect of Agency and Communality on Self-Esteem: Gender Differences in Longitudinal Data." *Sex Roles* 26 (11): 465–83.

Steiner, J., A. Bächtiger, M. Sporndli, and M. R. Steenbergen. 2004. *Deliberative Politics in Action*. Cambridge: Cambridge University Press.

Streib, Jessi. 2011. "Class Reproduction by Four Year Olds." *Qualitative Sociology* 2: 337–52.

Strodtbeck, Fred L., Rita M. James, and Charles Hawkins. 1957. "Social Status in Jury Deliberations." *American Sociological Review* 22: 713–19.

Strolovitch, Dara Z. 2008. *Affirmative Advocacy: Race, Class, and Gender in Interest Group Politics*. Chicago: University of Chicago Press.

Stromer-Galley, J. 2007. "Measuring Deliberation's Content: A Coding Scheme." *Journal of Public Deliberation* 3 (1): article 12.

Stromer-Galley, Jennifer, and Peter Muhlberger. 2009. "Agreement and Disagreement in Group Deliberation: Effects on Deliberation, Satisfaction, Future Engagement, and Decision Legitimacy." *Political Communication* 26 (2): 173–92.

Studlar, Donley T., and Ian McAllister. 2002. "Does a Critical Mass Exist? A Comparative Analysis of Women's Legislative Representation since 1950." *European Journal of Political Research* 41 (2): 233–53.

Sunstein, Cass. 2000. "Deliberative Trouble? Why Groups Go to Extremes." *Yale Law Review* 110 (71): 71–119.

———. 2002a. *Designing Democracy: What Constitutions Do*. London: Oxford University Press.

———. 2002b. "The Law of Group Polarization." *Journal of Political Philosophy* 10 (2): 175–95.

Svaleryd, H. 2002. "Female Representation—Is It of Importance for Policy Decisions?" Working Paper, Department of Economics, Stockholm University.

Swers, Michele. 1998. "Are Women More Likely to Vote for Women's Issue Bills Than Their Male Colleagues?" *Legislative Studies Quarterly* 23 (4): 435–48.

———. 2002. *The Difference Women Make: The Policy Impact of Women in Congress.* Chicago: University of Chicago Press.

———. 2013. *Women in the Club: Gender and Policy Making in the Senate.* Chicago: University of Chicago Press.

Tannen, Deborah. 1981. "The Machine-Gun Question: An Example of Conversational Style." *Journal of Pragmatics* 5: 383–97.

———. 1990. *You Just Don't Understand: Women and Men in Conversation.* New York: Ballantine Books.

———. 1993. "The Relativity of Linguistic Strategies." In *Gender and Conversational Interaction*, edited by Deborah Tannen. New York: Oxford University Press.

———. 1994. *Talking from 9 to 5: How Women's and Men's Conversational Styles Affect Who Gets Heard, Who Gets Credit, and What Gets Done at Work.* New York: William Morrow.

———. 2009. "Framing and Face: The Relevance of the Presentation of Self to Linguistic Discourse Analysis." *Social Psychology Quarterly* 72 (4): 300–305.

Taps, Judith, and Patricia Y. Martin. 1990. "Gender Composition, Attributional Accounts, and Women's Influence and Likability in Task Groups." *Small Group Research* 21 (4): 471–91.

Ten Velden, Femke S., Bianca Beersma, and Carsten K. W. De Dreu. 2007. "Majority and Minority Influence in Group Negotiation: The Moderating Effects of Social Motivation and Decision Rules." *Journal of Applied Psychology* 92 (1): 259–68.

Thatcher, Margaret. 1995. *The Path to Power.* London: HarperCollins.

Thomas, D. 1990. "Intra-Household Resource Allocation: An Inferential Approach." *Journal of Human Resources* 25: 625–64.

Thomas, Sue. 1991. "The Impact of Women on State Legislative Policies." *Journal of Politics* 53: 958–76.

———. 1994. *How Women Legislate.* New York: Oxford University Press.

———. 2005. "Cracking the Glass Ceiling: The Status, Significance, and Prospects of Women in Legislative Office." In *Gender and American Politics*, 2nd ed., edited by Sue Tolleson-Rinehart and Jyl J. Josephson. Armonk, NY: M.E. Sharpe.

Thomas, Sue, and Susan Welch. 1991. "Women Legislators: Legislative Styles and Policy Priorities." *Western Political Quarterly* 10: 125–34.

———. 2001. "The Impact of Women in State Legislatures: Numerical and Organizational Strength." In *The Impact of Women in Public Office*, edited by Sue Carroll, 166–81. Bloomington: Indiana University Press.

Thompson, Dennis. 2008. "Deliberative Democratic Theory and Empirical Political Science." *Annual Review of Political Science* 11: 497–520.

Thompson, L. L., E. A. Mannix, and M. H. Bazerman. 1988. "Group Negotiation: Effects of Decision Rule, Agenda, and Aspiration." *Journal of Personality and Social Psychology* 54 (1): 86–95.

Thompson, Mark, and Ludmilla Lennartz. 2006. "The Making of Chancellor Merkel." *German Politics* 15 (1): 99–110.

Thorne, B., and Z. Luria. 1986. "Sexuality and Gender in Children's Daily Worlds." *Social Problems* 33: 176–90.

Thunder, David. 2006. "A Rawlsian Argument against the Duty of Civility." *American Journal of Political Science* 50 (3): 676–90.

Tocqueville, Alexis de. [1835] 2006. *Democracy in America.* Volume 1, book 1.

Tolbert, C., and G. Steuernagal. 2001. "Women Lawmakers, State Mandates, and Women's Health." *Women and Politics* 22 (2): 1–39.

Tolbert, P. S., T. Simons, A. O. Andrews, and J. Rhee. 1995. "The Effects of Gender Composition in Academic Departments on Faculty Turnover." *Industrial Labor Relations Review* 48: 562–79.

Tolleson-Rinehart, Sue, and Jyl J. Josephson, eds. 2005. *Gender and American Politics: Women, Men, and the Political Process.* Revised and expanded 2nd ed. Armonk, NY: M. E. Sharpe.

Tönnies, Ferdinand. [1887] 1988. *Community and Society.* New Brunswick, NJ: Transaction.

Trenel, Matthias. 2009. "Facilitation and Inclusive Deliberation." In *Online Deliberation: Design, Research, and Practice*, edited by Todd Davies and Seeta Peña Gangadharan. Stanford, CA: CSLI Publications.

Tyler, Tom. 2006. *Why People Obey the Law.* Princeton, NJ: Princeton University Press.

UN Economic and Social Council. 1995. *Report: The United Nations Fourth World Conference on Women.* Beijing, China. Available at http://www.un.org/womenwatch/daw/beijing/platform/decision.htm. Accessed June 14, 2013.

Uphoff, Norman. 1989. "Distinguishing Power, Authority, and Legitimacy: Taking Max Weber at His Words by Using Resource-Exchange Analysis." *Polity* 22 (2): 295–322.

US Census Bureau. 1998. *Statistical Abstract of the United States: 1997.* Washington, DC: US Department of Commerce.

US Department of Commerce. 2011. *Women In America: Indicators of Social and Economic Well-Being.* Washington, DC: US Department of Commerce.

US Department of Labor. 2011. *Women's Employment during the Recovery.* Washington, DC: US Department of Labor.

van Knippenberg, Daan, and Michaela C. Schippers. 2007. "Work Group Diversity." *Annual Review of Psychology* 58: 515–41.

Van Lange, Paul A. M., Wilma Otten, Ellen M. N. De Bruin, and Jeffrey A. Joireman. 1997. "Development of Prosocial, Individualistic, and Competitive Orientations: Theory and Preliminary Evidence." *Journal of Personality and Social Psychology* 73 (4): 733–46.

van Swol, Lyn M., and Emily Seinfeld. 2006. "Differences between Minority, Majority, and Unanimous Group Members in the Communication of Information." *Human Communication Research* 32: 178–97.

Verba, Sidney. 1961. *Small Groups and Political Behavior.* Princeton, NJ: Princeton University Press.

Verba, Sidney, and Norman H. Nie. 1972. *Participation in America.* New York: Harper and Row.

Verba, Sidney, Kay Lehman Schlozman, and Henry E. Brady. 1995. *Voice and Equality: Civic Voluntarism in American Politics.* Cambridge, MA: Harvard University Press.

Wagner, H. L., Ross Buck, and Meg Winterbotham. 1993. "Communication of Specific Emotions: Gender Differences in Sending Accuracy and Communication Measures." *Journal of Nonverbal Behavior* 17: 29–53.

Walker, Alice. 1984. *In Search of Our Mothers' Gardens: Womanist Prose*. San Diego: Harcourt Brace Jovanovich.

Walker, Thomas, and Deborah Barrow. 1985. "The Diversification of the Federal Bench: Policy and Process Ramifications." *Journal of Politics* 47: 596–617.

Walsh, Denise. 2012. "Centralization and Debate Conditions in South Africa" In *The Impact of Gender Quotas*, edited by Susan Franceschet, Mona Lena Krook, and Jennifer M. Piscopo, 119–35. New York: Oxford University Press.

Walsh, Katherine Cramer. 2002. "Enlarging Representation: Women Bringing Marginalized Perspectives to Floor Debate in the House of Representatives." In *Women Transforming Congress*, edited by Cindy Simon Rosenthal, 370–98. Norman: University of Oklahoma Press.

———. 2007. *Talking about Race: Community Dialogues and the Politics of Difference*. Chicago: University of Chicago Press.

Wantchekon, Leonard. 2011. "Deliberative Electoral Campaigns and Transition from Clientelism: Evidence from a Field Experiment in Benin." Princeton University working paper.

Warner, Rebecca L., and Brent S. Steel. 1999. "Child Rearing as a Mechanism for Social Change: The Relationship of Child Gender to Parents' Commitment to Gender Equity." *Gender and Society* 13 (4): 503–17.

Warren, Mark E. 2000. *Democracy and Association*. Princeton, NJ: Princeton University Press.

Warren, Mark E., and Hillary Pearse. 2008. *Designing Deliberative Democracy: The British Columbia Citizens' Assembly*. Cambridge: Cambridge University Press.

Washington, Ebonya L. 2008. "Female Socialization: How Daughters Affect Their Legislator Fathers." *American Economic Review* 98 (1): 311–32.

Watson, Robert P., and Ann Gordon, eds. 2003. *Anticipating Madam President*. Boulder, CO: Lynne Rienner.

Weber, Max. 1947. *The Theory of Social and Economic Organization*. Translated by A. M. Henderson and Talcott Parsons. Edited with an introduction by Talcott Parsons. New York: Oxford University Press.

Weekes, Karen. 2007. *Women Know Everything!: 3,241 Quips, Quotes, and Brilliant Remarks*. Philadelphia: Quirk Books.

Welch, Susan, and Albert Karnig. 1979. "Correlates of Female Office Holding in City Politics." *Journal of Politics* 41: 478–91.

Weldon, S. Laurel. 2002. "Beyond Bodies: Institutional Sources of Representation for Women in Democratic Policymaking." *Journal of Politics* 64 (4): 1153–74.

West, Candace. 1984. "When the Doctor Is a 'Lady': Power, Status, and Gender in Physician-Patient Encounters." *Social Problems* 24: 521–29.

West, Candace, and Don Zimmerman. 1987. "Doing Gender." *Gender and Society* 1 (2): 125–51.

Williams, Melissa S. 2000. "The Uneasy Alliance of Group Representation in Deliberative Democracy." In *Citizenship in Diverse Societies*, edited by Will Kymlicka and Wayne Norman. London: Oxford University Press.

Winthrop, Delba. 1986. "Tocqueville's American Woman and 'The True Conception of Democratic Progress.'" *Political Theory* 14 (2): 239–61.

Wharton, A. S., T. Rotolo, and S. R. Bird. 2000. "Social Context at Work: A Multilevel Analysis of Job Satisfaction." *Sociological Forum* 15 (1): 65–90.

White, Melanie. 2006. "An Ambivalent Civility." *Canadian Journal of Sociology* 31 (4): 445–60.

Whitt, J. Elizabeth. 1994. "'I Can Be Anything': Student Leadership in Three Women's Colleges." *Journal of College Student Development* 35 (3): 198–207.

Wigfield, Allan, Jacquelynne S. Eccles, and Paul R. Pintrich. 1996. "Development between the Ages of 11 and 25." In *Handbook of Educational Psychology*, edited by David Berliner and Robert Calfee, 148–85. New York: Macmillan Library Reference.

Williams, Melissa. 2000. "The Uneasy Alliance of Group Representation and Deliberative Democracy." In *Citizenship in Diverse Societies*, edited by Will Kymlicka and Wayne Norman, 124–54. Oxford: Oxford University Press.

Winter, Nicholas. 2008. *Dangerous Frames*. Chicago: University of Chicago Press.

Wolbrecht, Christina. 2008. "Introduction: What We Saw at the Revolution: Women in American Politics and Political Science." In *Political Women and American Democracy*, edited by Christina Wolbrecht, Karen Beckwith, and Lisa Baldez, 1–11. New York: Cambridge University Press.

Wolbrecht, Christina, and David E. Campbell. 2007. "Leading by Example: Female Members of Parliament as Political Role Models." *American Journal of Political Science* 51 (4): 921–39.

Wolfinger, Raymond E., and Steven J. Rosenstone. 1980. *Who Votes?* New Haven, CT: Yale University Press.

Wood, Wendy, and Stephen J. Karten. 1986. "Sex Differences in Interaction Style as a Product of Perceived Sex Differences in Competence." *Journal of Personality and Social Psychology* 50: 341–47.

Woolley, Anita W., Christopher F. Chabris, Alex Pentland, Nada Hasmi, and Thomas W. Malone. 2010. "Evidence for a Collective Intelligence Factor in the Performance of Human Groups." *Science* 330 (6004): 686–88.

Young, Alfred F. 2011. "The People and the Patriots: Who Led Whom in the American Revolution." *Boston Review* 36 (6).

Young, Iris M. 1996. "Communication and the Other: Beyond Deliberative Democracy." In *Democracy and Difference: Contesting the Boundaries of the Political*, edited by Seyla Benhabib. Princeton, NJ: Princeton University Press.

———. 2000. *Inclusion and Democracy*. New York: Oxford University Press.

———. 2001. "Activist Challenges to Deliberative Democracy." *Political Theory* 29: 670–90.

Young, G. 2001. *Study of Parliament Group Newsletter* 30 (Summer).

Zimmerman, D. H., and C. West. 1975. "Sex Roles, Interruptions, and Silences in Conversation." In *Language and Sex: Difference and Dominance*, edited by B. Thorne and N. Henley. Rowley, MA: Newbury House.

Zimmerman, Joseph. 1999. *The New England Town Meeting: Democracy in Action*. Westport, CT: Praeger Publishers.

Zukin, Cliff, Scott Keeter, Molly Andolina, Krista Jenkins, and Michael X. Delli Carpini. 2006. *A New Engagement? Political Participation, Civic Life, and the Changing American Citizen*. New York: Oxford University Press.

Index